Yu-Gi-Oh!
THE MOVIE
ANI-MANGA

D0017844

Original Story by
Kazuki Takahashi

YU-GI-OH! THE MOVIE
SHONEN JUMP ANI-MANGA

Original Story by Kazuki Takahashi

Editing/KISOUSHA
Tetsuo Daitoku, Michiyo Tsutsumi,
Yoshihiko Tozawa, Natsuo Funatsu

Design/BANANA GROVE STUDIO
Yoko Iwasa, Ayano Yamamoto, Chizuru Mae, Yoko Nose,
Takako Abukawa, Misato Shibakai, Akihito Matsubara,
Tomofumi Nakano, Emi Nakano, Kazumi Yamamoto

Cover Design/Veronica Casson
Senior Editor/Jason Thompson

Managing Editor/Masumi Washington
Director of Production/Noboru Watanabe
Editorial Director/Alvin Lu
Executive Vice President & Editor in Chief/Hyoe Narita
Sr. Director of Licensing & Acquisitions/Rika Inouye
Vice President of Sales & Marketing/Liza Coppola
Vice President of Strategic Development/Yumi Hoashi
Publisher/Seiji Horibuchi

©1996 Kazuki Takahashi

TV TOKYO   NAS   SHUEISHA

4Kids ENTERTAINMENT

Printed in the U.S.A.

Published by VIZ, LLC
P.O. Box 77010
San Francisco, CA 94107

SHONEN JUMP ANI-MANGA
10 9 8 7 6 5 4 3 2 1
First printing, October 2004

www.viz.com

RATED
A
FOR
ALL AGES

YU-GI-OH! THE MOVIE
ANI-MANGA is rated A
for All Ages.
It is recommended for
any age group.

THE WORLD'S
MOST POPULAR MANGA

SHONEN JUMP
ANI-MANGA
www.shonenjump.com

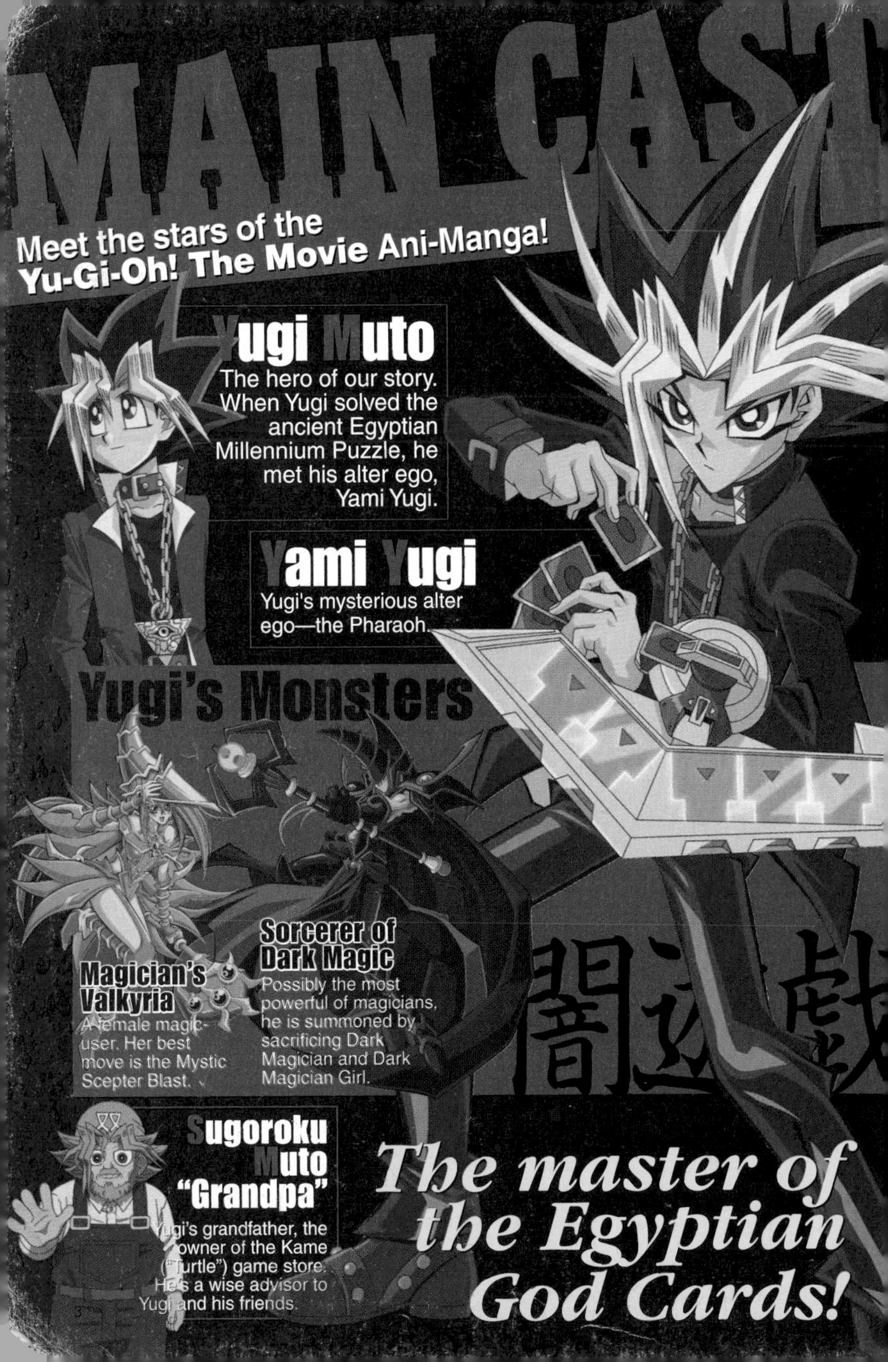
MAIN CAST
Meet the stars of the Yu-Gi-Oh! The Movie Ani-Manga!
Yugi Muto
The hero of our story. When Yugi solved the ancient Egyptian Millennium Puzzle, he met his alter ego, Yami Yugi.
Yami Yugi
Yugi's mysterious alter ego—the Pharaoh.
Yugi's Monsters
Magician's Valkyria
A female magic-user. Her best move is the Mystic Scepter Blast.
Sorcerer of Dark Magic
Possibly the most powerful of magicians, he is summoned by sacrificing Dark Magician and Dark Magician Girl.
闇遊戯
Sugoroku Muto "Grandpa"
Yugi's grandfather, the owner of the Kame ("Turtle") game store. He's a wise advisor to Yugi and his friends.
The master of the Egyptian God Cards!

Seto Kaiba

The teenage president of Kaiba Corporation, Kaiba vows to defeat Yugi and become the world champion duelist. His current goal: to find a way to beat Yugi's almost unstoppable Egyptian God Cards!

海馬

Yugi's eternal rival!

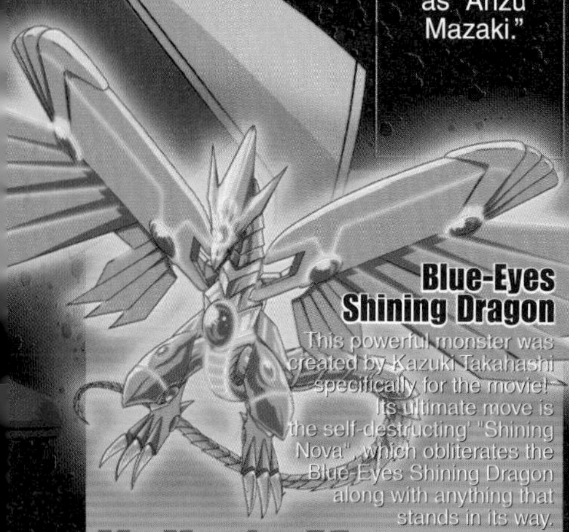

Blue-Eyes Shining Dragon

This powerful monster was created by Kazuki Takahashi specifically for the movie! Its ultimate move is the self-destructing "Shining Nova", which obliterates the Blue-Eyes Shining Dragon along with anything that stands in its way.

Kaiba's Monsters

Yugi's Friends

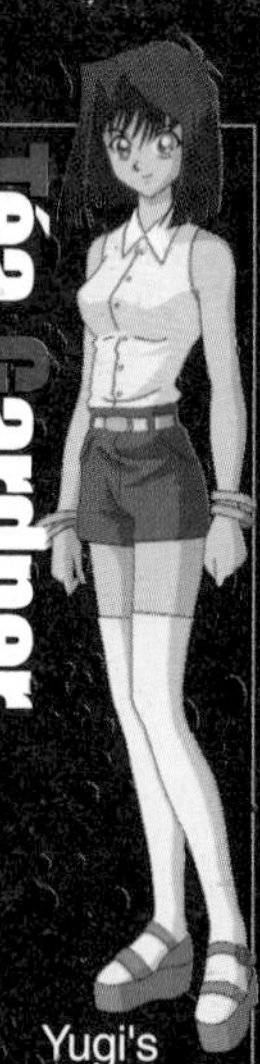

Téa Gardner

Yugi's classmate and childhood friend. She may have a crush on Yami Yugi. In Japanese she's known as "Anzu Mazaki."

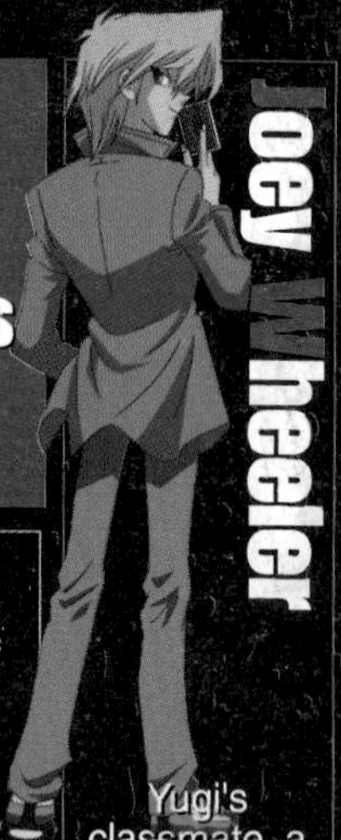

Joey Wheeler

Yugi's classmate, a tough guy who used to get in a lot of fights. He initially thought Yugi was a wimp, but now he is one of his best friends. In Japanese he's known as "Katsuya Jonouchi."

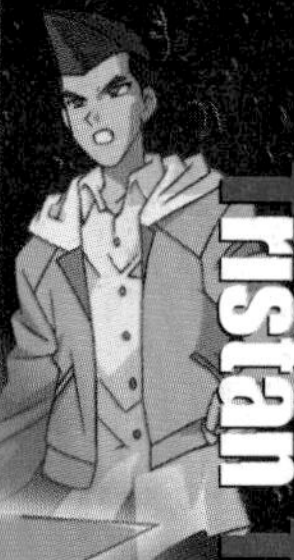

Tristan Taylor

Yugi's classmate and one of Yugi's best friends. Like Joey, he used to get in a lot of fights. In Japanese he's known as "Hiroto Honda."

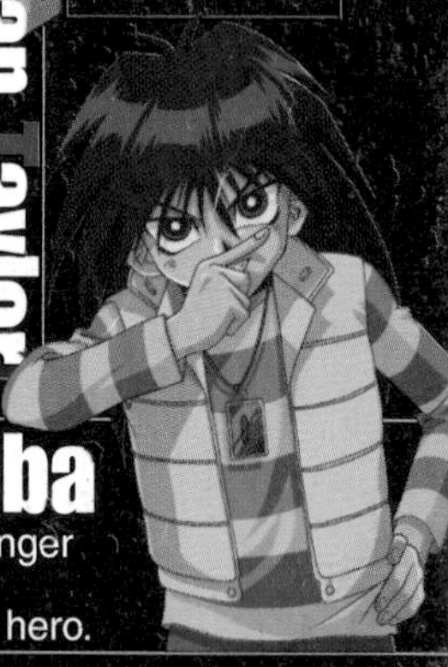

Mokuba

Kaiba's younger brother. Kaiba is his hero.

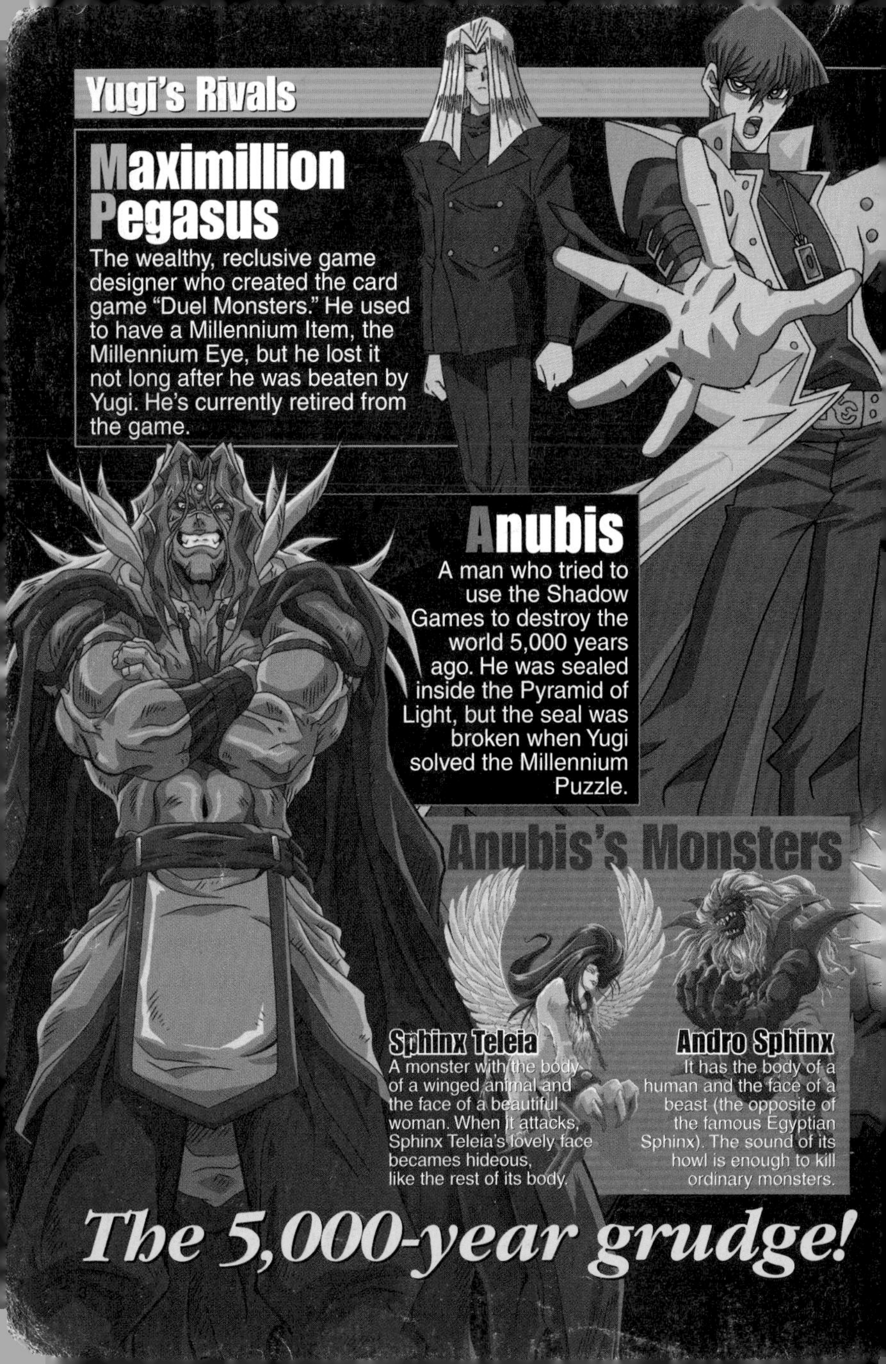

Yugi's Rivals

Maximillion Pegasus

The wealthy, reclusive game designer who created the card game "Duel Monsters." He used to have a Millennium Item, the Millennium Eye, but he lost it not long after he was beaten by Yugi. He's currently retired from the game.

Anubis

A man who tried to use the Shadow Games to destroy the world 5,000 years ago. He was sealed inside the Pyramid of Light, but the seal was broken when Yugi solved the Millennium Puzzle.

Anubis's Monsters

Sphinx Teleia

A monster with the body of a winged animal and the face of a beautiful woman. When it attacks, Sphinx Teleia's lovely face becames hideous, like the rest of its body.

Andro Sphinx

It has the body of a human and the face of a beast (the opposite of the famous Egyptian Sphinx). The sound of its howl is enough to kill ordinary monsters.

The 5,000-year grudge!

YU-GI-OH!™ THE MOVIE

ANI-MANGA™

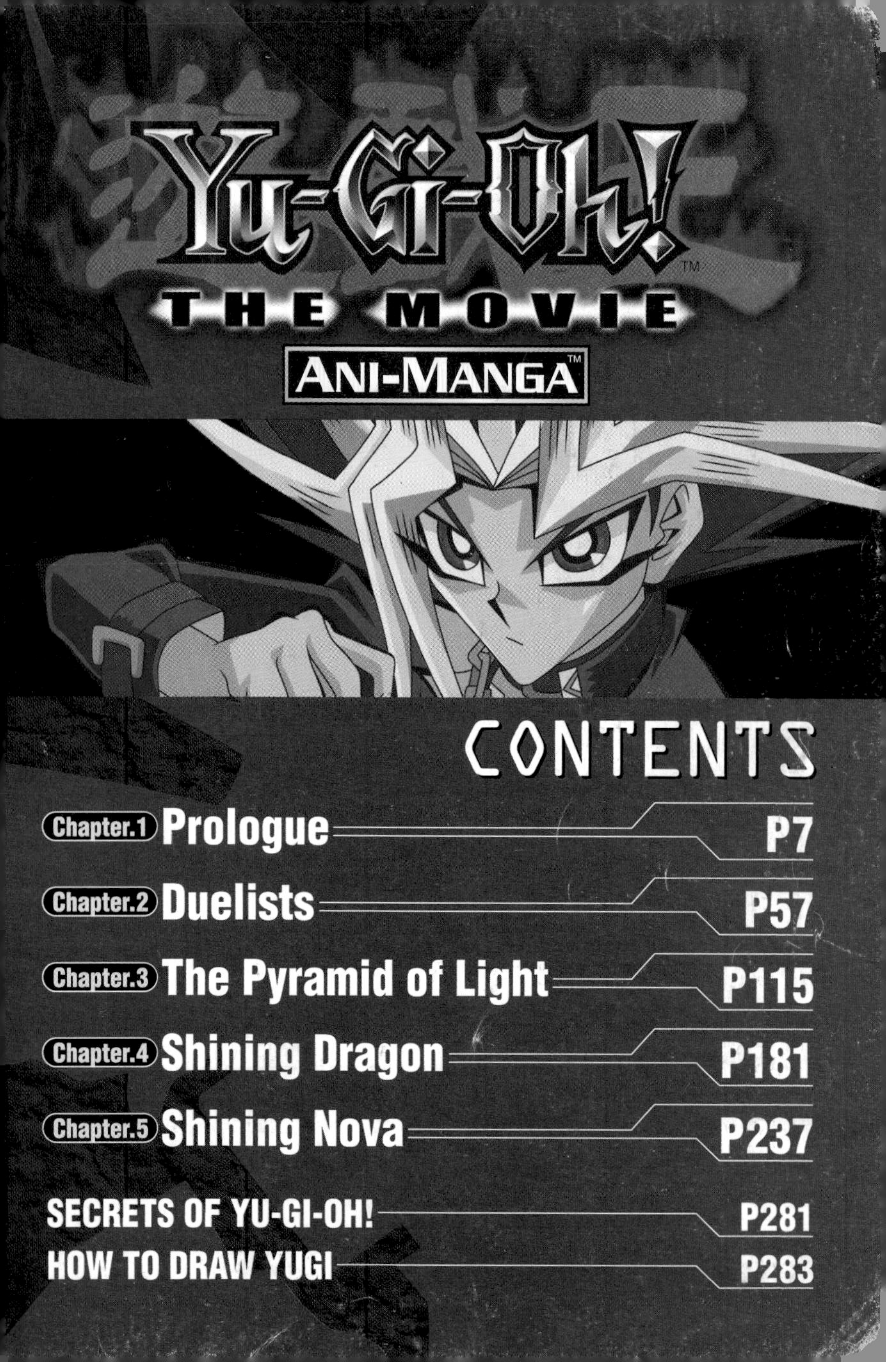

CONTENTS

READ THIS WAY

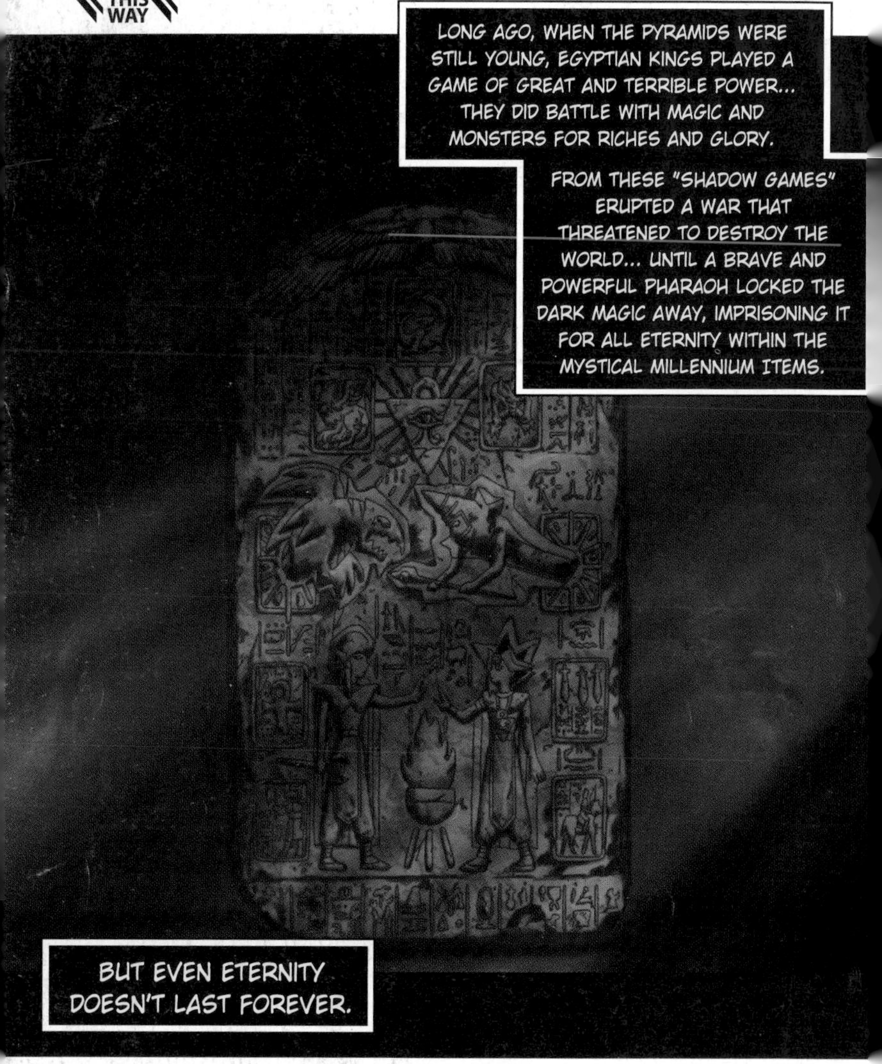
LONG AGO, WHEN THE PYRAMIDS WERE STILL YOUNG, EGYPTIAN KINGS PLAYED A GAME OF GREAT AND TERRIBLE POWER... THEY DID BATTLE WITH MAGIC AND MONSTERS FOR RICHES AND GLORY.
FROM THESE "SHADOW GAMES" ERUPTED A WAR THAT THREATENED TO DESTROY THE WORLD... UNTIL A BRAVE AND POWERFUL PHARAOH LOCKED THE DARK MAGIC AWAY, IMPRISONING IT FOR ALL ETERNITY WITHIN THE MYSTICAL MILLENNIUM ITEMS.
BUT EVEN ETERNITY DOESN'T LAST FOREVER.

Chapter. 1

Prologue

READ THIS WAY

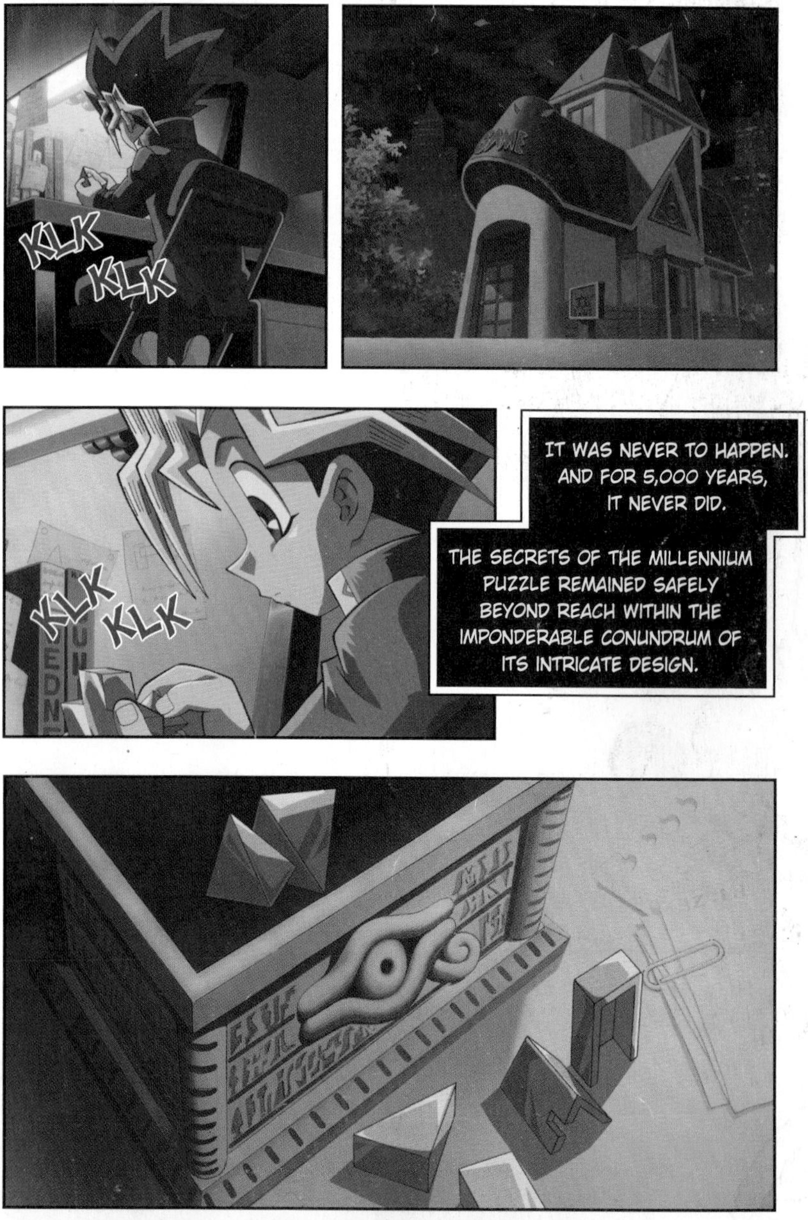
KLK
KLK
IT WAS NEVER TO HAPPEN. AND FOR 5,000 YEARS, IT NEVER DID.
THE SECRETS OF THE MILLENNIUM PUZZLE REMAINED SAFELY BEYOND REACH WITHIN THE IMPONDERABLE CONUNDRUM OF ITS INTRICATE DESIGN.
KLK
KLK

READ THIS WAY

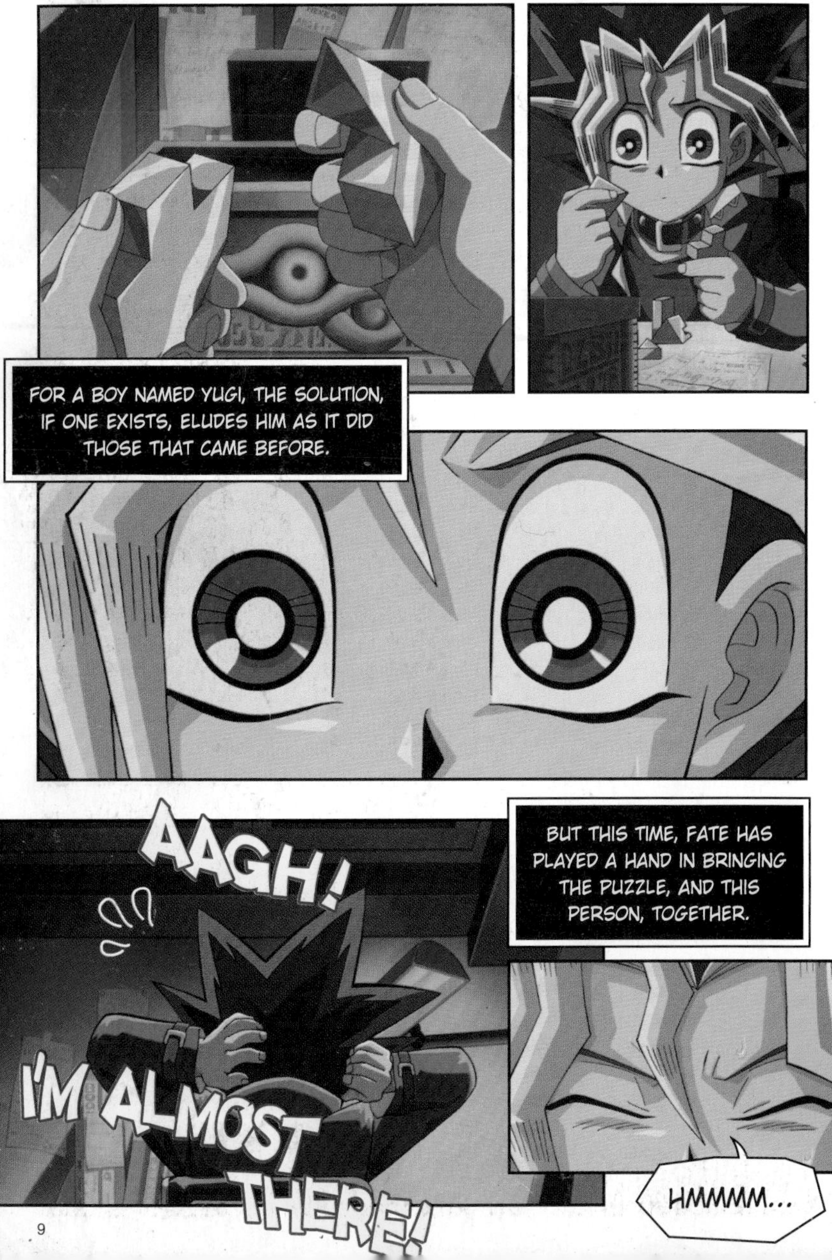
FOR A BOY NAMED YUGI, THE SOLUTION, IF ONE EXISTS, ELUDES HIM AS IT DID THOSE THAT CAME BEFORE.
BUT THIS TIME, FATE HAS PLAYED A HAND IN BRINGING THE PUZZLE, AND THIS PERSON, TOGETHER.
HMMMM...
AAGH!
I'M ALMOST THERE!

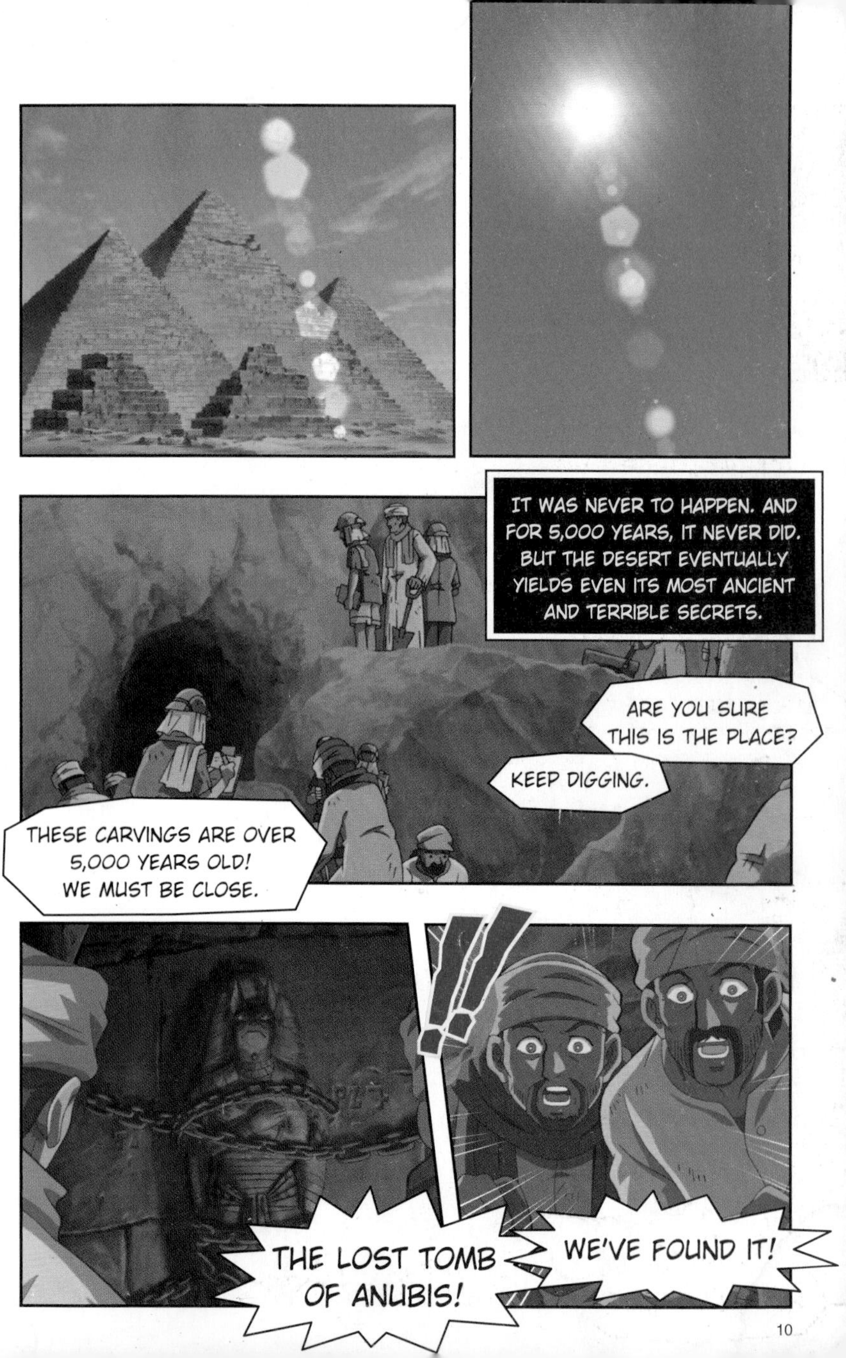
IT WAS NEVER TO HAPPEN. AND FOR 5,000 YEARS, IT NEVER DID. BUT THE DESERT EVENTUALLY YIELDS EVEN ITS MOST ANCIENT AND TERRIBLE SECRETS.
ARE YOU SURE THIS IS THE PLACE?
KEEP DIGGING.
THESE CARVINGS ARE OVER 5,000 YEARS OLD! WE MUST BE CLOSE.
!!
WE'VE FOUND IT!
THE LOST TOMB OF ANUBIS!

READ THIS WAY

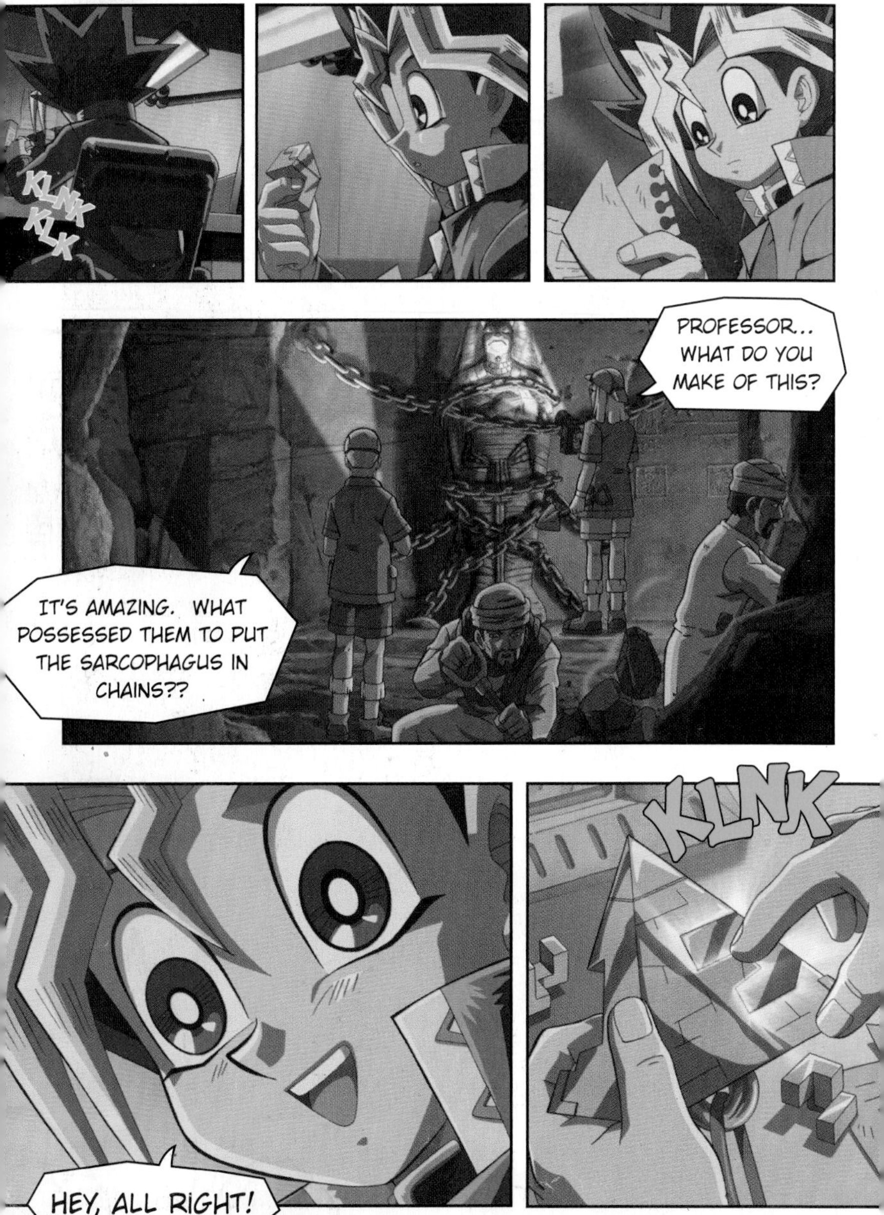
KLNK KLK
PROFESSOR... WHAT DO YOU MAKE OF THIS?
IT'S AMAZING. WHAT POSSESSED THEM TO PUT THE SARCOPHAGUS IN CHAINS??
KLNK
HEY, ALL RIGHT!

READ THIS WAY

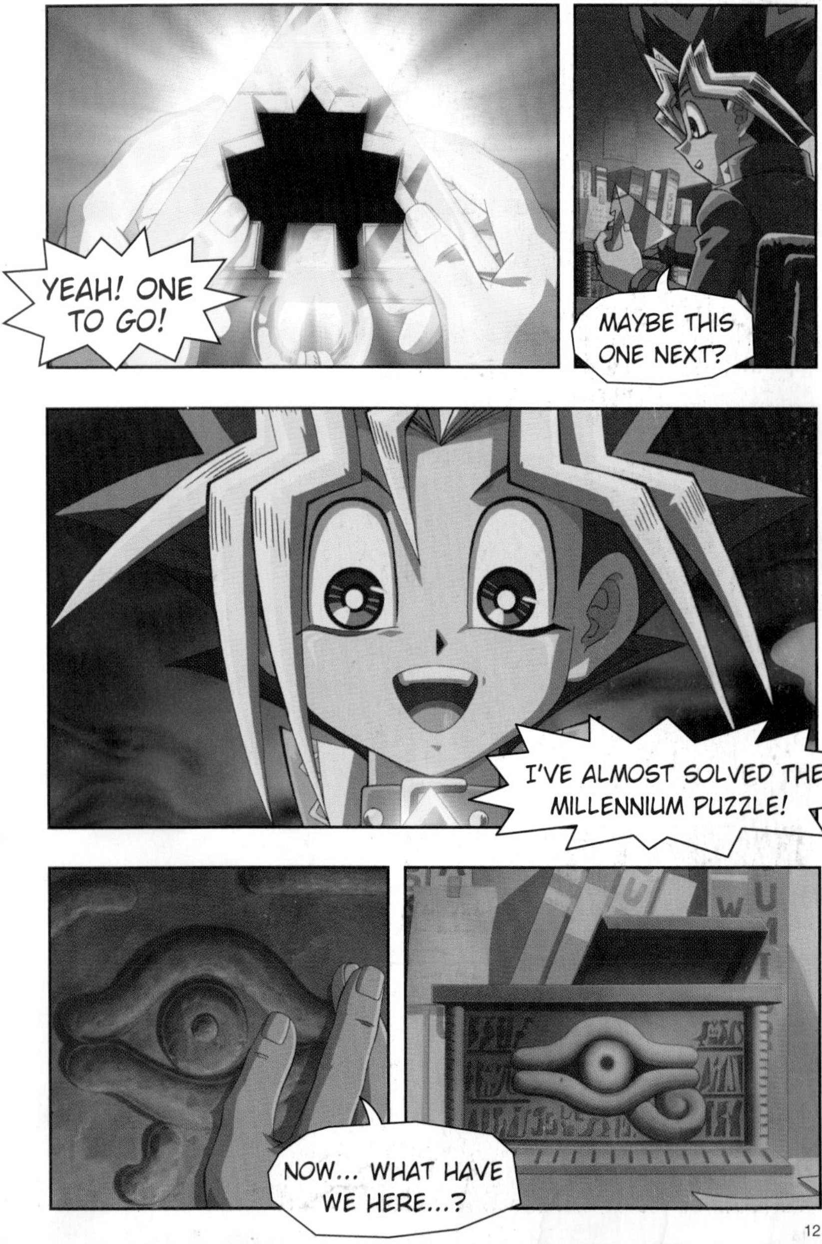
MAYBE THIS ONE NEXT?
YEAH! ONE TO GO!
I'VE ALMOST SOLVED THE MILLENNIUM PUZZLE!
NOW... WHAT HAVE WE HERE...?

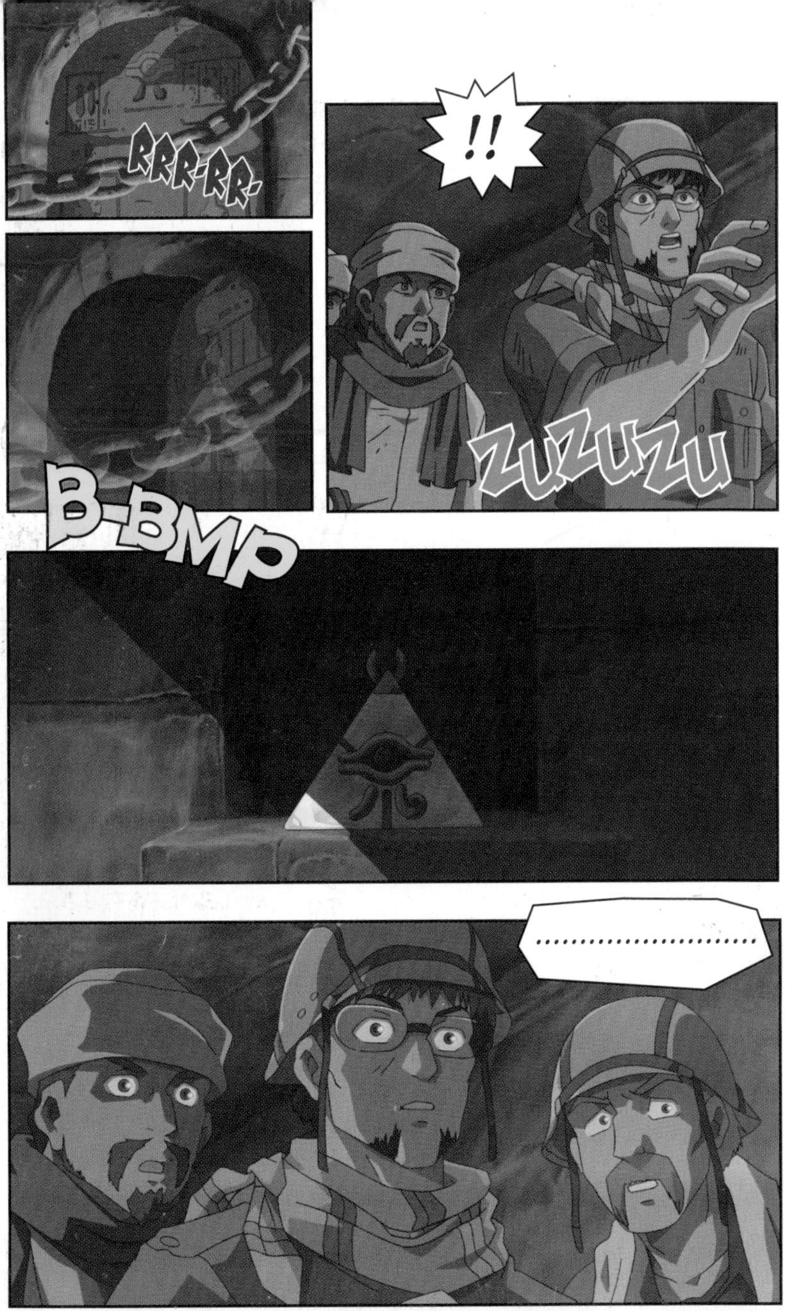
!!
ZUZUZU
RRR-RR-
B-BMP
....

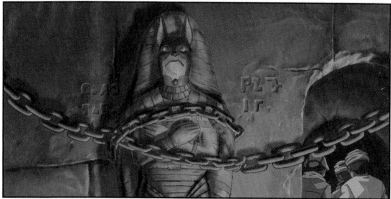

GRANDPA'S SURE GONNA BE SURPRISED WHEN HE SEES I FIGURED THIS PUZZLE OUT ALL BY MYSELF!

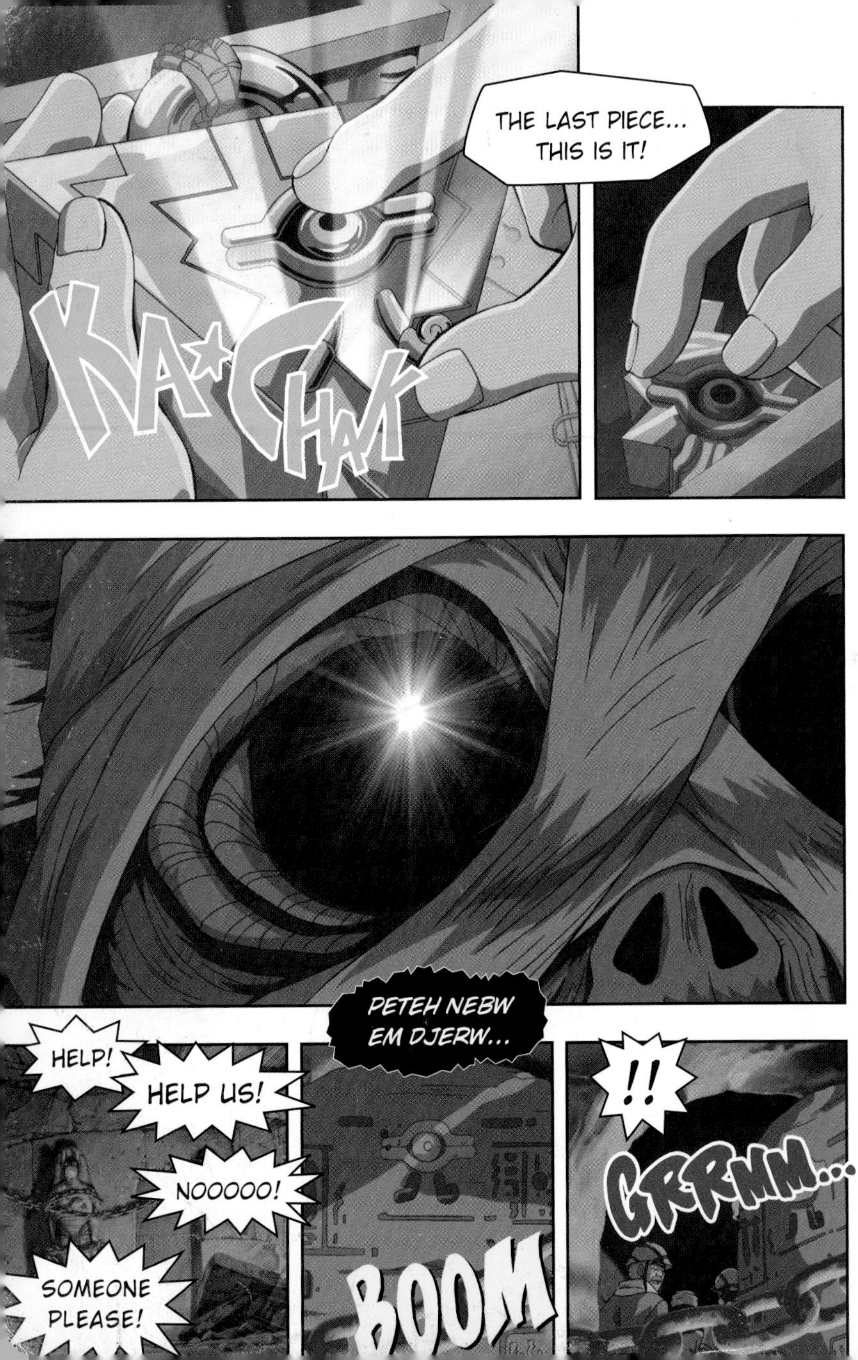
THE LAST PIECE... THIS IS IT!
KA*CHAK
!!
GRRMM...
PETEH NEBW EM DJERW...
BOOM
HELP!
HELP US!
NOOOOO!
SOMEONE PLEASE!

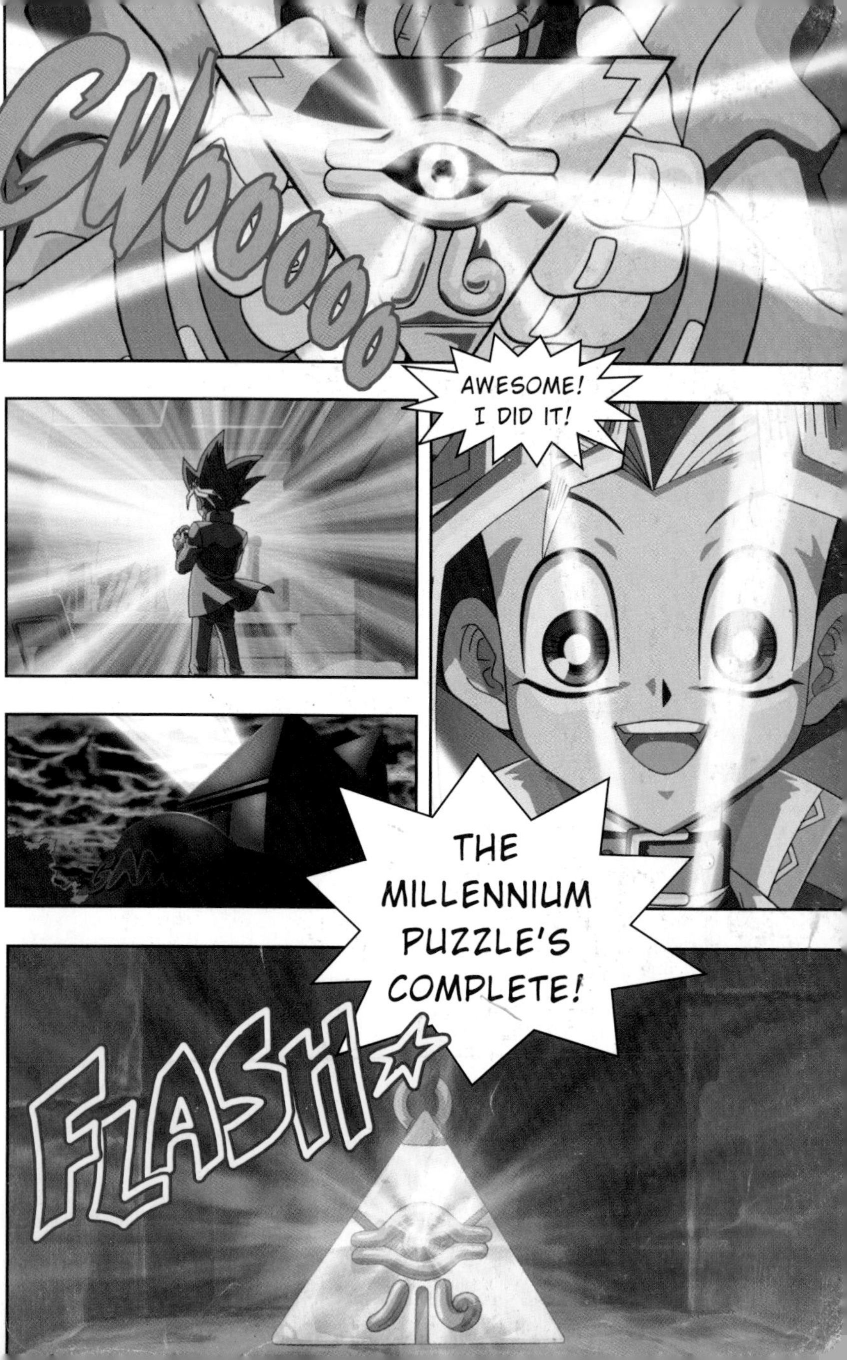
GWOOOOO
AWESOME! I DID IT!
THE MILLENNIUM PUZZLE'S COMPLETE!
FLASH

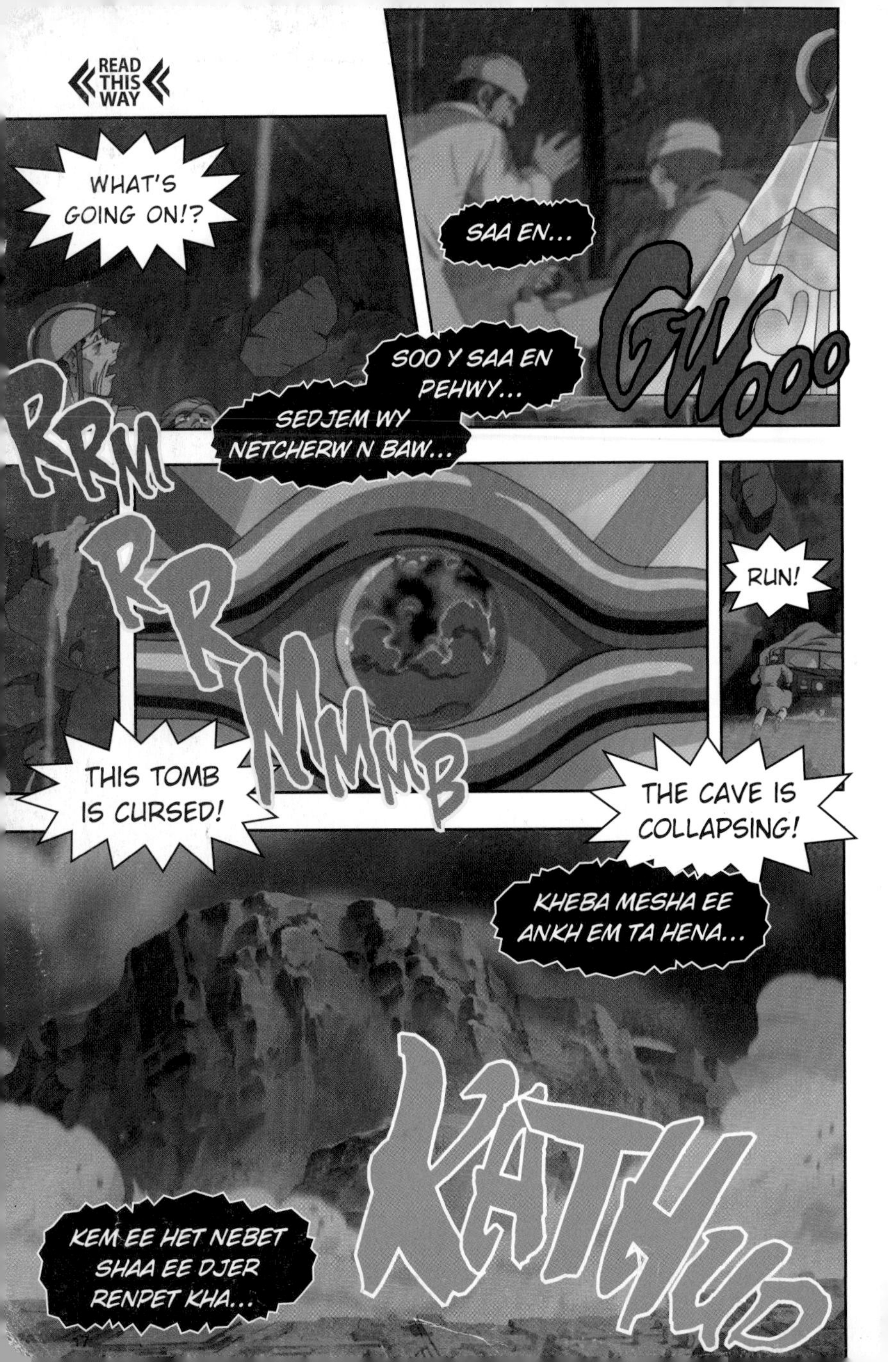
READ THIS WAY
SAA EN...
GWOOO
SOO Y SAA EN PEHWY...
SEDJEM WY NETCHERW N BAW...
WHAT'S GOING ON!?
RRM
RUN!
RRMMMMB
THIS TOMB IS CURSED!
THE CAVE IS COLLAPSING!
KHEBA MESHA EE ANKH EM TA HENA...
KATHUD
KEM EE HET NEBET SHAA EE DJER RENPET KHA...

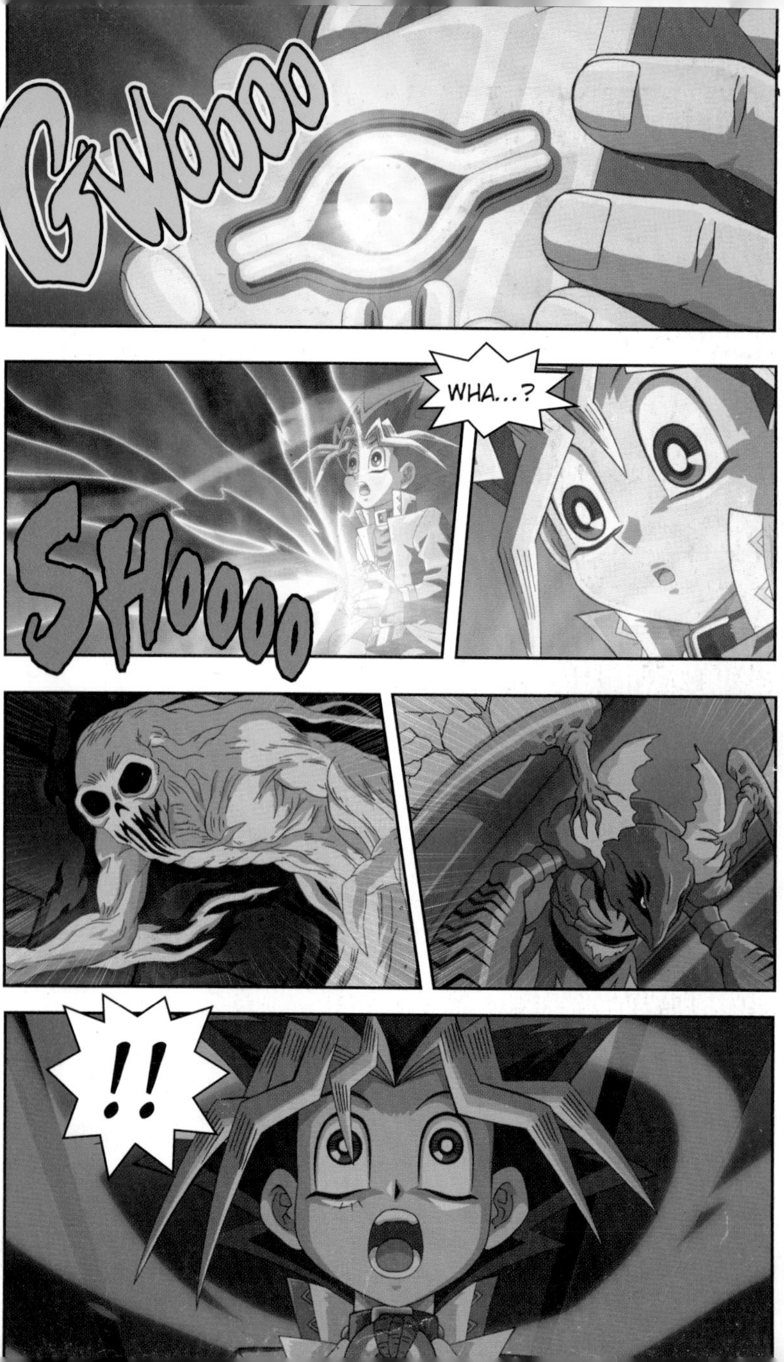
GWOOOO
WHA...?
SHOOOO
!!

READ THIS WAY

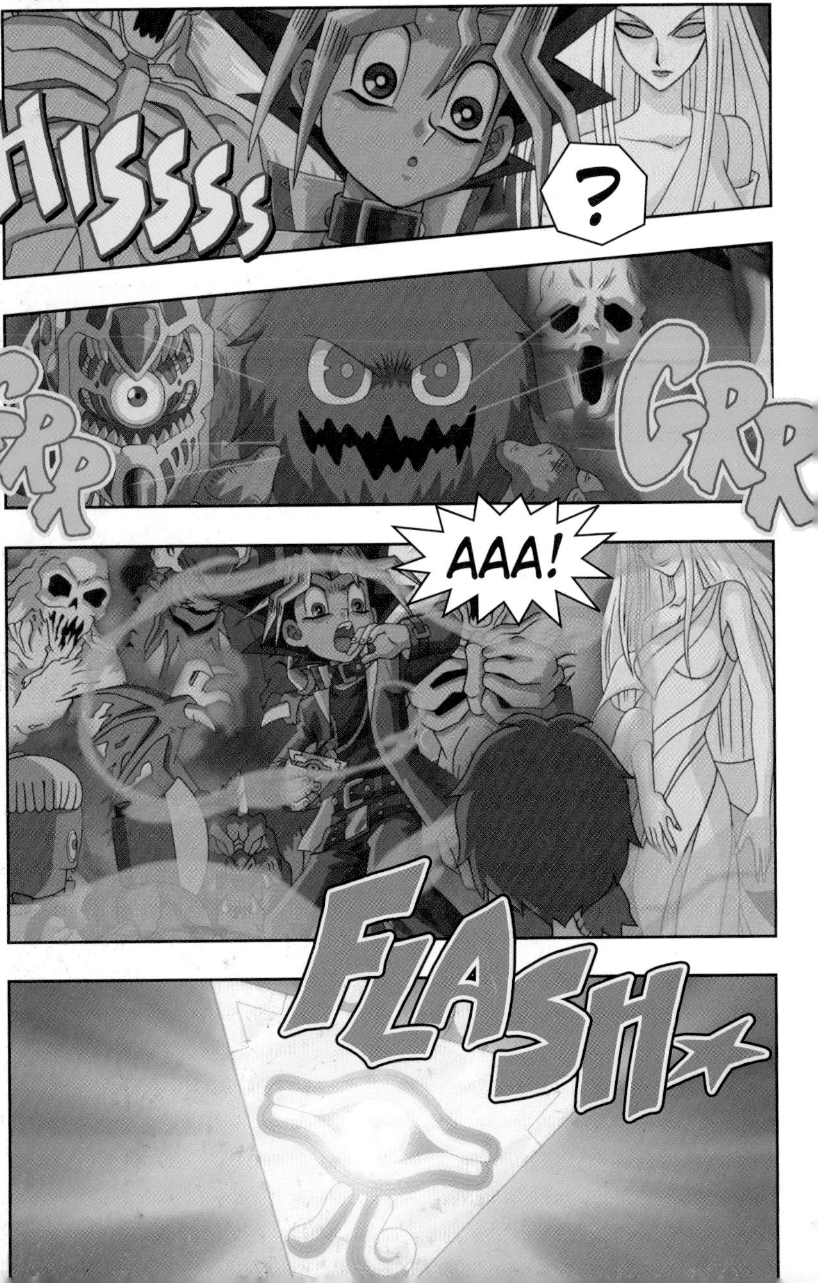
?
HISSSss
GRR
GRR
AAA!
FLASH

READ THIS WAY

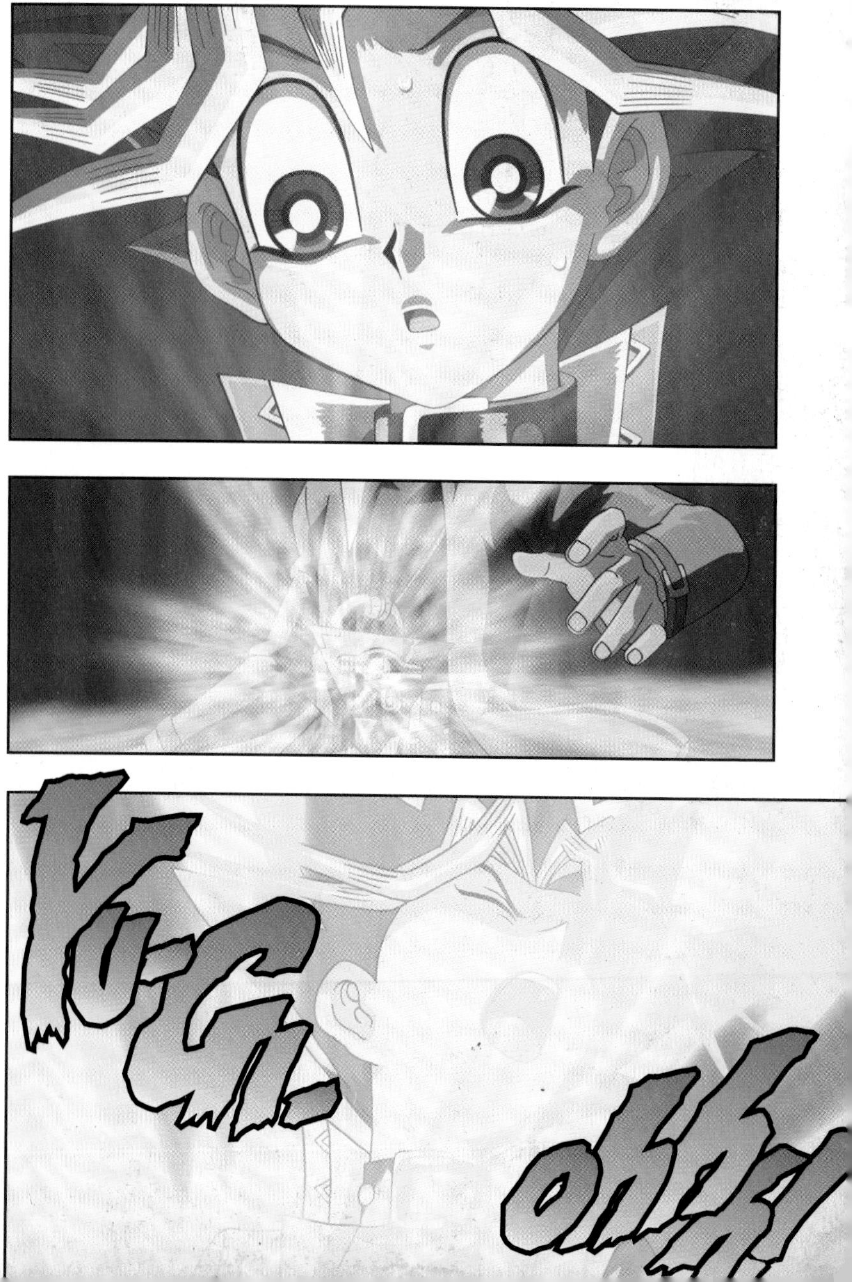
YU-GI-OHH!

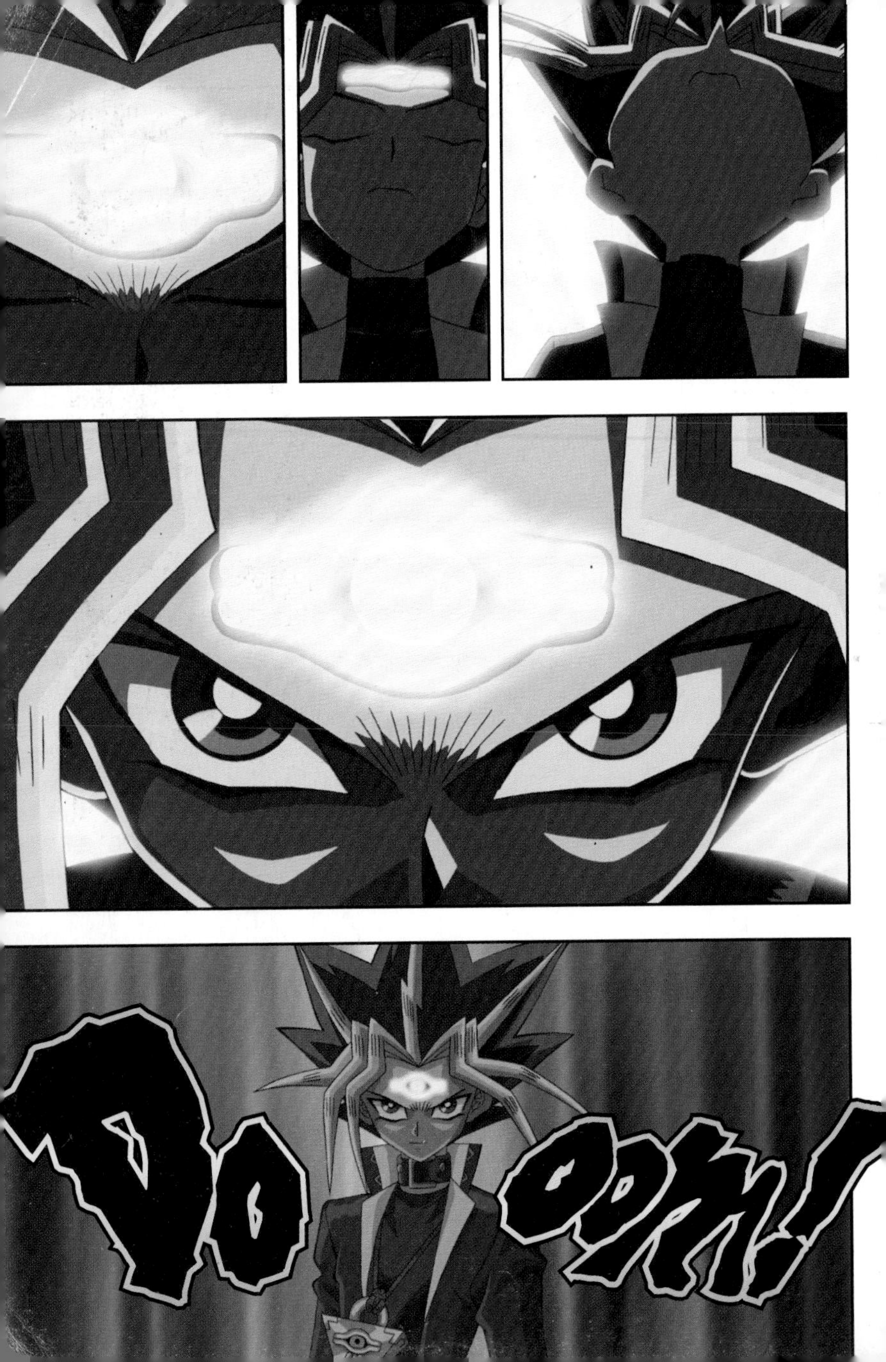
DOOOM!

READ THIS WAY

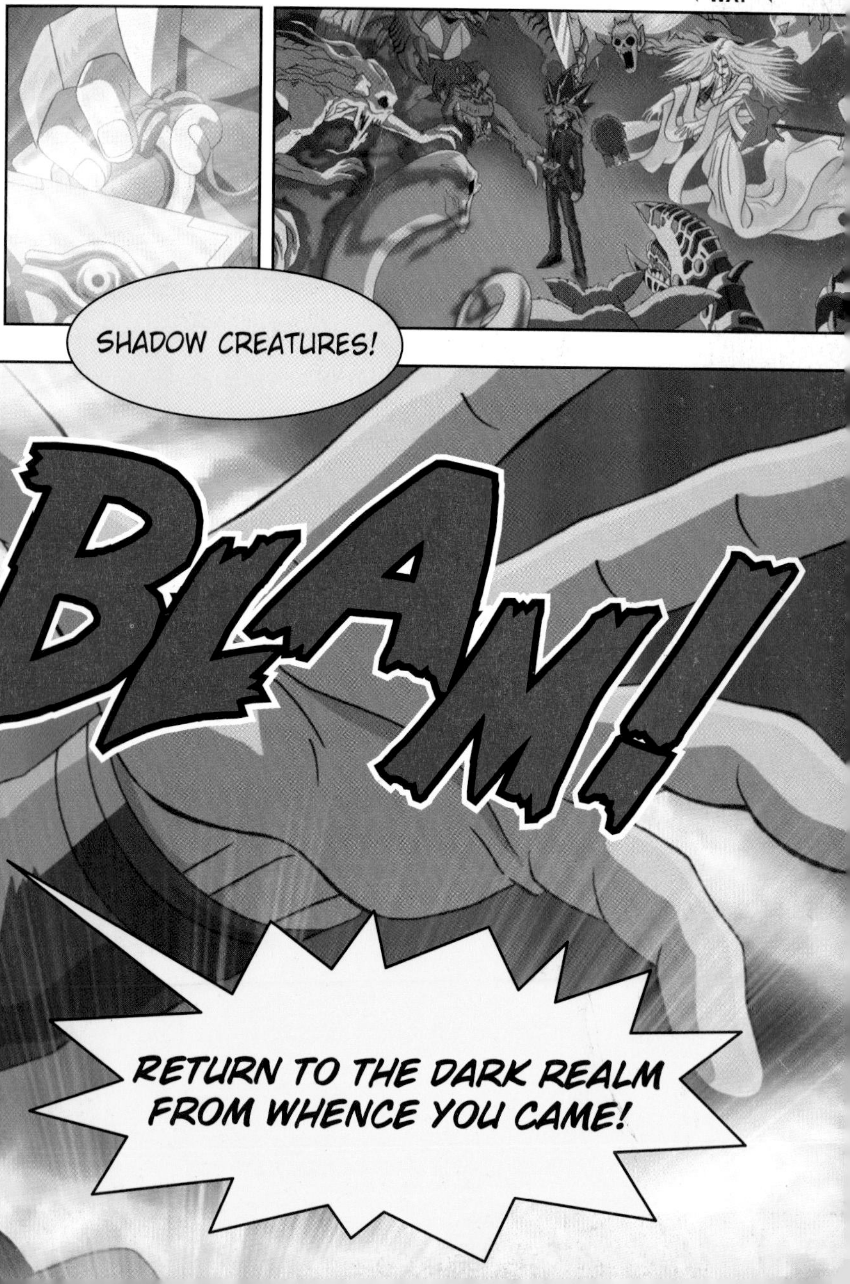
SHADOW CREATURES!
BLAM!
RETURN TO THE DARK REALM FROM WHENCE YOU CAME!

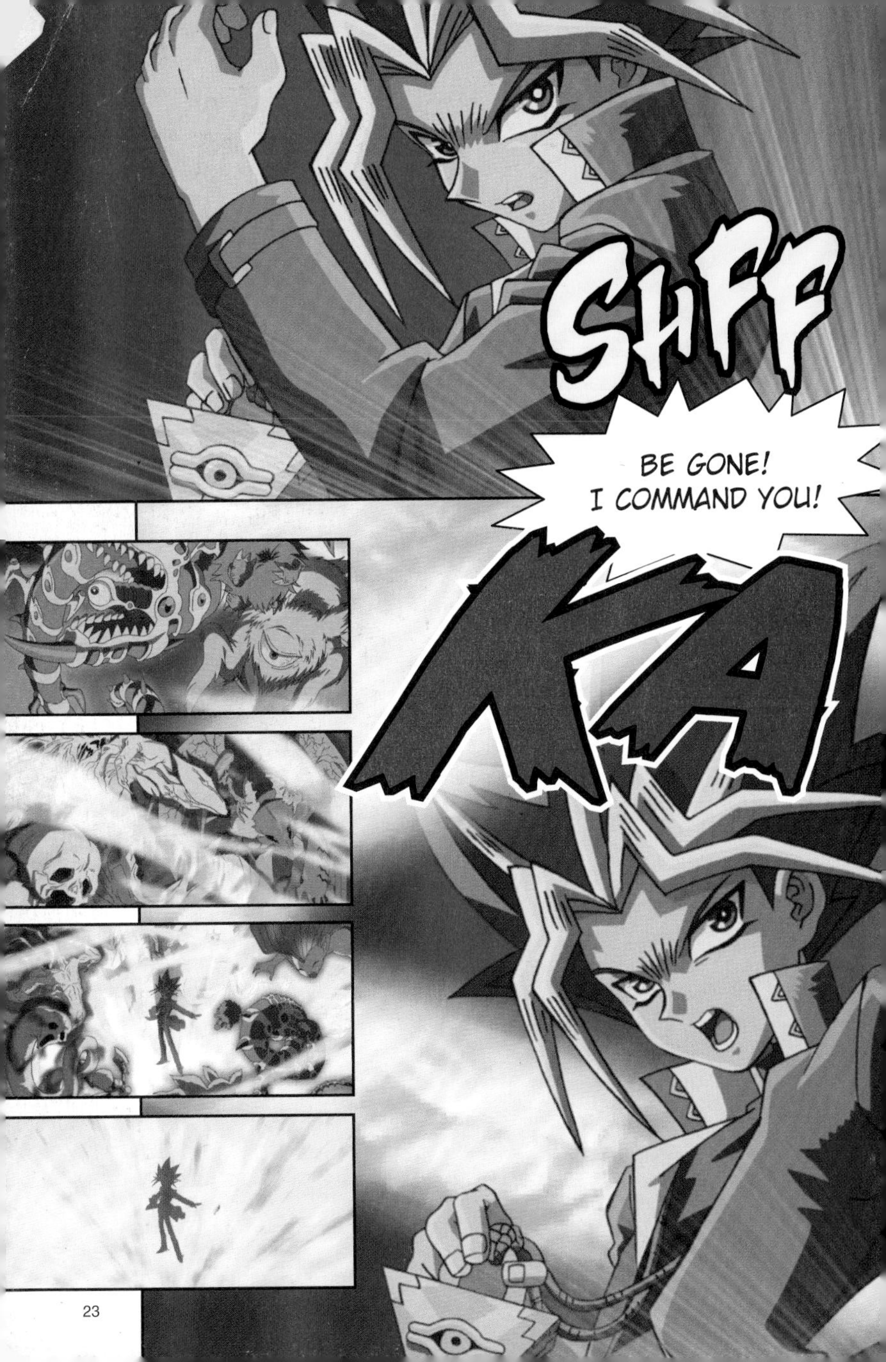
SHFF
BE GONE!
I COMMAND YOU!
KA

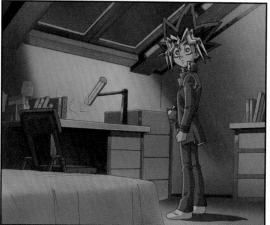

IT WAS NEVER TO HAPPEN. BUT AFTER 5,000 YEARS, IT DID. AND WITH IT... THE SHADOW GAMES BEGIN AGAIN.

?

READ THIS WAY

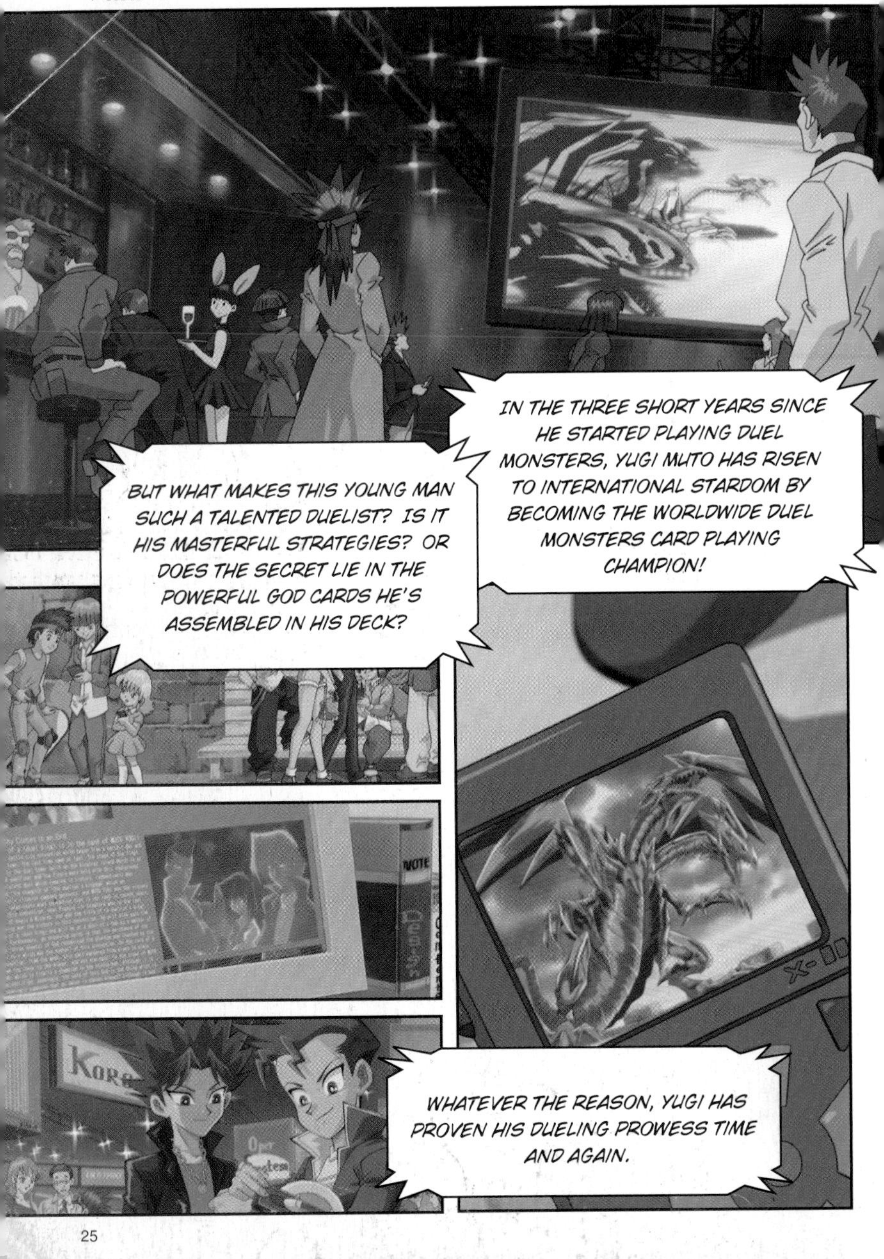
IN THE THREE SHORT YEARS SINCE HE STARTED PLAYING DUEL MONSTERS, YUGI MUTO HAS RISEN TO INTERNATIONAL STARDOM BY BECOMING THE WORLDWIDE DUEL MONSTERS CARD PLAYING CHAMPION!
BUT WHAT MAKES THIS YOUNG MAN SUCH A TALENTED DUELIST? IS IT HIS MASTERFUL STRATEGIES? OR DOES THE SECRET LIE IN THE POWERFUL GOD CARDS HE'S ASSEMBLED IN HIS DECK?
WHATEVER THE REASON, YUGI HAS PROVEN HIS DUELING PROWESS TIME AND AGAIN.

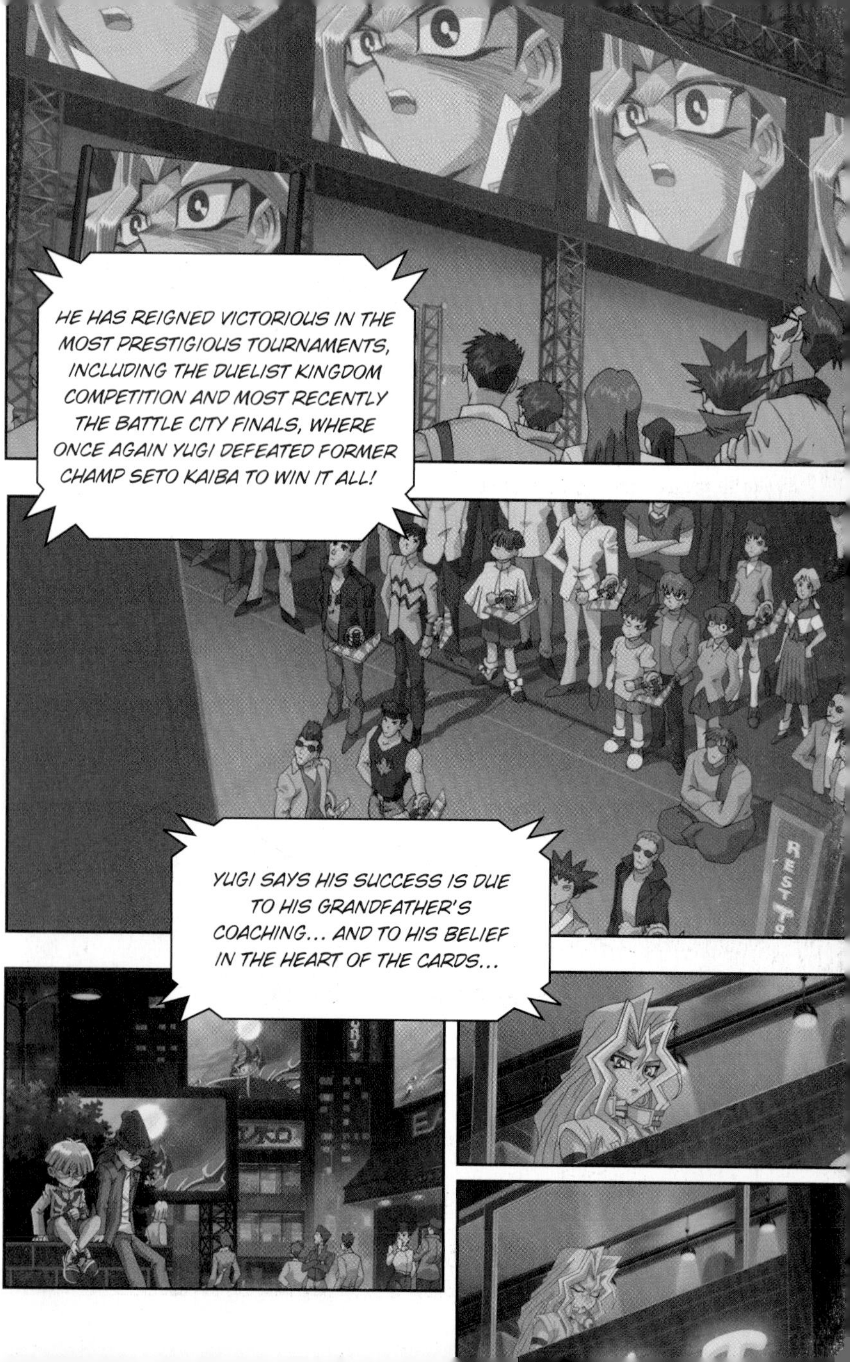
HE HAS REIGNED VICTORIOUS IN THE MOST PRESTIGIOUS TOURNAMENTS, INCLUDING THE DUELIST KINGDOM COMPETITION AND MOST RECENTLY THE BATTLE CITY FINALS, WHERE ONCE AGAIN YUGI DEFEATED FORMER CHAMP SETO KAIBA TO WIN IT ALL!
YUGI SAYS HIS SUCCESS IS DUE TO HIS GRANDFATHER'S COACHING... AND TO HIS BELIEF IN THE HEART OF THE CARDS...

READ THIS WAY

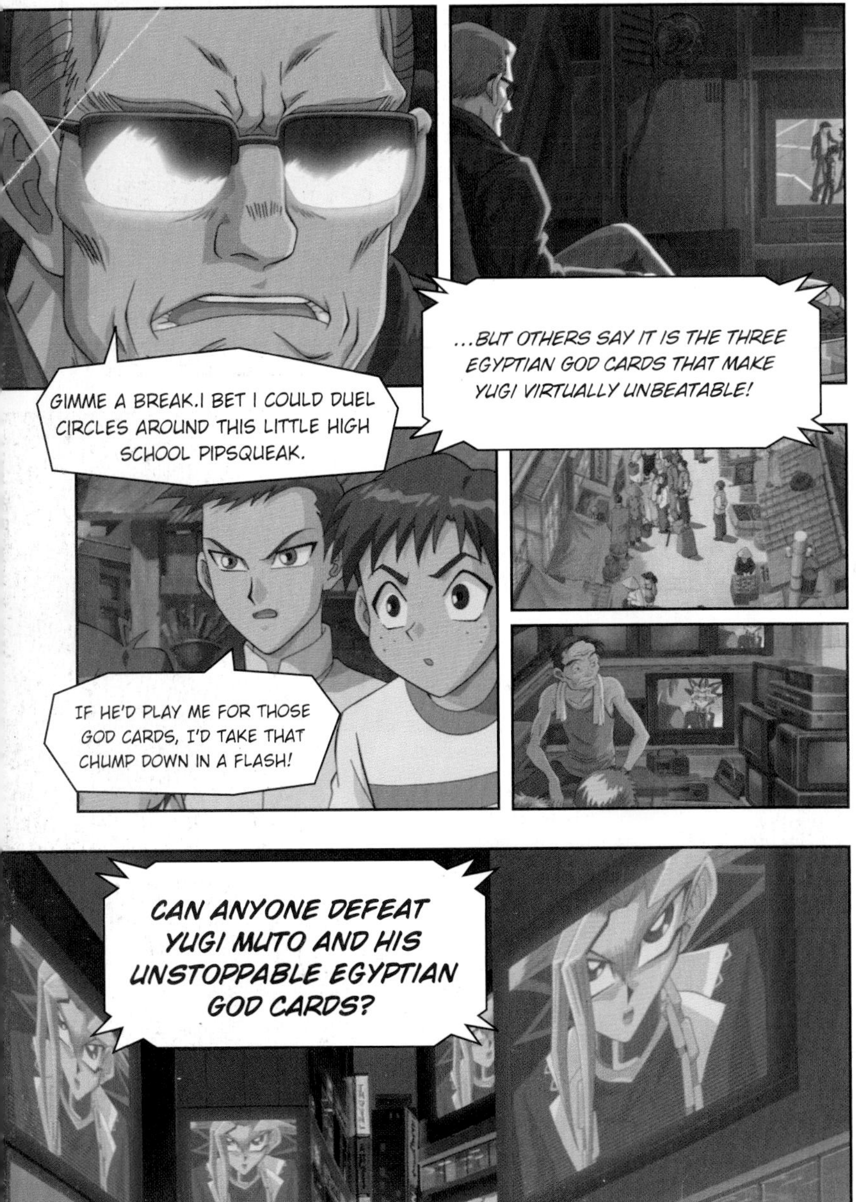
...BUT OTHERS SAY IT IS THE THREE EGYPTIAN GOD CARDS THAT MAKE YUGI VIRTUALLY UNBEATABLE!
GIMME A BREAK. I BET I COULD DUEL CIRCLES AROUND THIS LITTLE HIGH SCHOOL PIPSQUEAK.
IF HE'D PLAY ME FOR THOSE GOD CARDS, I'D TAKE THAT CHUMP DOWN IN A FLASH!
CAN ANYONE DEFEAT YUGI MUTO AND HIS UNSTOPPABLE EGYPTIAN GOD CARDS?

READ THIS WAY

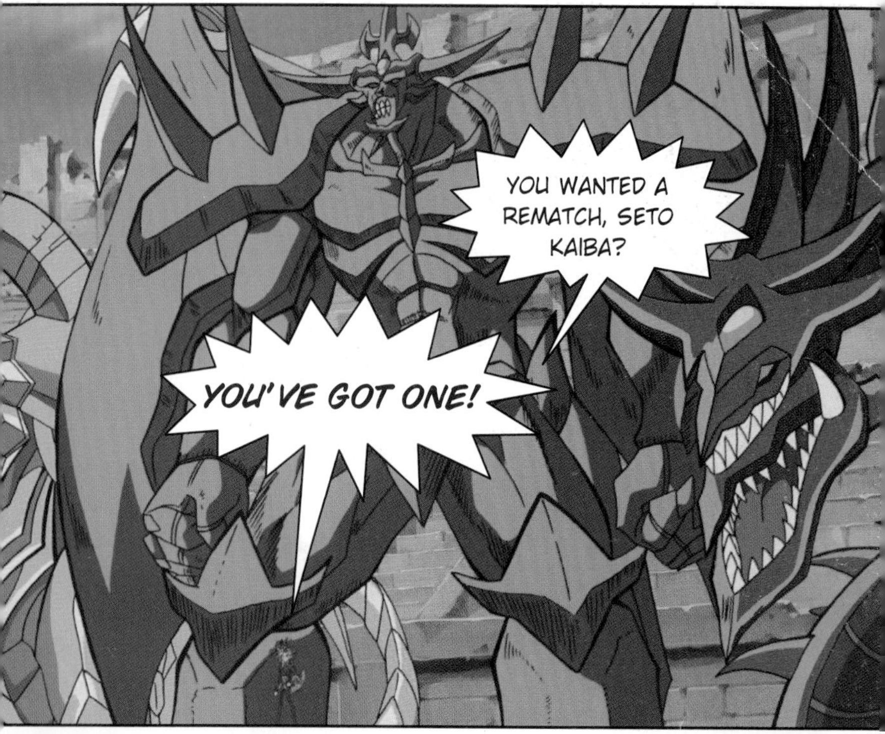
YOU WANTED A REMATCH, SETO KAIBA?
YOU'VE GOT ONE!

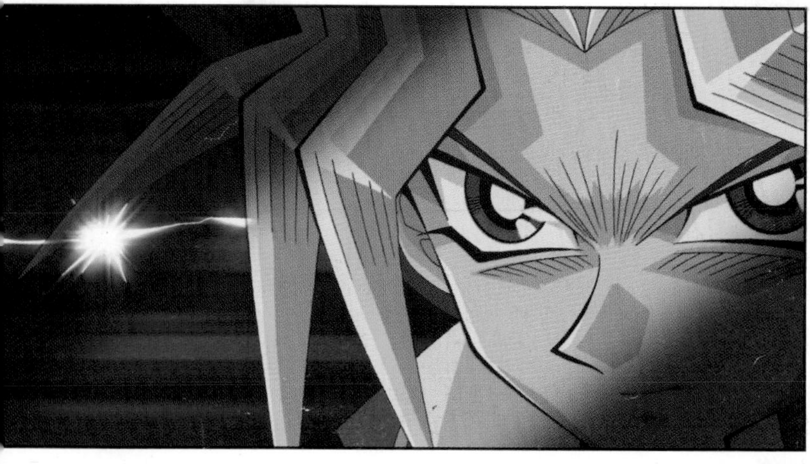

READ THIS WAY

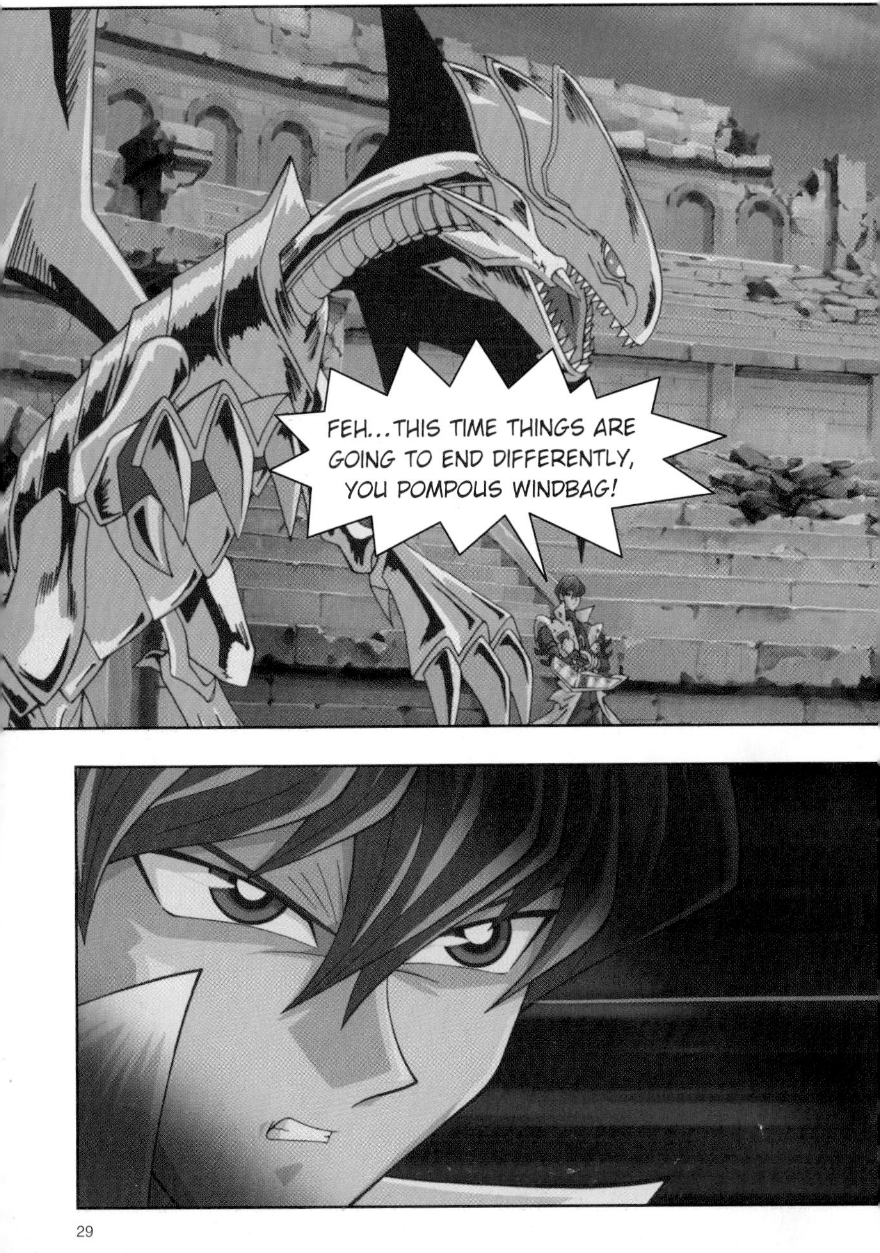
FEH...THIS TIME THINGS ARE GOING TO END DIFFERENTLY, YOU POMPOUS WINDBAG!

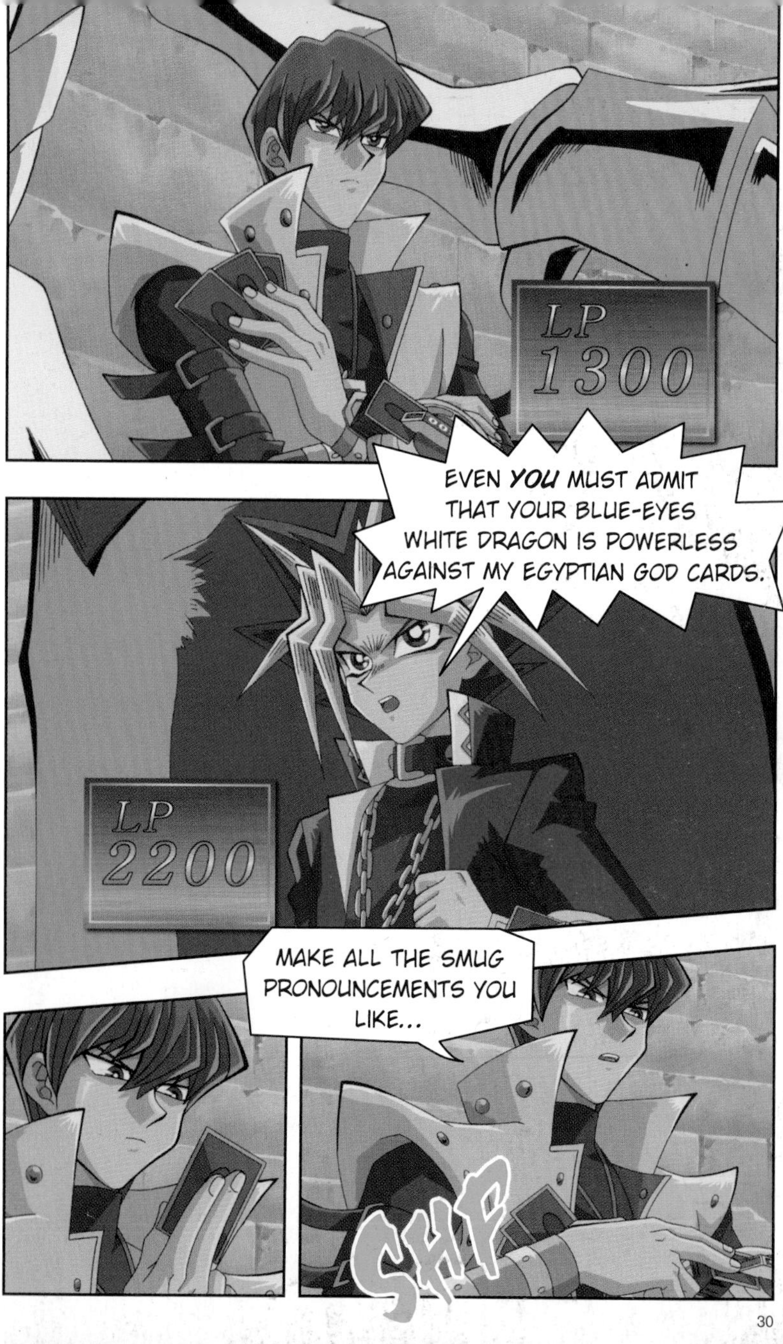
LP 1300
EVEN ***YOU*** MUST ADMIT THAT YOUR BLUE-EYES WHITE DRAGON IS POWERLESS AGAINST MY EGYPTIAN GOD CARDS.
LP 2200
MAKE ALL THE SMUG PRONOUNCEMENTS YOU LIKE...
SHP

READ THIS WAY

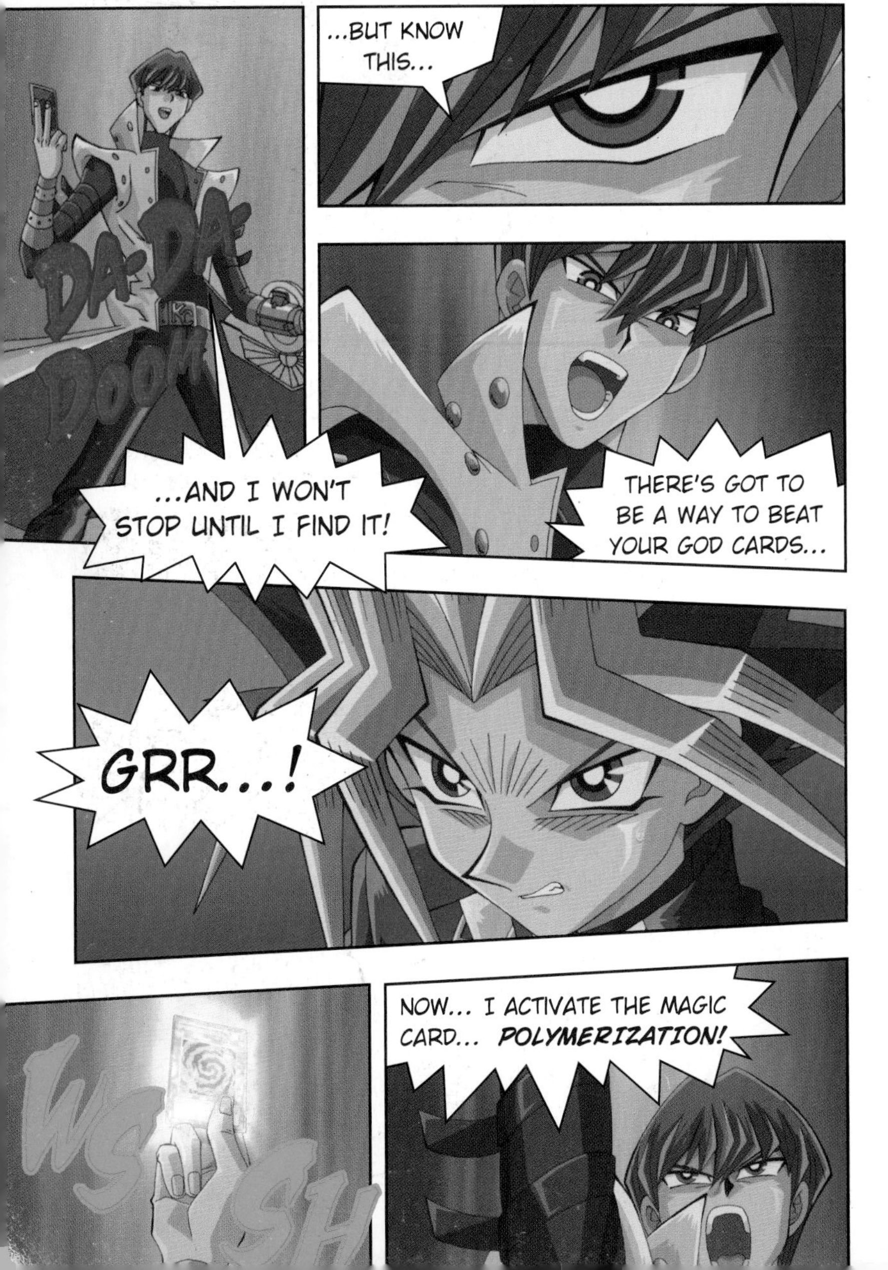
...BUT KNOW THIS...
THERE'S GOT TO BE A WAY TO BEAT YOUR GOD CARDS...
...AND I WON'T STOP UNTIL I FIND IT!
DA-DA-DOOM
GRR...!
NOW... I ACTIVATE THE MAGIC CARD... ***POLYMERIZATION!***

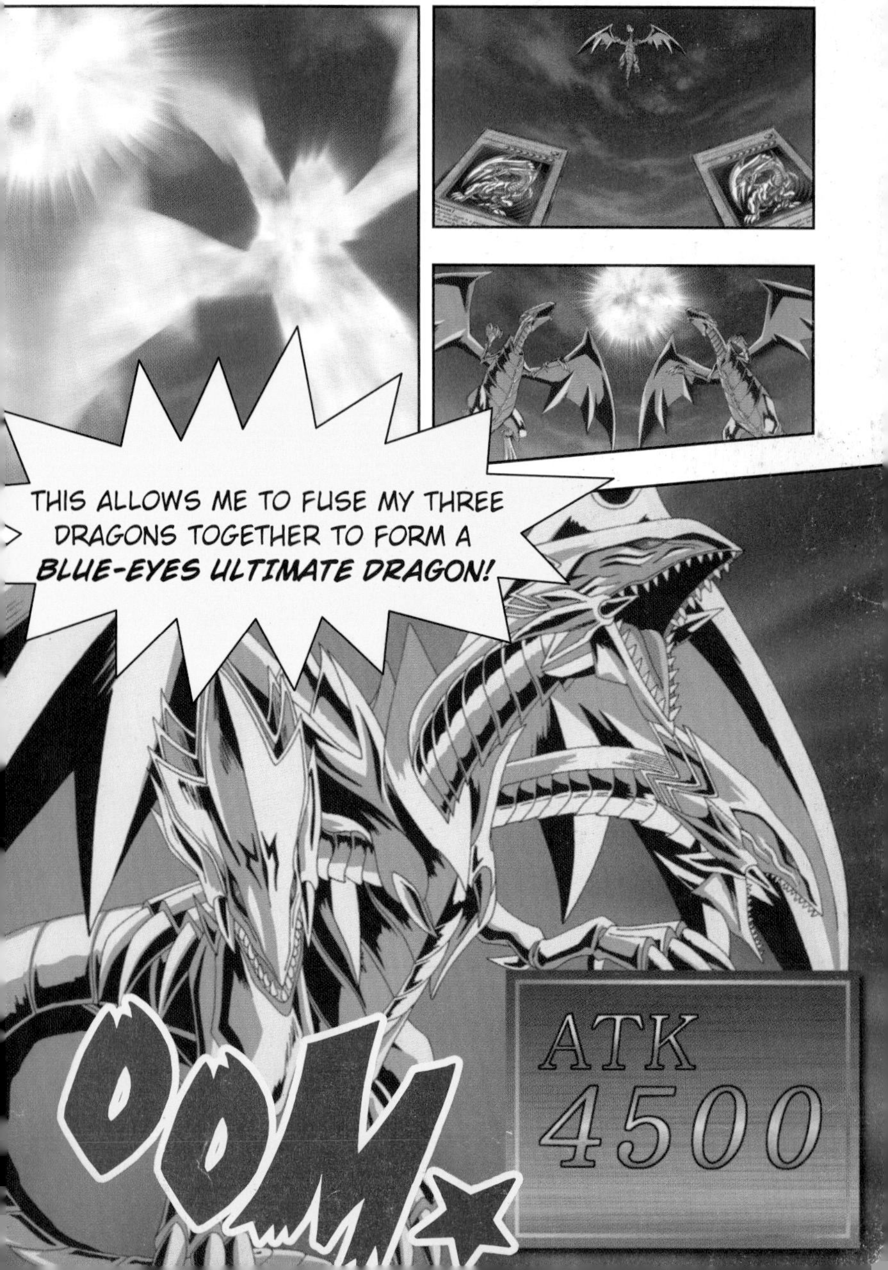
READ THIS WAY
THIS ALLOWS ME TO FUSE MY THREE DRAGONS TOGETHER TO FORM A *BLUE-EYES ULTIMATE DRAGON!*
ATK 4500

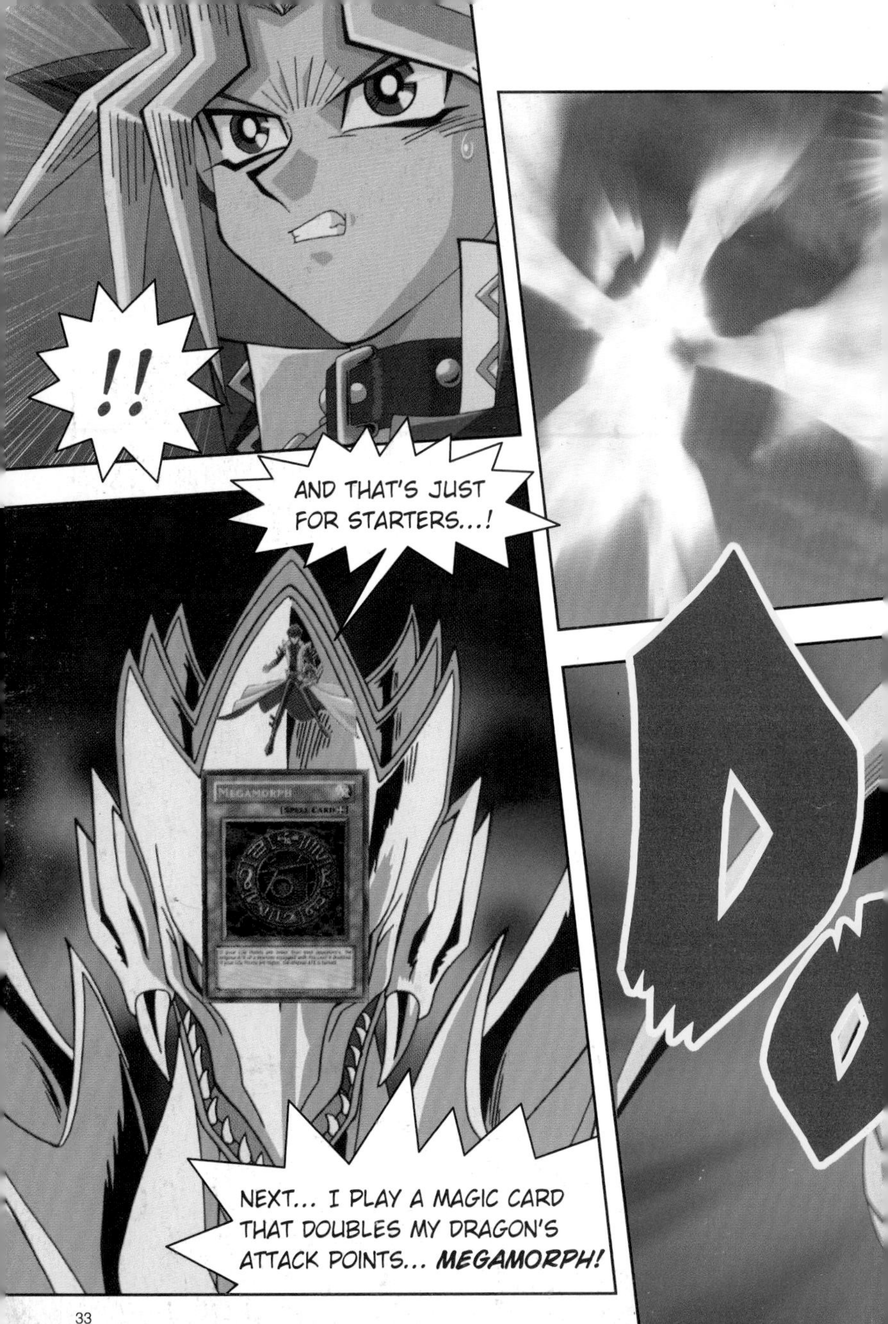
!!
AND THAT'S JUST FOR STARTERS...!
NEXT... I PLAY A MAGIC CARD THAT DOUBLES MY DRAGON'S ATTACK POINTS... MEGAMORPH!

READ THIS WAY

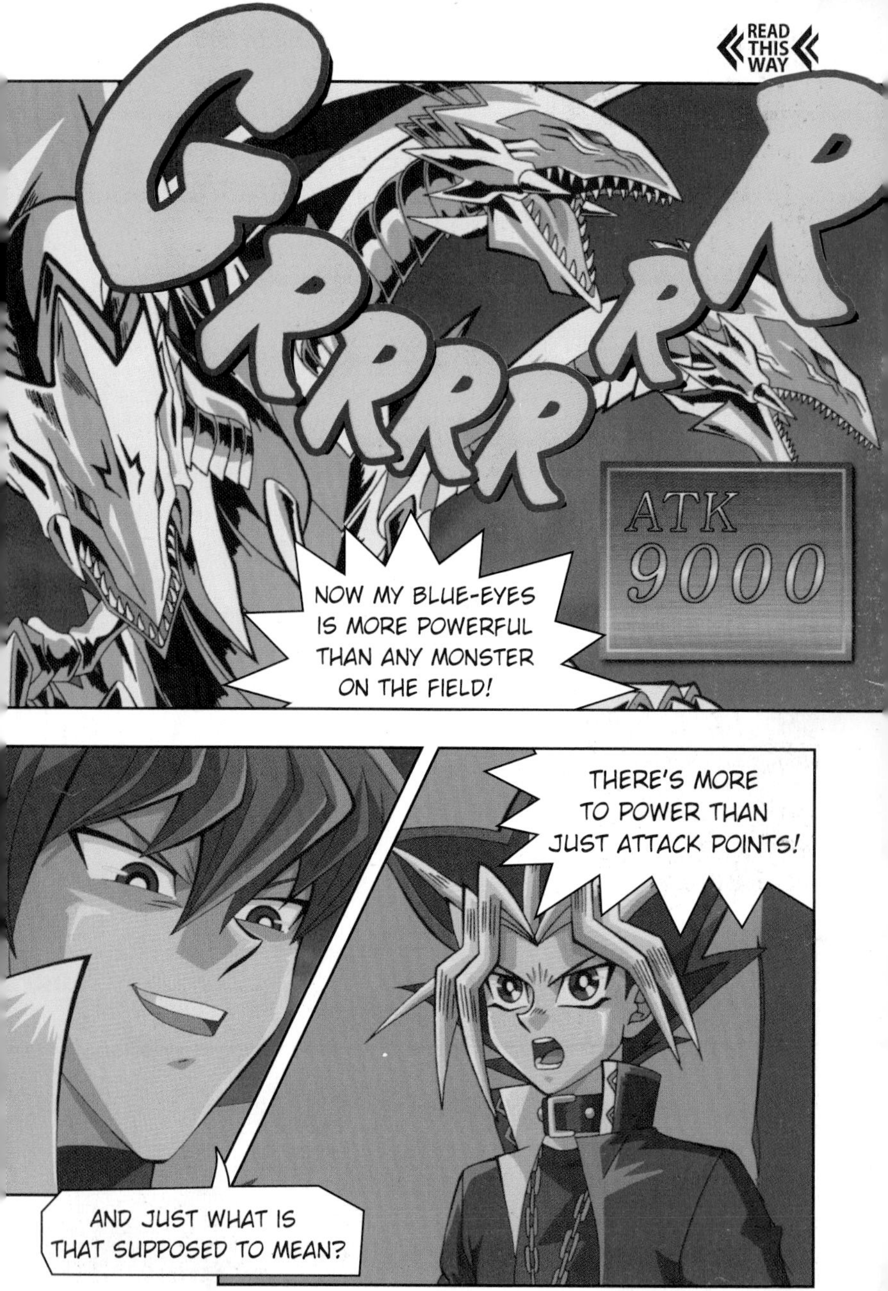
CRRRRRR
ATK 9000
NOW MY BLUE-EYES IS MORE POWERFUL THAN ANY MONSTER ON THE FIELD!
THERE'S MORE TO POWER THAN JUST ATTACK POINTS!
AND JUST WHAT IS THAT SUPPOSED TO MEAN?

READ THIS WAY

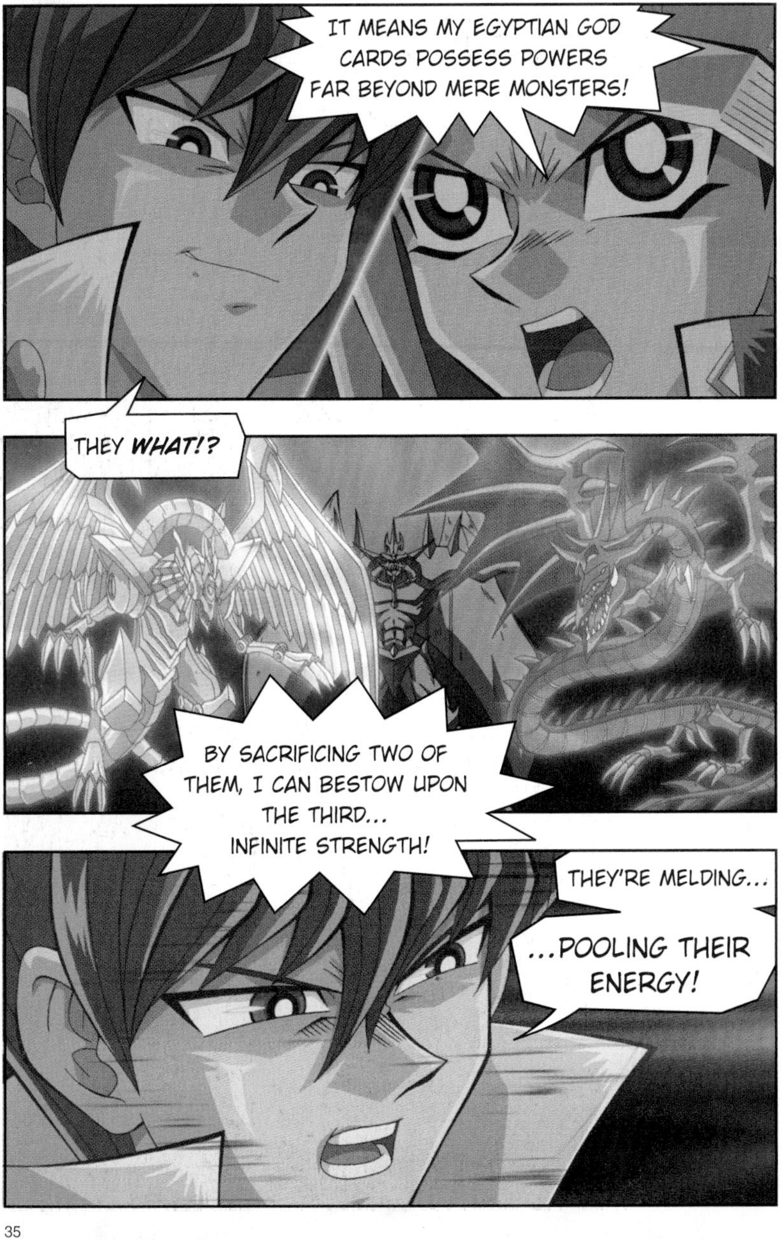
IT MEANS MY EGYPTIAN GOD CARDS POSSESS POWERS FAR BEYOND MERE MONSTERS!
THEY *WHAT!?*
BY SACRIFICING TWO OF THEM, I CAN BESTOW UPON THE THIRD... INFINITE STRENGTH!
THEY'RE MELDING...
...POOLING THEIR ENERGY!

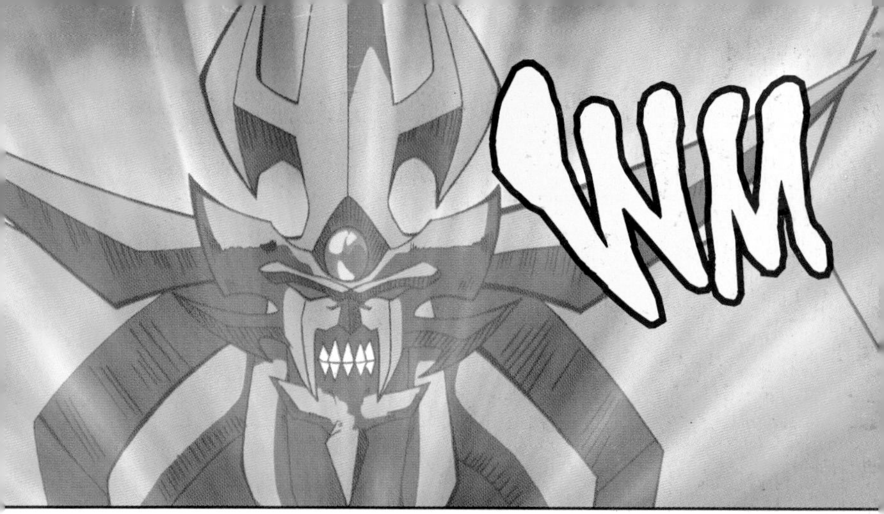
WM

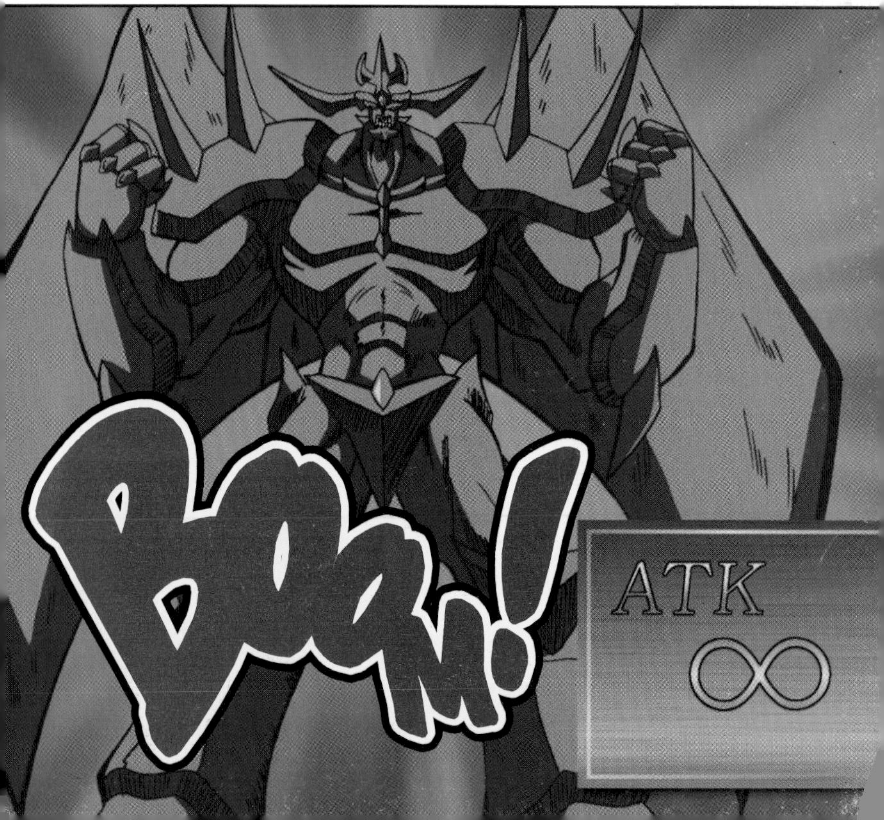
BOOM!
ATK
∞

READ THIS WAY

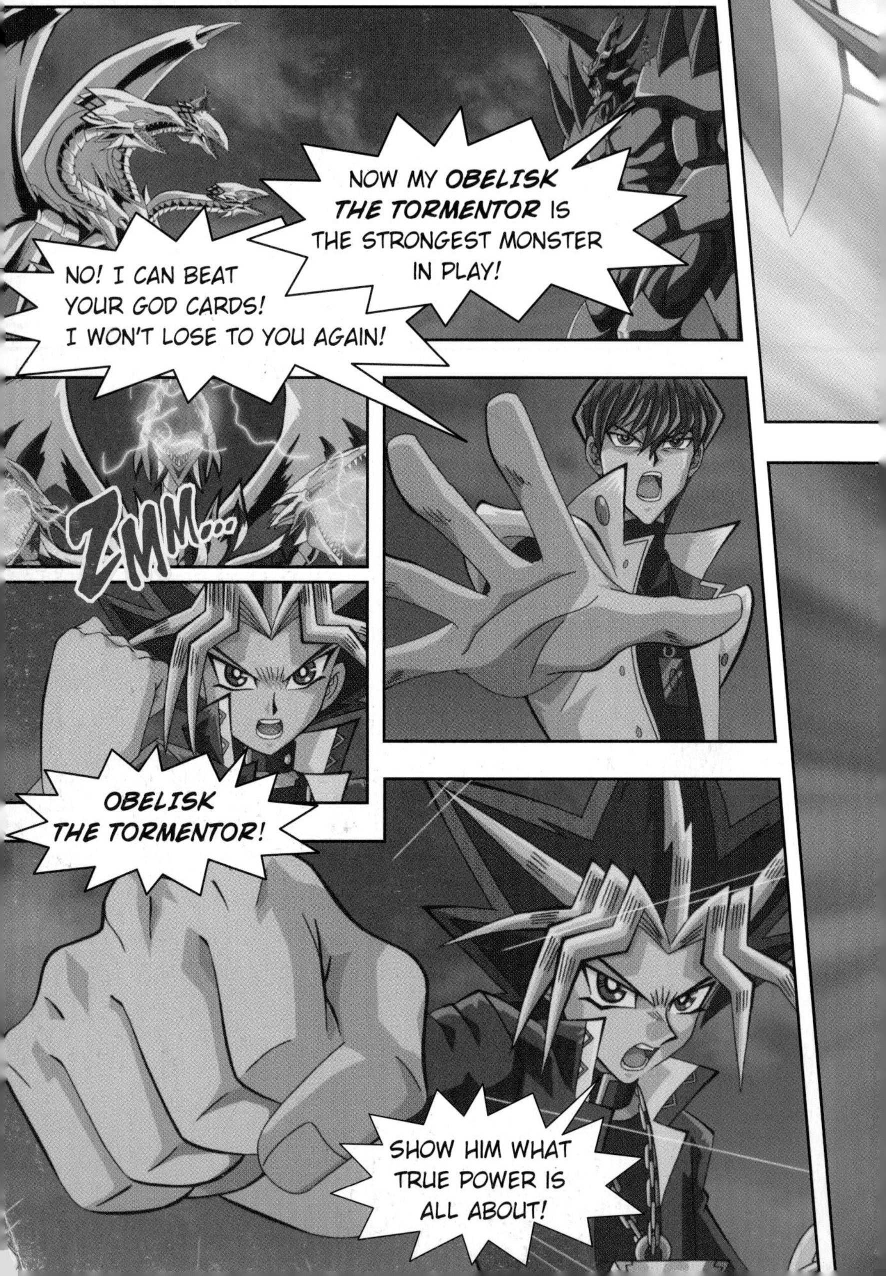
NOW MY *OBELISK THE TORMENTOR* IS THE STRONGEST MONSTER IN PLAY!
NO! I CAN BEAT YOUR GOD CARDS! I WON'T LOSE TO YOU AGAIN!
ZMM...
OBELISK THE TORMENTOR!
SHOW HIM WHAT TRUE POWER IS ALL ABOUT!

READ THIS WAY

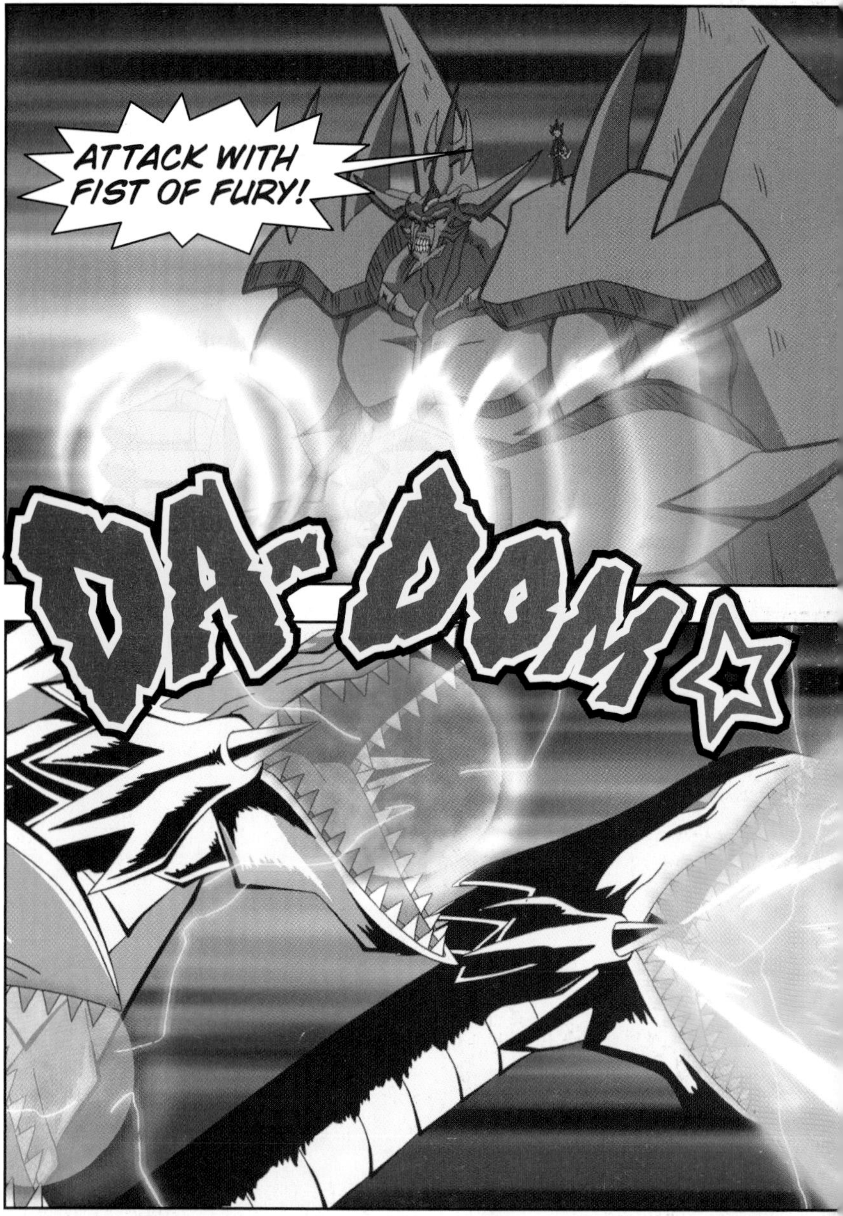
ATTACK WITH FIST OF FURY!
DA-DOOM

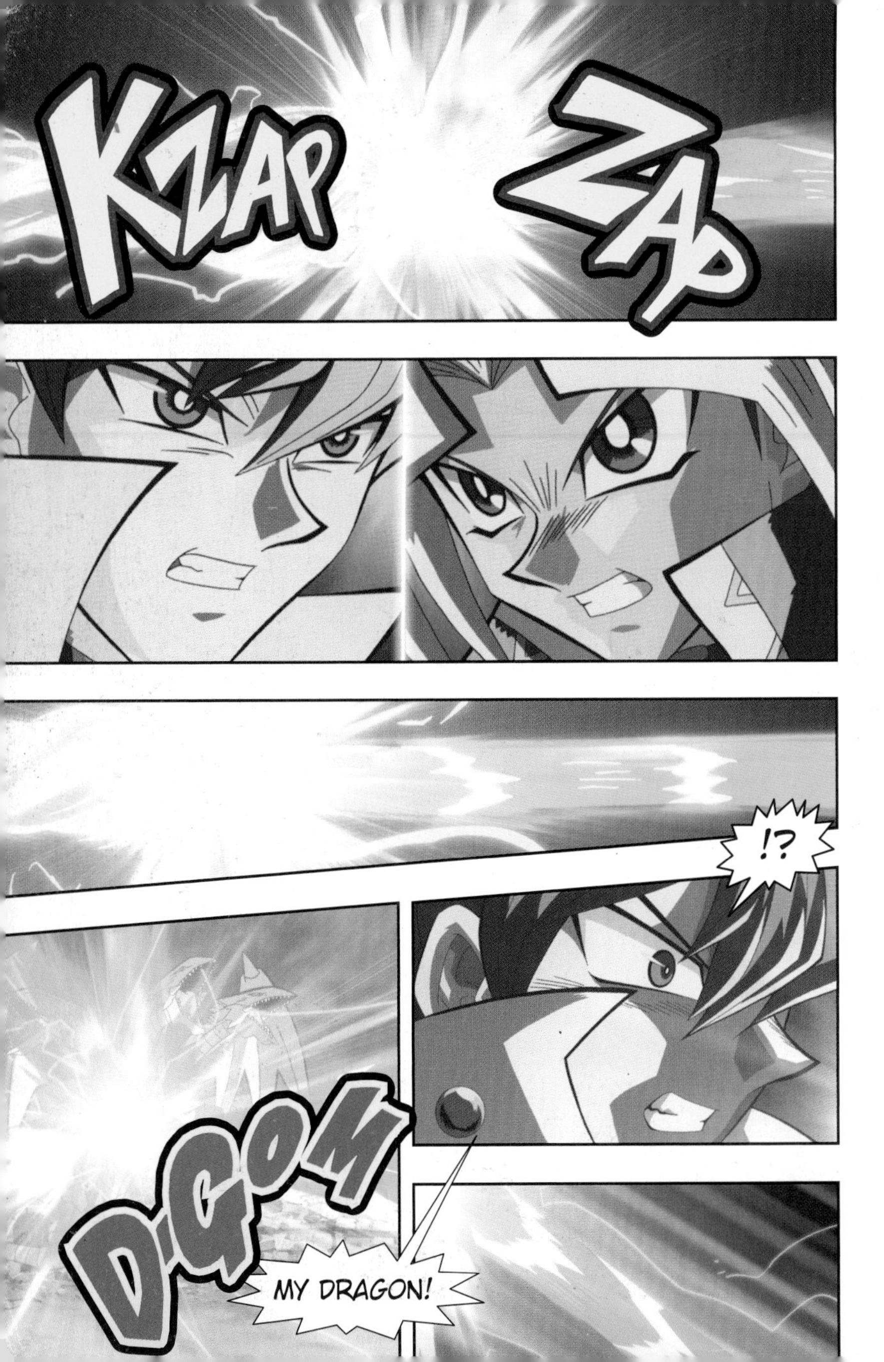
ZAP
KZZAP
!?
D-GOM
MY DRAGON!

READ THIS WAY

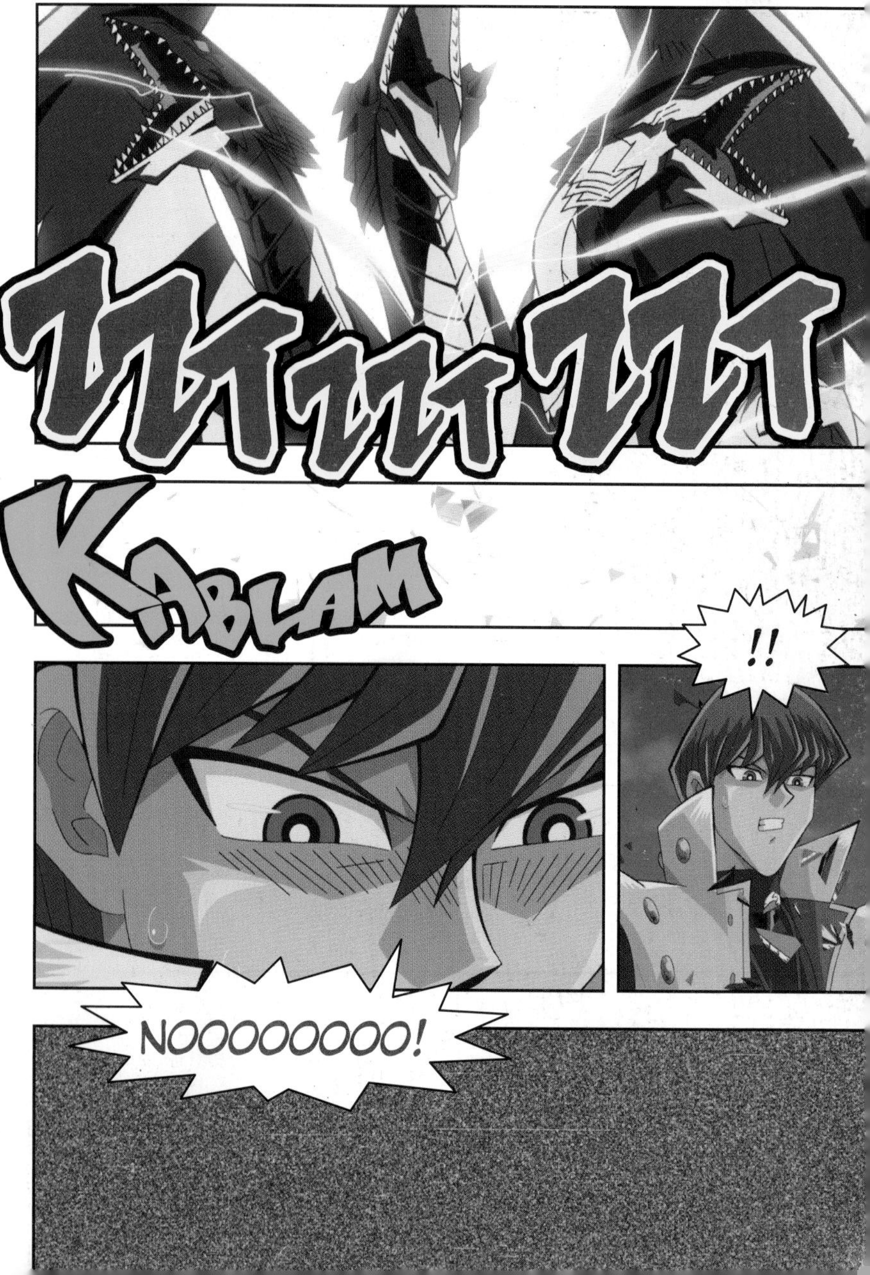
KABLAM
!!
NOOOOOOOO!

READ THIS WAY

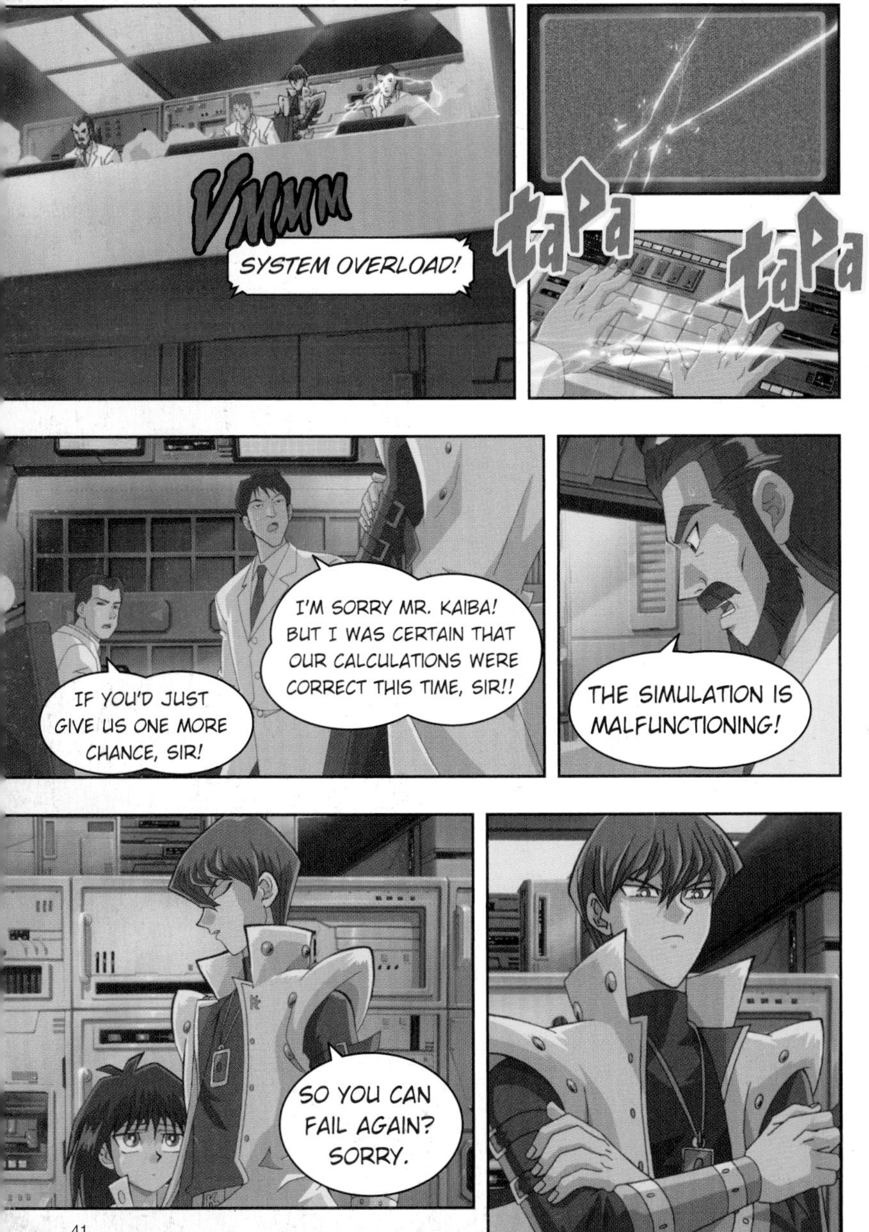

taPa
taPa
VMMM
SYSTEM OVERLOAD!
THE SIMULATION IS MALFUNCTIONING!
I'M SORRY MR. KAIBA! BUT I WAS CERTAIN THAT OUR CALCULATIONS WERE CORRECT THIS TIME, SIR!!
IF YOU'D JUST GIVE US ONE MORE CHANCE, SIR!
SO YOU CAN FAIL AGAIN? SORRY.

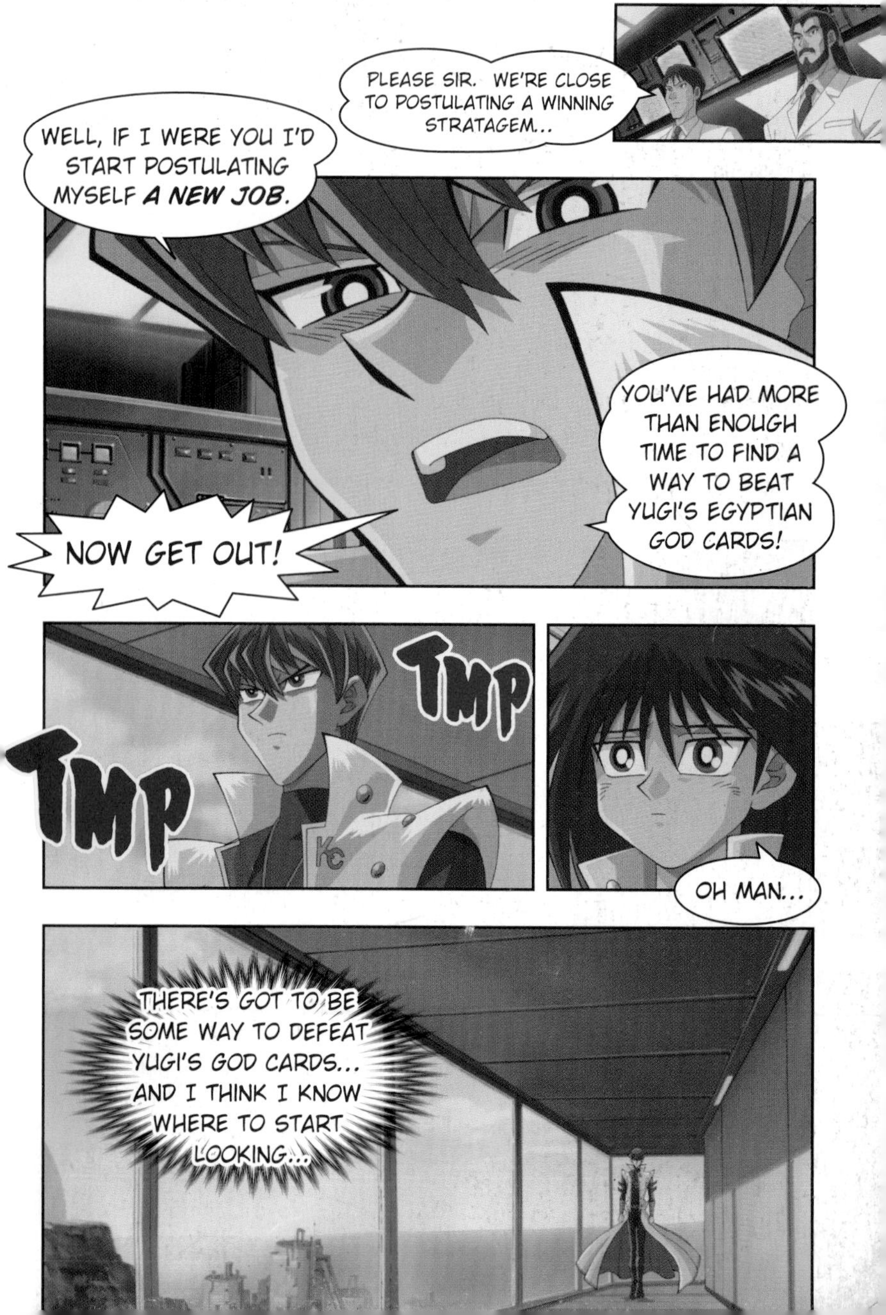
PLEASE SIR. WE'RE CLOSE TO POSTULATING A WINNING STRATAGEM...
WELL, IF I WERE YOU I'D START POSTULATING MYSELF A NEW JOB.
YOU'VE HAD MORE THAN ENOUGH TIME TO FIND A WAY TO BEAT YUGI'S EGYPTIAN GOD CARDS!
NOW GET OUT!
OH MAN...
TMP
TMP
THERE'S GOT TO BE SOME WAY TO DEFEAT YUGI'S GOD CARDS... AND I THINK I KNOW WHERE TO START LOOKING...

READ THIS WAY

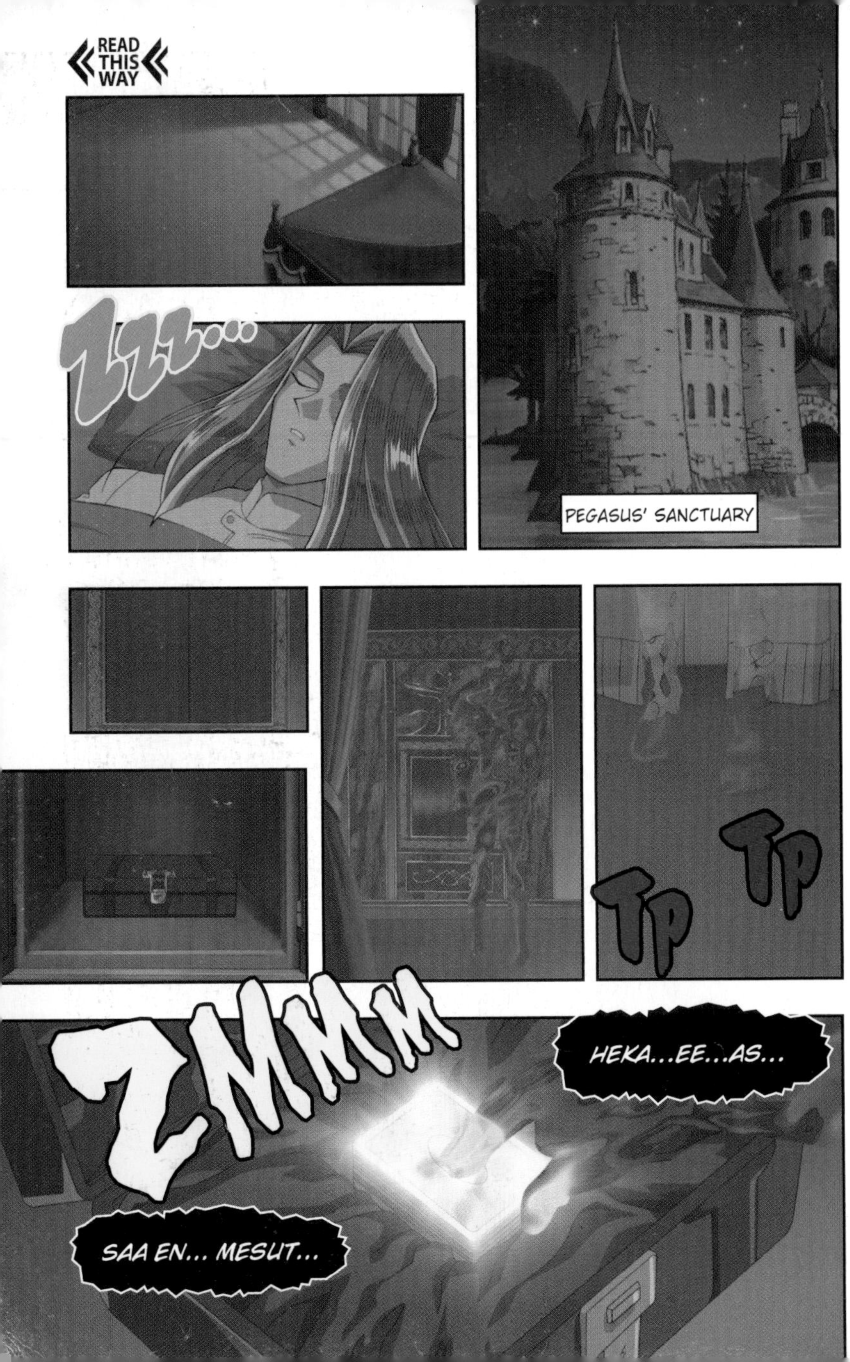
PEGASUS' SANCTUARY
ZZZ...
TP
TP
HEKA...EE...AS...
ZMMM
SAA EN... MESUT...

READ THIS WAY

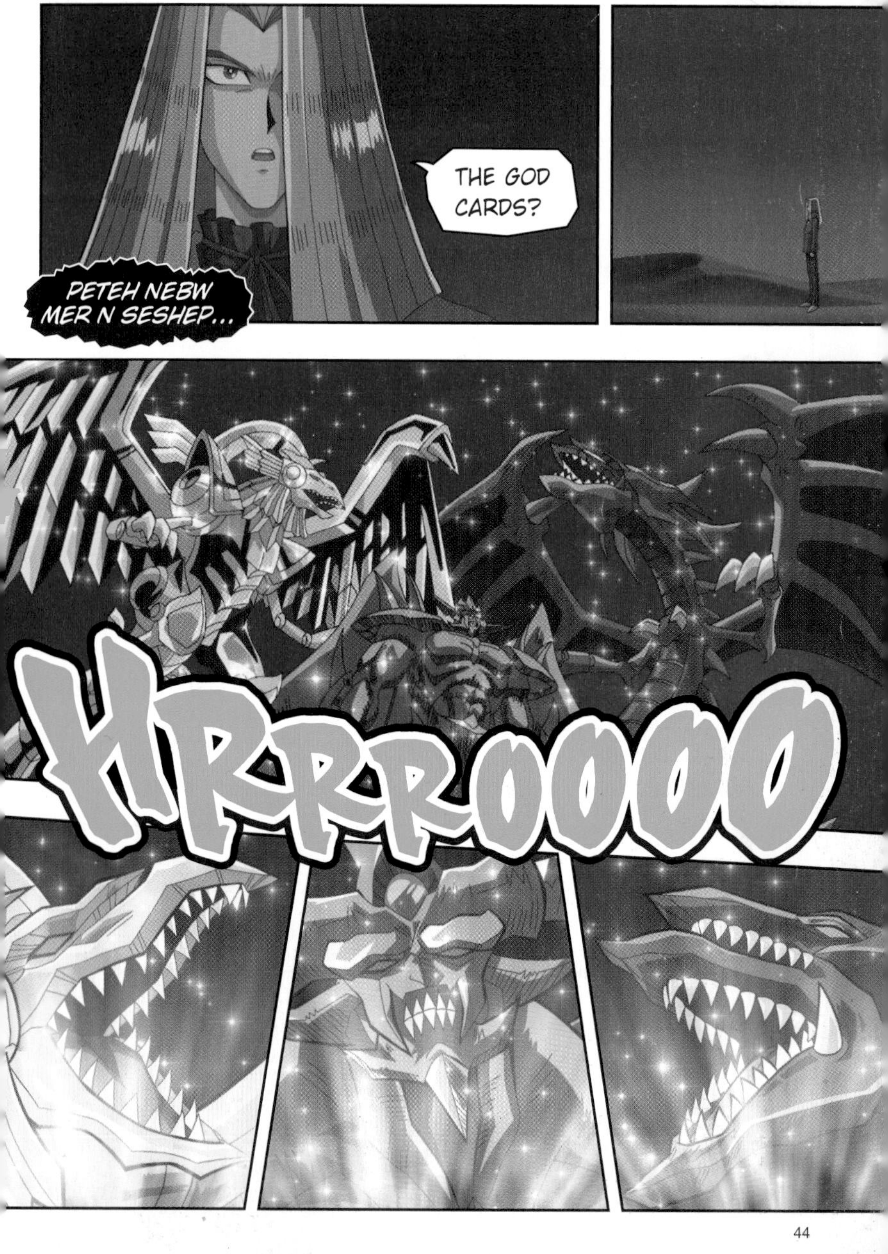

THE GOD CARDS?
PETEH NEBW MER N SESHEP...
HRRROOOO

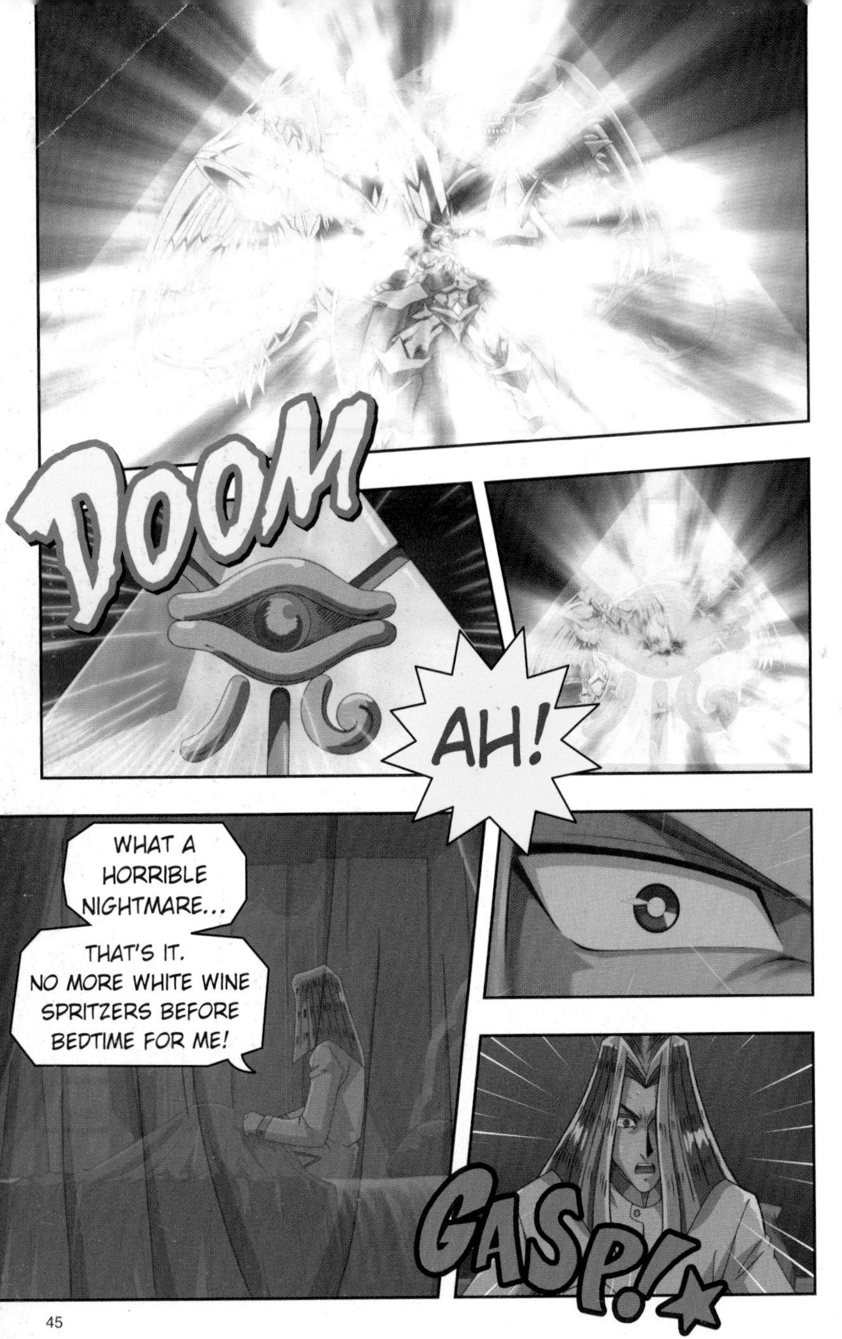
DOOM
AH!
GASP!
WHAT A HORRIBLE NIGHTMARE...
THAT'S IT. NO MORE WHITE WINE SPRITZERS BEFORE BEDTIME FOR ME!

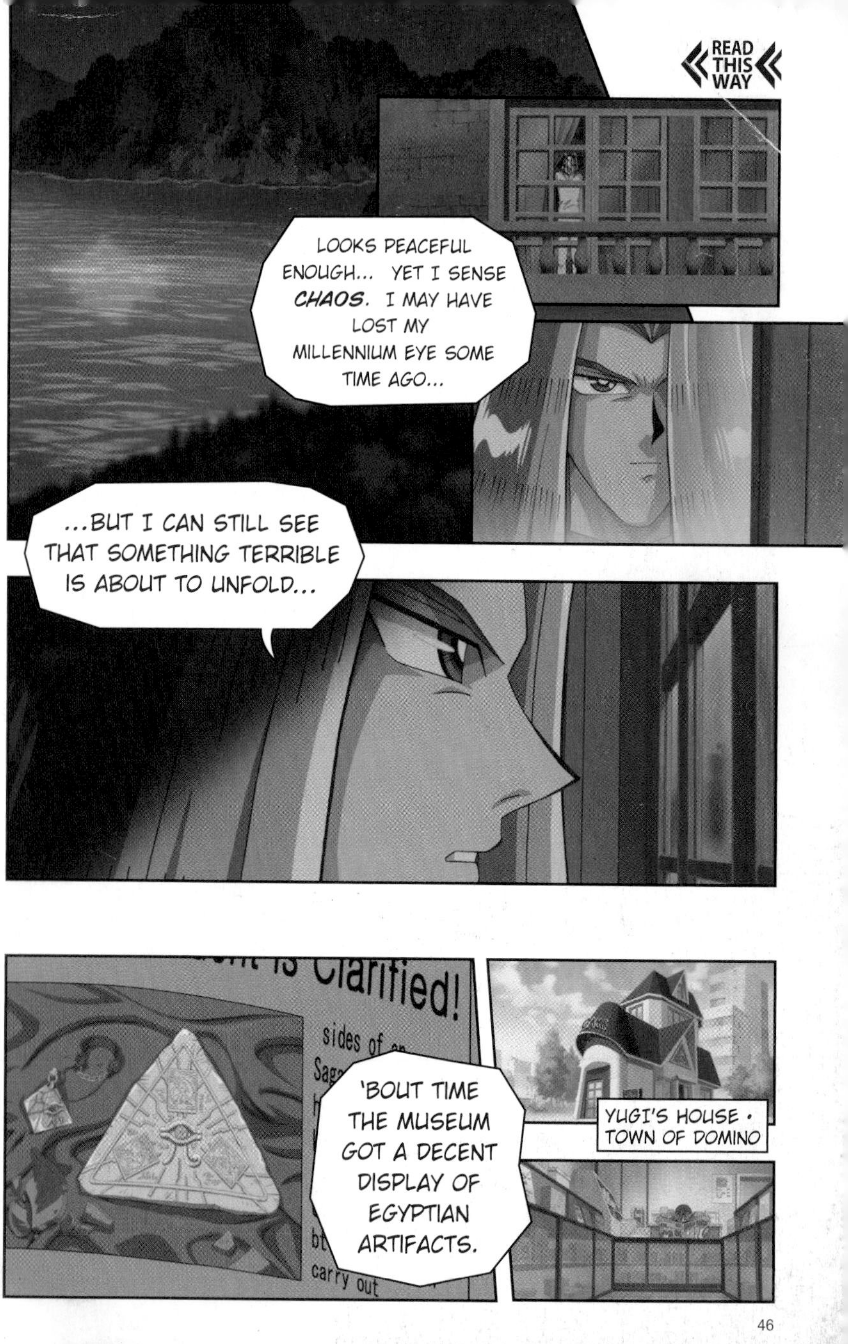
READ THIS WAY
LOOKS PEACEFUL ENOUGH... YET I SENSE *CHAOS*. I MAY HAVE LOST MY MILLENNIUM EYE SOME TIME AGO...
...BUT I CAN STILL SEE THAT SOMETHING TERRIBLE IS ABOUT TO UNFOLD...
YUGI'S HOUSE • TOWN OF DOMINO
'BOUT TIME THE MUSEUM GOT A DECENT DISPLAY OF EGYPTIAN ARTIFACTS.
Clarified!
sides of an
carry out

READ THIS WAY

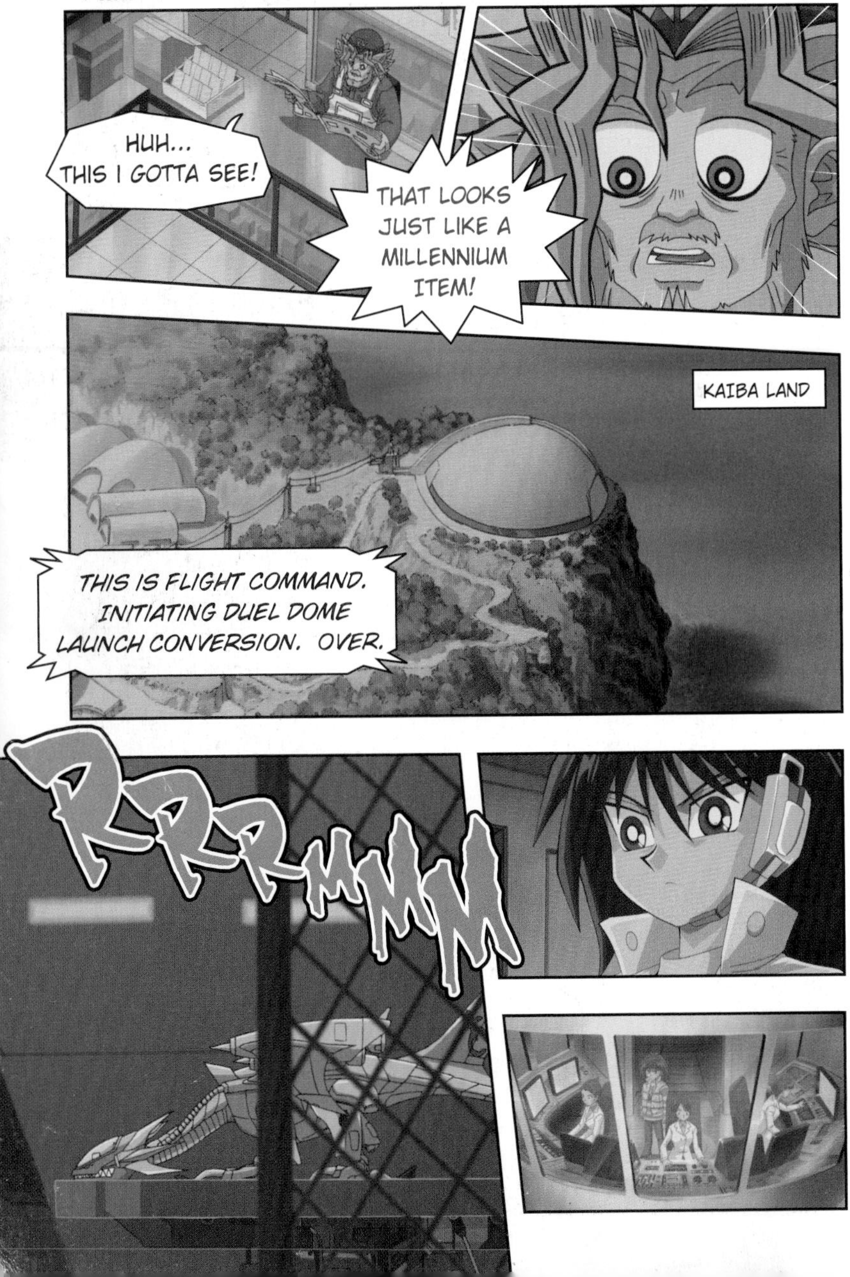
THAT LOOKS JUST LIKE A MILLENNIUM ITEM!
HUH... THIS I GOTTA SEE!
KAIBA LAND
THIS IS FLIGHT COMMAND. INITIATING DUEL DOME LAUNCH CONVERSION. OVER.
RRRMMM

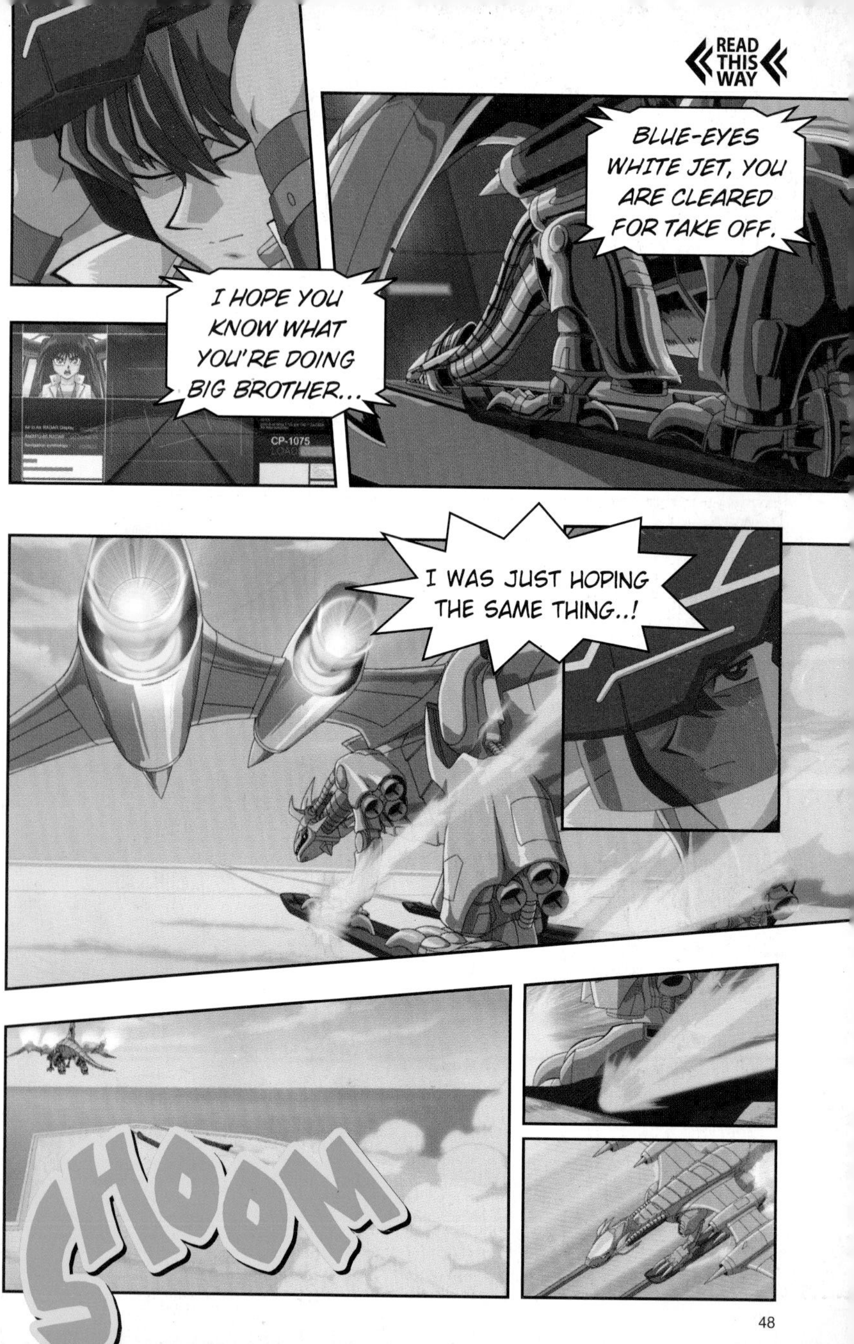
READ THIS WAY
BLUE-EYES WHITE JET, YOU ARE CLEARED FOR TAKE OFF.
I HOPE YOU KNOW WHAT YOU'RE DOING BIG BROTHER...
CP-1075
I WAS JUST HOPING THE SAME THING..!
SHOOM

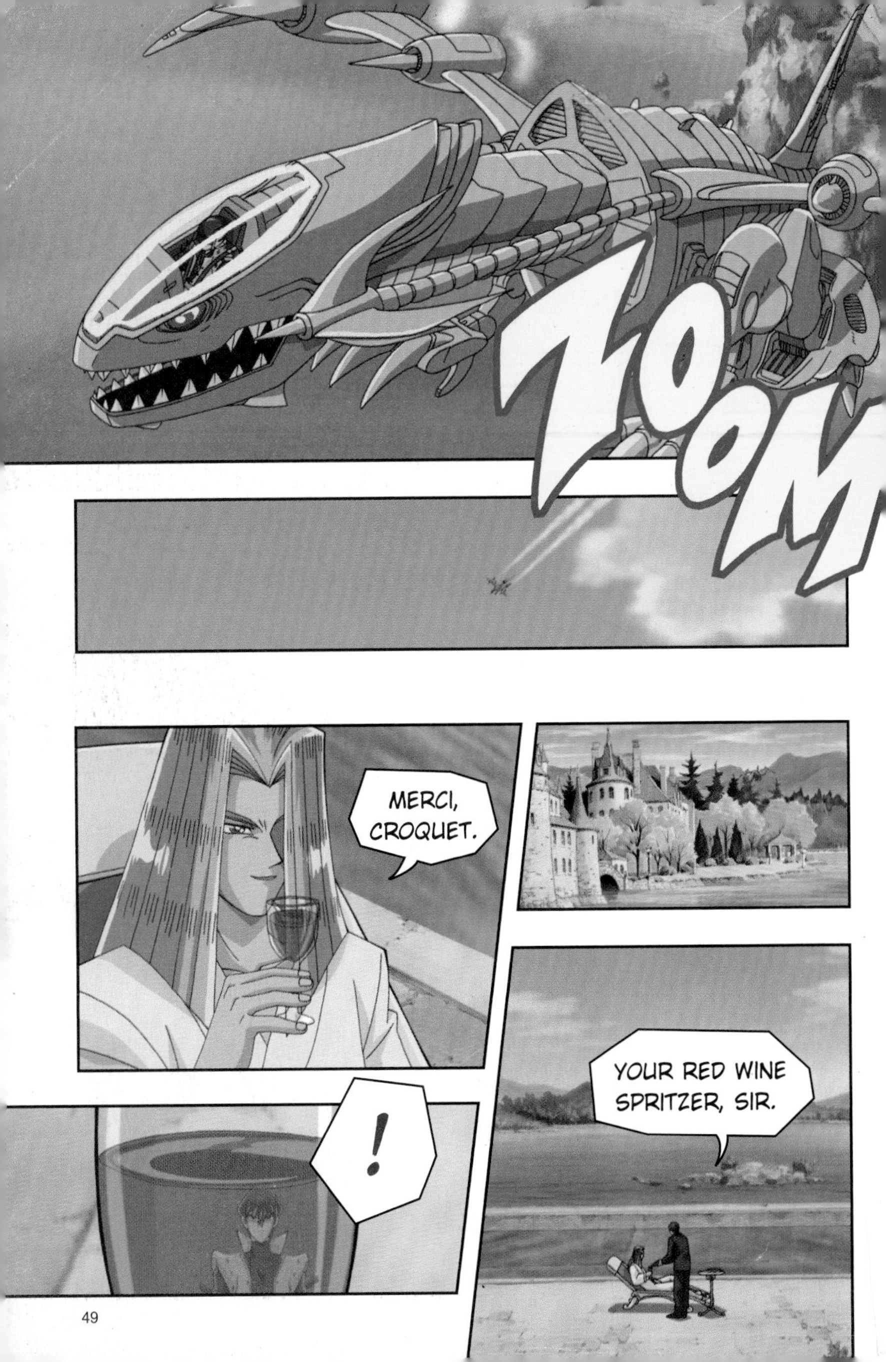
ZOOM
YOUR RED WINE SPRITZER, SIR.
MERCI, CROQUET.
!

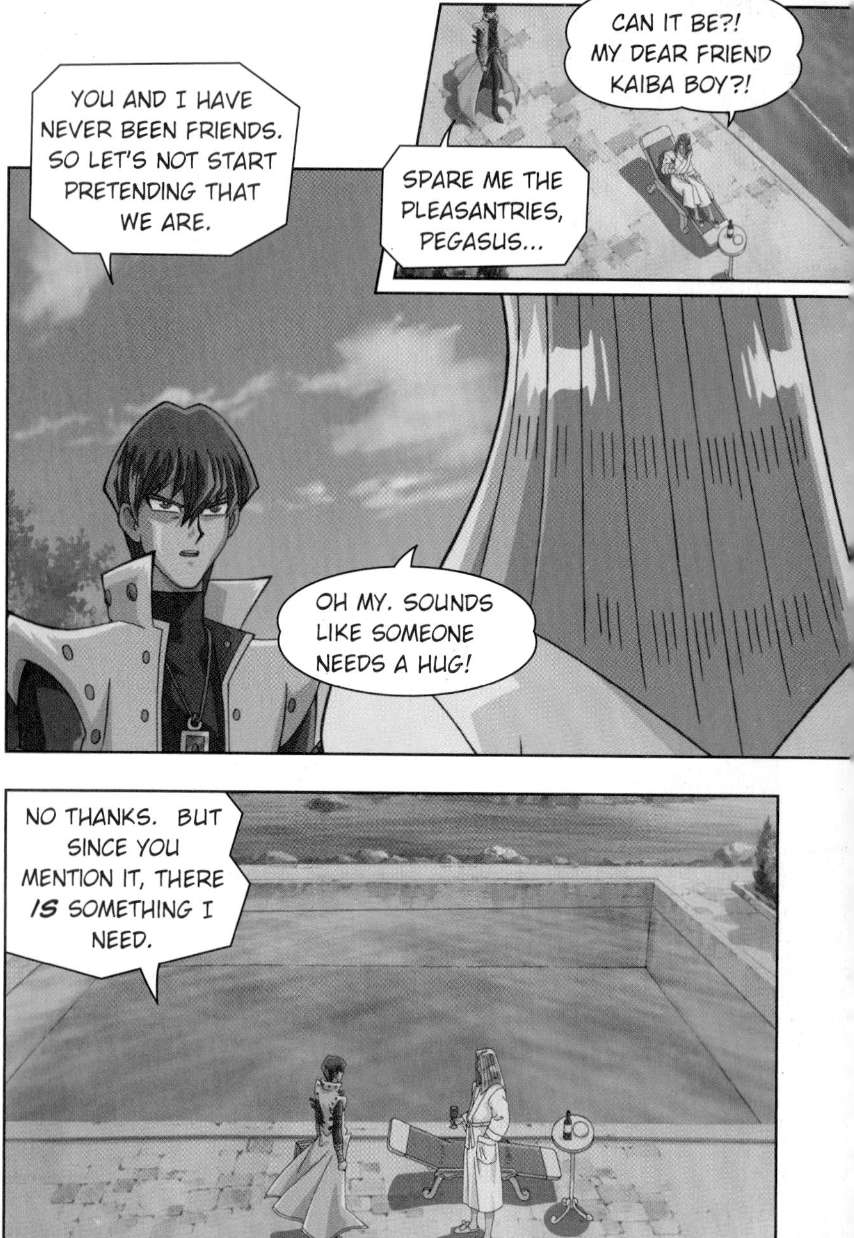
CAN IT BE?! MY DEAR FRIEND KAIBA BOY?!
SPARE ME THE PLEASANTRIES, PEGASUS...
YOU AND I HAVE NEVER BEEN FRIENDS. SO LET'S NOT START PRETENDING THAT WE ARE.
OH MY. SOUNDS LIKE SOMEONE NEEDS A HUG!
NO THANKS. BUT SINCE YOU MENTION IT, THERE *IS* SOMETHING I NEED.

READ THIS WAY

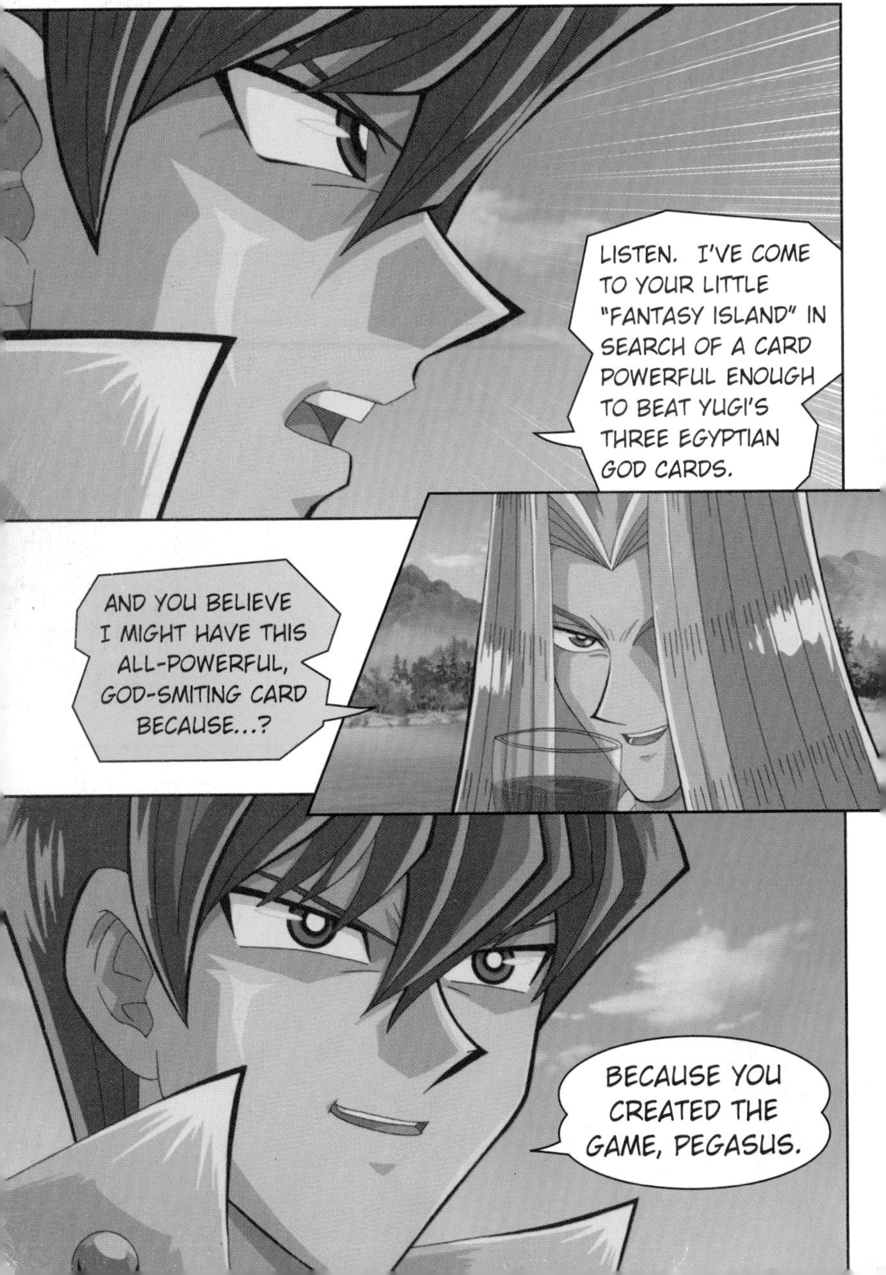
LISTEN. I'VE COME TO YOUR LITTLE "FANTASY ISLAND" IN SEARCH OF A CARD POWERFUL ENOUGH TO BEAT YUGI'S THREE EGYPTIAN GOD CARDS.
AND YOU BELIEVE I MIGHT HAVE THIS ALL-POWERFUL, GOD-SMITING CARD BECAUSE...?
BECAUSE YOU CREATED THE GAME, PEGASUS.

READ THIS WAY

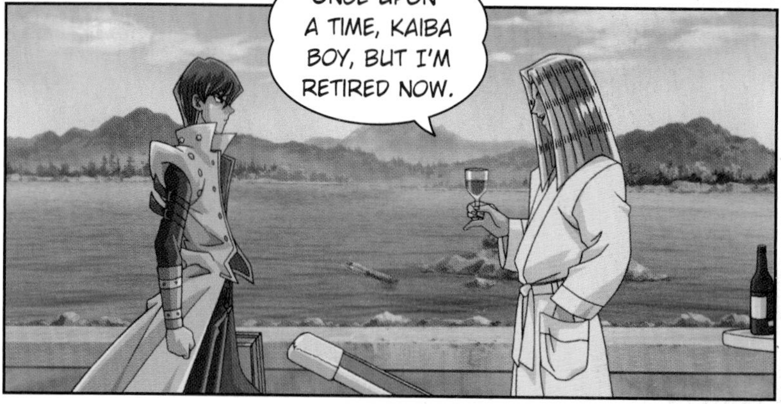
ONCE UPON A TIME, KAIBA BOY, BUT I'M RETIRED NOW.

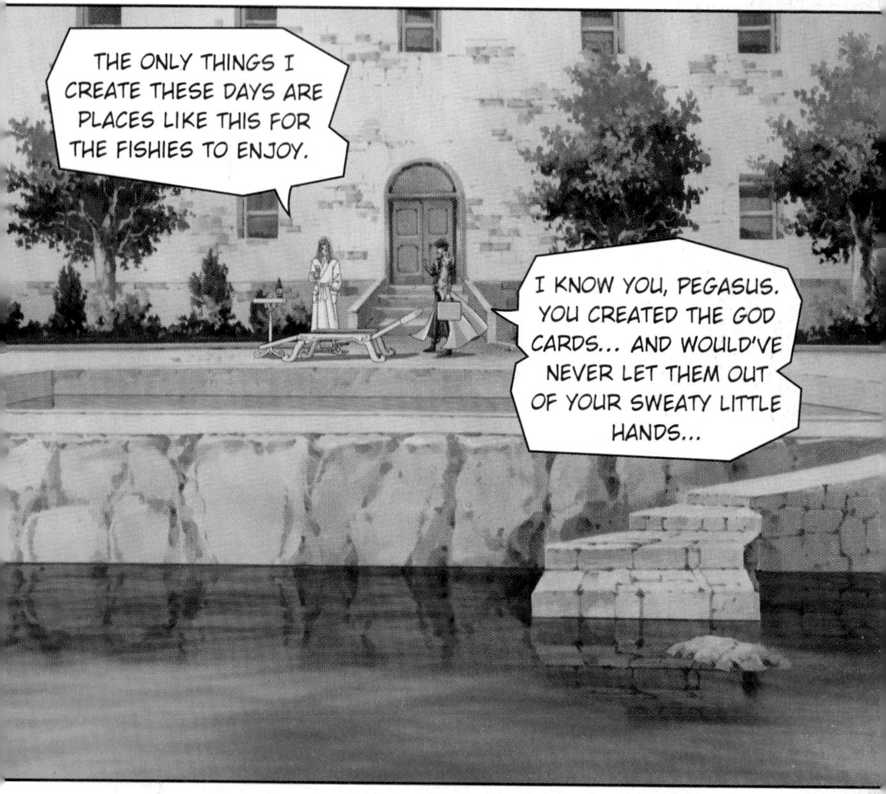
THE ONLY THINGS I CREATE THESE DAYS ARE PLACES LIKE THIS FOR THE FISHIES TO ENJOY.
I KNOW YOU, PEGASUS. YOU CREATED THE GOD CARDS... AND WOULD'VE NEVER LET THEM OUT OF YOUR SWEATY LITTLE HANDS...

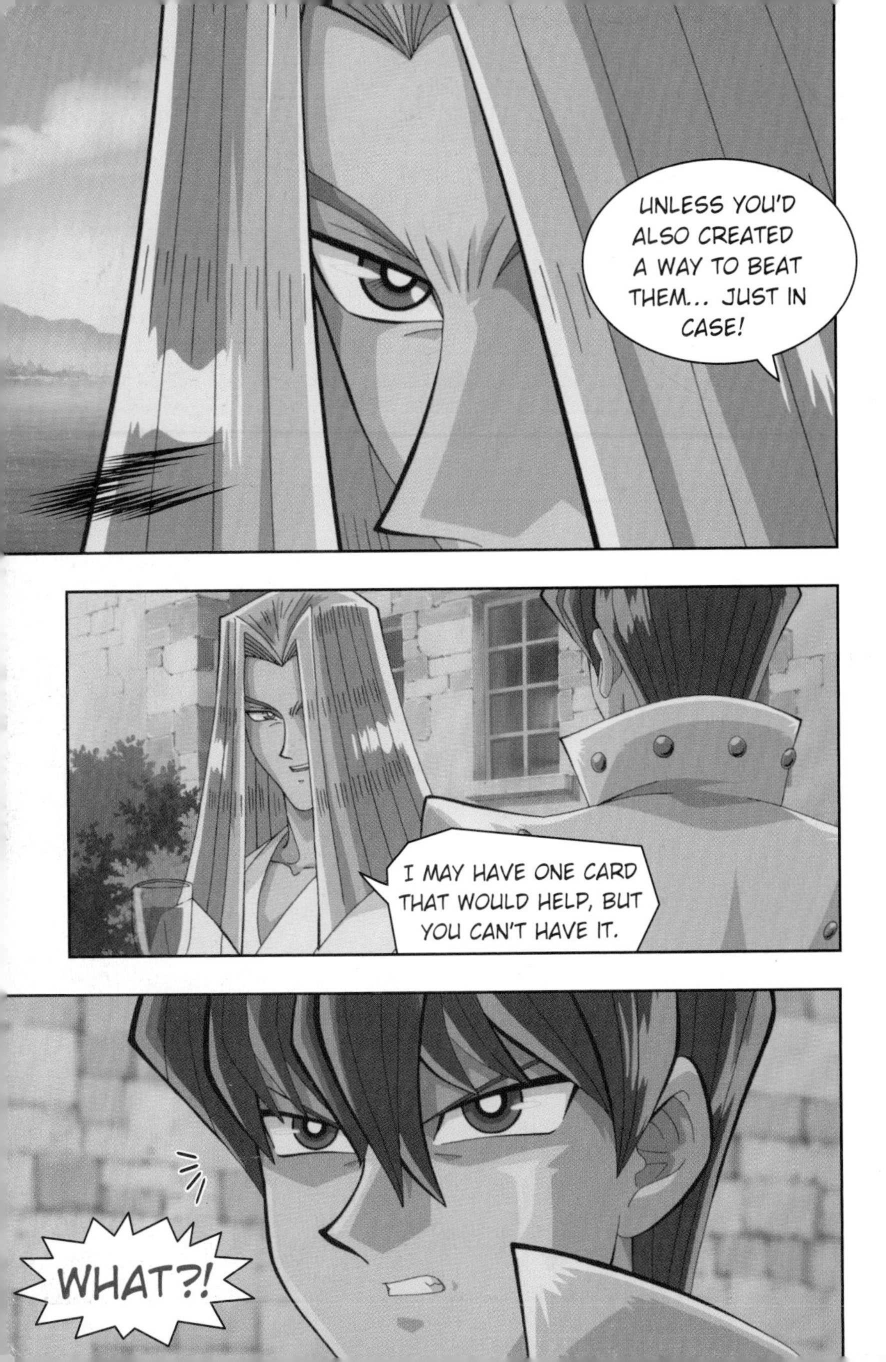
UNLESS YOU'D ALSO CREATED A WAY TO BEAT THEM... JUST IN CASE!
I MAY HAVE ONE CARD THAT WOULD HELP, BUT YOU CAN'T HAVE IT.
WHAT?!

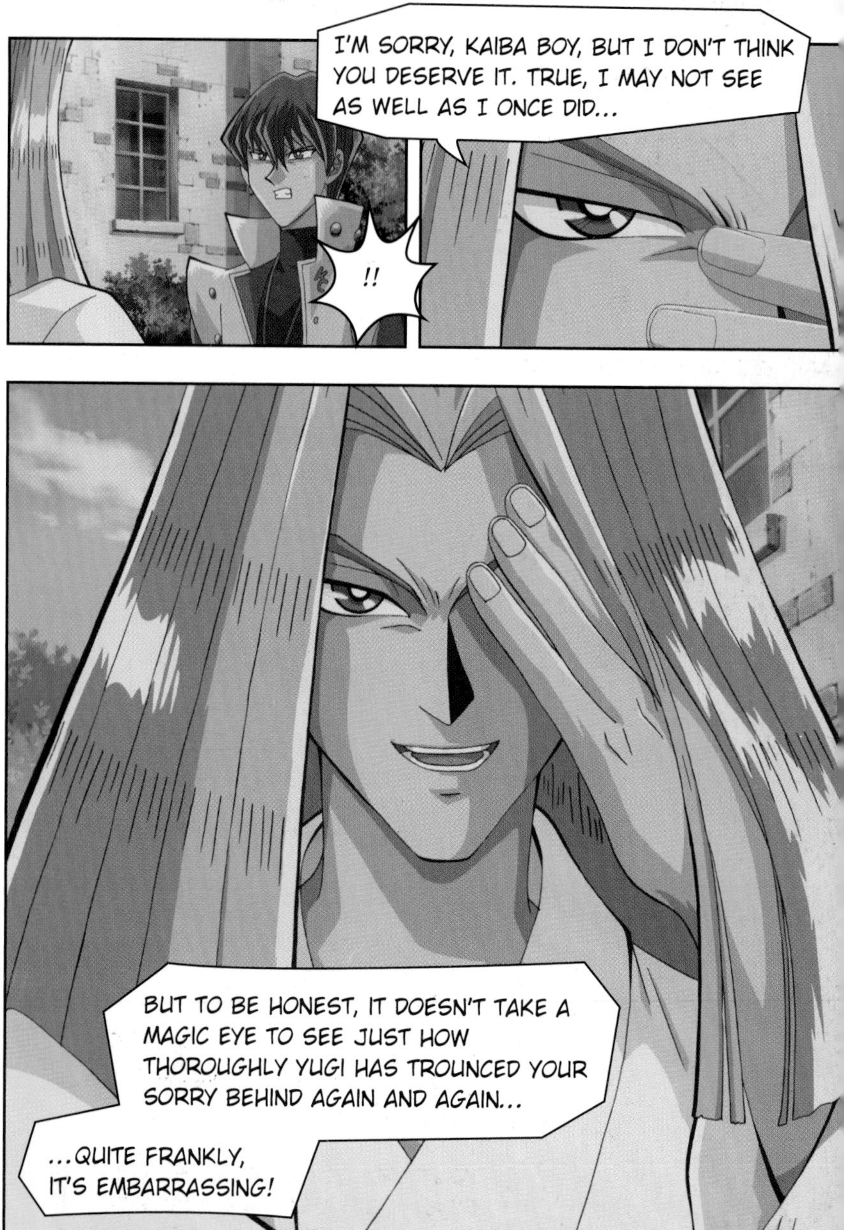
I'M SORRY, KAIBA BOY, BUT I DON'T THINK YOU DESERVE IT. TRUE, I MAY NOT SEE AS WELL AS I ONCE DID...
!!
BUT TO BE HONEST, IT DOESN'T TAKE A MAGIC EYE TO SEE JUST HOW THOROUGHLY YUGI HAS TROUNCED YOUR SORRY BEHIND AGAIN AND AGAIN...
...QUITE FRANKLY, IT'S EMBARRASSING!

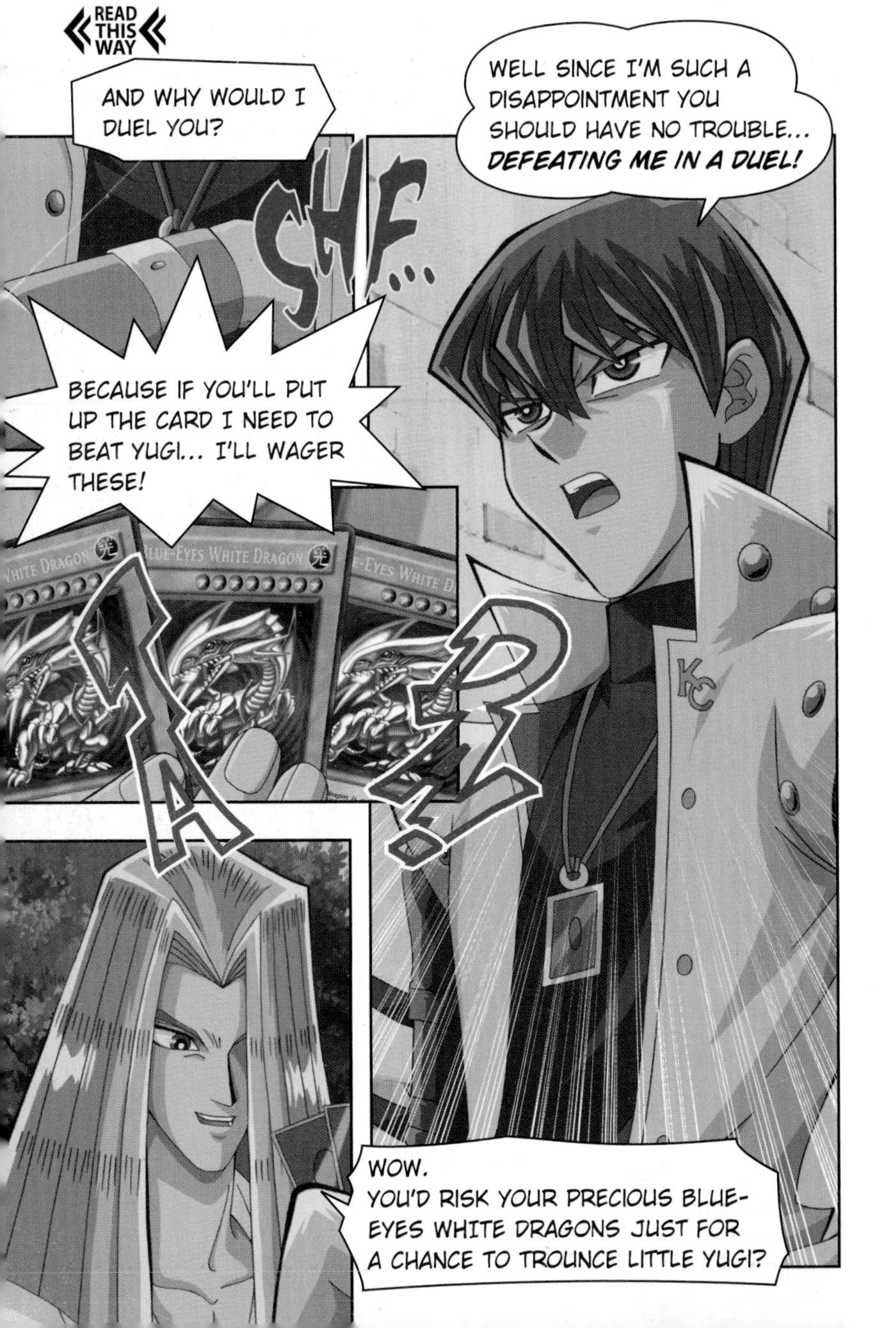
READ THIS WAY
WELL SINCE I'M SUCH A DISAPPOINTMENT YOU SHOULD HAVE NO TROUBLE... ***DEFEATING ME IN A DUEL!***
AND WHY WOULD I DUEL YOU?
SHF...
BECAUSE IF YOU'LL PUT UP THE CARD I NEED TO BEAT YUGI... I'LL WAGER THESE!
WOW.
YOU'D RISK YOUR PRECIOUS BLUE-EYES WHITE DRAGONS JUST FOR A CHANCE TO TROUNCE LITTLE YUGI?

READ THIS WAY

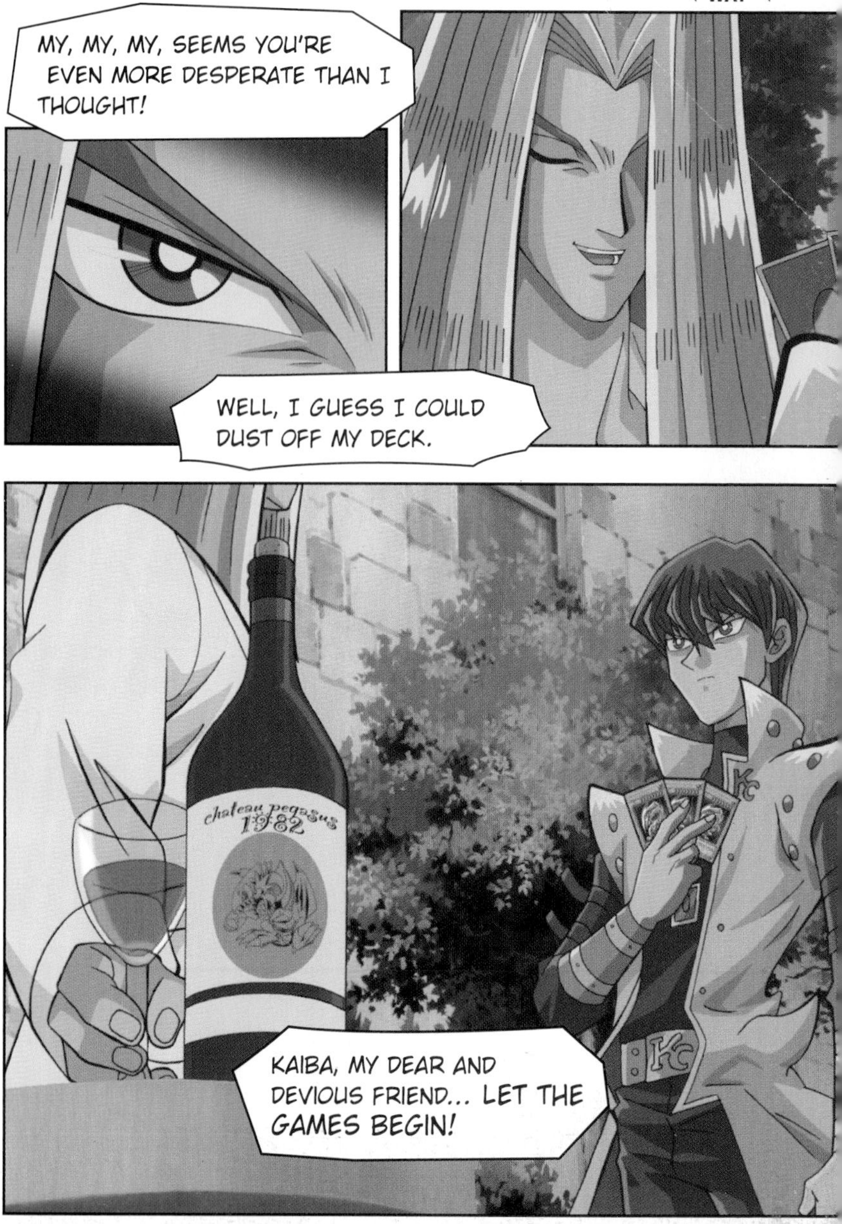
MY, MY, MY, SEEMS YOU'RE EVEN MORE DESPERATE THAN I THOUGHT!
WELL, I GUESS I COULD DUST OFF MY DECK.
chateau pegasus 1982
KAIBA, MY DEAR AND DEVIOUS FRIEND... LET THE GAMES BEGIN!

DING DONG...

Chapter. **2**

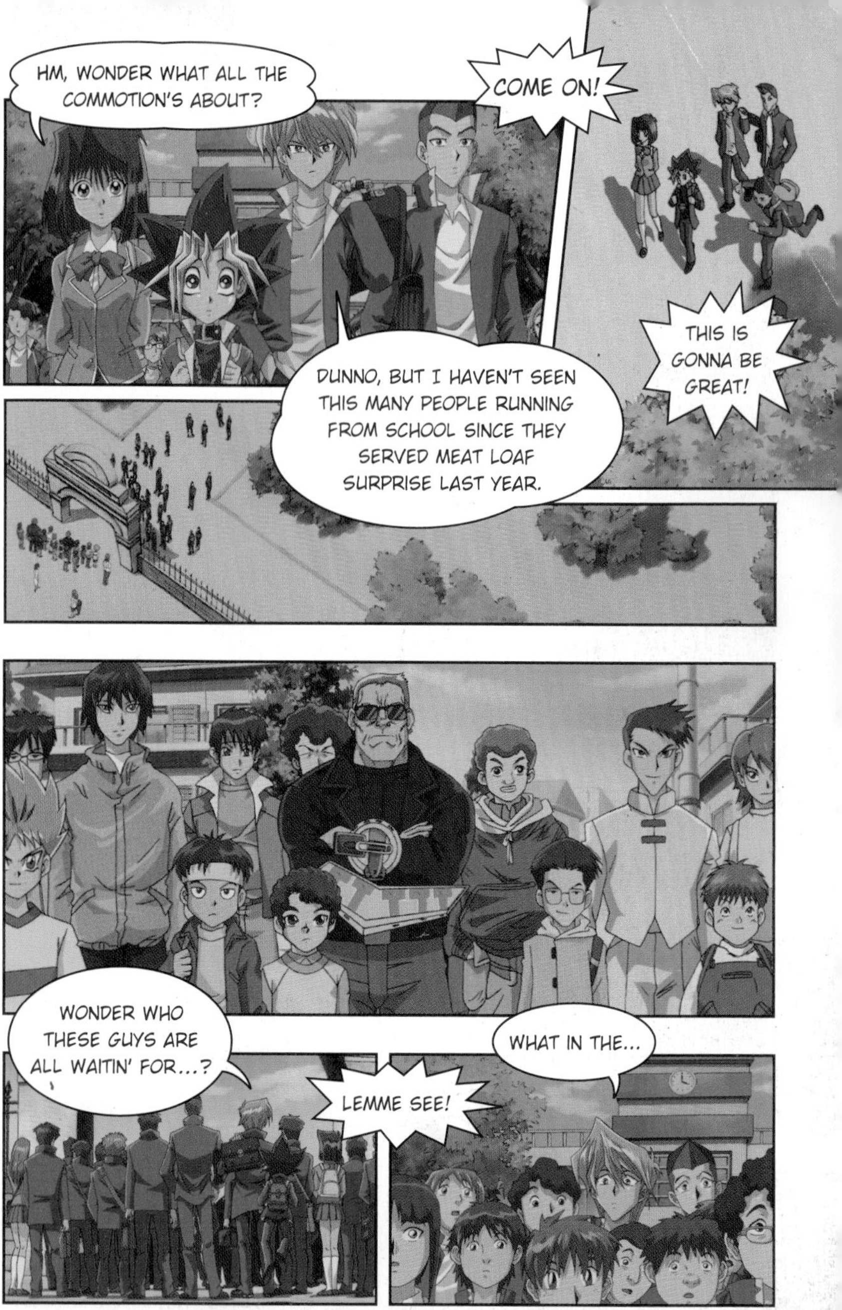
COME ON!
THIS IS GONNA BE GREAT!
HM, WONDER WHAT ALL THE COMMOTION'S ABOUT?
DUNNO, BUT I HAVEN'T SEEN THIS MANY PEOPLE RUNNING FROM SCHOOL SINCE THEY SERVED MEAT LOAF SURPRISE LAST YEAR.
WHAT IN THE...
WONDER WHO THESE GUYS ARE ALL WAITIN' FOR...?
LEMME SEE!

READ THIS WAY

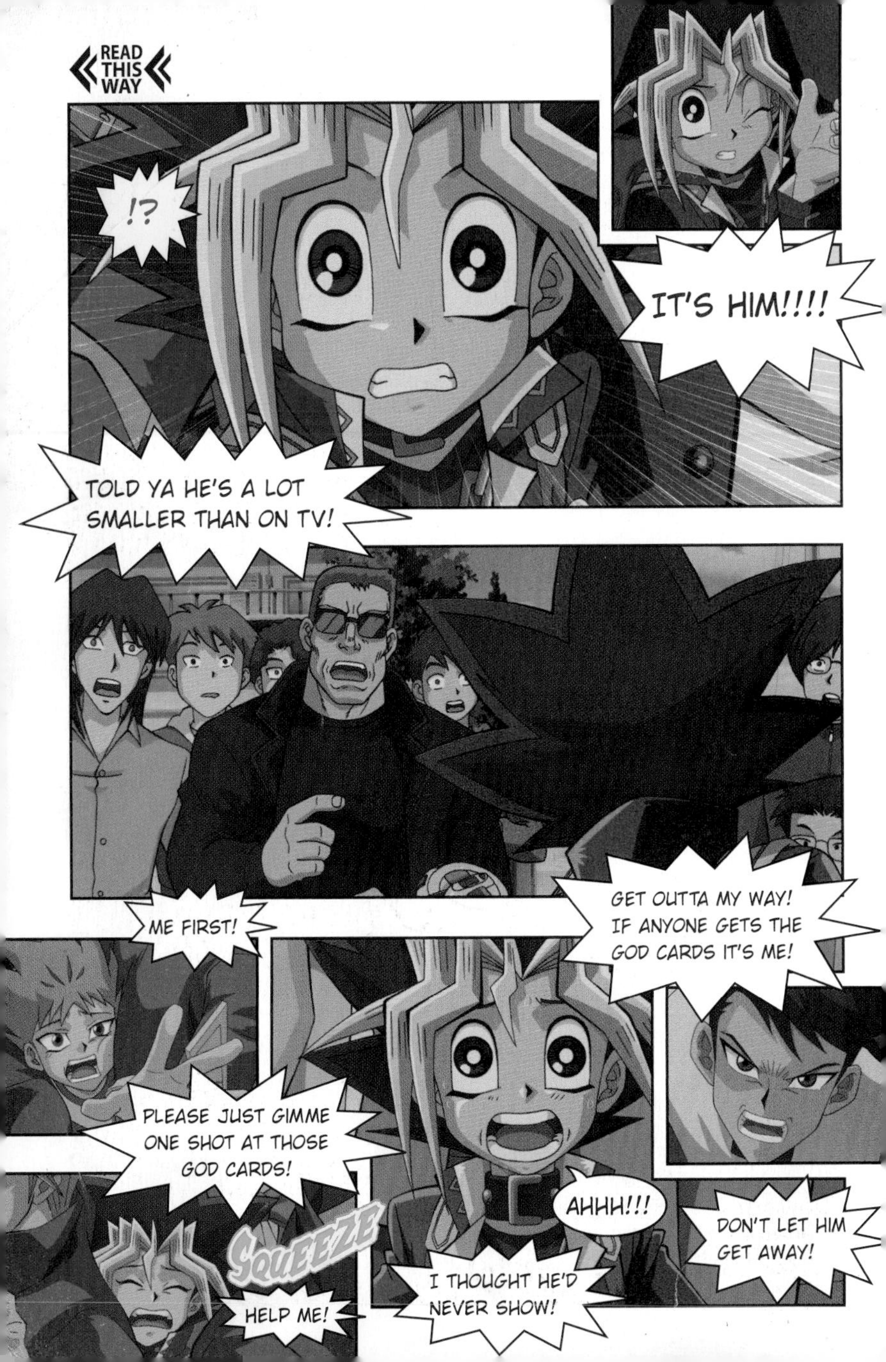

IT'S HIM!!!!
!?
TOLD YA HE'S A LOT SMALLER THAN ON TV!
GET OUTTA MY WAY! IF ANYONE GETS THE GOD CARDS IT'S ME!
ME FIRST!
DON'T LET HIM GET AWAY!
AHHH!!!
I THOUGHT HE'D NEVER SHOW!
PLEASE JUST GIMME ONE SHOT AT THOSE GOD CARDS!
SQUEEZE
HELP ME!

READ THIS WAY

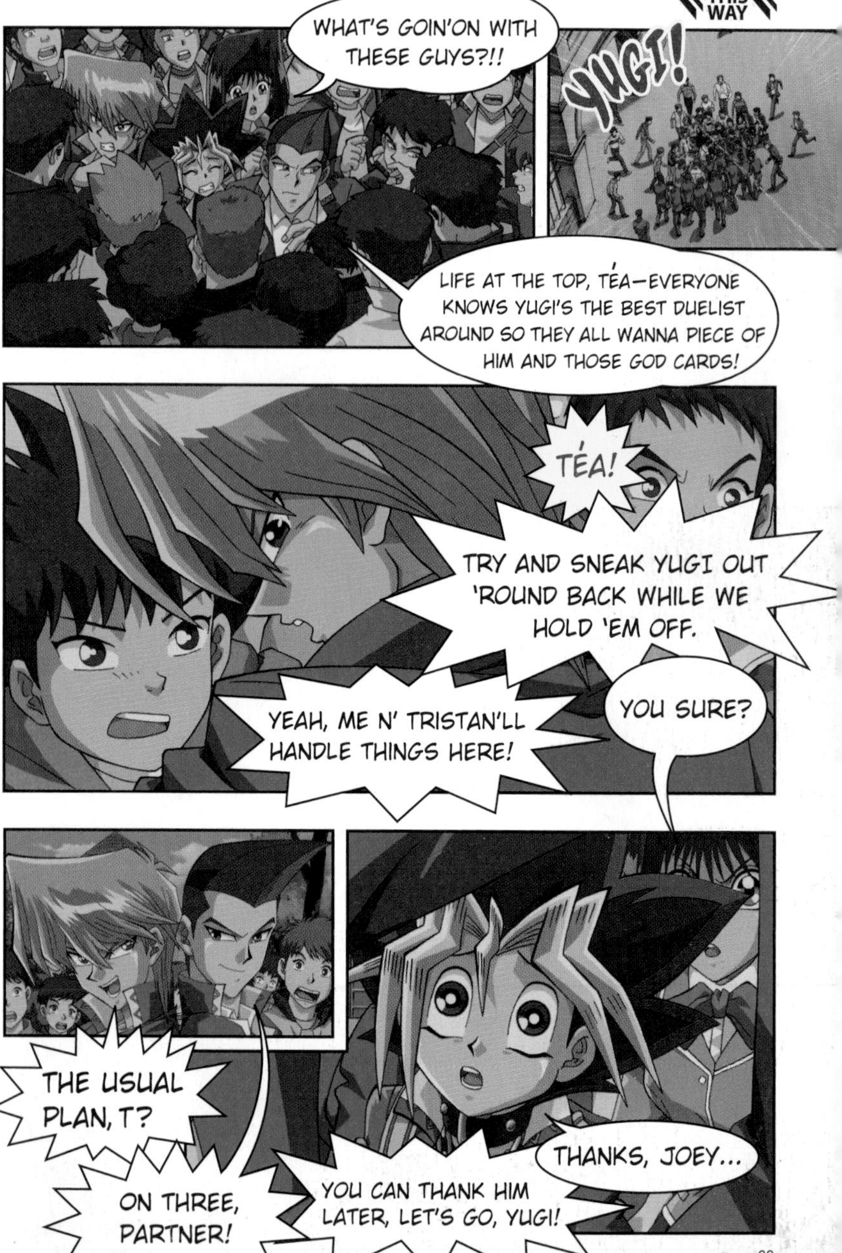
YUGI!
WHAT'S GOIN'ON WITH THESE GUYS?!!
LIFE AT THE TOP, TÉA—EVERYONE KNOWS YUGI'S THE BEST DUELIST AROUND SO THEY ALL WANNA PIECE OF HIM AND THOSE GOD CARDS!
TÉA!
TRY AND SNEAK YUGI OUT 'ROUND BACK WHILE WE HOLD 'EM OFF.
YEAH, ME N' TRISTAN'LL HANDLE THINGS HERE!
YOU SURE?
THANKS, JOEY...
YOU CAN THANK HIM LATER, LET'S GO, YUGI!
THE USUAL PLAN, T?
ON THREE, PARTNER!

READ THIS WAY

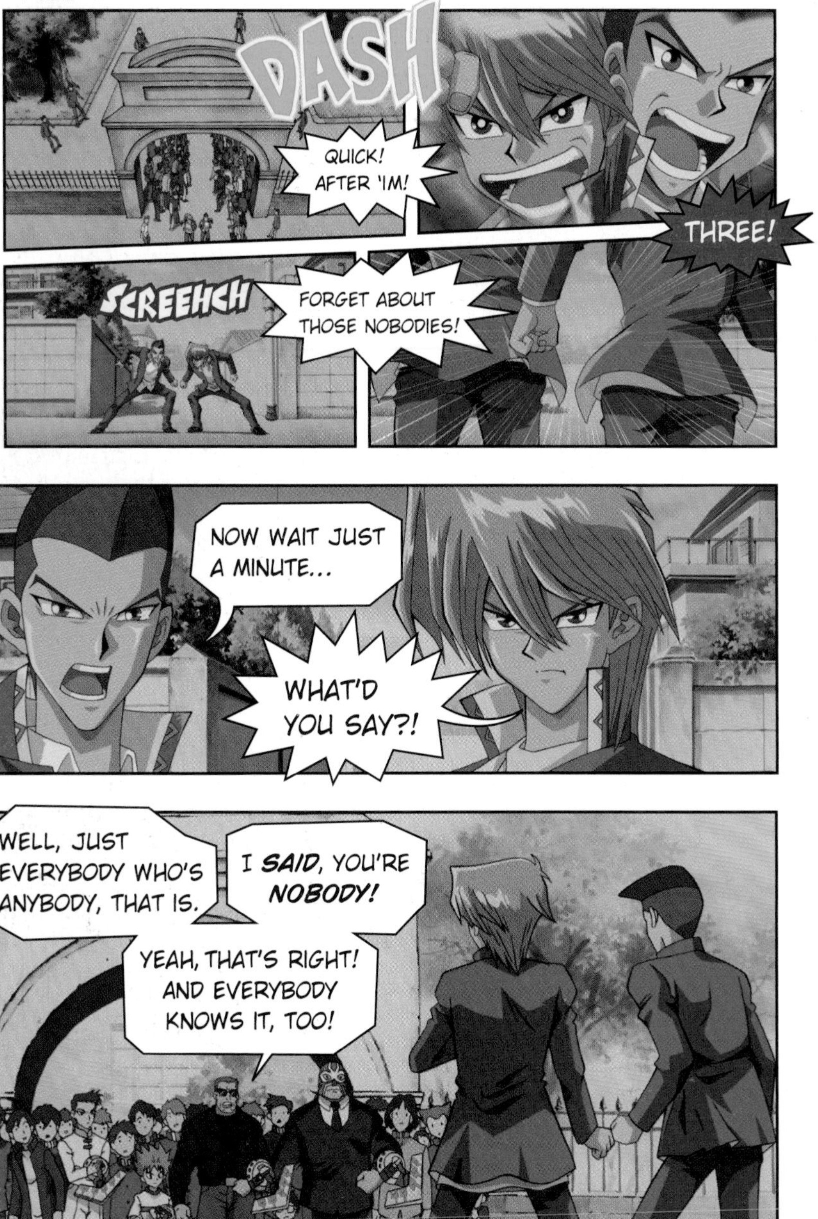

DASH
QUICK! AFTER 'IM!
THREE!
SCREEHCH
FORGET ABOUT THOSE NOBODIES!
NOW WAIT JUST A MINUTE...
WHAT'D YOU SAY?!
I *SAID*, YOU'RE *NOBODY!*
WELL, JUST EVERYBODY WHO'S ANYBODY, THAT IS.
YEAH, THAT'S RIGHT! AND EVERYBODY KNOWS IT, TOO!

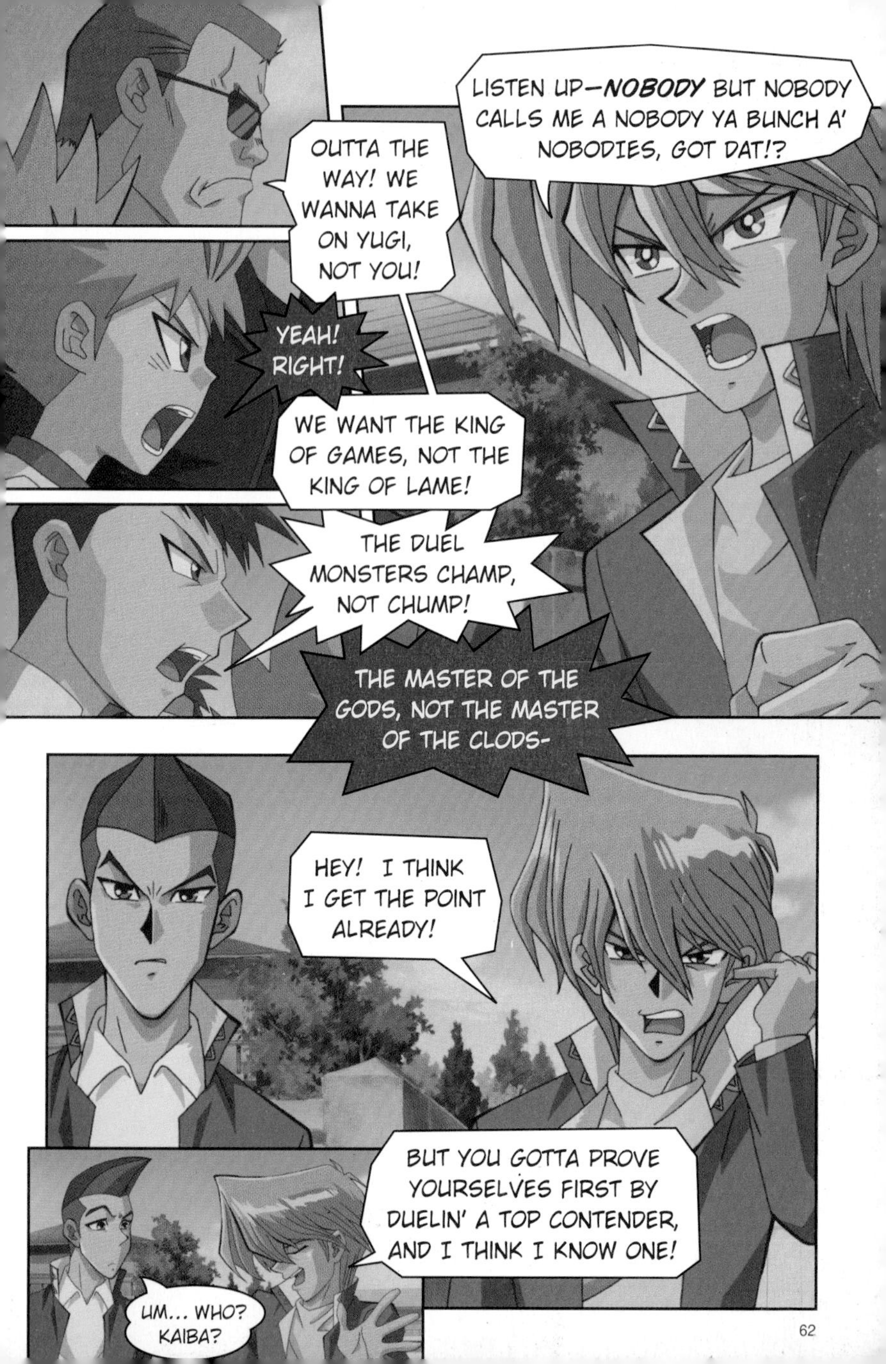
LISTEN UP—**NOBODY** BUT NOBODY CALLS ME A NOBODY YA BUNCH A' NOBODIES, GOT DAT!?
OUTTA THE WAY! WE WANNA TAKE ON YUGI, NOT YOU!
YEAH! RIGHT!
WE WANT THE KING OF GAMES, NOT THE KING OF LAME!
THE DUEL MONSTERS CHAMP, NOT CHUMP!
THE MASTER OF THE GODS, NOT THE MASTER OF THE CLODS-
HEY! I THINK I GET THE POINT ALREADY!
BUT YOU GOTTA PROVE YOURSELVES FIRST BY DUELIN' A TOP CONTENDER, AND I THINK I KNOW ONE!
UM... WHO? KAIBA?

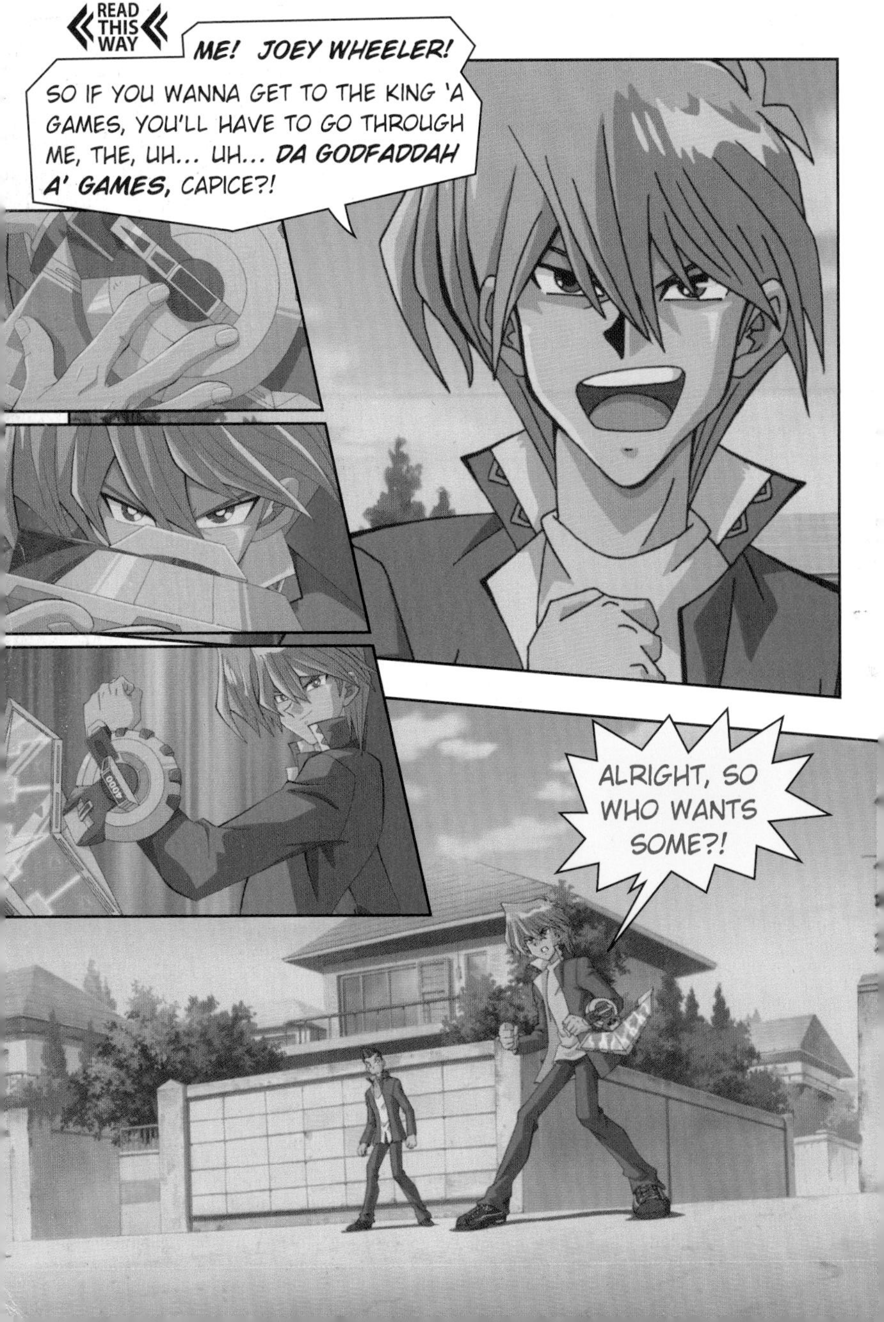
READ THIS WAY
ME! JOEY WHEELER!
SO IF YOU WANNA GET TO THE KING 'A GAMES, YOU'LL HAVE TO GO THROUGH ME, THE, UH... UH... DA GODFADDAH A' GAMES, CAPICE?!
ALRIGHT, SO WHO WANTS SOME?!

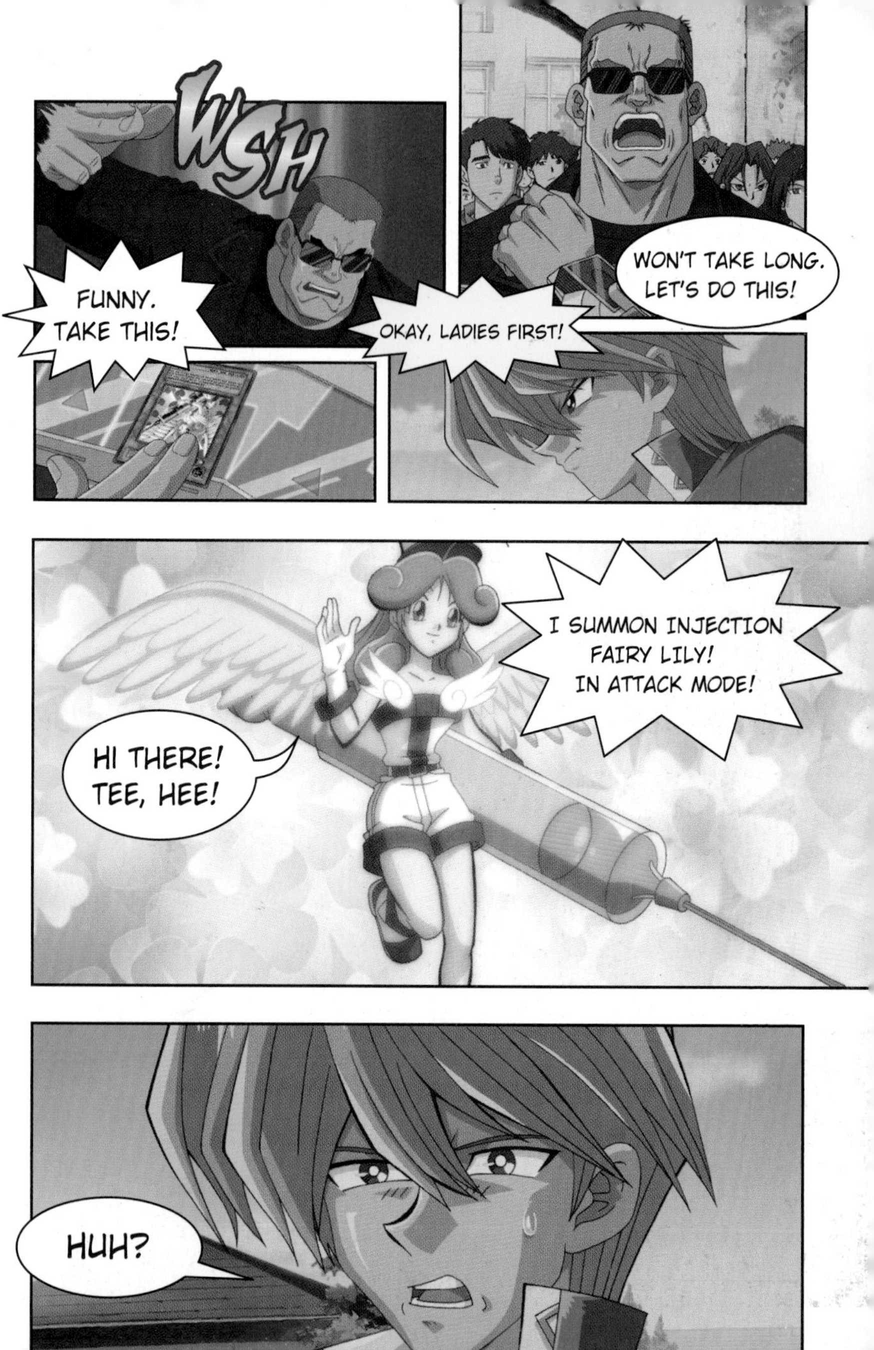
WON'T TAKE LONG. LET'S DO THIS!
WSH
FUNNY. TAKE THIS!
OKAY, LADIES FIRST!
I SUMMON INJECTION FAIRY LILY! IN ATTACK MODE!
HI THERE! TEE, HEE!
HUH?

READ THIS WAY

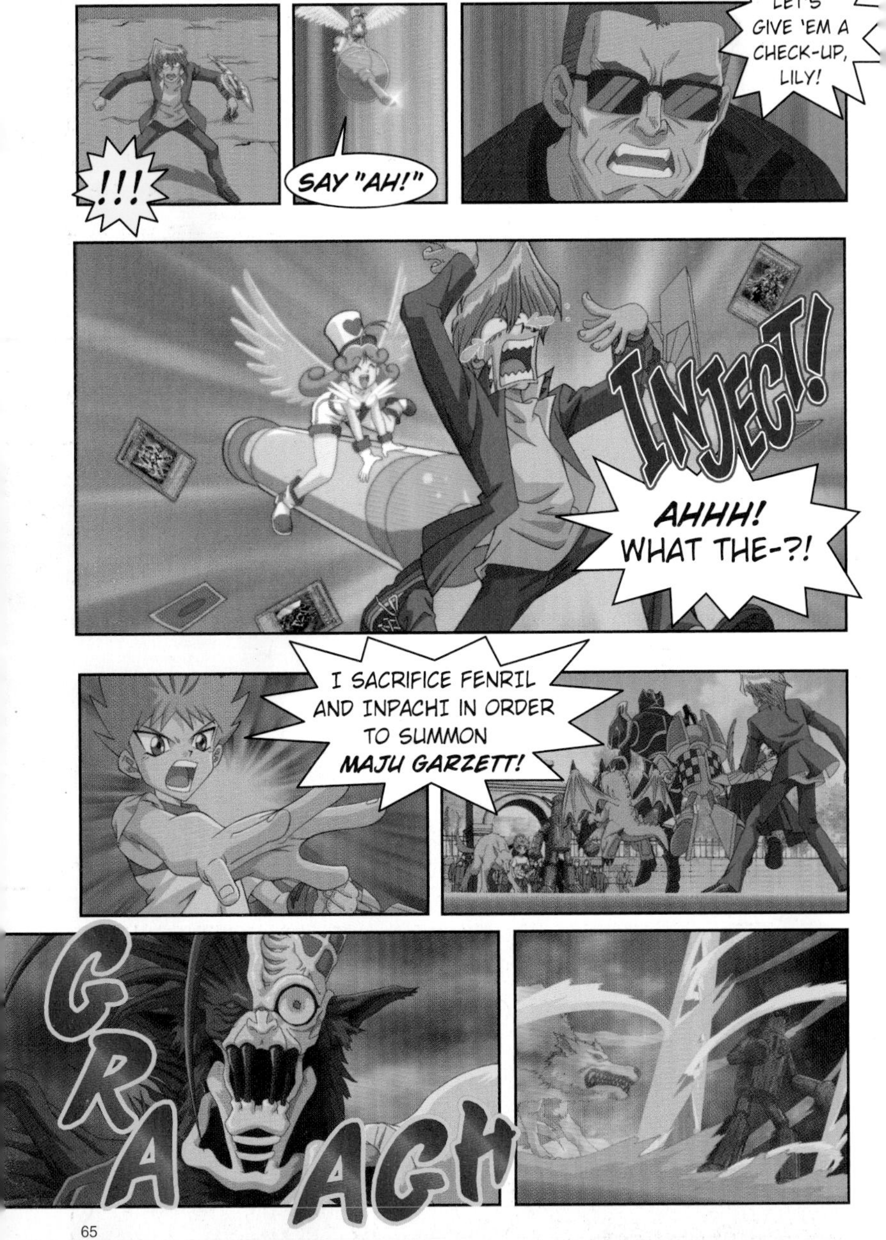

LET'S GIVE 'EM A CHECK-UP, LILY!
SAY "AH!"
!!!
INJECT!
AHHH! WHAT THE-?!
I SACRIFICE FENRIL AND INPACHI IN ORDER TO SUMMON MAJU GARZETT!
GRAAGH

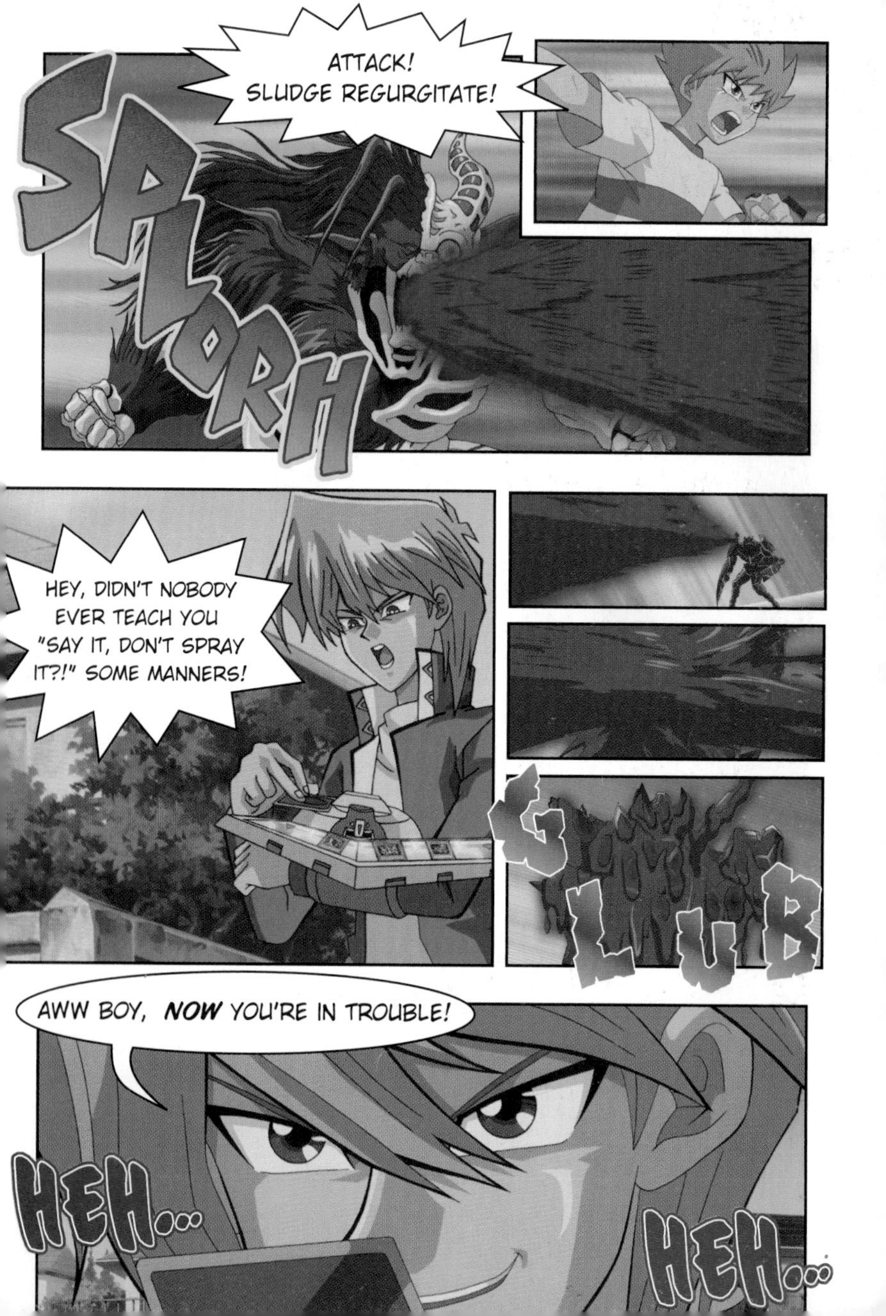
ATTACK! SLUDGE REGURGITATE!
SPLORH
GLUB
HEY, DIDN'T NOBODY EVER TEACH YOU "SAY IT, DON'T SPRAY IT?!" SOME MANNERS!
AWW BOY, **NOW** YOU'RE IN TROUBLE!
HEH...
HEH...

READ THIS WAY

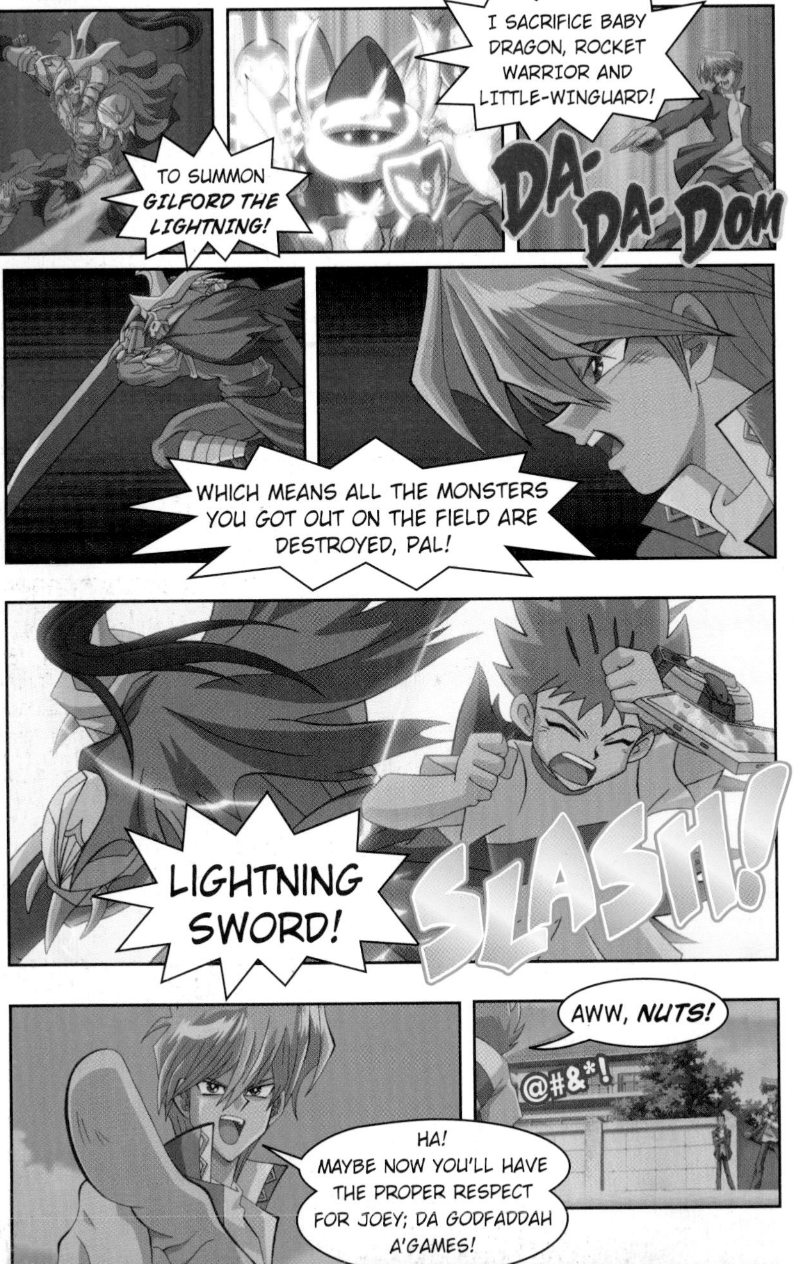
I SACRIFICE BABY DRAGON, ROCKET WARRIOR AND LITTLE-WINGUARD!
DA-DA-DOM
TO SUMMON GILFORD THE LIGHTNING!
WHICH MEANS ALL THE MONSTERS YOU GOT OUT ON THE FIELD ARE DESTROYED, PAL!
SLASH!
LIGHTNING SWORD!
AWW, NUTS!
@#&*!
HA! MAYBE NOW YOU'LL HAVE THE PROPER RESPECT FOR JOEY; DA GODFADDAH A'GAMES!

READ THIS WAY

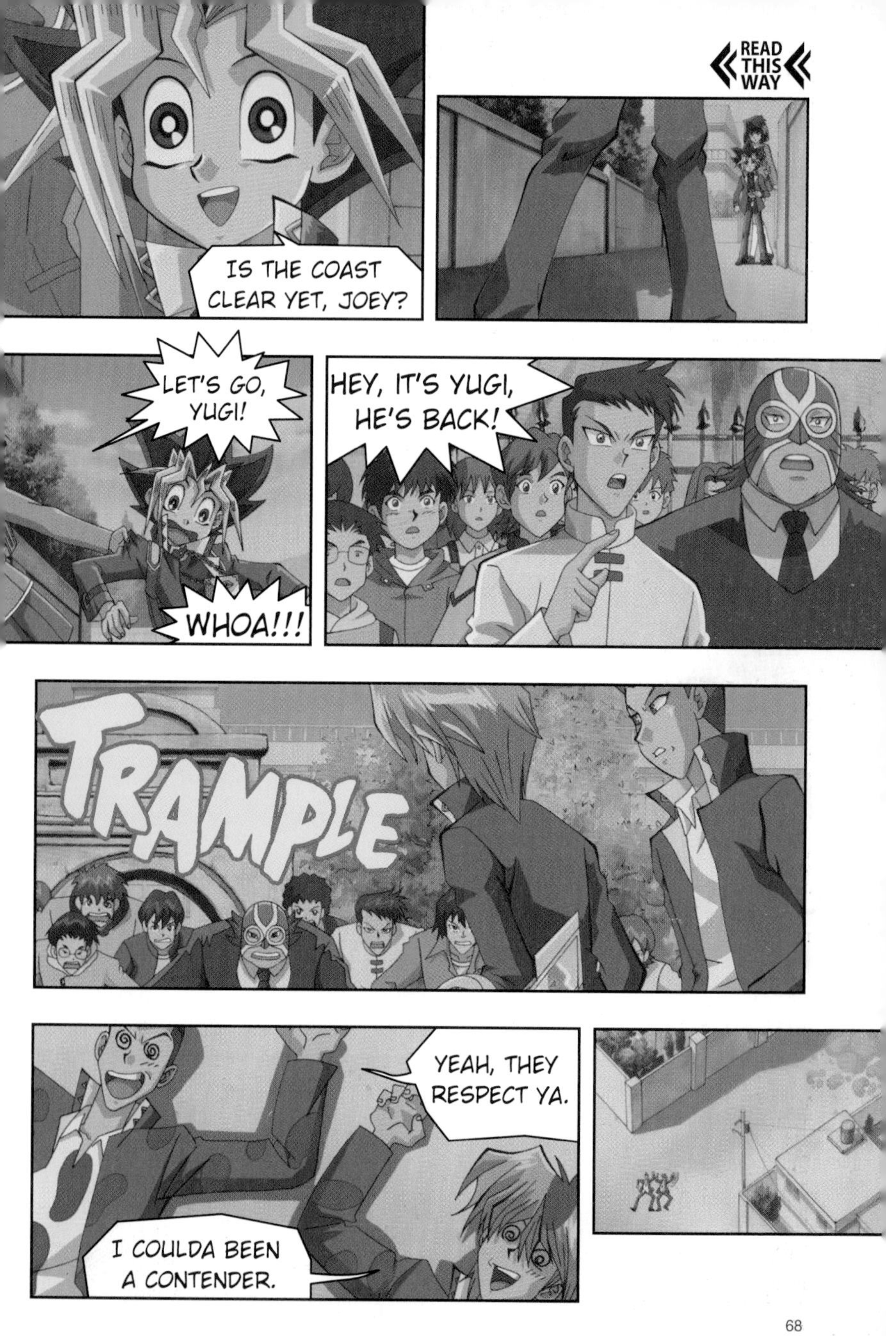

IS THE COAST CLEAR YET, JOEY?
HEY, IT'S YUGI, HE'S BACK!
LET'S GO, YUGI!
WHOA!!!
TRAMPLE
YEAH, THEY RESPECT YA.
I COULDA BEEN A CONTENDER.

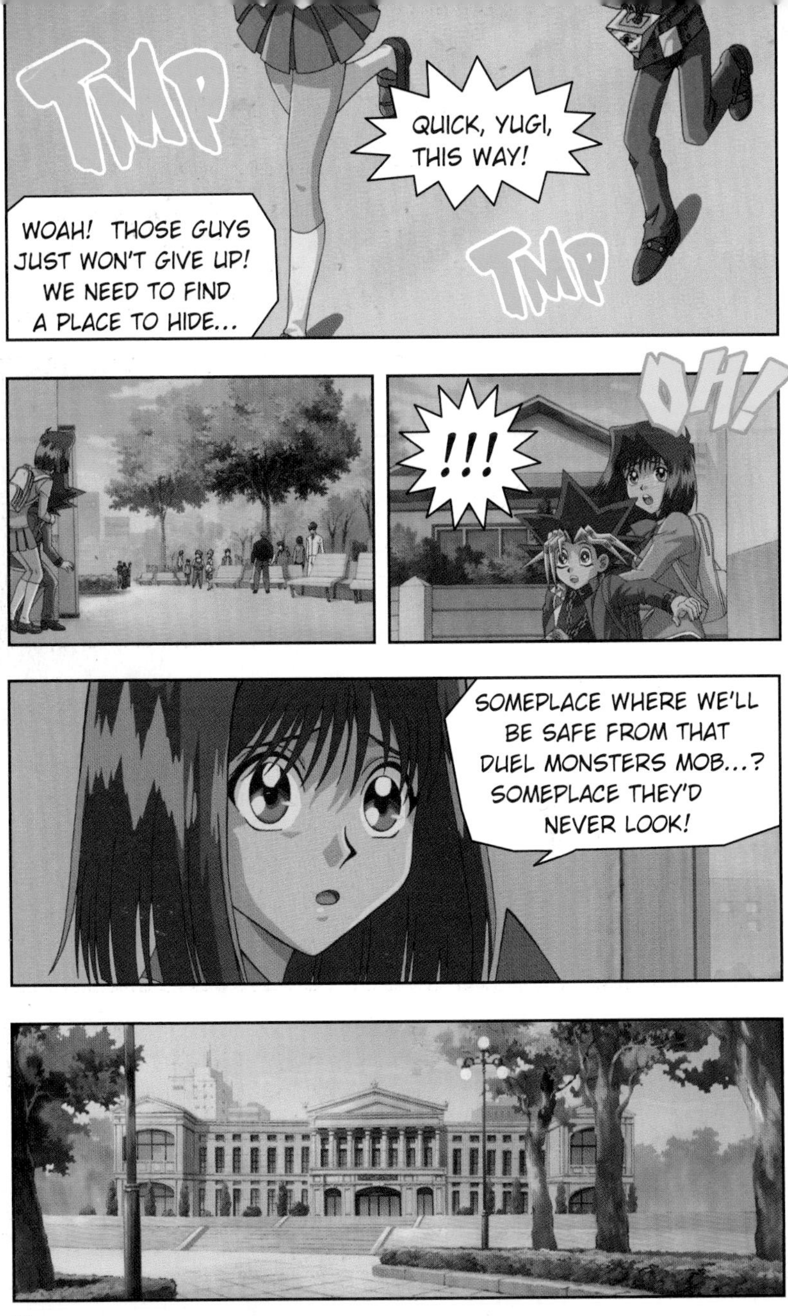

QUICK, YUGI, THIS WAY!
TMP
TMP
WOAH! THOSE GUYS JUST WON'T GIVE UP! WE NEED TO FIND A PLACE TO HIDE...
OH!
!!!
SOMEPLACE WHERE WE'LL BE SAFE FROM THAT DUEL MONSTERS MOB...? SOMEPLACE THEY'D NEVER LOOK!

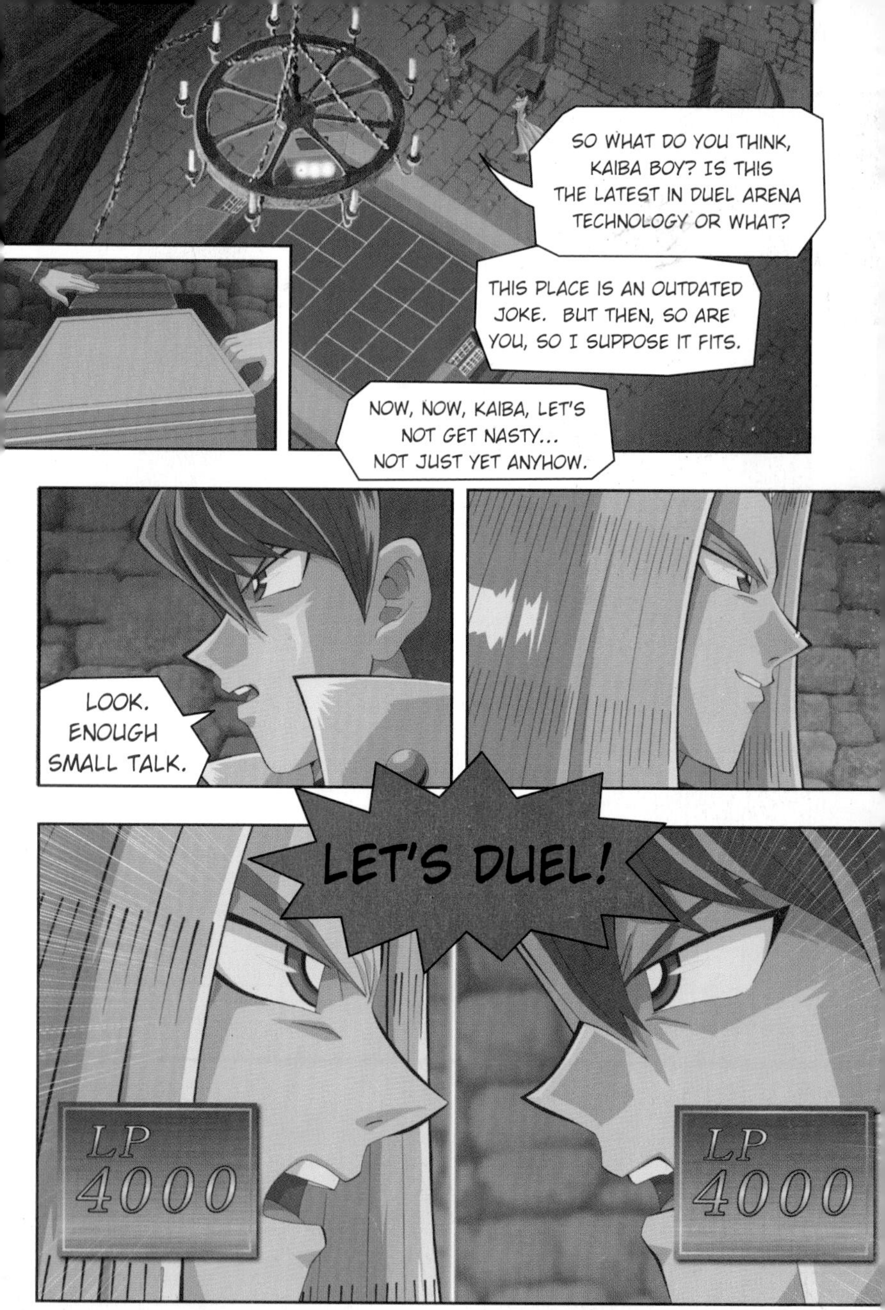
SO WHAT DO YOU THINK, KAIBA BOY? IS THIS THE LATEST IN DUEL ARENA TECHNOLOGY OR WHAT?
THIS PLACE IS AN OUTDATED JOKE. BUT THEN, SO ARE YOU, SO I SUPPOSE IT FITS.
NOW, NOW, KAIBA, LET'S NOT GET NASTY... NOT JUST YET ANYHOW.
LOOK. ENOUGH SMALL TALK.
LET'S DUEL!
LP 4000
LP 4000

READ THIS WAY

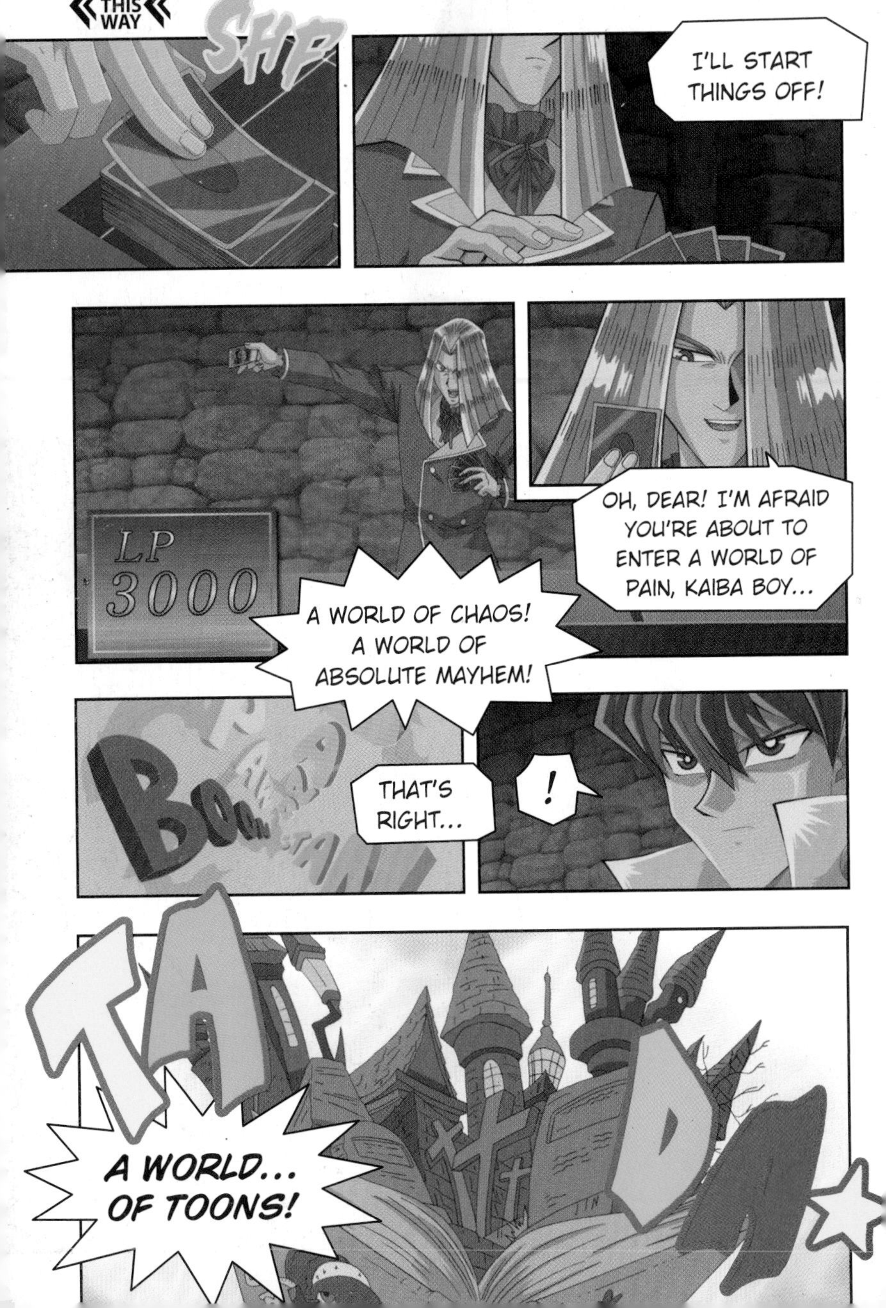
I'LL START THINGS OFF!
SHP
OH, DEAR! I'M AFRAID YOU'RE ABOUT TO ENTER A WORLD OF PAIN, KAIBA BOY...
LP 3000
A WORLD OF CHAOS! A WORLD OF ABSOLUTE MAYHEM!
!
THAT'S RIGHT...
TA DA
A WORLD... OF TOONS!

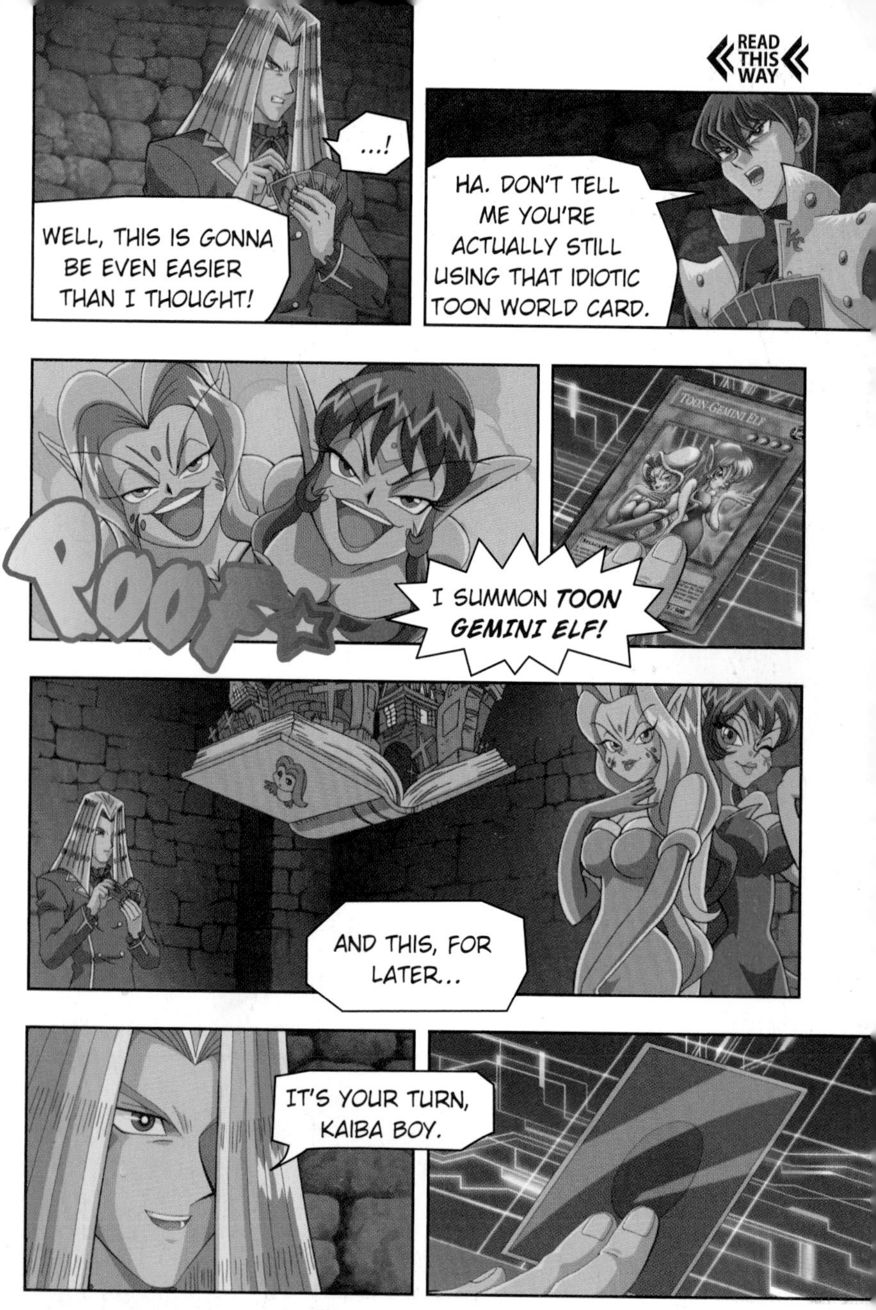
READ THIS WAY
HA. DON'T TELL ME YOU'RE ACTUALLY STILL USING THAT IDIOTIC TOON WORLD CARD.
...!
WELL, THIS IS GONNA BE EVEN EASIER THAN I THOUGHT!
I SUMMON *TOON GEMINI ELF!*
POOF
AND THIS, FOR LATER...
IT'S YOUR TURN, KAIBA BOY.

READ THIS WAY

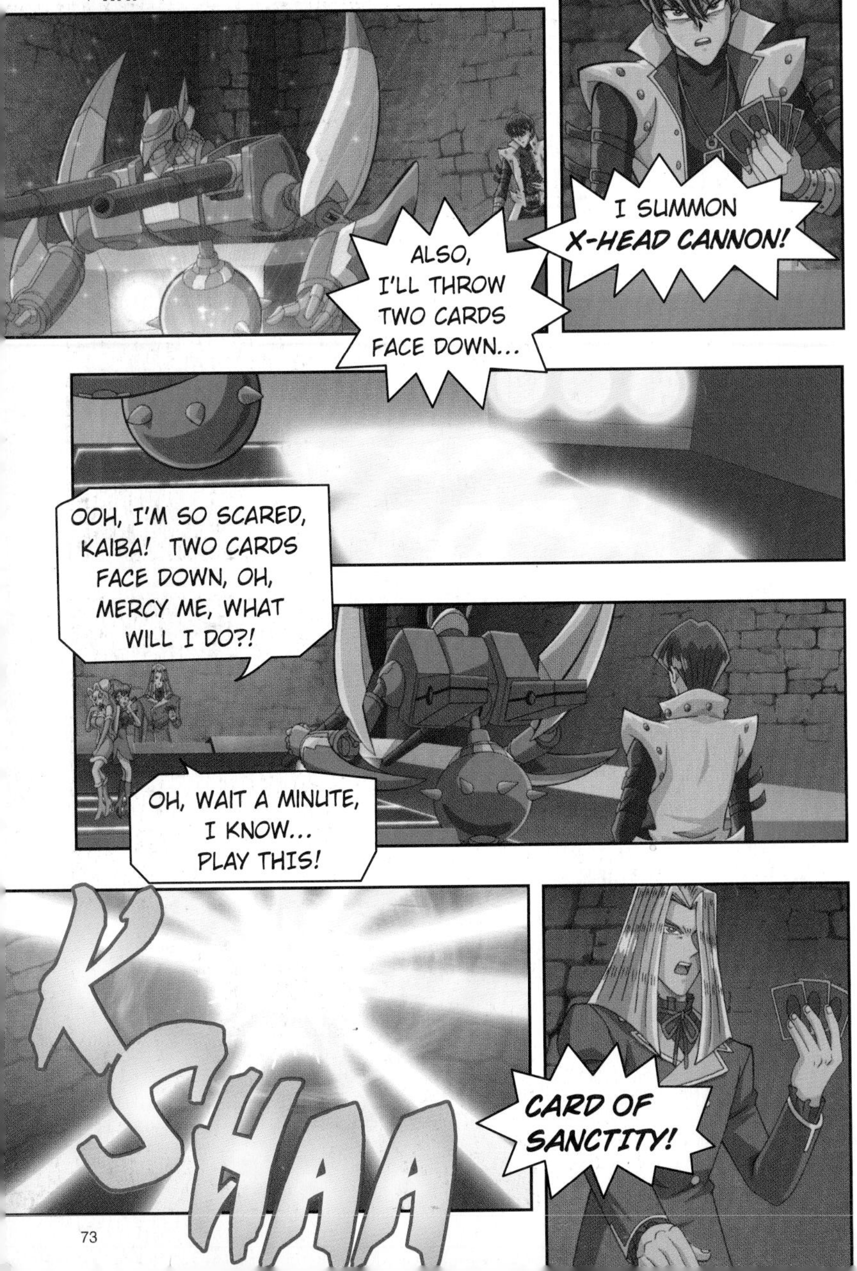

I SUMMON X-HEAD CANNON!
ALSO, I'LL THROW TWO CARDS FACE DOWN...
OOH, I'M SO SCARED, KAIBA! TWO CARDS FACE DOWN, OH, MERCY ME, WHAT WILL I DO?!
OH, WAIT A MINUTE, I KNOW... PLAY THIS!
CARD OF SANCTITY!
K'SHAA

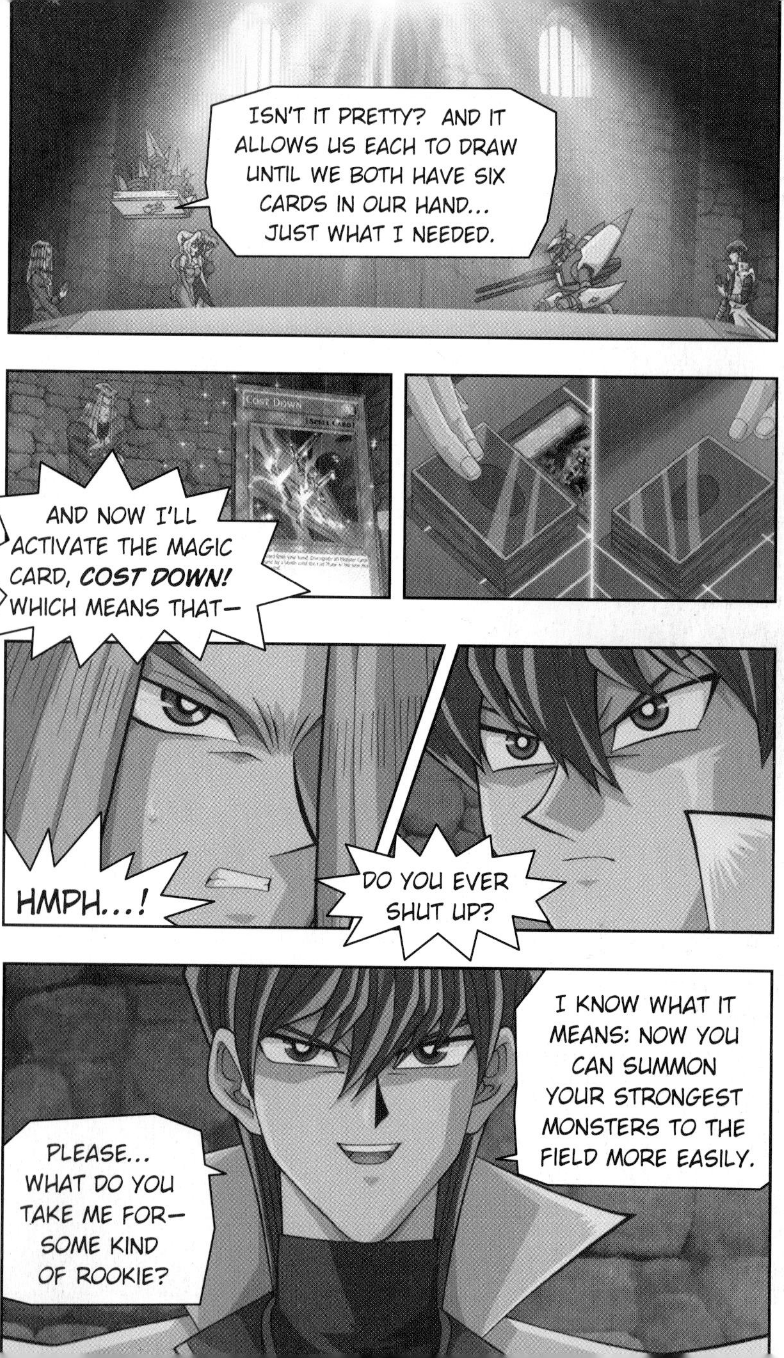
ISN'T IT PRETTY? AND IT ALLOWS US EACH TO DRAW UNTIL WE BOTH HAVE SIX CARDS IN OUR HAND... JUST WHAT I NEEDED.
COST DOWN
[SPELL CARD]
AND NOW I'LL ACTIVATE THE MAGIC CARD, **COST DOWN!** WHICH MEANS THAT—
DO YOU EVER SHUT UP?
HMPH...!
I KNOW WHAT IT MEANS: NOW YOU CAN SUMMON YOUR STRONGEST MONSTERS TO THE FIELD MORE EASILY.
PLEASE... WHAT DO YOU TAKE ME FOR— SOME KIND OF ROOKIE?

READ THIS WAY

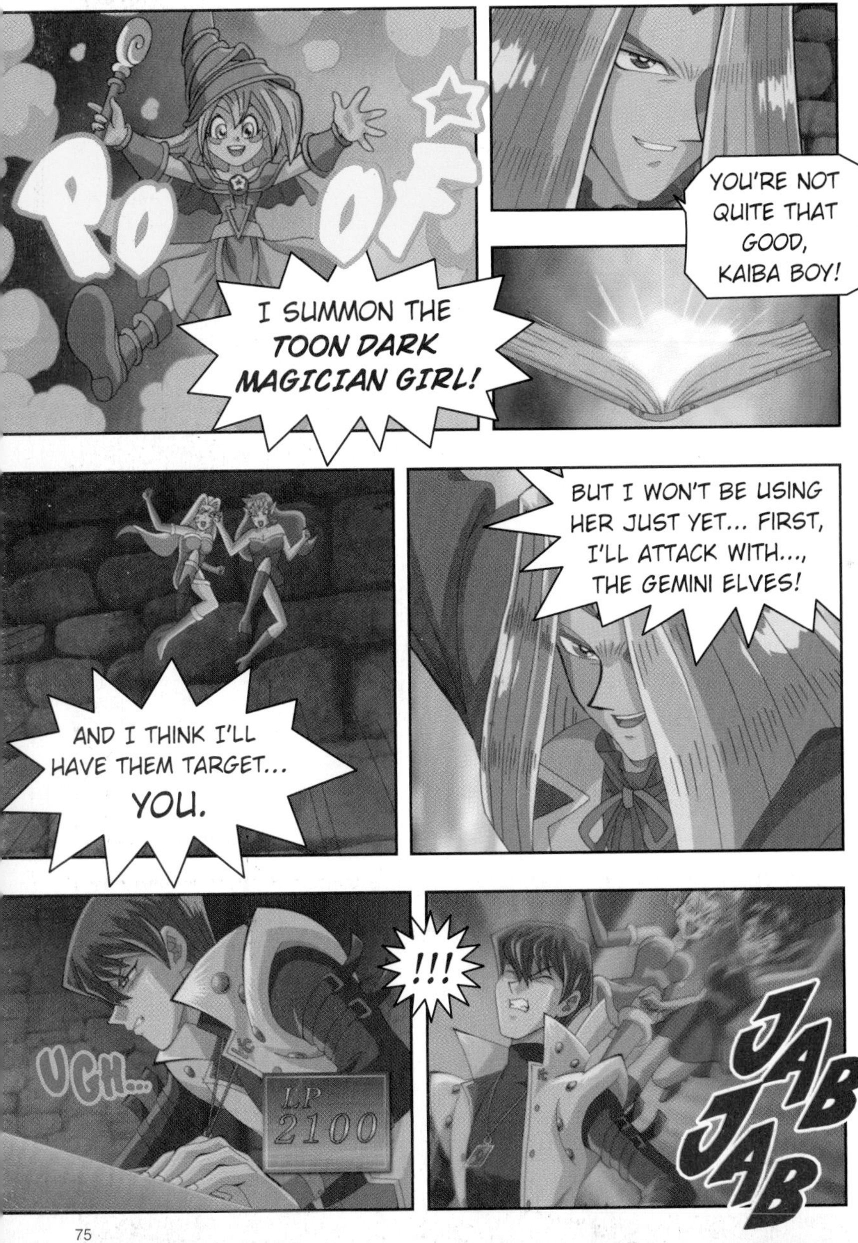

YOU'RE NOT QUITE THAT GOOD, KAIBA BOY!
POOF
I SUMMON THE *TOON DARK MAGICIAN GIRL!*
BUT I WON'T BE USING HER JUST YET... FIRST, I'LL ATTACK WITH..., THE GEMINI ELVES!
AND I THINK I'LL HAVE THEM TARGET... YOU.
!!!
JAB JAB
UGH...
LP 2100

READ THIS WAY

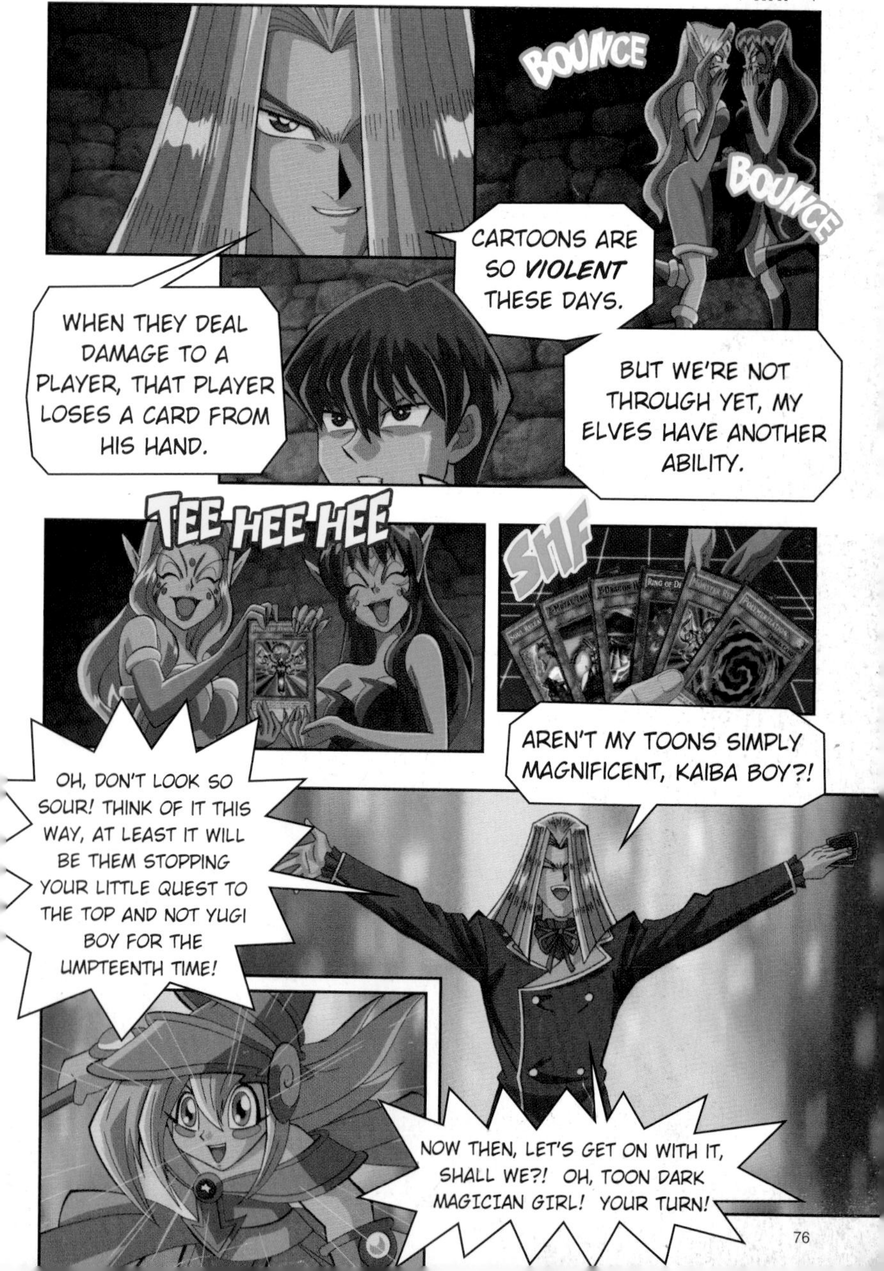

BOUNCE
BOUNCE
CARTOONS ARE SO *VIOLENT* THESE DAYS.
WHEN THEY DEAL DAMAGE TO A PLAYER, THAT PLAYER LOSES A CARD FROM HIS HAND.
BUT WE'RE NOT THROUGH YET, MY ELVES HAVE ANOTHER ABILITY.
SHF
AREN'T MY TOONS SIMPLY MAGNIFICENT, KAIBA BOY?!
TEE HEE HEE
OH, DON'T LOOK SO SOUR! THINK OF IT THIS WAY, AT LEAST IT WILL BE THEM STOPPING YOUR LITTLE QUEST TO THE TOP AND NOT YUGI BOY FOR THE UMPTEENTH TIME!
NOW THEN, LET'S GET ON WITH IT, SHALL WE?! OH, TOON DARK MAGICIAN GIRL! YOUR TURN!

READ THIS WAY

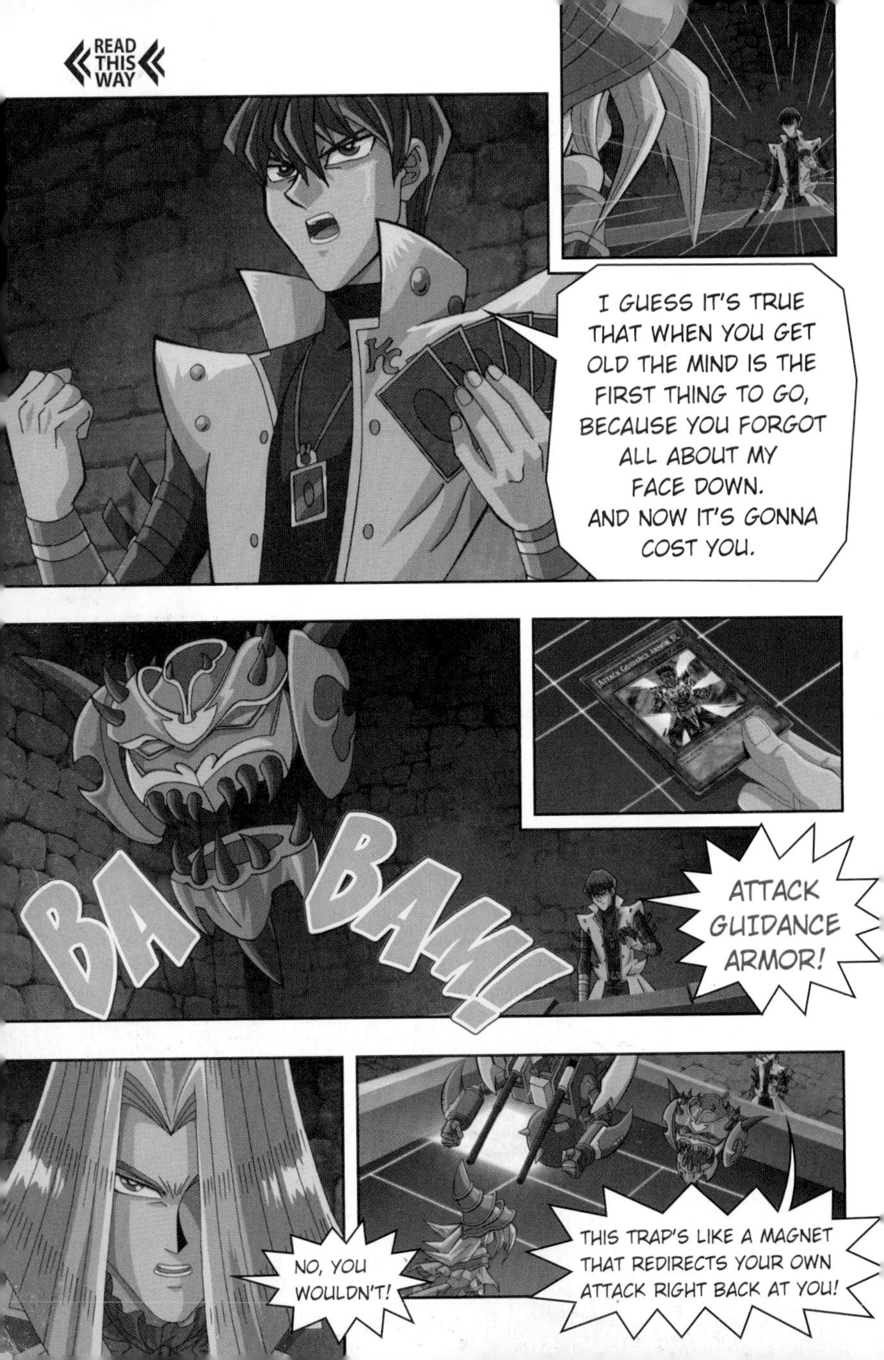
I GUESS IT'S TRUE THAT WHEN YOU GET OLD THE MIND IS THE FIRST THING TO GO, BECAUSE YOU FORGOT ALL ABOUT MY FACE DOWN. AND NOW IT'S GONNA COST YOU.
ATTACK GUIDANCE ARMOR!
BA BAM!!
THIS TRAP'S LIKE A MAGNET THAT REDIRECTS YOUR OWN ATTACK RIGHT BACK AT YOU!
NO, YOU WOULDN'T!

READ THIS WAY

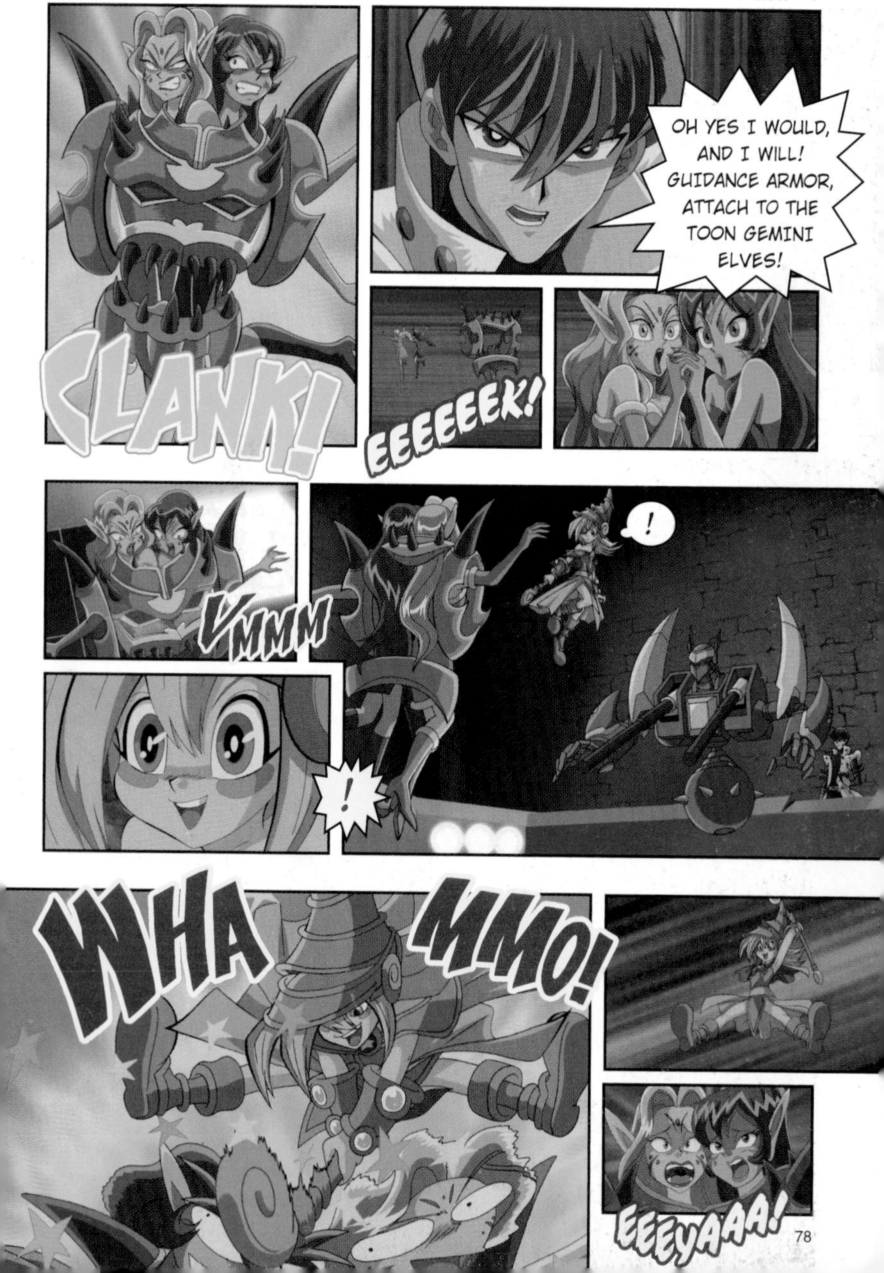

OH YES I WOULD, AND I WILL! GUIDANCE ARMOR, ATTACH TO THE TOON GEMINI ELVES!
EEEEEEK!
CLANK!
!
VMMM
!
EEEYAAA!
WHAMMO!

READ THIS WAY

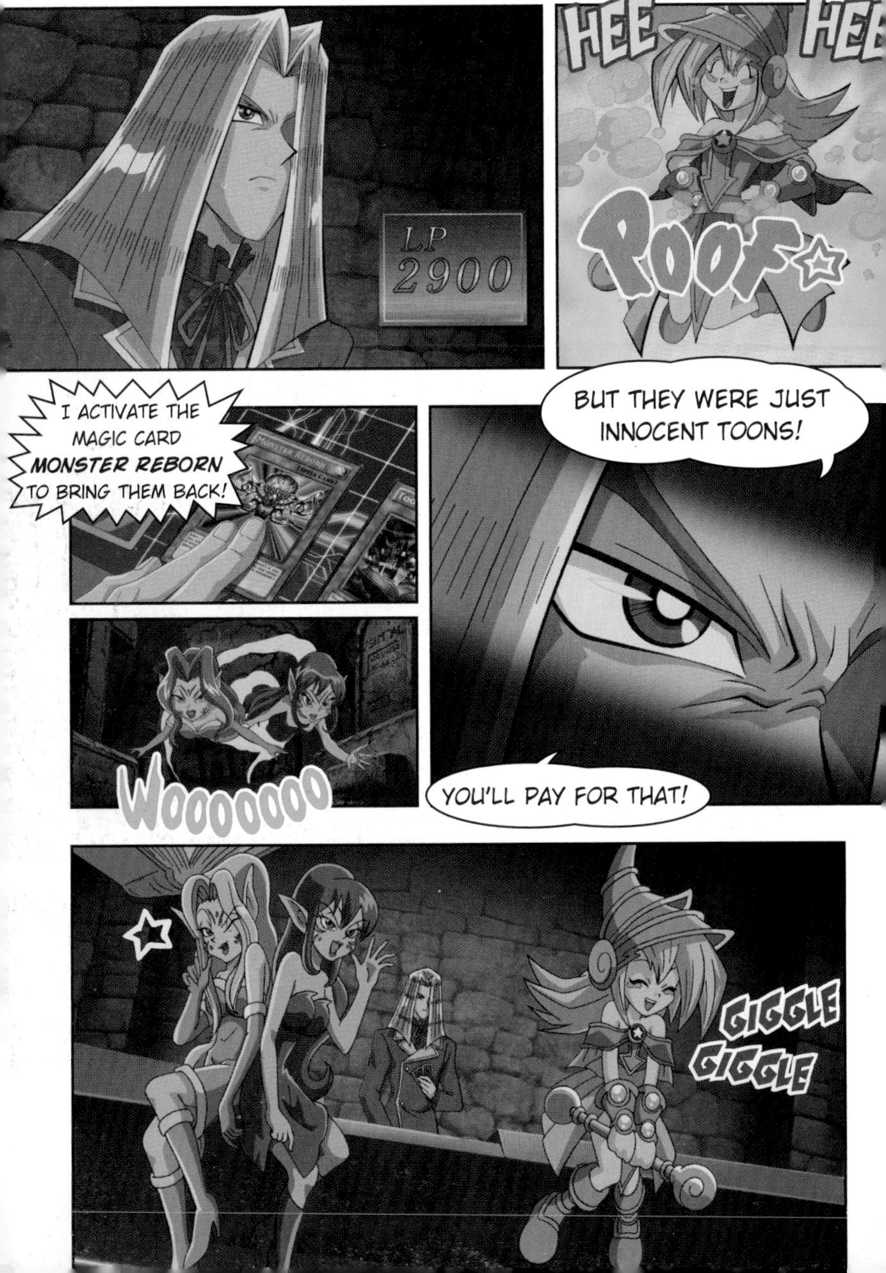
HEE HEE
POOF
LP 2900
BUT THEY WERE JUST INNOCENT TOONS!
YOU'LL PAY FOR THAT!
I ACTIVATE THE MAGIC CARD **MONSTER REBORN** TO BRING THEM BACK!
WOOOOOOO
GIGGLE GIGGLE

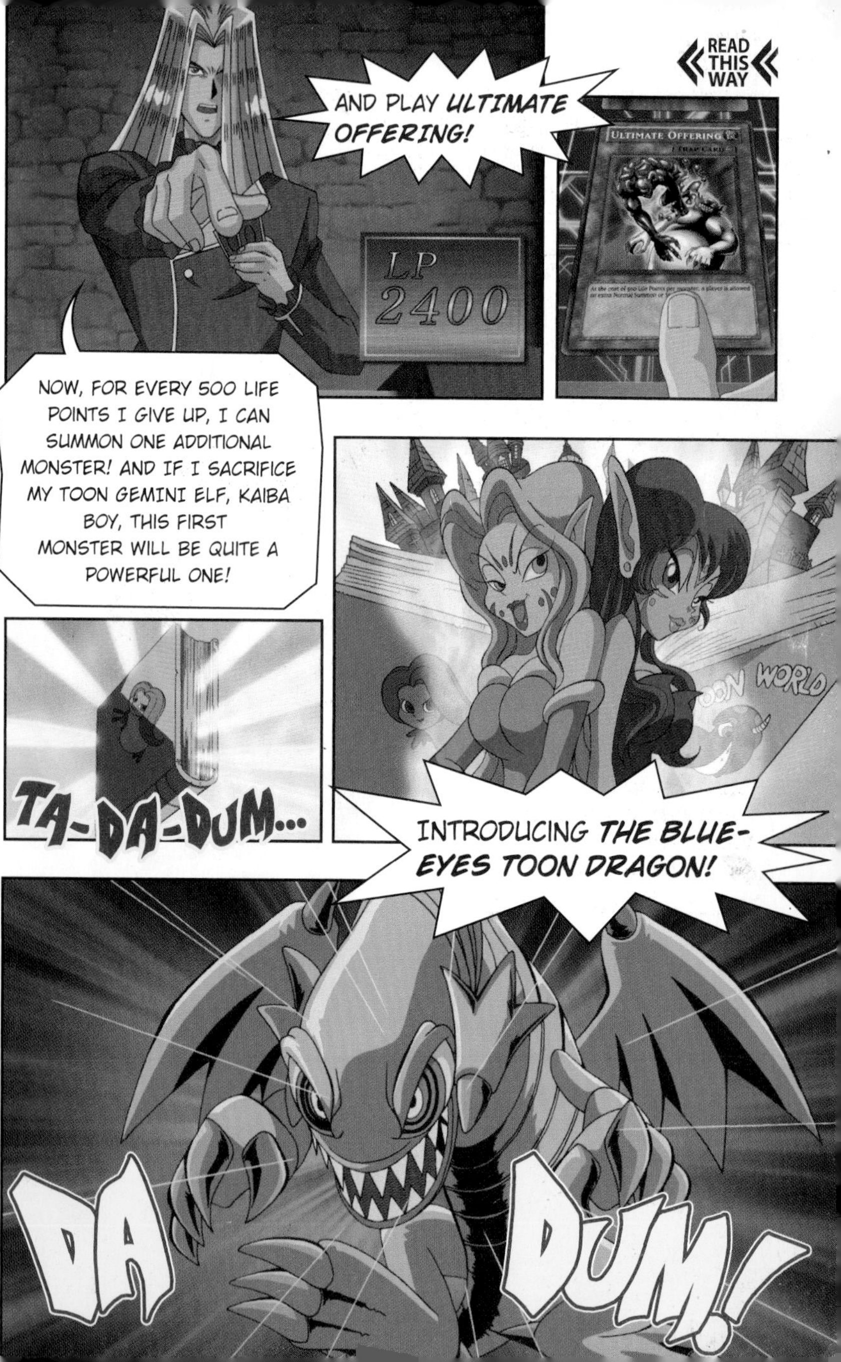
READ THIS WAY
AND PLAY ULTIMATE OFFERING!
ULTIMATE OFFERING
LP 2400
NOW, FOR EVERY 500 LIFE POINTS I GIVE UP, I CAN SUMMON ONE ADDITIONAL MONSTER! AND IF I SACRIFICE MY TOON GEMINI ELF, KAIBA BOY, THIS FIRST MONSTER WILL BE QUITE A POWERFUL ONE!
TOON WORLD
INTRODUCING THE BLUE-EYES TOON DRAGON!
TA-DA-DUM...
DA DUM!

READ THIS WAY

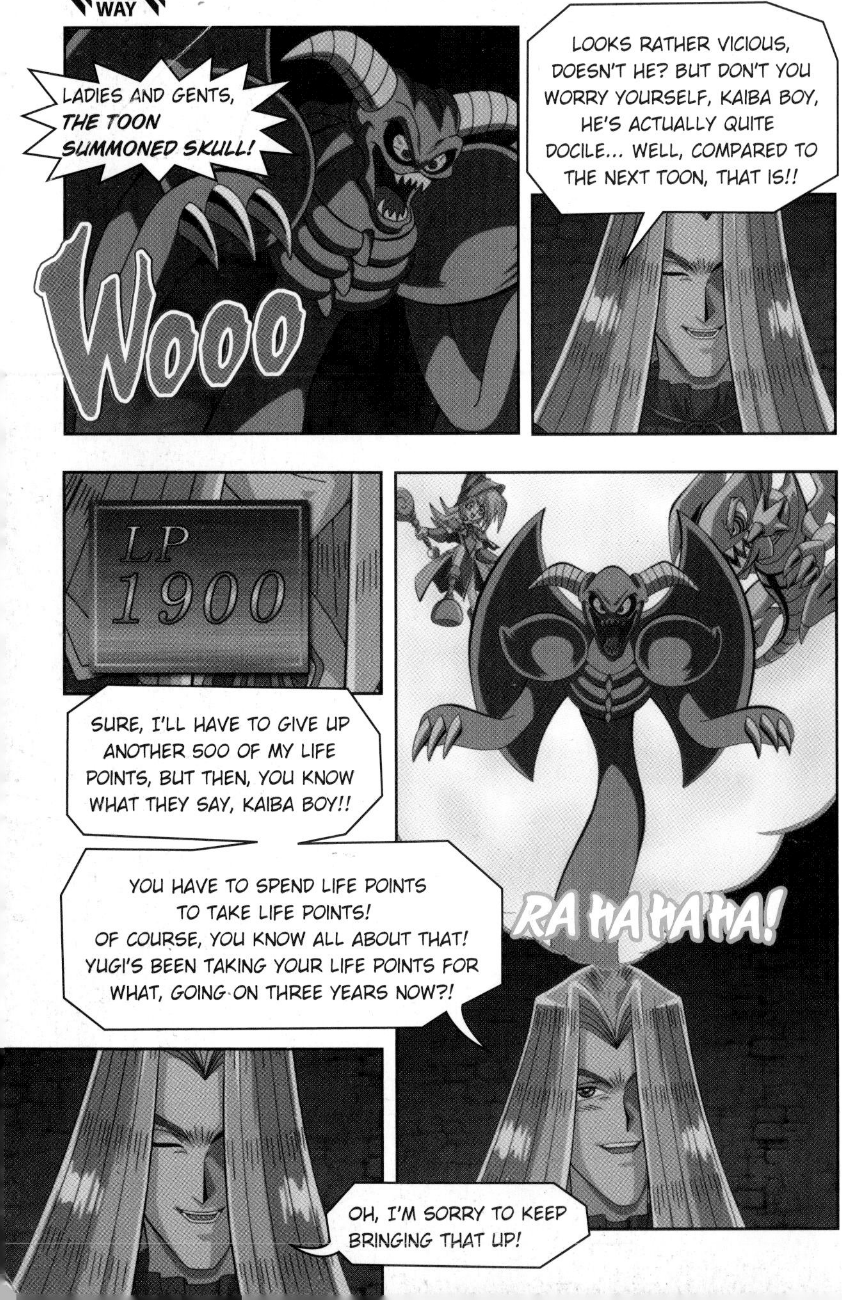
LOOKS RATHER VICIOUS, DOESN'T HE? BUT DON'T YOU WORRY YOURSELF, KAIBA BOY, HE'S ACTUALLY QUITE DOCILE... WELL, COMPARED TO THE NEXT TOON, THAT IS!!
LADIES AND GENTS, THE TOON SUMMONED SKULL!
WOOO
LP 1900
SURE, I'LL HAVE TO GIVE UP ANOTHER 500 OF MY LIFE POINTS, BUT THEN, YOU KNOW WHAT THEY SAY, KAIBA BOY!!
YOU HAVE TO SPEND LIFE POINTS TO TAKE LIFE POINTS! OF COURSE, YOU KNOW ALL ABOUT THAT! YUGI'S BEEN TAKING YOUR LIFE POINTS FOR WHAT, GOING ON THREE YEARS NOW?!
RA HA HA HA!
OH, I'M SORRY TO KEEP BRINGING THAT UP!

READ THIS WAY

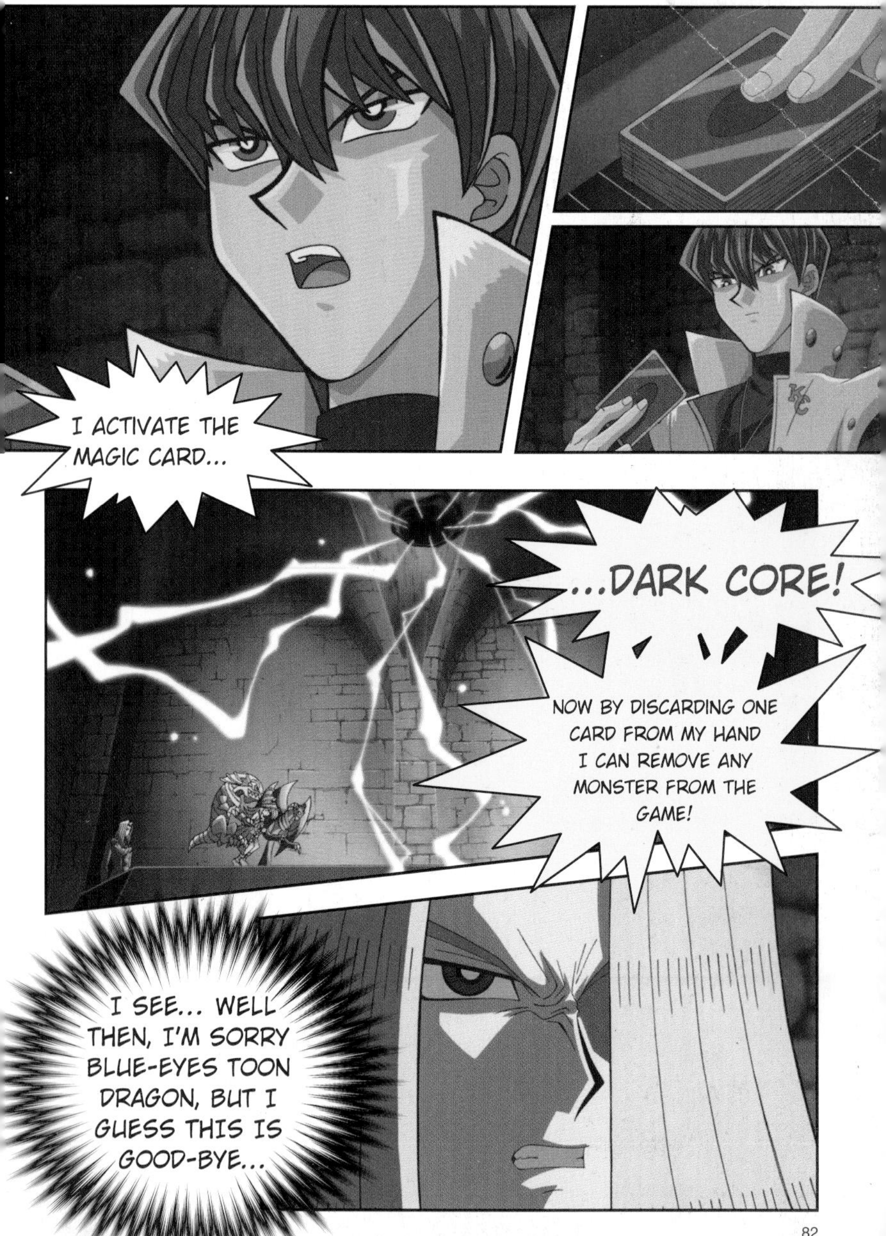
I ACTIVATE THE MAGIC CARD...
...DARK CORE!
NOW BY DISCARDING ONE CARD FROM MY HAND I CAN REMOVE ANY MONSTER FROM THE GAME!
I SEE... WELL THEN, I'M SORRY BLUE-EYES TOON DRAGON, BUT I GUESS THIS IS GOOD-BYE...

READ THIS WAY

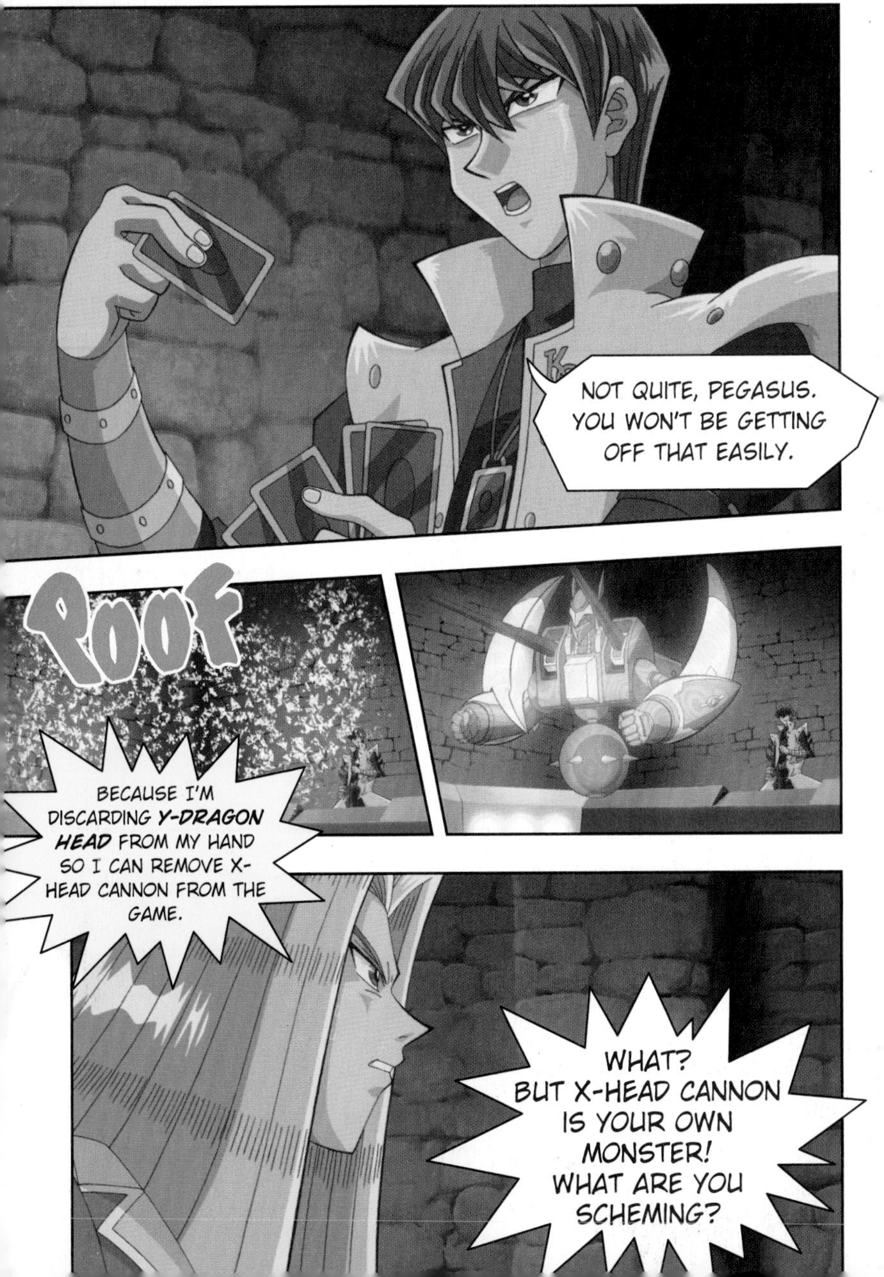
NOT QUITE, PEGASUS. YOU WON'T BE GETTING OFF THAT EASILY.
POOF
BECAUSE I'M DISCARDING ***Y-DRAGON HEAD*** FROM MY HAND SO I CAN REMOVE X-HEAD CANNON FROM THE GAME.
WHAT? BUT X-HEAD CANNON IS YOUR OWN MONSTER! WHAT ARE YOU SCHEMING?

READ THIS WAY

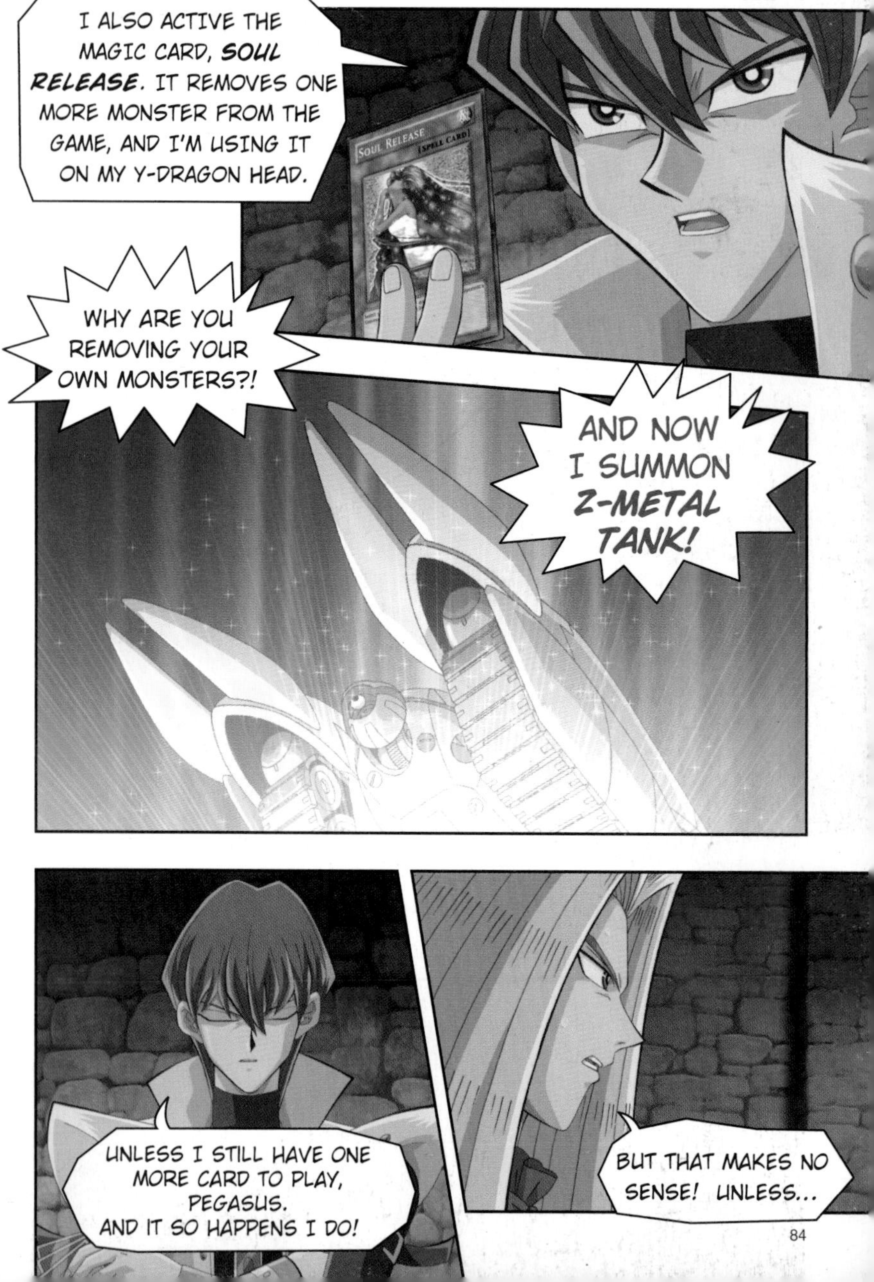
I ALSO ACTIVE THE MAGIC CARD, ***SOUL RELEASE***. IT REMOVES ONE MORE MONSTER FROM THE GAME, AND I'M USING IT ON MY Y-DRAGON HEAD.
SOUL RELEASE
[SPELL CARD]
WHY ARE YOU REMOVING YOUR OWN MONSTERS?!
AND NOW I SUMMON ***Z-METAL TANK!***
BUT THAT MAKES NO SENSE! UNLESS...
UNLESS I STILL HAVE ONE MORE CARD TO PLAY, PEGASUS. AND IT SO HAPPENS I DO!

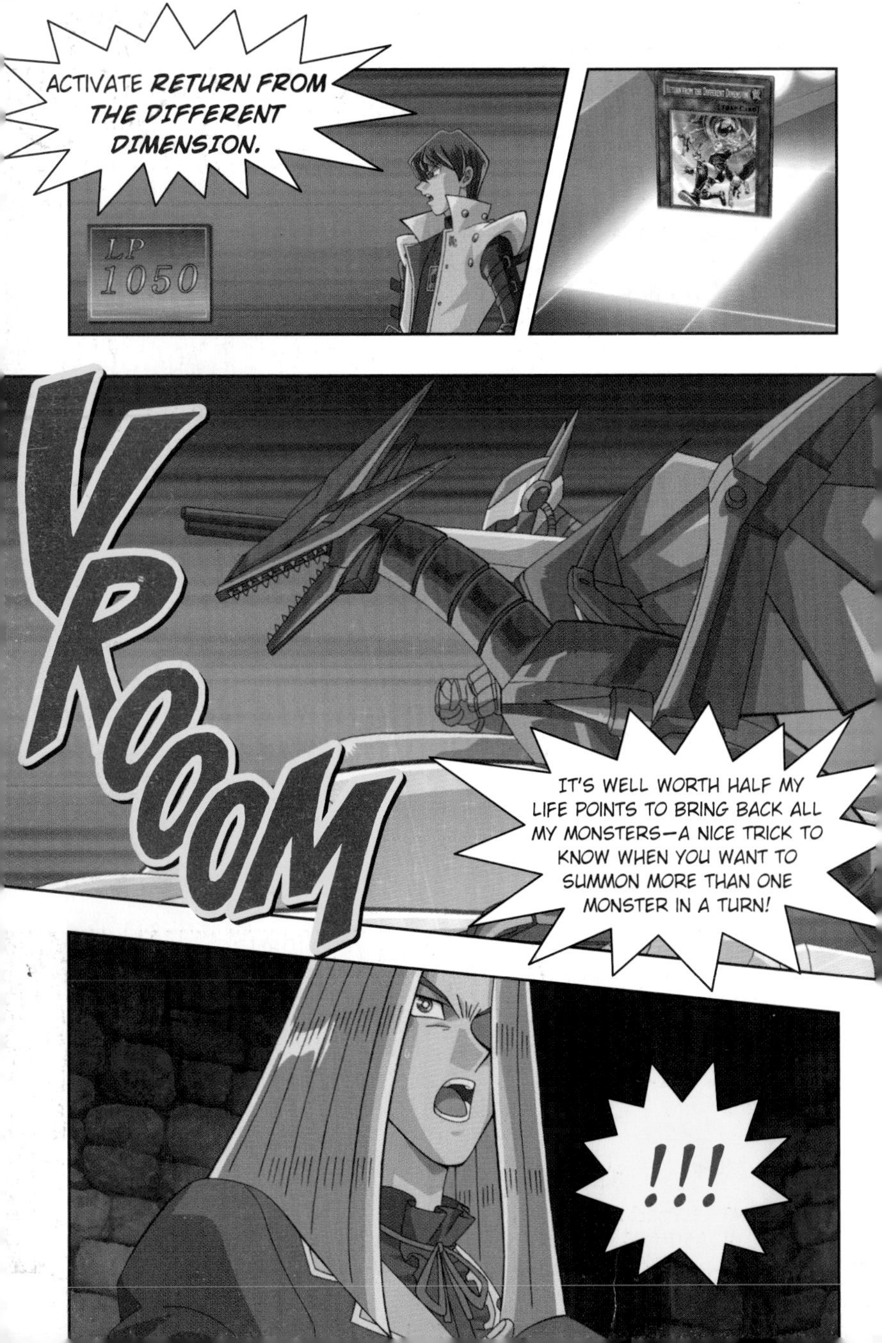
ACTIVATE RETURN FROM THE DIFFERENT DIMENSION.
LP 1050
VROOOM
IT'S WELL WORTH HALF MY LIFE POINTS TO BRING BACK ALL MY MONSTERS—A NICE TRICK TO KNOW WHEN YOU WANT TO SUMMON MORE THAN ONE MONSTER IN A TURN!
!!!

READ THIS WAY

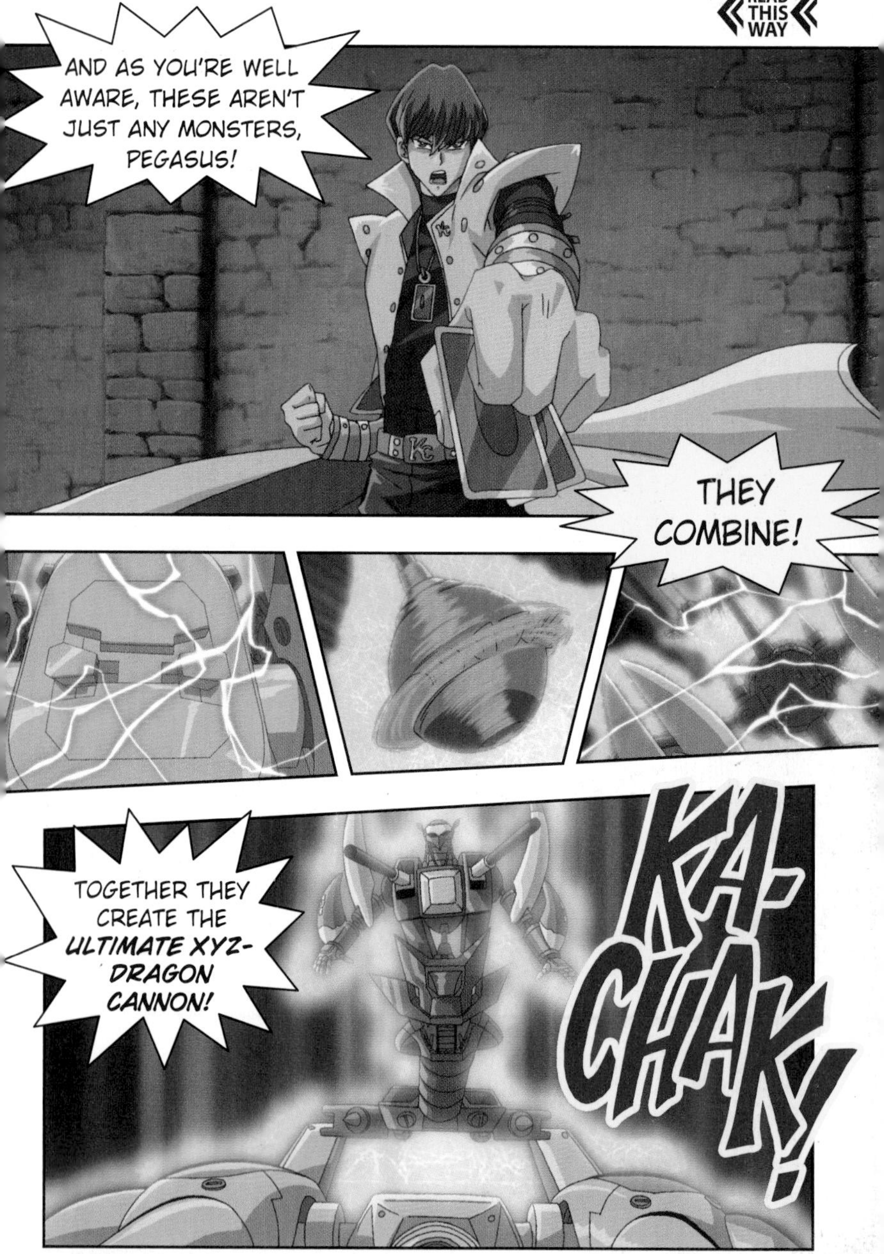
AND AS YOU'RE WELL AWARE, THESE AREN'T JUST ANY MONSTERS, PEGASUS!
THEY COMBINE!
KA-CHAK!
TOGETHER THEY CREATE THE ULTIMATE XYZ-DRAGON CANNON!

READ THIS WAY

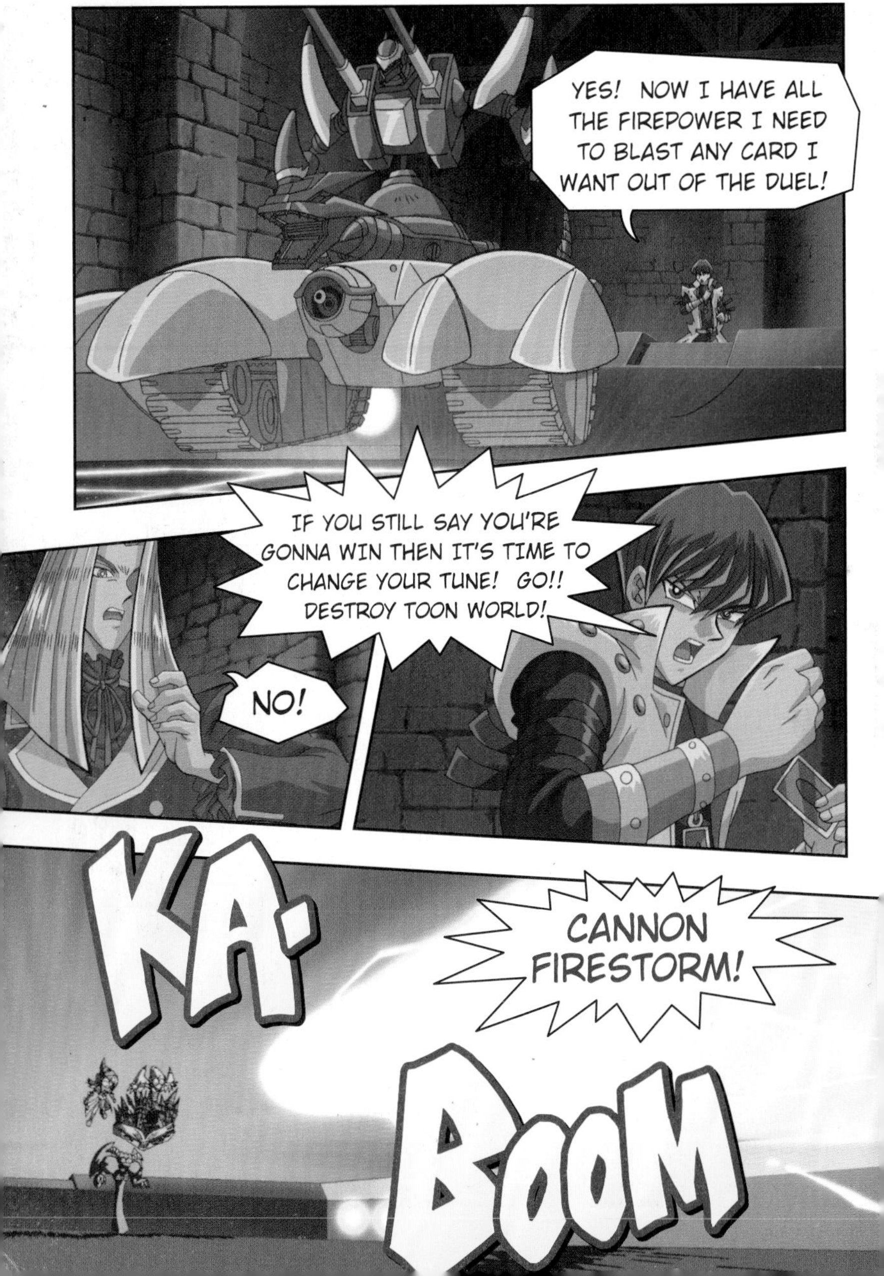

YES! NOW I HAVE ALL THE FIREPOWER I NEED TO BLAST ANY CARD I WANT OUT OF THE DUEL!
IF YOU STILL SAY YOU'RE GONNA WIN THEN IT'S TIME TO CHANGE YOUR TUNE! GO!! DESTROY TOON WORLD!
NO!
CANNON FIRESTORM!
KA-
BOOM

READ THIS WAY

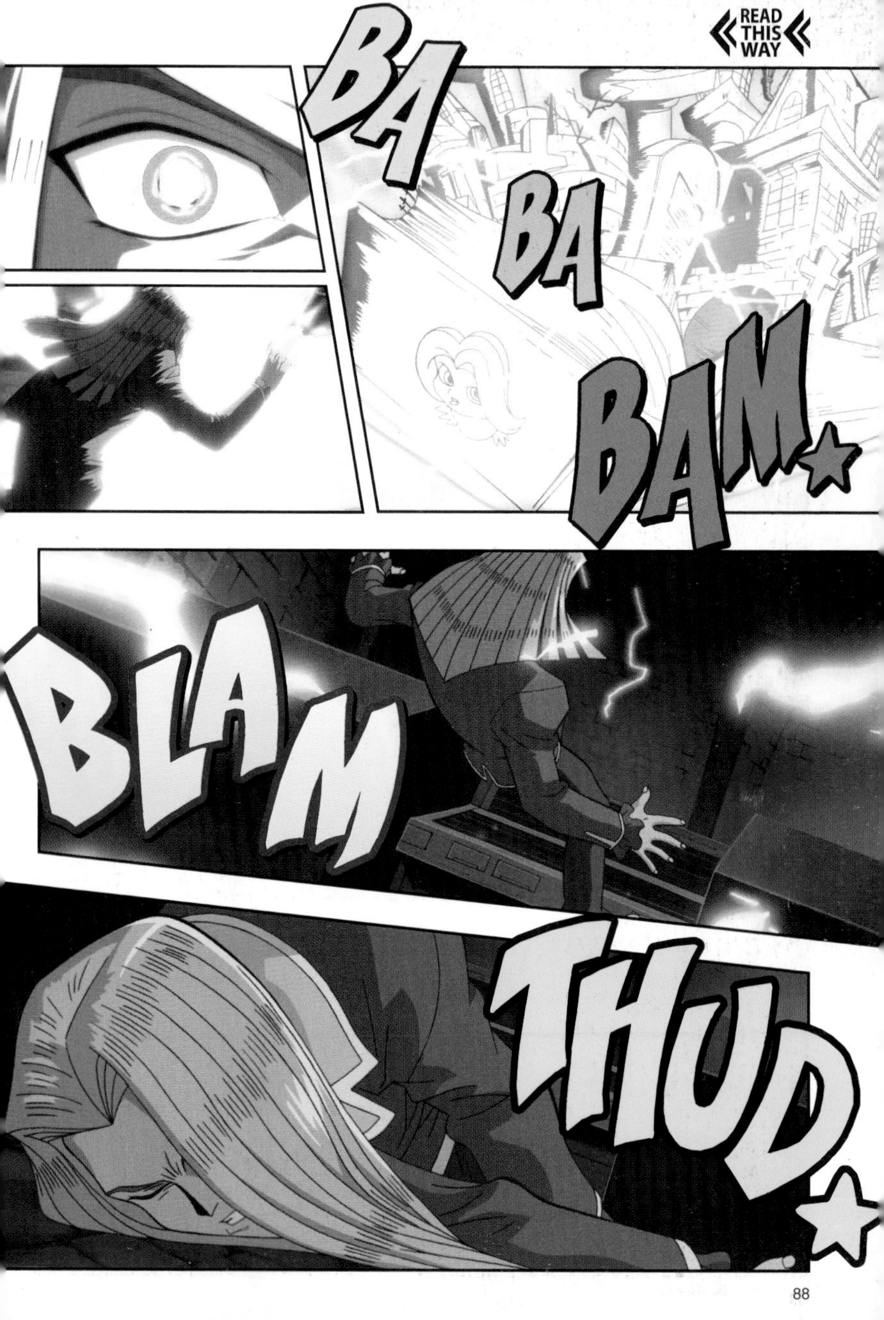
BA
BA
BAM
BLAM
THUD

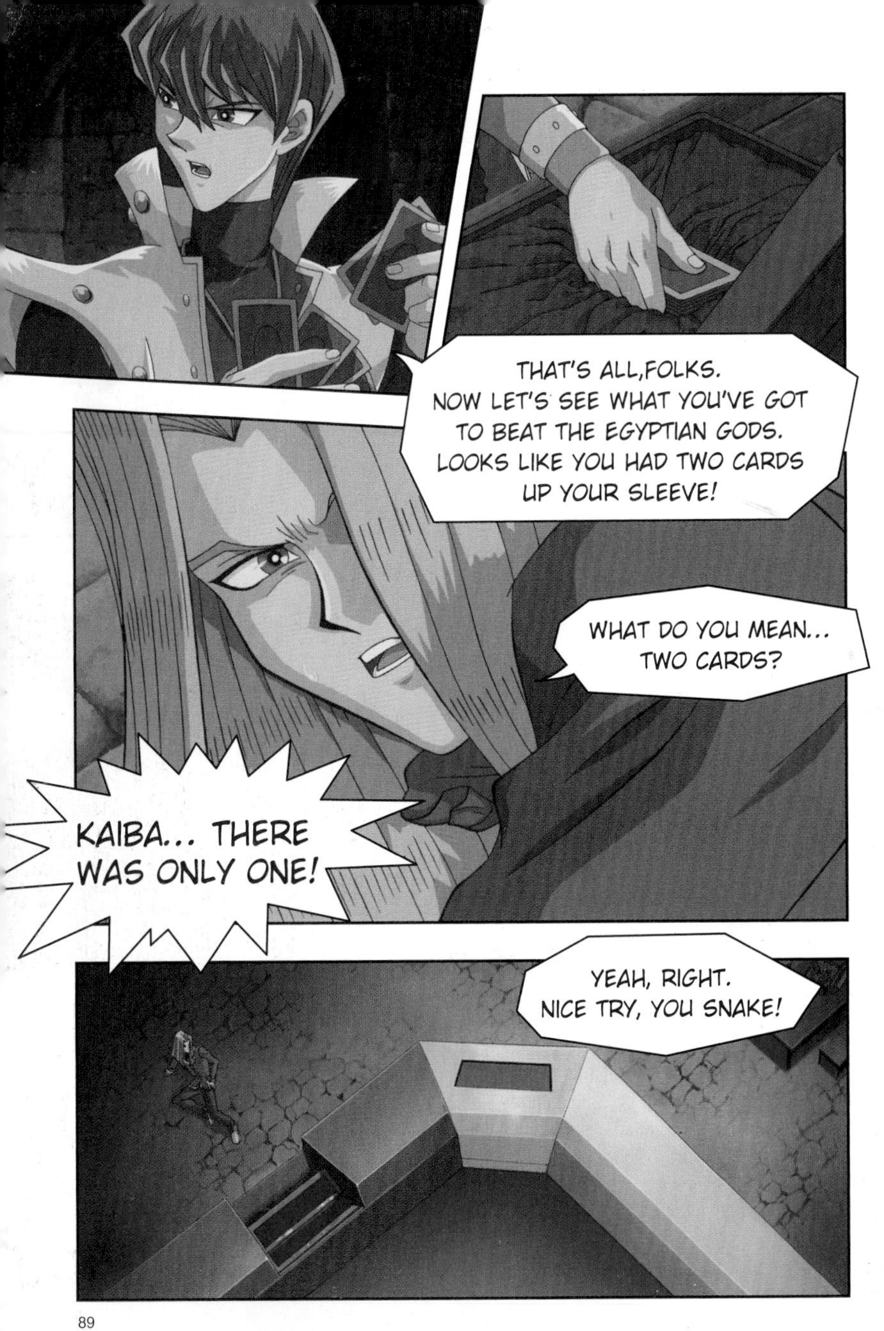
THAT'S ALL,FOLKS. NOW LET'S SEE WHAT YOU'VE GOT TO BEAT THE EGYPTIAN GODS. LOOKS LIKE YOU HAD TWO CARDS UP YOUR SLEEVE!
WHAT DO YOU MEAN... TWO CARDS?
KAIBA... THERE WAS ONLY ONE!
YEAH, RIGHT. NICE TRY, YOU SNAKE!

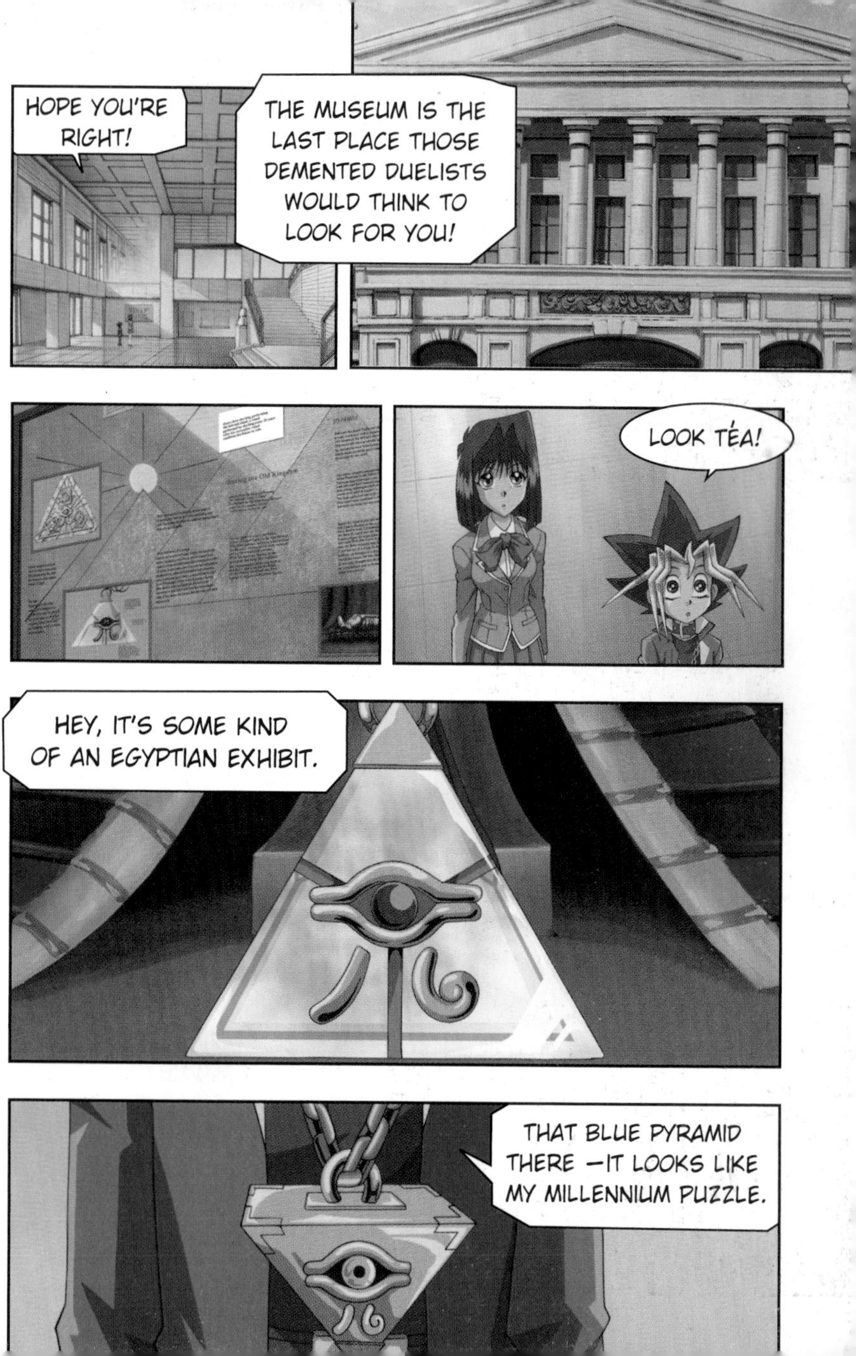
THE MUSEUM IS THE LAST PLACE THOSE DEMENTED DUELISTS WOULD THINK TO LOOK FOR YOU!
HOPE YOU'RE RIGHT!
LOOK TÉA!
HEY, IT'S SOME KIND OF AN EGYPTIAN EXHIBIT.
THAT BLUE PYRAMID THERE —IT LOOKS LIKE MY MILLENNIUM PUZZLE.

READ THIS WAY

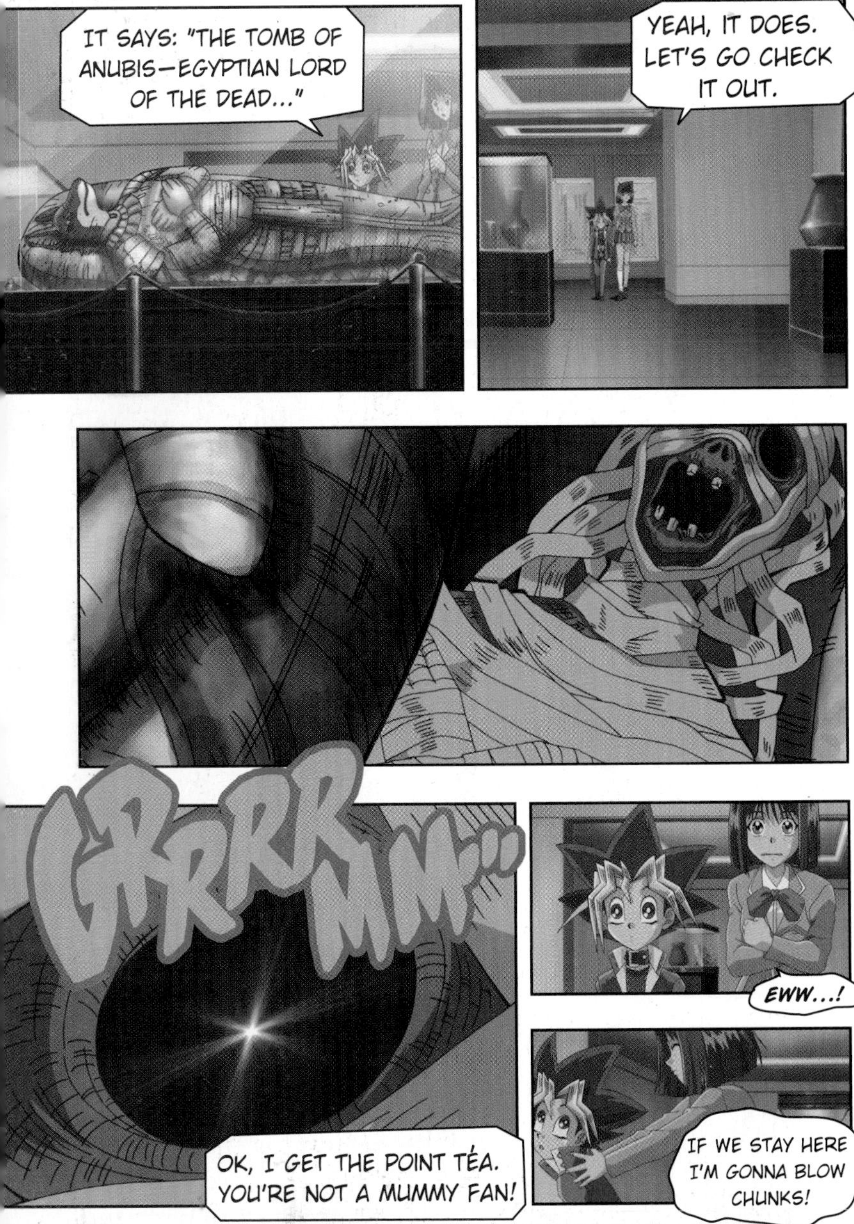
YEAH, IT DOES. LET'S GO CHECK IT OUT.
IT SAYS: "THE TOMB OF ANUBIS—EGYPTIAN LORD OF THE DEAD..."
EWW...!
IF WE STAY HERE I'M GONNA BLOW CHUNKS!
GRRRR MM...
OK, I GET THE POINT TÉA. YOU'RE NOT A MUMMY FAN!

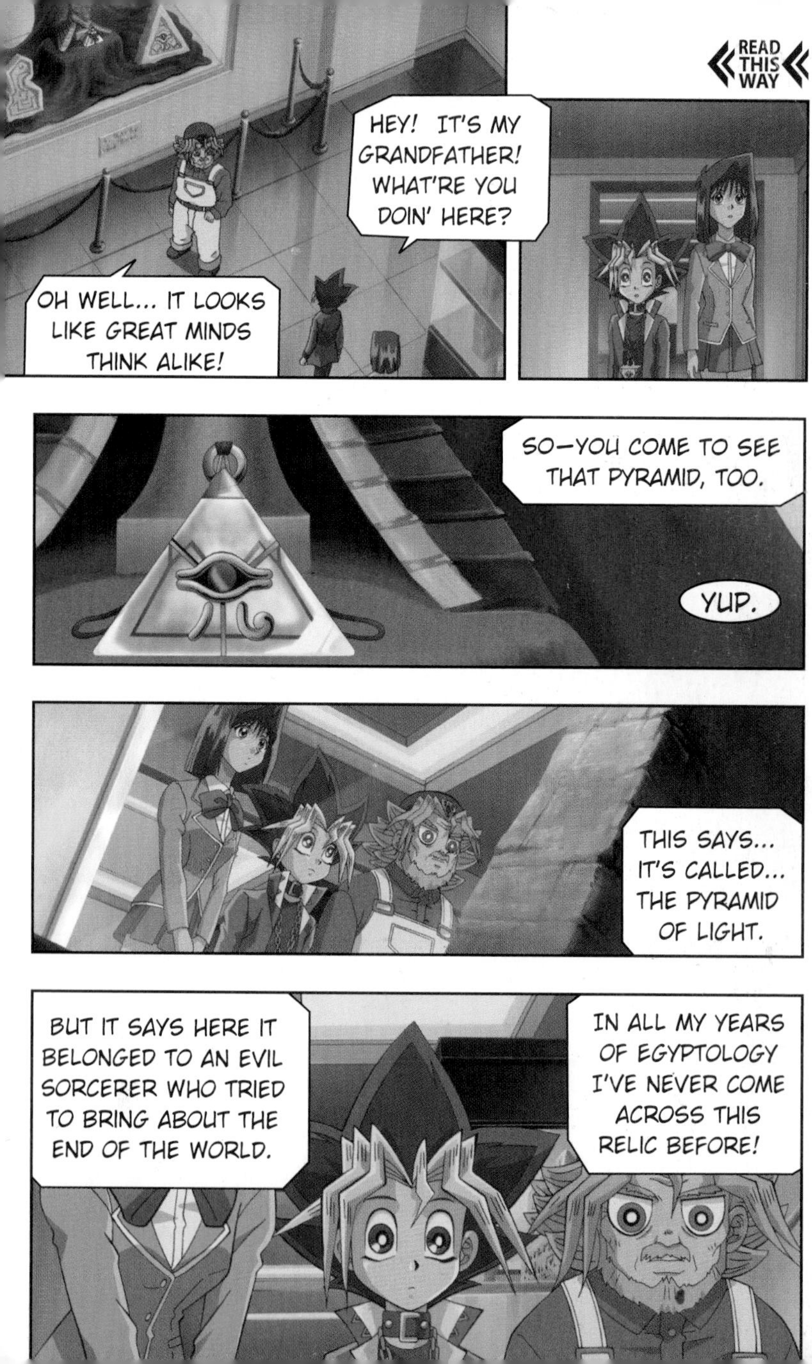
READ THIS WAY
HEY! IT'S MY GRANDFATHER! WHAT'RE YOU DOIN' HERE?
OH WELL... IT LOOKS LIKE GREAT MINDS THINK ALIKE!
SO—YOU COME TO SEE THAT PYRAMID, TOO.
YUP.
THIS SAYS... IT'S CALLED... THE PYRAMID OF LIGHT.
IN ALL MY YEARS OF EGYPTOLOGY I'VE NEVER COME ACROSS THIS RELIC BEFORE!
BUT IT SAYS HERE IT BELONGED TO AN EVIL SORCERER WHO TRIED TO BRING ABOUT THE END OF THE WORLD.

READ THIS WAY

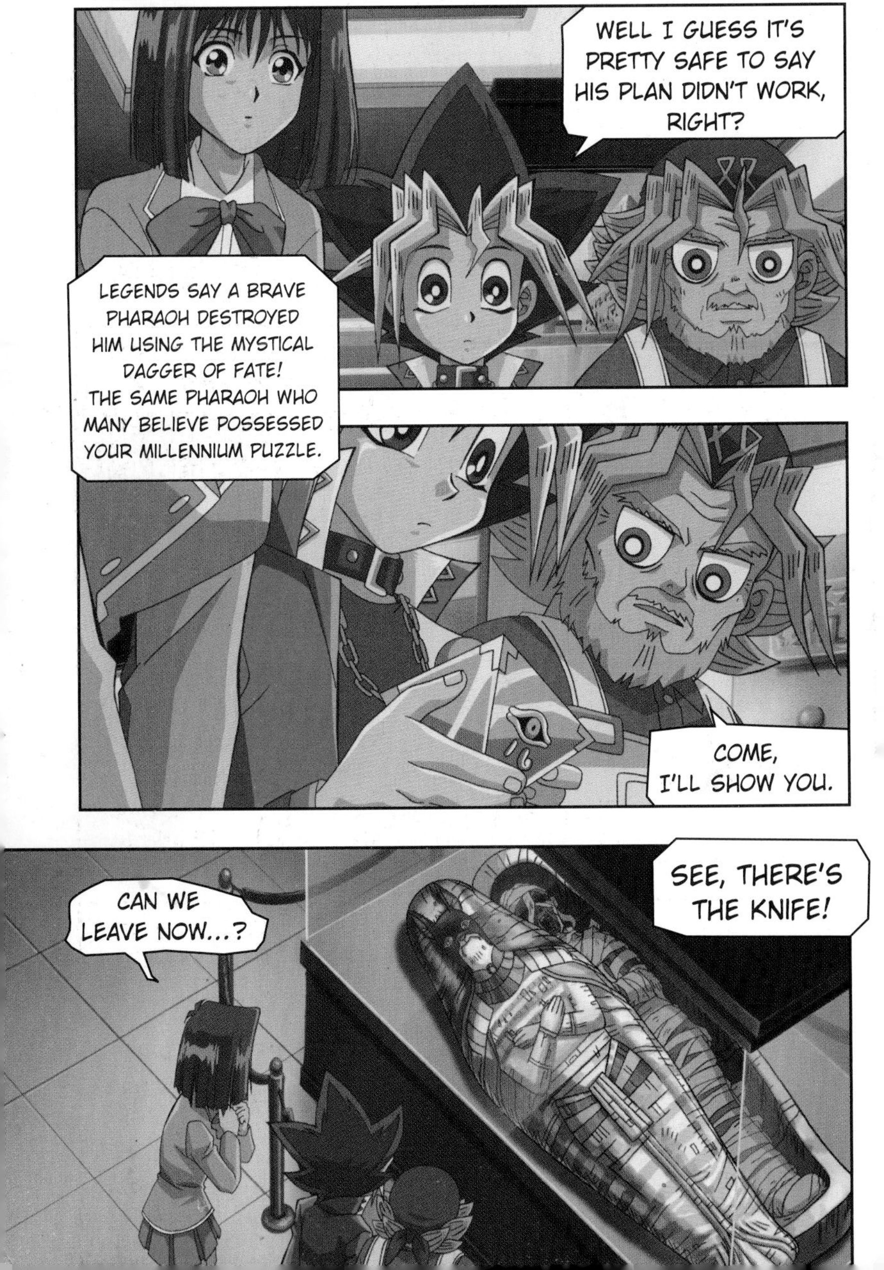

WELL I GUESS IT'S PRETTY SAFE TO SAY HIS PLAN DIDN'T WORK, RIGHT?
LEGENDS SAY A BRAVE PHARAOH DESTROYED HIM USING THE MYSTICAL DAGGER OF FATE! THE SAME PHARAOH WHO MANY BELIEVE POSSESSED YOUR MILLENNIUM PUZZLE.
COME, I'LL SHOW YOU.
SEE, THERE'S THE KNIFE!
CAN WE LEAVE NOW...?

READ THIS WAY

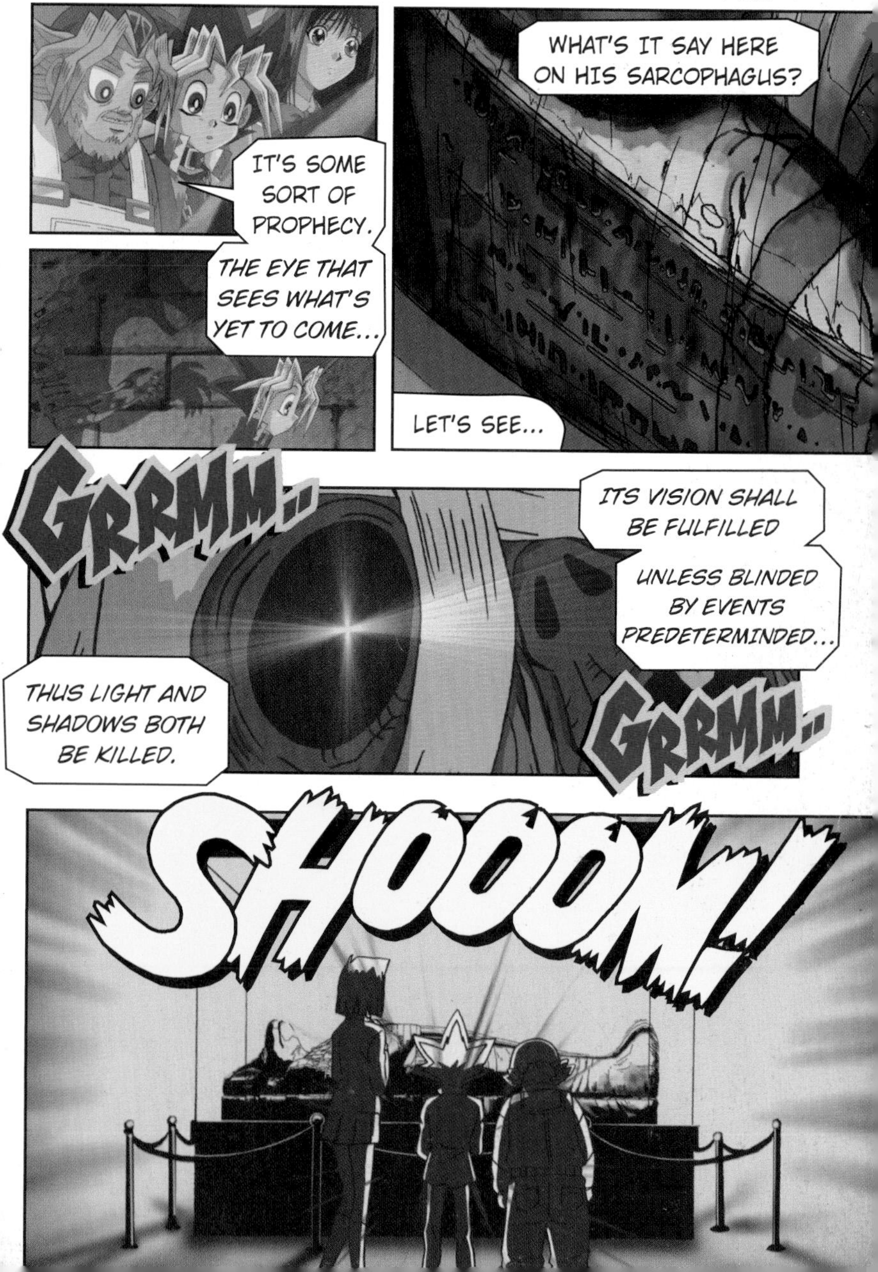

WHAT'S IT SAY HERE ON HIS SARCOPHAGUS?
LET'S SEE...
IT'S SOME SORT OF PROPHECY.
THE EYE THAT SEES WHAT'S YET TO COME...
ITS VISION SHALL BE FULFILLED
UNLESS BLINDED BY EVENTS PREDETERMINDED...
GRRMM..
GRRMM..
THUS LIGHT AND SHADOWS BOTH BE KILLED.
SHOOOM!

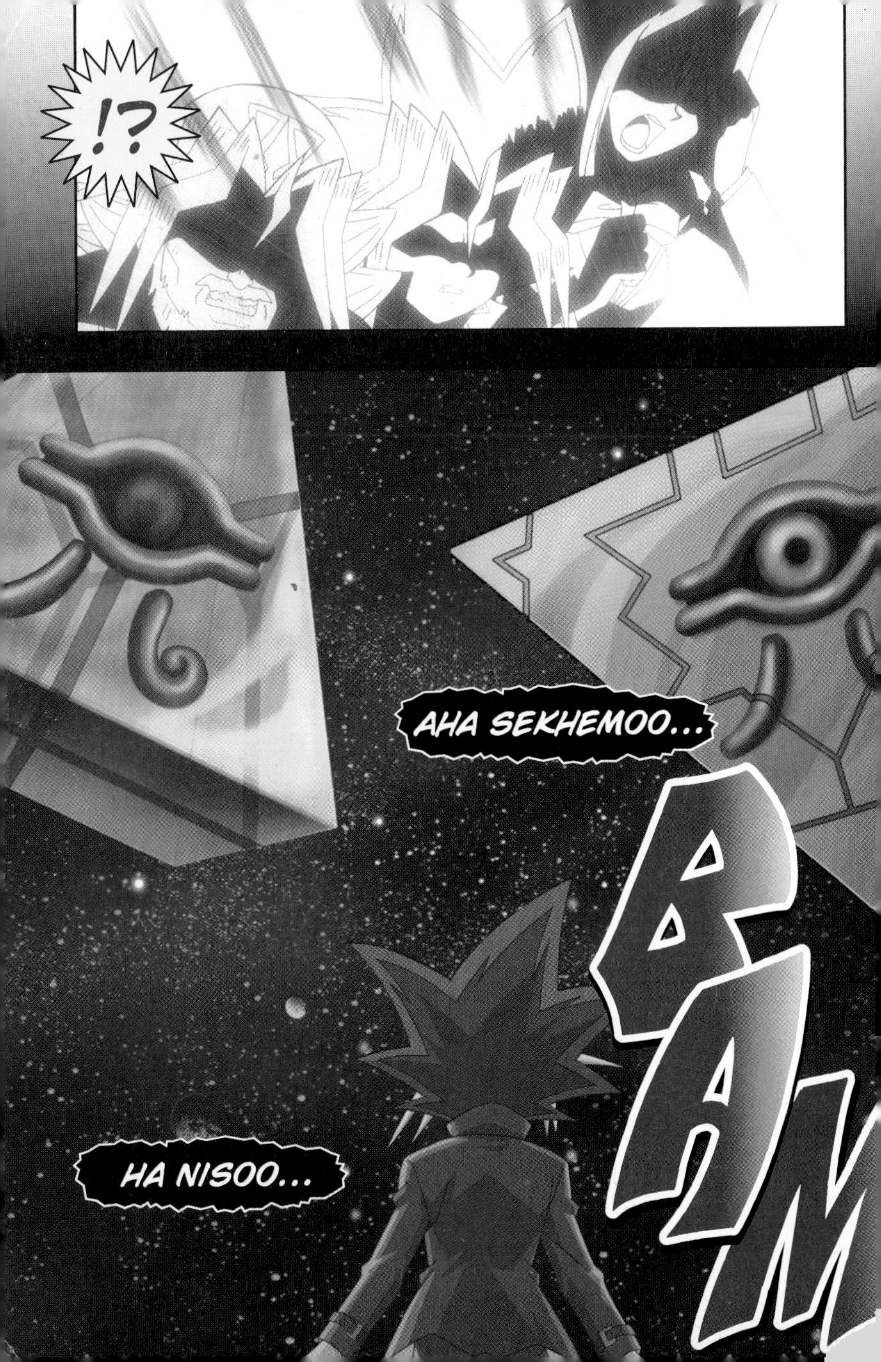
!?
AHA SEKHEMOO...
BAM
HA NISOO...

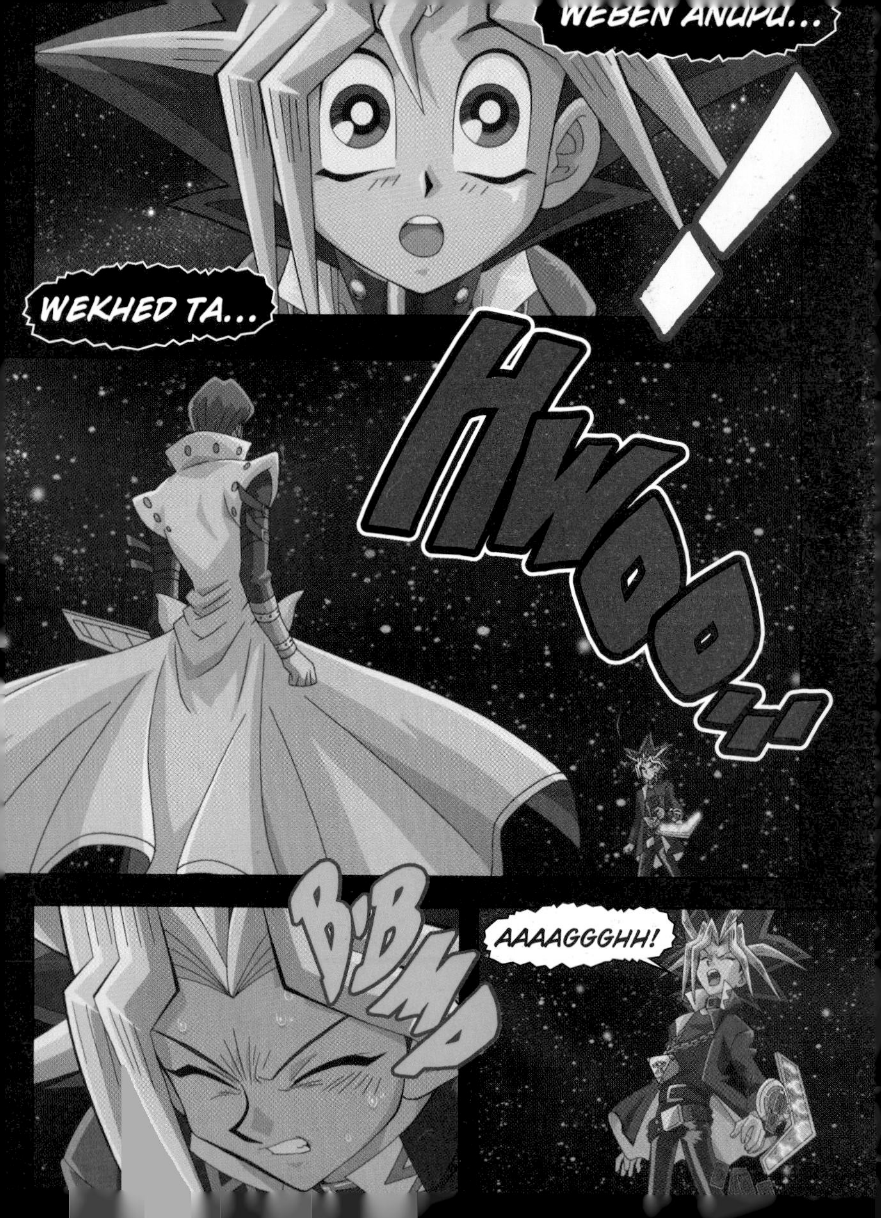
WEBEN ANUPU...
!
WEKHED TA...
HWOO...
AAAAGGGHH!
B-BMP

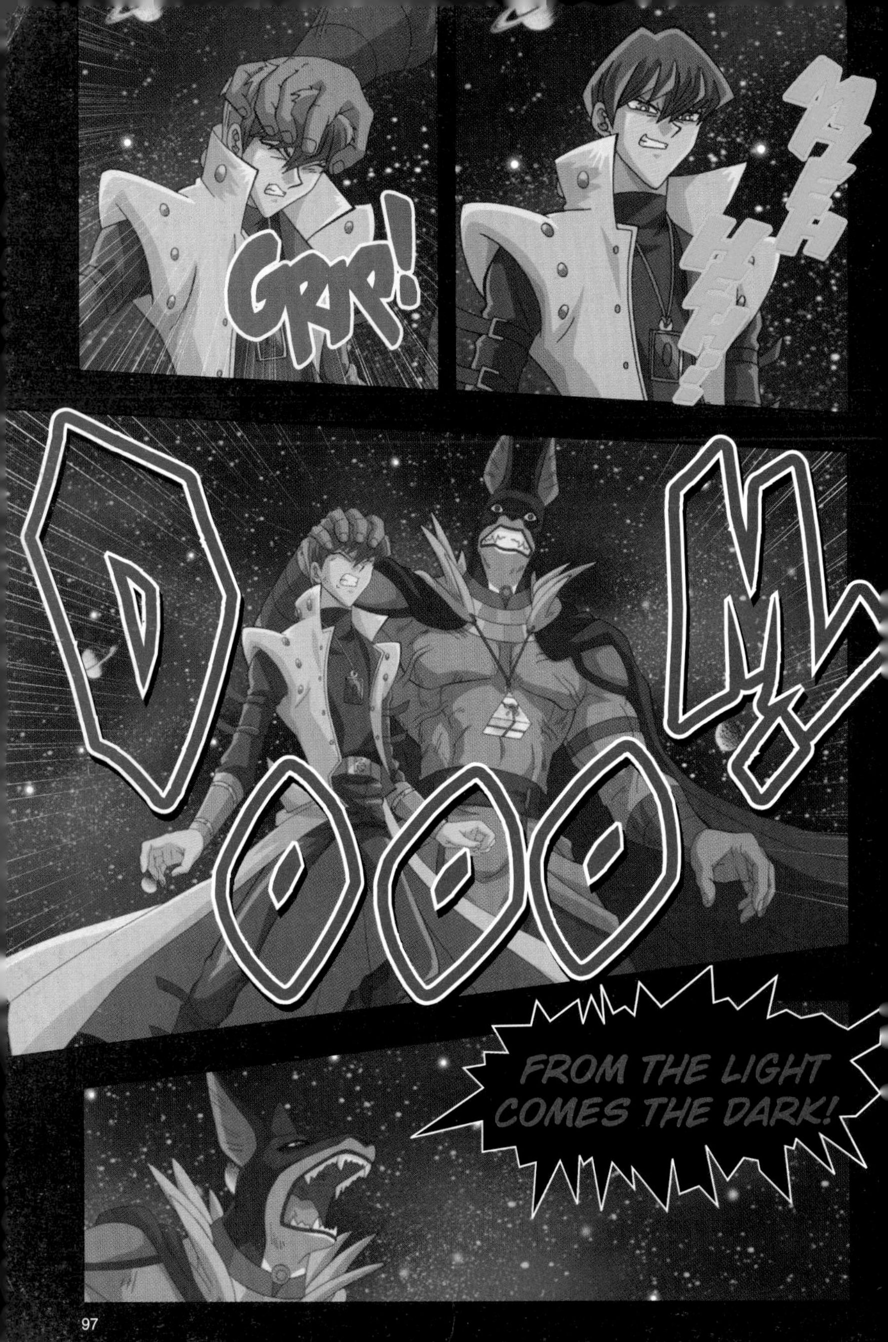
GRRR!
DOOOM!
FROM THE LIGHT COMES THE DARK!

READ THIS WAY

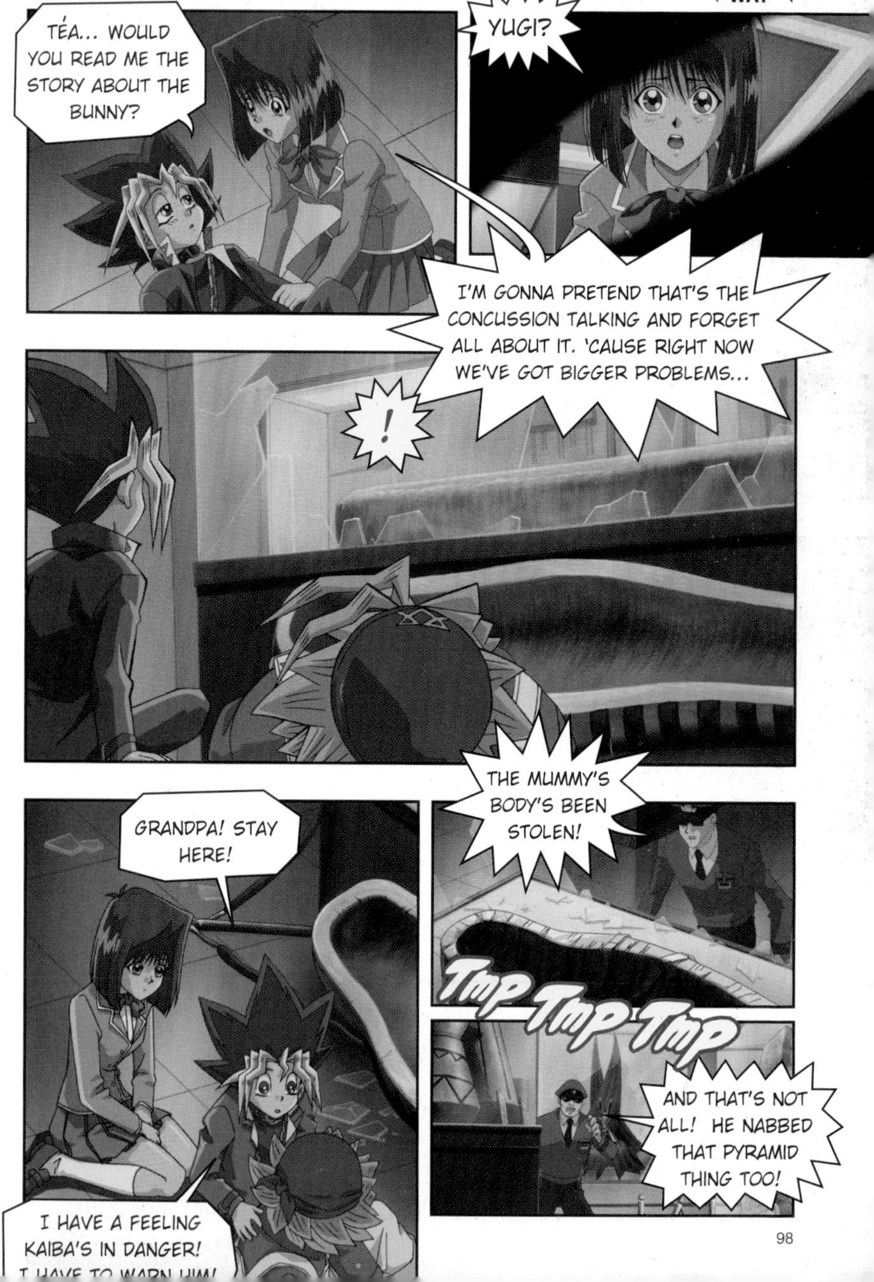

YUGI?
TÉA... WOULD YOU READ ME THE STORY ABOUT THE BUNNY?
I'M GONNA PRETEND THAT'S THE CONCUSSION TALKING AND FORGET ALL ABOUT IT. 'CAUSE RIGHT NOW WE'VE GOT BIGGER PROBLEMS...
!
THE MUMMY'S BODY'S BEEN STOLEN!
Tmp Tmp Tmp
AND THAT'S NOT ALL! HE NABBED THAT PYRAMID THING TOO!
GRANDPA! STAY HERE!
I HAVE A FEELING KAIBA'S IN DANGER! I HAVE TO WARN HIM!

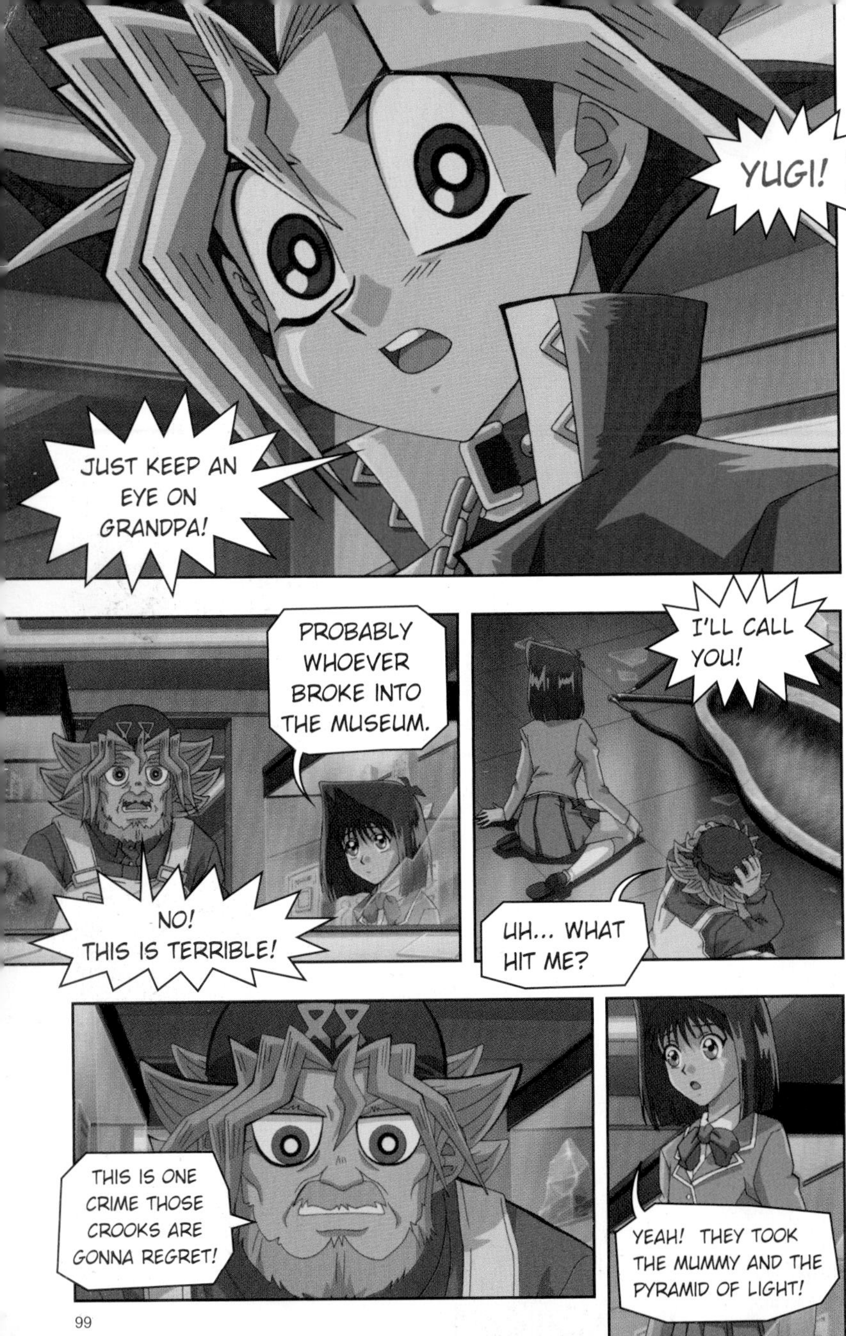
YUGI!
JUST KEEP AN EYE ON GRANDPA!
I'LL CALL YOU!
UH... WHAT HIT ME?
PROBABLY WHOEVER BROKE INTO THE MUSEUM.
NO! THIS IS TERRIBLE!
YEAH! THEY TOOK THE MUMMY AND THE PYRAMID OF LIGHT!
THIS IS ONE CRIME THOSE CROOKS ARE GONNA REGRET!

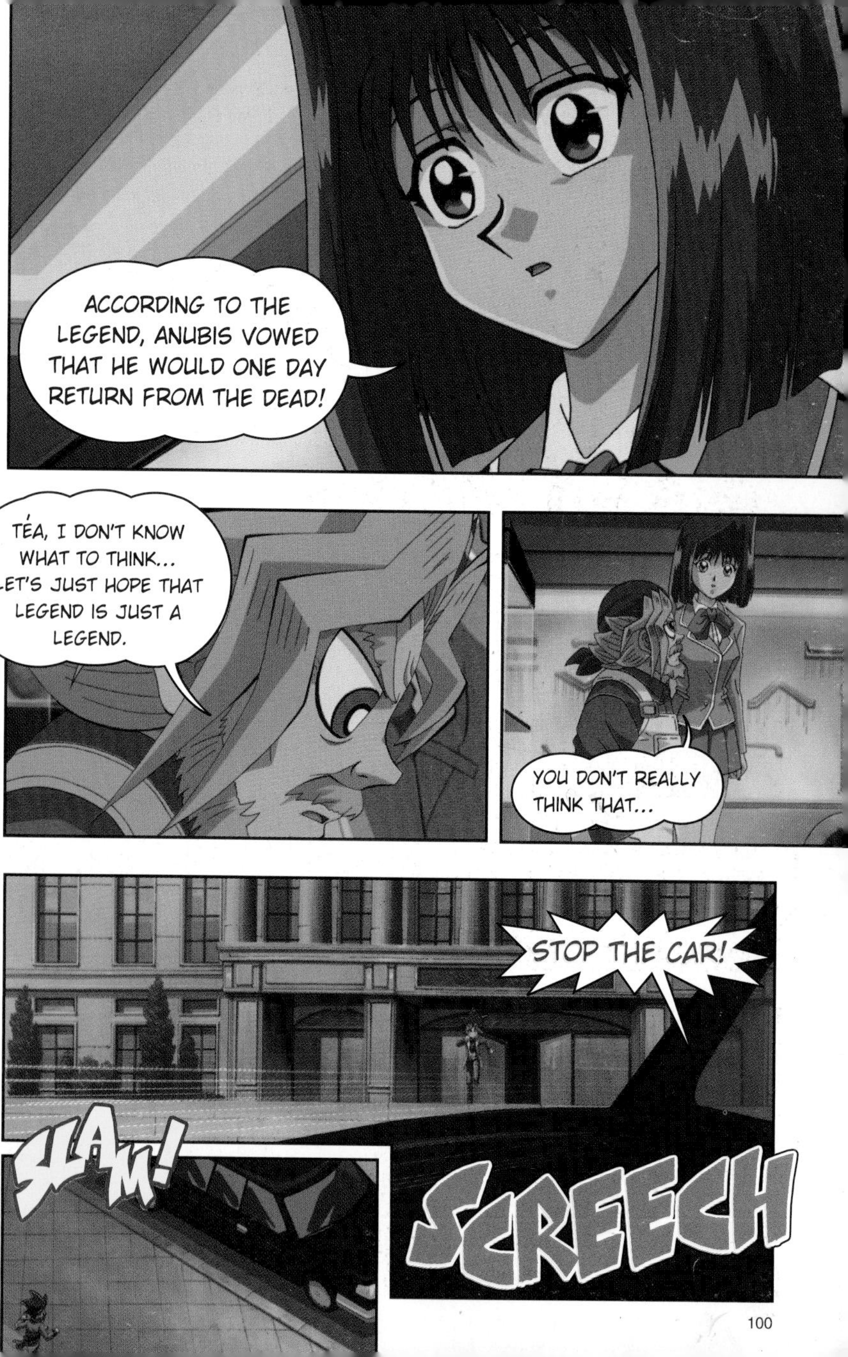
ACCORDING TO THE LEGEND, ANUBIS VOWED THAT HE WOULD ONE DAY RETURN FROM THE DEAD!
YOU DON'T REALLY THINK THAT...
TÉA, I DON'T KNOW WHAT TO THINK... LET'S JUST HOPE THAT LEGEND IS JUST A LEGEND.
STOP THE CAR!
SCREECH
SLAM!

READ THIS WAY

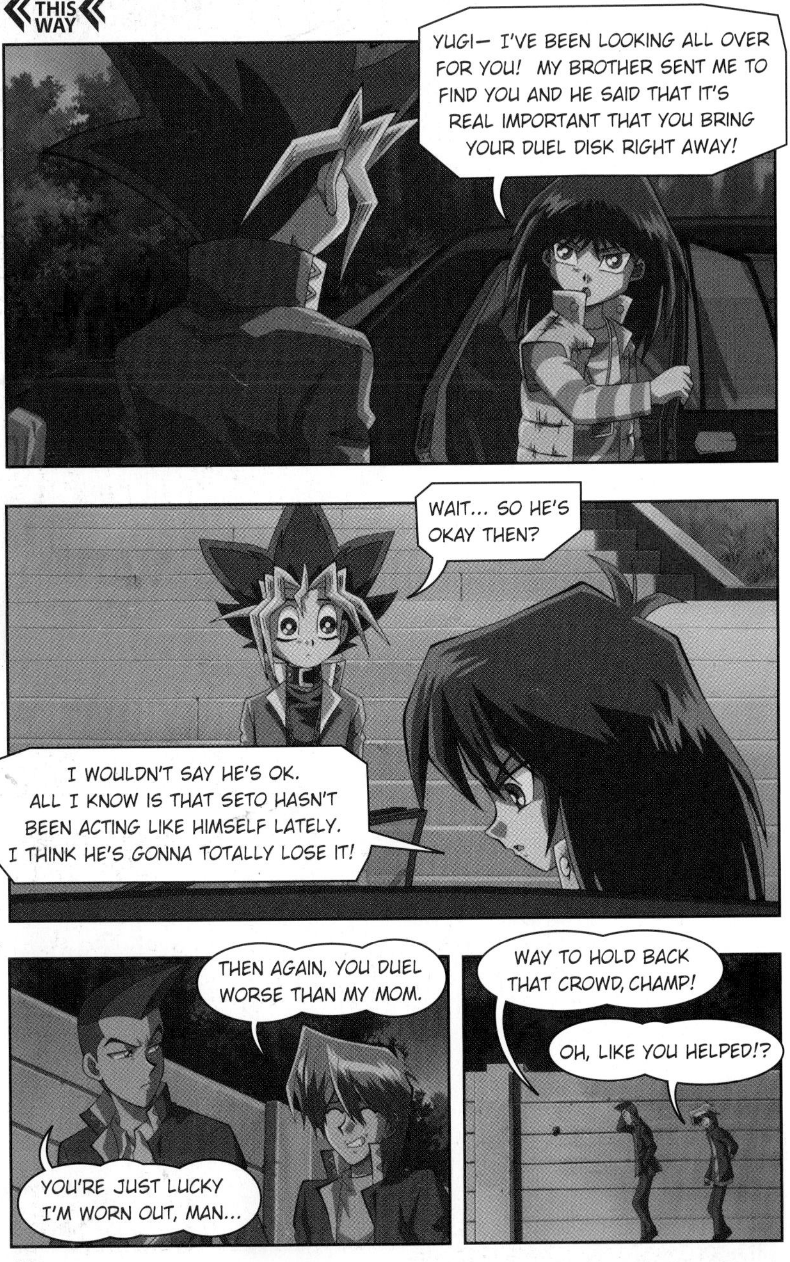
YUGI— I'VE BEEN LOOKING ALL OVER FOR YOU! MY BROTHER SENT ME TO FIND YOU AND HE SAID THAT IT'S REAL IMPORTANT THAT YOU BRING YOUR DUEL DISK RIGHT AWAY!
WAIT... SO HE'S OKAY THEN?
I WOULDN'T SAY HE'S OK. ALL I KNOW IS THAT SETO HASN'T BEEN ACTING LIKE HIMSELF LATELY. I THINK HE'S GONNA TOTALLY LOSE IT!
WAY TO HOLD BACK THAT CROWD, CHAMP!
OH, LIKE YOU HELPED!?
THEN AGAIN, YOU DUEL WORSE THAN MY MOM.
YOU'RE JUST LUCKY I'M WORN OUT, MAN...

READ THIS WAY

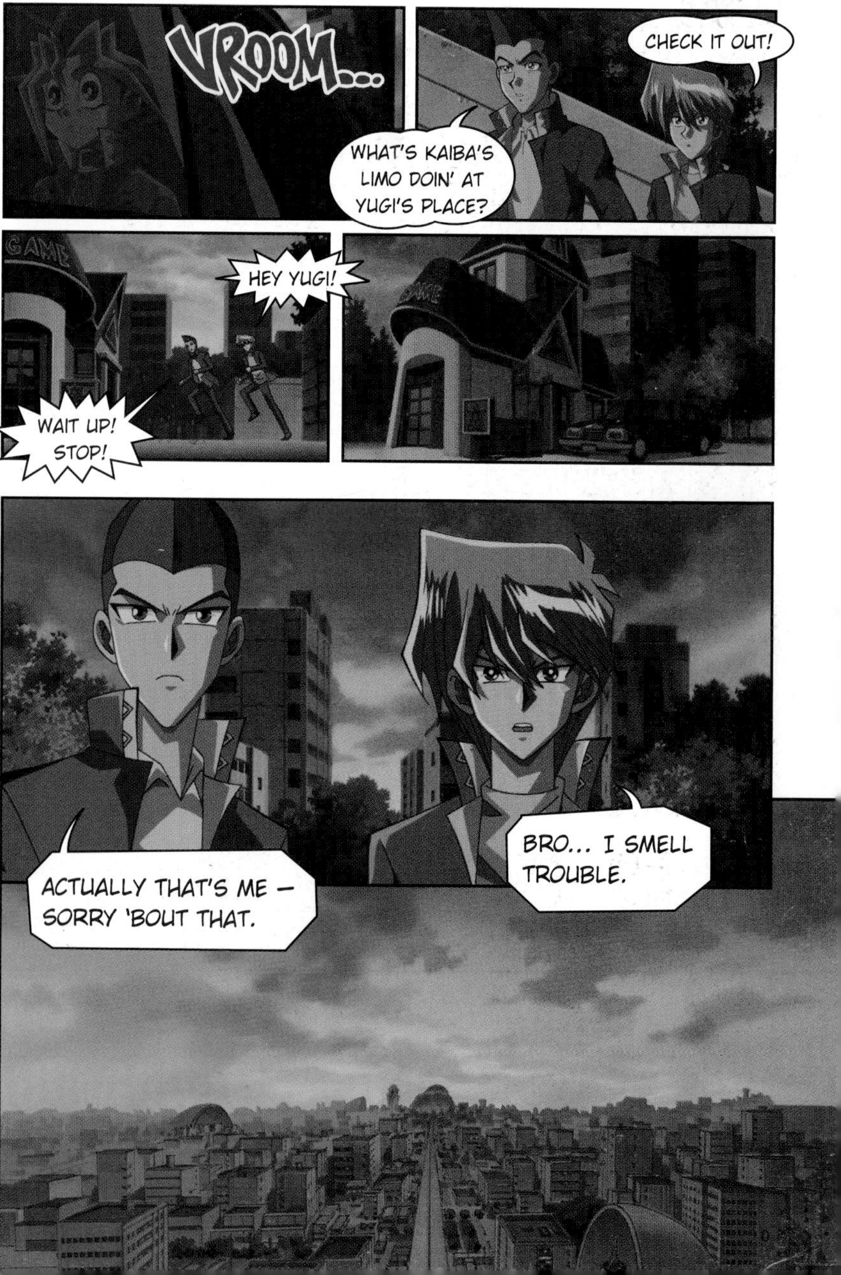
CHECK IT OUT!
WHAT'S KAIBA'S LIMO DOIN' AT YUGI'S PLACE?
VROOM...
HEY YUGI!
WAIT UP! STOP!
BRO... I SMELL TROUBLE.
ACTUALLY THAT'S ME — SORRY 'BOUT THAT.

READ THIS WAY

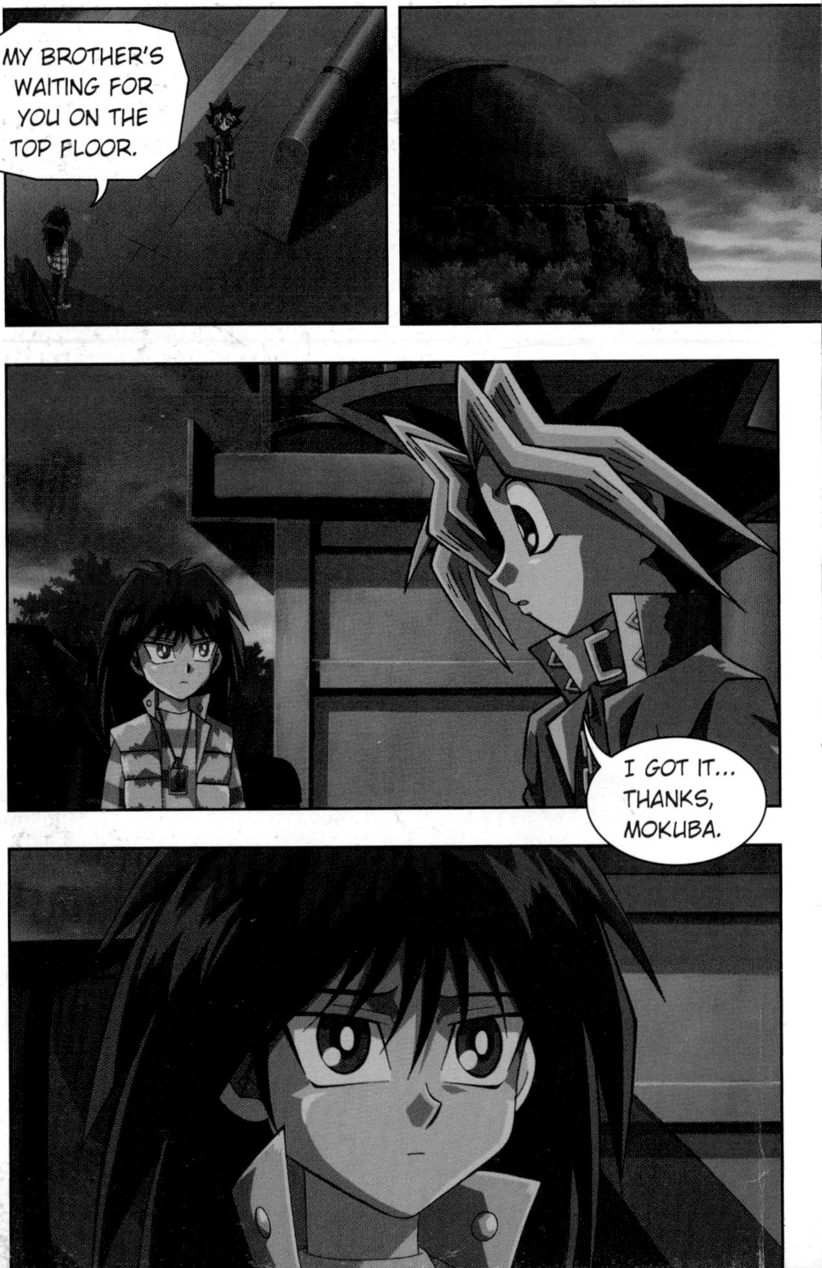
MY BROTHER'S WAITING FOR YOU ON THE TOP FLOOR.
I GOT IT... THANKS, MOKUBA.

READ THIS WAY

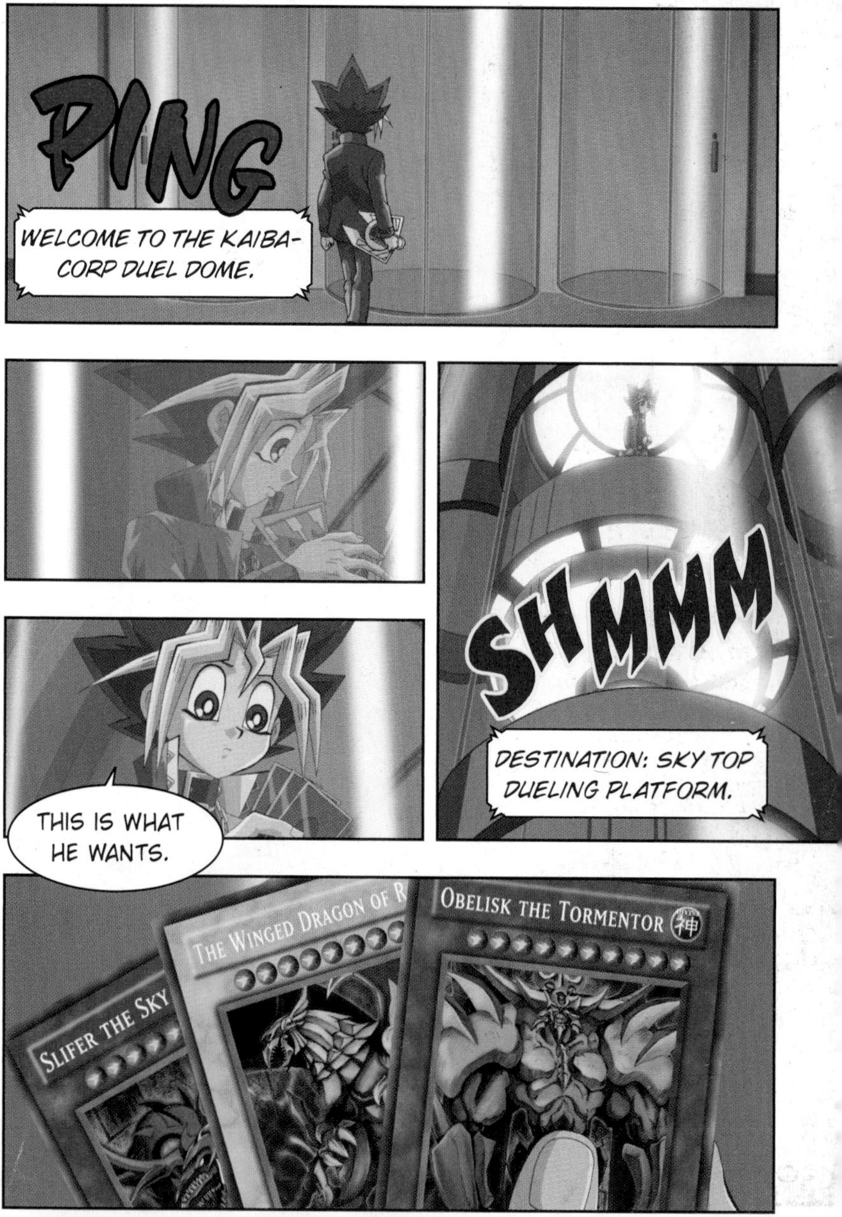
PING
WELCOME TO THE KAIBA-CORP DUEL DOME.
SHMMM
DESTINATION: SKY TOP DUELING PLATFORM.
THIS IS WHAT HE WANTS.
OBELISK THE TORMENTOR
THE WINGED DRAGON OF R
SLIFER THE SKY

READ THIS WAY

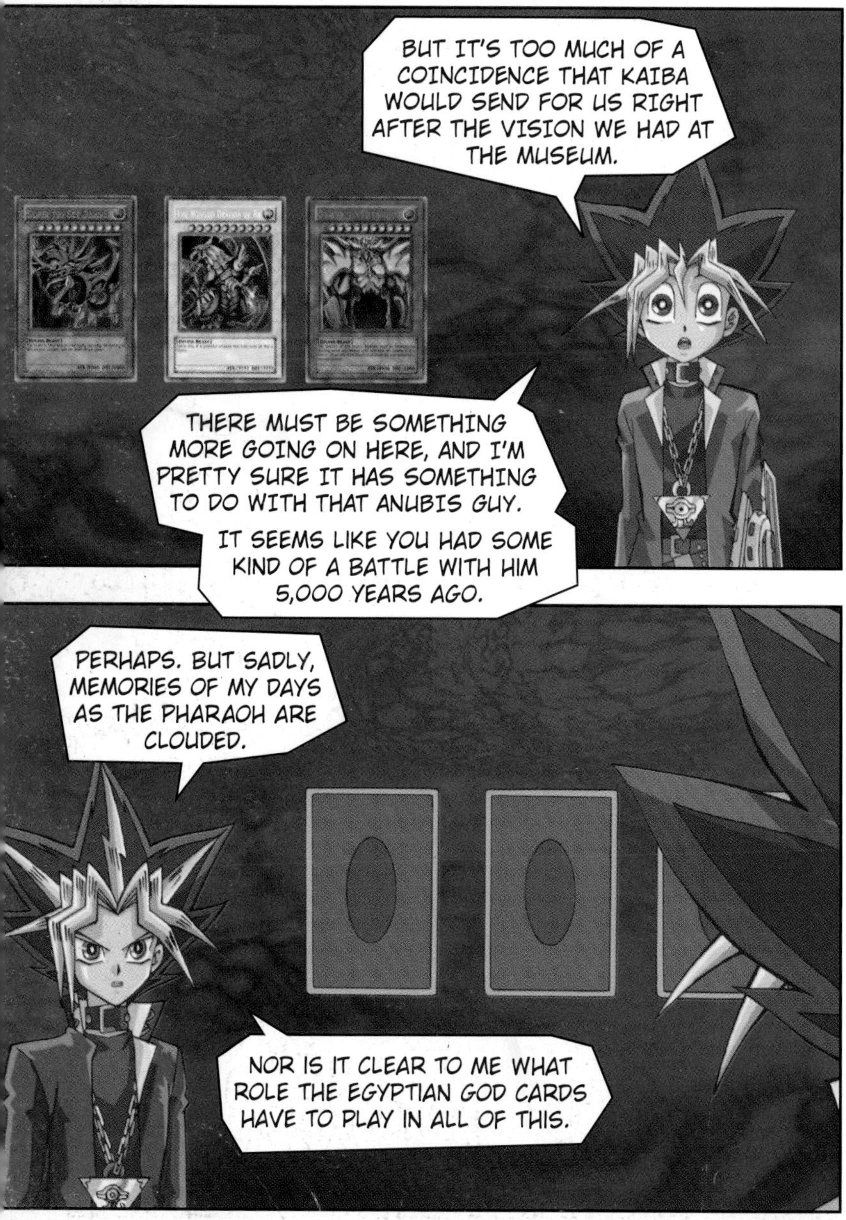

BUT IT'S TOO MUCH OF A COINCIDENCE THAT KAIBA WOULD SEND FOR US RIGHT AFTER THE VISION WE HAD AT THE MUSEUM.
THERE MUST BE SOMETHING MORE GOING ON HERE, AND I'M PRETTY SURE IT HAS SOMETHING TO DO WITH THAT ANUBIS GUY.
IT SEEMS LIKE YOU HAD SOME KIND OF A BATTLE WITH HIM 5,000 YEARS AGO.
PERHAPS. BUT SADLY, MEMORIES OF MY DAYS AS THE PHARAOH ARE CLOUDED.
NOR IS IT CLEAR TO ME WHAT ROLE THE EGYPTIAN GOD CARDS HAVE TO PLAY IN ALL OF THIS.

READ THIS WAY

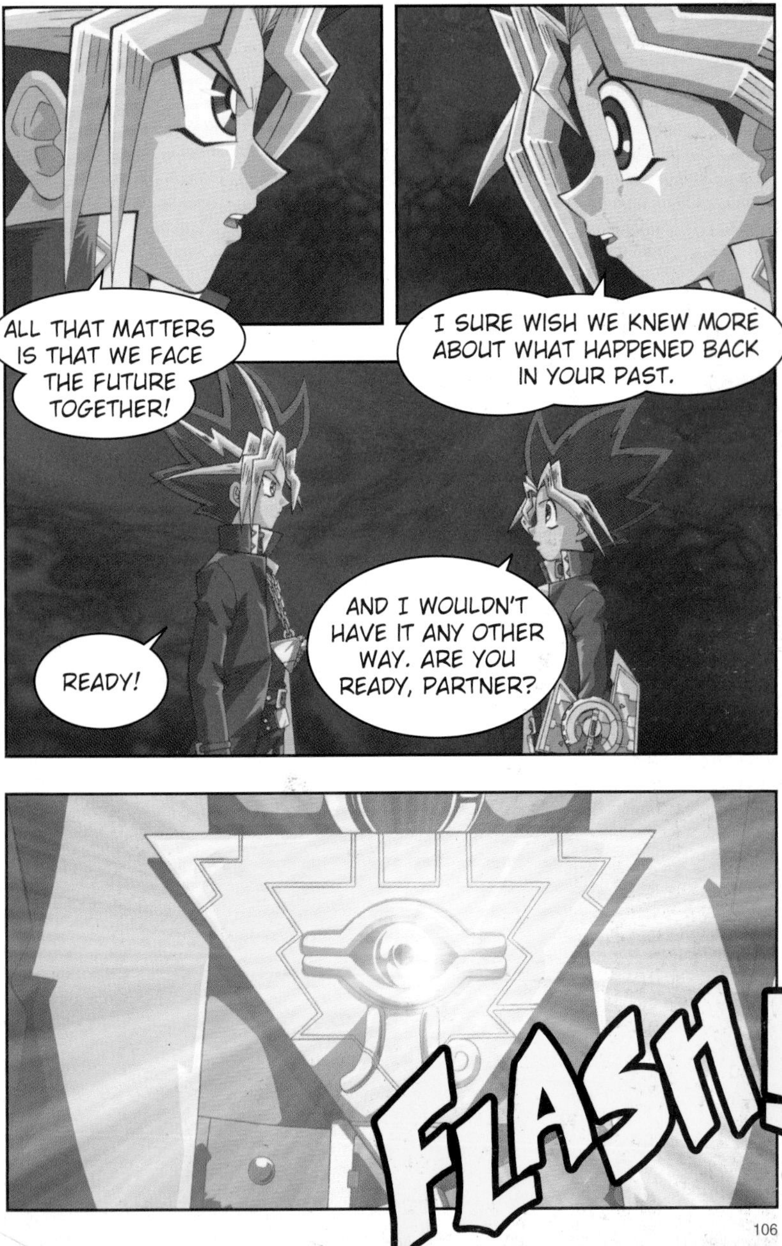
I SURE WISH WE KNEW MORE ABOUT WHAT HAPPENED BACK IN YOUR PAST.
ALL THAT MATTERS IS THAT WE FACE THE FUTURE TOGETHER!
AND I WOULDN'T HAVE IT ANY OTHER WAY. ARE YOU READY, PARTNER?
READY!
FLASH!

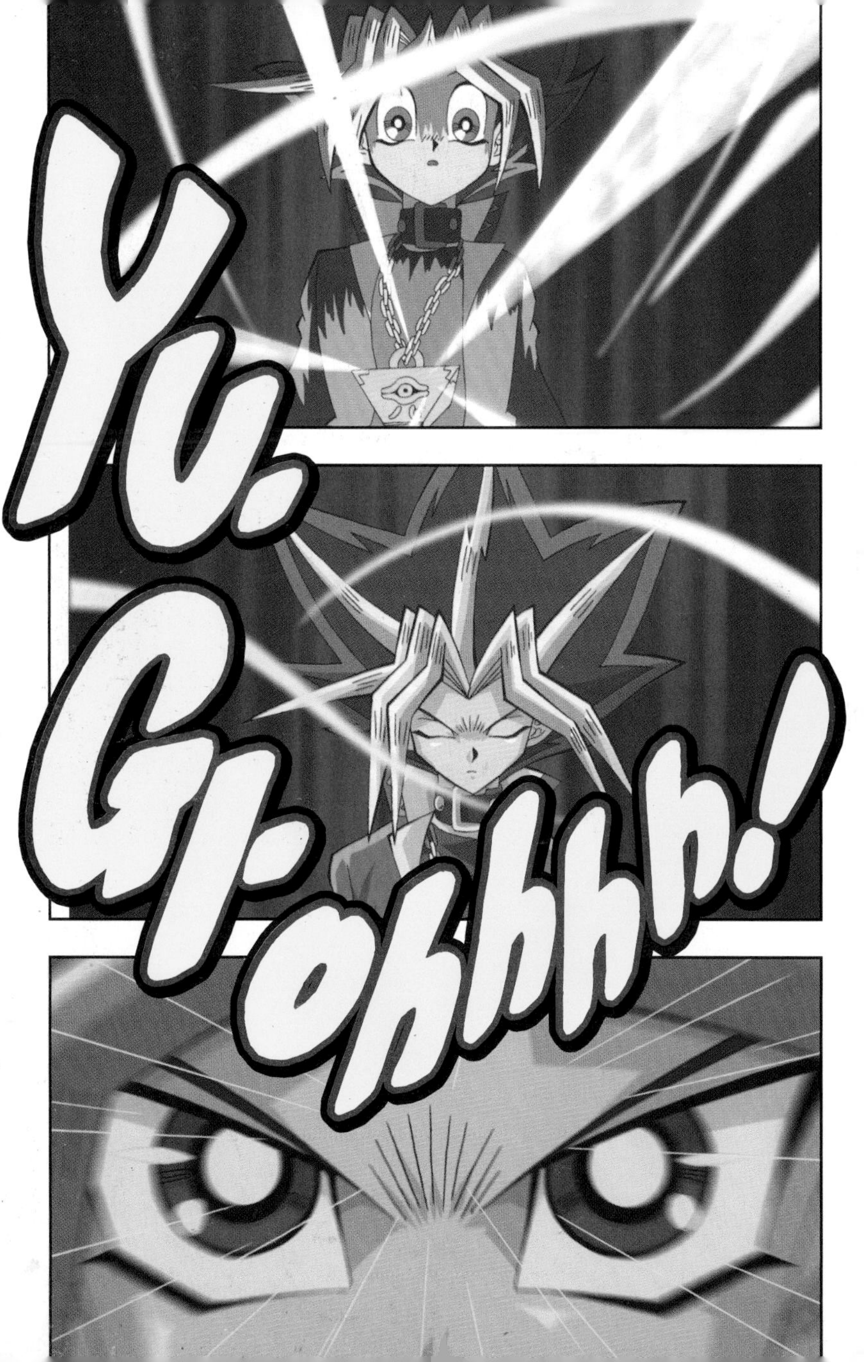
YU-GI-OHHHH!

READ THIS WAY

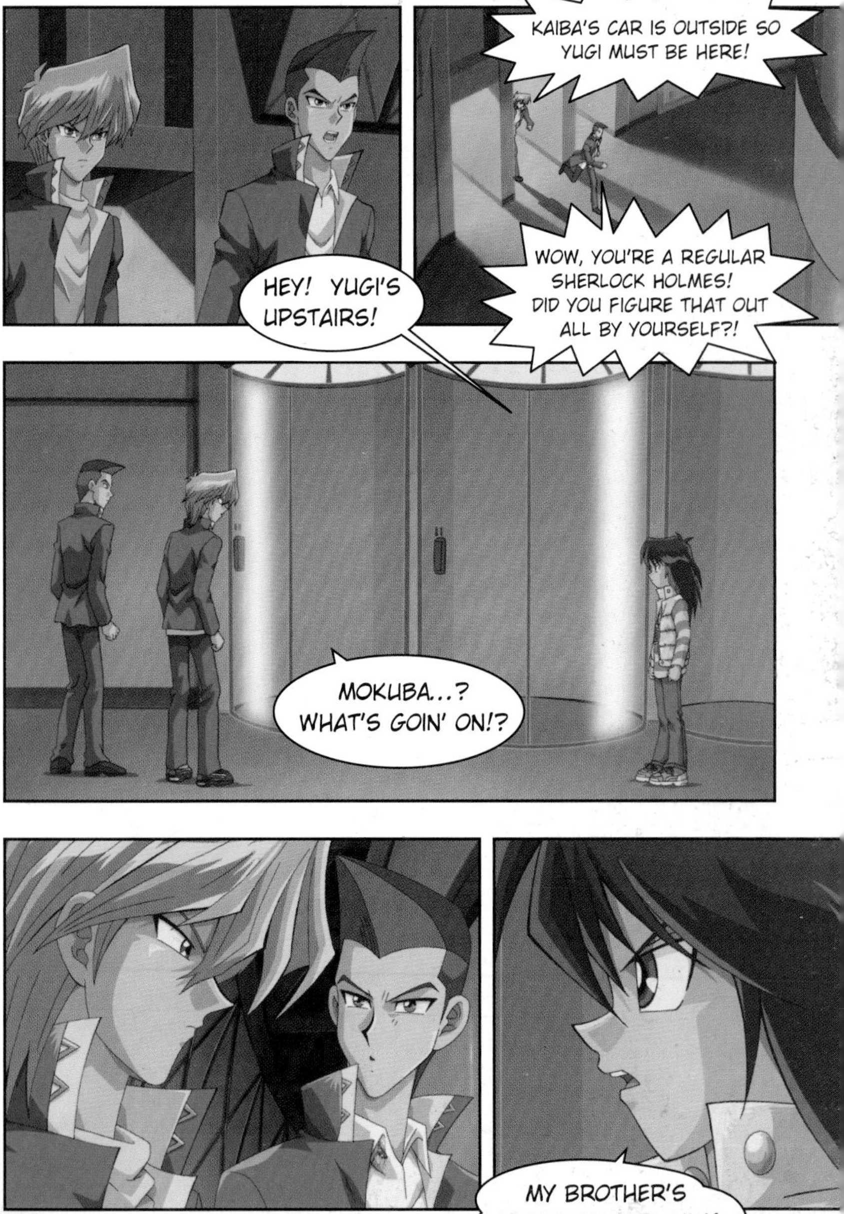
KAIBA'S CAR IS OUTSIDE SO YUGI MUST BE HERE!
WOW, YOU'RE A REGULAR SHERLOCK HOLMES! DID YOU FIGURE THAT OUT ALL BY YOURSELF?!
HEY! YUGI'S UPSTAIRS!
MOKUBA...? WHAT'S GOIN' ON!?
MY BROTHER'S ABOUT TO DUEL HIM!

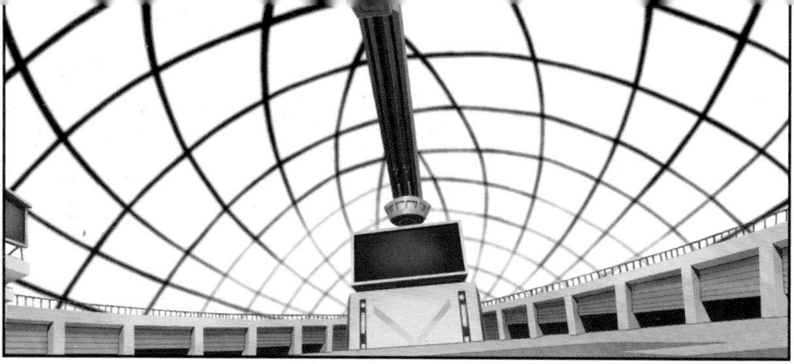

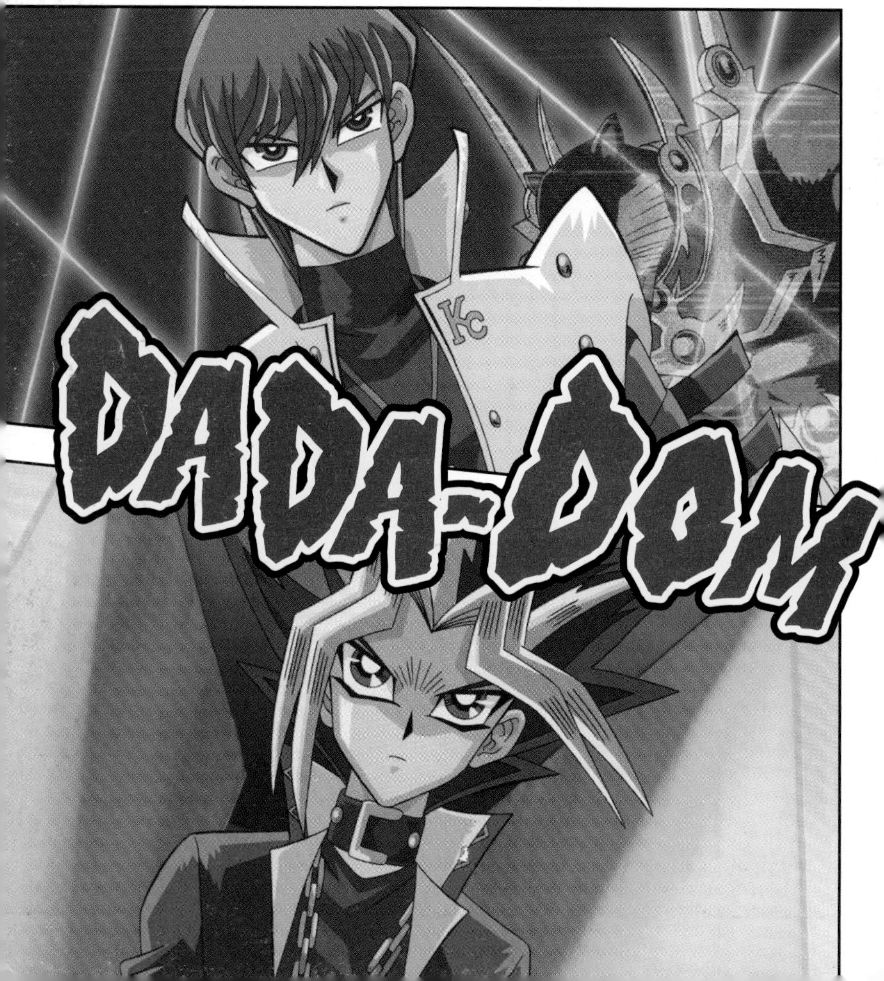
DADA-DOM

READ THIS WAY

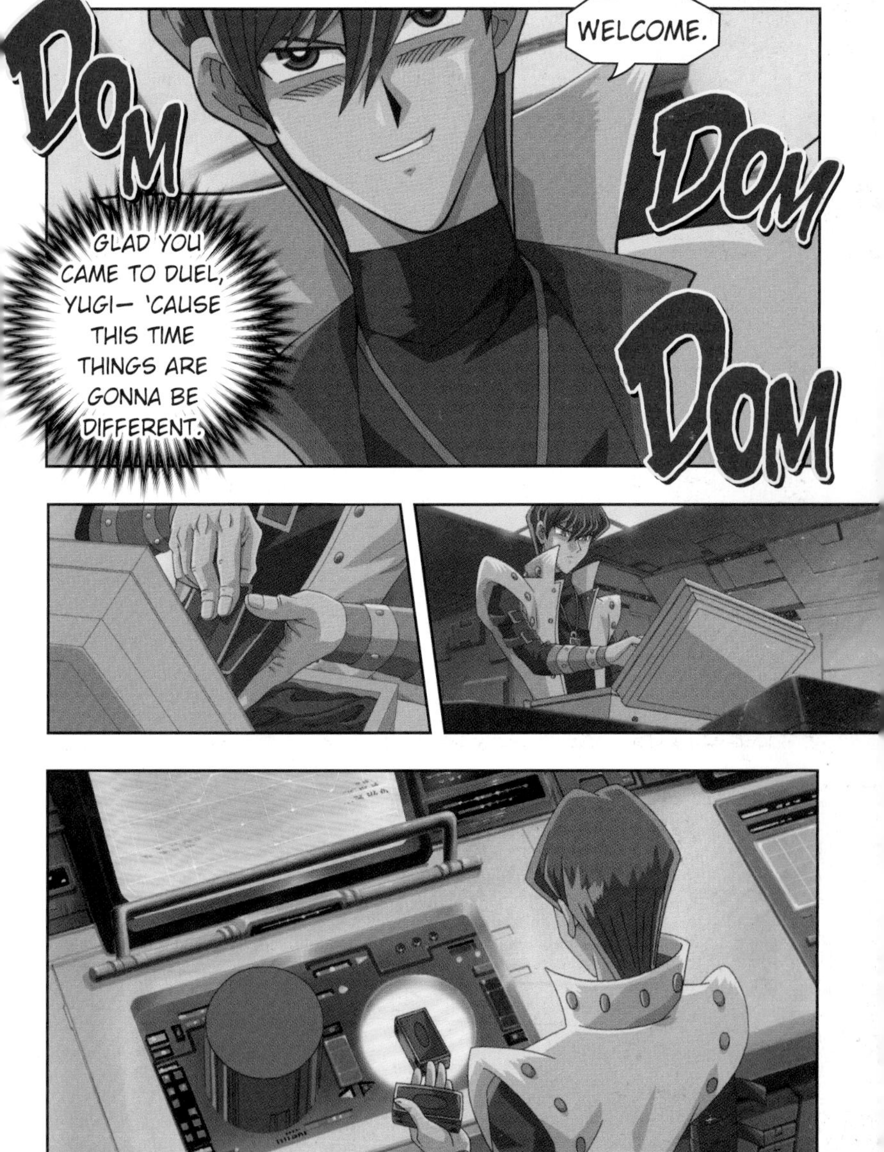
WELCOME.
DOM
DOM
DOM
GLAD YOU CAME TO DUEL, YUGI— 'CAUSE THIS TIME THINGS ARE GONNA BE DIFFERENT.

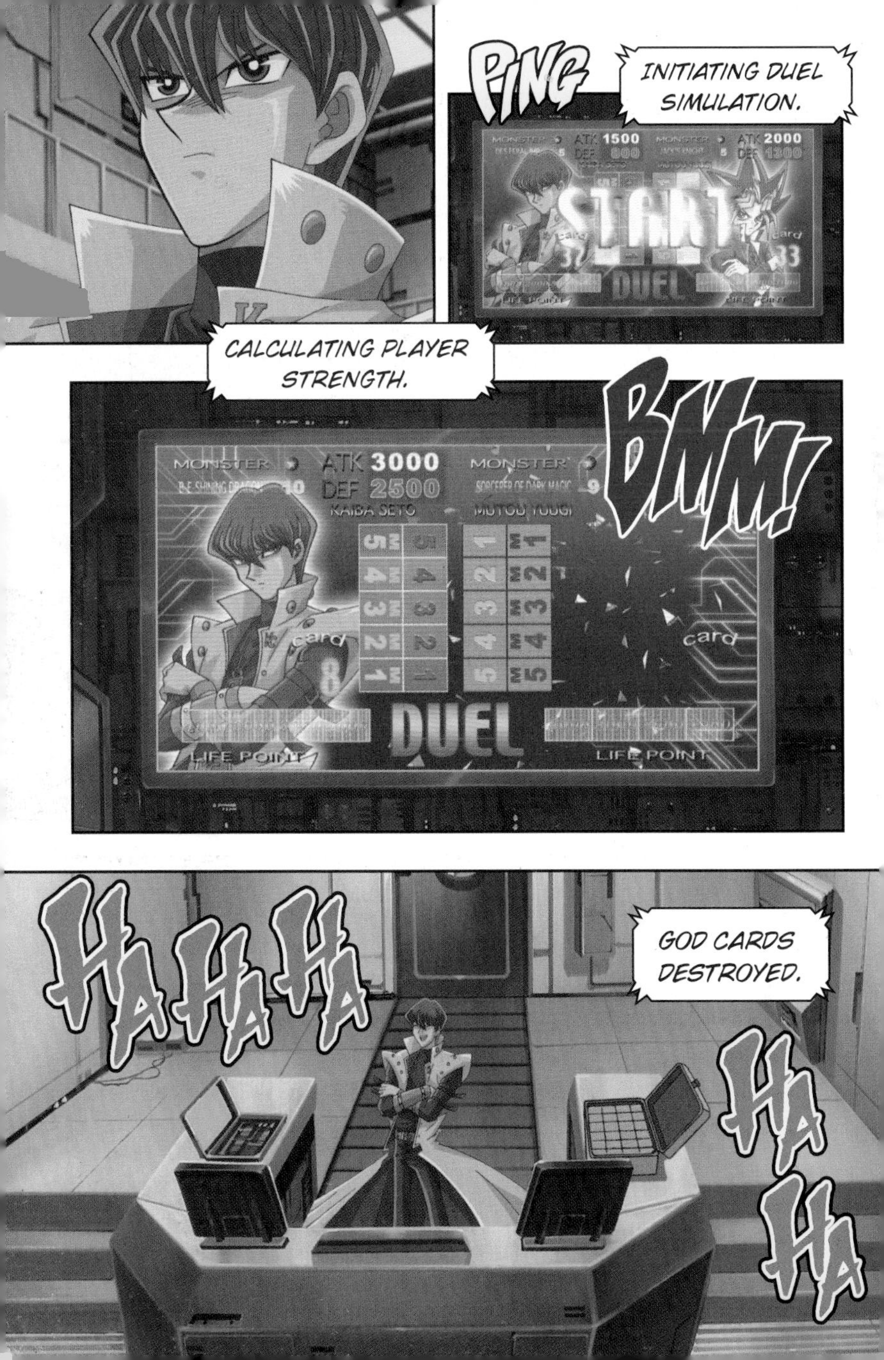
PING
INITIATING DUEL SIMULATION.
MONSTER
ATK 1500
DEF 800
MONSTER
ATK 2000
DEF 1300
START
card
33
DUEL
CALCULATING PLAYER STRENGTH.
BMM!
MONSTER
ATK 3000
DEF 2500
KAIBA SETO
MONSTER
SORCERER OF DARK MAGIC
9
MUTOU YUUGI
card
card
DUEL
LIFE POINT
LIFE POINT
GOD CARDS DESTROYED.
HA HA HA
HA HA

READ THIS WAY

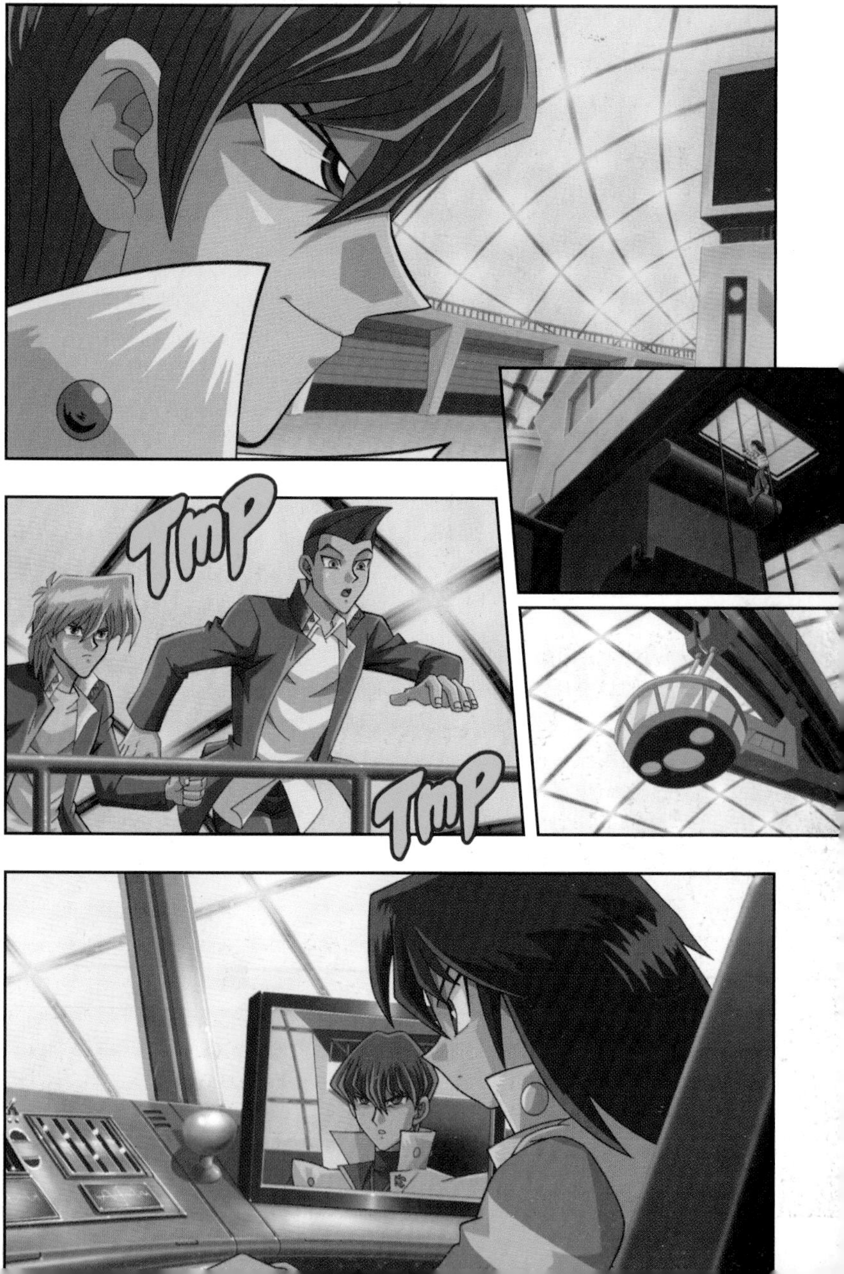
TMP
TMP

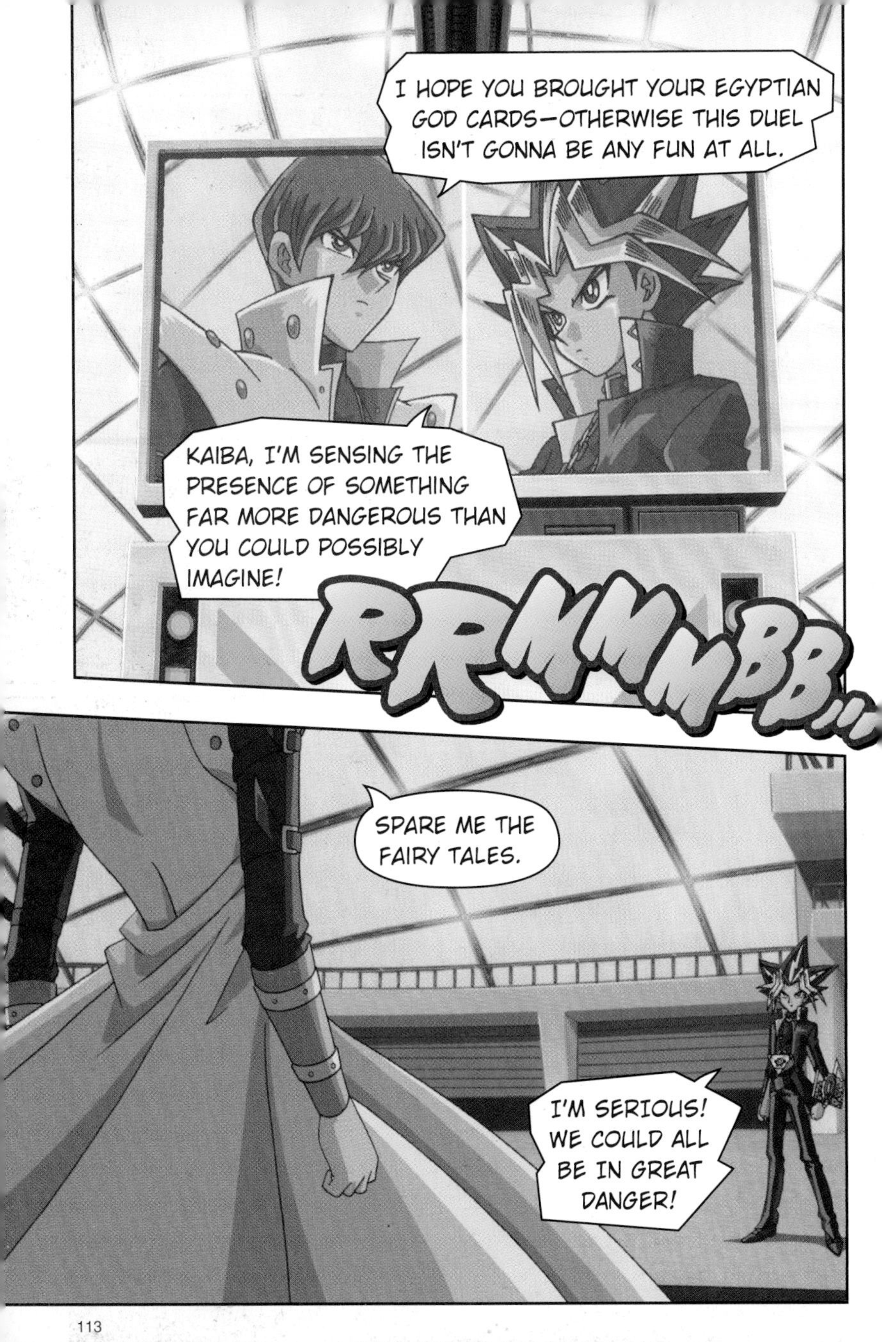
I HOPE YOU BROUGHT YOUR EGYPTIAN GOD CARDS—OTHERWISE THIS DUEL ISN'T GONNA BE ANY FUN AT ALL.
KAIBA, I'M SENSING THE PRESENCE OF SOMETHING FAR MORE DANGEROUS THAN YOU COULD POSSIBLY IMAGINE!
RRMMMBB...
SPARE ME THE FAIRY TALES.
I'M SERIOUS! WE COULD ALL BE IN GREAT DANGER!

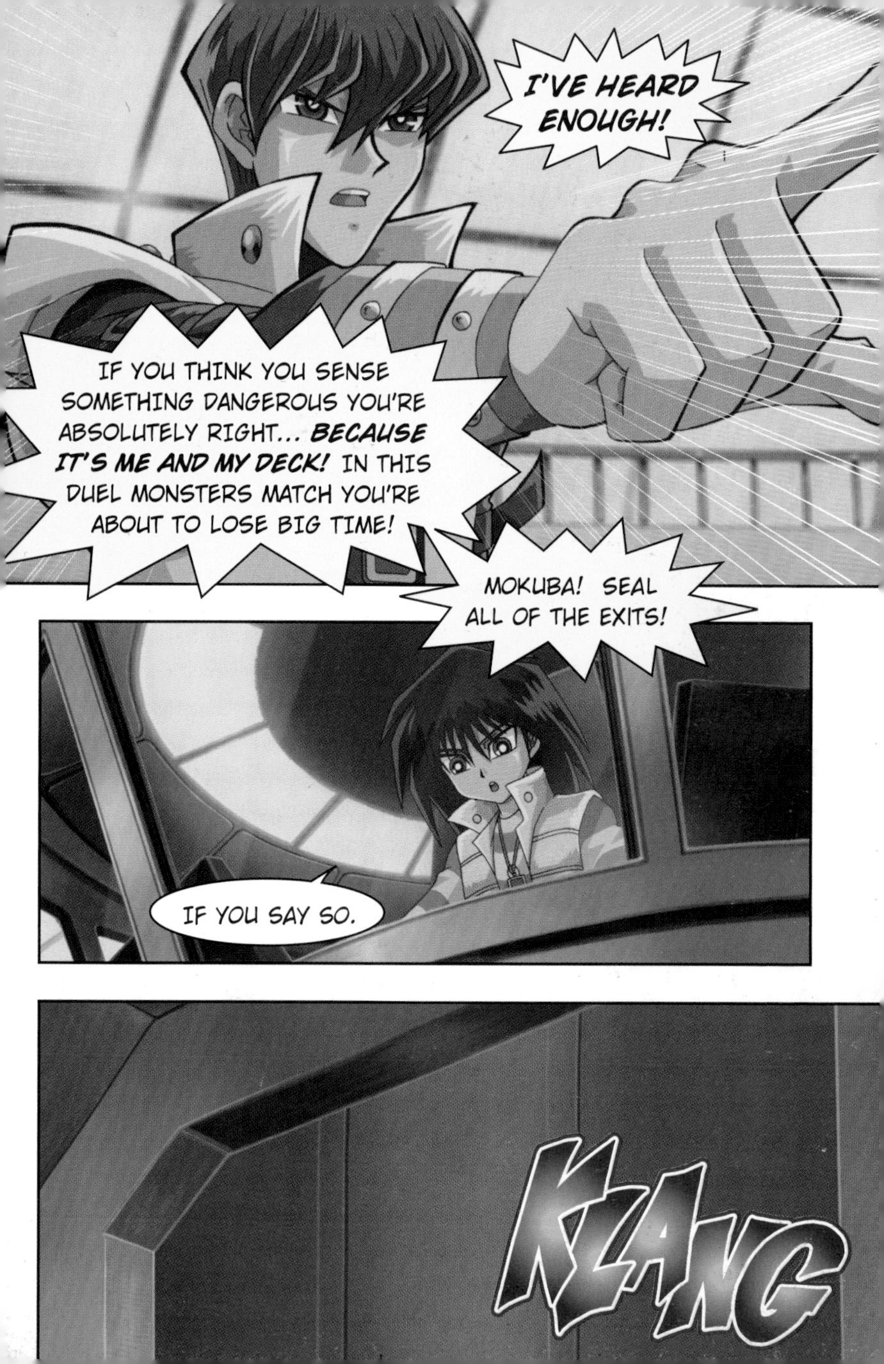
I'VE HEARD ENOUGH!
IF YOU THINK YOU SENSE SOMETHING DANGEROUS YOU'RE ABSOLUTELY RIGHT... **BECAUSE IT'S ME AND MY DECK!** IN THIS DUEL MONSTERS MATCH YOU'RE ABOUT TO LOSE BIG TIME!
MOKUBA! SEAL ALL OF THE EXITS!
IF YOU SAY SO.
KLANG

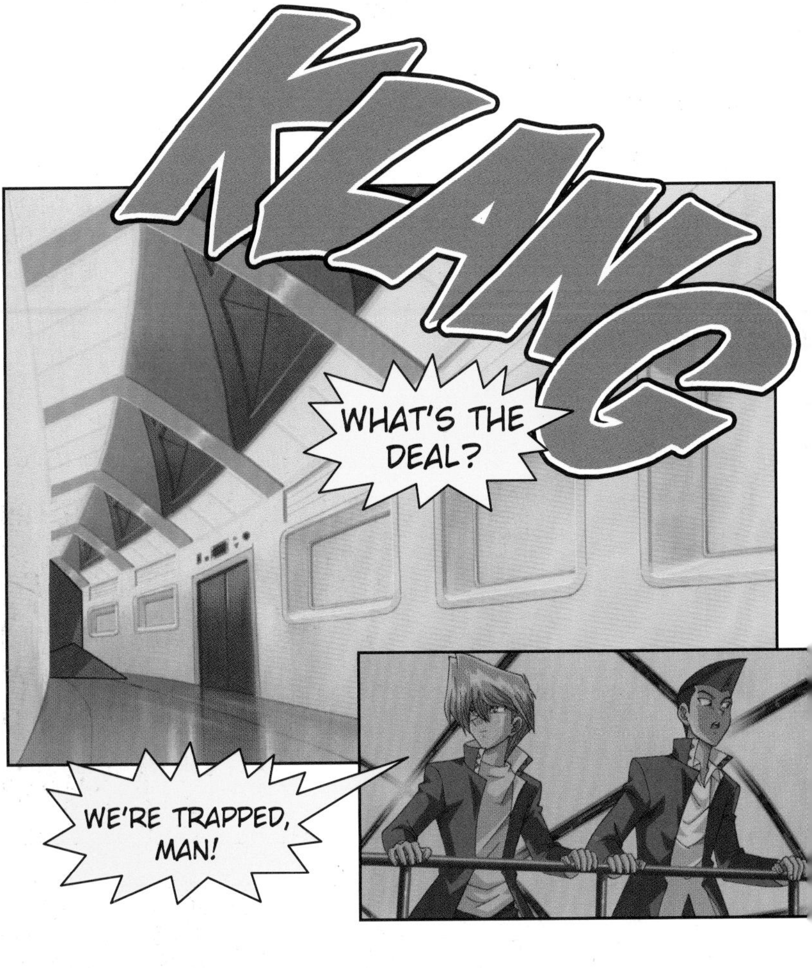
KLANG
WHAT'S THE DEAL?
WE'RE TRAPPED, MAN!

Chapter. 3 The Pyramid of Light

READ THIS WAY

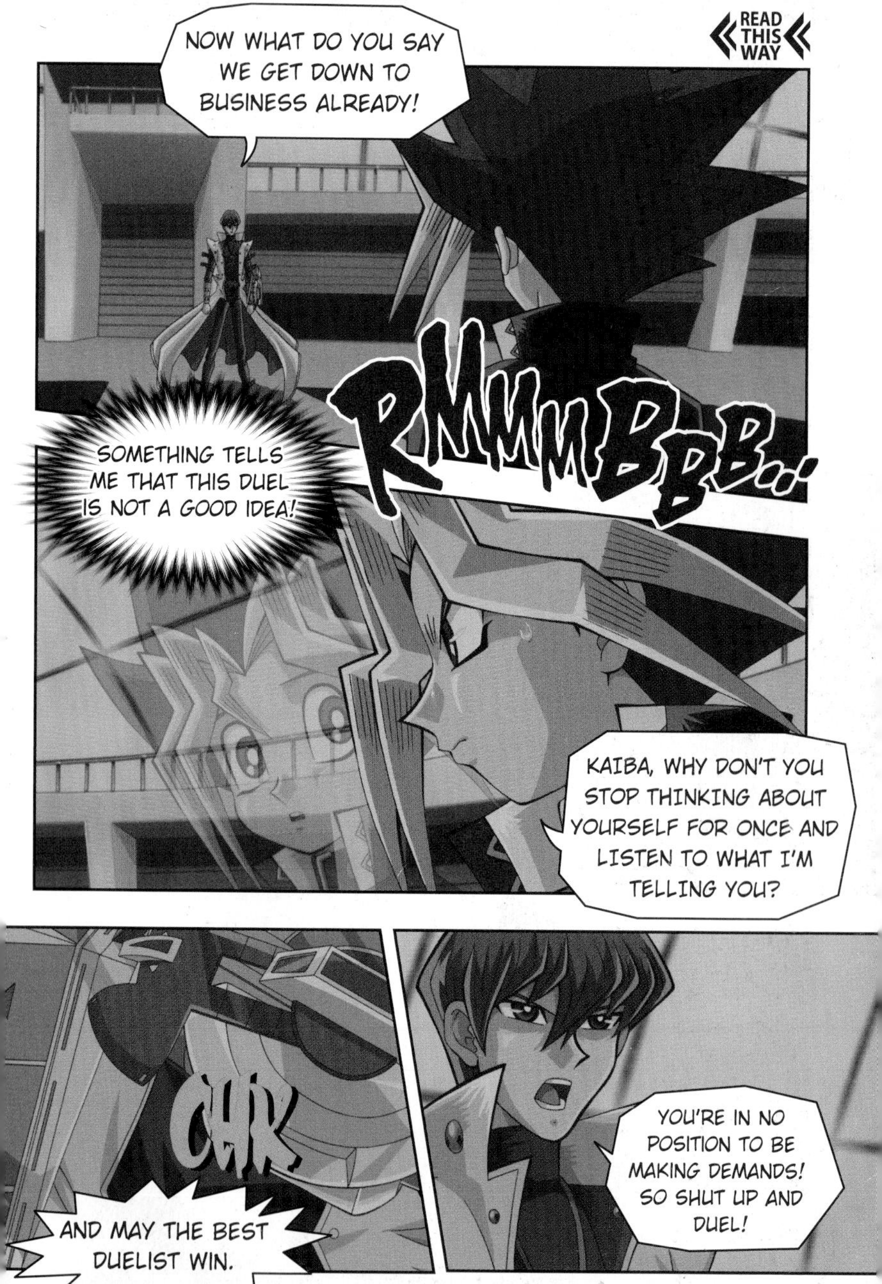

NOW WHAT DO YOU SAY WE GET DOWN TO BUSINESS ALREADY!
RMMMBBB...
SOMETHING TELLS ME THAT THIS DUEL IS NOT A GOOD IDEA!
KAIBA, WHY DON'T YOU STOP THINKING ABOUT YOURSELF FOR ONCE AND LISTEN TO WHAT I'M TELLING YOU?
YOU'RE IN NO POSITION TO BE MAKING DEMANDS! SO SHUT UP AND DUEL!
CHK
AND MAY THE BEST DUELIST WIN.

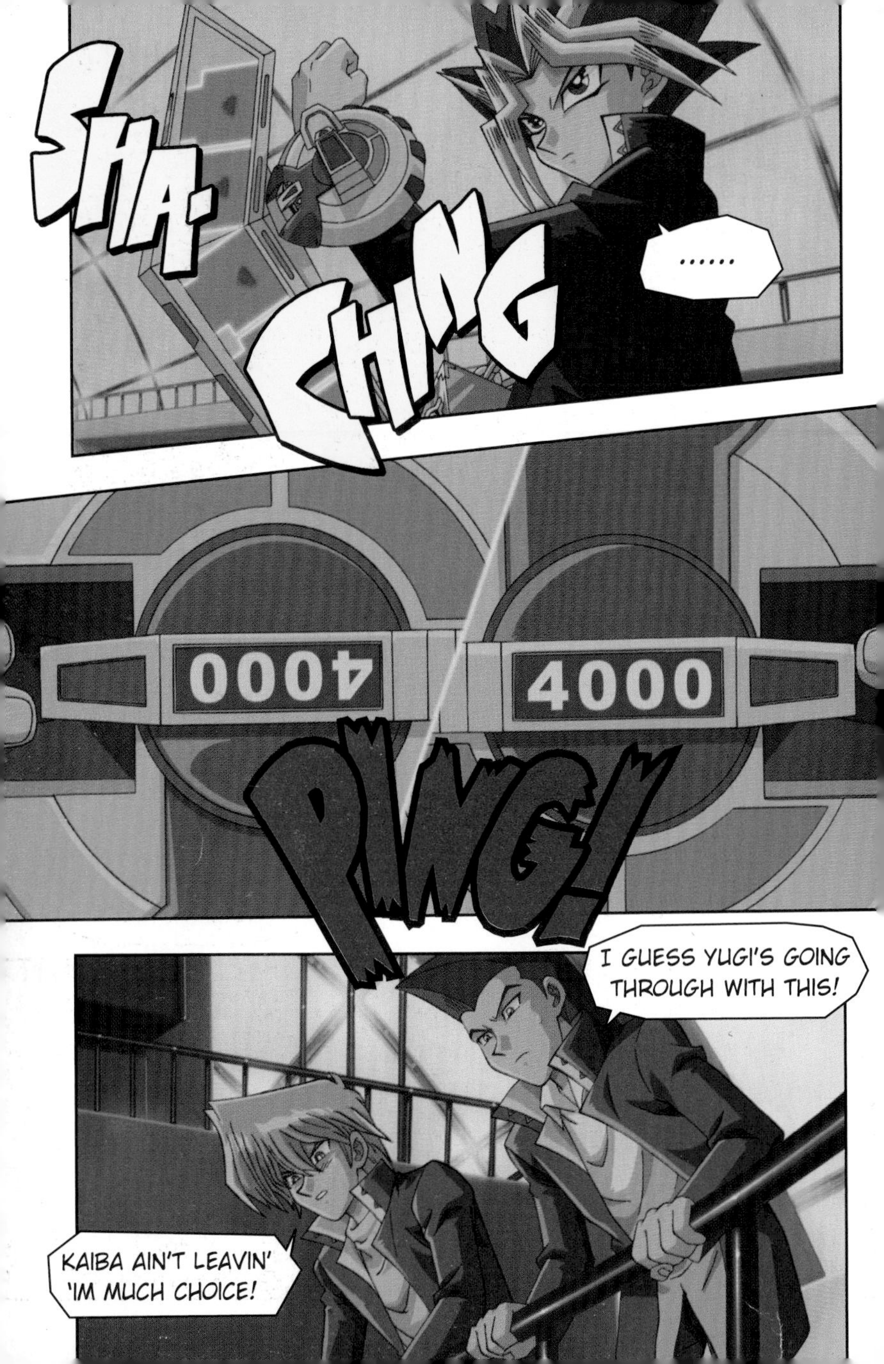
SHA-CHING
......
4000
0004
PING!
I GUESS YUGI'S GOING THROUGH WITH THIS!
KAIBA AIN'T LEAVIN' 'IM MUCH CHOICE!

READ THIS WAY

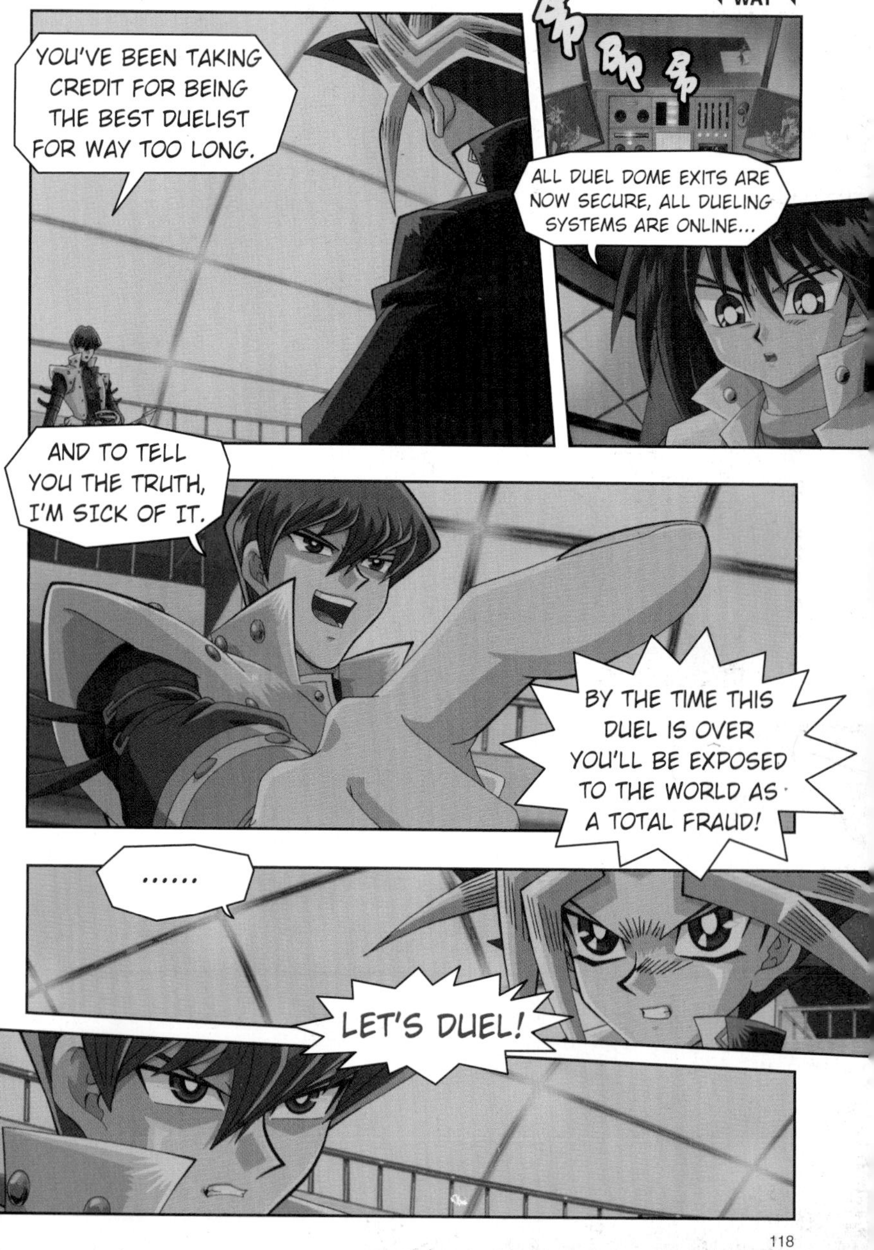
ALL DUEL DOME EXITS ARE NOW SECURE, ALL DUELING SYSTEMS ARE ONLINE...
YOU'VE BEEN TAKING CREDIT FOR BEING THE BEST DUELIST FOR WAY TOO LONG.
AND TO TELL YOU THE TRUTH, I'M SICK OF IT.
BY THE TIME THIS DUEL IS OVER YOU'LL BE EXPOSED TO THE WORLD AS A TOTAL FRAUD!
......
LET'S DUEL!

READ THIS WAY

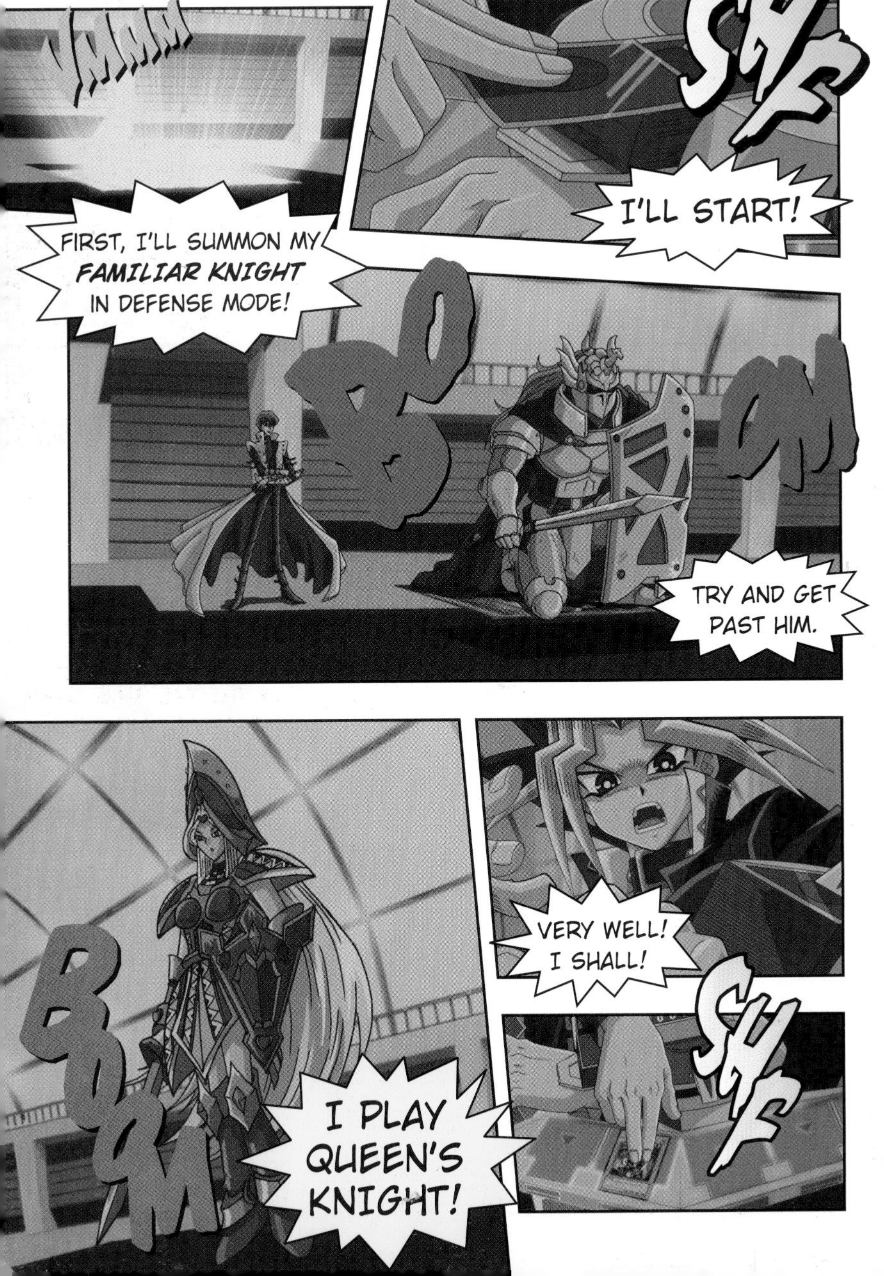

SHF
I'LL START!
VMMM
FIRST, I'LL SUMMON MY *FAMILIAR KNIGHT* IN DEFENSE MODE!
BOOM
TRY AND GET PAST HIM.
VERY WELL! I SHALL!
SHF
BOOM
I PLAY QUEEN'S KNIGHT!

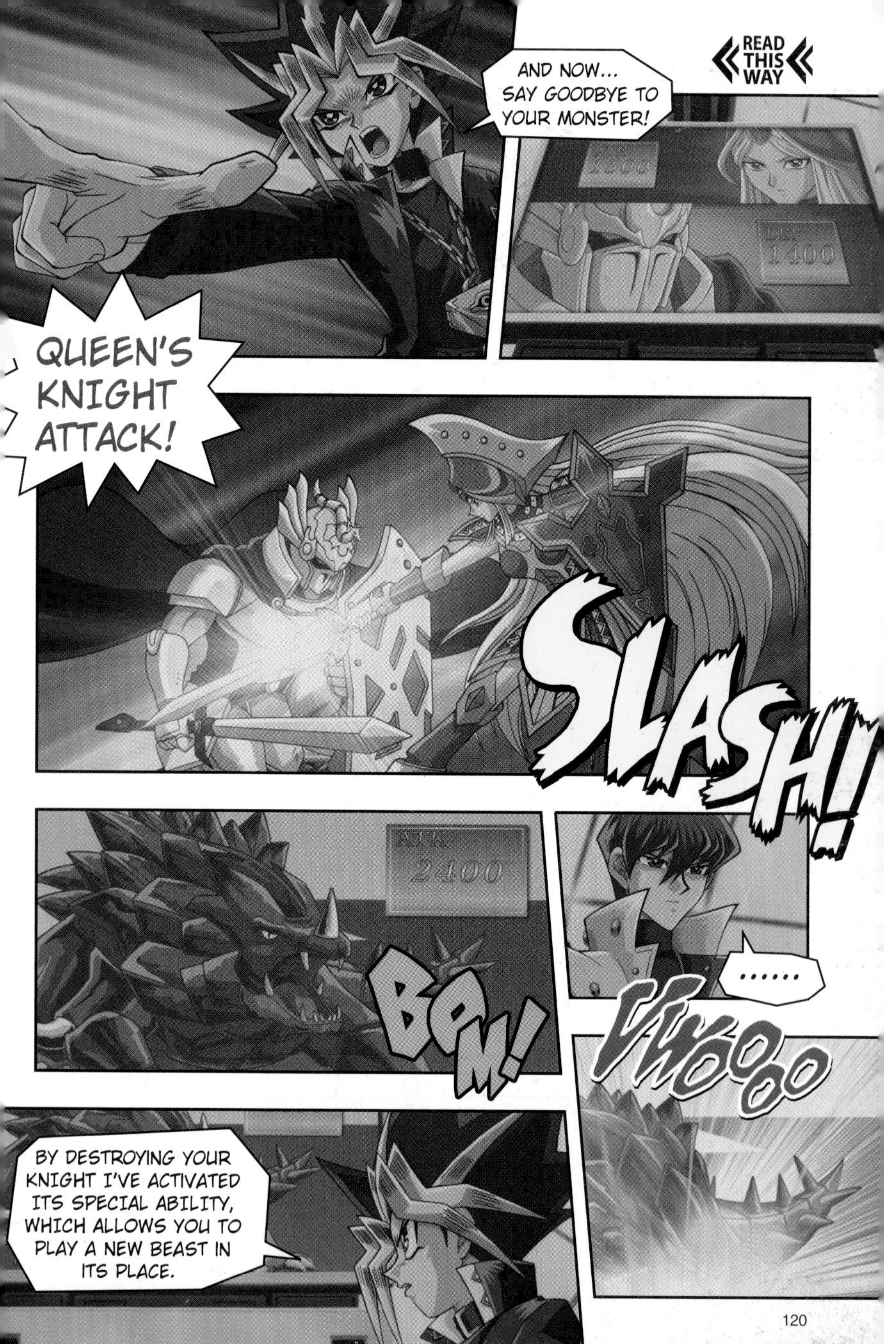
READ THIS WAY
AND NOW... SAY GOODBYE TO YOUR MONSTER!
QUEEN'S KNIGHT ATTACK!
ATK 1500
DEF 1400
SLASH!
......
ATK 2400
BOOM!
VHOOOO
BY DESTROYING YOUR KNIGHT I'VE ACTIVATED ITS SPECIAL ABILITY, WHICH ALLOWS YOU TO PLAY A NEW BEAST IN ITS PLACE.

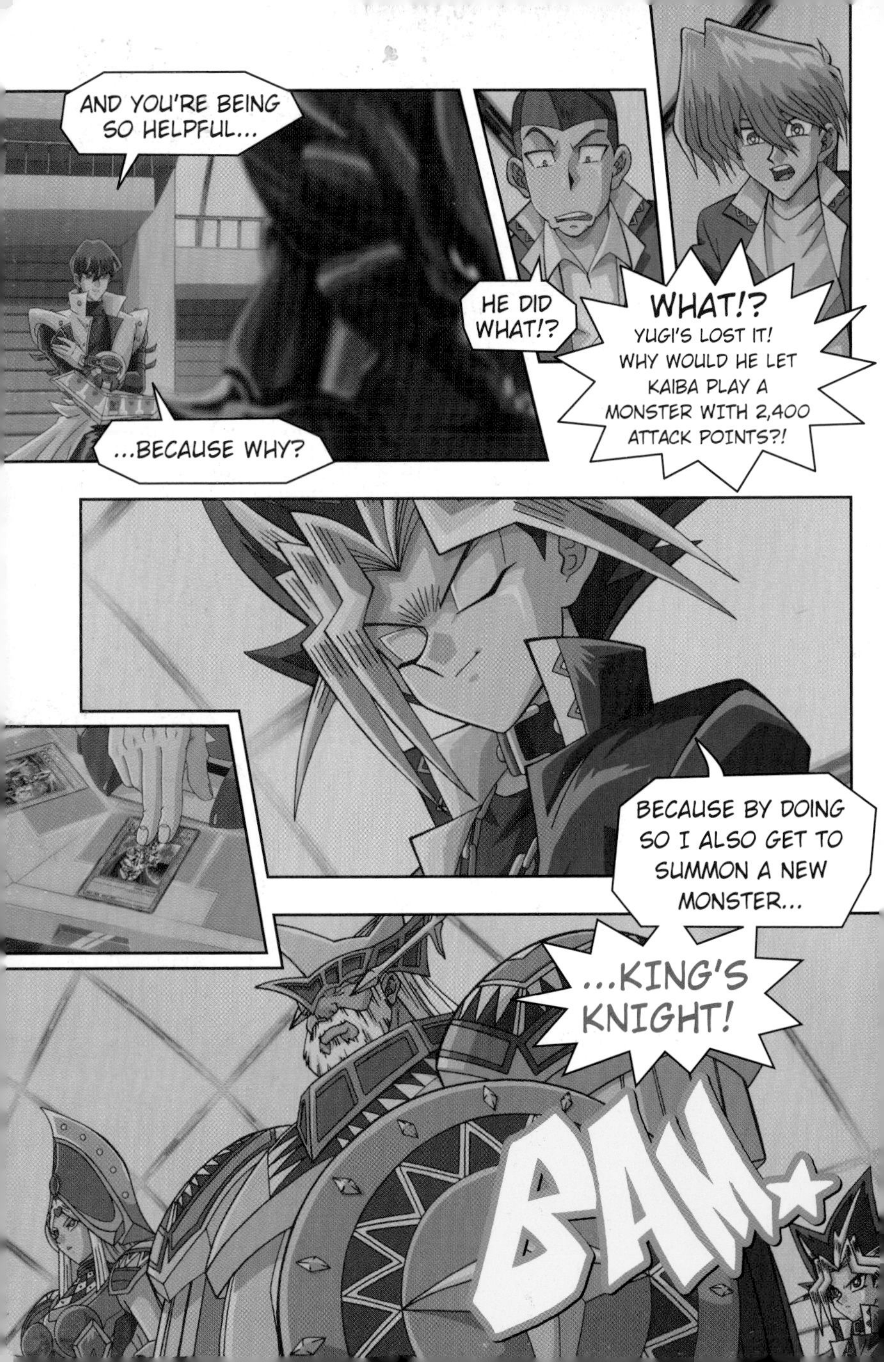
WHAT!? YUGI'S LOST IT! WHY WOULD HE LET KAIBA PLAY A MONSTER WITH 2,400 ATTACK POINTS?!
HE DID WHAT!?
AND YOU'RE BEING SO HELPFUL...
...BECAUSE WHY?
BECAUSE BY DOING SO I ALSO GET TO SUMMON A NEW MONSTER...
...KING'S KNIGHT!
BAM

READ THIS WAY

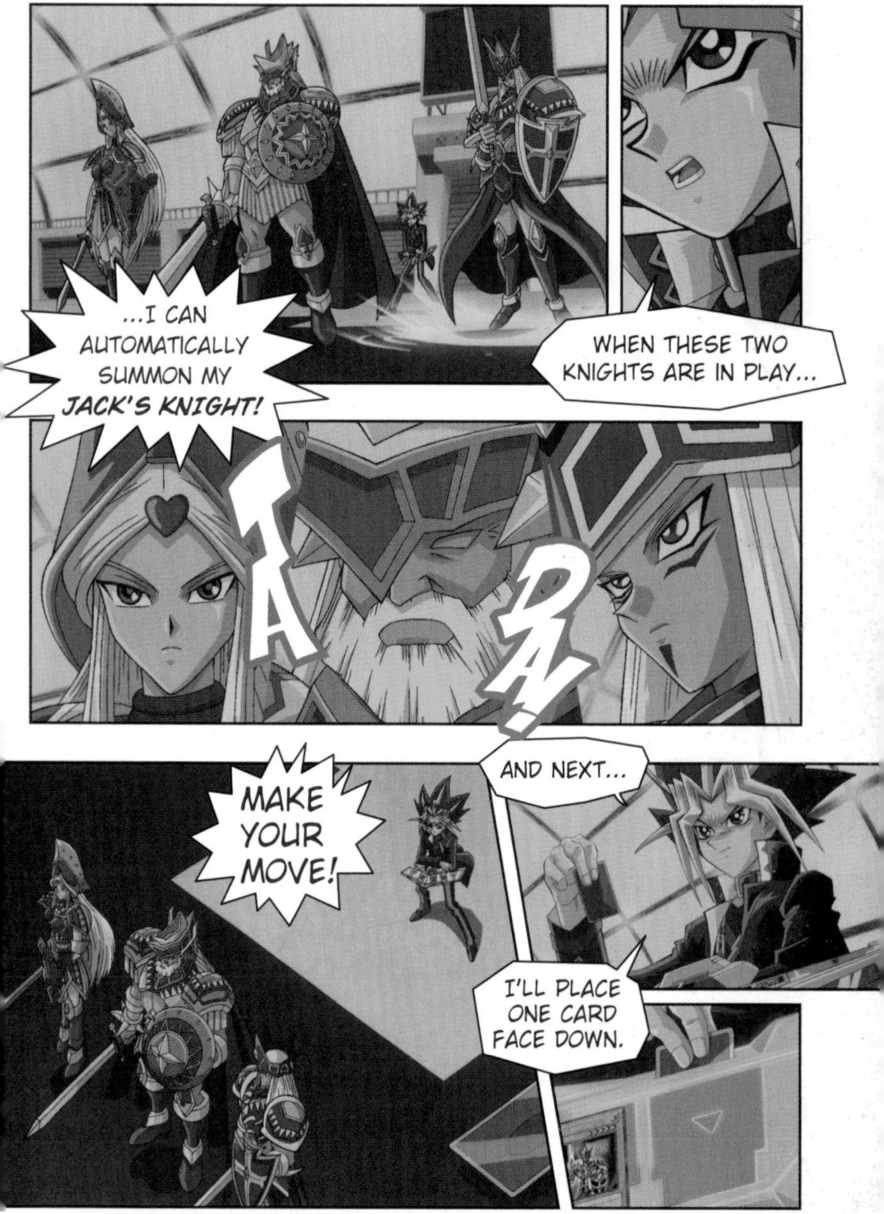

WHEN THESE TWO KNIGHTS ARE IN PLAY...
...I CAN AUTOMATICALLY SUMMON MY JACK'S KNIGHT!
TA DA
AND NEXT...
I'LL PLACE ONE CARD FACE DOWN.
MAKE YOUR MOVE!

....

WAS EMA TCHEN...

SHMMM

PYRAMID OF LIGHT

[TRAP CARD]

All God Cards on the ... ...er play

LOOKS LIKE YOUR LUCK'S FINALLY RUN OUT.

I'LL KEEP THIS CARD FACE DOWN ON THE FIELD UNTIL THE TIME IS RIGHT.

RIGHT FOR *ME*, THAT IS. AND THEN NOTHING IN YOUR DECK WILL MAKE A DIFFERENCE.

YOUR MOVE, YUGI.

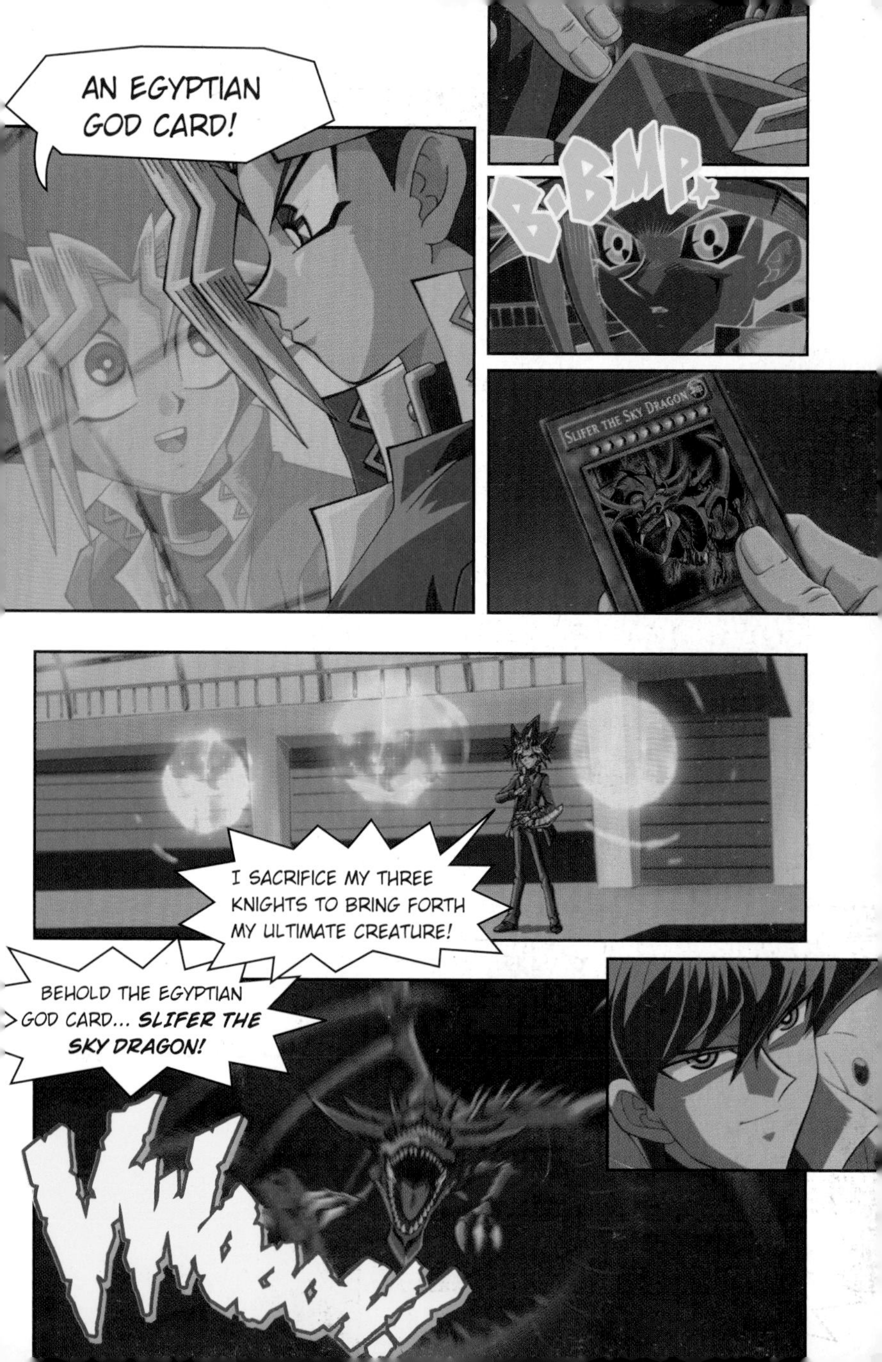

B-BMP
SLIFER THE SKY DRAGON
AN EGYPTIAN GOD CARD!
I SACRIFICE MY THREE KNIGHTS TO BRING FORTH MY ULTIMATE CREATURE!
BEHOLD THE EGYPTIAN GOD CARD... **SLIFER THE SKY DRAGON!**

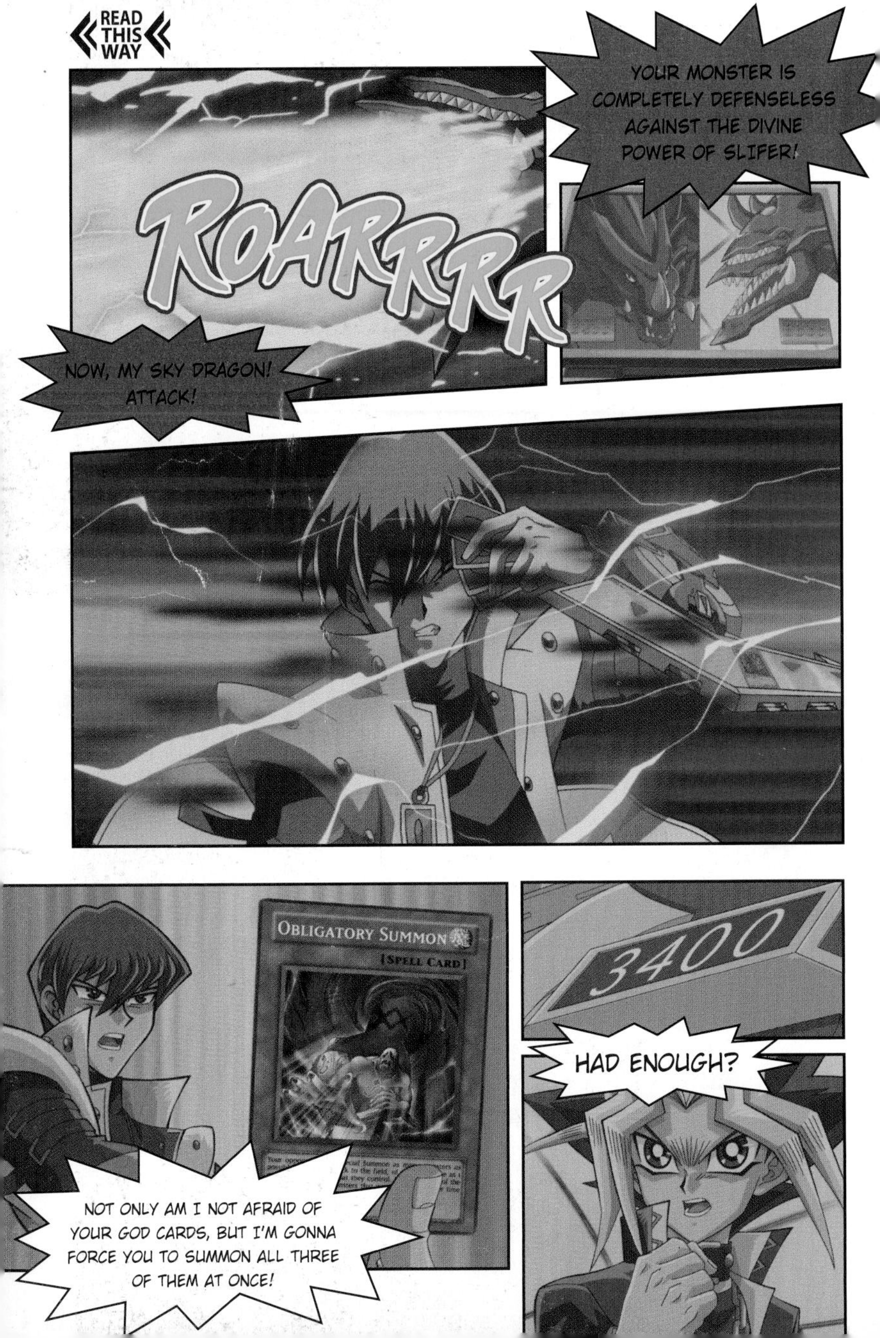
READ THIS WAY
YOUR MONSTER IS COMPLETELY DEFENSELESS AGAINST THE DIVINE POWER OF SLIFER!
ROARRRR
NOW, MY SKY DRAGON! ATTACK!
3400
HAD ENOUGH?
OBLIGATORY SUMMON
[SPELL CARD]
NOT ONLY AM I NOT AFRAID OF YOUR GOD CARDS, BUT I'M GONNA FORCE YOU TO SUMMON ALL THREE OF THEM AT ONCE!

READ THIS WAY

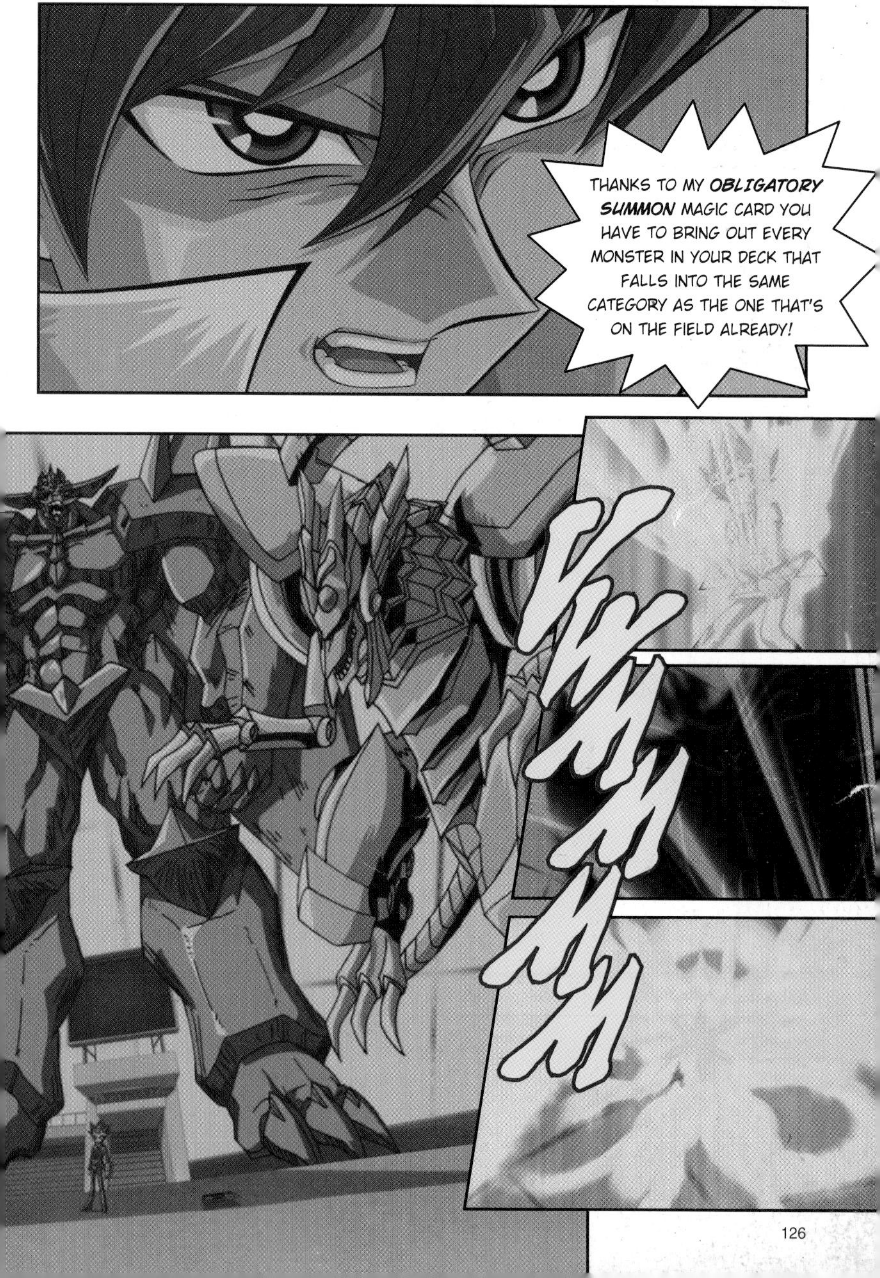
THANKS TO MY ***OBLIGATORY SUMMON*** MAGIC CARD YOU HAVE TO BRING OUT EVERY MONSTER IN YOUR DECK THAT FALLS INTO THE SAME CATEGORY AS THE ONE THAT'S ON THE FIELD ALREADY!

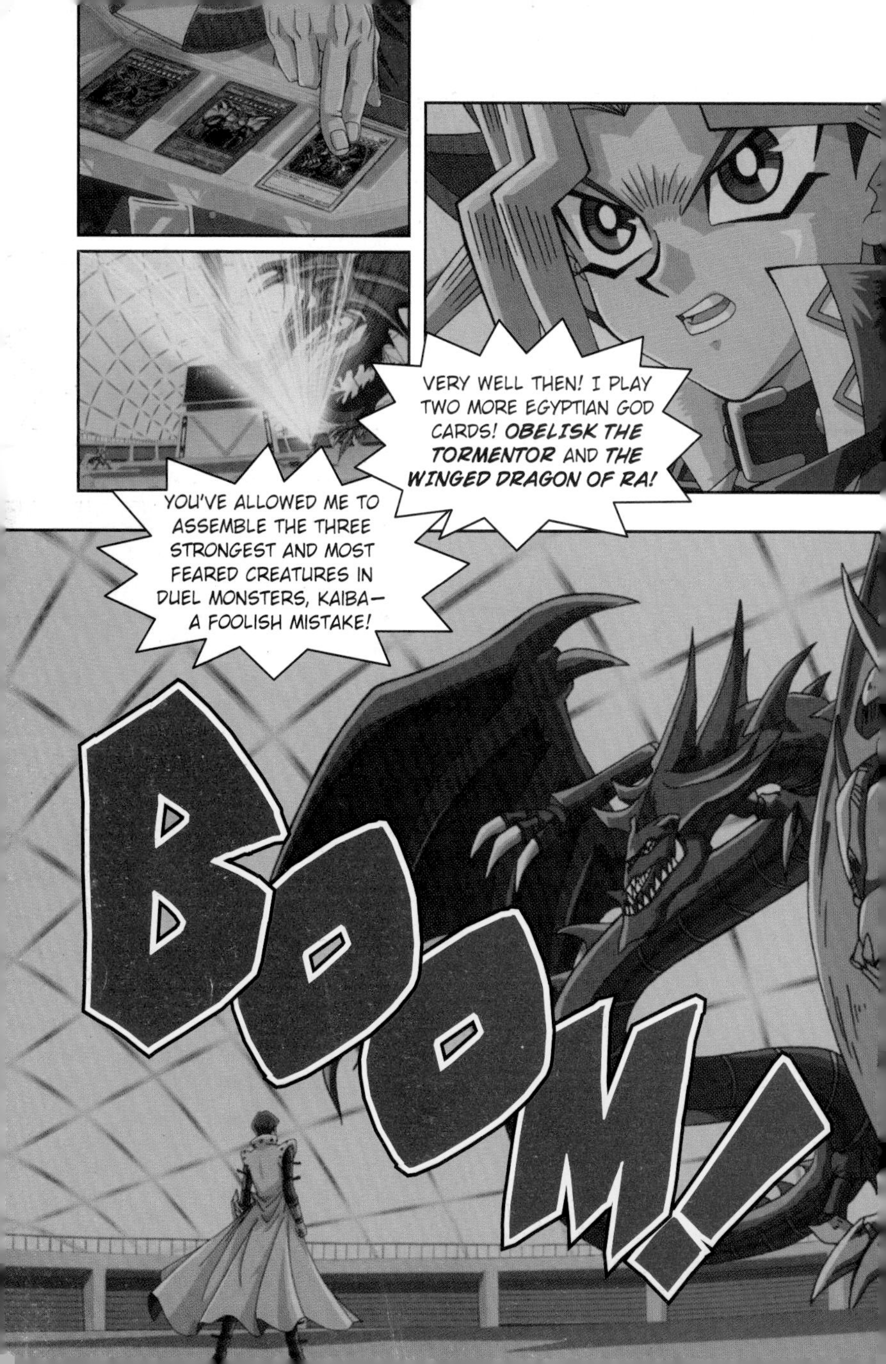
VERY WELL THEN! I PLAY TWO MORE EGYPTIAN GOD CARDS! ***OBELISK THE TORMENTOR*** AND ***THE WINGED DRAGON OF RA!***
YOU'VE ALLOWED ME TO ASSEMBLE THE THREE STRONGEST AND MOST FEARED CREATURES IN DUEL MONSTERS, KAIBA— A FOOLISH MISTAKE!
BOOM!

READ THIS WAY

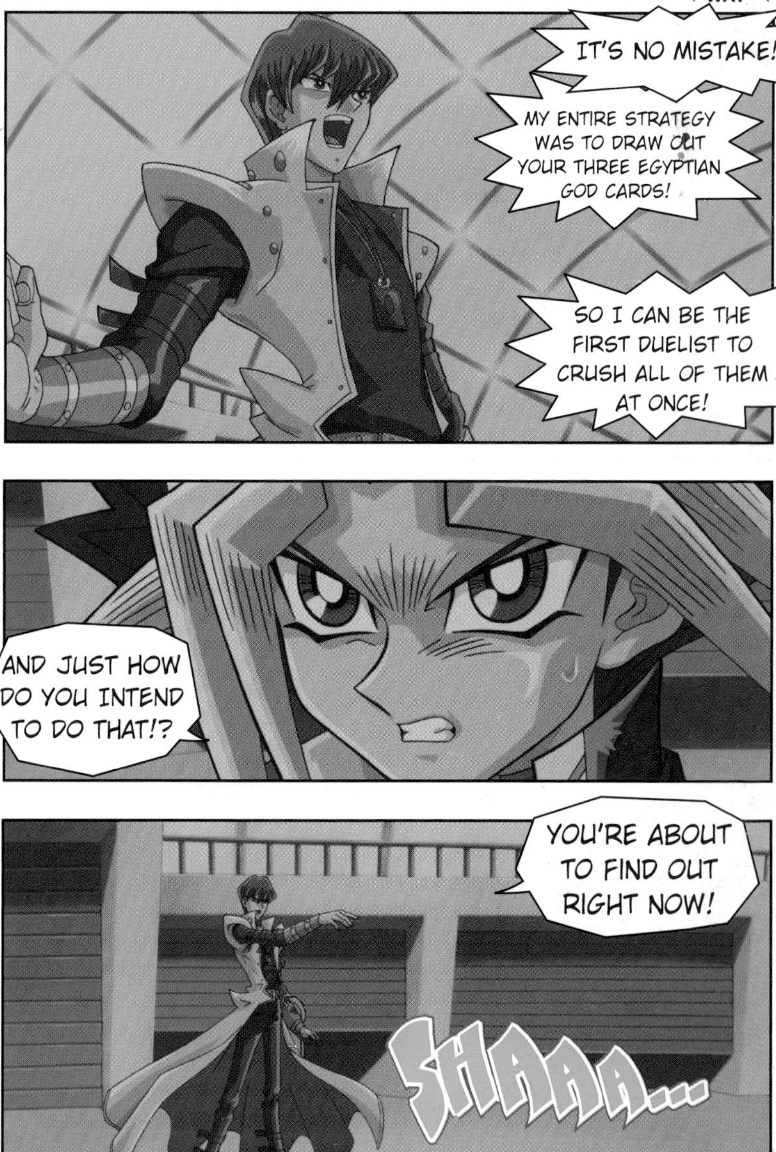
IT'S NO MISTAKE!
MY ENTIRE STRATEGY WAS TO DRAW OUT YOUR THREE EGYPTIAN GOD CARDS!
SO I CAN BE THE FIRST DUELIST TO CRUSH ALL OF THEM AT ONCE!
AND JUST HOW DO YOU INTEND TO DO THAT!?
YOU'RE ABOUT TO FIND OUT RIGHT NOW!
SHAAA...

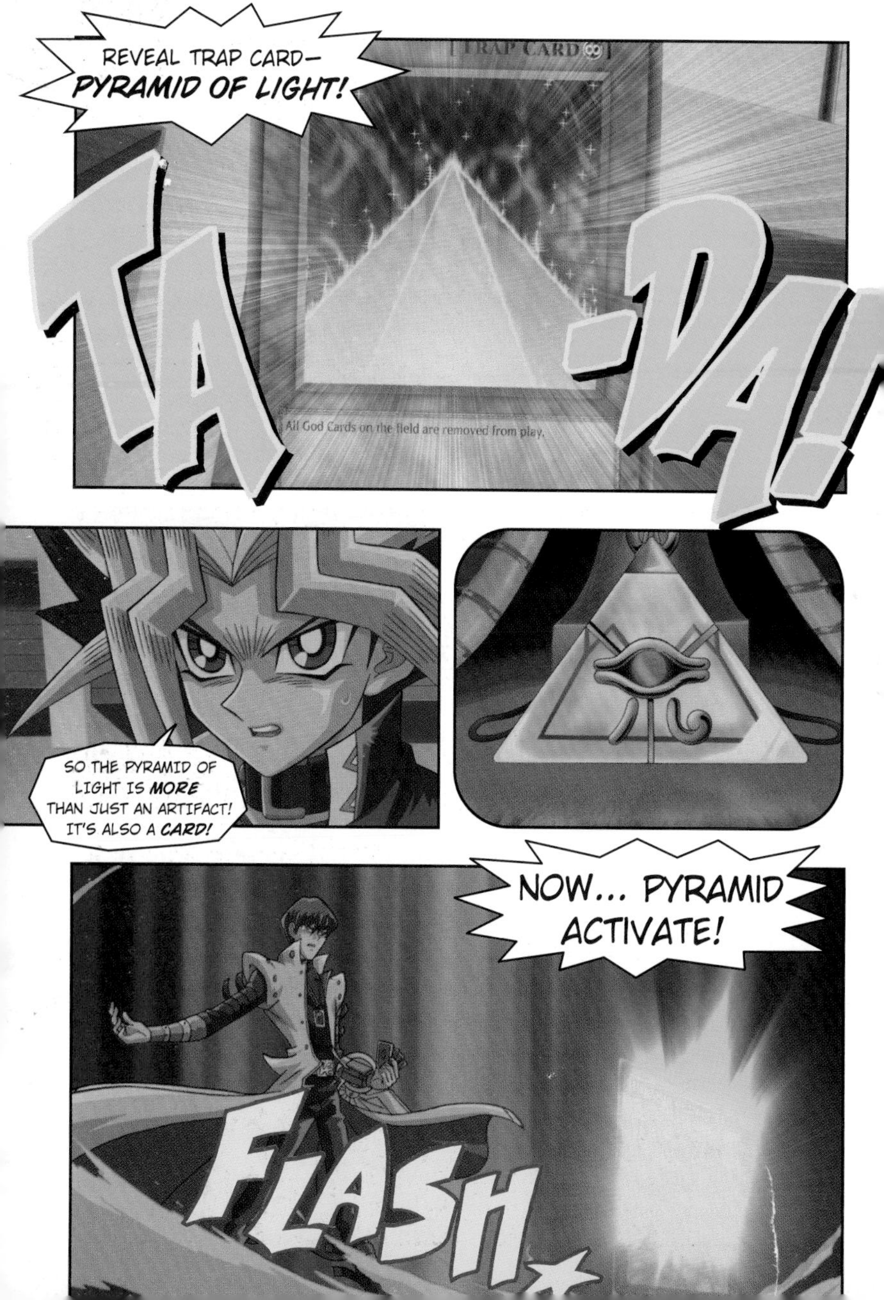
REVEAL TRAP CARD—PYRAMID OF LIGHT!
[TRAP CARD]
All God Cards on the field are removed from play.
TA-DA!
SO THE PYRAMID OF LIGHT IS MORE THAN JUST AN ARTIFACT! IT'S ALSO A CARD!
NOW... PYRAMID ACTIVATE!
FLASH

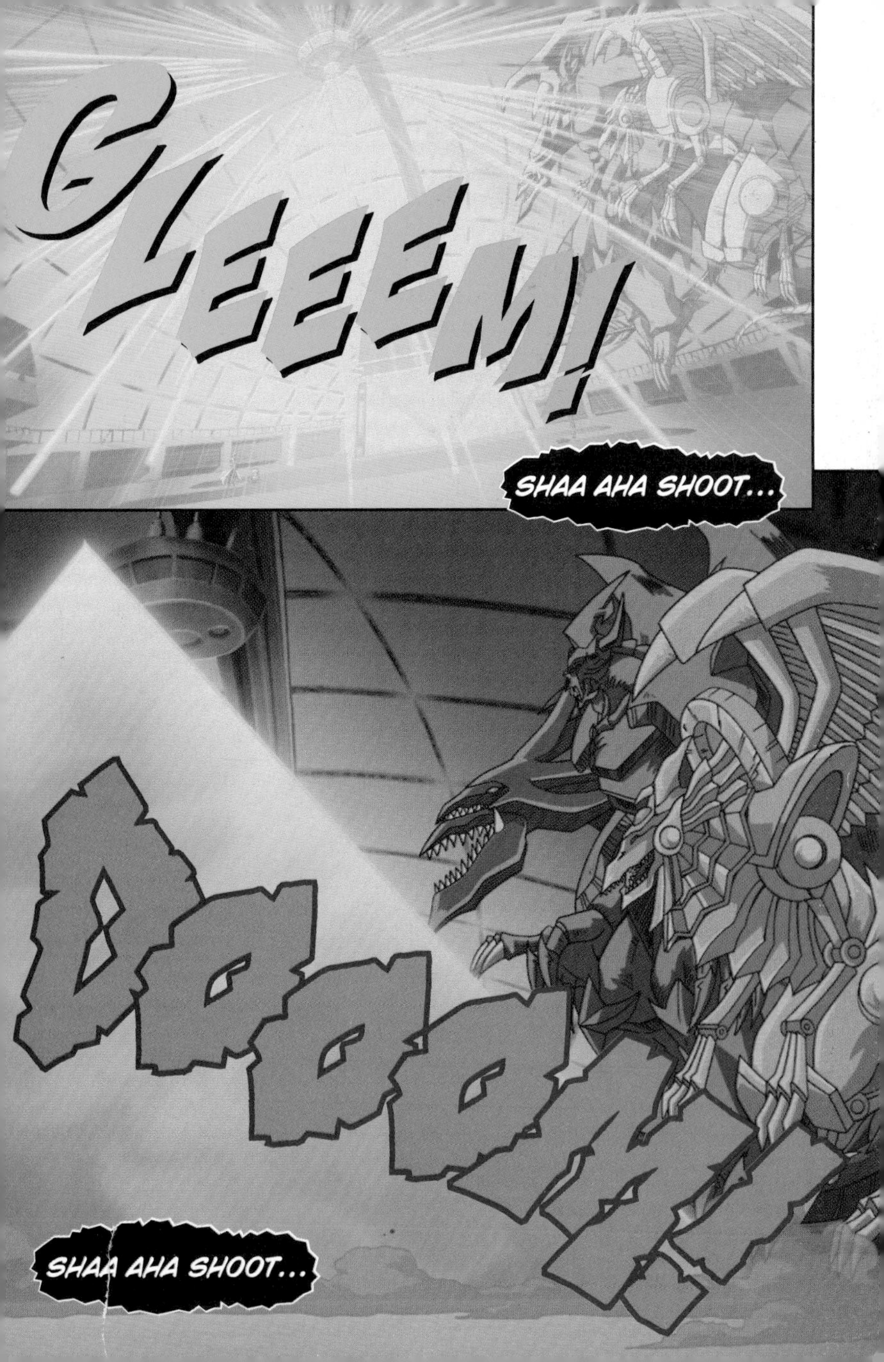
GLEEEM!
SHAA AHA SHOOT...
DOOOM!!
SHAA AHA SHOOT...

READ THIS WAY

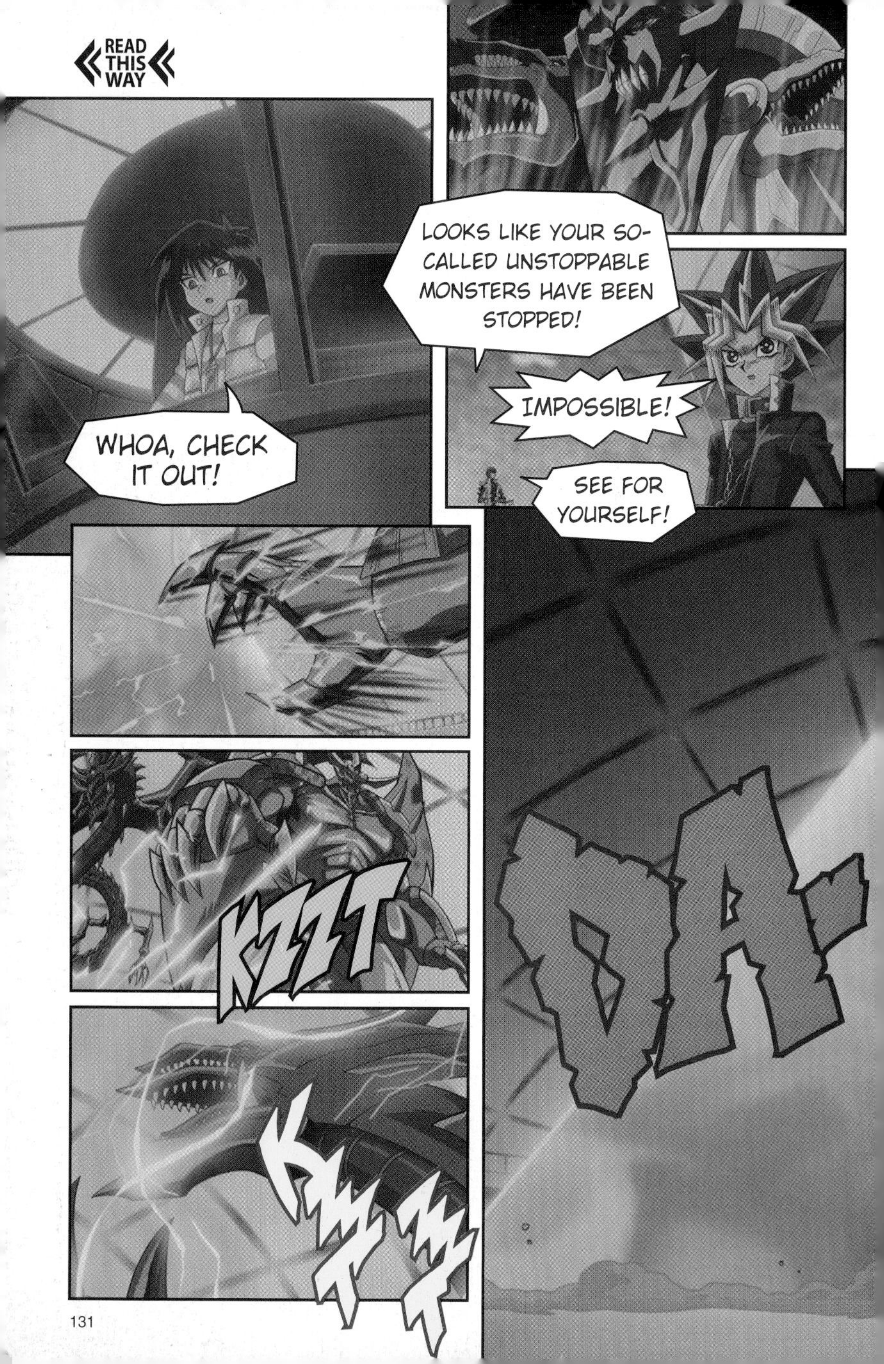

LOOKS LIKE YOUR SO-CALLED UNSTOPPABLE MONSTERS HAVE BEEN STOPPED!
IMPOSSIBLE!
SEE FOR YOURSELF!
WHOA, CHECK IT OUT!
DA
KZZT
KZZT

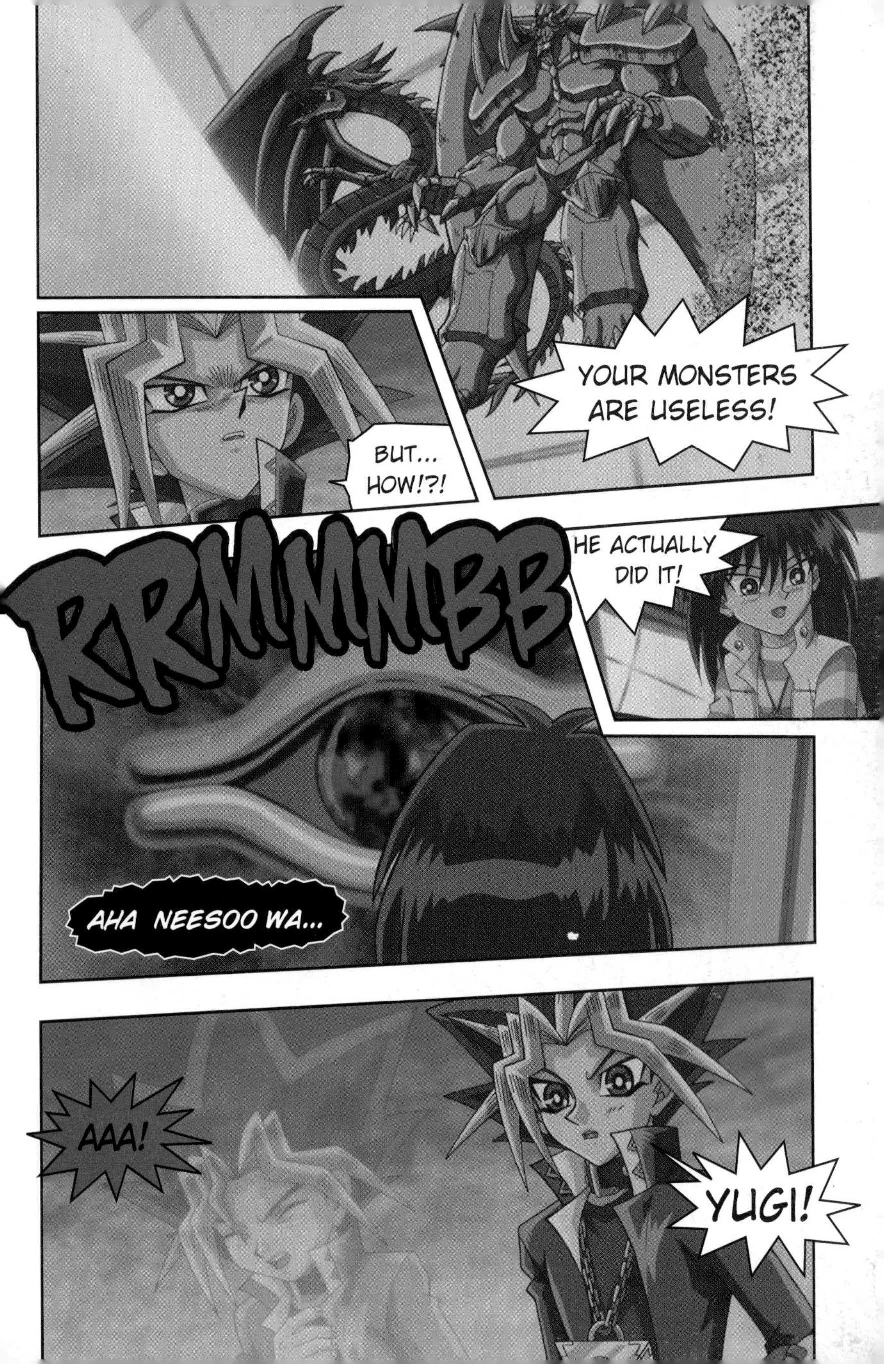

YOUR MONSTERS ARE USELESS!
BUT... HOW!?!
HE ACTUALLY DID IT!
RRMMMBB
AHA NEESOO WA...
YUGI!
AAA!

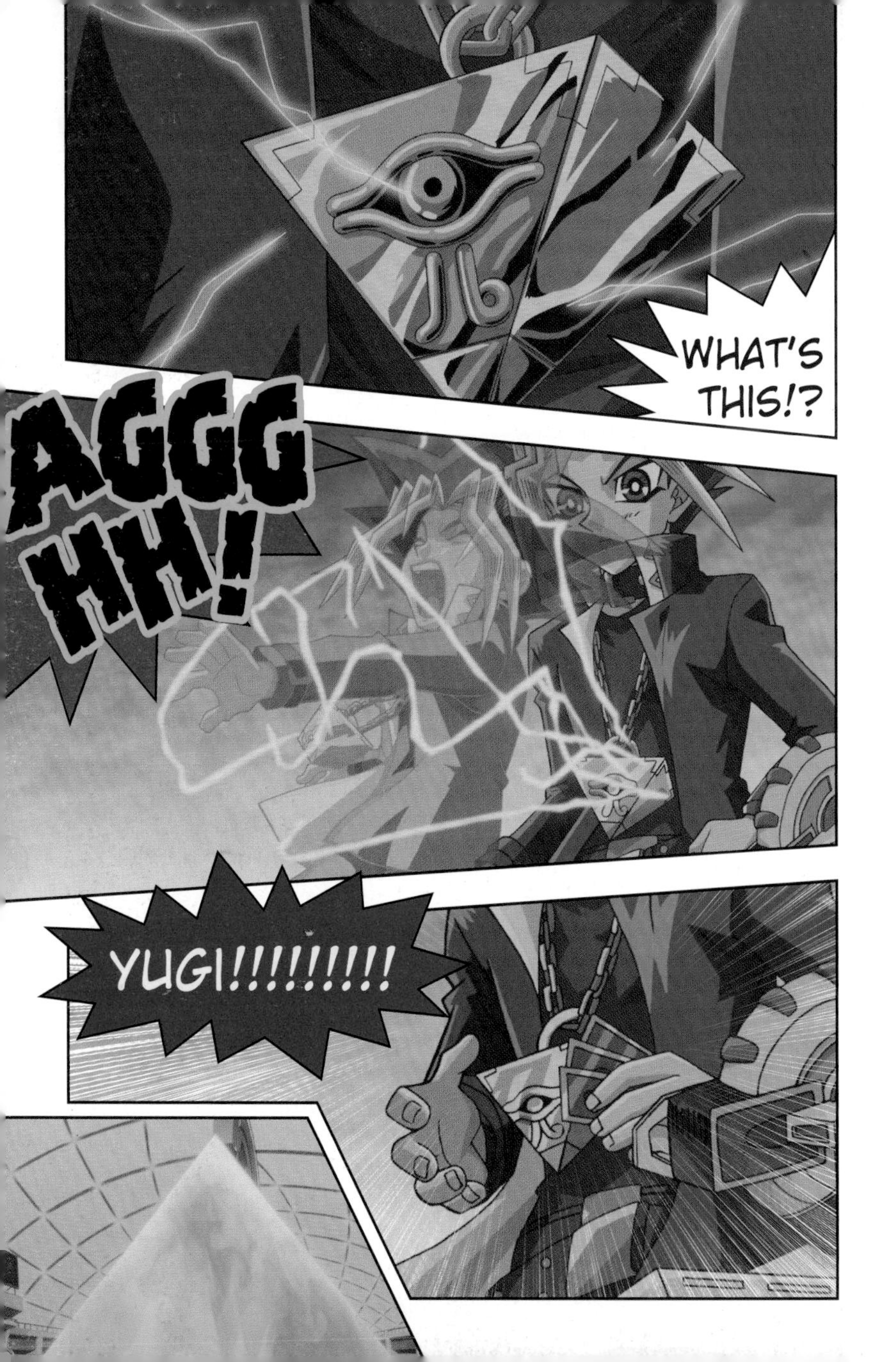
WHAT'S THIS!?
AGGGHH!
YUGI!!!!!!!!!!

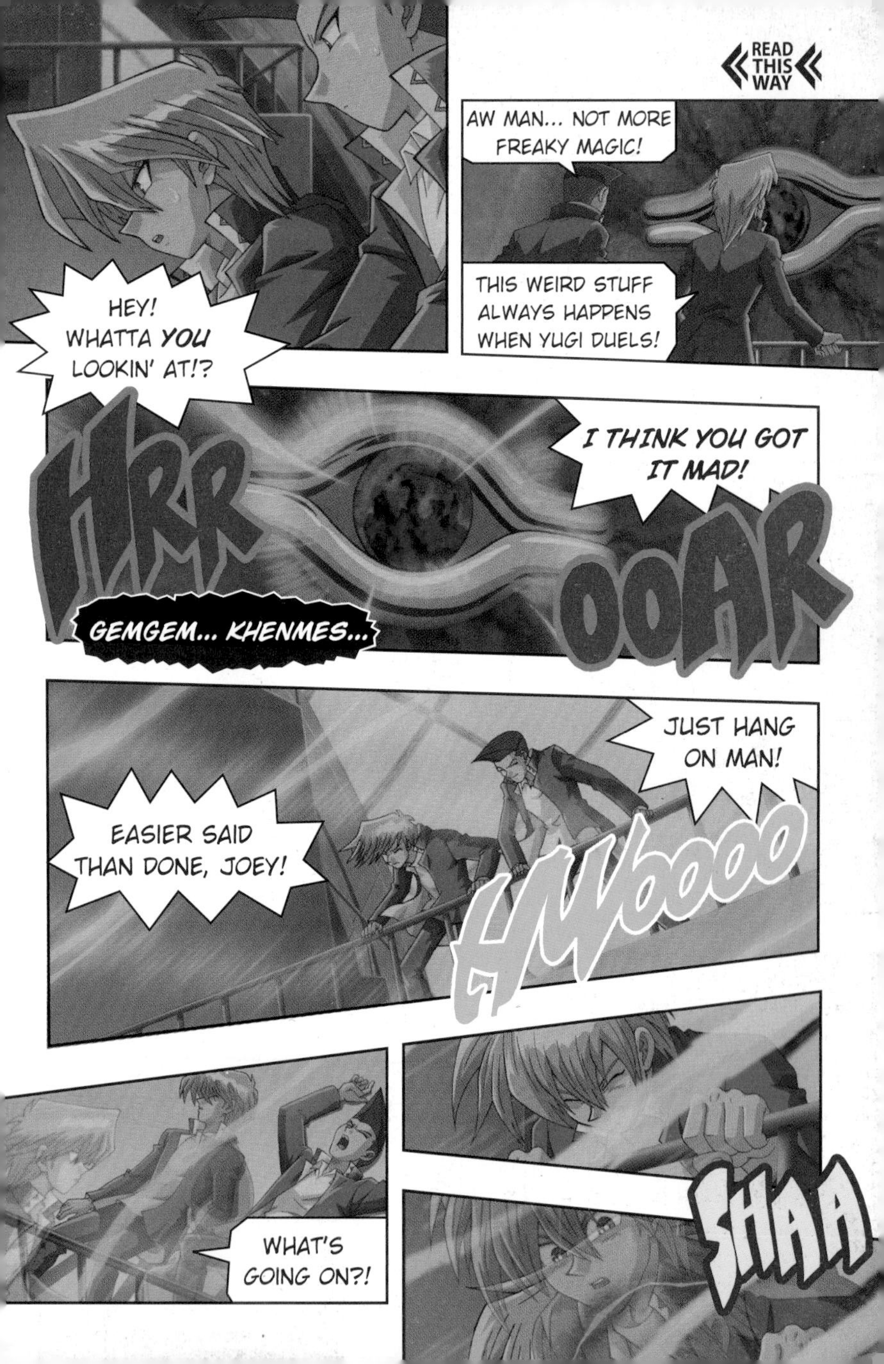

READ THIS WAY
AW MAN... NOT MORE FREAKY MAGIC!
THIS WEIRD STUFF ALWAYS HAPPENS WHEN YUGI DUELS!
HEY! WHATTA *YOU* LOOKIN' AT!?
I THINK YOU GOT IT MAD!
HRR
OOAR
GEMGEM... KHENMES...
JUST HANG ON MAN!
EASIER SAID THAN DONE, JOEY!
HWOOOO
SHAA
WHAT'S GOING ON?!

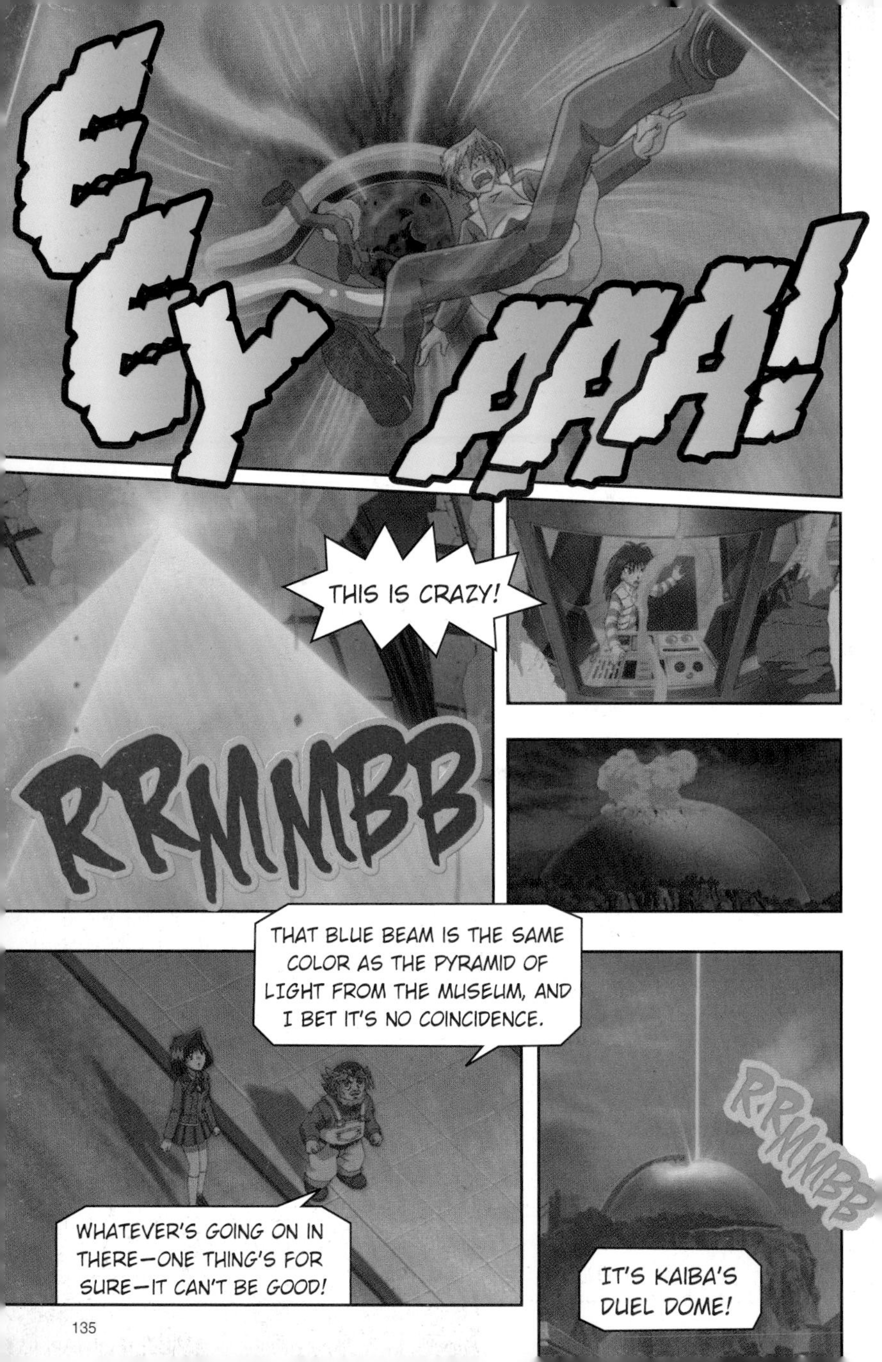
EEYAAA!
THIS IS CRAZY!
RRMMBB
RRMMBB
IT'S KAIBA'S DUEL DOME!
THAT BLUE BEAM IS THE SAME COLOR AS THE PYRAMID OF LIGHT FROM THE MUSEUM, AND I BET IT'S NO COINCIDENCE.
WHATEVER'S GOING ON IN THERE—ONE THING'S FOR SURE—IT CAN'T BE GOOD!

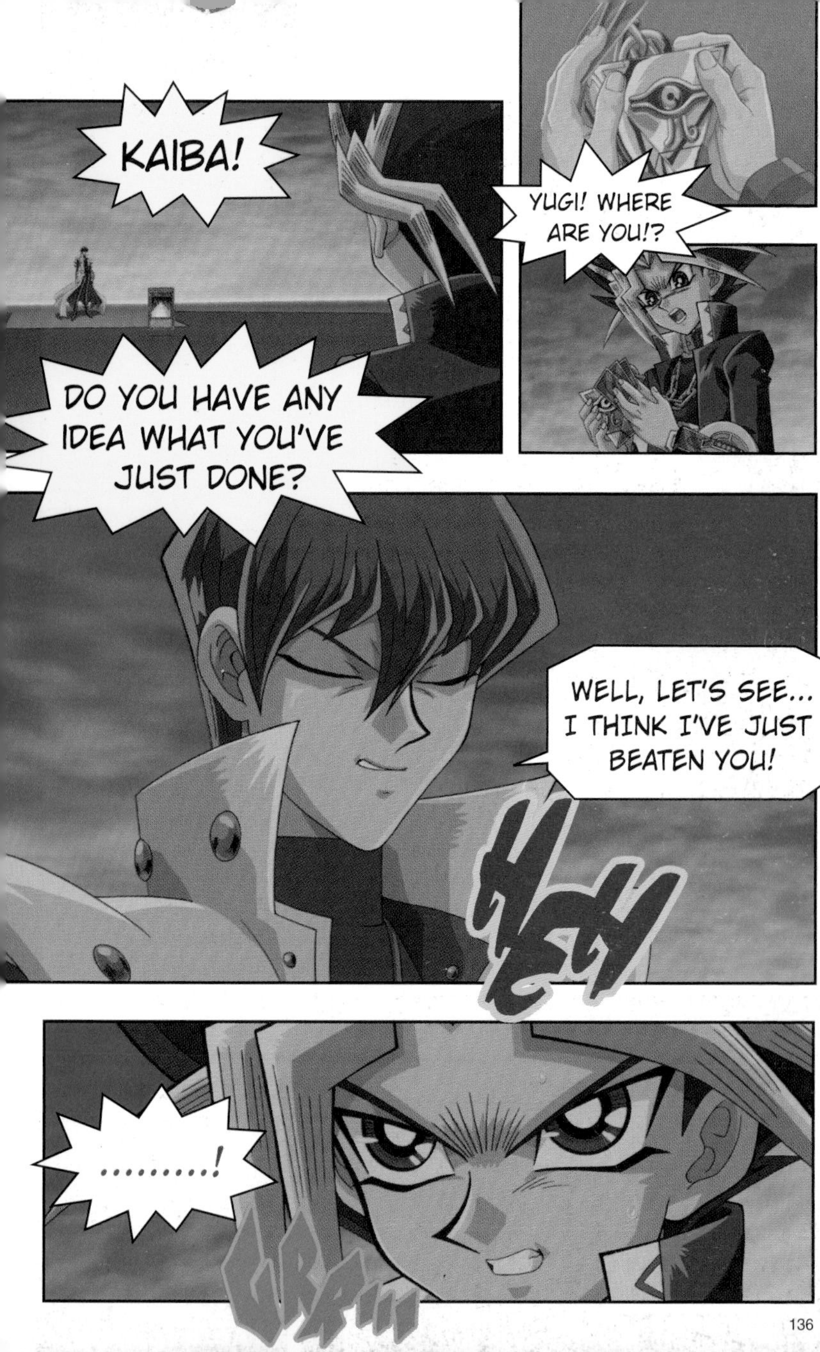
YUGI! WHERE ARE YOU!?
KAIBA!
DO YOU HAVE ANY IDEA WHAT YOU'VE JUST DONE?
WELL, LET'S SEE... I THINK I'VE JUST BEATEN YOU!
HEH
.........!
GRR...

READ THIS WAY

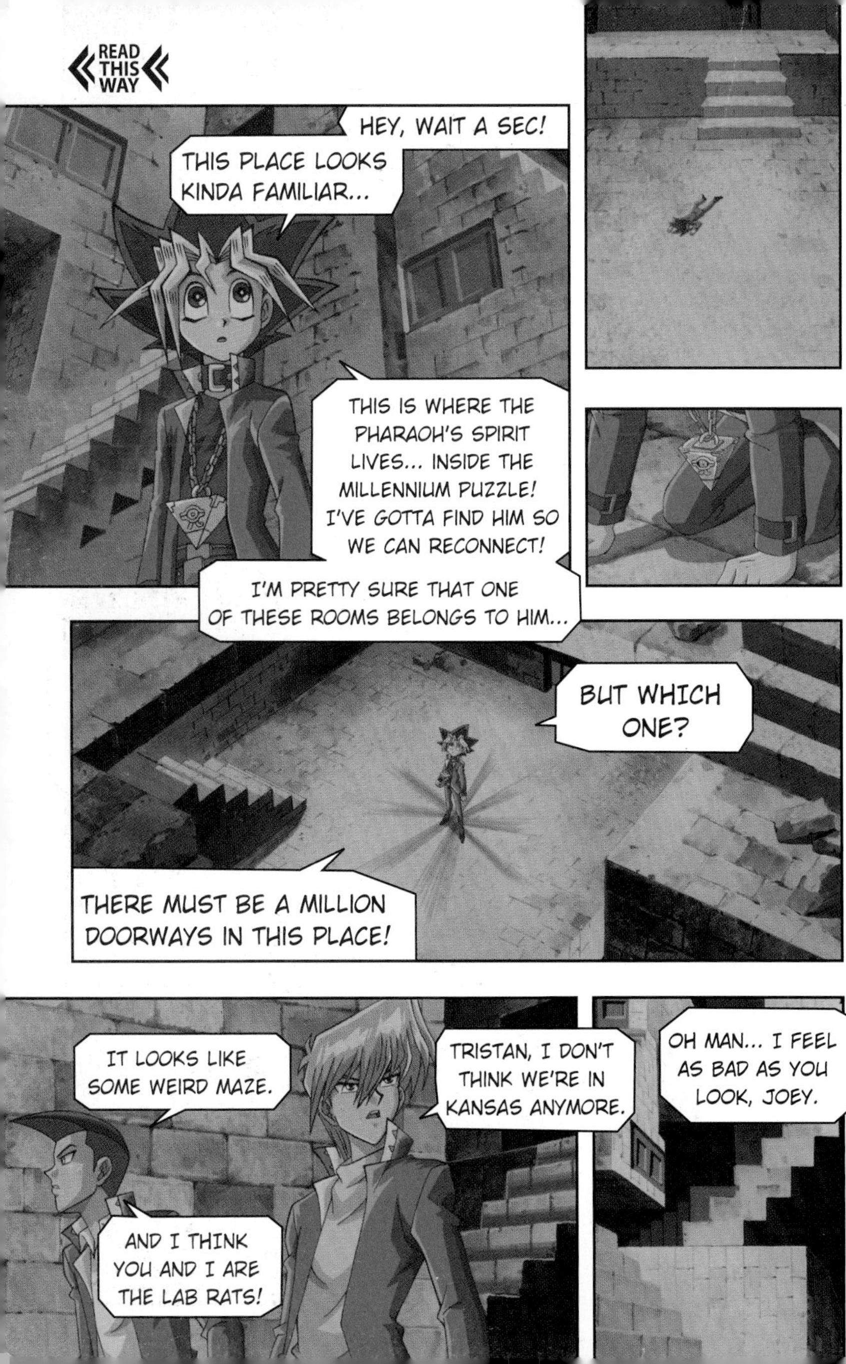
HEY, WAIT A SEC!
THIS PLACE LOOKS KINDA FAMILIAR...
THIS IS WHERE THE PHARAOH'S SPIRIT LIVES... INSIDE THE MILLENNIUM PUZZLE! I'VE GOTTA FIND HIM SO WE CAN RECONNECT!
I'M PRETTY SURE THAT ONE OF THESE ROOMS BELONGS TO HIM...
BUT WHICH ONE?
THERE MUST BE A MILLION DOORWAYS IN THIS PLACE!
OH MAN... I FEEL AS BAD AS YOU LOOK, JOEY.
TRISTAN, I DON'T THINK WE'RE IN KANSAS ANYMORE.
IT LOOKS LIKE SOME WEIRD MAZE.
AND I THINK YOU AND I ARE THE LAB RATS!

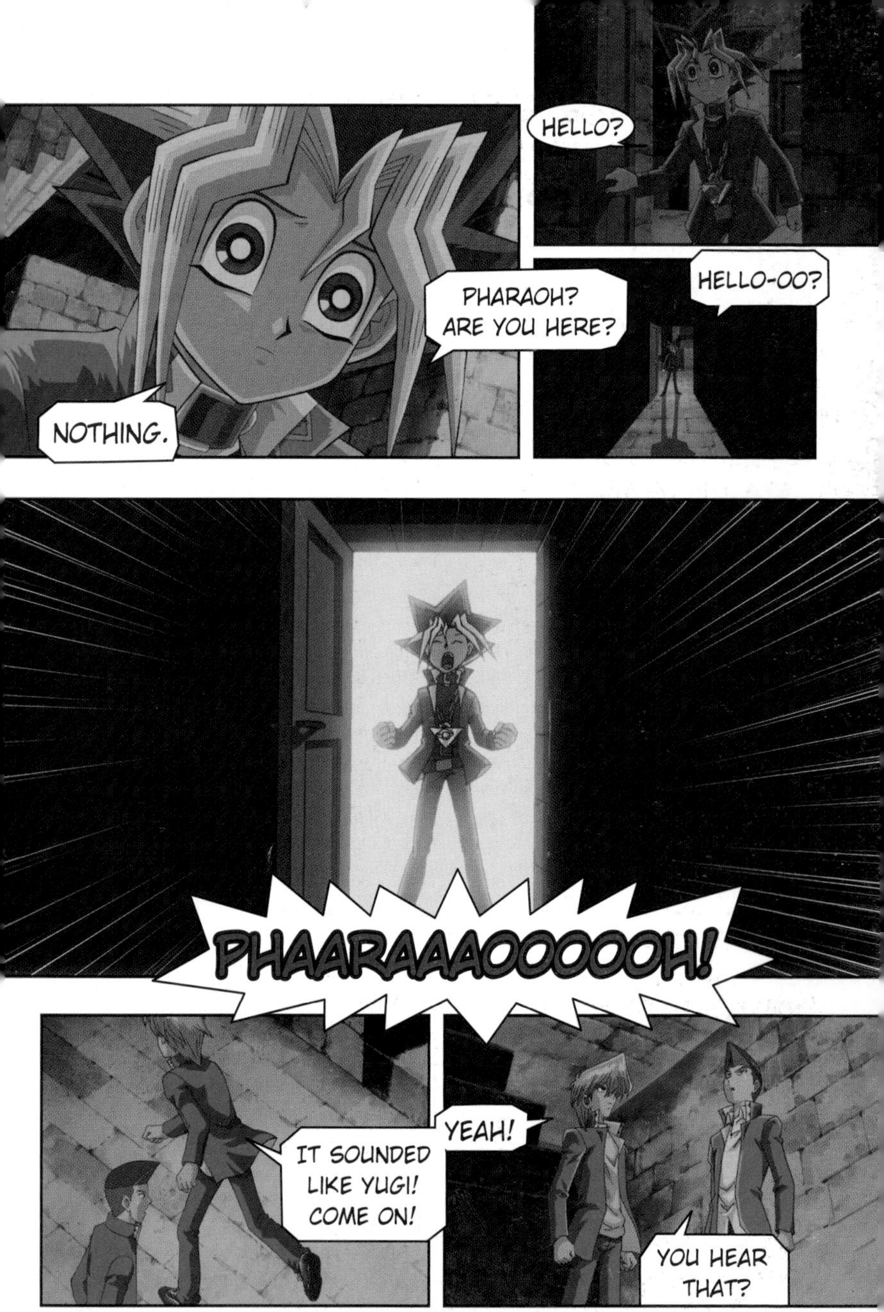

HELLO?
HELLO-OO?
PHARAOH? ARE YOU HERE?
NOTHING.
PHAARAAAOOOOOH!
YOU HEAR THAT?
YEAH!
IT SOUNDED LIKE YUGI! COME ON!

READ THIS WAY

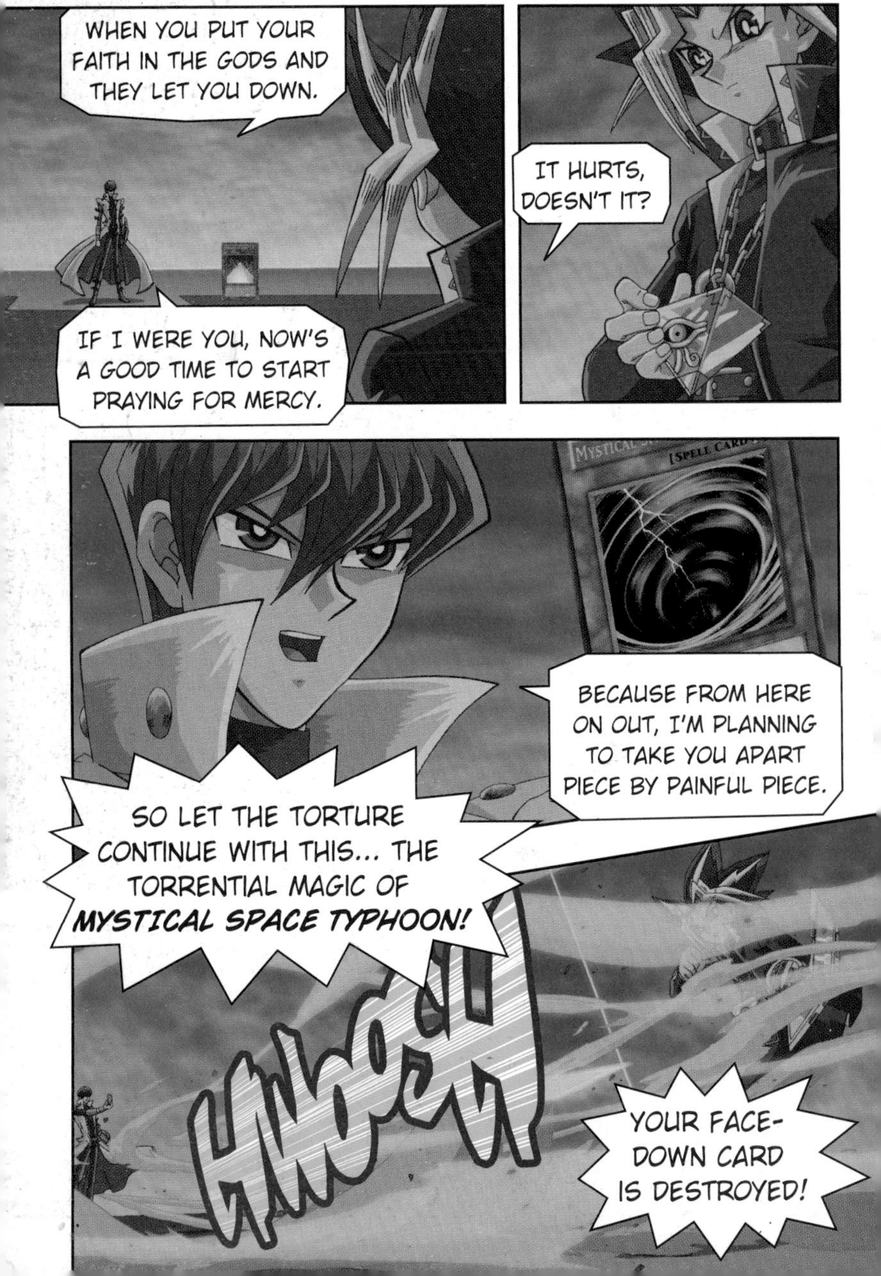
IT HURTS, DOESN'T IT?
WHEN YOU PUT YOUR FAITH IN THE GODS AND THEY LET YOU DOWN.
IF I WERE YOU, NOW'S A GOOD TIME TO START PRAYING FOR MERCY.
BECAUSE FROM HERE ON OUT, I'M PLANNING TO TAKE YOU APART PIECE BY PAINFUL PIECE.
SO LET THE TORTURE CONTINUE WITH THIS... THE TORRENTIAL MAGIC OF ***MYSTICAL SPACE TYPHOON!***
YOUR FACE-DOWN CARD IS DESTROYED!

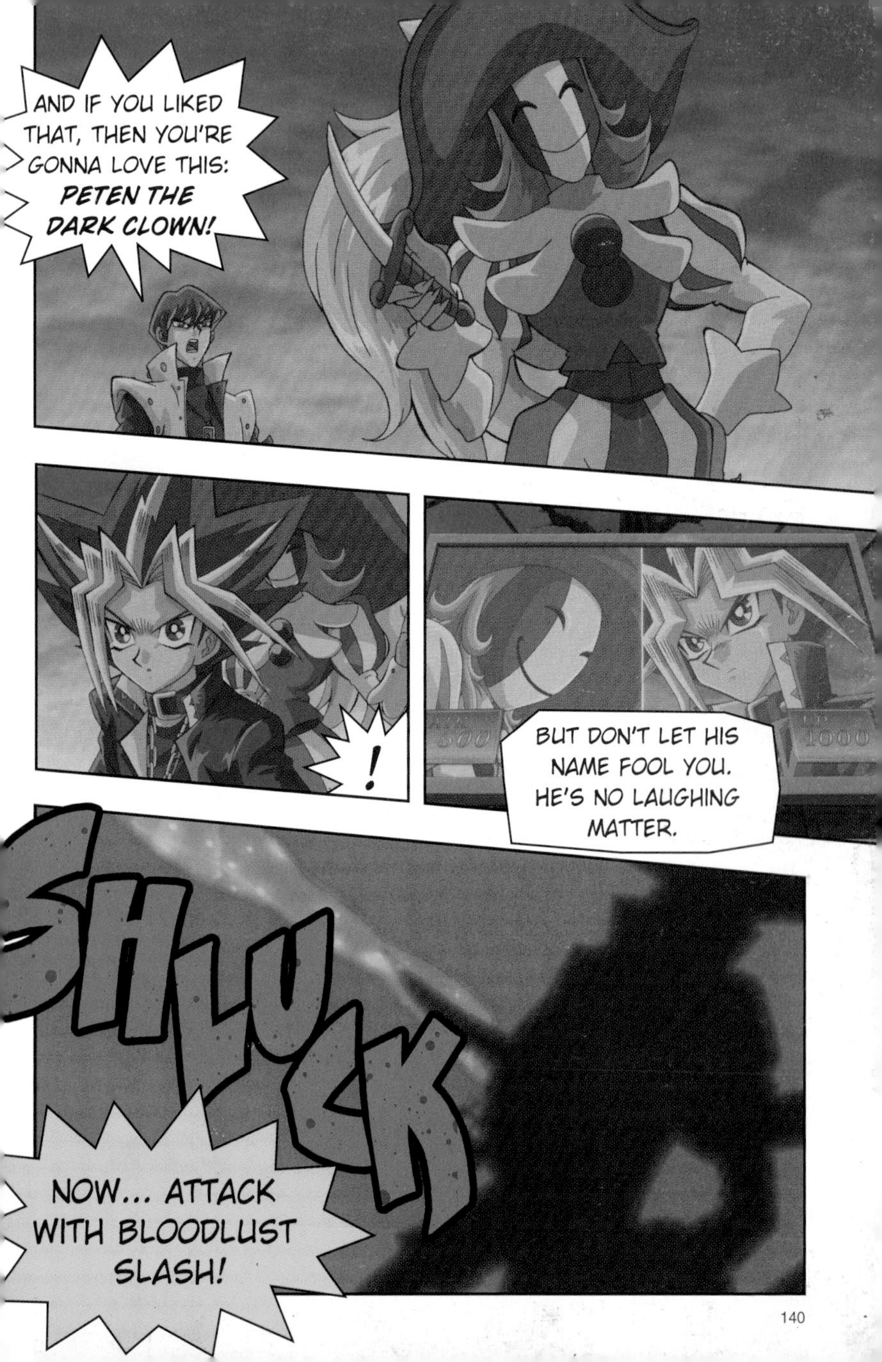
AND IF YOU LIKED THAT, THEN YOU'RE GONNA LOVE THIS: *PETEN THE DARK CLOWN!*
BUT DON'T LET HIS NAME FOOL YOU. HE'S NO LAUGHING MATTER.
!
SHLUCK
NOW... ATTACK WITH BLOODLUST SLASH!

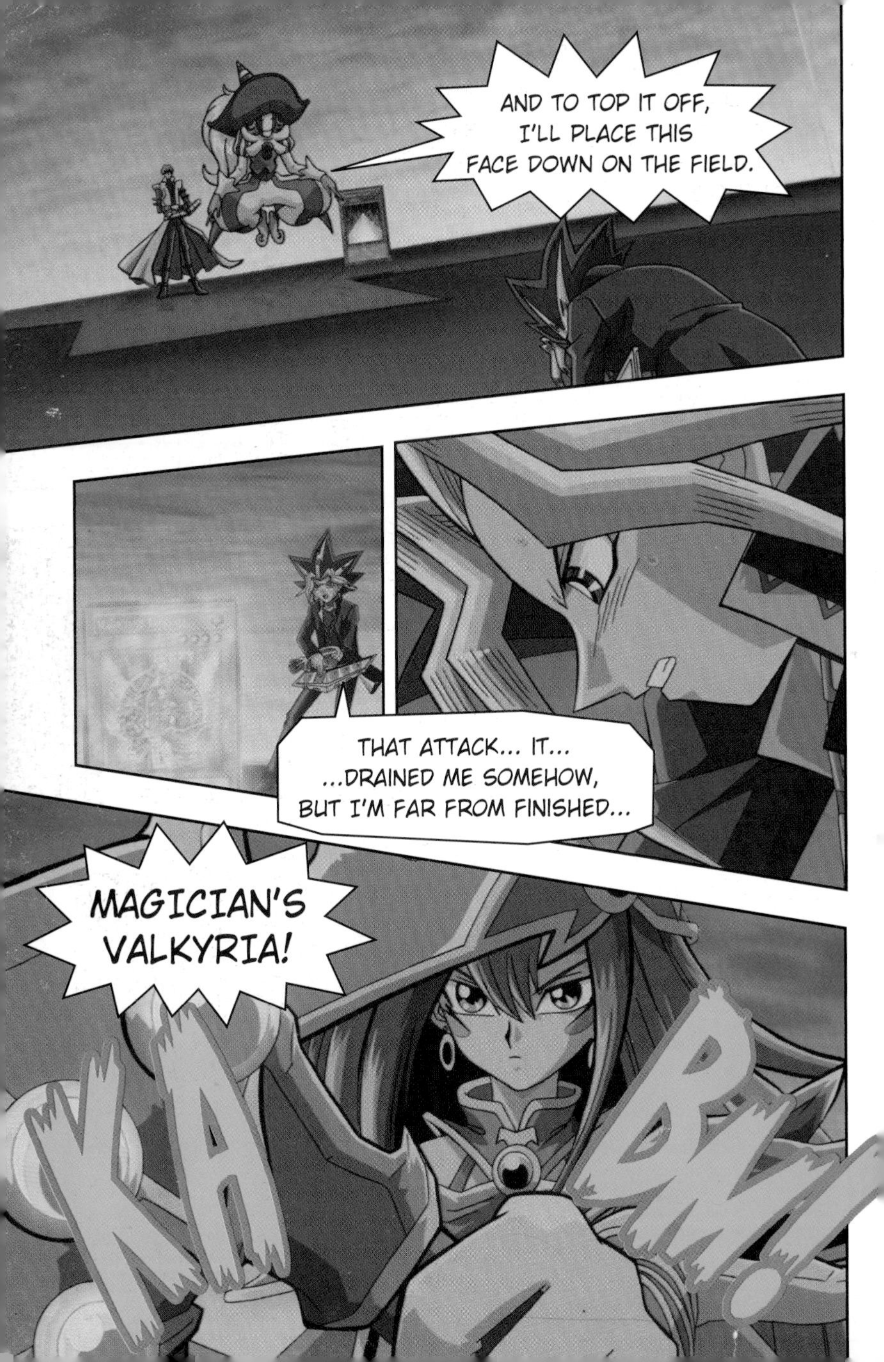
AND TO TOP IT OFF, I'LL PLACE THIS FACE DOWN ON THE FIELD.
THAT ATTACK... IT... ...DRAINED ME SOMEHOW, BUT I'M FAR FROM FINISHED...
MAGICIAN'S VALKYRIA!
KA BM!

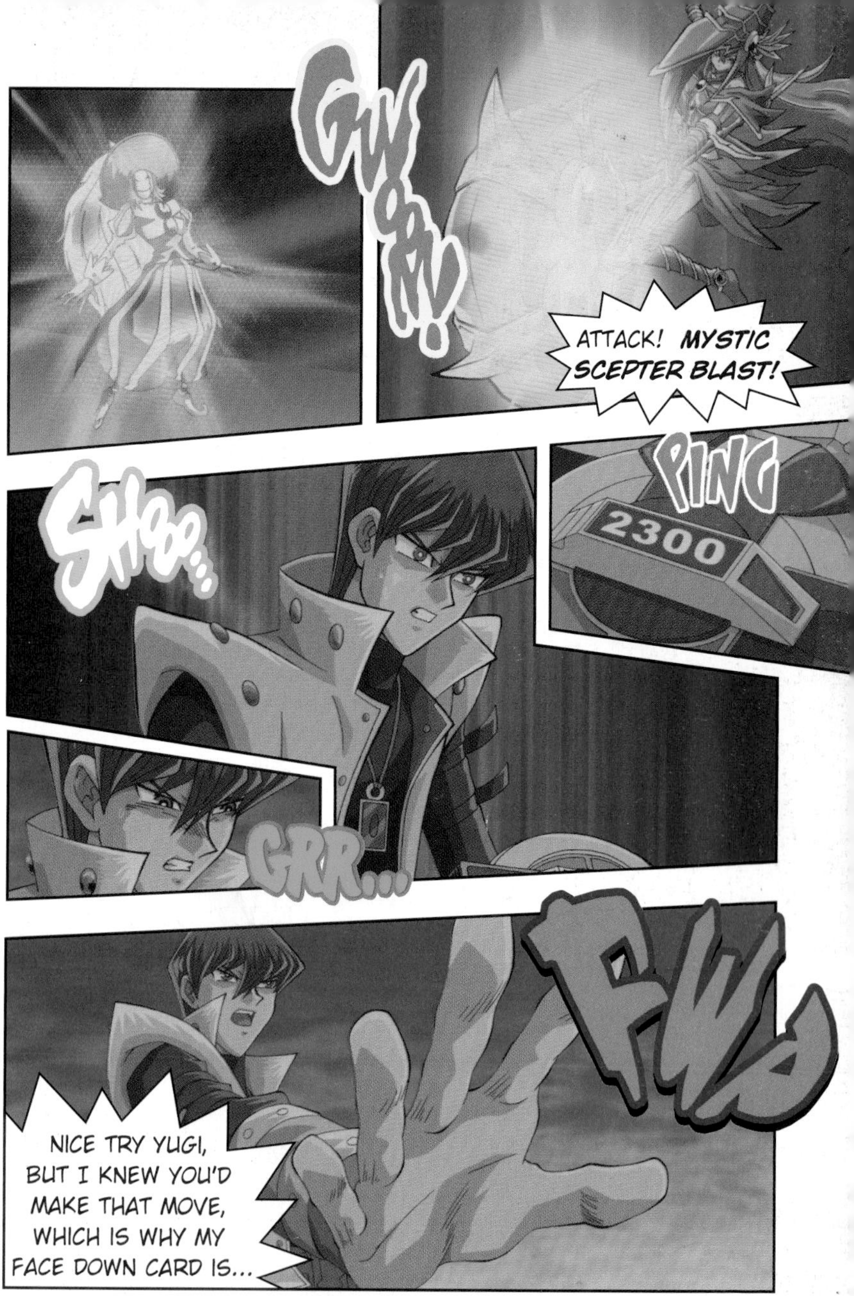

GWOOM!
ATTACK! MYSTIC SCEPTER BLAST!
PING
2300
SHOO...
GRR...
FWA
NICE TRY YUGI, BUT I KNEW YOU'D MAKE THAT MOVE, WHICH IS WHY MY FACE DOWN CARD IS...

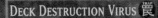

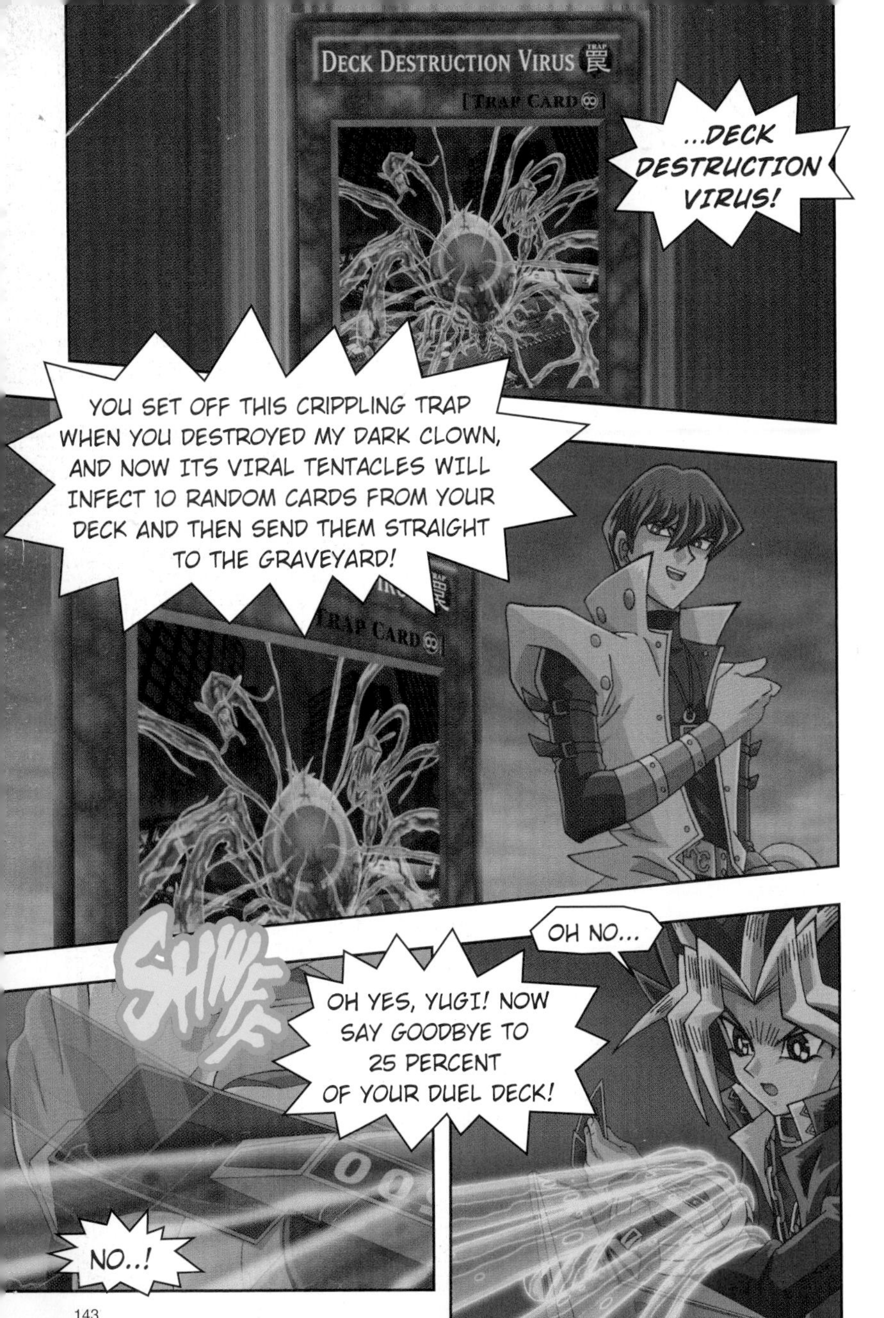

DECK DESTRUCTION VIRUS 罠

[TRAP CARD ⊙]

...DECK DESTRUCTION VIRUS!

YOU SET OFF THIS CRIPPLING TRAP WHEN YOU DESTROYED MY DARK CLOWN, AND NOW ITS VIRAL TENTACLES WILL INFECT 10 RANDOM CARDS FROM YOUR DECK AND THEN SEND THEM STRAIGHT TO THE GRAVEYARD!

TRAP CARD ⊙

OH NO...

SHWF

OH YES, YUGI! NOW SAY GOODBYE TO 25 PERCENT OF YOUR DUEL DECK!

NO..!

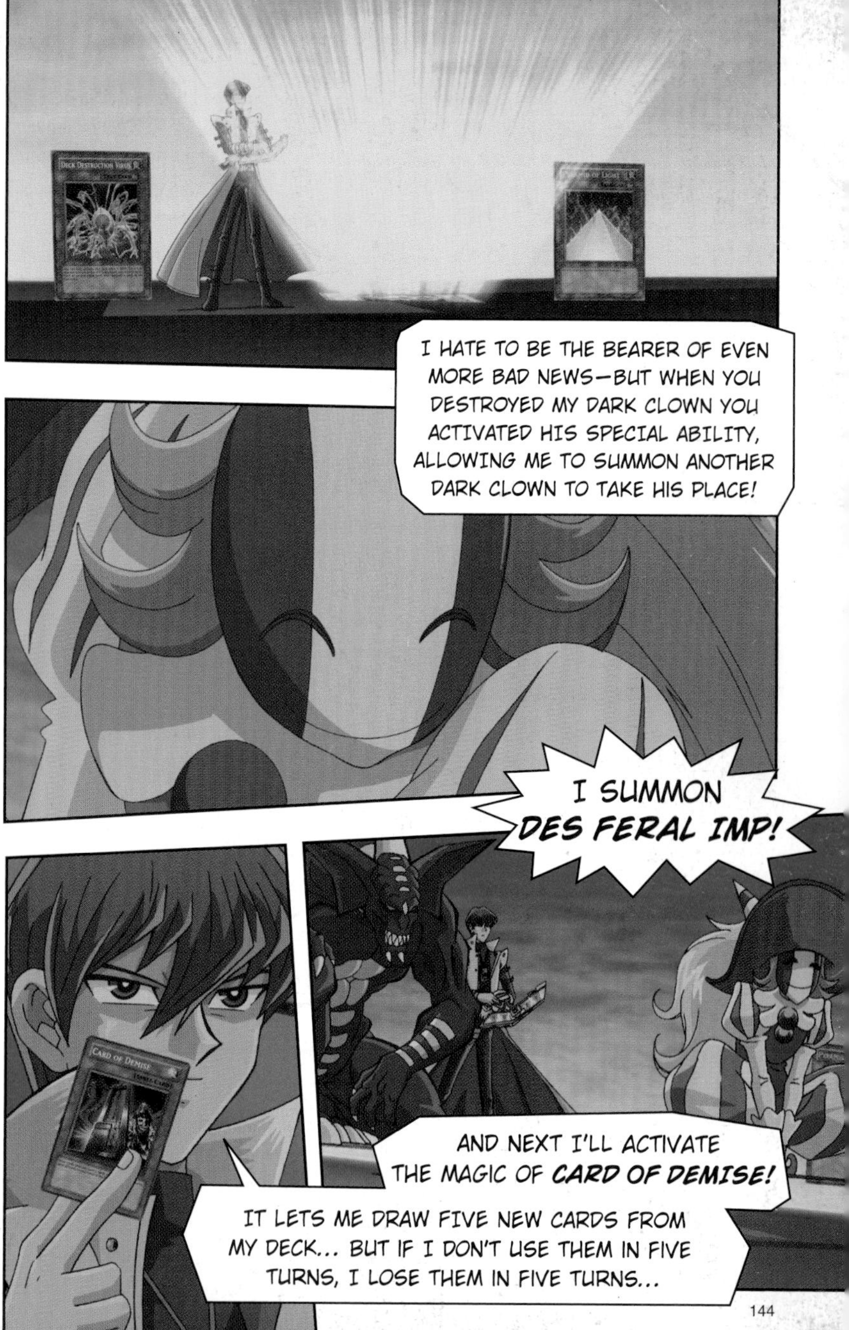
I HATE TO BE THE BEARER OF EVEN MORE BAD NEWS—BUT WHEN YOU DESTROYED MY DARK CLOWN YOU ACTIVATED HIS SPECIAL ABILITY, ALLOWING ME TO SUMMON ANOTHER DARK CLOWN TO TAKE HIS PLACE!
I SUMMON ***DES FERAL IMP!***
AND NEXT I'LL ACTIVATE THE MAGIC OF ***CARD OF DEMISE!***
IT LETS ME DRAW FIVE NEW CARDS FROM MY DECK... BUT IF I DON'T USE THEM IN FIVE TURNS, I LOSE THEM IN FIVE TURNS...

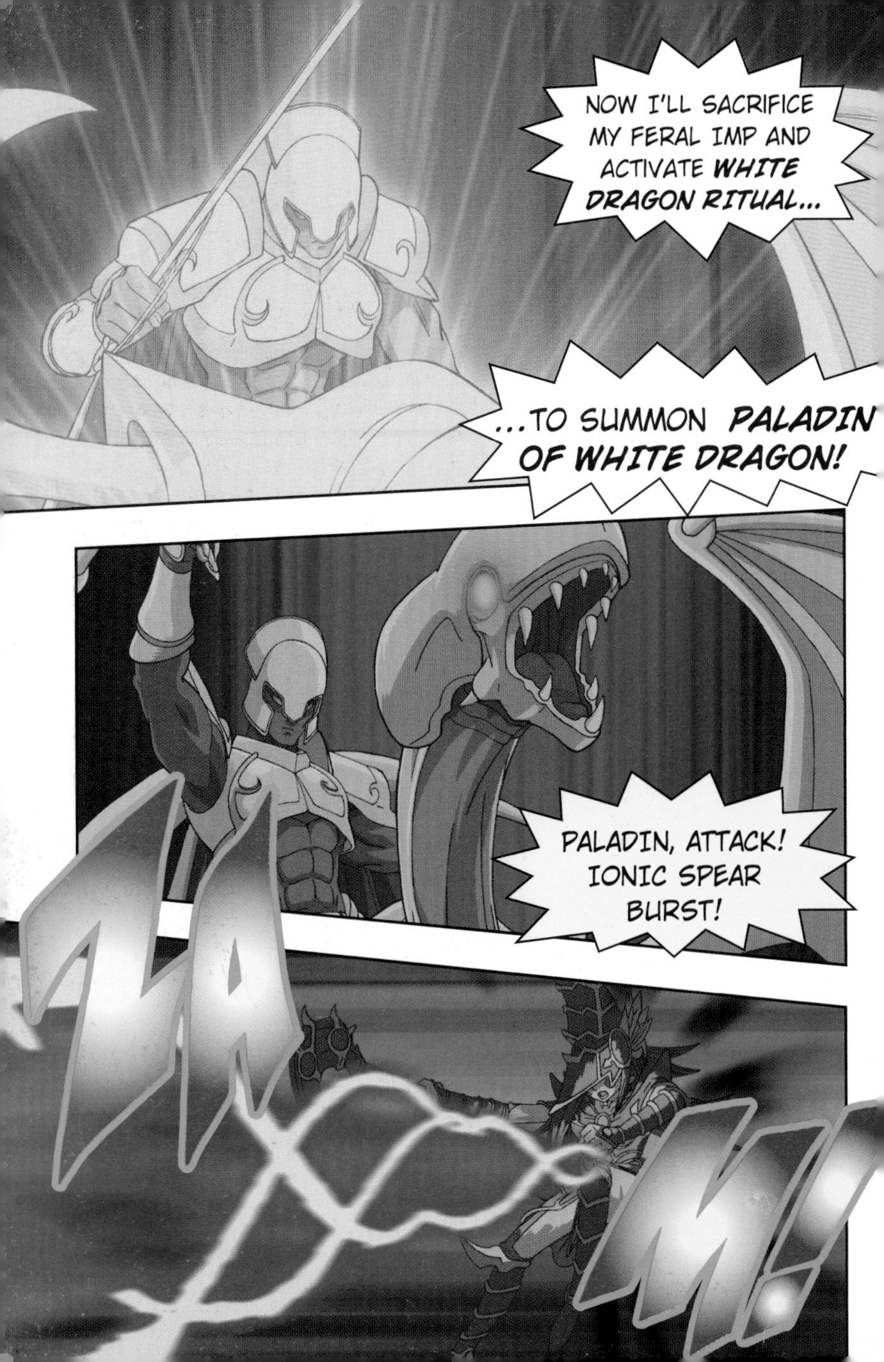
NOW I'LL SACRIFICE MY FERAL IMP AND ACTIVATE ***WHITE DRAGON RITUAL...***
...TO SUMMON ***PALADIN OF WHITE DRAGON!***
PALADIN, ATTACK! IONIC SPEAR BURST!
ZAM!

READ THIS WAY

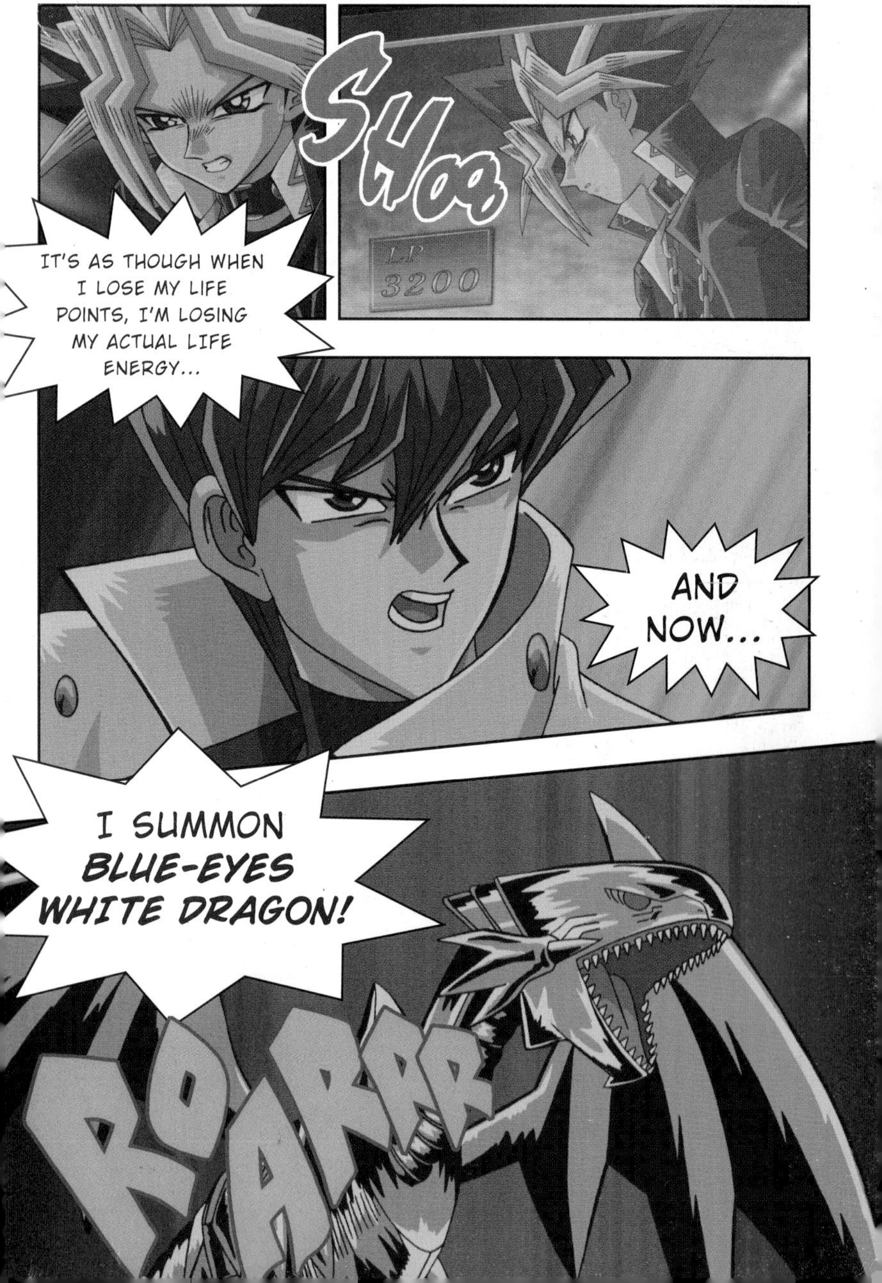
SHOO
LP 3200
IT'S AS THOUGH WHEN I LOSE MY LIFE POINTS, I'M LOSING MY ACTUAL LIFE ENERGY...
AND NOW...
I SUMMON BLUE-EYES WHITE DRAGON!
ROARRR

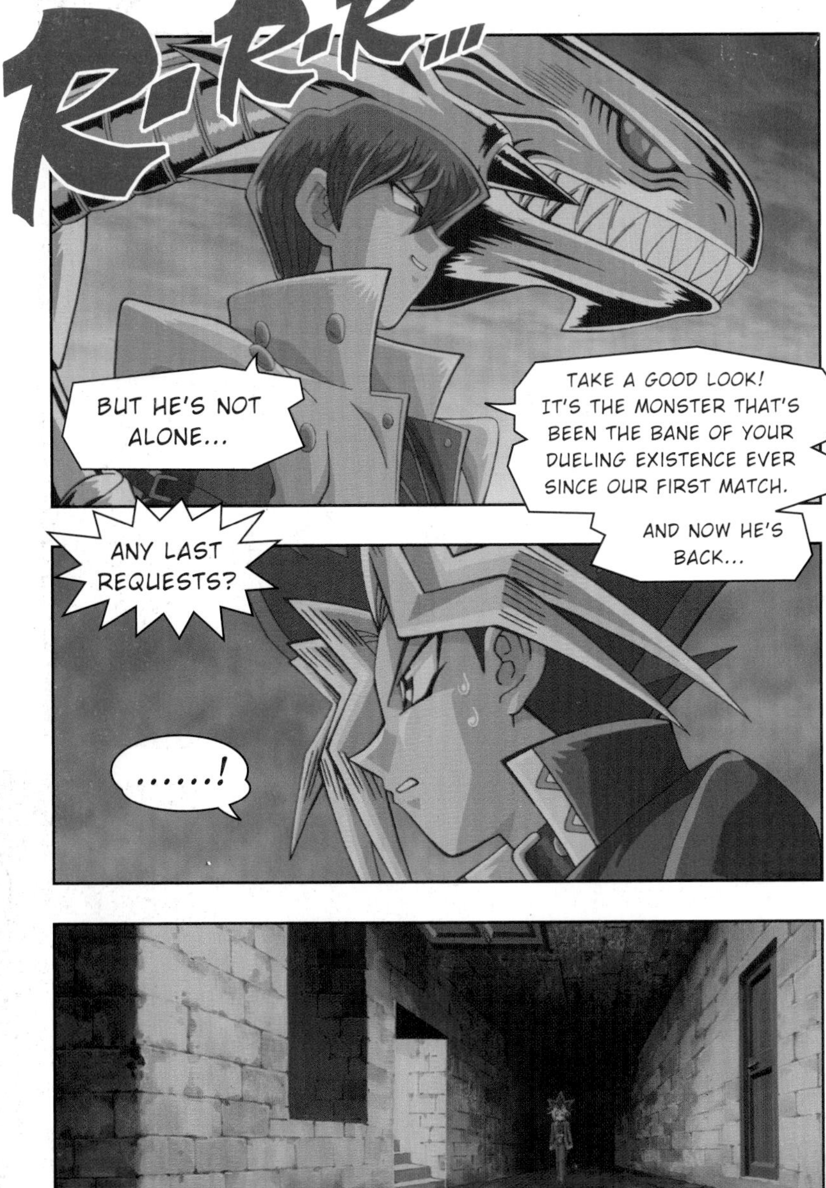
R..R..R...
TAKE A GOOD LOOK! IT'S THE MONSTER THAT'S BEEN THE BANE OF YOUR DUELING EXISTENCE EVER SINCE OUR FIRST MATCH.
AND NOW HE'S BACK...
BUT HE'S NOT ALONE...
ANY LAST REQUESTS?
......!

READ THIS WAY

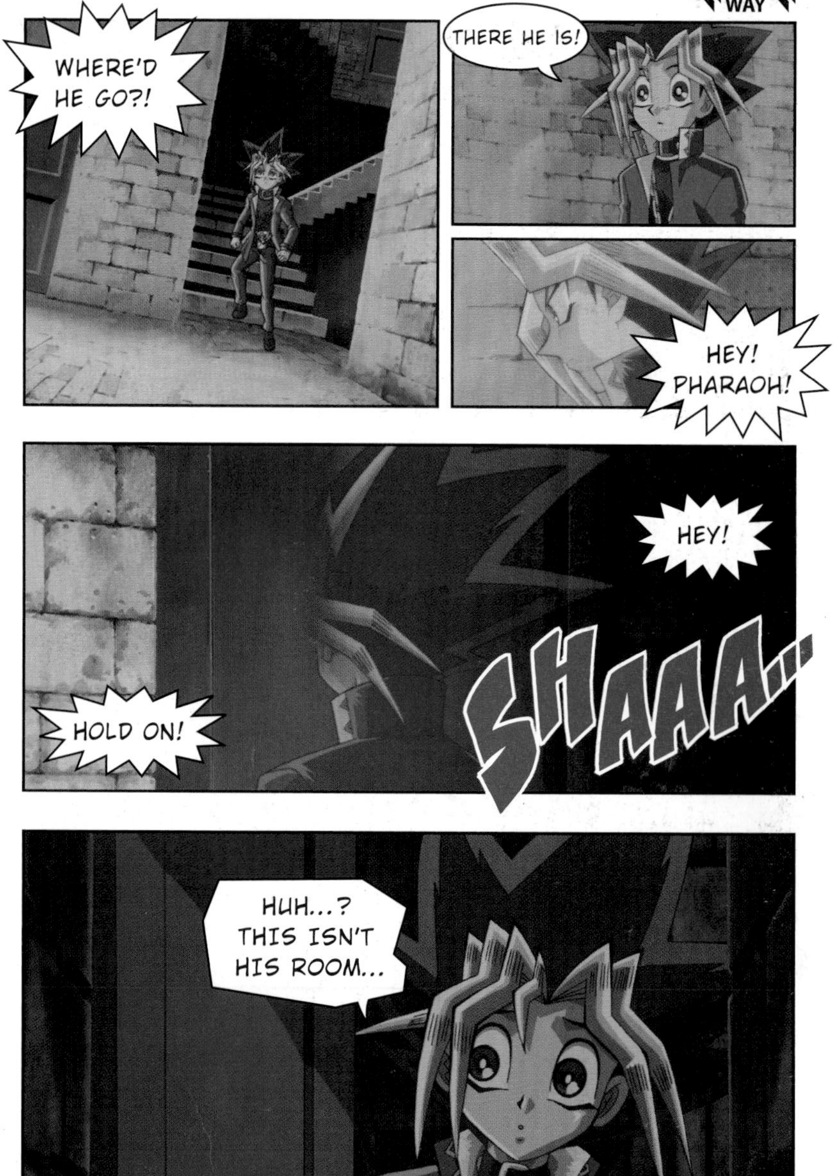
THERE HE IS!
HEY! PHARAOH!
WHERE'D HE GO?!
HEY!
SHAAA...
HOLD ON!
HUH...? THIS ISN'T HIS ROOM...

READ THIS WAY

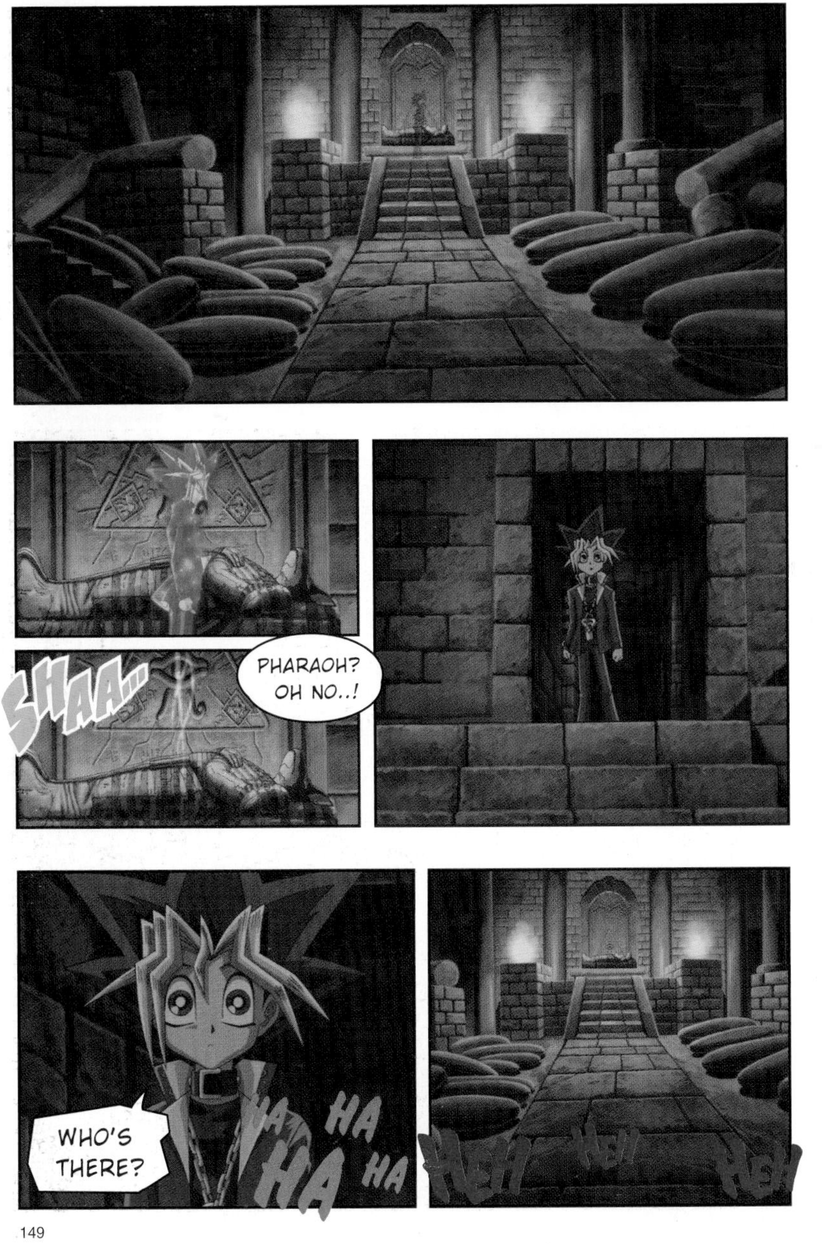
PHARAOH? OH NO..!
SHAA...
HEH HEH HEH
HA HA HA HA HA
WHO'S THERE?

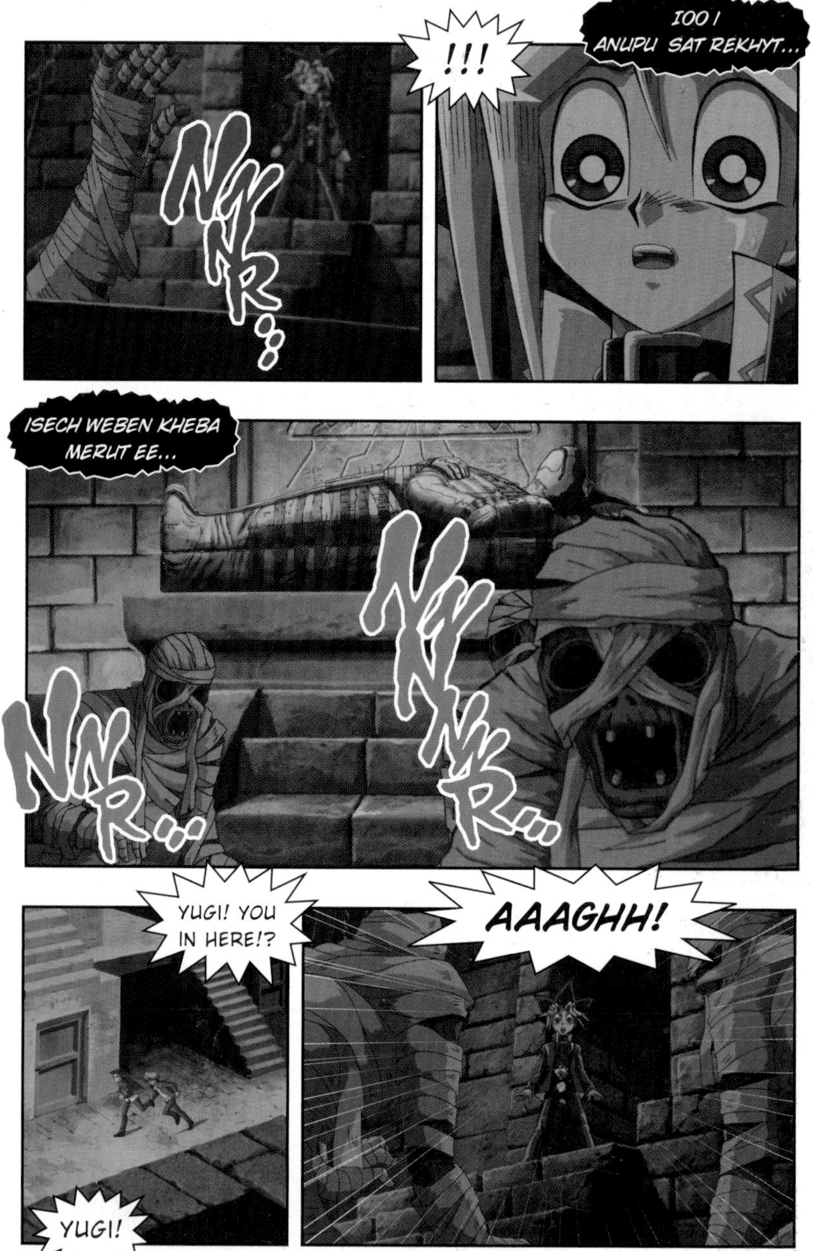
IOO I
ANUPU SAT REKHYT...
!!!
NNNR..
ISECH WEBEN KHEBA
MERUT EE...
NNNNR...
NNR...
AAAGHH!
YUGI! YOU
IN HERE!?
YUGI!

READ THIS WAY

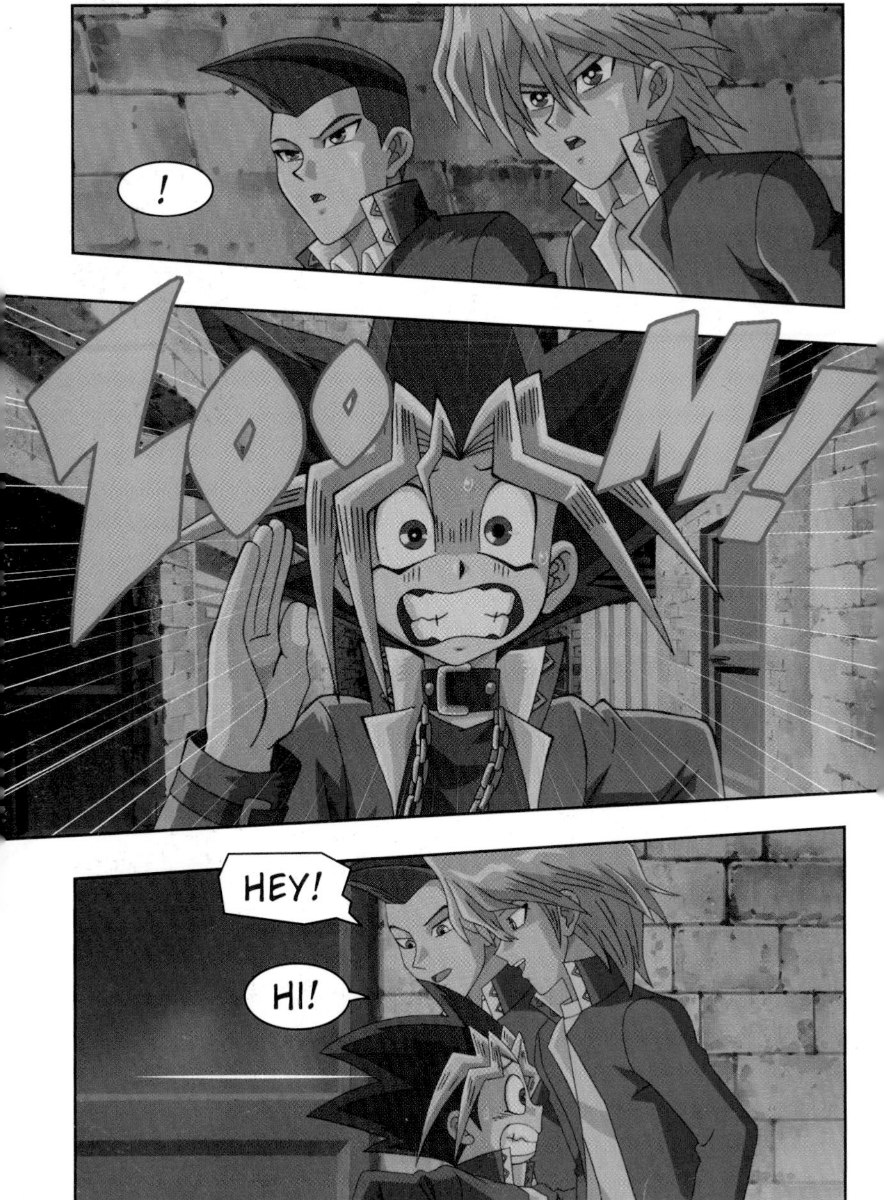
!
ZOOM!!
HEY!
HI!

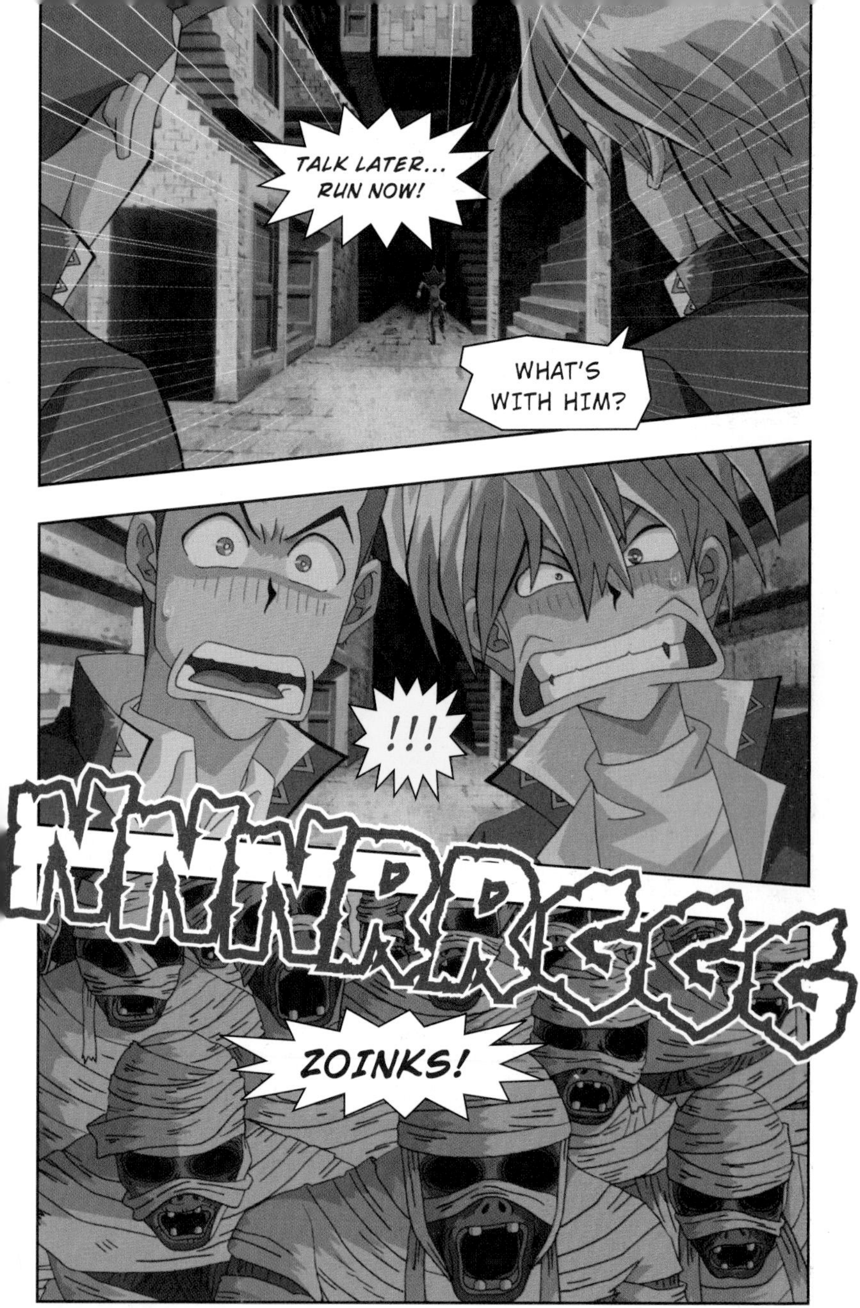
TALK LATER...
RUN NOW!
WHAT'S
WITH HIM?
!!!
NNNRRGGG
ZOINKS!

READ THIS WAY

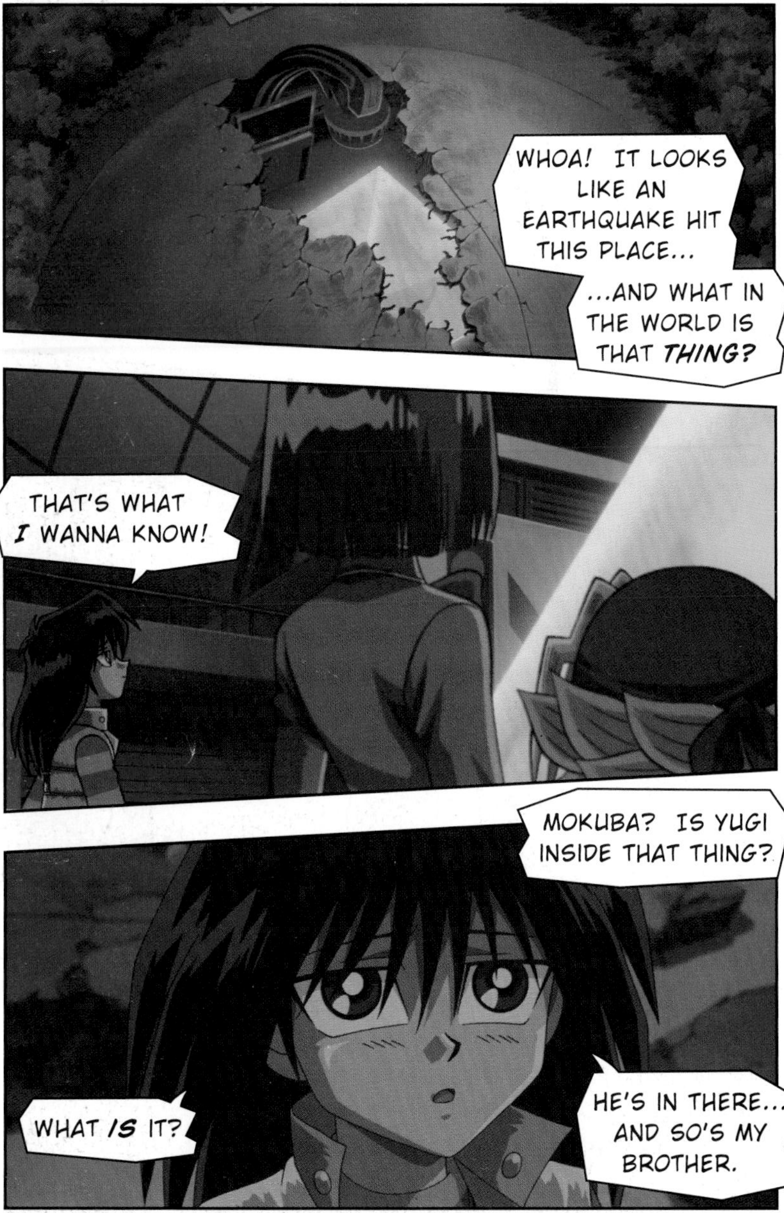
WHOA! IT LOOKS LIKE AN EARTHQUAKE HIT THIS PLACE...
...AND WHAT IN THE WORLD IS THAT *THING?*
THAT'S WHAT *I* WANNA KNOW!
MOKUBA? IS YUGI INSIDE THAT THING?
HE'S IN THERE... AND SO'S MY BROTHER.
WHAT *IS* IT?

READ THIS WAY

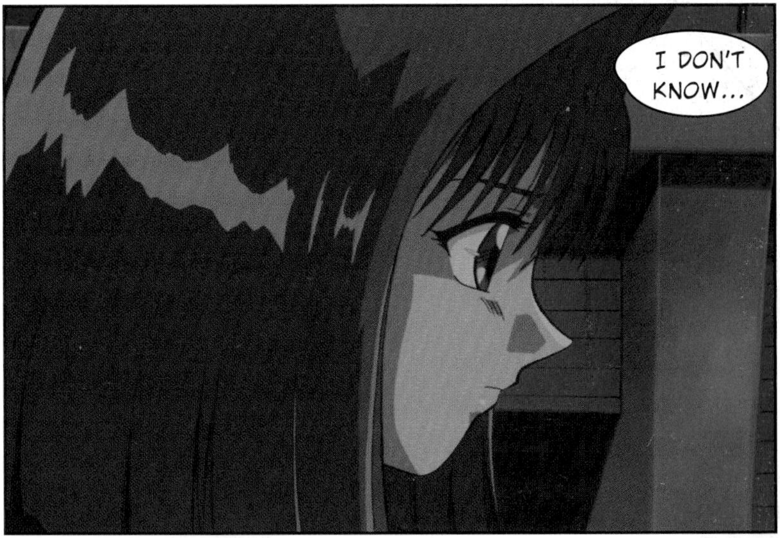
I DON'T KNOW...

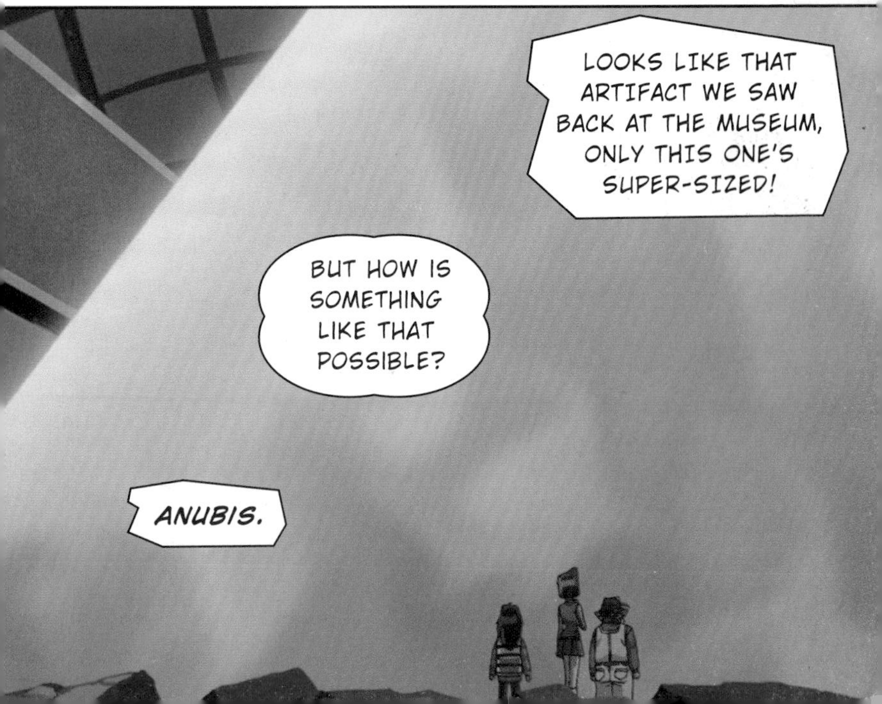
LOOKS LIKE THAT ARTIFACT WE SAW BACK AT THE MUSEUM, ONLY THIS ONE'S SUPER-SIZED!
BUT HOW IS SOMETHING LIKE THAT POSSIBLE?
ANUBIS.

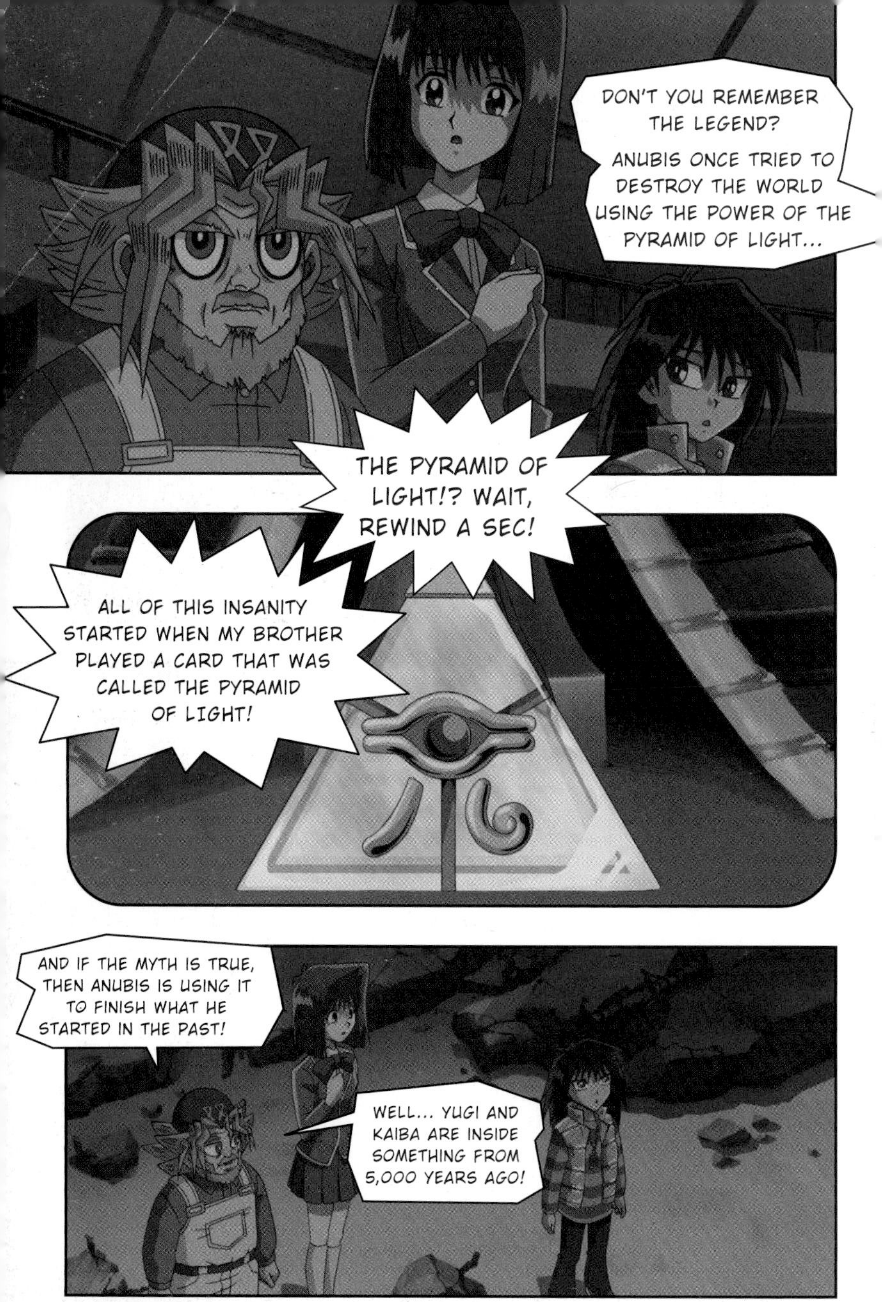

DON'T YOU REMEMBER THE LEGEND?
ANUBIS ONCE TRIED TO DESTROY THE WORLD USING THE POWER OF THE PYRAMID OF LIGHT...
THE PYRAMID OF LIGHT!? WAIT, REWIND A SEC!
ALL OF THIS INSANITY STARTED WHEN MY BROTHER PLAYED A CARD THAT WAS CALLED THE PYRAMID OF LIGHT!
AND IF THE MYTH IS TRUE, THEN ANUBIS IS USING IT TO FINISH WHAT HE STARTED IN THE PAST!
WELL... YUGI AND KAIBA ARE INSIDE SOMETHING FROM 5,000 YEARS AGO!

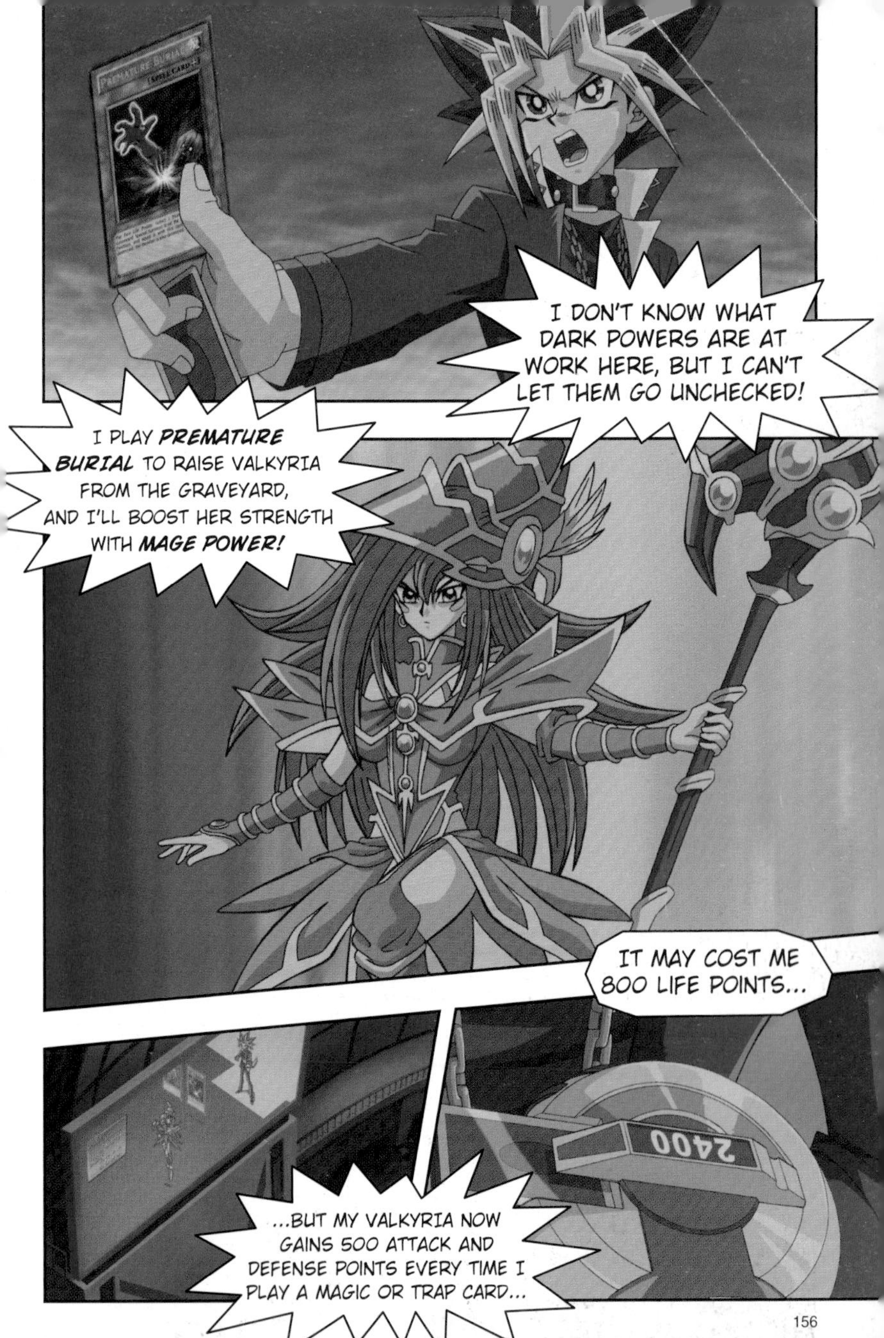
I DON'T KNOW WHAT DARK POWERS ARE AT WORK HERE, BUT I CAN'T LET THEM GO UNCHECKED!
I PLAY ***PREMATURE BURIAL*** TO RAISE VALKYRIA FROM THE GRAVEYARD, AND I'LL BOOST HER STRENGTH WITH ***MAGE POWER!***
IT MAY COST ME 800 LIFE POINTS...
2400
...BUT MY VALKYRIA NOW GAINS 500 ATTACK AND DEFENSE POINTS EVERY TIME I PLAY A MAGIC OR TRAP CARD...

READ THIS WAY

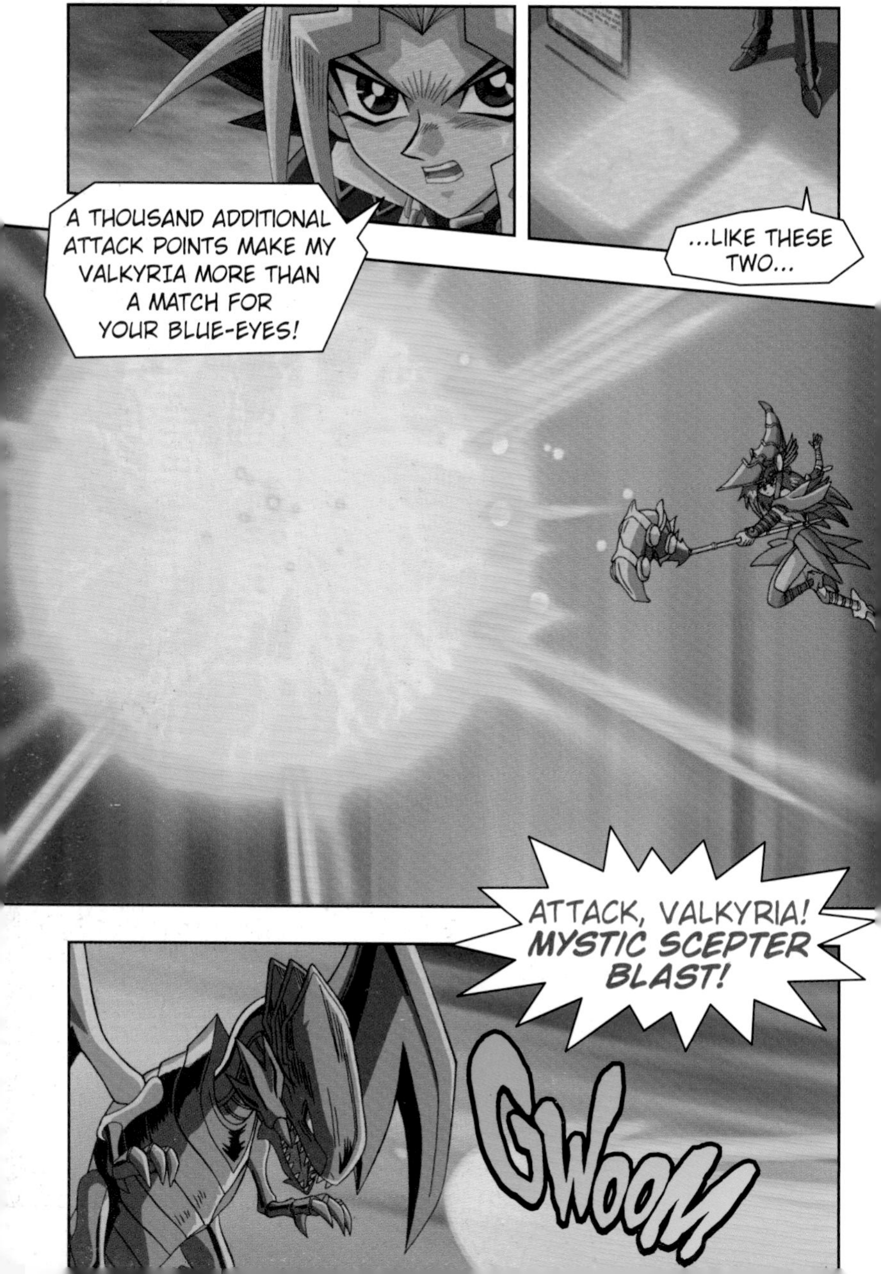
...LIKE THESE TWO...
A THOUSAND ADDITIONAL ATTACK POINTS MAKE MY VALKYRIA MORE THAN A MATCH FOR YOUR BLUE-EYES!
ATTACK, VALKYRIA! MYSTIC SCEPTER BLAST!
GWOOM

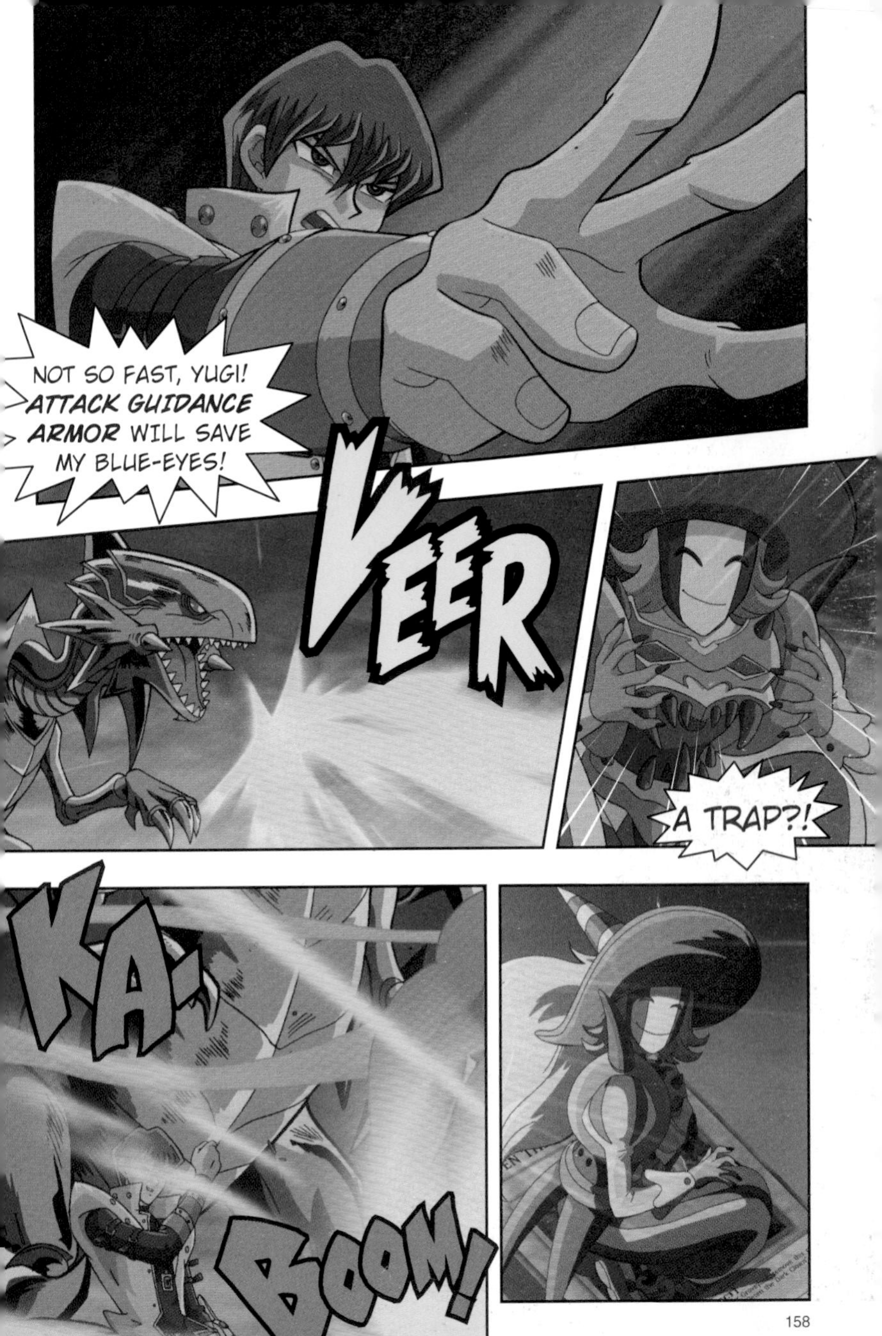
NOT SO FAST, YUGI! **ATTACK GUIDANCE ARMOR** WILL SAVE MY BLUE-EYES!
A TRAP?!
VEER
KA-
BOOM!

READ THIS WAY

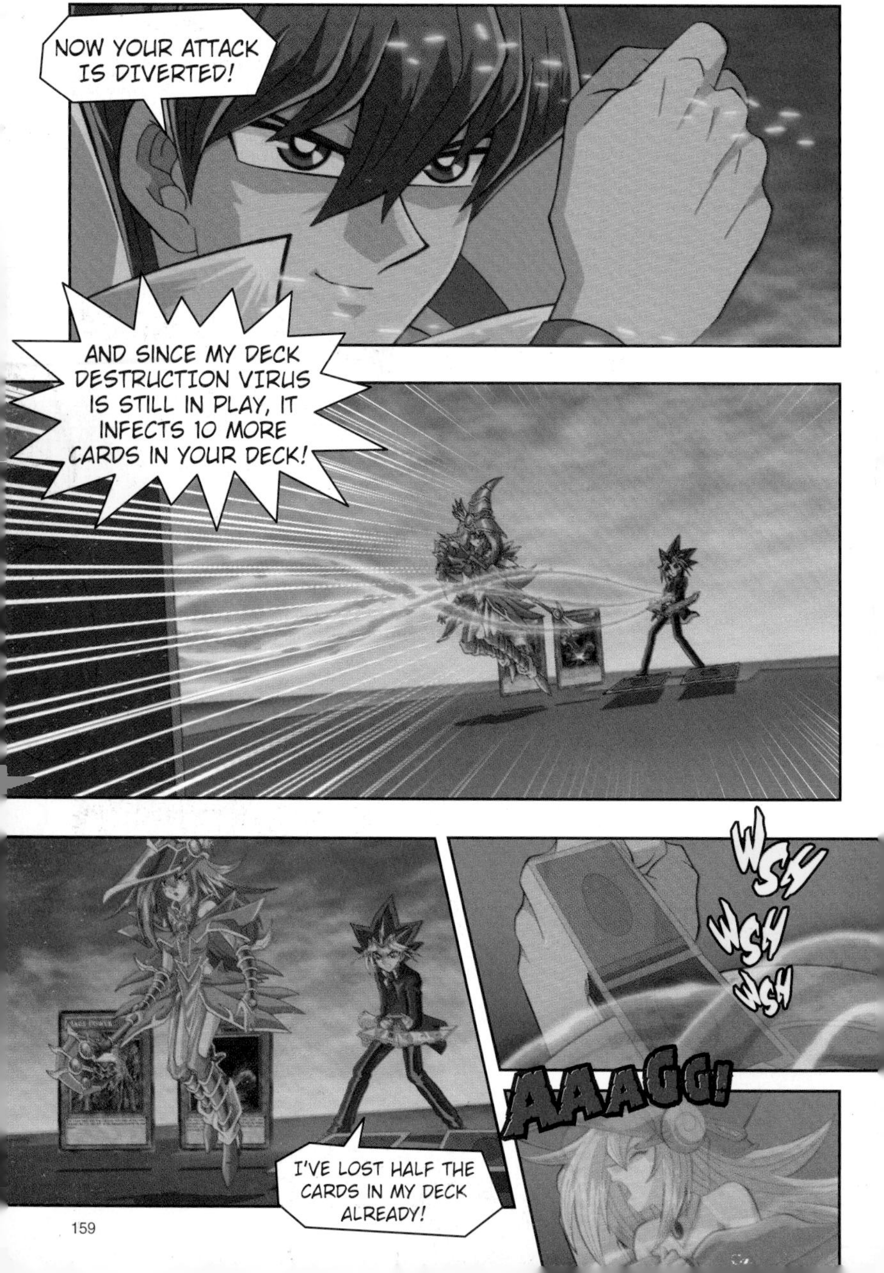

NOW YOUR ATTACK IS DIVERTED!
AND SINCE MY DECK DESTRUCTION VIRUS IS STILL IN PLAY, IT INFECTS 10 MORE CARDS IN YOUR DECK!
WSH
WSH
WSH
AAAGG!
I'VE LOST HALF THE CARDS IN MY DECK ALREADY!

READ THIS WAY

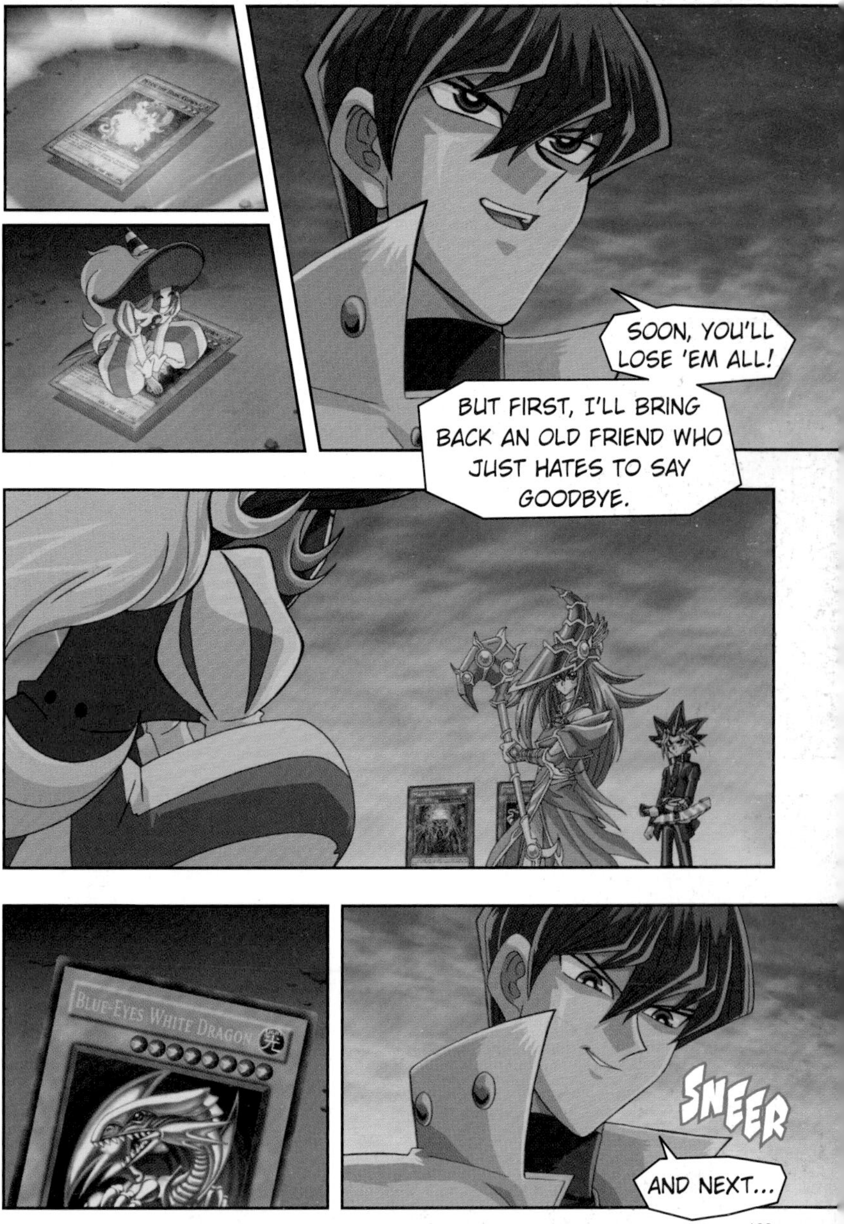
SOON, YOU'LL LOSE 'EM ALL!
BUT FIRST, I'LL BRING BACK AN OLD FRIEND WHO JUST HATES TO SAY GOODBYE.
SNEER
AND NEXT...
Blue-Eyes White Dragon

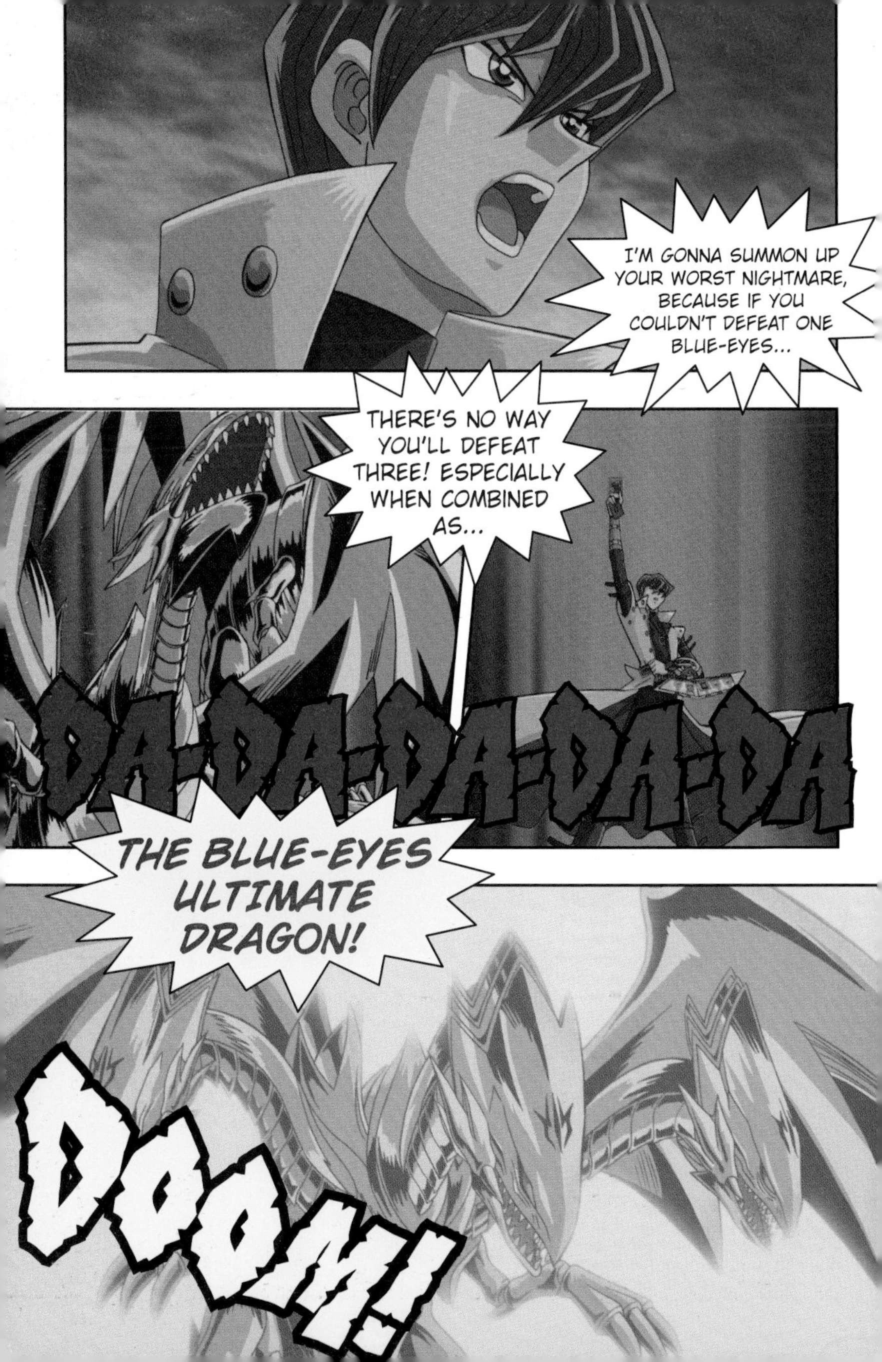
I'M GONNA SUMMON UP YOUR WORST NIGHTMARE, BECAUSE IF YOU COULDN'T DEFEAT ONE BLUE-EYES...
THERE'S NO WAY YOU'LL DEFEAT THREE! ESPECIALLY WHEN COMBINED AS...
DA-DA-DA-DA-DA-DA
THE BLUE-EYES ULTIMATE DRAGON!
DOOM!

READ THIS WAY

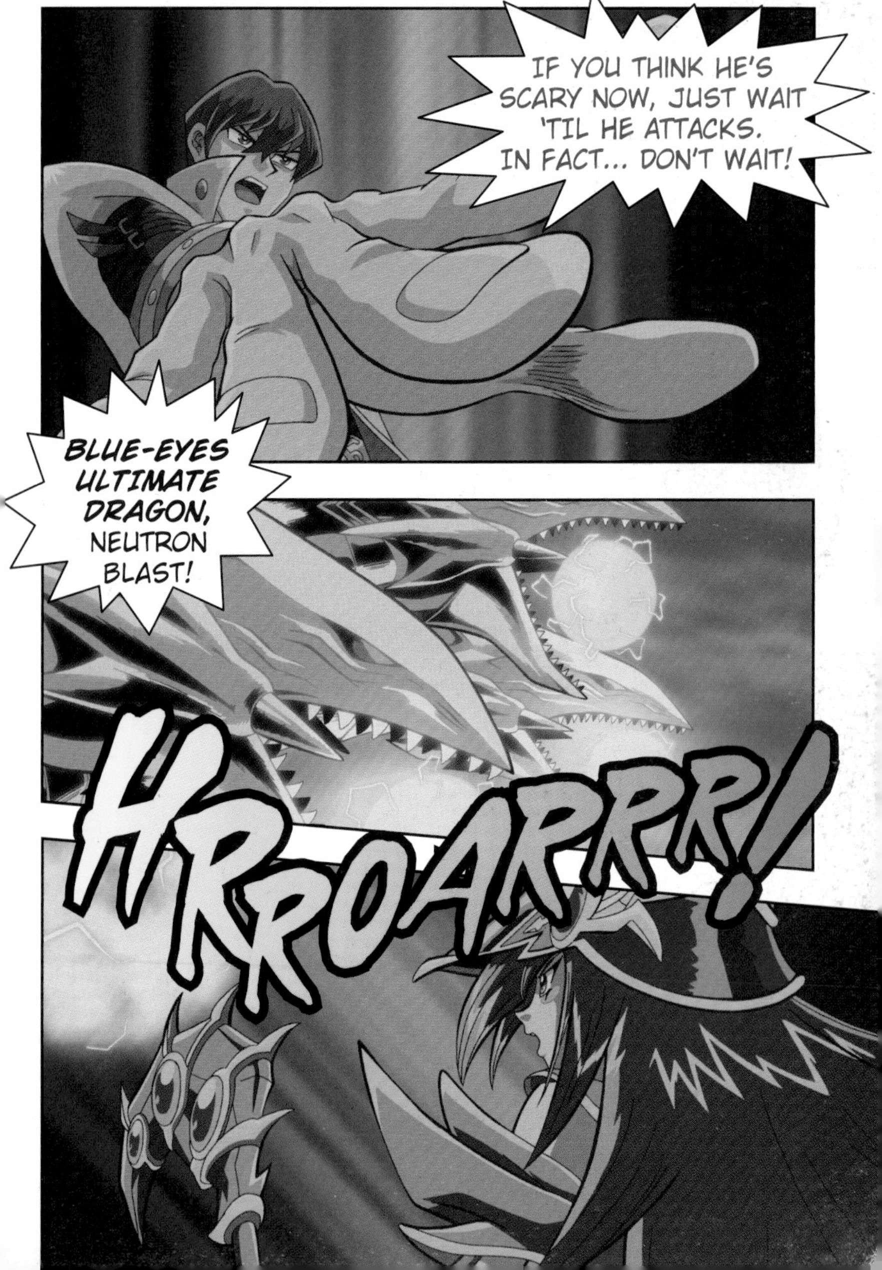
IF YOU THINK HE'S SCARY NOW, JUST WAIT 'TIL HE ATTACKS. IN FACT... DON'T WAIT!
BLUE-EYES ULTIMATE DRAGON, NEUTRON BLAST!
HRROARRR!

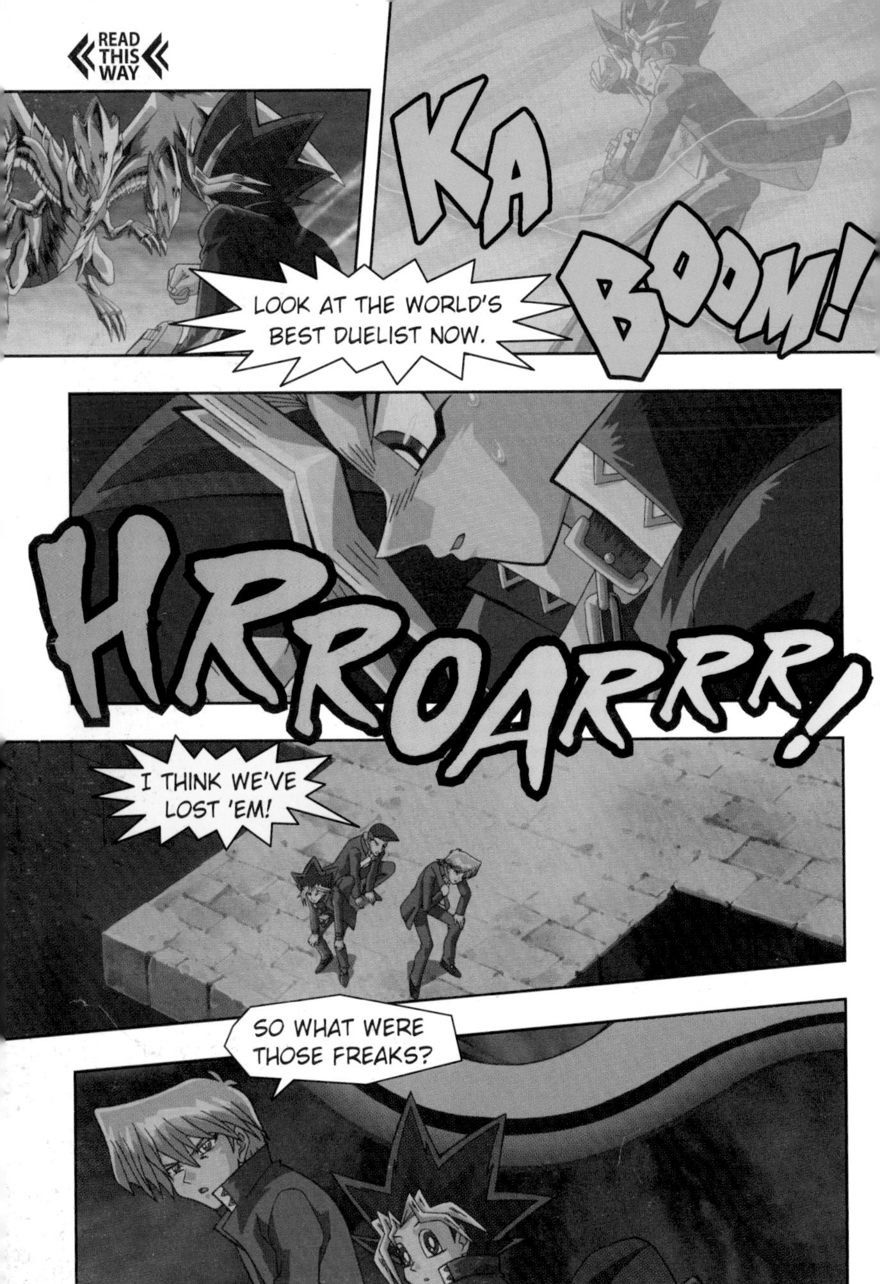
READ THIS WAY
KA BOOM!
LOOK AT THE WORLD'S BEST DUELIST NOW.
HRROARRR!
I THINK WE'VE LOST 'EM!
SO WHAT WERE THOSE FREAKS?

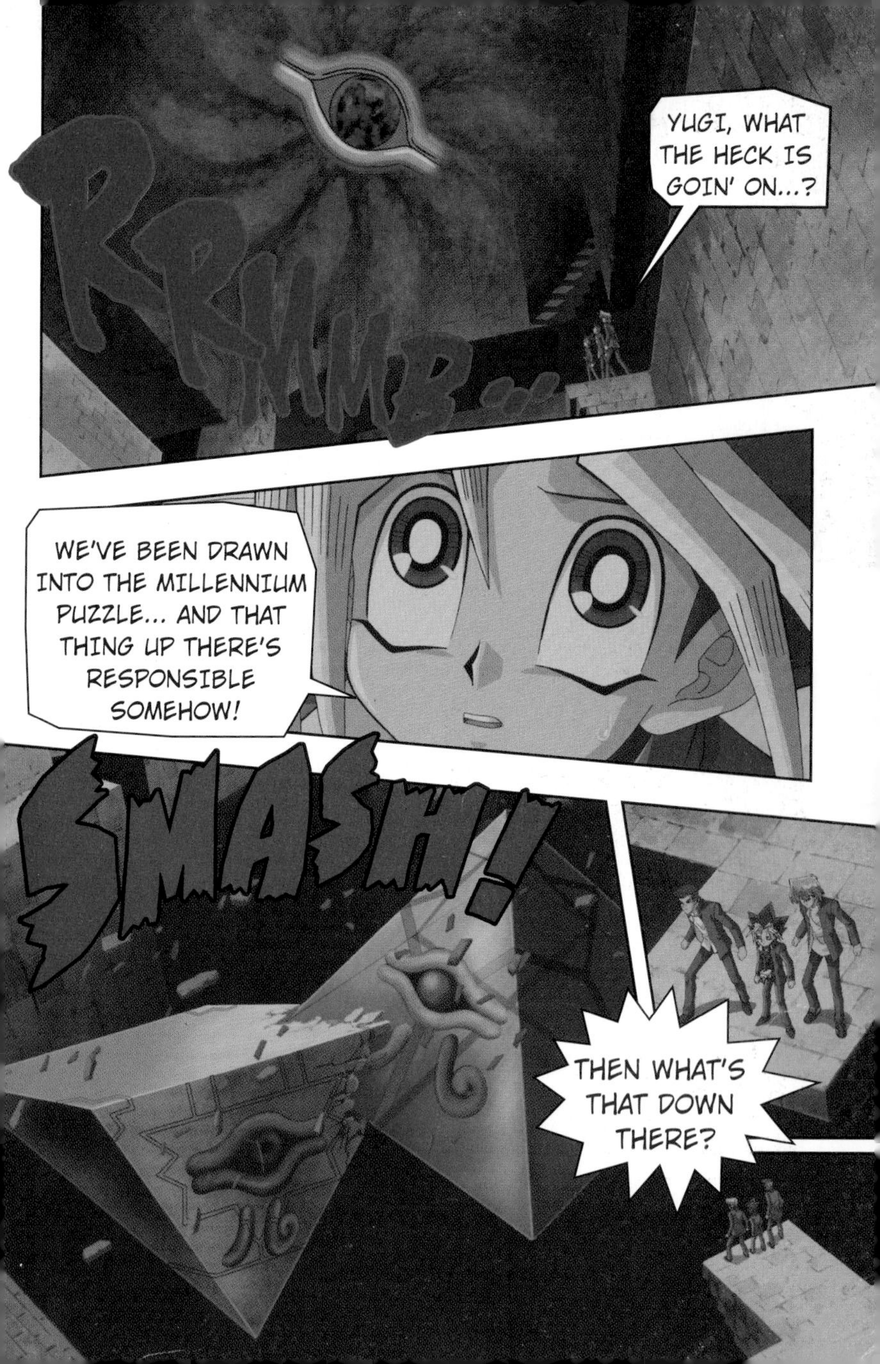
YUGI, WHAT THE HECK IS GOIN' ON...?
RRRUMB...
WE'VE BEEN DRAWN INTO THE MILLENNIUM PUZZLE... AND THAT THING UP THERE'S RESPONSIBLE SOMEHOW!
SMASH!
THEN WHAT'S THAT DOWN THERE?

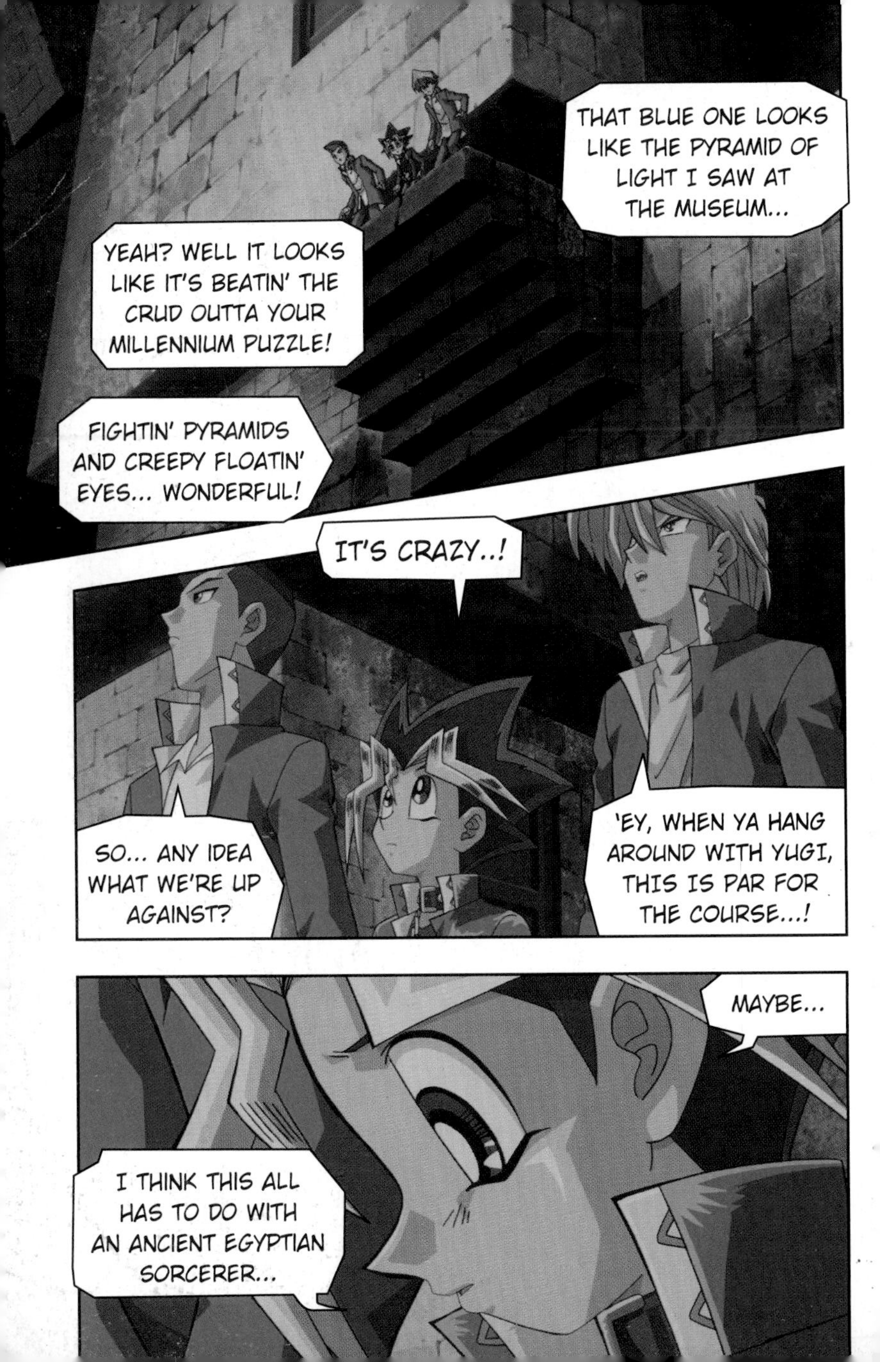
THAT BLUE ONE LOOKS LIKE THE PYRAMID OF LIGHT I SAW AT THE MUSEUM...
YEAH? WELL IT LOOKS LIKE IT'S BEATIN' THE CRUD OUTTA YOUR MILLENNIUM PUZZLE!
FIGHTIN' PYRAMIDS AND CREEPY FLOATIN' EYES... WONDERFUL!
IT'S CRAZY..!
'EY, WHEN YA HANG AROUND WITH YUGI, THIS IS PAR FOR THE COURSE...!
SO... ANY IDEA WHAT WE'RE UP AGAINST?
MAYBE...
I THINK THIS ALL HAS TO DO WITH AN ANCIENT EGYPTIAN SORCERER...

READ THIS WAY

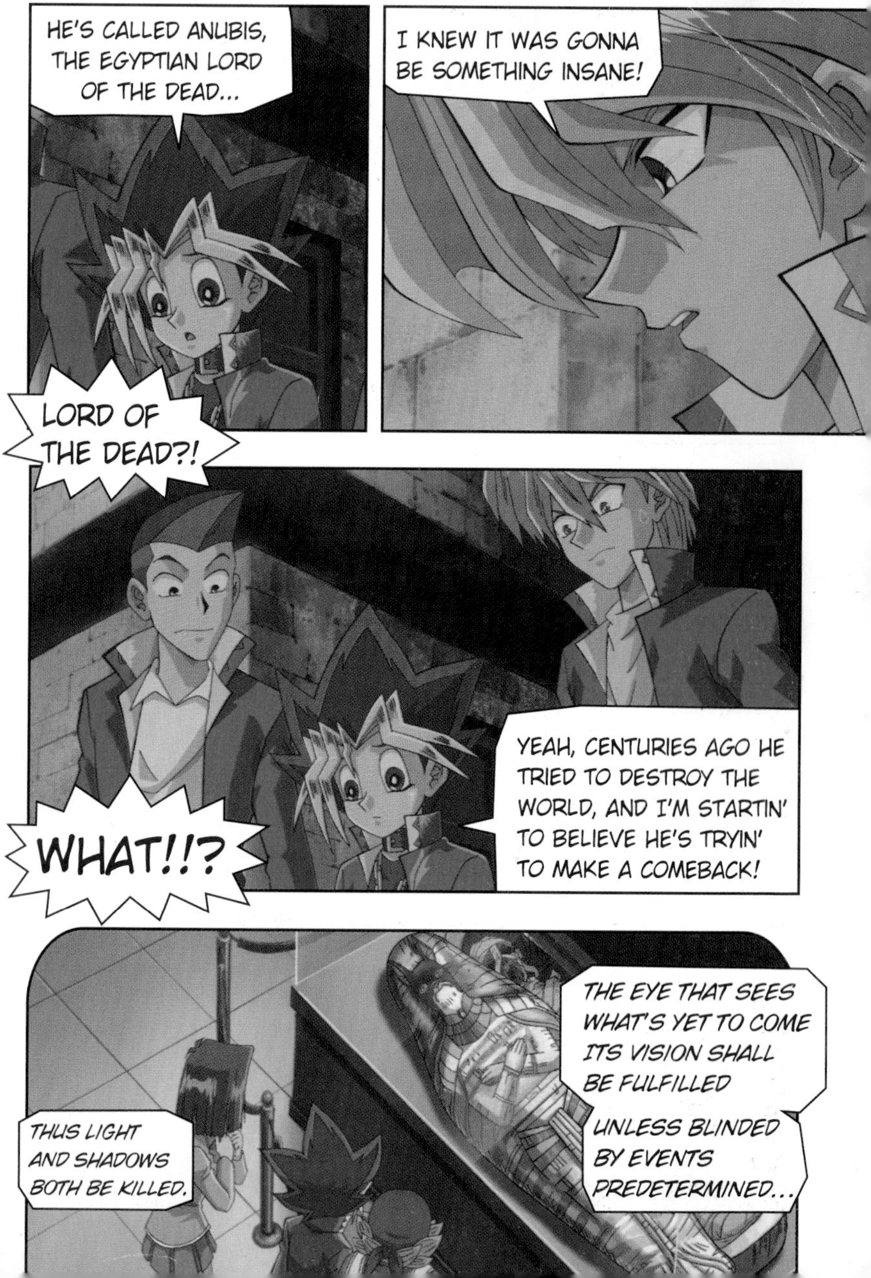
I KNEW IT WAS GONNA BE SOMETHING INSANE!
HE'S CALLED ANUBIS, THE EGYPTIAN LORD OF THE DEAD...
LORD OF THE DEAD?!
YEAH, CENTURIES AGO HE TRIED TO DESTROY THE WORLD, AND I'M STARTIN' TO BELIEVE HE'S TRYIN' TO MAKE A COMEBACK!
WHAT!!?
THE EYE THAT SEES WHAT'S YET TO COME ITS VISION SHALL BE FULFILLED
UNLESS BLINDED BY EVENTS PREDETERMINED...
THUS LIGHT AND SHADOWS BOTH BE KILLED.

READ THIS WAY

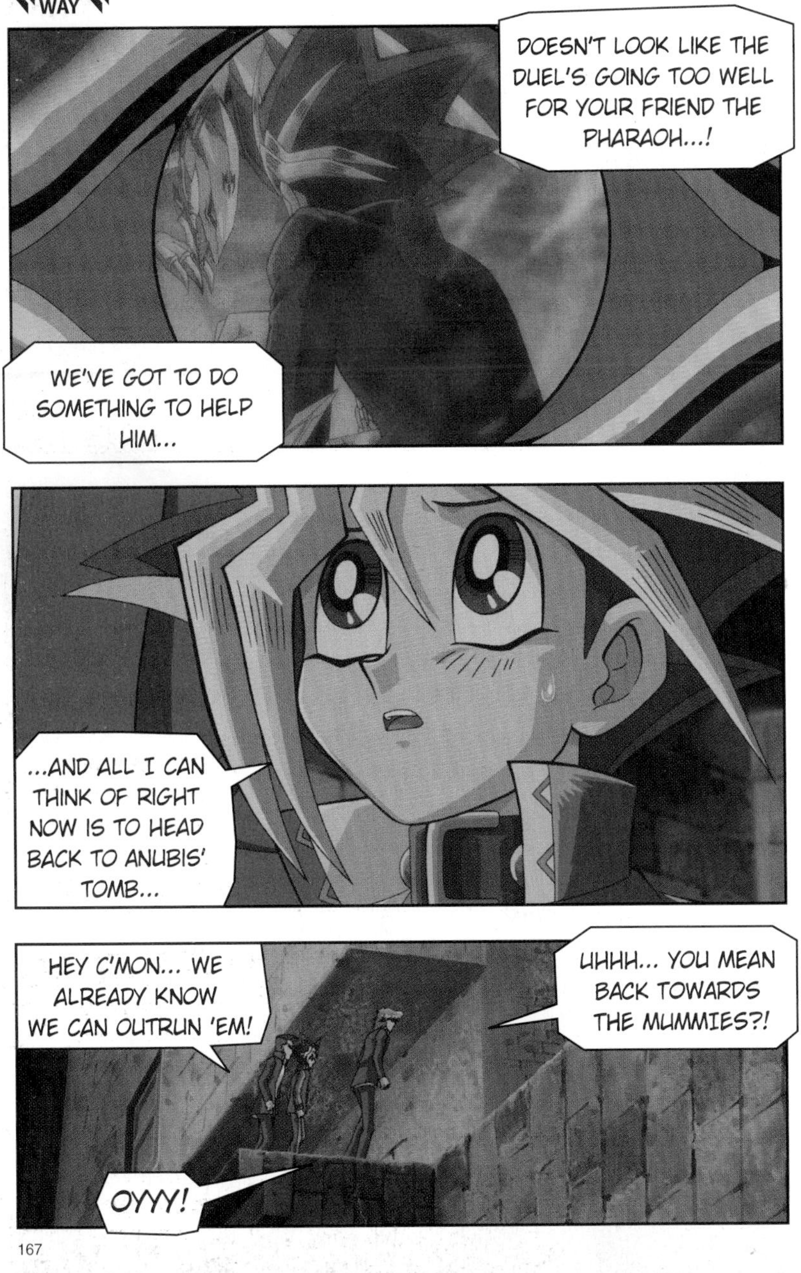

DOESN'T LOOK LIKE THE DUEL'S GOING TOO WELL FOR YOUR FRIEND THE PHARAOH...!
WE'VE GOT TO DO SOMETHING TO HELP HIM...
...AND ALL I CAN THINK OF RIGHT NOW IS TO HEAD BACK TO ANUBIS' TOMB...
UHHH... YOU MEAN BACK TOWARDS THE MUMMIES?!
HEY C'MON... WE ALREADY KNOW WE CAN OUTRUN 'EM!
OYYY!

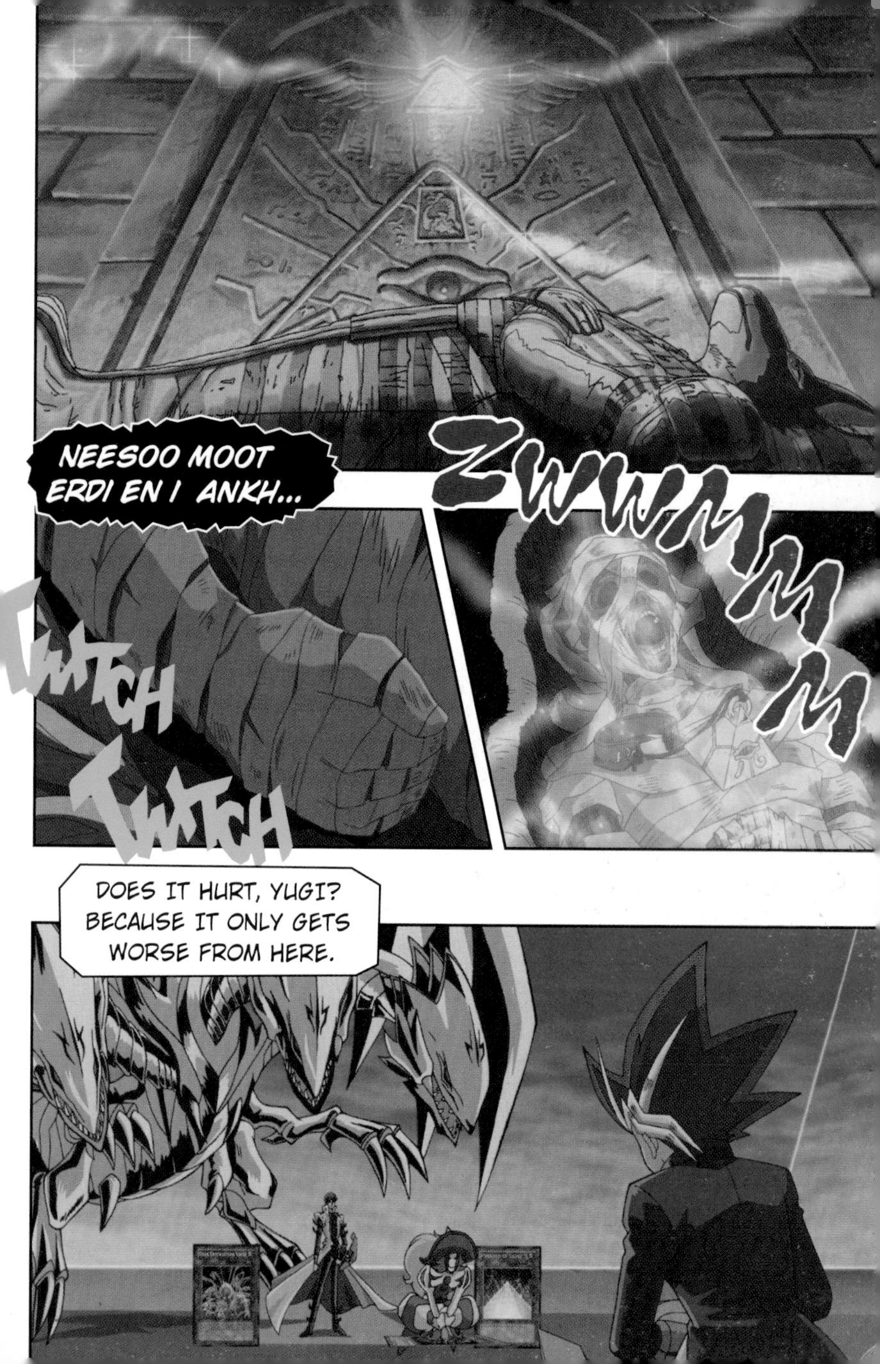
NEESOO MOOT ERDI EN I ANKH...
ZWWMMMM
TWITCH
TWITCH
DOES IT HURT, YUGI? BECAUSE IT ONLY GETS WORSE FROM HERE.

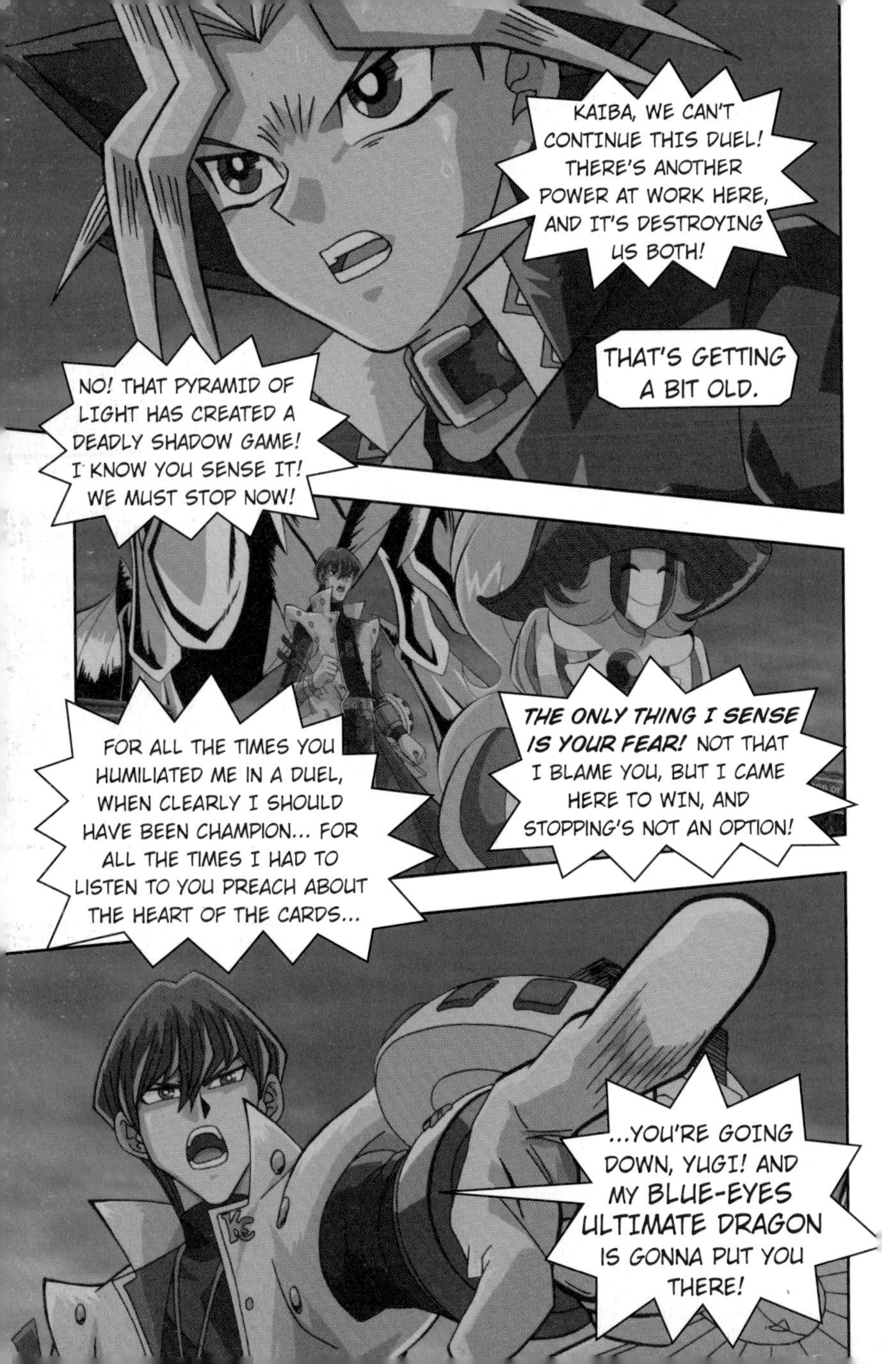
KAIBA, WE CAN'T CONTINUE THIS DUEL! THERE'S ANOTHER POWER AT WORK HERE, AND IT'S DESTROYING US BOTH!
THAT'S GETTING A BIT OLD.
NO! THAT PYRAMID OF LIGHT HAS CREATED A DEADLY SHADOW GAME! I KNOW YOU SENSE IT! WE MUST STOP NOW!
THE ONLY THING I SENSE IS YOUR FEAR! NOT THAT I BLAME YOU, BUT I CAME HERE TO WIN, AND STOPPING'S NOT AN OPTION!
FOR ALL THE TIMES YOU HUMILIATED ME IN A DUEL, WHEN CLEARLY I SHOULD HAVE BEEN CHAMPION... FOR ALL THE TIMES I HAD TO LISTEN TO YOU PREACH ABOUT THE HEART OF THE CARDS...
...YOU'RE GOING DOWN, YUGI! AND MY BLUE-EYES ULTIMATE DRAGON IS GONNA PUT YOU THERE!

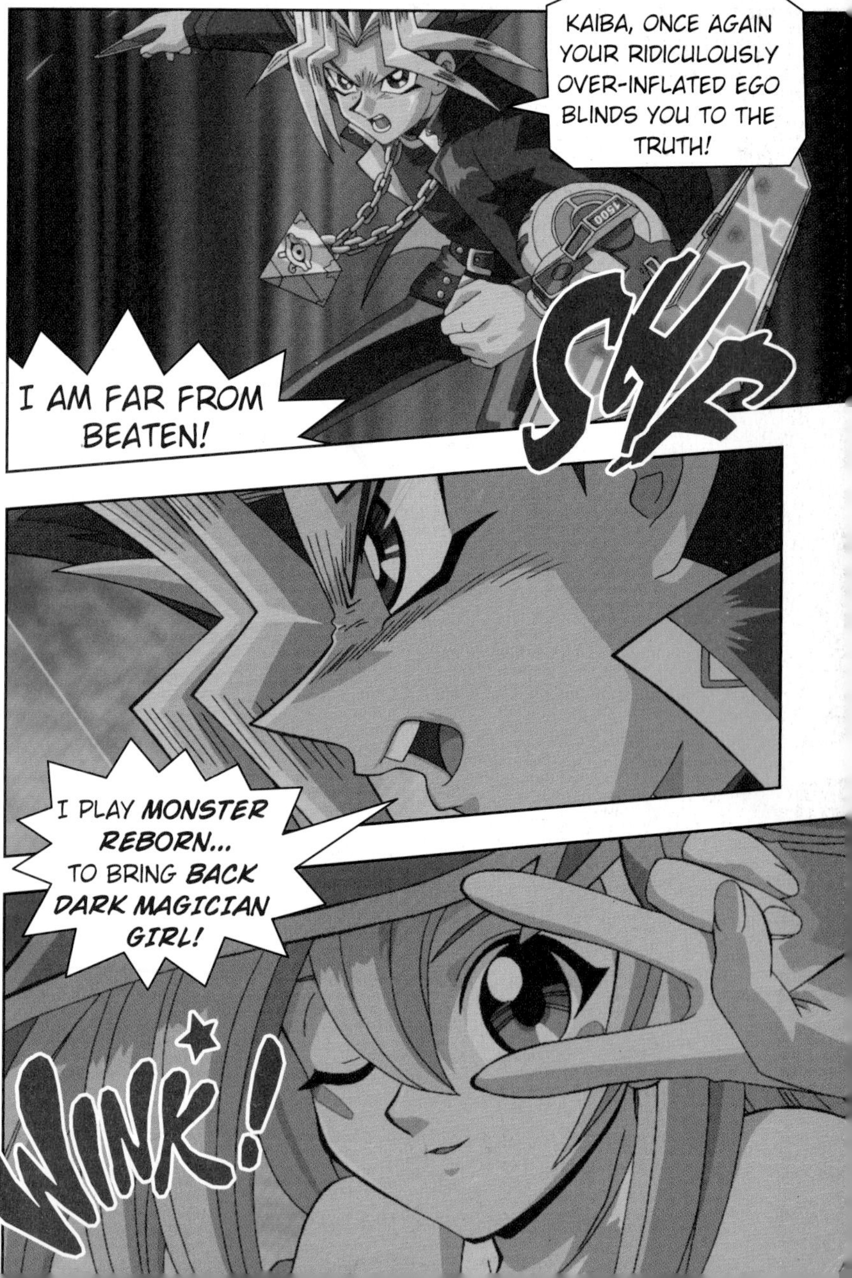
KAIBA, ONCE AGAIN YOUR RIDICULOUSLY OVER-INFLATED EGO BLINDS YOU TO THE TRUTH!
I AM FAR FROM BEATEN!
SHK
I PLAY MONSTER REBORN... TO BRING BACK DARK MAGICIAN GIRL!
WINK!

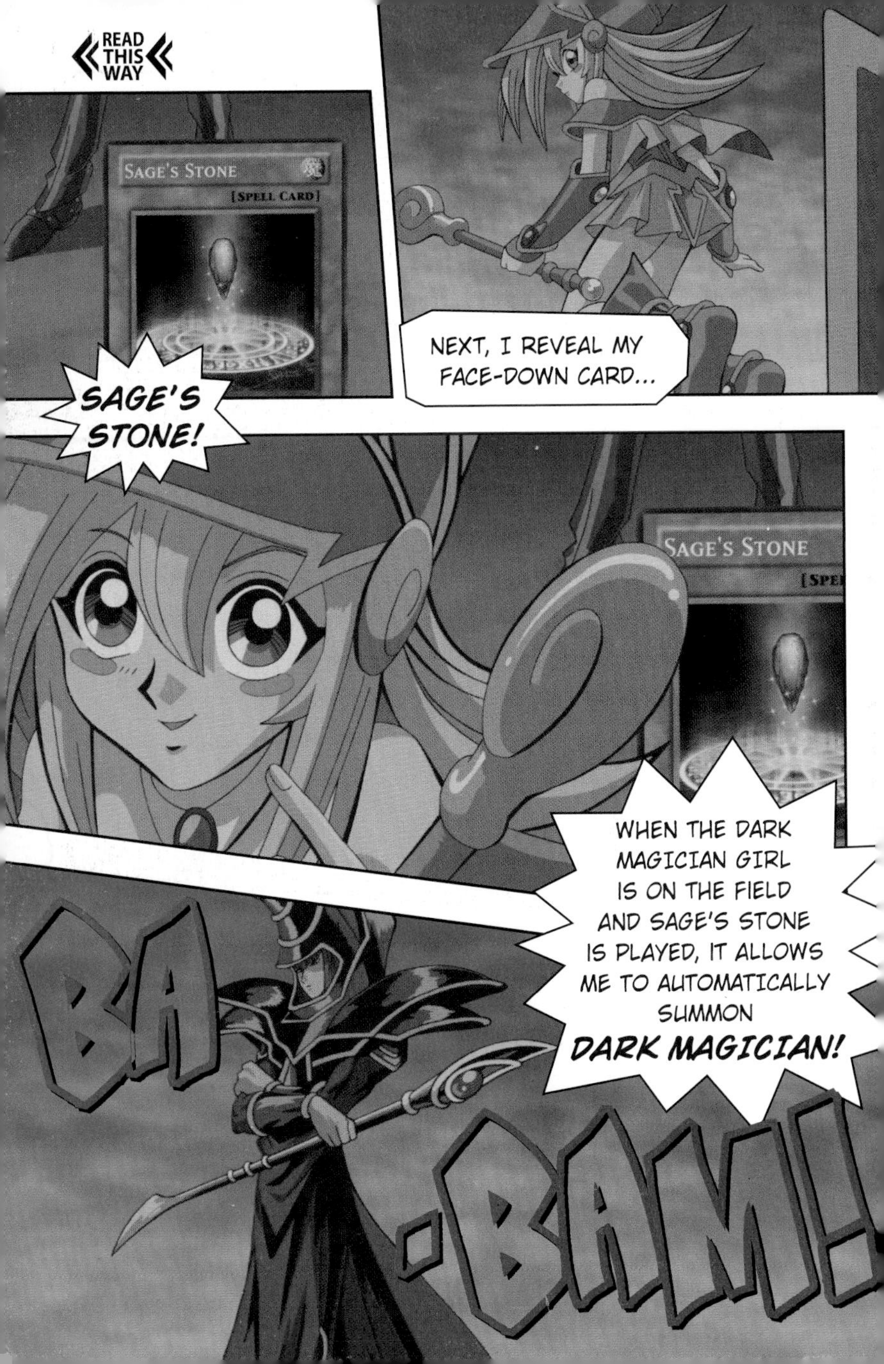
READ THIS WAY
NEXT, I REVEAL MY FACE-DOWN CARD...
Sage's Stone
[SPELL CARD]
SAGE'S STONE!
Sage's Stone
WHEN THE DARK MAGICIAN GIRL IS ON THE FIELD AND SAGE'S STONE IS PLAYED, IT ALLOWS ME TO AUTOMATICALLY SUMMON DARK MAGICIAN!
BA-BAM!

READ THIS WAY

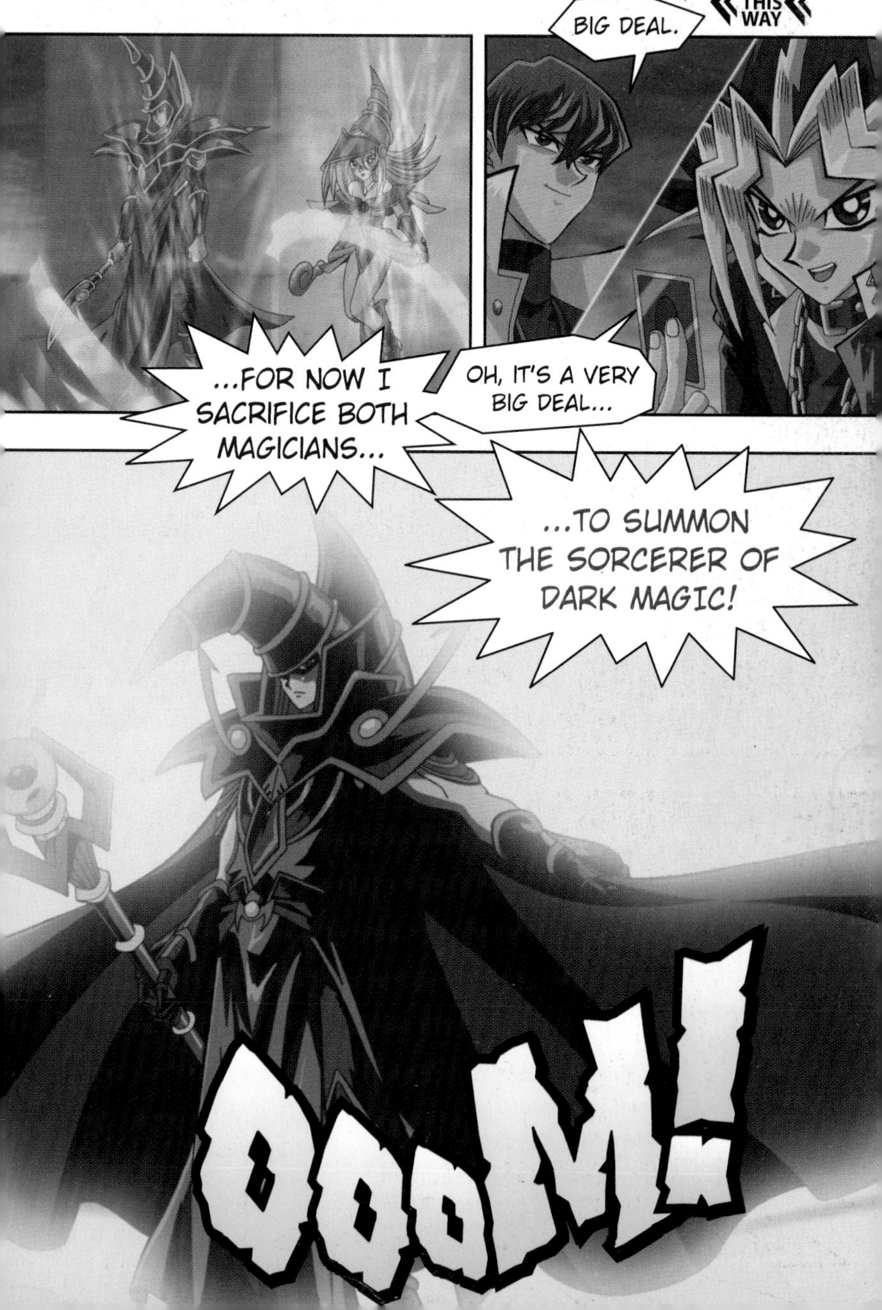
BIG DEAL.
OH, IT'S A VERY BIG DEAL...
...FOR NOW I SACRIFICE BOTH MAGICIANS...
...TO SUMMON THE SORCERER OF DARK MAGIC!
DOOM!

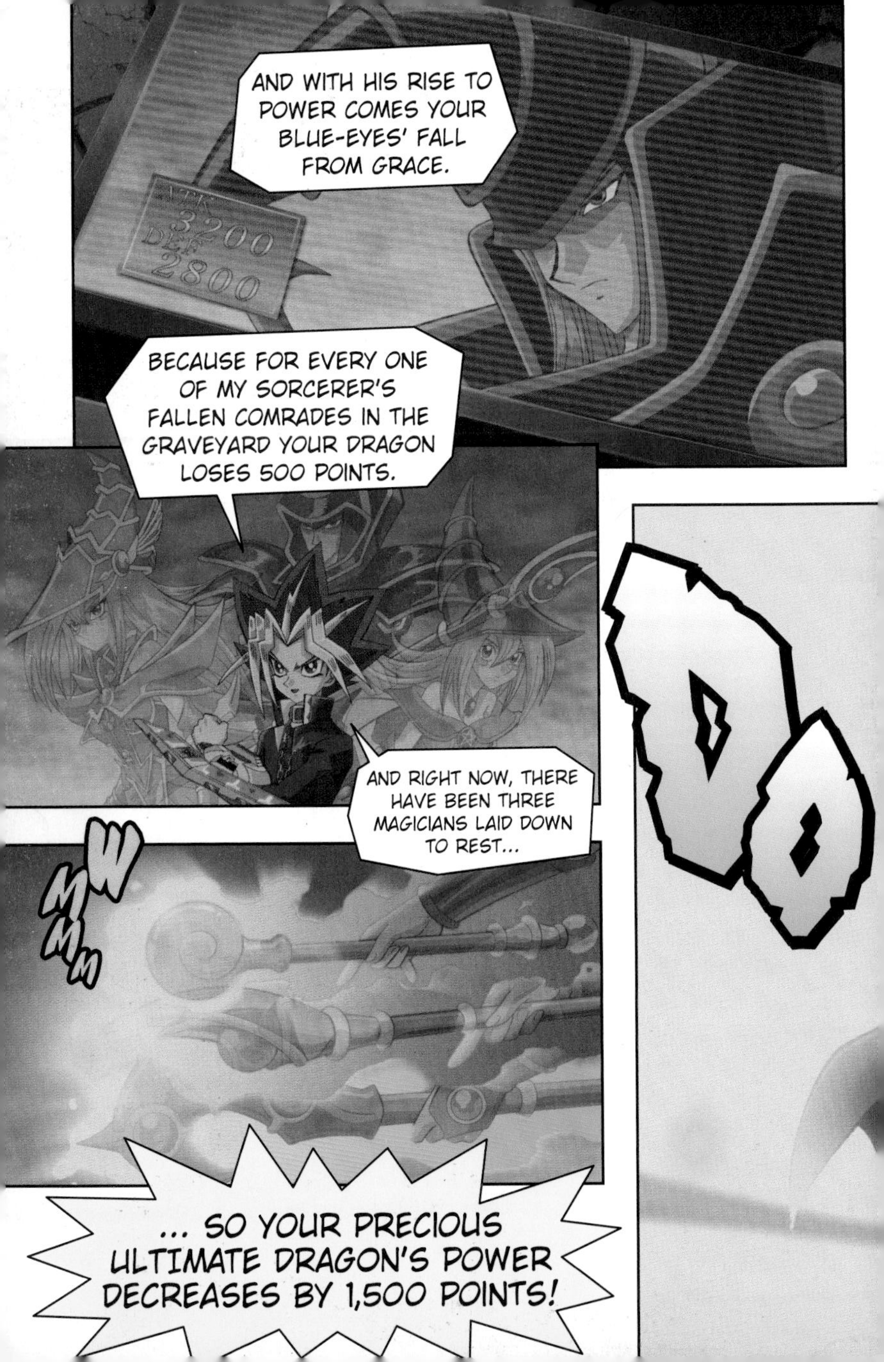
AND WITH HIS RISE TO POWER COMES YOUR BLUE-EYES' FALL FROM GRACE.
BECAUSE FOR EVERY ONE OF MY SORCERER'S FALLEN COMRADES IN THE GRAVEYARD YOUR DRAGON LOSES 500 POINTS.
AND RIGHT NOW, THERE HAVE BEEN THREE MAGICIANS LAID DOWN TO REST...
... SO YOUR PRECIOUS ULTIMATE DRAGON'S POWER DECREASES BY 1,500 POINTS!

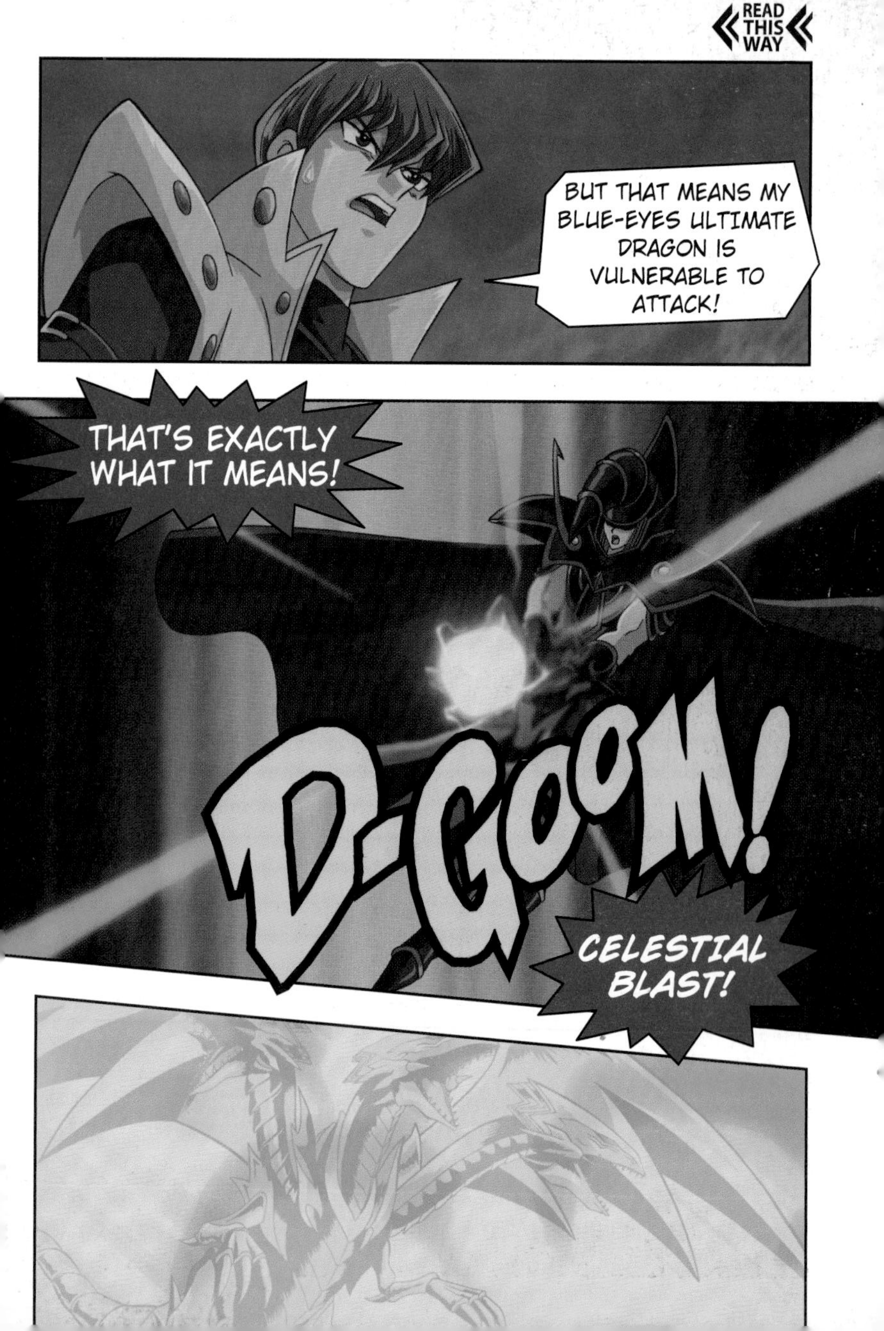
READ THIS WAY
BUT THAT MEANS MY BLUE-EYES ULTIMATE DRAGON IS VULNERABLE TO ATTACK!
THAT'S EXACTLY WHAT IT MEANS!
D-GOOM!
CELESTIAL BLAST!

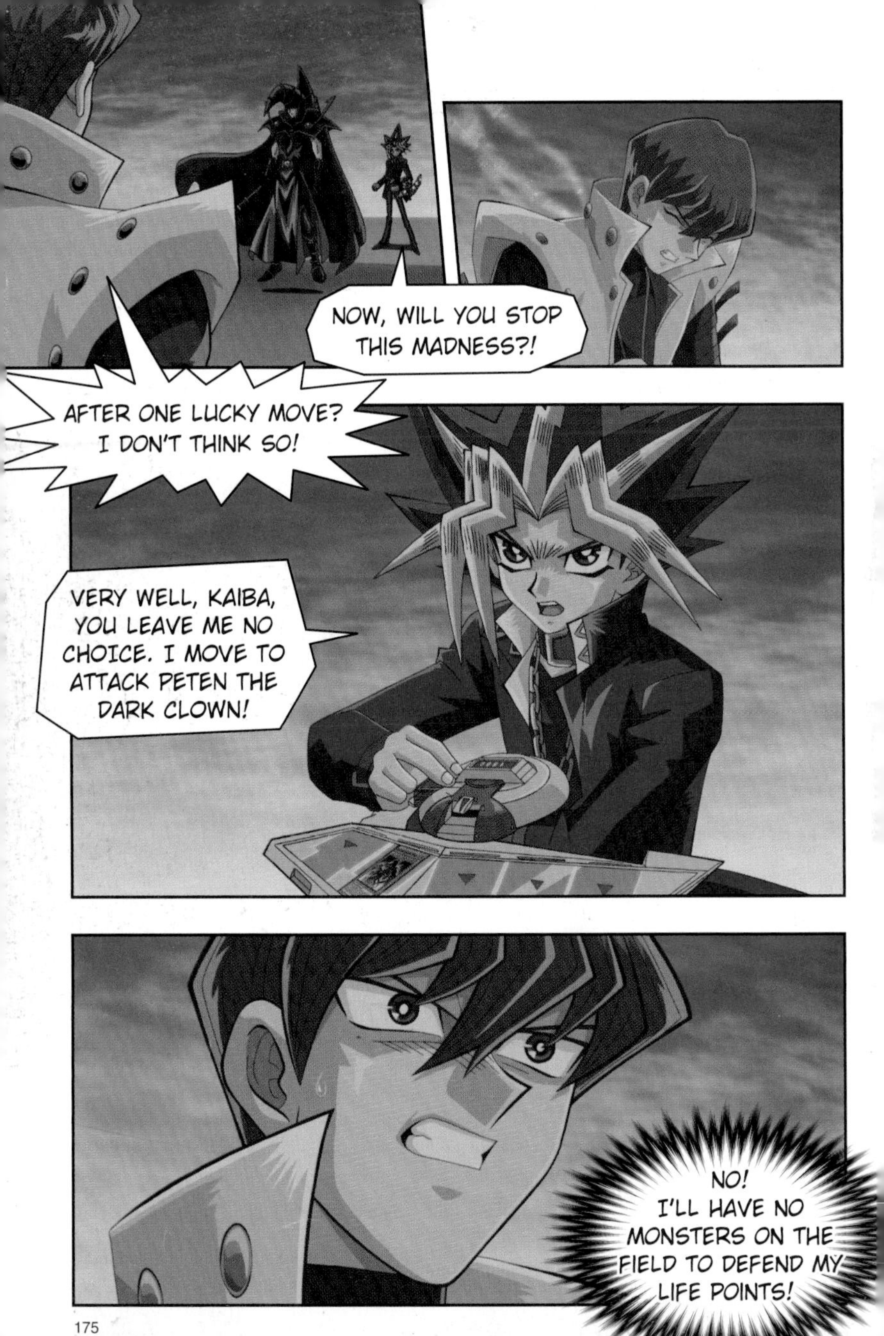
NOW, WILL YOU STOP THIS MADNESS?!
AFTER ONE LUCKY MOVE? I DON'T THINK SO!
VERY WELL, KAIBA, YOU LEAVE ME NO CHOICE. I MOVE TO ATTACK PETEN THE DARK CLOWN!
NO! I'LL HAVE NO MONSTERS ON THE FIELD TO DEFEND MY LIFE POINTS!

READ THIS WAY

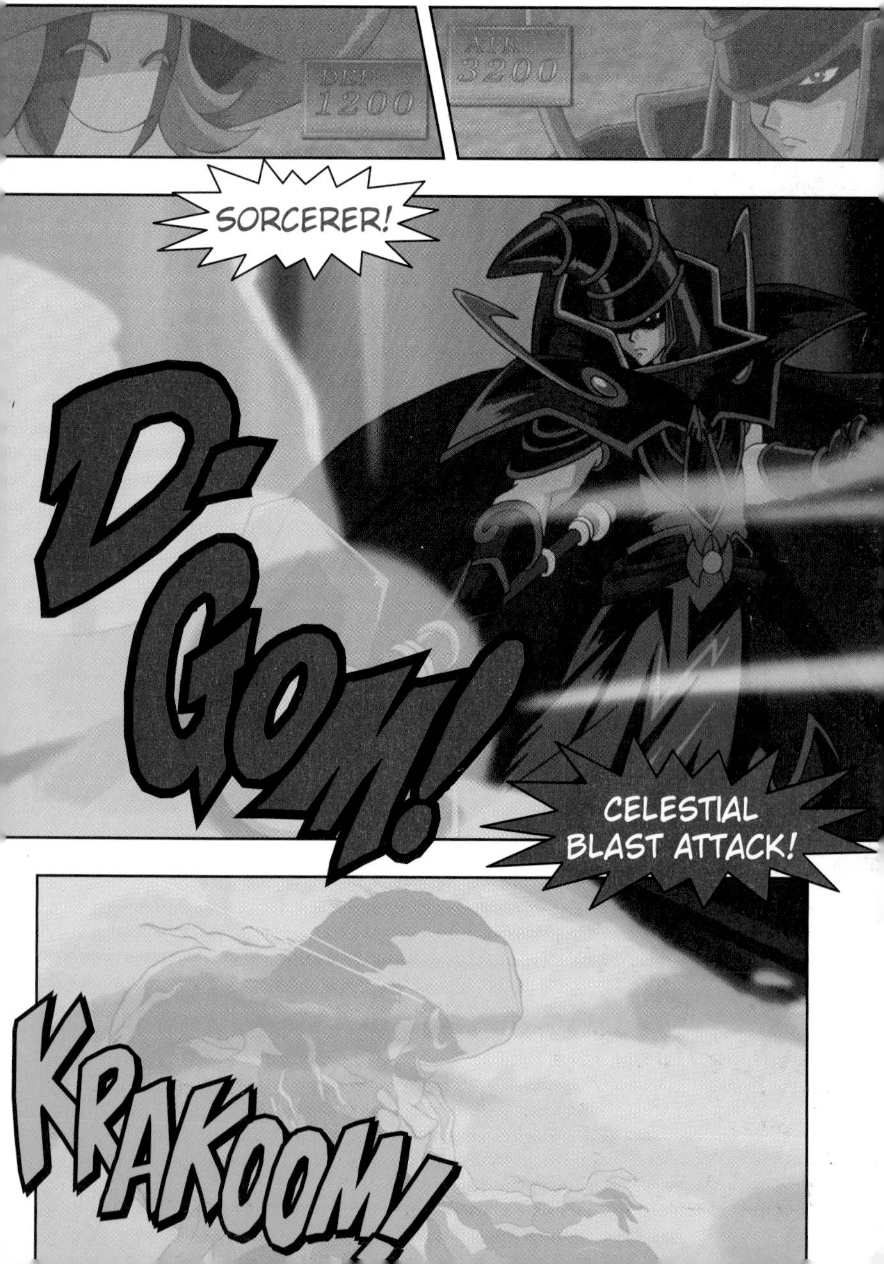
ATK
3200
DEF
1200
SORCERER!
CELESTIAL BLAST ATTACK!
D-GOM!
KRAKOOM!

READ THIS WAY

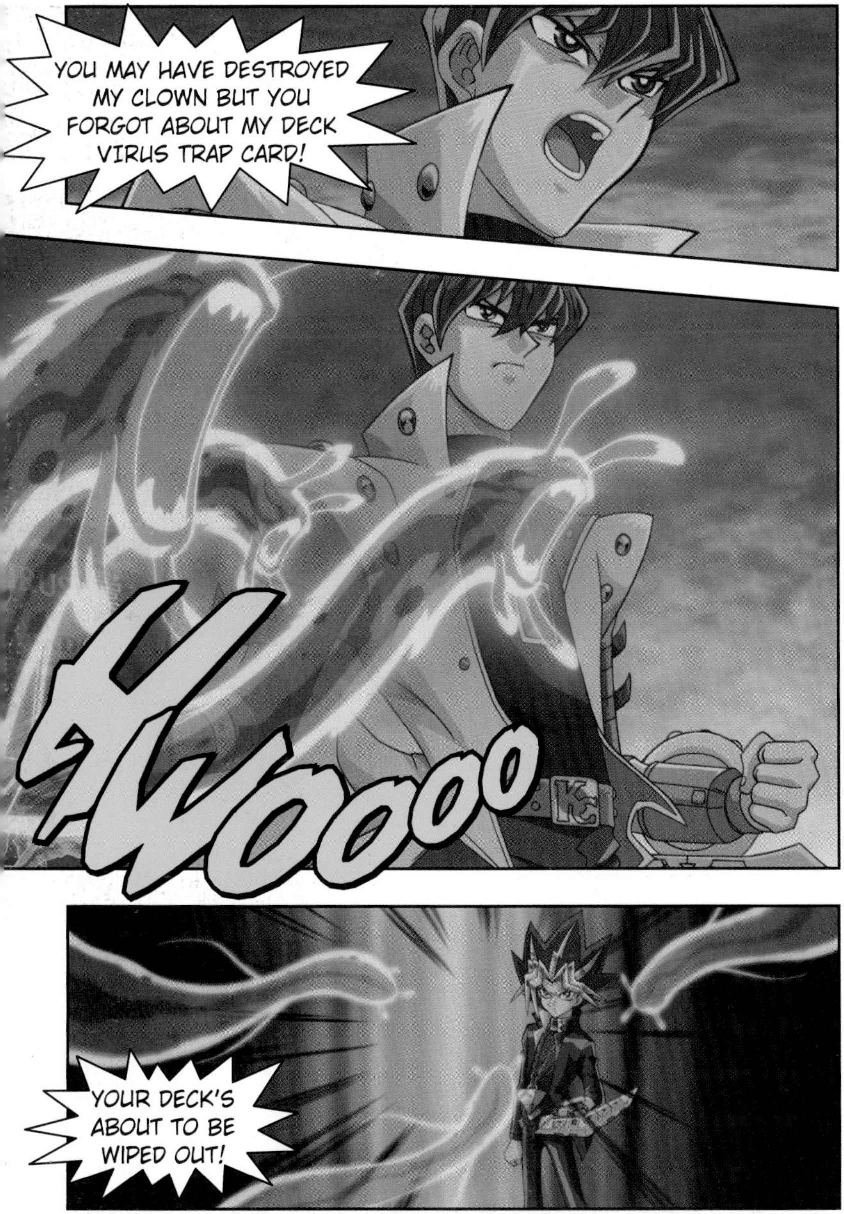
YOU MAY HAVE DESTROYED MY CLOWN BUT YOU FORGOT ABOUT MY DECK VIRUS TRAP CARD!
HWOOOO
YOUR DECK'S ABOUT TO BE WIPED OUT!

ZAM!

WHAT!?

SORRY KAIBA, BUT MY SORCERER OF DARK MAGIC'S MYSTIC POWERS ARE SO MIGHTY, HE CAN STOP THE ACTIVATION OF TRAP CARDS LIKE YOUR DECK VIRUS AND DESTROY THEM!

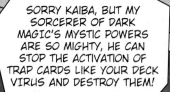

READ THIS WAY

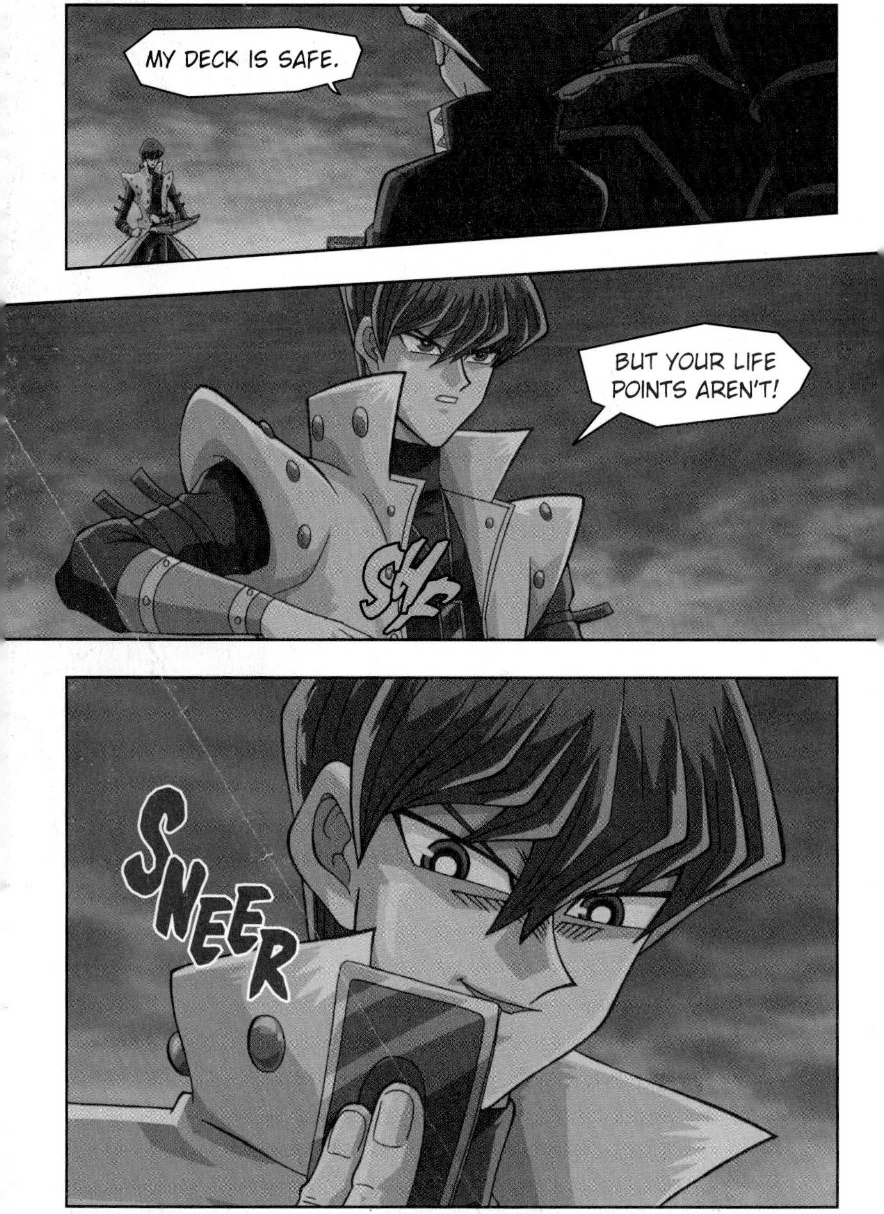
MY DECK IS SAFE.
BUT YOUR LIFE POINTS AREN'T!
SNEER

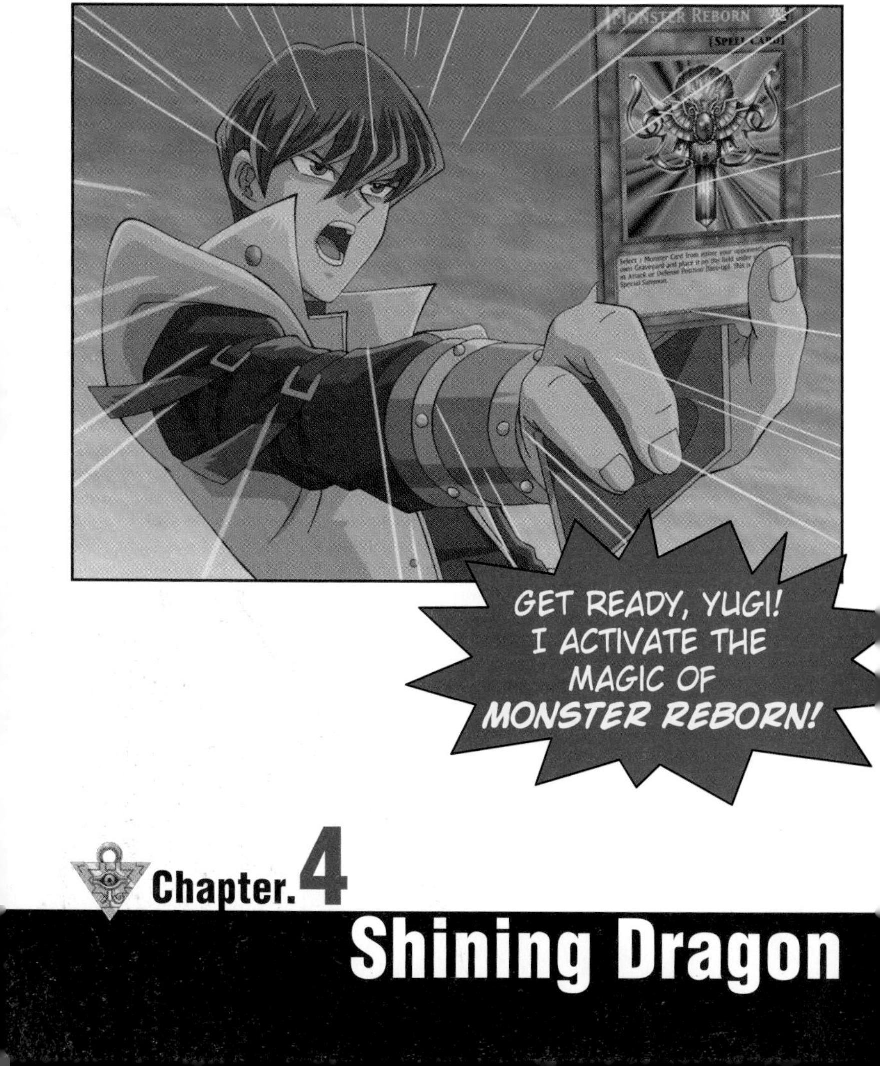
MONSTER REBORN
GET READY, YUGI! I ACTIVATE THE MAGIC OF MONSTER REBORN!

Chapter. 4
Shining Dragon

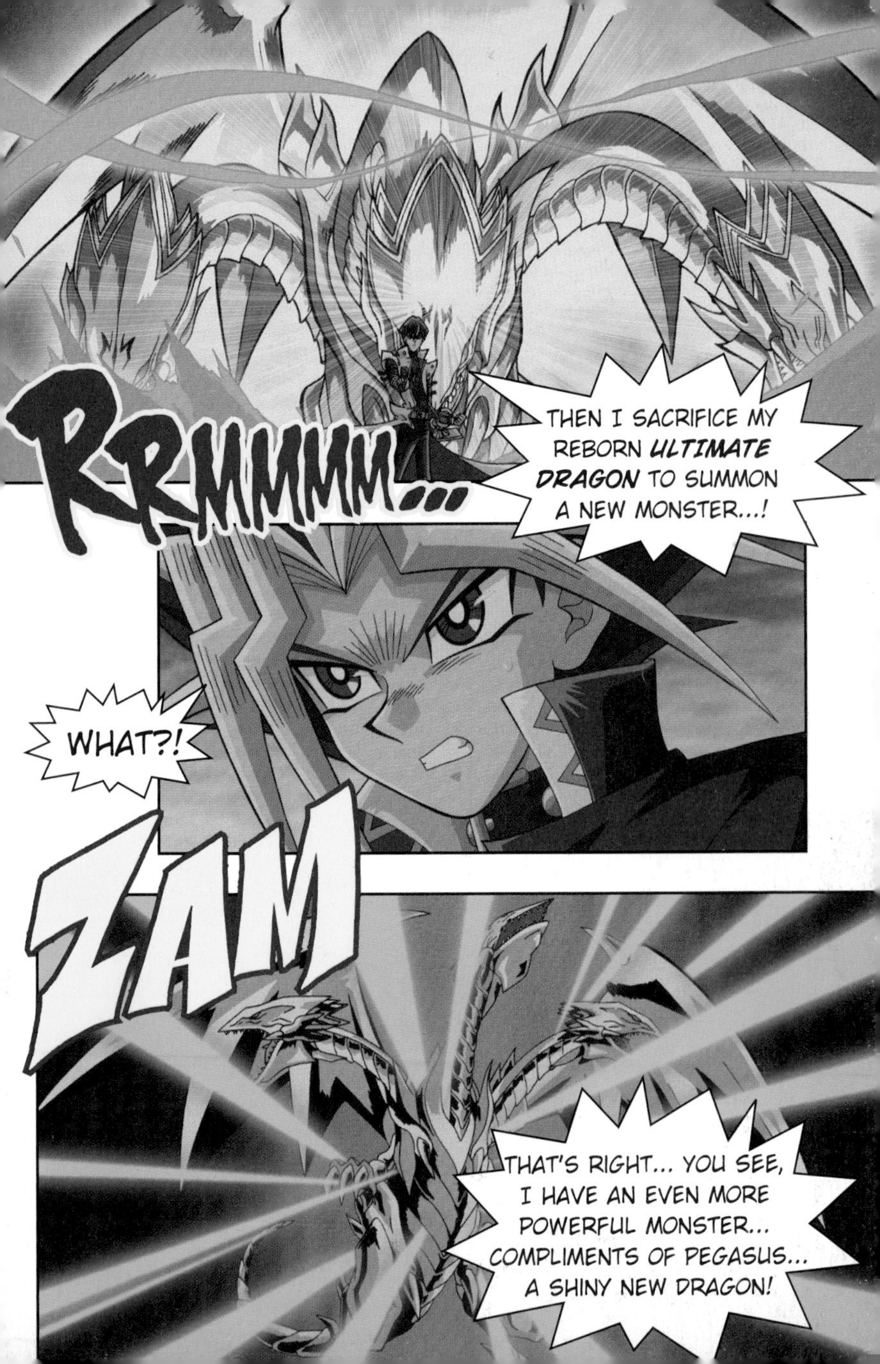
THEN I SACRIFICE MY REBORN *ULTIMATE DRAGON* TO SUMMON A NEW MONSTER...!
RRMMMM...
WHAT?!
ZAM
THAT'S RIGHT... YOU SEE, I HAVE AN EVEN MORE POWERFUL MONSTER... COMPLIMENTS OF PEGASUS... A SHINY NEW DRAGON!

READ THIS WAY

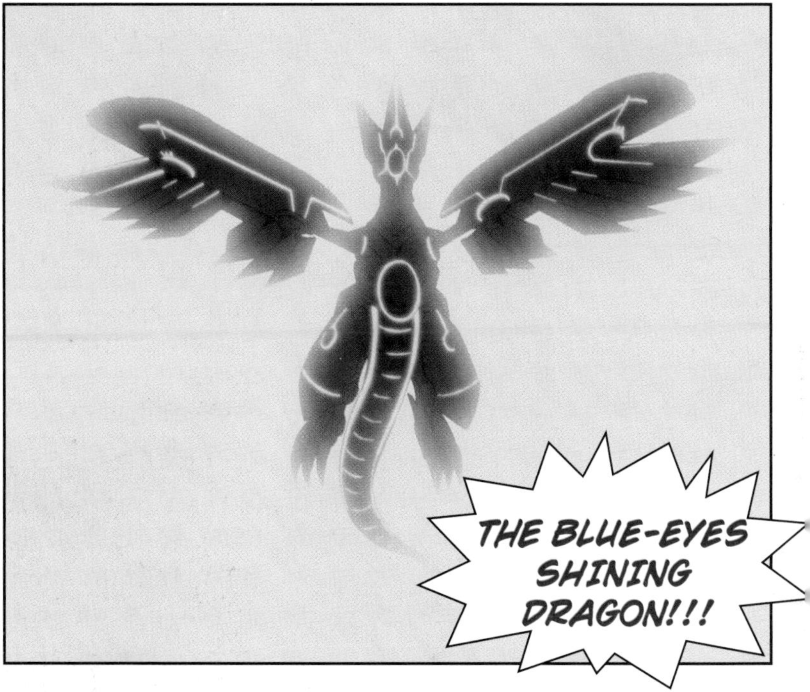
THE BLUE-EYES SHINING DRAGON!!!

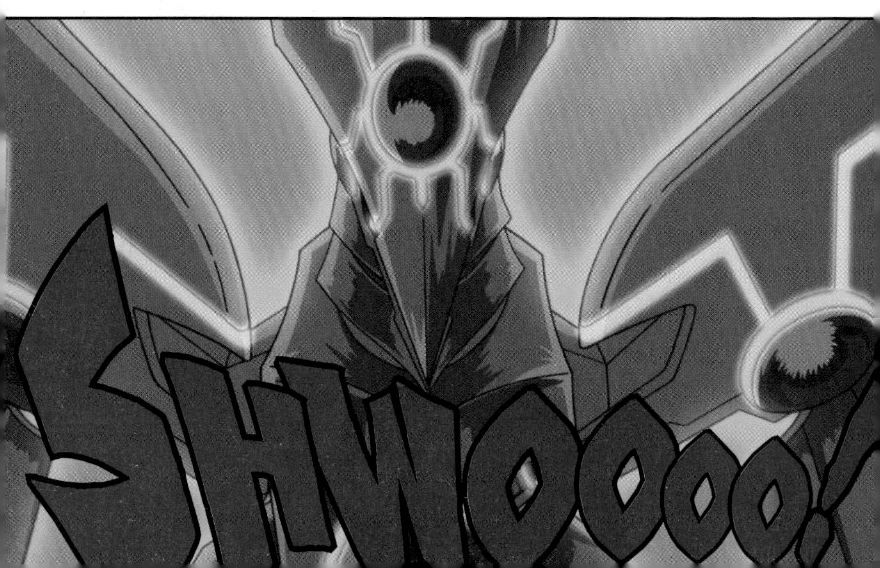
SHWOOOO!

READ THIS WAY

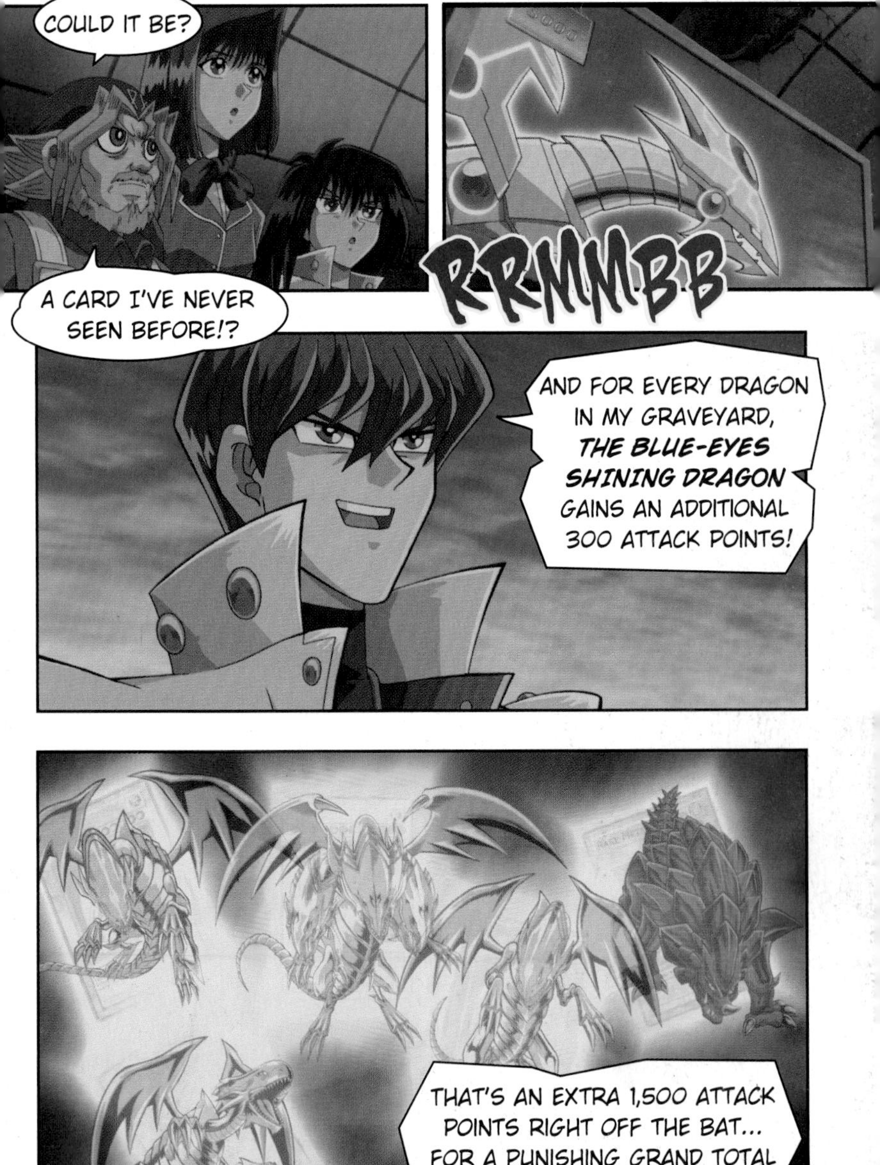
RRMMBB
COULD IT BE?
A CARD I'VE NEVER SEEN BEFORE!?
AND FOR EVERY DRAGON IN MY GRAVEYARD, ***THE BLUE-EYES SHINING DRAGON*** GAINS AN ADDITIONAL 300 ATTACK POINTS!
THAT'S AN EXTRA 1,500 ATTACK POINTS RIGHT OFF THE BAT... FOR A PUNISHING GRAND TOTAL OF 4,500 POINTS!

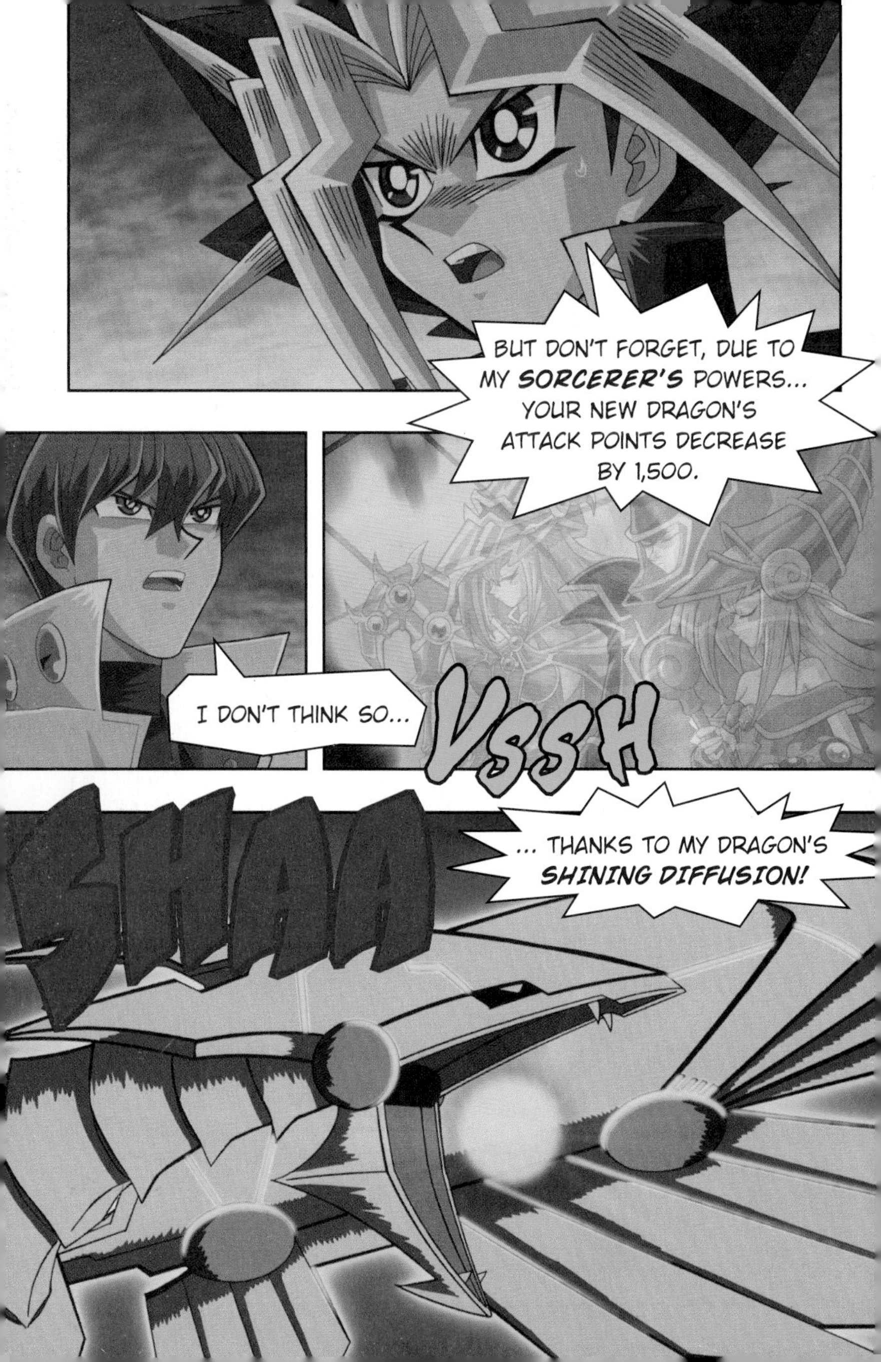
BUT DON'T FORGET, DUE TO MY **SORCERER'S** POWERS... YOUR NEW DRAGON'S ATTACK POINTS DECREASE BY 1,500.
VSSH
I DON'T THINK SO...
... THANKS TO MY DRAGON'S **SHINING DIFFUSION!**
SHAA

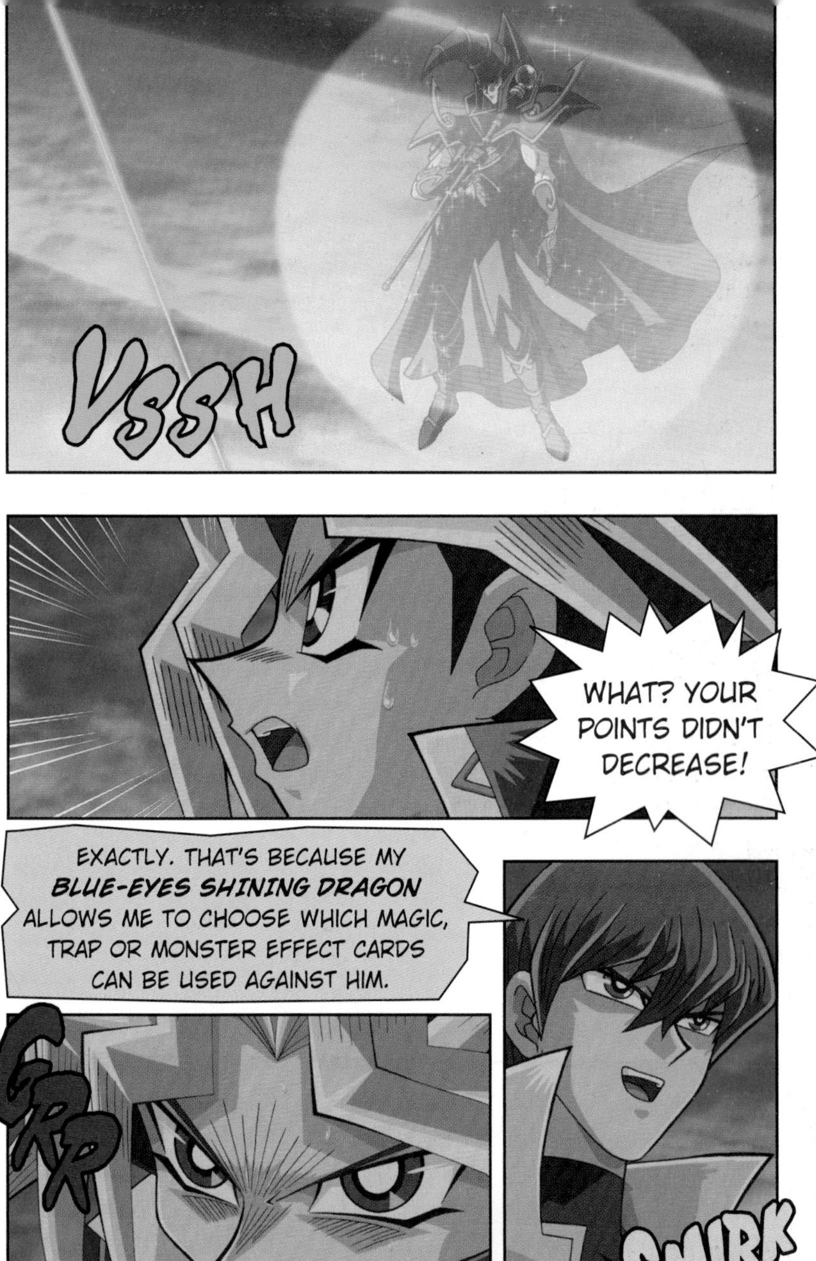
VSSH
WHAT? YOUR POINTS DIDN'T DECREASE!
EXACTLY. THAT'S BECAUSE MY ***BLUE-EYES SHINING DRAGON*** ALLOWS ME TO CHOOSE WHICH MAGIC, TRAP OR MONSTER EFFECT CARDS CAN BE USED AGAINST HIM.
SMIRK
GRR

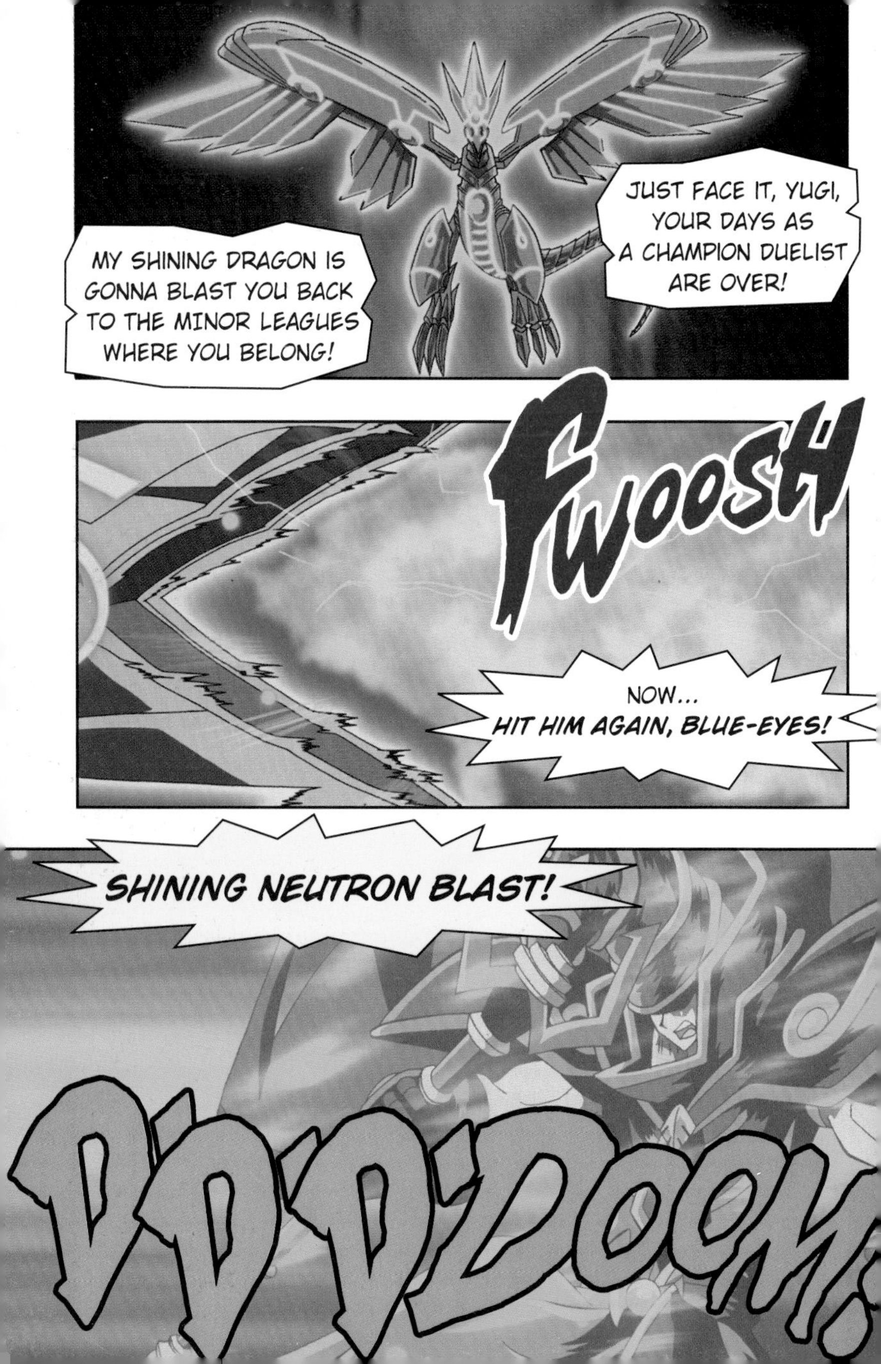
JUST FACE IT, YUGI, YOUR DAYS AS A CHAMPION DUELIST ARE OVER!
MY SHINING DRAGON IS GONNA BLAST YOU BACK TO THE MINOR LEAGUES WHERE YOU BELONG!
FWOOSH
NOW... HIT HIM AGAIN, BLUE-EYES!
SHINING NEUTRON BLAST!
D'D'DOOM

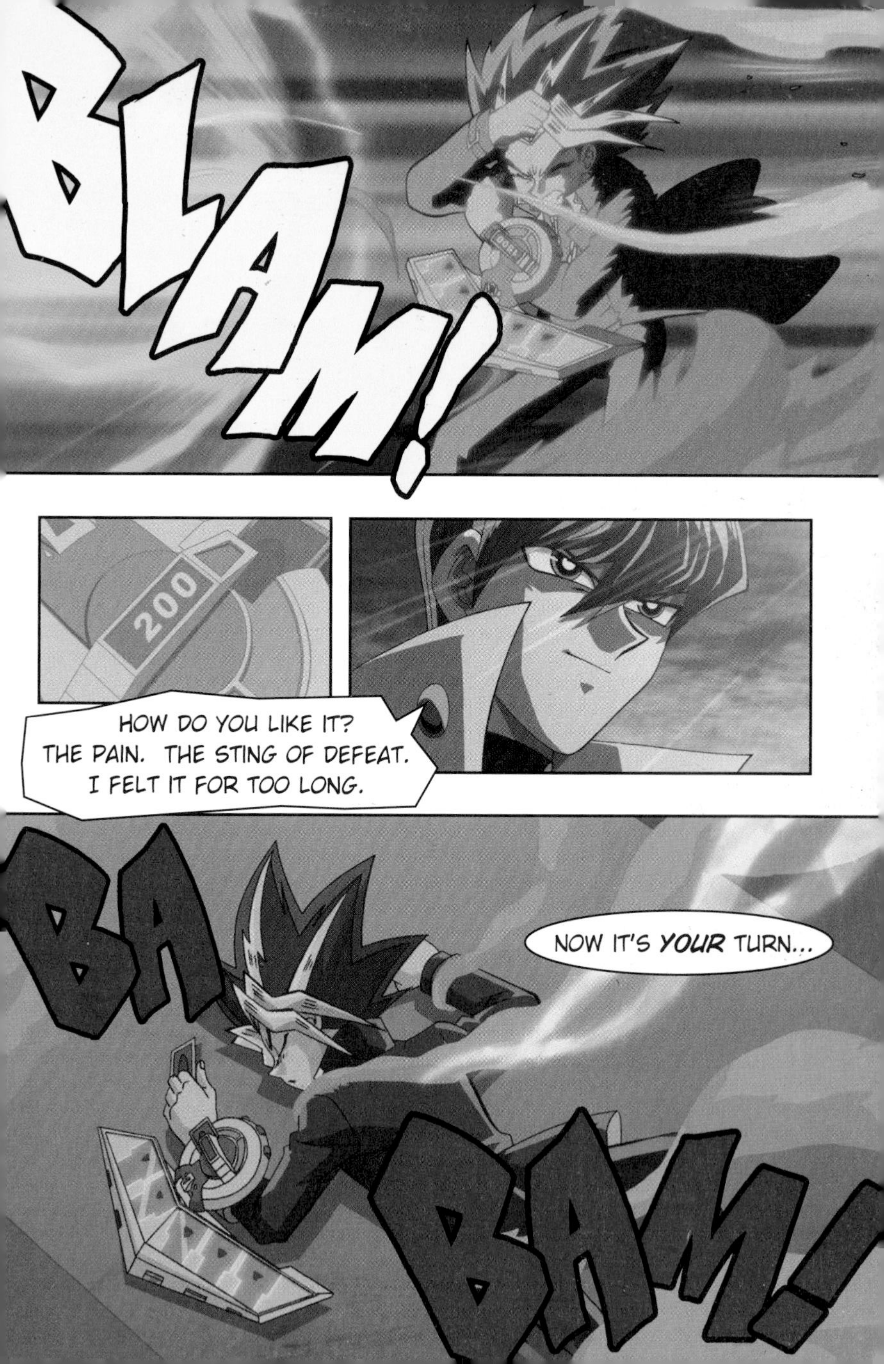
BLAM!
HOW DO YOU LIKE IT? THE PAIN. THE STING OF DEFEAT. I FELT IT FOR TOO LONG.
200
NOW IT'S ***YOUR*** TURN...
BA
BAM!

READ THIS WAY

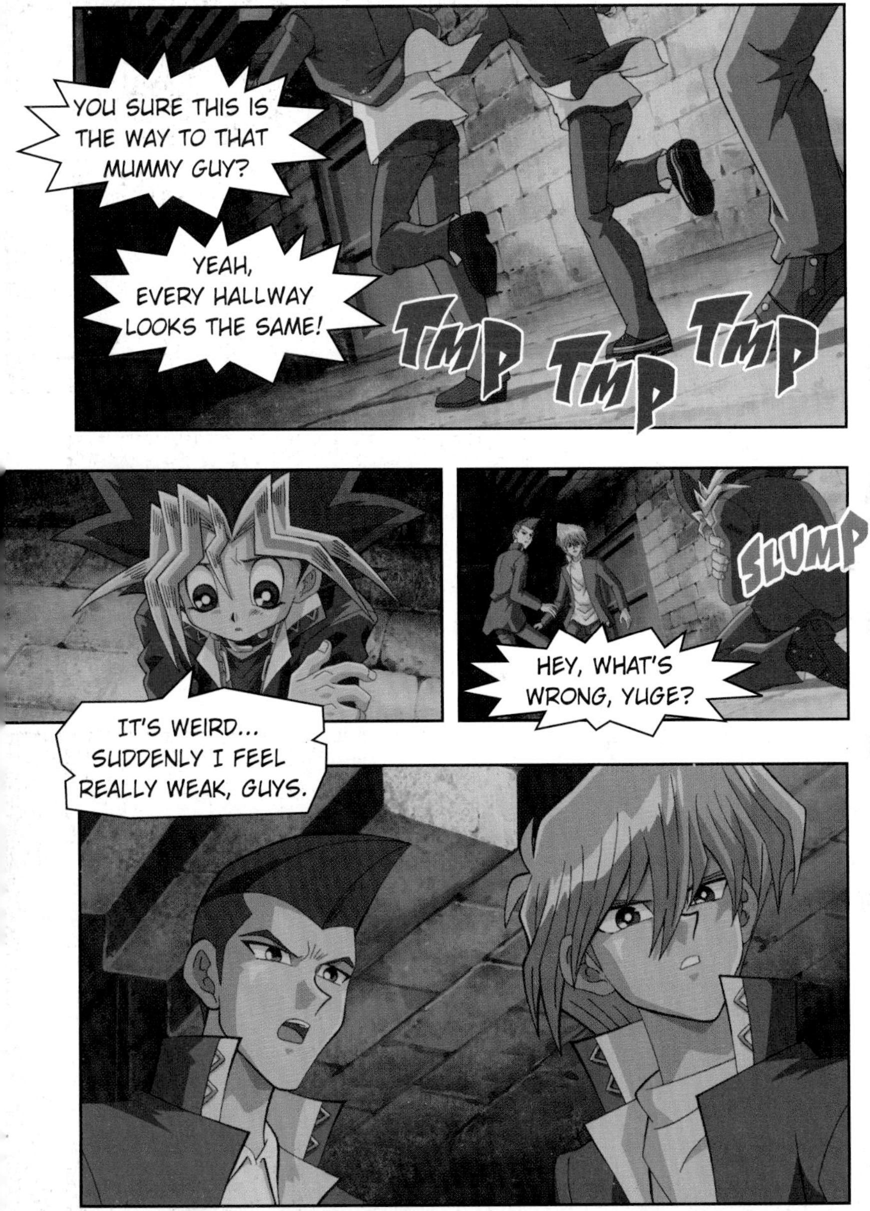

YOU SURE THIS IS THE WAY TO THAT MUMMY GUY?
YEAH, EVERY HALLWAY LOOKS THE SAME!
TMP TMP TMP
SLUMP
HEY, WHAT'S WRONG, YUGE?
IT'S WEIRD... SUDDENLY I FEEL REALLY WEAK, GUYS.

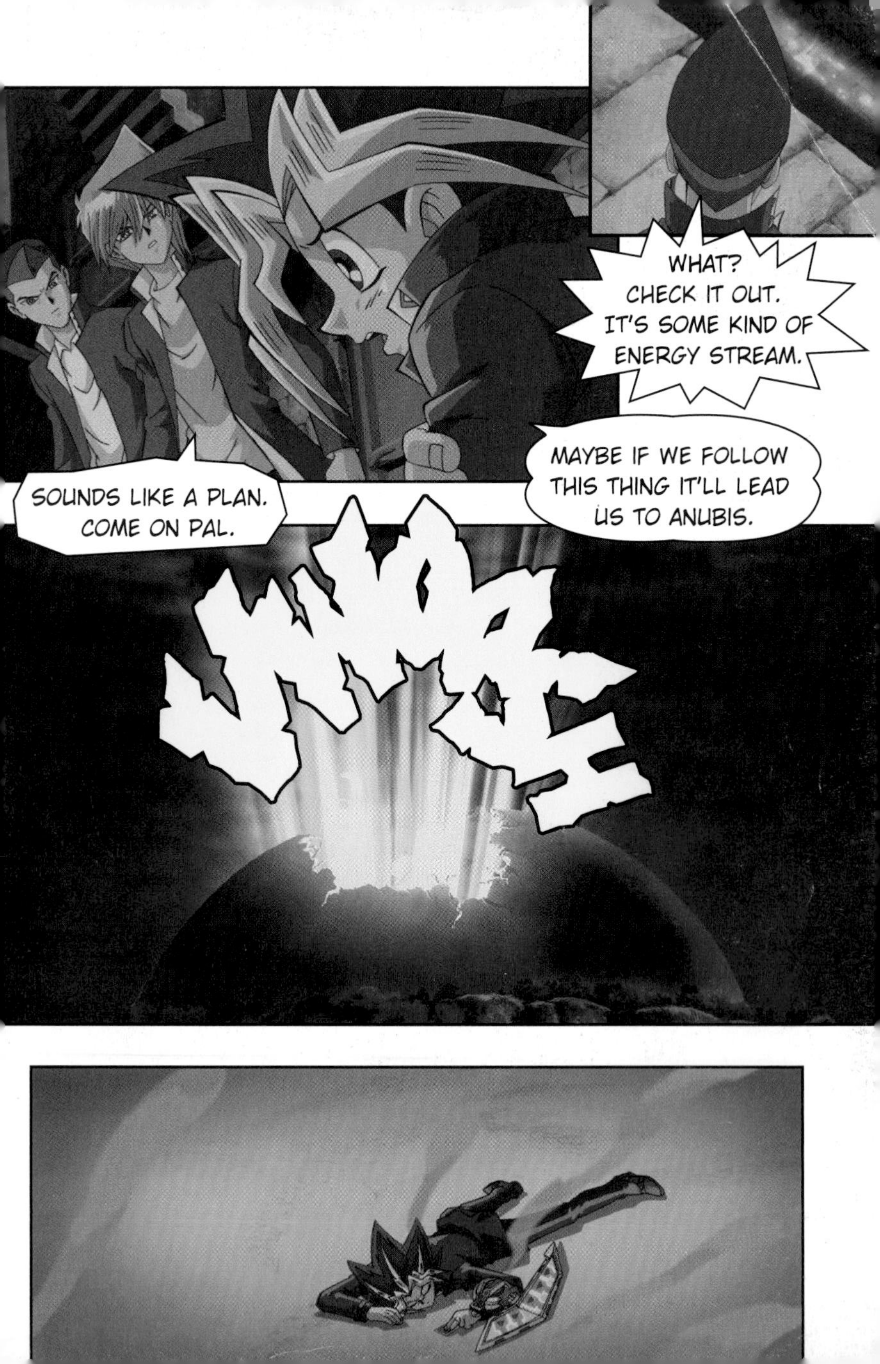
WHAT? CHECK IT OUT. IT'S SOME KIND OF ENERGY STREAM.
MAYBE IF WE FOLLOW THIS THING IT'LL LEAD US TO ANUBIS.
SOUNDS LIKE A PLAN. COME ON PAL.

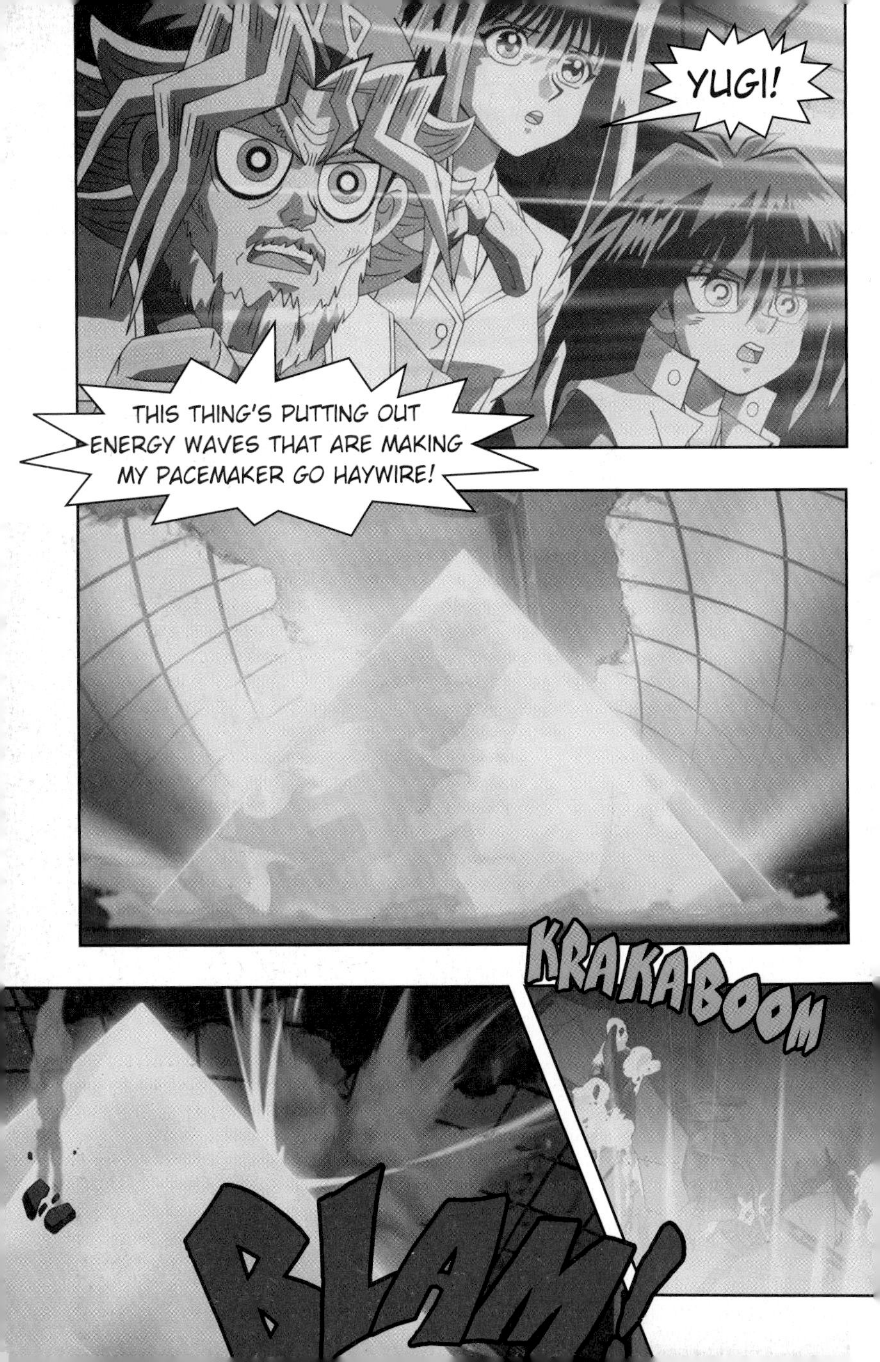
YUGI!
THIS THING'S PUTTING OUT ENERGY WAVES THAT ARE MAKING MY PACEMAKER GO HAYWIRE!
KRAKABOOM
BLAM!

READ THIS WAY

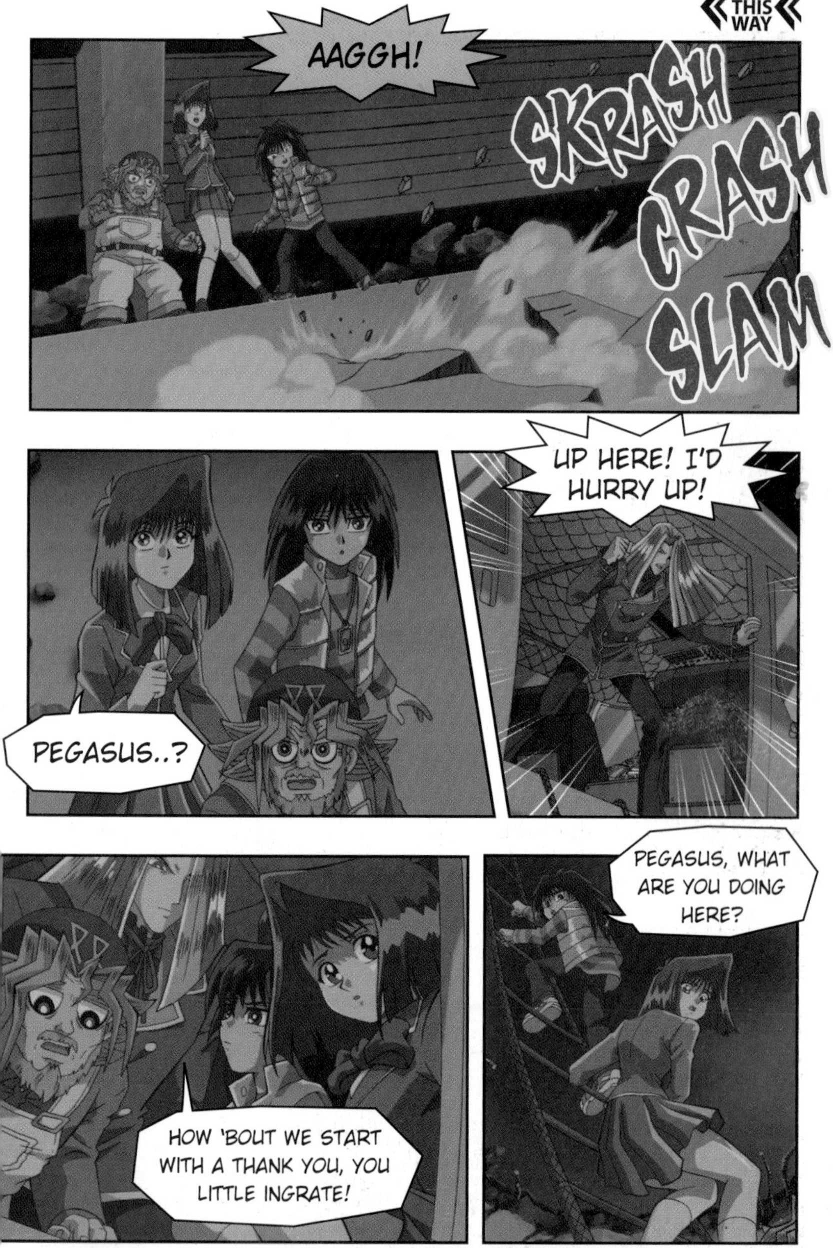
AAGGH!
SKRASH
CRASH
SLAM
UP HERE! I'D HURRY UP!
PEGASUS..?
PEGASUS, WHAT ARE YOU DOING HERE?
HOW 'BOUT WE START WITH A THANK YOU, YOU LITTLE INGRATE!

READ THIS WAY

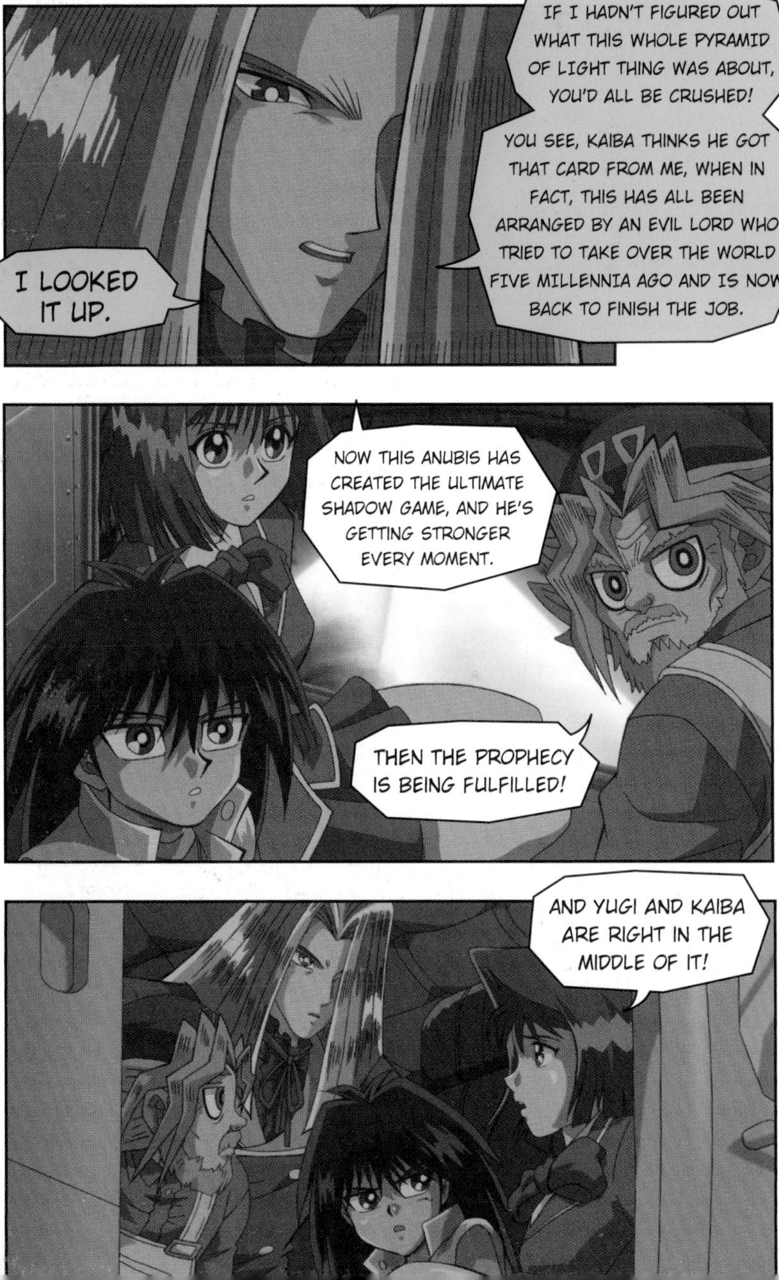
IF I HADN'T FIGURED OUT WHAT THIS WHOLE PYRAMID OF LIGHT THING WAS ABOUT, YOU'D ALL BE CRUSHED!
YOU SEE, KAIBA THINKS HE GOT THAT CARD FROM ME, WHEN IN FACT, THIS HAS ALL BEEN ARRANGED BY AN EVIL LORD WHO TRIED TO TAKE OVER THE WORLD FIVE MILLENNIA AGO AND IS NOW BACK TO FINISH THE JOB.
I LOOKED IT UP.
NOW THIS ANUBIS HAS CREATED THE ULTIMATE SHADOW GAME, AND HE'S GETTING STRONGER EVERY MOMENT.
THEN THE PROPHECY IS BEING FULFILLED!
AND YUGI AND KAIBA ARE RIGHT IN THE MIDDLE OF IT!

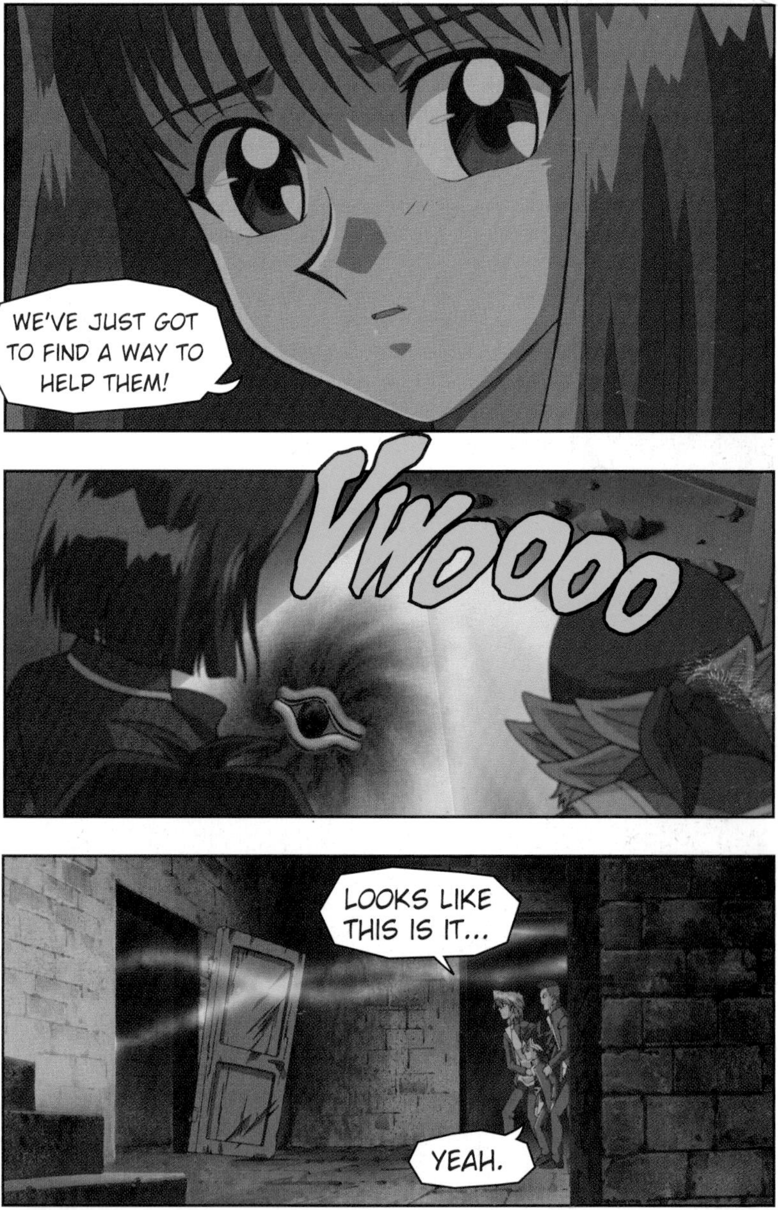
WE'VE JUST GOT TO FIND A WAY TO HELP THEM!
VWOOOO
LOOKS LIKE THIS IS IT...
YEAH.

FOOLISH MORTALS! THERE IS NOTHING YOU CAN DO TO STOP MY REBIRTH!

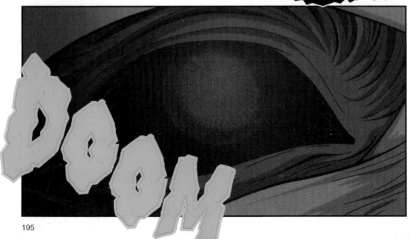

DOOM

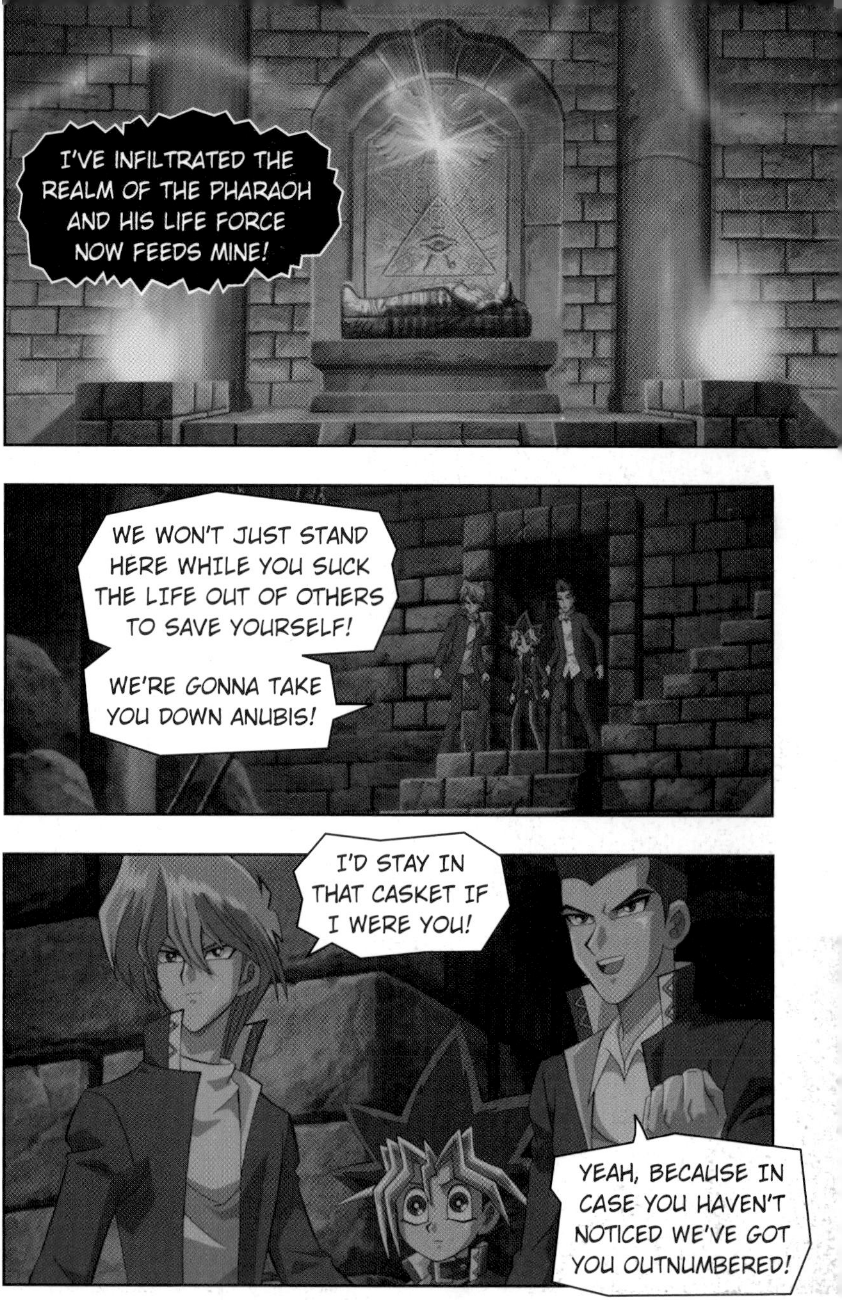
I'VE INFILTRATED THE REALM OF THE PHARAOH AND HIS LIFE FORCE NOW FEEDS MINE!
WE WON'T JUST STAND HERE WHILE YOU SUCK THE LIFE OUT OF OTHERS TO SAVE YOURSELF!
WE'RE GONNA TAKE YOU DOWN ANUBIS!
I'D STAY IN THAT CASKET IF I WERE YOU!
YEAH, BECAUSE IN CASE YOU HAVEN'T NOTICED WE'VE GOT YOU OUTNUMBERED!

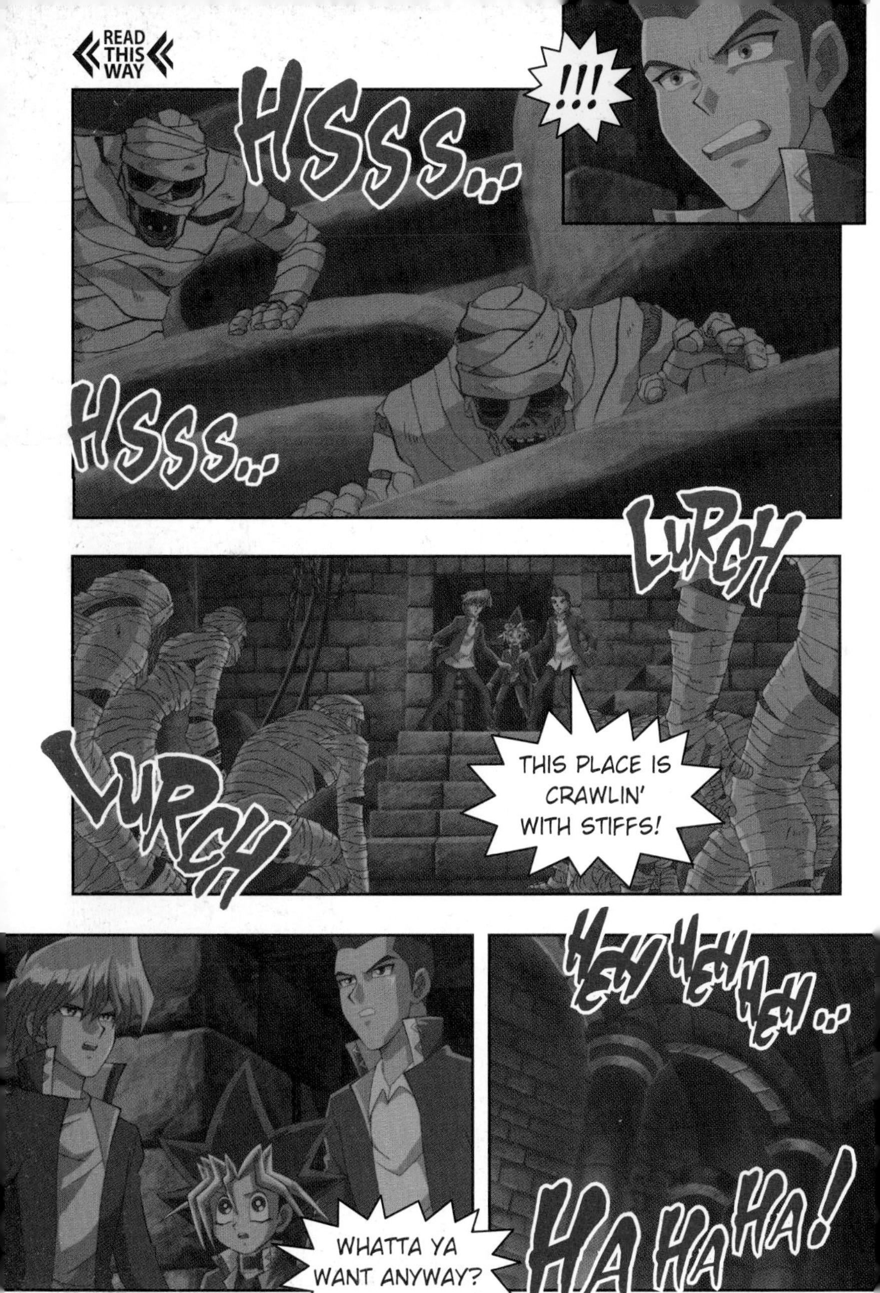
READ THIS WAY
!!!
HSSS..
HSSS..
LURCH
LURCH
THIS PLACE IS CRAWLIN' WITH STIFFS!
HEH HEH HEH..
HA HA HA HA!
WHATTA YA WANT ANYWAY?

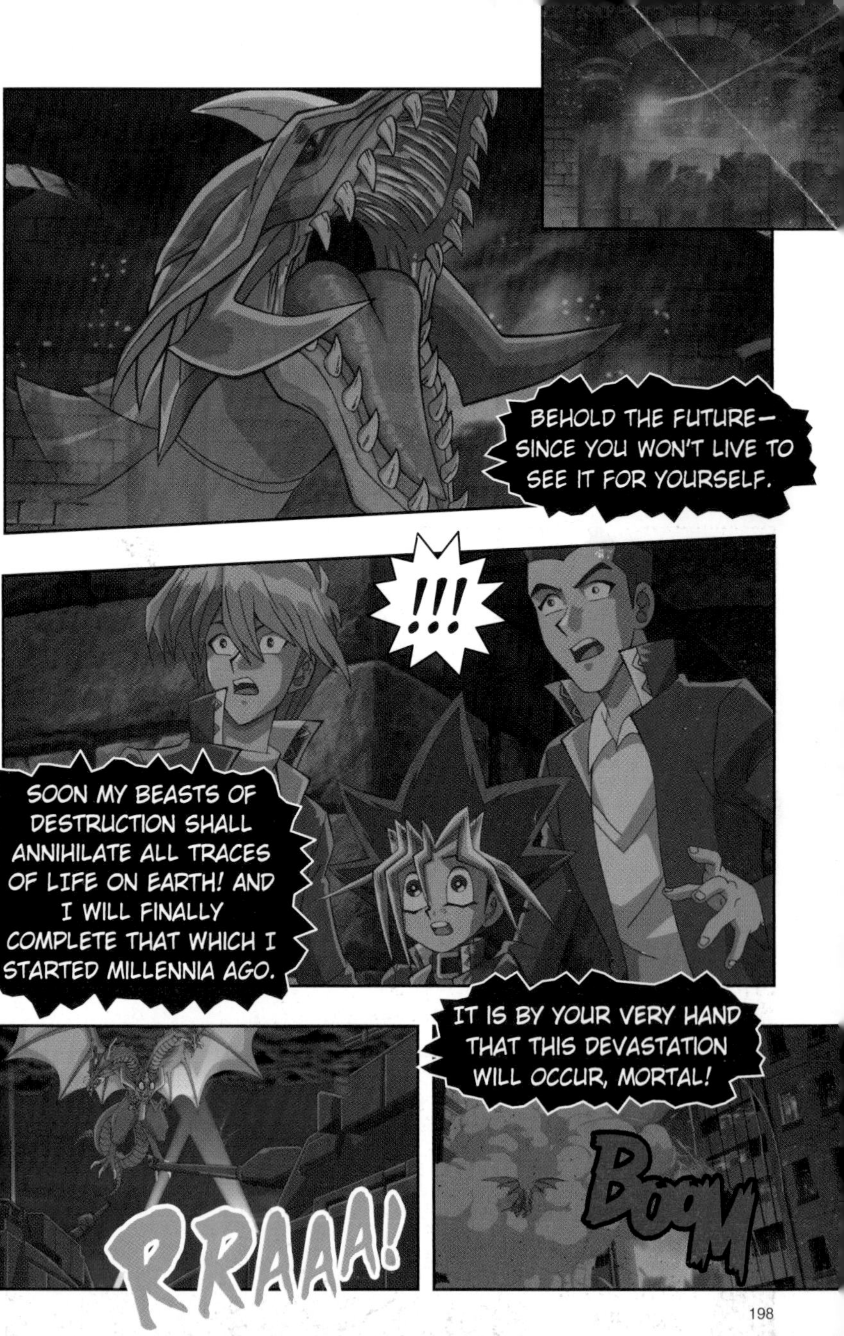
BEHOLD THE FUTURE—SINCE YOU WON'T LIVE TO SEE IT FOR YOURSELF.
!!!
SOON MY BEASTS OF DESTRUCTION SHALL ANNIHILATE ALL TRACES OF LIFE ON EARTH! AND I WILL FINALLY COMPLETE THAT WHICH I STARTED MILLENNIA AGO.
IT IS BY YOUR VERY HAND THAT THIS DEVASTATION WILL OCCUR, MORTAL!
BOOM
RRAAA!

READ THIS WAY

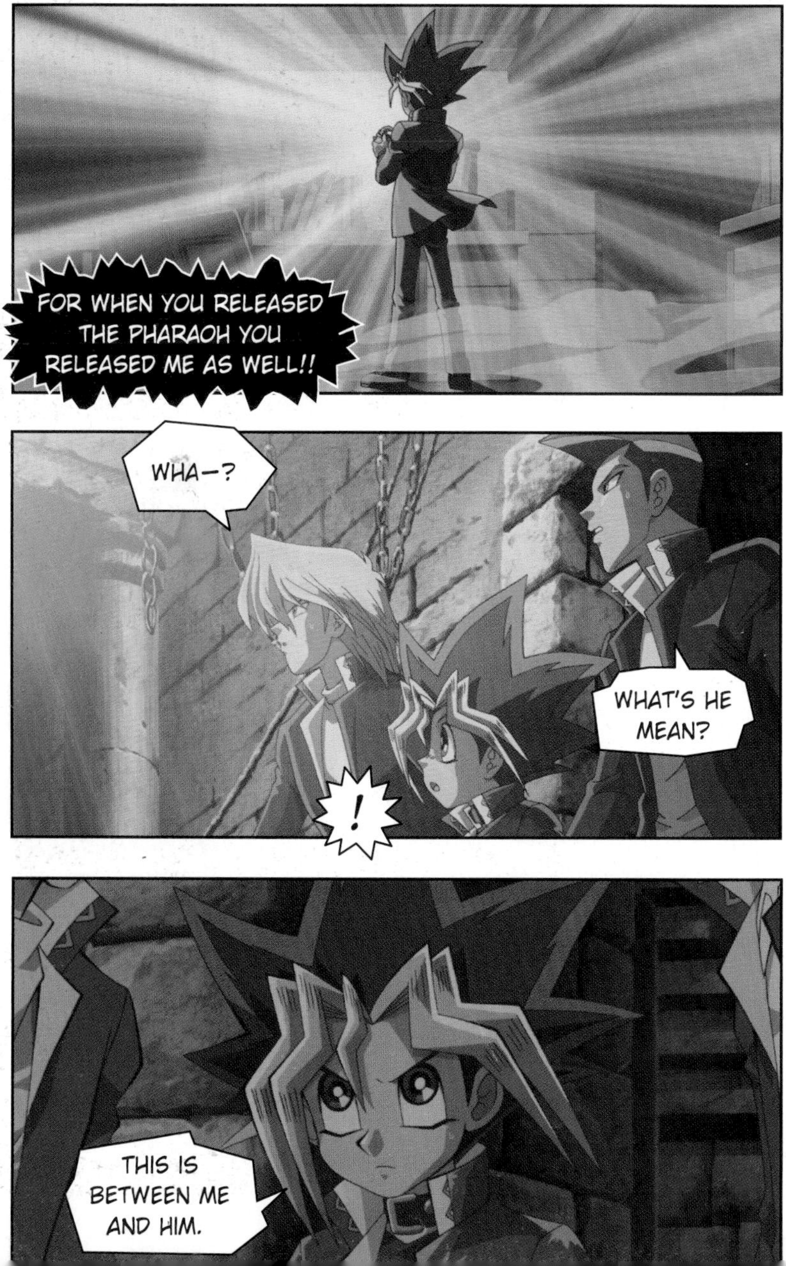
FOR WHEN YOU RELEASED THE PHARAOH YOU RELEASED ME AS WELL!!
WHA—?
WHAT'S HE MEAN?
!
THIS IS BETWEEN ME AND HIM.

READ THIS WAY

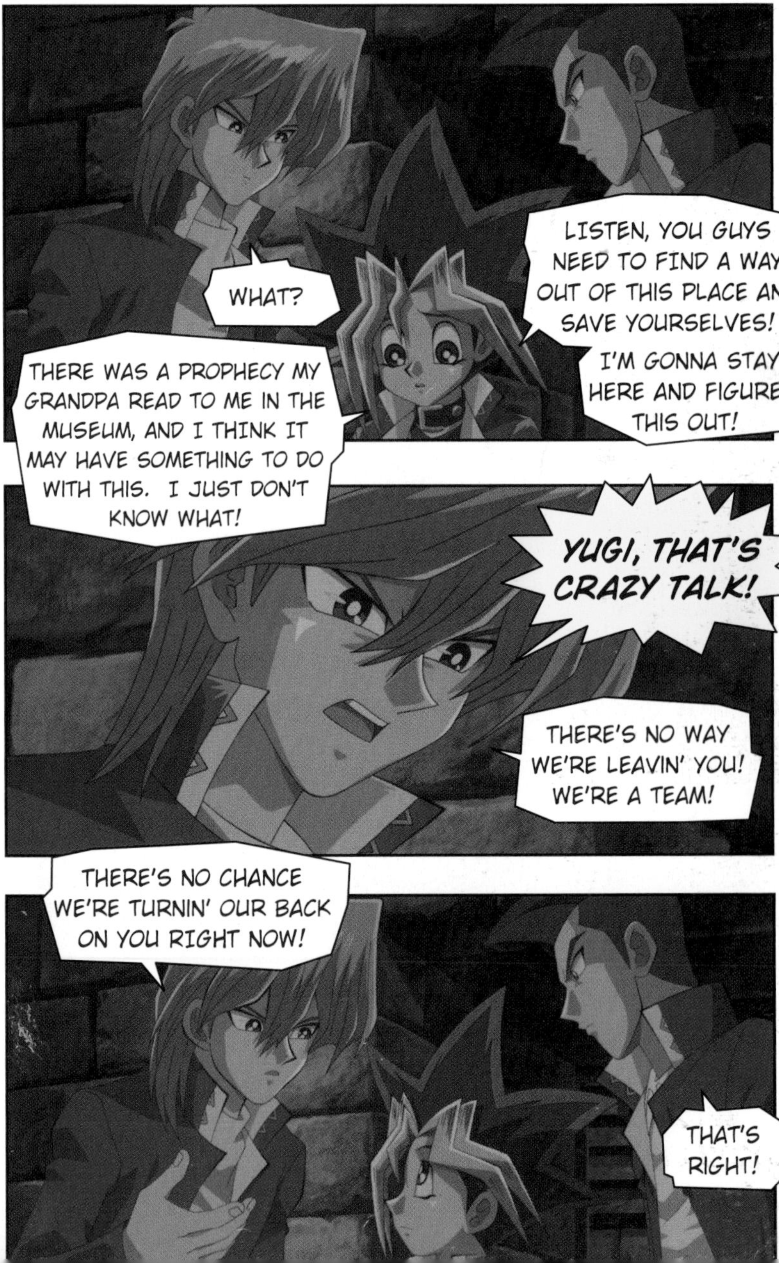
LISTEN, YOU GUYS NEED TO FIND A WAY OUT OF THIS PLACE AND SAVE YOURSELVES!
WHAT?
I'M GONNA STAY HERE AND FIGURE THIS OUT!
THERE WAS A PROPHECY MY GRANDPA READ TO ME IN THE MUSEUM, AND I THINK IT MAY HAVE SOMETHING TO DO WITH THIS. I JUST DON'T KNOW WHAT!
YUGI, THAT'S CRAZY TALK!
THERE'S NO WAY WE'RE LEAVIN' YOU! WE'RE A TEAM!
THERE'S NO CHANCE WE'RE TURNIN' OUR BACK ON YOU RIGHT NOW!
THAT'S RIGHT!

READ THIS WAY

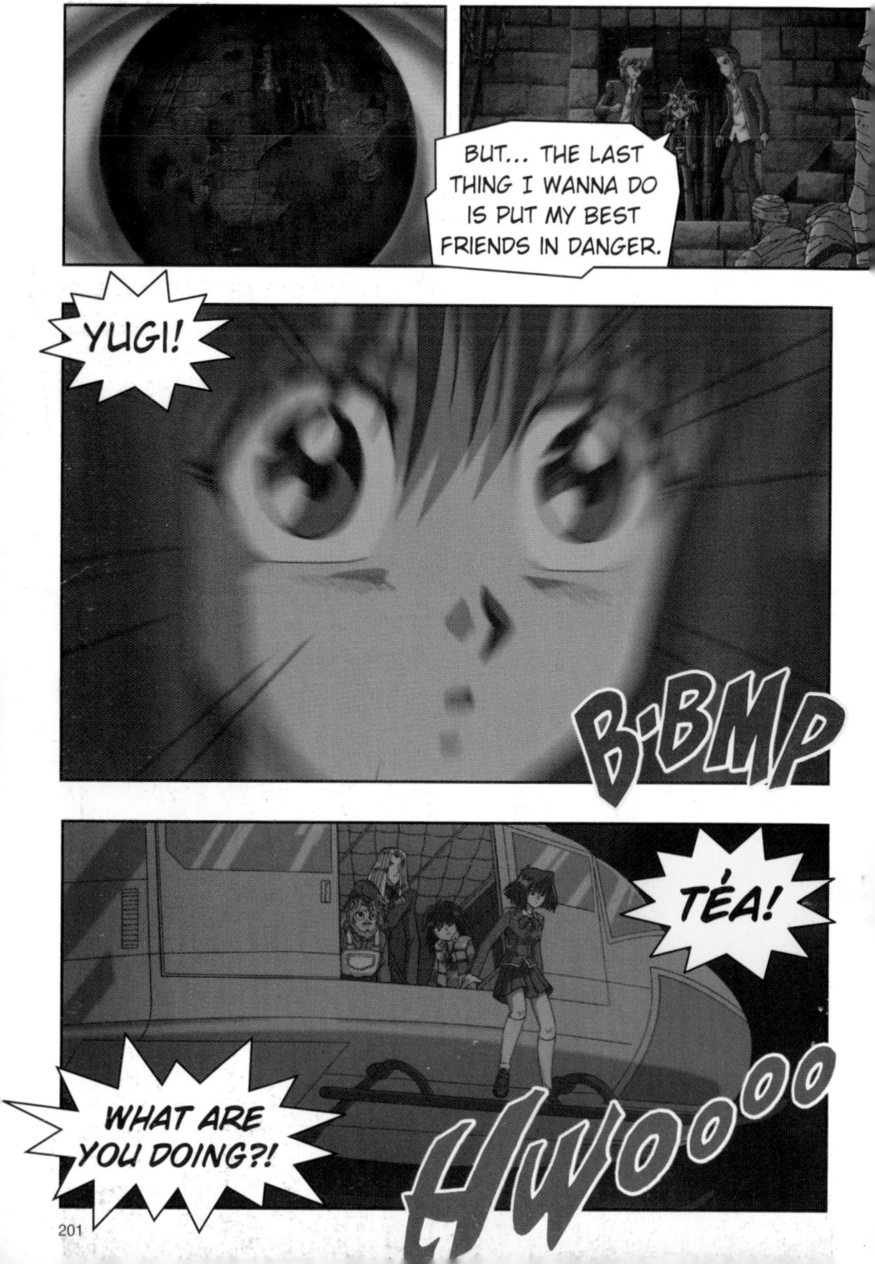
BUT... THE LAST THING I WANNA DO IS PUT MY BEST FRIENDS IN DANGER.
YUGI!
B-BMP
TÉA!
WHAT ARE YOU DOING?!
HWOOOOO

READ THIS WAY

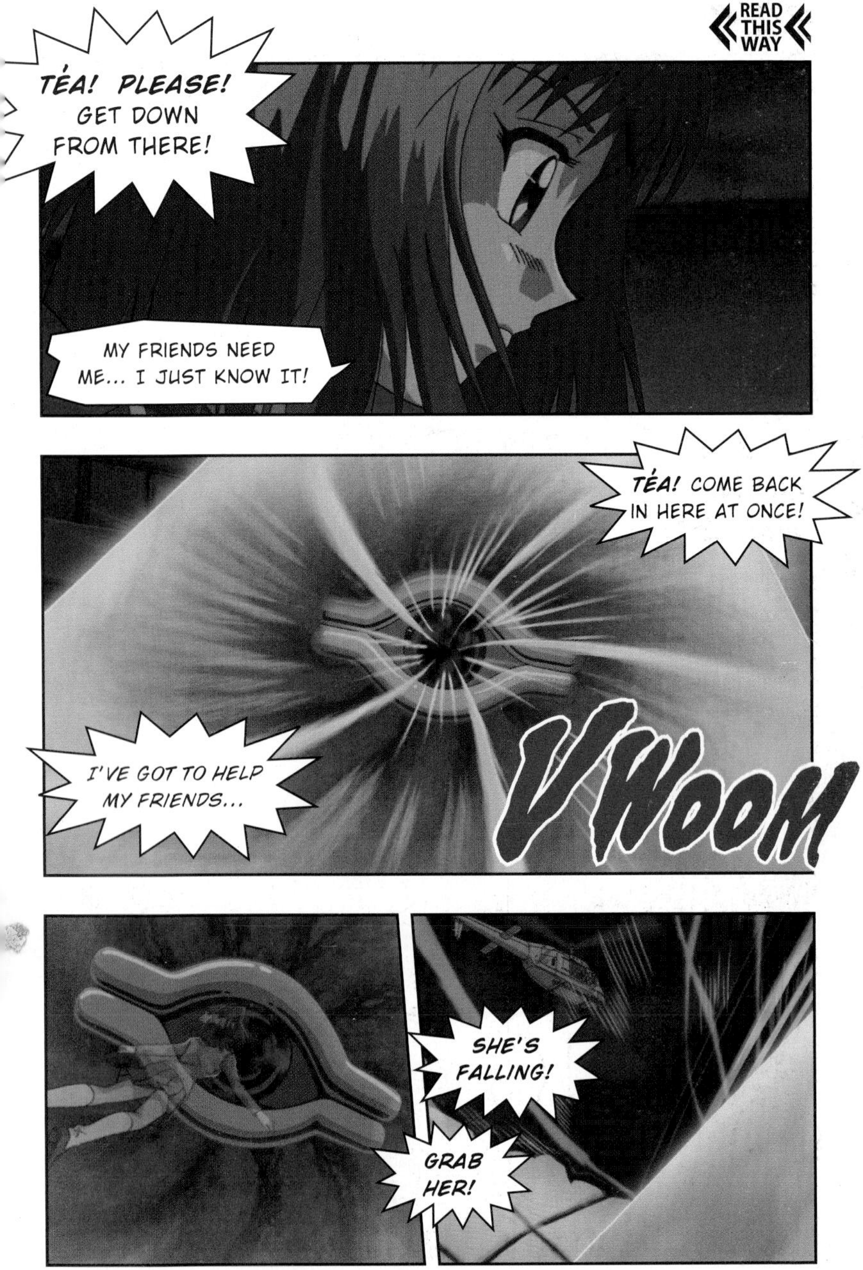
TÉA! PLEASE! GET DOWN FROM THERE!
MY FRIENDS NEED ME... I JUST KNOW IT!
TÉA! COME BACK IN HERE AT ONCE!
I'VE GOT TO HELP MY FRIENDS...
VWOOM
SHE'S FALLING!
GRAB HER!

READ THIS WAY

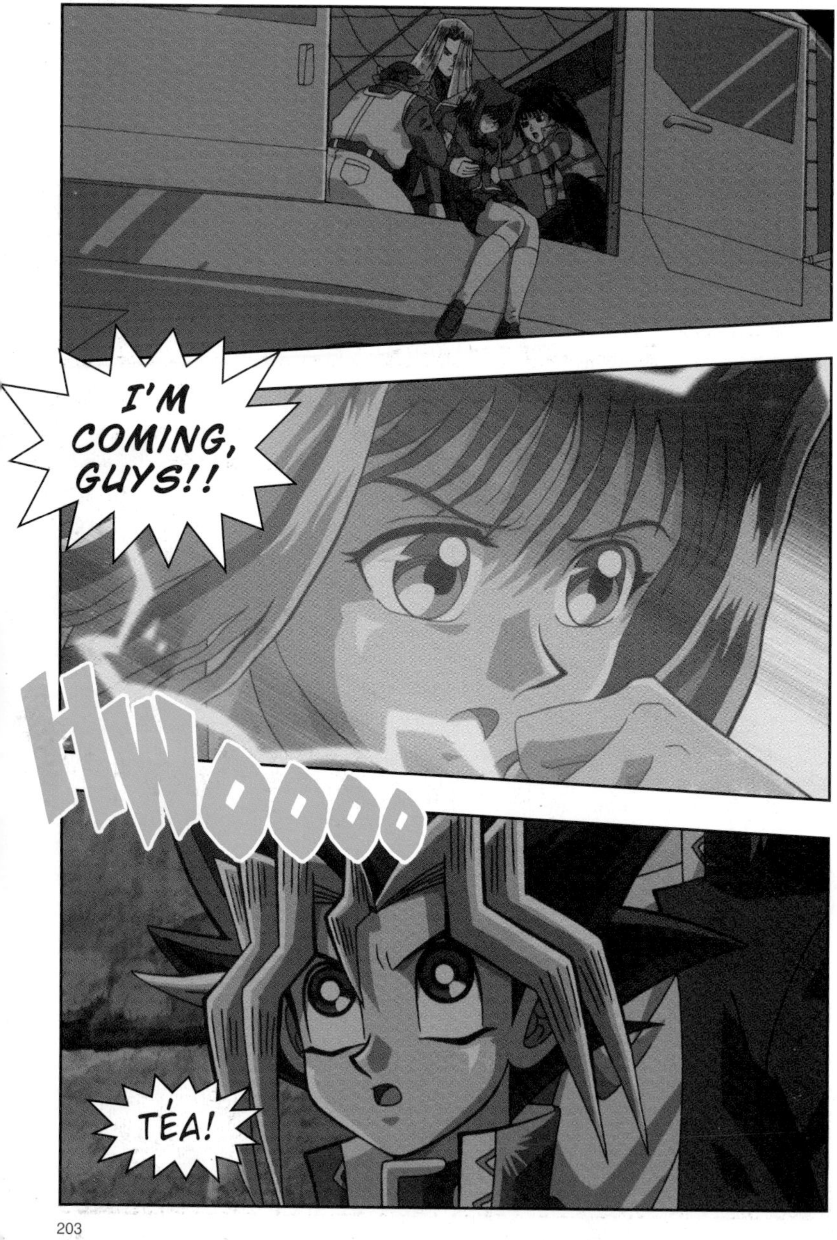
I'M COMING, GUYS!!
HWOOOO
TÉA!

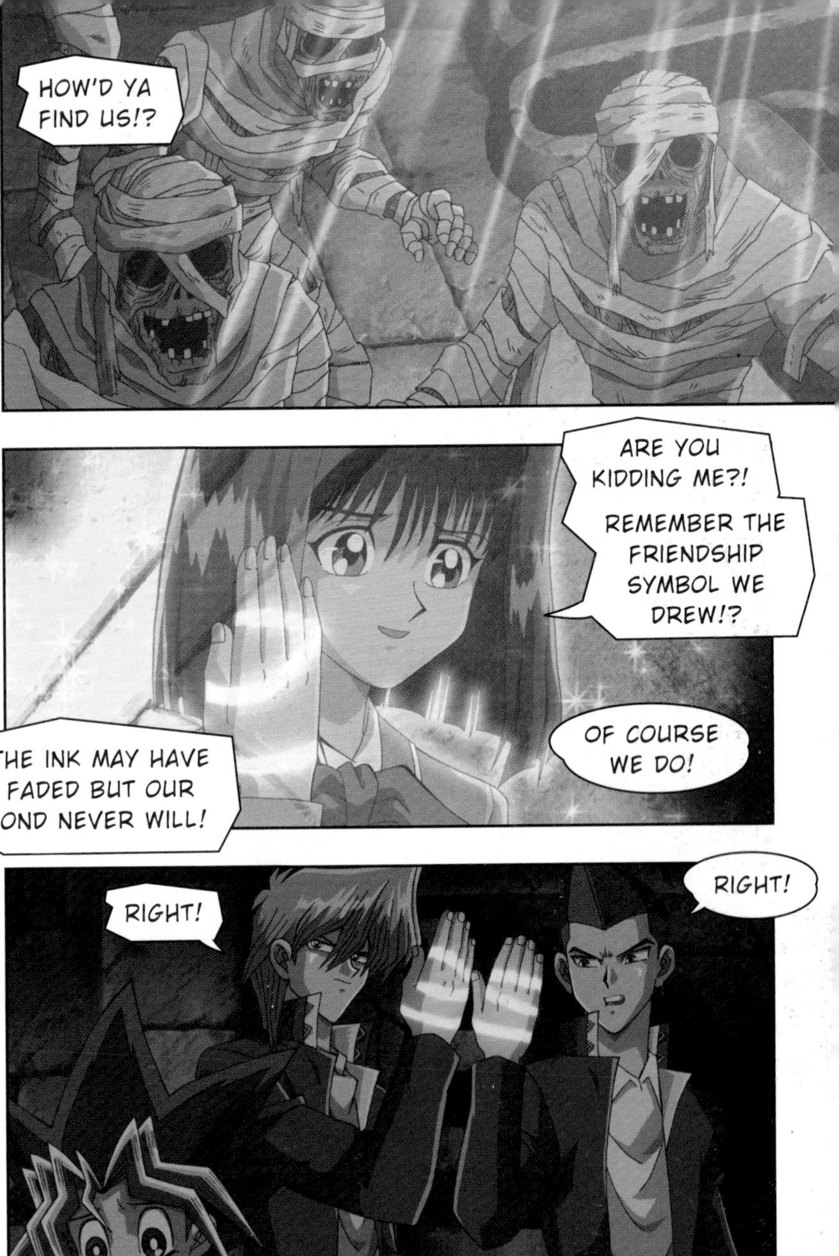
HOW'D YA FIND US!?
ARE YOU KIDDING ME?!
REMEMBER THE FRIENDSHIP SYMBOL WE DREW!?
OF COURSE WE DO!
THE INK MAY HAVE FADED BUT OUR BOND NEVER WILL!
RIGHT!
RIGHT!

READ THIS WAY

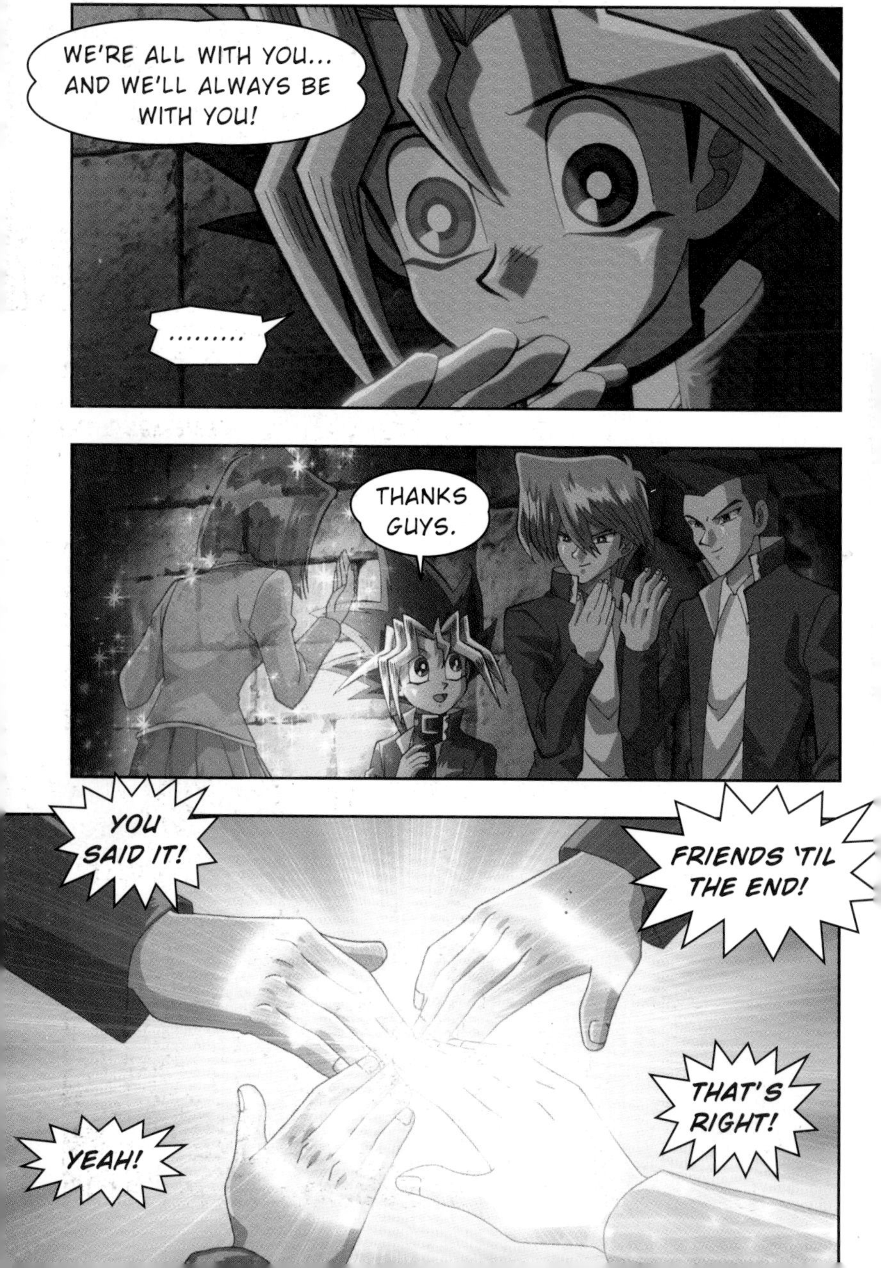
WE'RE ALL WITH YOU... AND WE'LL ALWAYS BE WITH YOU!
....
THANKS GUYS.
FRIENDS 'TIL THE END!
YOU SAID IT!
THAT'S RIGHT!
YEAH!

READ THIS WAY

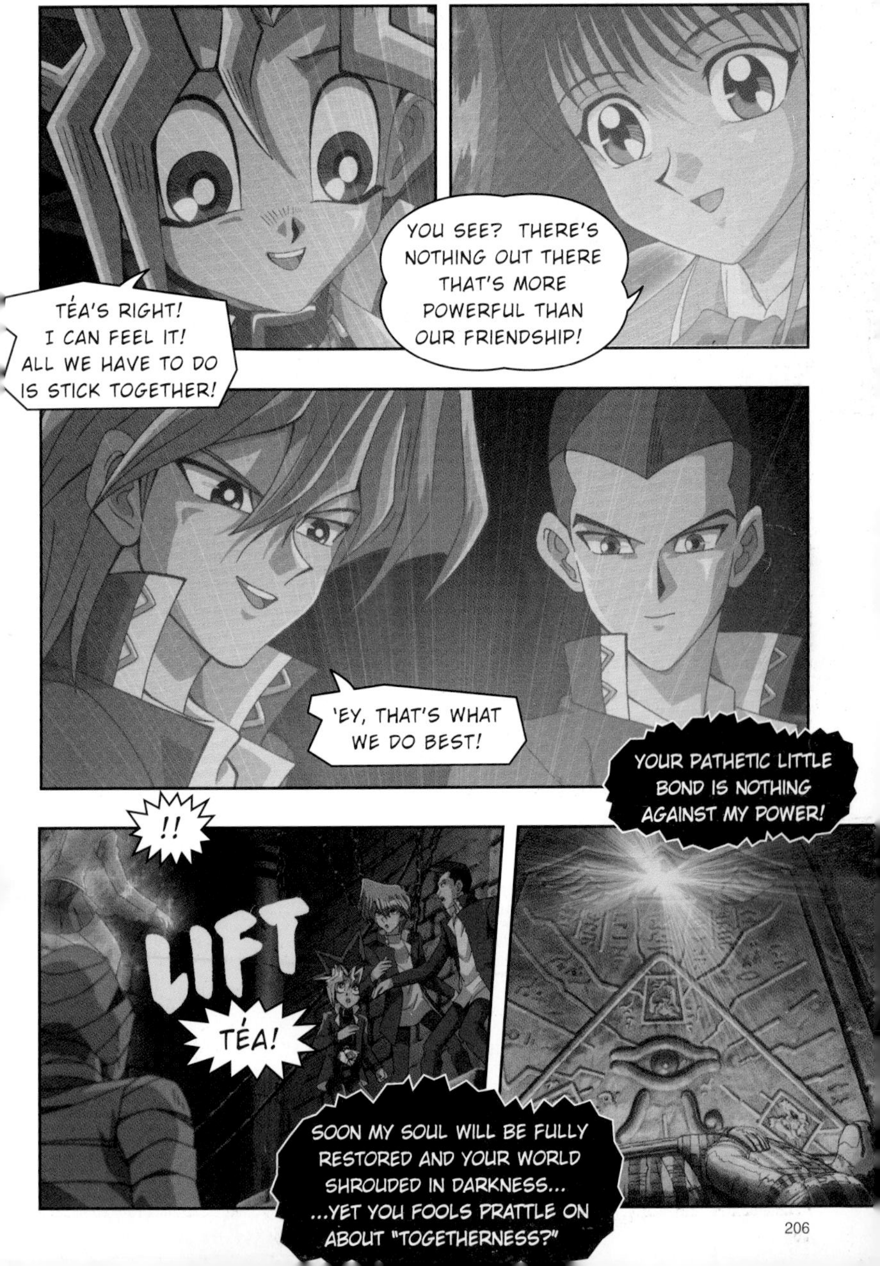
YOU SEE? THERE'S NOTHING OUT THERE THAT'S MORE POWERFUL THAN OUR FRIENDSHIP!
TÉA'S RIGHT! I CAN FEEL IT! ALL WE HAVE TO DO IS STICK TOGETHER!
'EY, THAT'S WHAT WE DO BEST!
YOUR PATHETIC LITTLE BOND IS NOTHING AGAINST MY POWER!
SOON MY SOUL WILL BE FULLY RESTORED AND YOUR WORLD SHROUDED IN DARKNESS... ...YET YOU FOOLS PRATTLE ON ABOUT "TOGETHERNESS?"
!!
LIFT
TÉA!

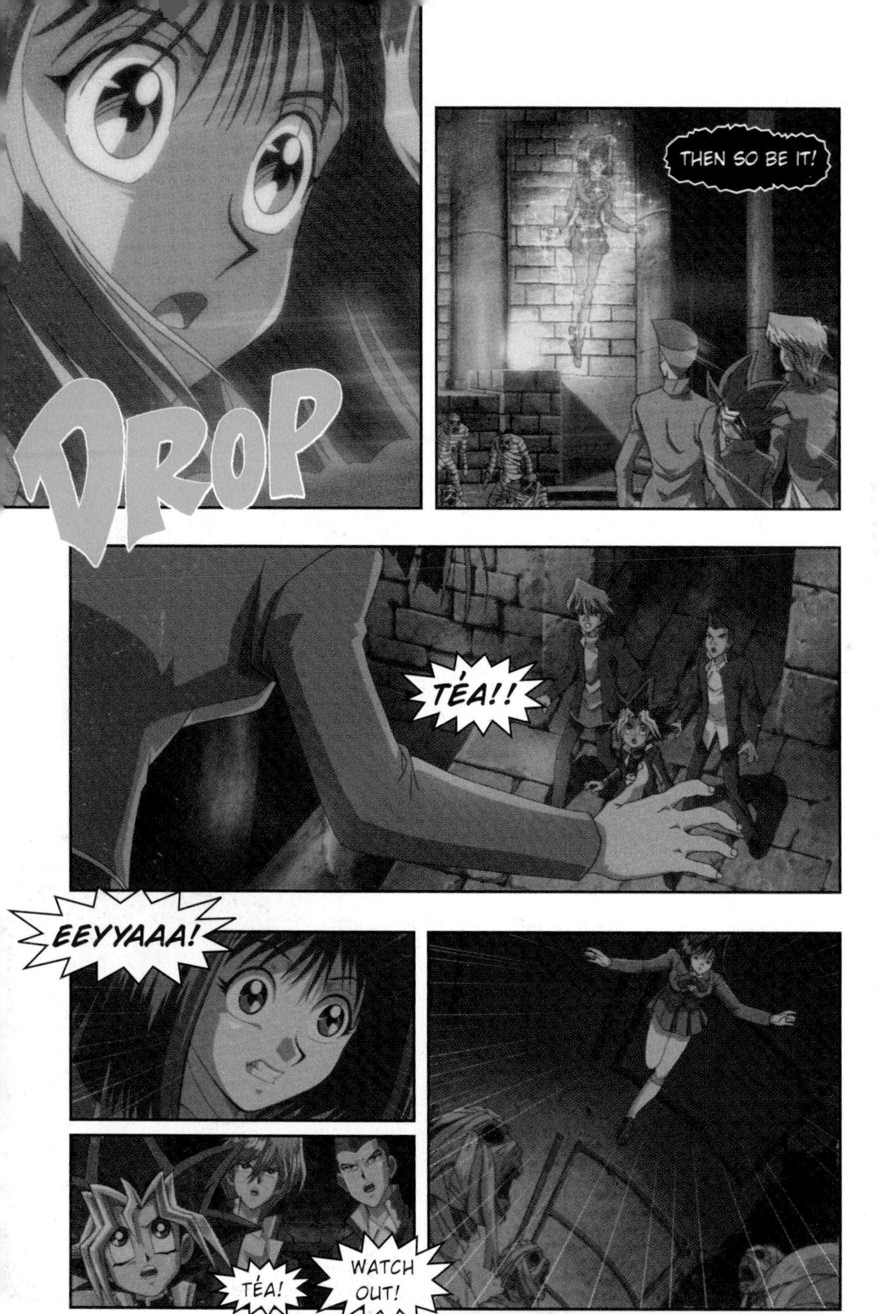
THEN SO BE IT!
DROP
TÉA!!
EEYYAAA!
WATCH OUT!
TÉA!

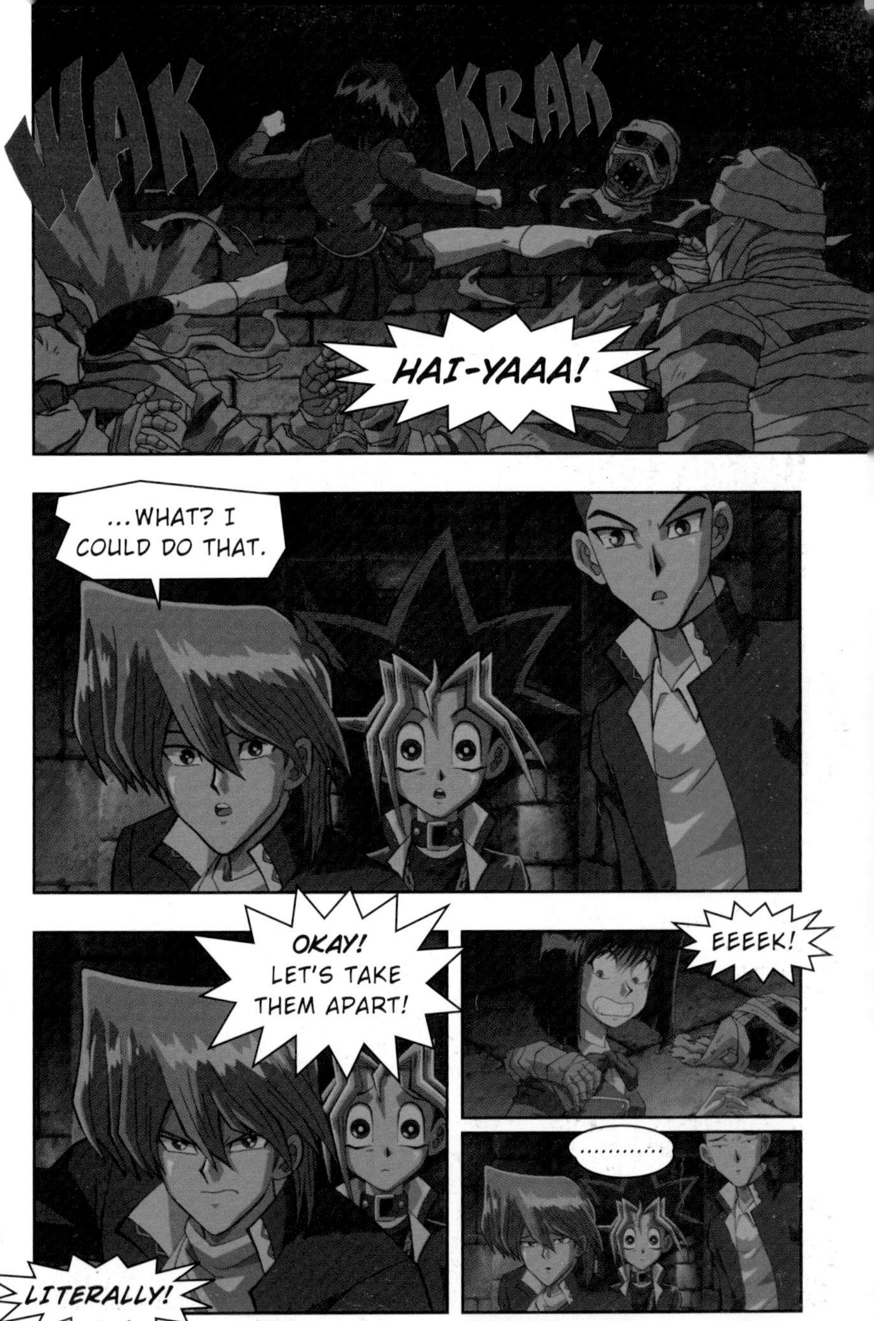
KRAK
WAK
HAI-YAAA!
...WHAT? I COULD DO THAT.
EEEEK!
....
OKAY! LET'S TAKE THEM APART!
LITERALLY!

READ THIS WAY

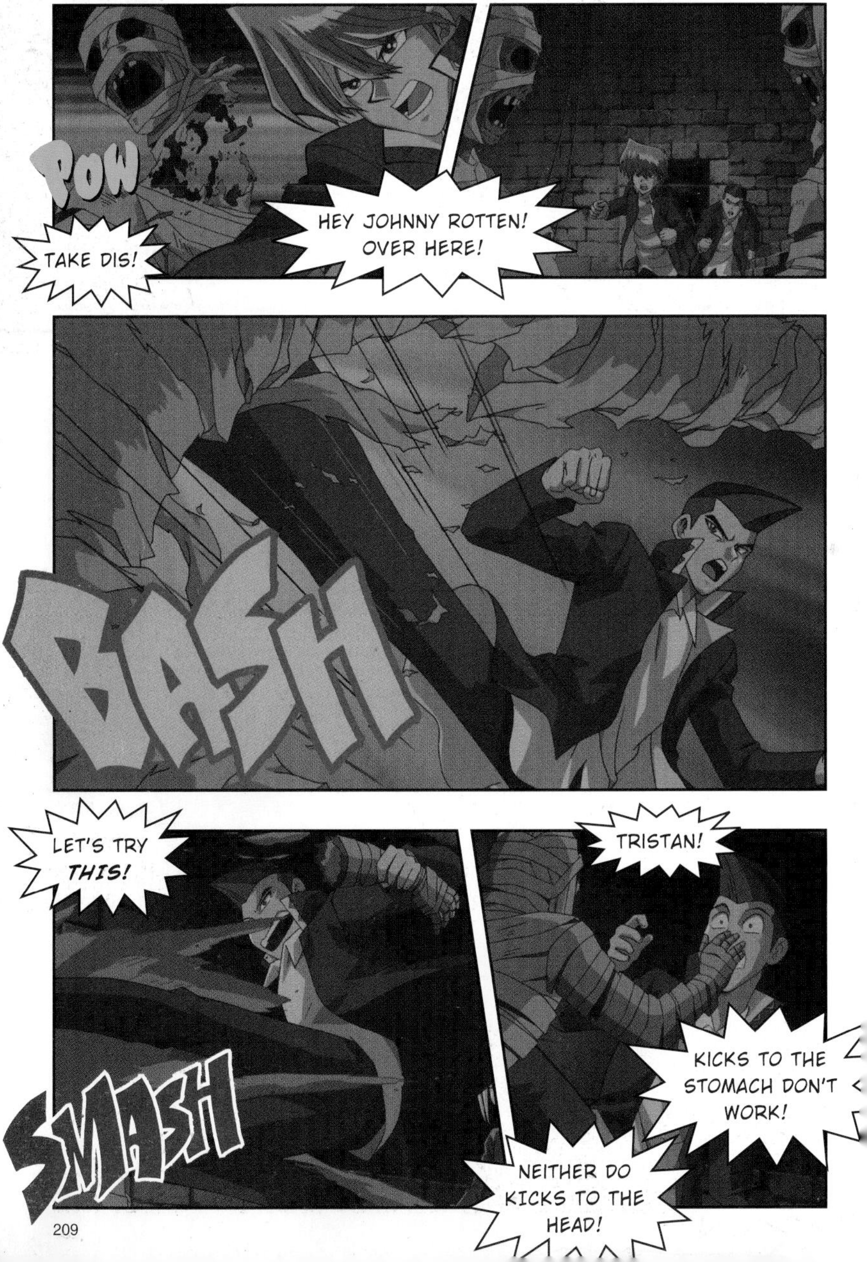
HEY JOHNNY ROTTEN! OVER HERE!
POW
TAKE DIS!
BASH
TRISTAN!
KICKS TO THE STOMACH DON'T WORK!
NEITHER DO KICKS TO THE HEAD!
LET'S TRY *THIS!*
SMASH

READ THIS WAY

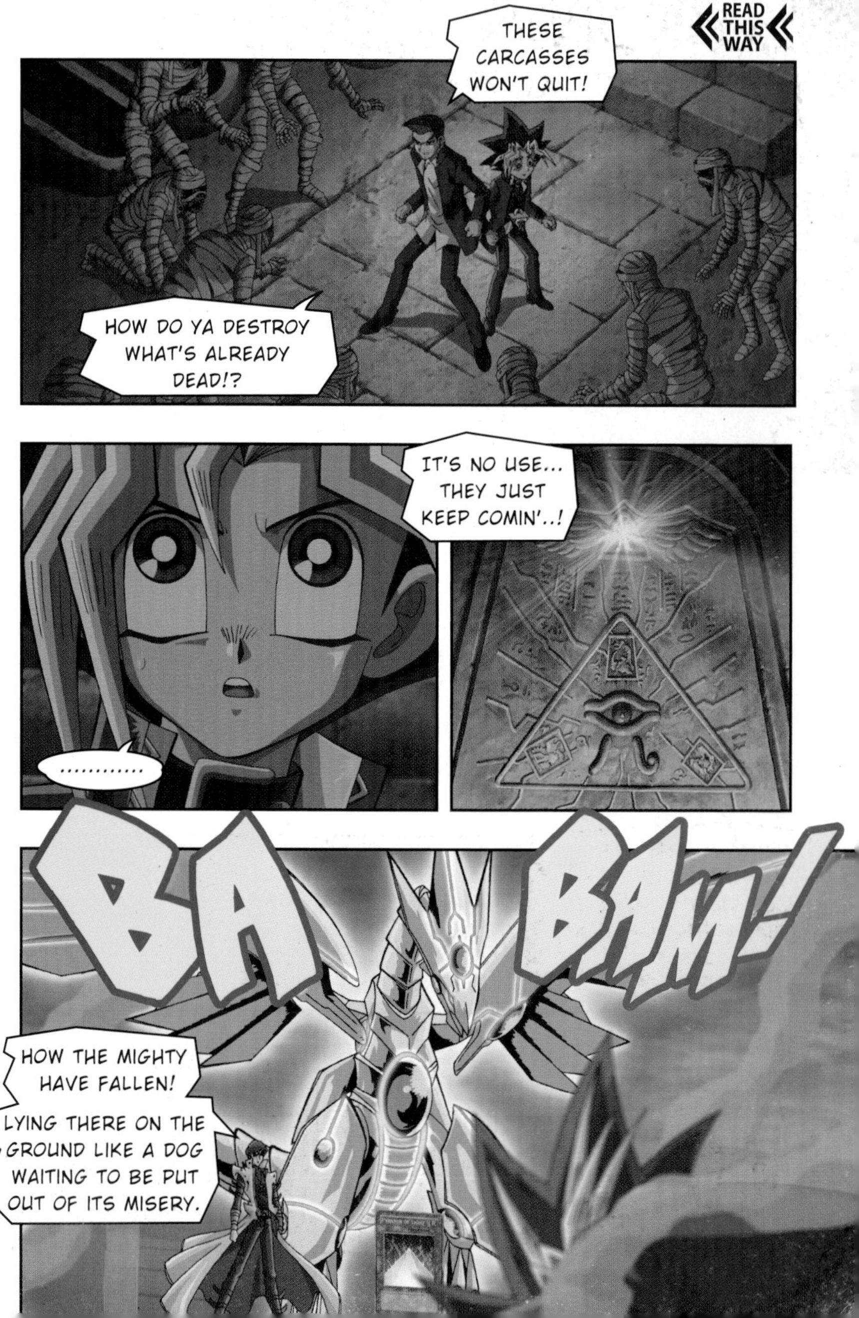
THESE CARCASSES WON'T QUIT!
HOW DO YA DESTROY WHAT'S ALREADY DEAD!?
IT'S NO USE... THEY JUST KEEP COMIN'..!
....
BA BAM!
HOW THE MIGHTY HAVE FALLEN!
LYING THERE ON THE GROUND LIKE A DOG WAITING TO BE PUT OUT OF ITS MISERY.

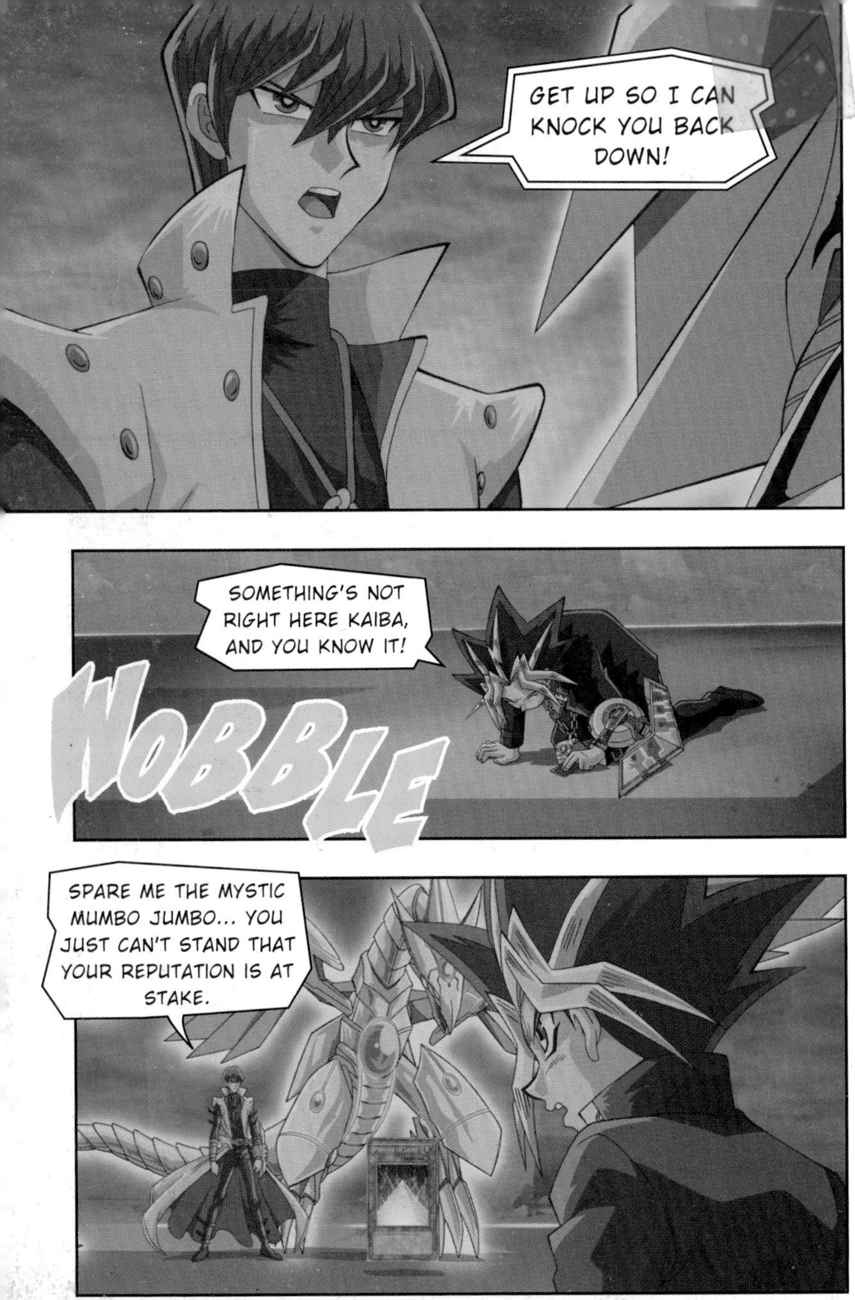
GET UP SO I CAN KNOCK YOU BACK DOWN!
SOMETHING'S NOT RIGHT HERE KAIBA, AND YOU KNOW IT!
WOBBLE
SPARE ME THE MYSTIC MUMBO JUMBO... YOU JUST CAN'T STAND THAT YOUR REPUTATION IS AT STAKE.

READ THIS WAY

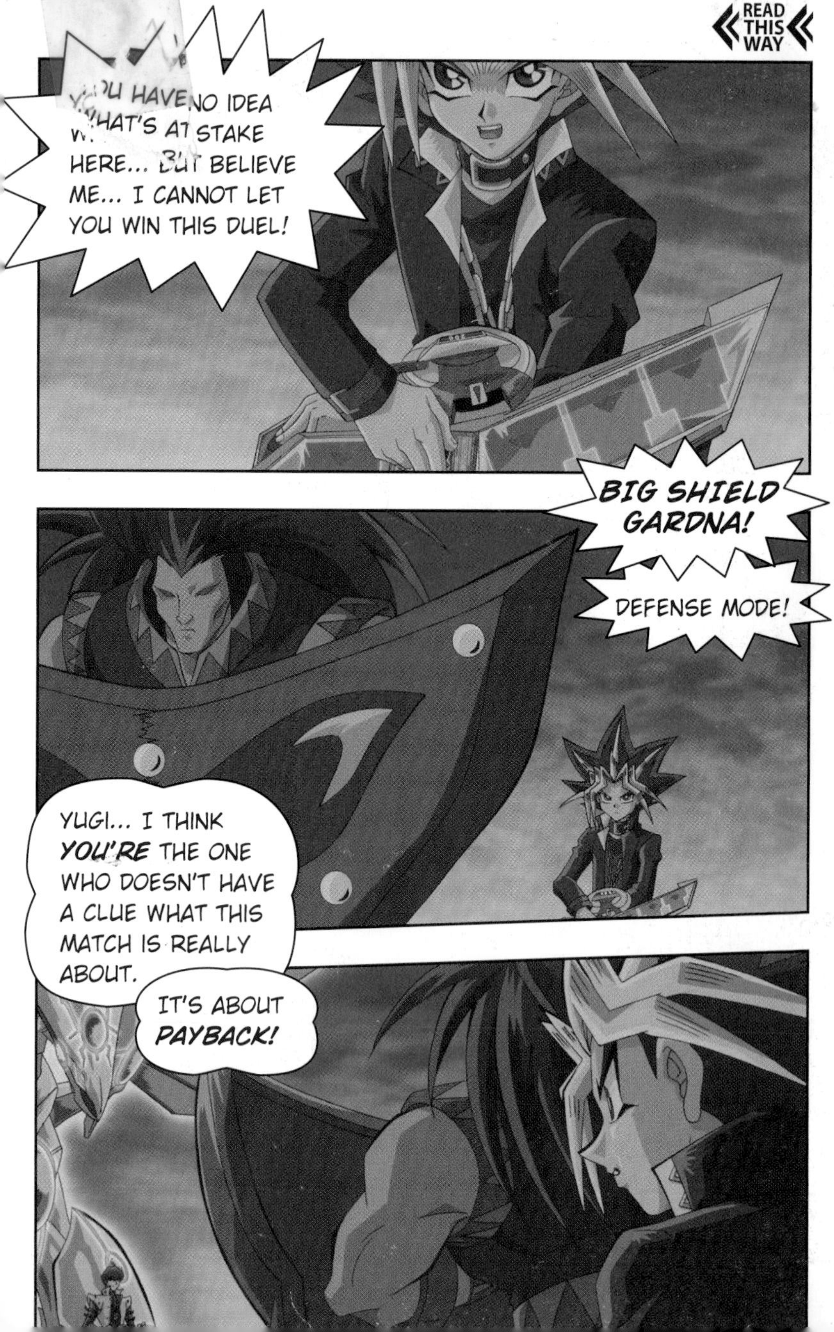
YOU HAVE NO IDEA WHAT'S AT STAKE HERE... BUT BELIEVE ME... I CANNOT LET YOU WIN THIS DUEL!
BIG SHIELD GARDNA!
DEFENSE MODE!
YUGI... I THINK YOU'RE THE ONE WHO DOESN'T HAVE A CLUE WHAT THIS MATCH IS REALLY ABOUT.
IT'S ABOUT PAYBACK!

READ THIS WAY

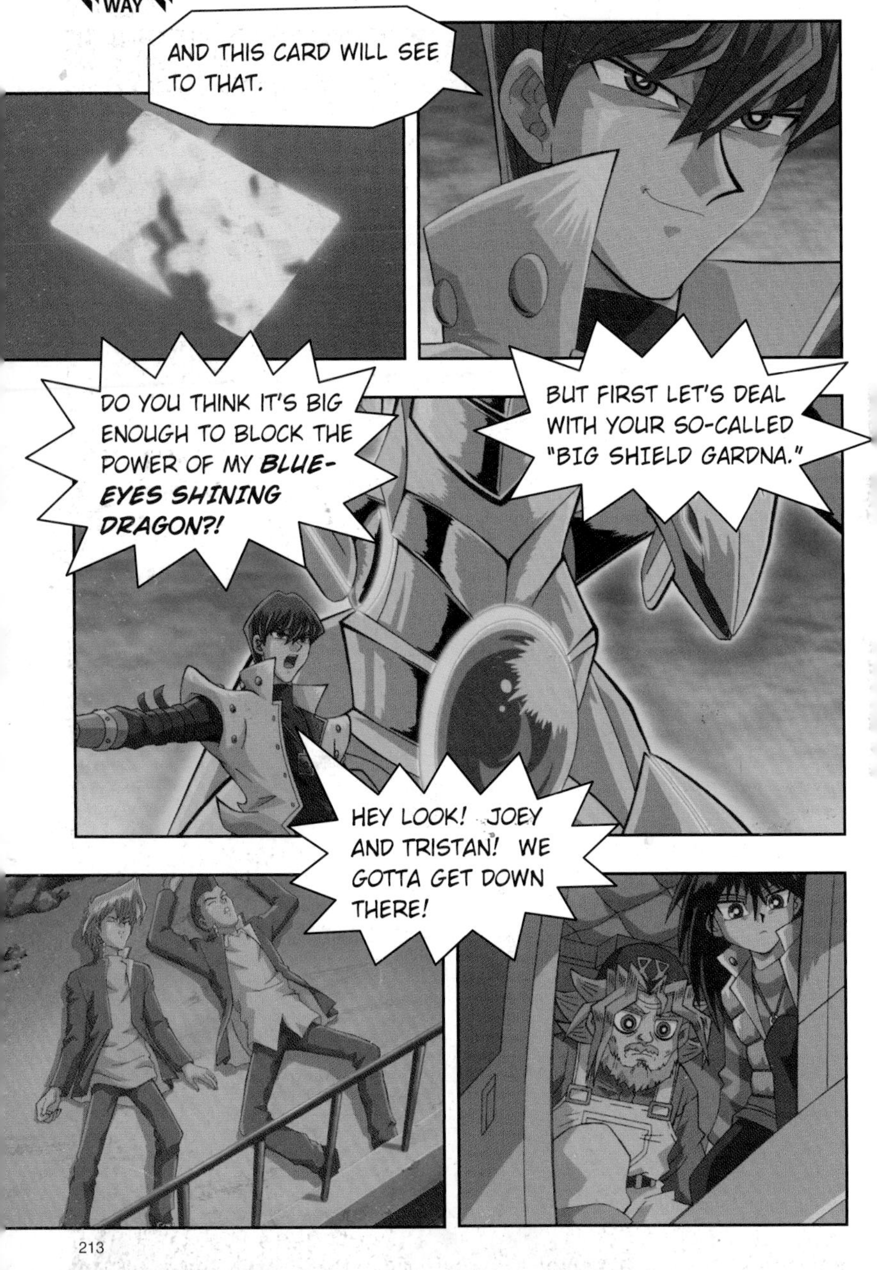
AND THIS CARD WILL SEE TO THAT.
BUT FIRST LET'S DEAL WITH YOUR SO-CALLED "BIG SHIELD GARDNA."
DO YOU THINK IT'S BIG ENOUGH TO BLOCK THE POWER OF MY **BLUE-EYES SHINING DRAGON?!**
HEY LOOK! JOEY AND TRISTAN! WE GOTTA GET DOWN THERE!

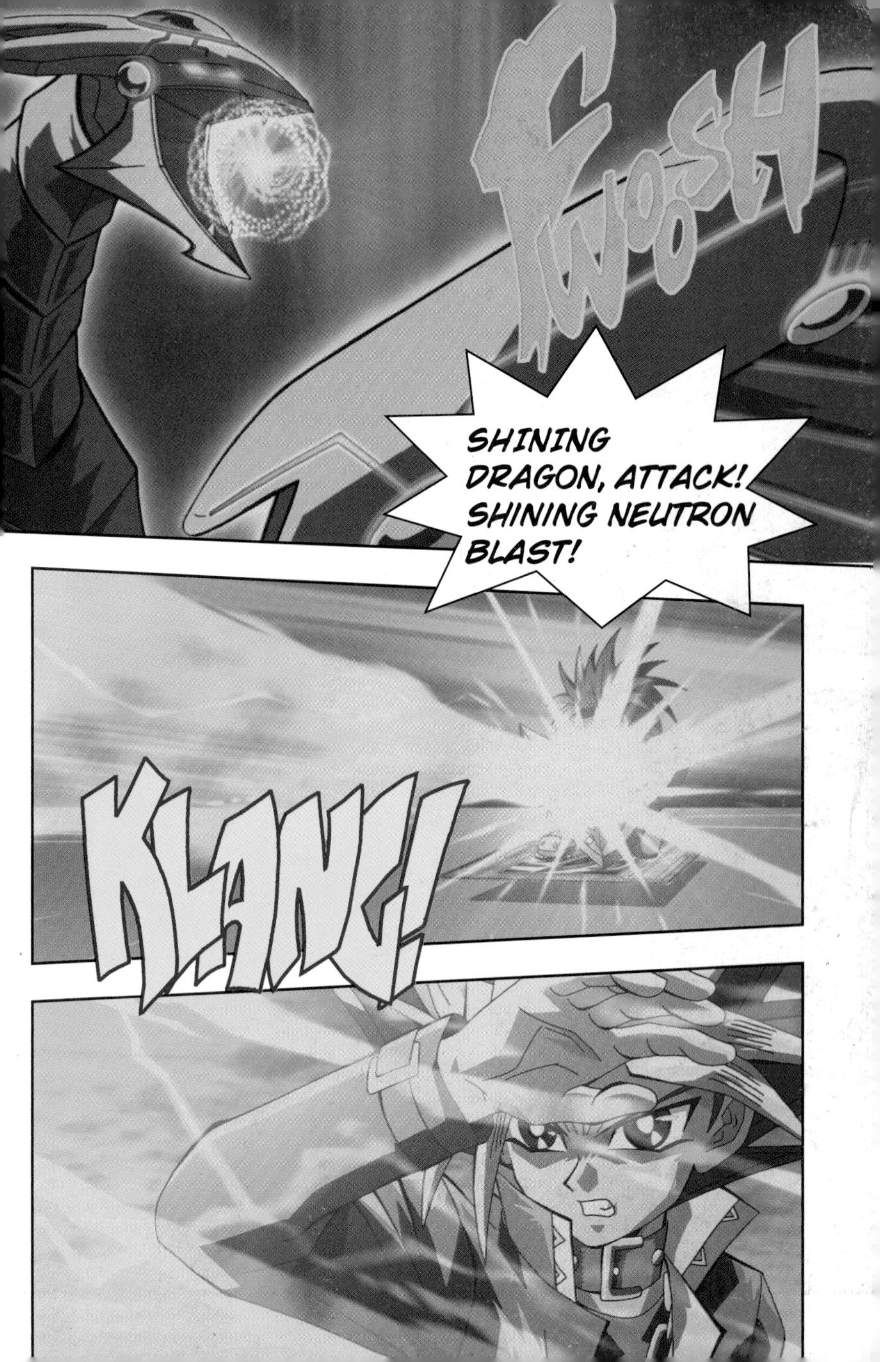
FWOOSH
SHINING DRAGON, ATTACK! SHINING NEUTRON BLAST!
KLANG!

READ THIS WAY

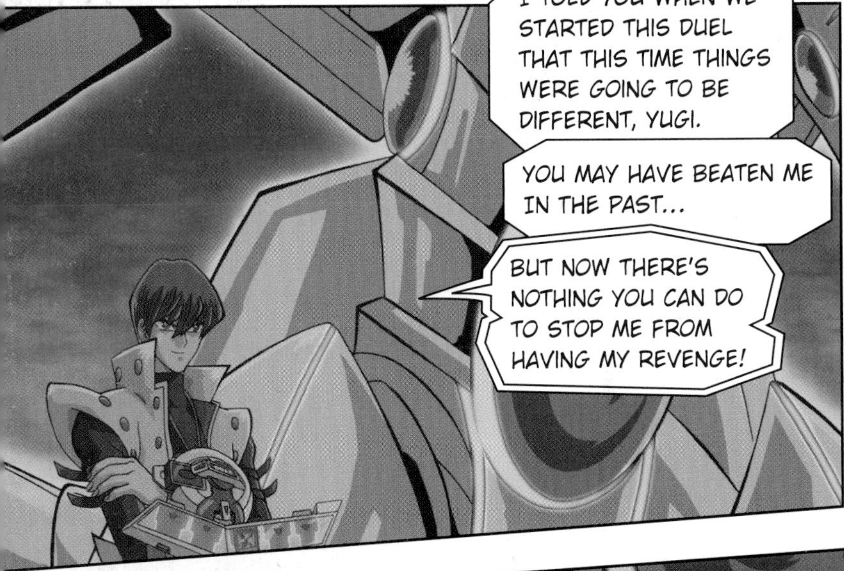
I TOLD YOU WHEN WE STARTED THIS DUEL THAT THIS TIME THINGS WERE GOING TO BE DIFFERENT, YUGI.
YOU MAY HAVE BEATEN ME IN THE PAST...
BUT NOW THERE'S NOTHING YOU CAN DO TO STOP ME FROM HAVING MY REVENGE!

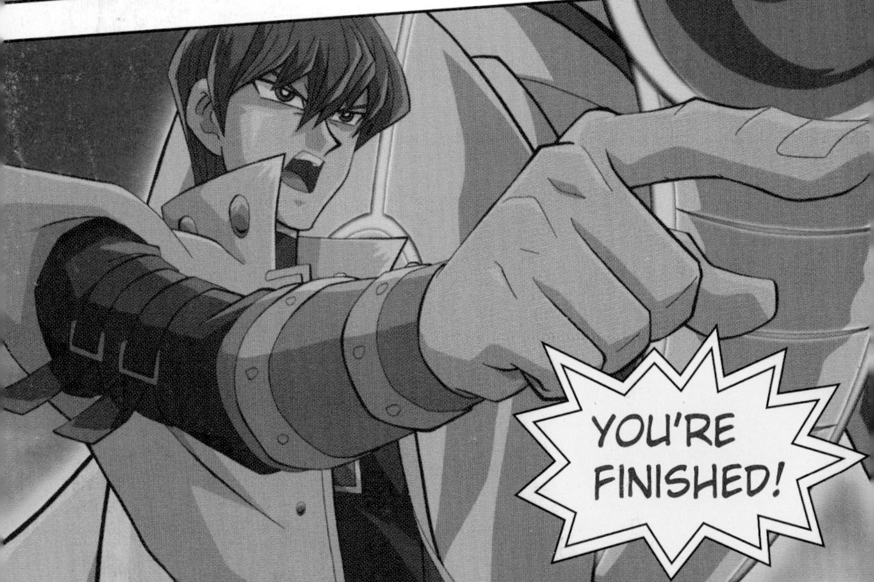
YOU'RE FINISHED!

READ THIS WAY

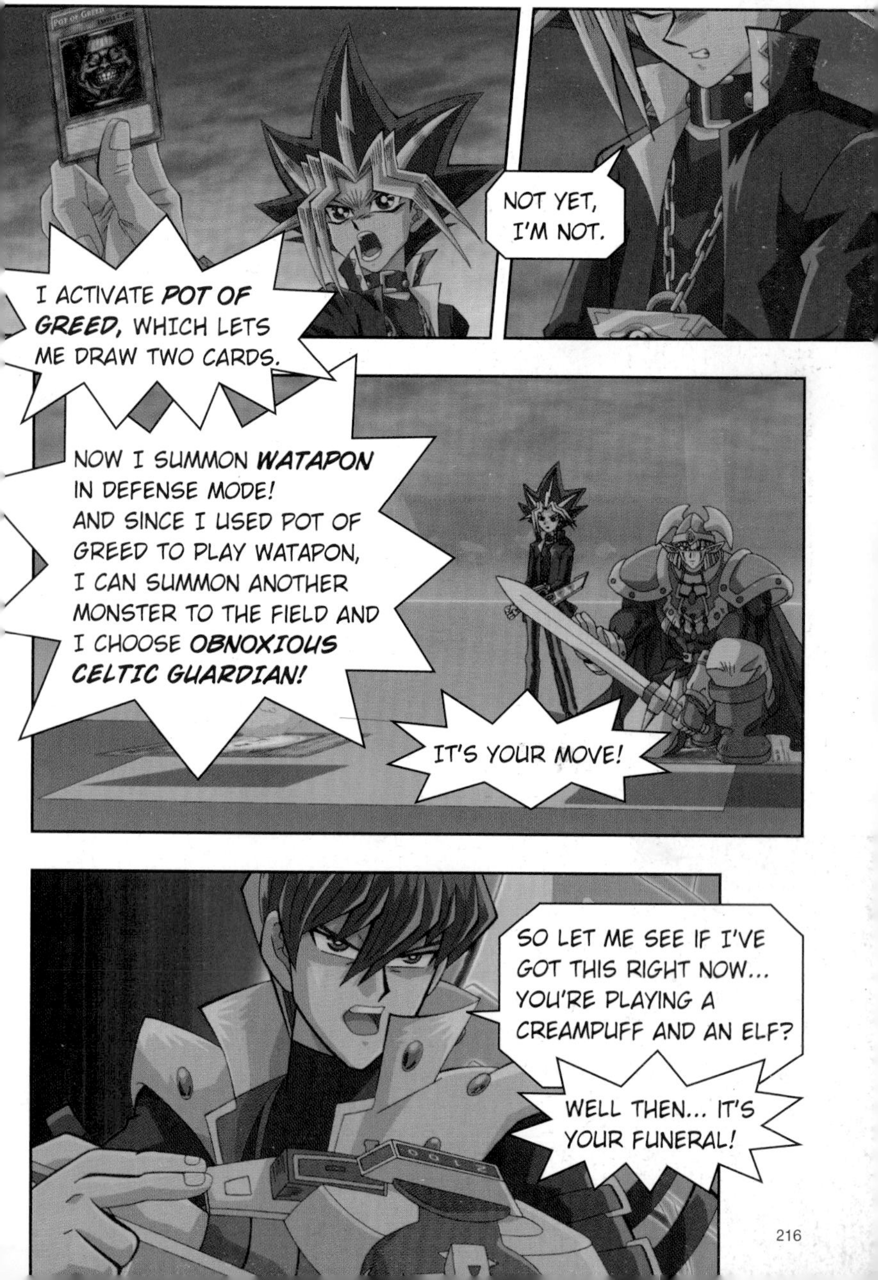
NOT YET, I'M NOT.
I ACTIVATE POT OF GREED, WHICH LETS ME DRAW TWO CARDS.
NOW I SUMMON WATAPON IN DEFENSE MODE! AND SINCE I USED POT OF GREED TO PLAY WATAPON, I CAN SUMMON ANOTHER MONSTER TO THE FIELD AND I CHOOSE OBNOXIOUS CELTIC GUARDIAN!
IT'S YOUR MOVE!
SO LET ME SEE IF I'VE GOT THIS RIGHT NOW... YOU'RE PLAYING A CREAMPUFF AND AN ELF?
WELL THEN... IT'S YOUR FUNERAL!

READ THIS WAY

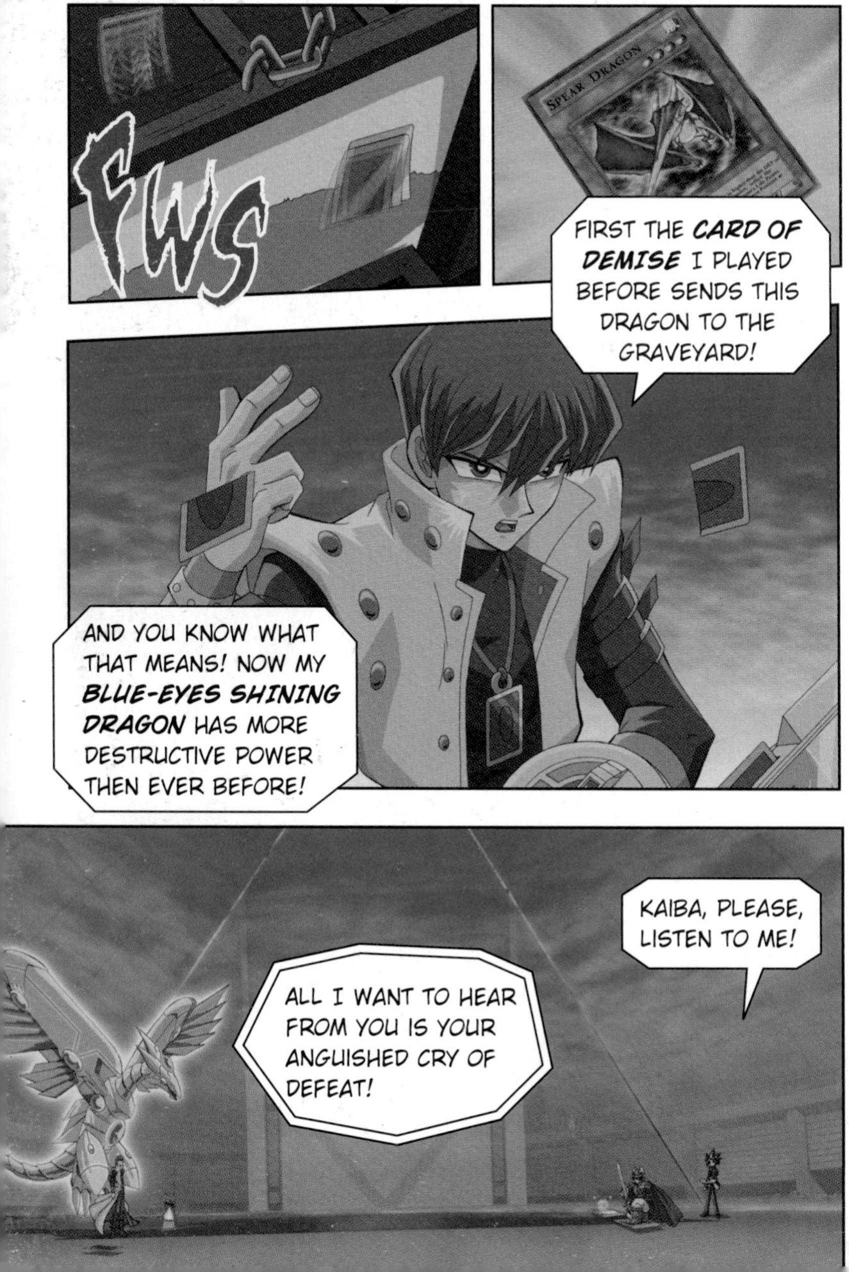
SPEAR DRAGON
FIRST THE ***CARD OF DEMISE*** I PLAYED BEFORE SENDS THIS DRAGON TO THE GRAVEYARD!
FWS
AND YOU KNOW WHAT THAT MEANS! NOW MY ***BLUE-EYES SHINING DRAGON*** HAS MORE DESTRUCTIVE POWER THEN EVER BEFORE!
KAIBA, PLEASE, LISTEN TO ME!
ALL I WANT TO HEAR FROM YOU IS YOUR ANGUISHED CRY OF DEFEAT!

READ THIS WAY

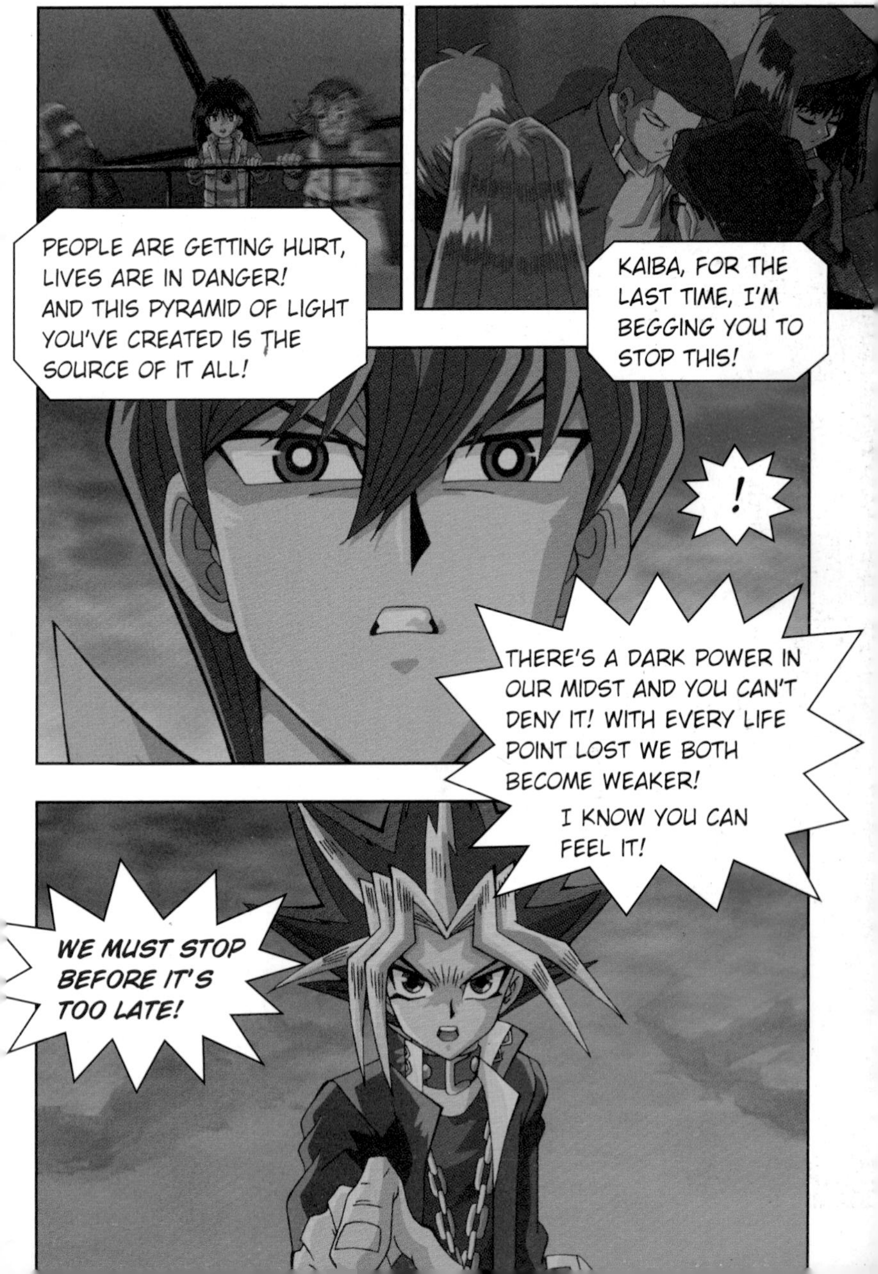
KAIBA, FOR THE LAST TIME, I'M BEGGING YOU TO STOP THIS!
PEOPLE ARE GETTING HURT, LIVES ARE IN DANGER! AND THIS PYRAMID OF LIGHT YOU'VE CREATED IS THE SOURCE OF IT ALL!
!
THERE'S A DARK POWER IN OUR MIDST AND YOU CAN'T DENY IT! WITH EVERY LIFE POINT LOST WE BOTH BECOME WEAKER!
I KNOW YOU CAN FEEL IT!
WE MUST STOP BEFORE IT'S TOO LATE!

READ THIS WAY

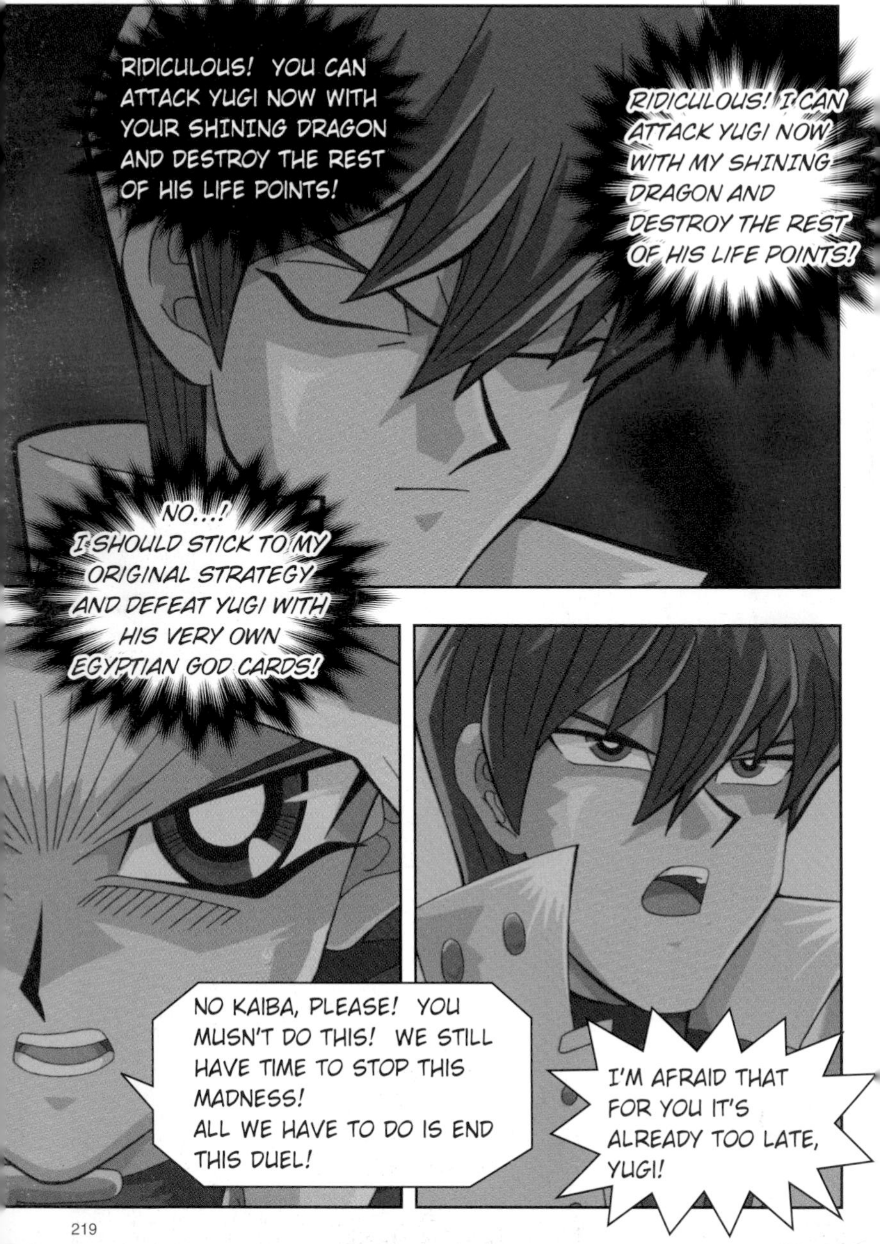
RIDICULOUS! I CAN ATTACK YUGI NOW WITH MY SHINING DRAGON AND DESTROY THE REST OF HIS LIFE POINTS!
RIDICULOUS! YOU CAN ATTACK YUGI NOW WITH YOUR SHINING DRAGON AND DESTROY THE REST OF HIS LIFE POINTS!
NO...! I SHOULD STICK TO MY ORIGINAL STRATEGY AND DEFEAT YUGI WITH HIS VERY OWN EGYPTIAN GOD CARDS!
I'M AFRAID THAT FOR YOU IT'S ALREADY TOO LATE, YUGI!
NO KAIBA, PLEASE! YOU MUSN'T DO THIS! WE STILL HAVE TIME TO STOP THIS MADNESS! ALL WE HAVE TO DO IS END THIS DUEL!

READ THIS WAY

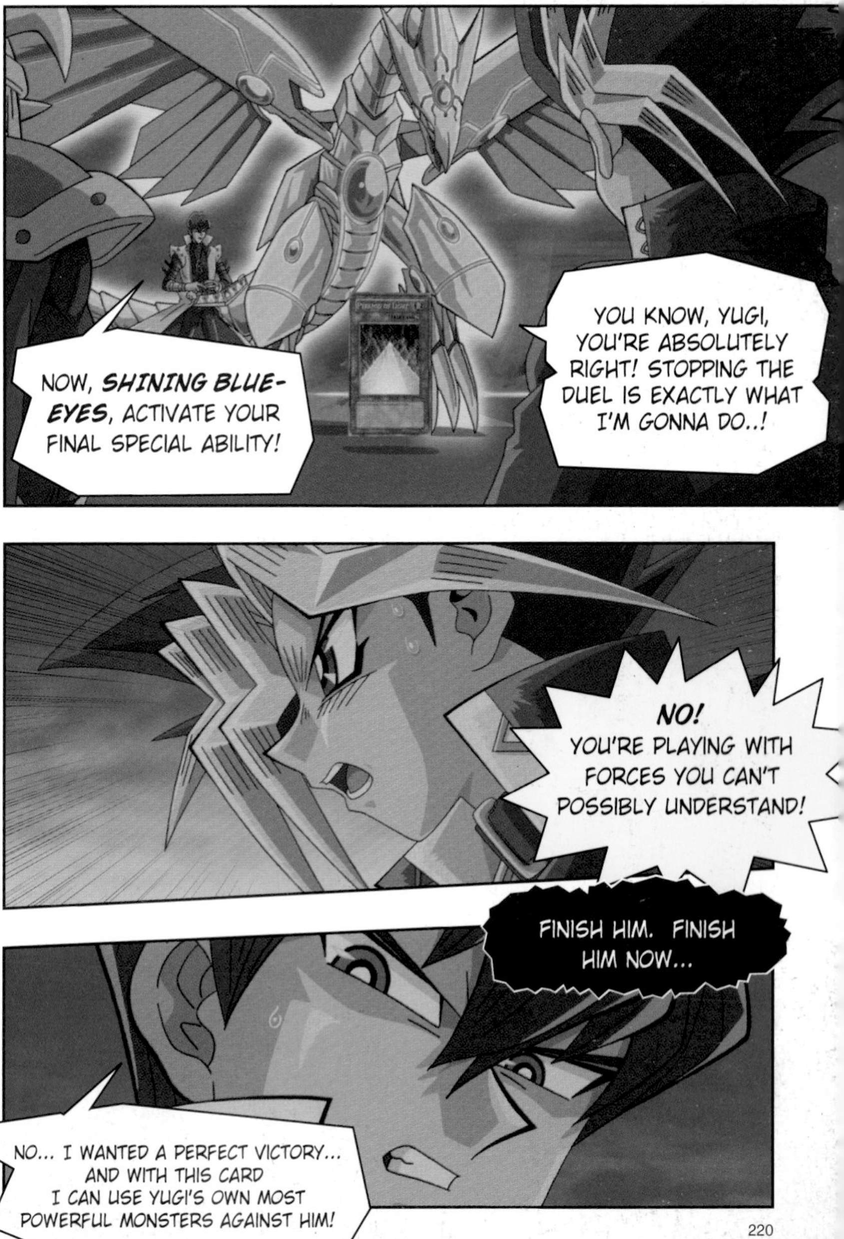

YOU KNOW, YUGI, YOU'RE ABSOLUTELY RIGHT! STOPPING THE DUEL IS EXACTLY WHAT I'M GONNA DO..!
NOW, ***SHINING BLUE-EYES***, ACTIVATE YOUR FINAL SPECIAL ABILITY!
NO! YOU'RE PLAYING WITH FORCES YOU CAN'T POSSIBLY UNDERSTAND!
FINISH HIM. FINISH HIM NOW...
NO... I WANTED A PERFECT VICTORY... AND WITH THIS CARD I CAN USE YUGI'S OWN MOST POWERFUL MONSTERS AGAINST HIM!

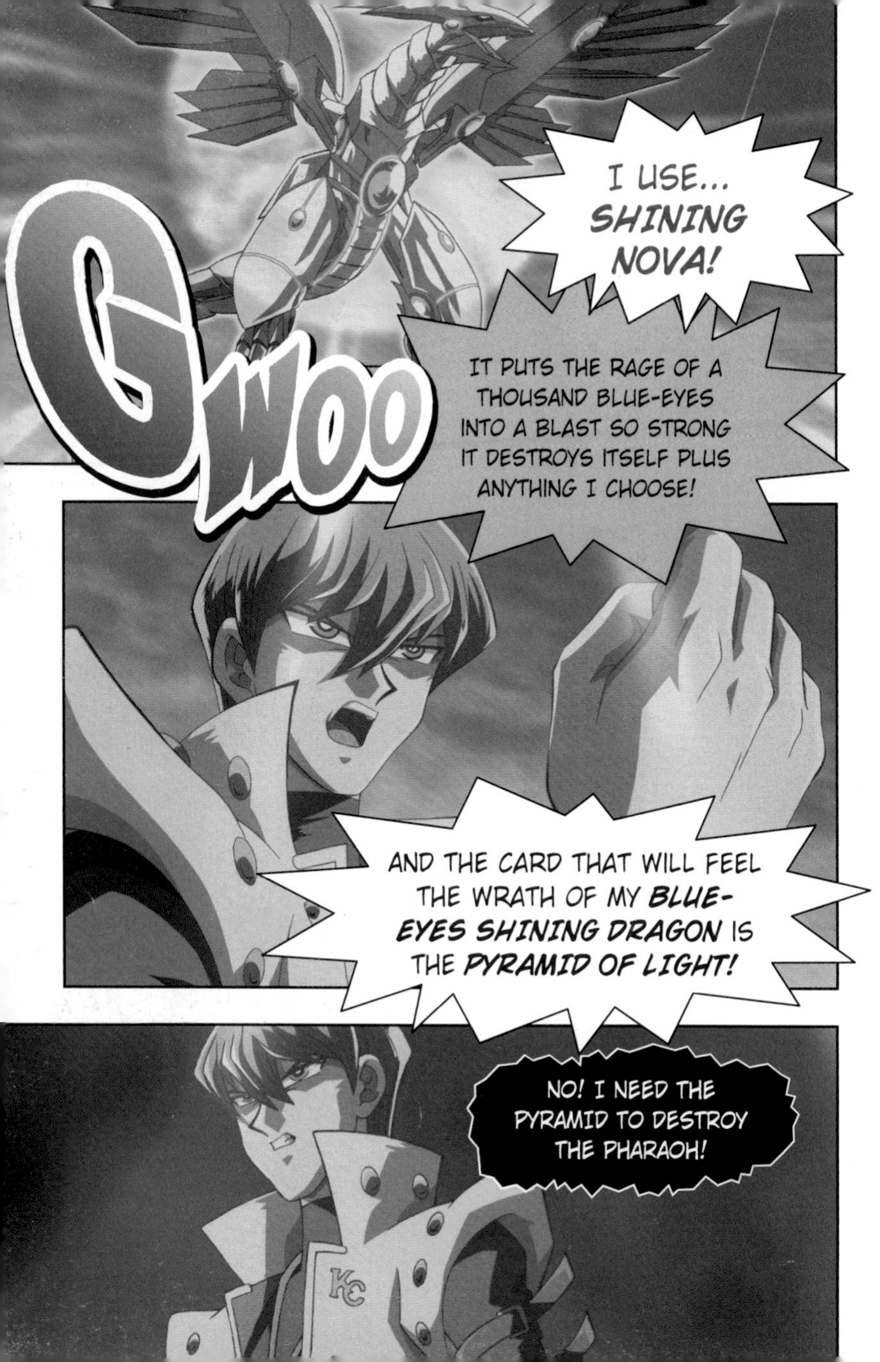
I USE... SHINING NOVA!
GWOO
IT PUTS THE RAGE OF A THOUSAND BLUE-EYES INTO A BLAST SO STRONG IT DESTROYS ITSELF PLUS ANYTHING I CHOOSE!
AND THE CARD THAT WILL FEEL THE WRATH OF MY BLUE-EYES SHINING DRAGON IS THE PYRAMID OF LIGHT!
NO! I NEED THE PYRAMID TO DESTROY THE PHARAOH!
KC

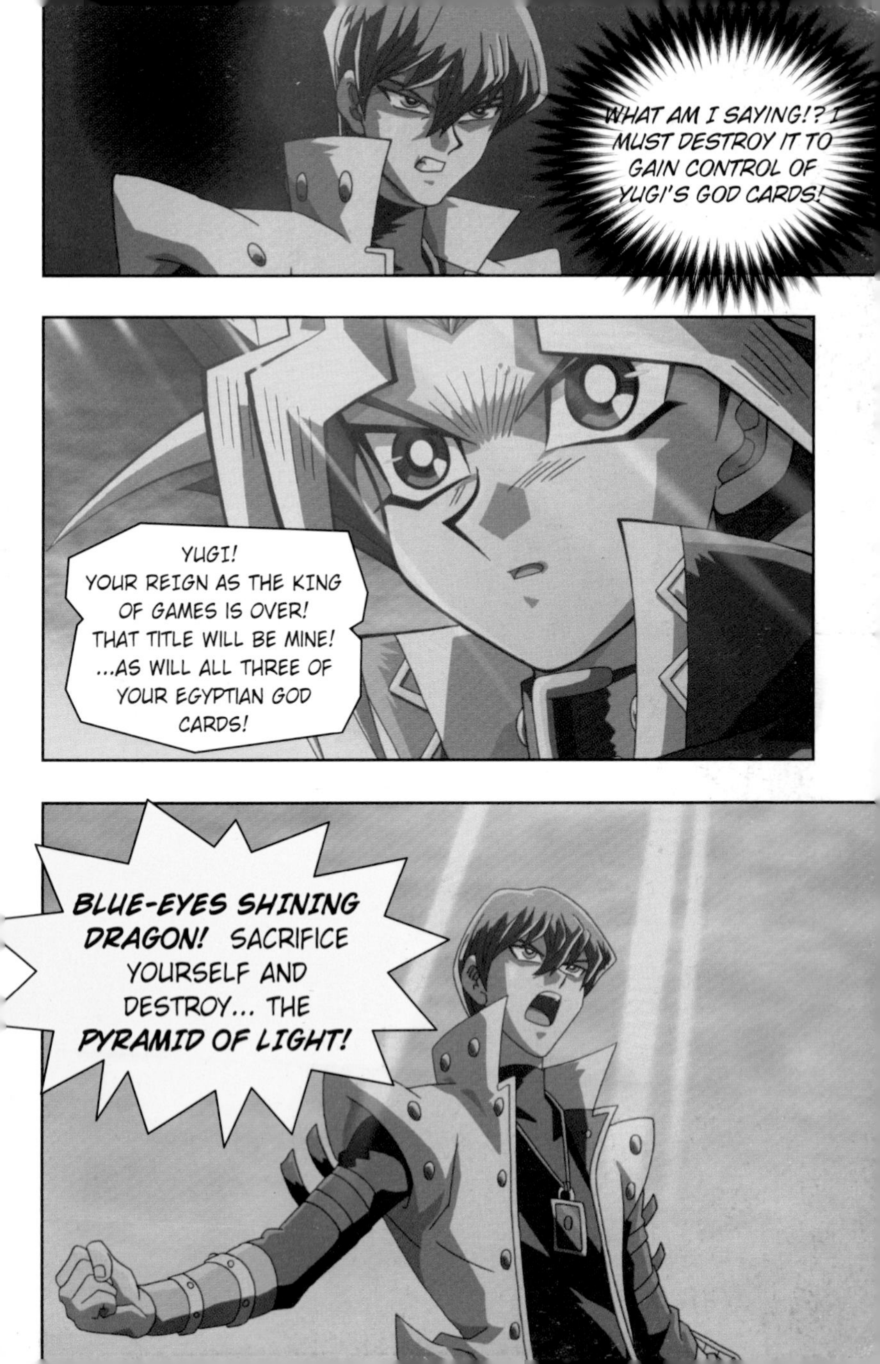
WHAT AM I SAYING!? I MUST DESTROY IT TO GAIN CONTROL OF YUGI'S GOD CARDS!
YUGI! YOUR REIGN AS THE KING OF GAMES IS OVER! THAT TITLE WILL BE MINE! ...AS WILL ALL THREE OF YOUR EGYPTIAN GOD CARDS!
BLUE-EYES SHINING DRAGON! SACRIFICE YOURSELF AND DESTROY... THE PYRAMID OF LIGHT!

READ THIS WAY

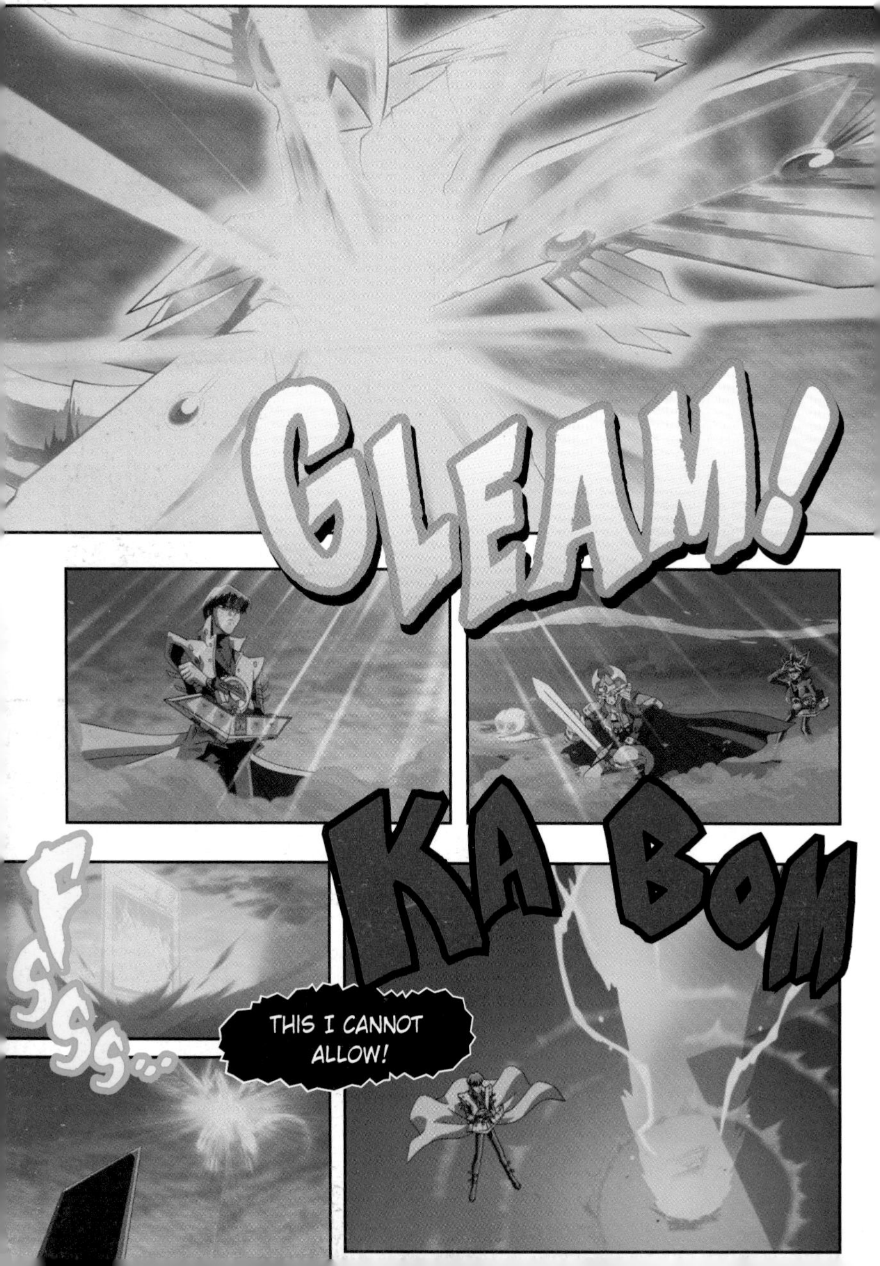
GLEAM!
KA BOM
THIS I CANNOT ALLOW!
FSSS...

READ THIS WAY

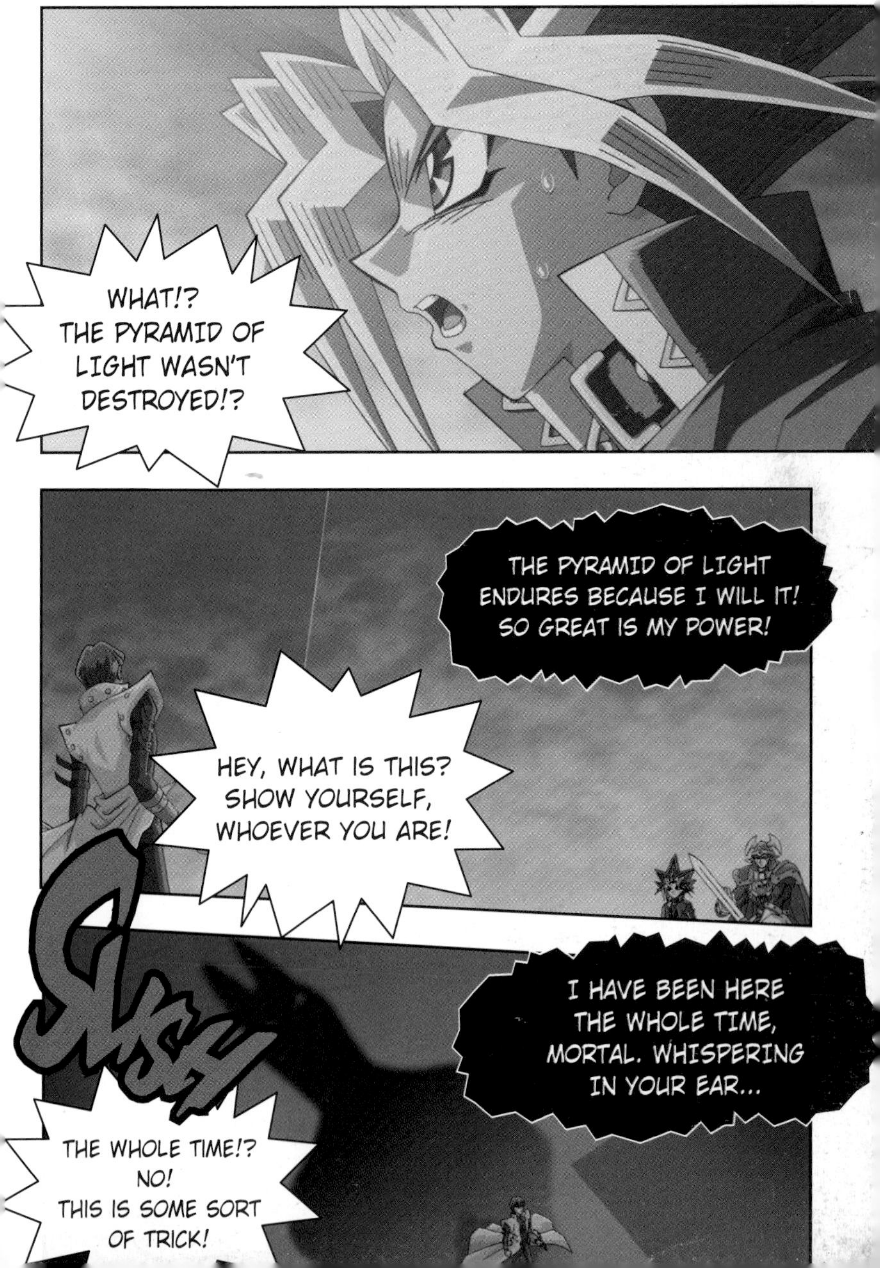
WHAT!? THE PYRAMID OF LIGHT WASN'T DESTROYED!?
THE PYRAMID OF LIGHT ENDURES BECAUSE I WILL IT! SO GREAT IS MY POWER!
HEY, WHAT IS THIS? SHOW YOURSELF, WHOEVER YOU ARE!
I HAVE BEEN HERE THE WHOLE TIME, MORTAL. WHISPERING IN YOUR EAR...
THE WHOLE TIME!? NO! THIS IS SOME SORT OF TRICK!

READ THIS WAY

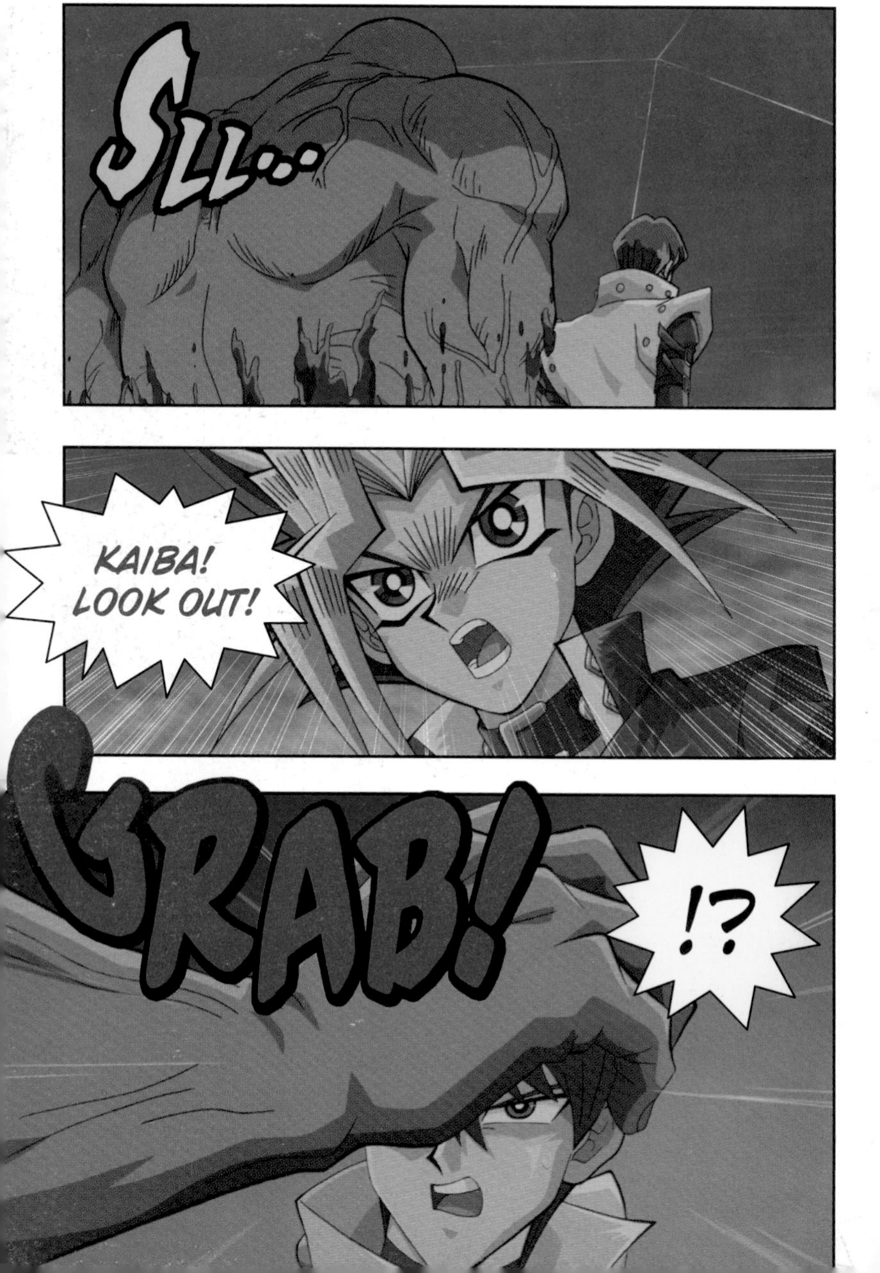
SLL...
KAIBA! LOOK OUT!
GRAB!
!?

READ THIS WAY

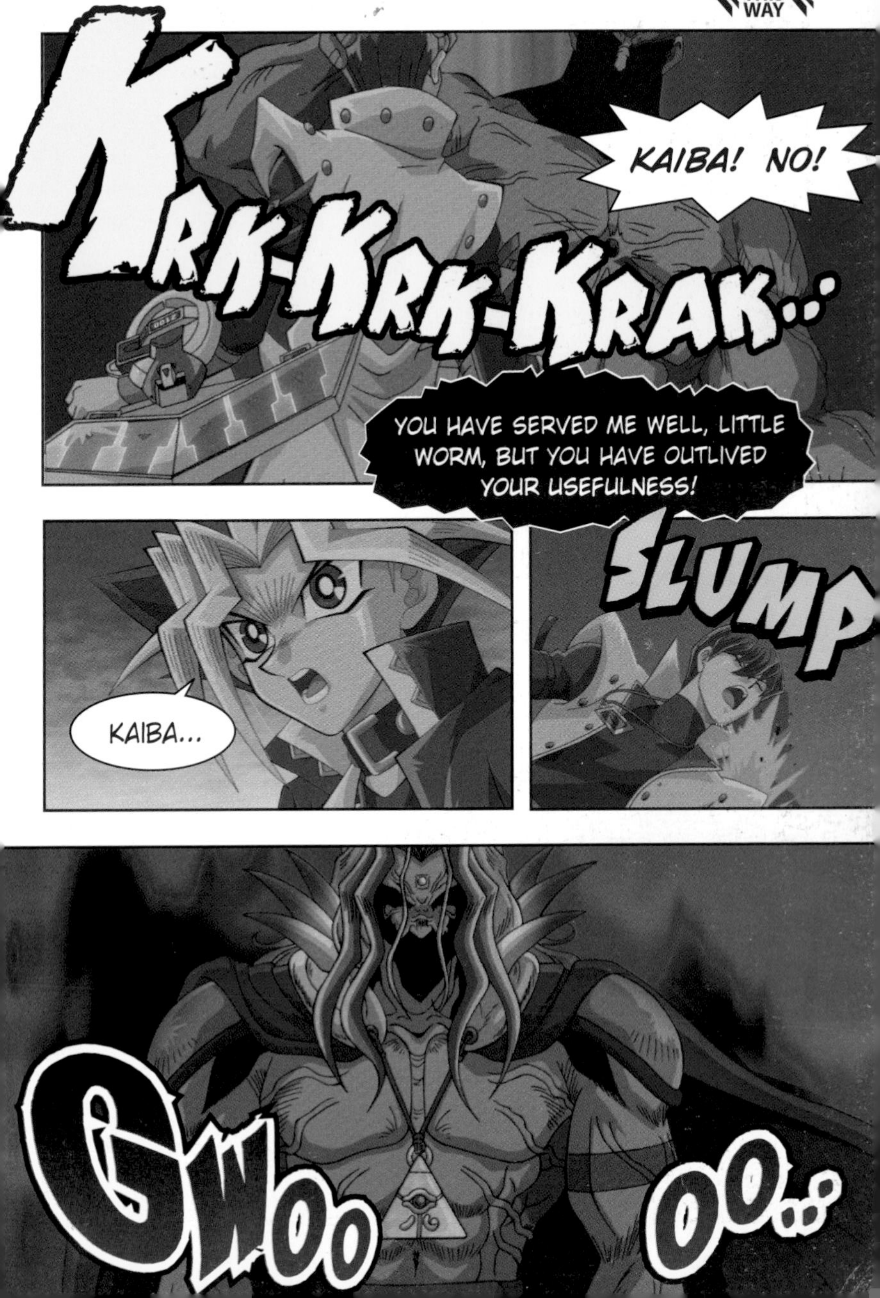
KAIBA! NO!
KRK-KRK-KRAK...
YOU HAVE SERVED ME WELL, LITTLE WORM, BUT YOU HAVE OUTLIVED YOUR USEFULNESS!
SLUMP
KAIBA...
GWOO OO...

READ THIS WAY

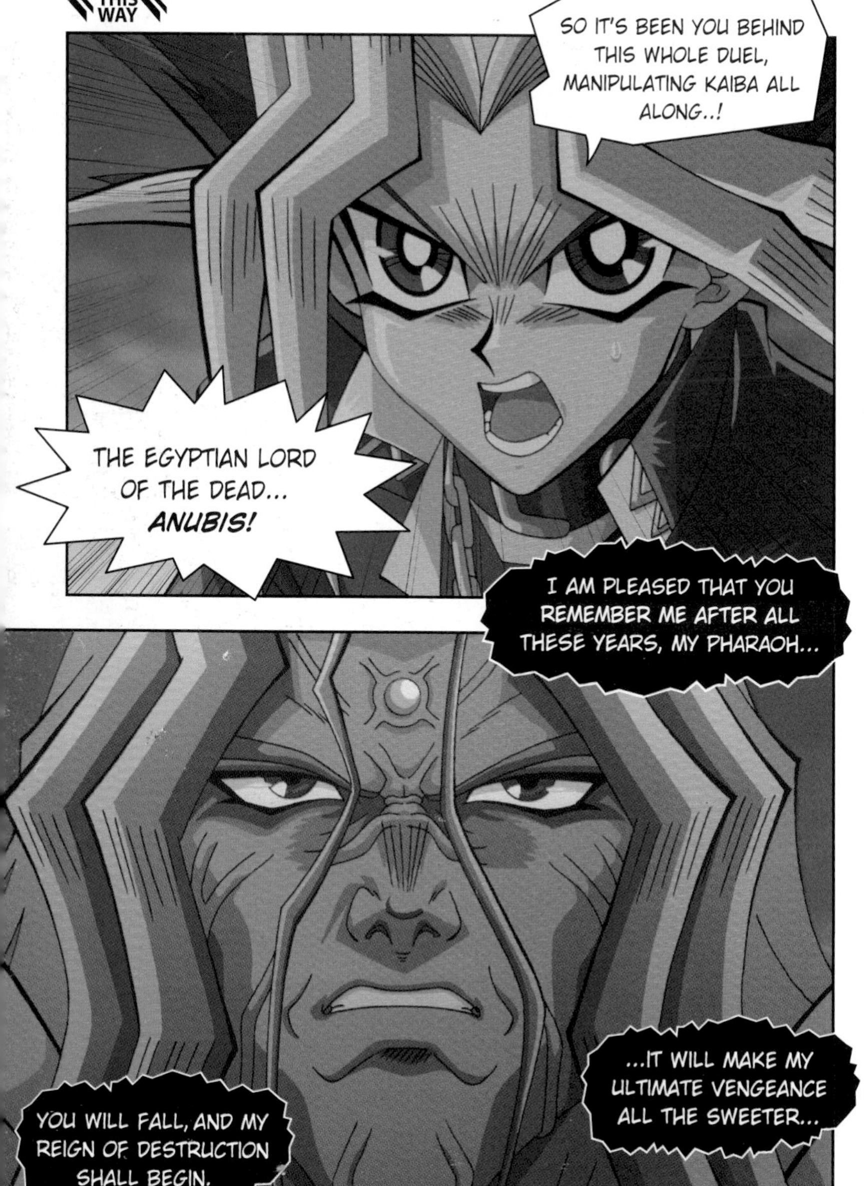

SO IT'S BEEN YOU BEHIND THIS WHOLE DUEL, MANIPULATING KAIBA ALL ALONG..!
THE EGYPTIAN LORD OF THE DEAD... *ANUBIS!*
I AM PLEASED THAT YOU REMEMBER ME AFTER ALL THESE YEARS, MY PHARAOH...
...IT WILL MAKE MY ULTIMATE VENGEANCE ALL THE SWEETER...
YOU WILL FALL, AND MY REIGN OF DESTRUCTION SHALL BEGIN.

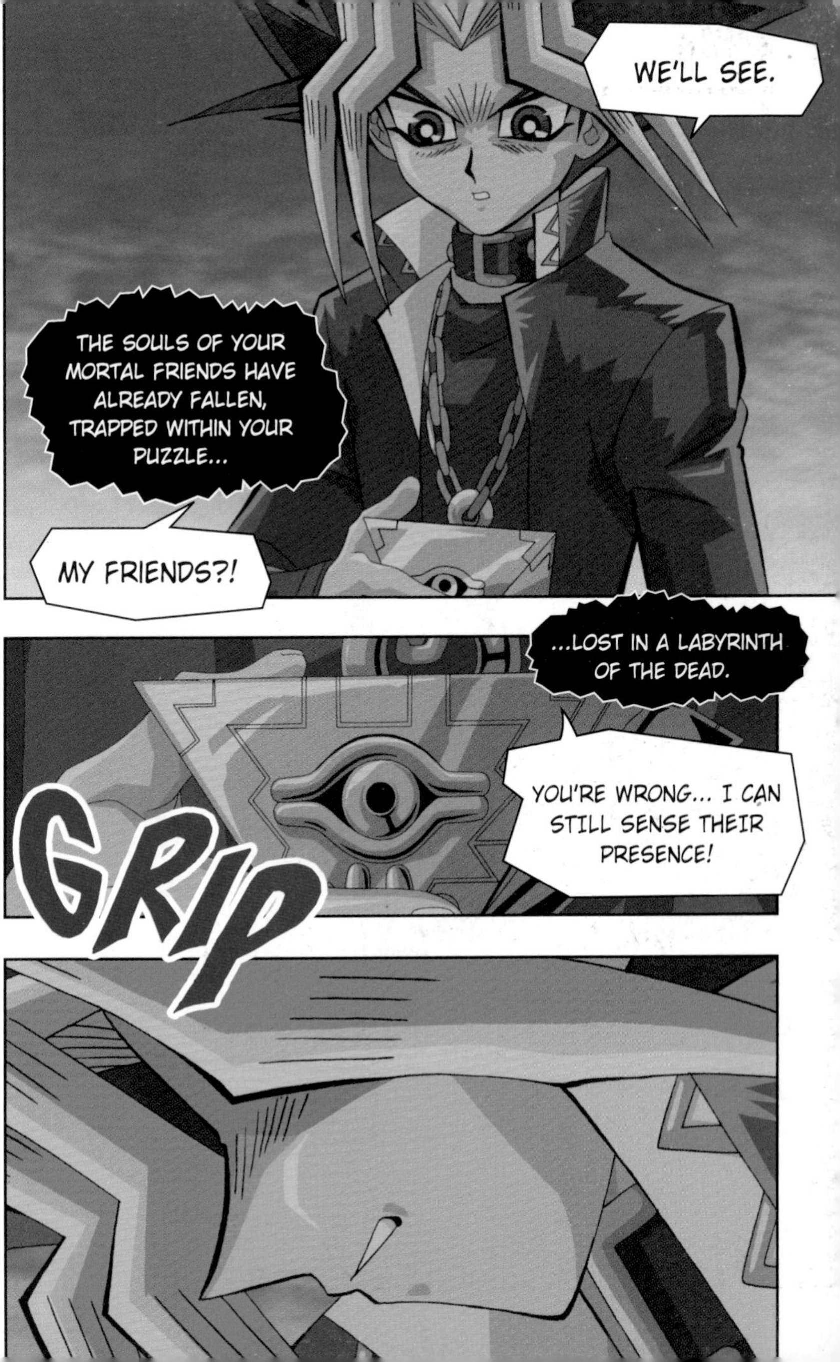
WE'LL SEE.
THE SOULS OF YOUR MORTAL FRIENDS HAVE ALREADY FALLEN, TRAPPED WITHIN YOUR PUZZLE...
MY FRIENDS?!
...LOST IN A LABYRINTH OF THE DEAD.
YOU'RE WRONG... I CAN STILL SENSE THEIR PRESENCE!
GRIP

READ THIS WAY

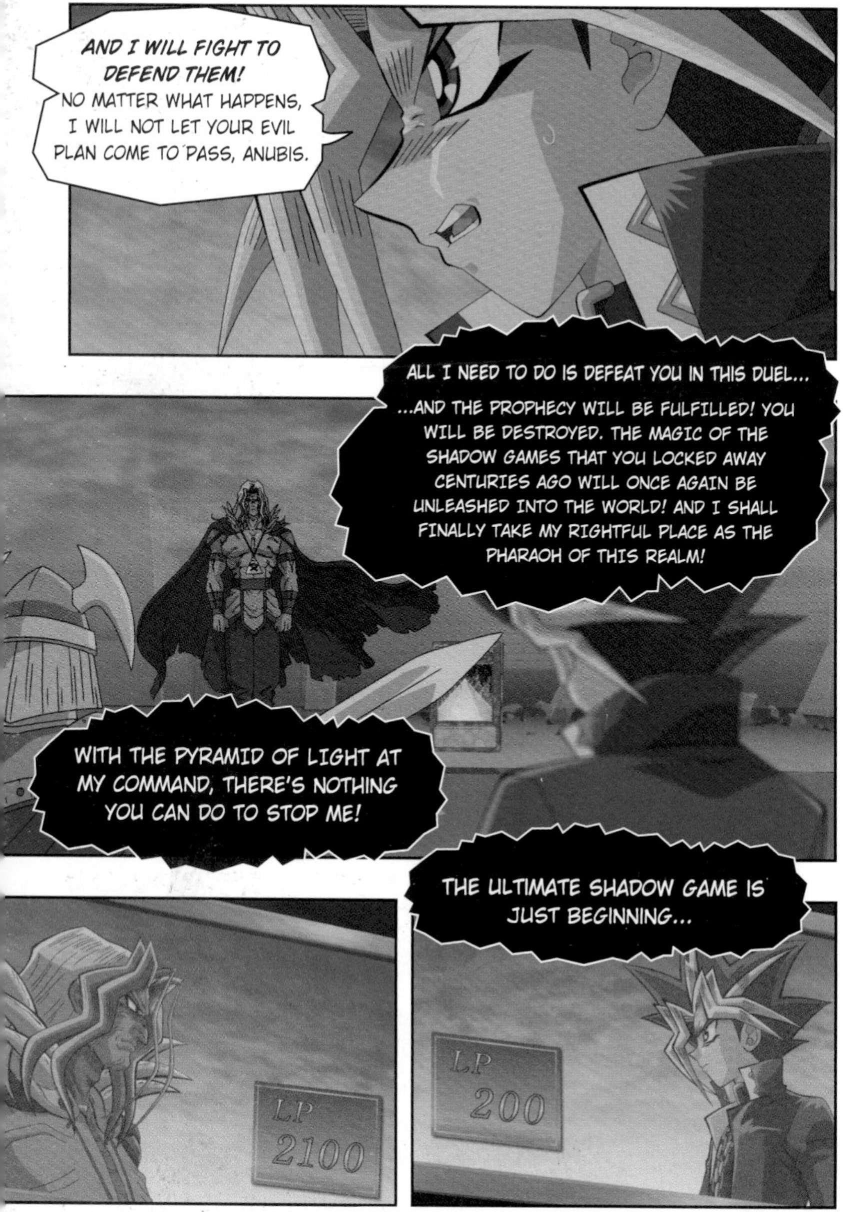

AND I WILL FIGHT TO DEFEND THEM! NO MATTER WHAT HAPPENS, I WILL NOT LET YOUR EVIL PLAN COME TO PASS, ANUBIS.
ALL I NEED TO DO IS DEFEAT YOU IN THIS DUEL...
...AND THE PROPHECY WILL BE FULFILLED! YOU WILL BE DESTROYED. THE MAGIC OF THE SHADOW GAMES THAT YOU LOCKED AWAY CENTURIES AGO WILL ONCE AGAIN BE UNLEASHED INTO THE WORLD! AND I SHALL FINALLY TAKE MY RIGHTFUL PLACE AS THE PHARAOH OF THIS REALM!
WITH THE PYRAMID OF LIGHT AT MY COMMAND, THERE'S NOTHING YOU CAN DO TO STOP ME!
THE ULTIMATE SHADOW GAME IS JUST BEGINNING...
LP 200
LP 2100

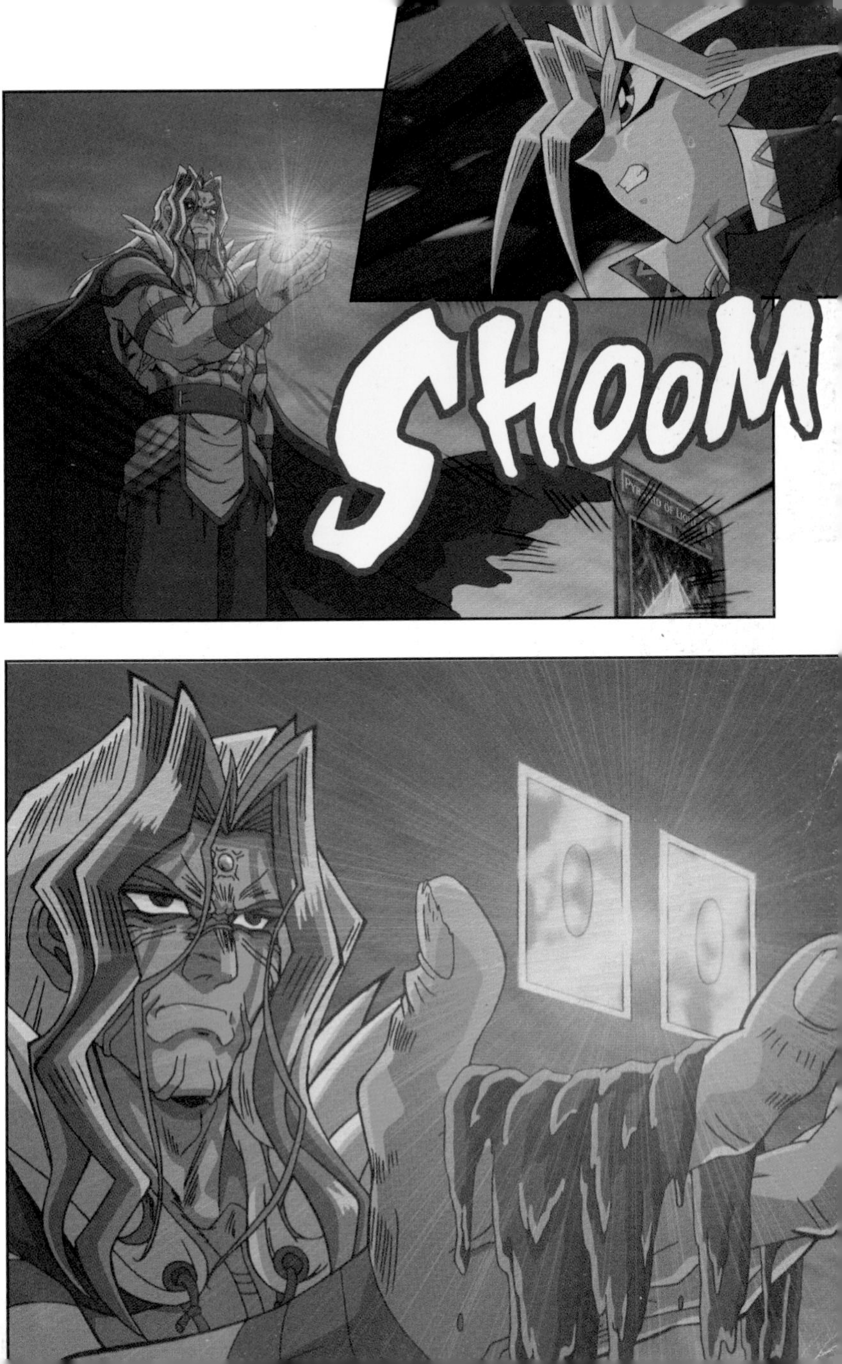
SHOOM

READ THIS WAY

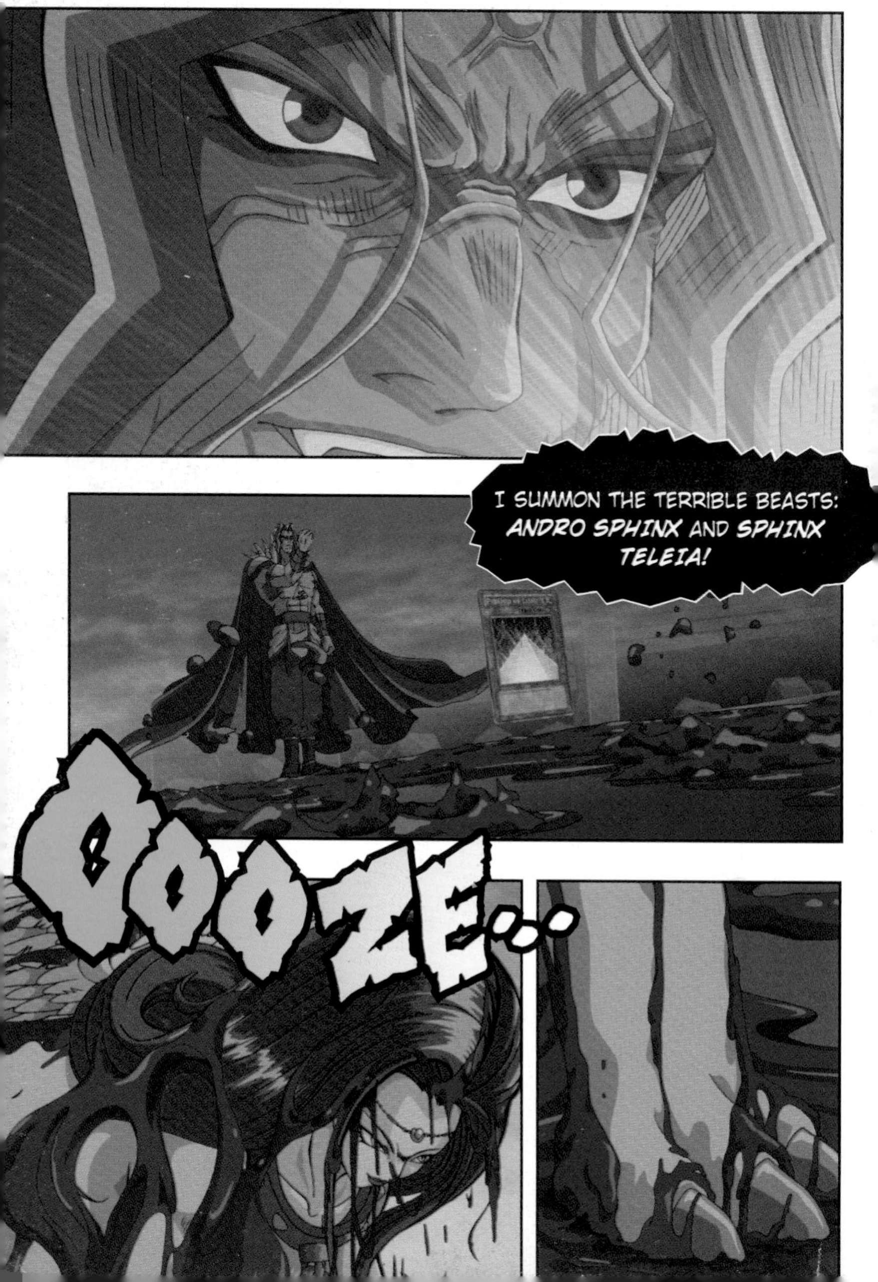
I SUMMON THE TERRIBLE BEASTS: ANDRO SPHINX AND SPHINX TELEIA!
OOOZE...

READ THIS WAY

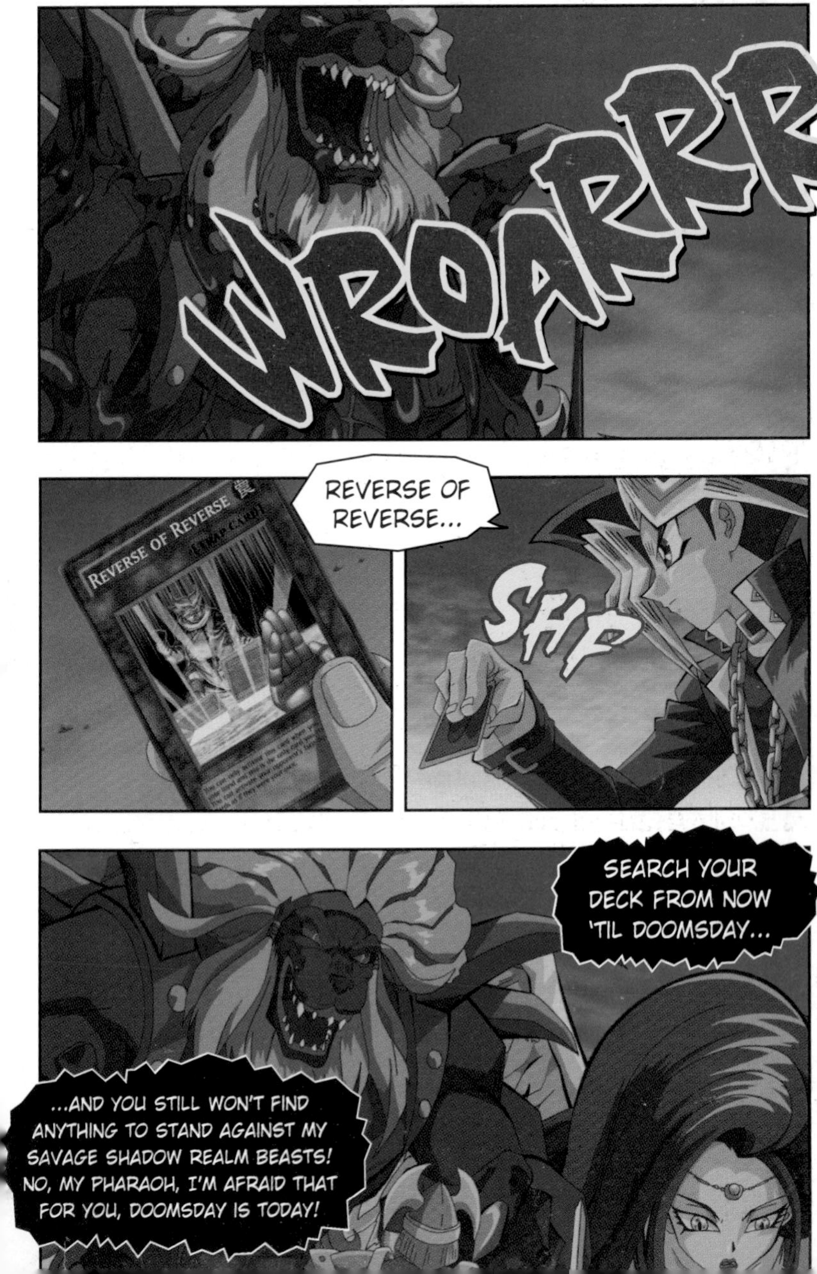
WROARRR
REVERSE OF REVERSE...
SHIP
REVERSE OF REVERSE
SEARCH YOUR DECK FROM NOW 'TIL DOOMSDAY...
...AND YOU STILL WON'T FIND ANYTHING TO STAND AGAINST MY SAVAGE SHADOW REALM BEASTS! NO, MY PHARAOH, I'M AFRAID THAT FOR YOU, DOOMSDAY IS TODAY!

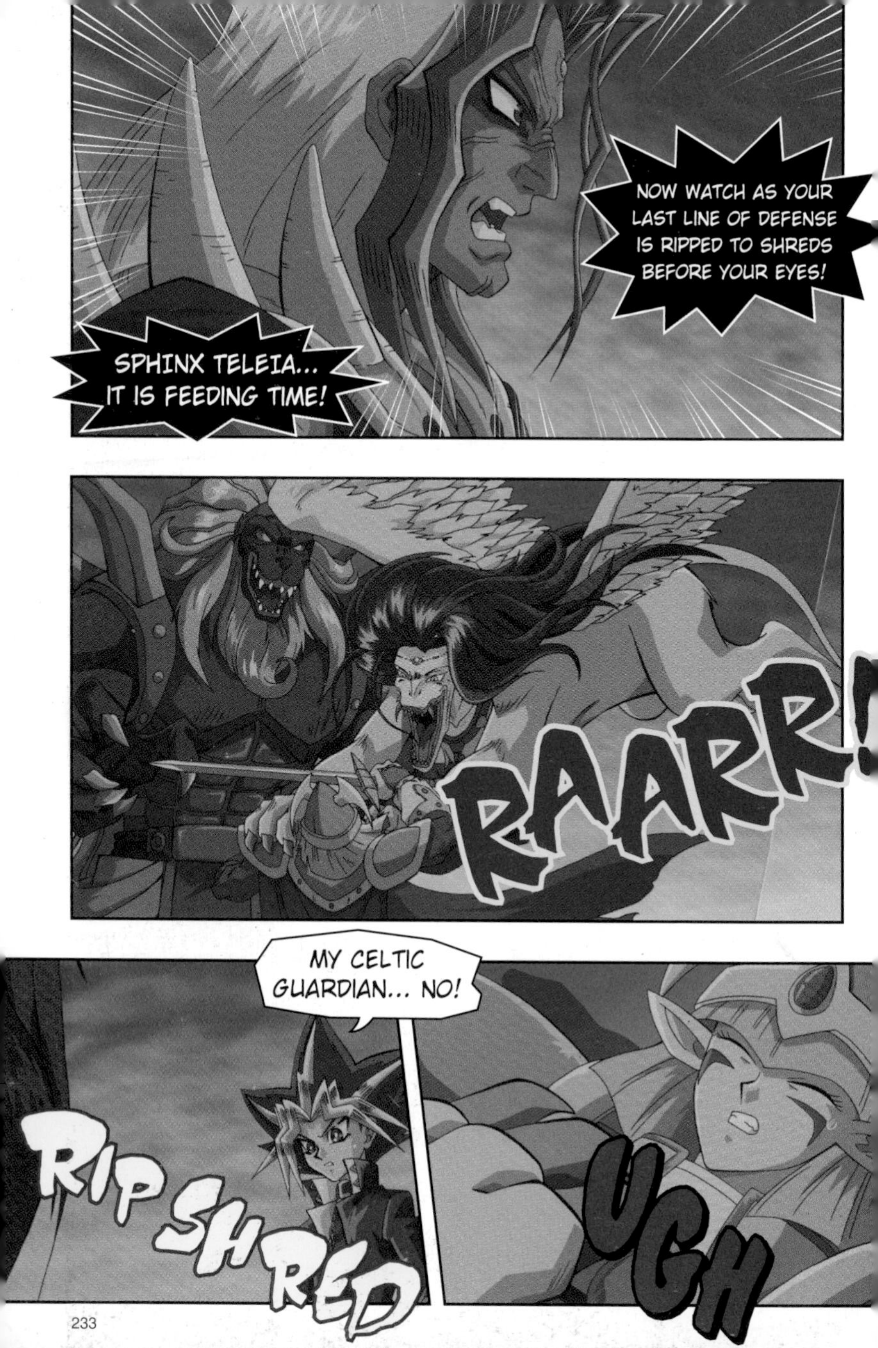
NOW WATCH AS YOUR LAST LINE OF DEFENSE IS RIPPED TO SHREDS BEFORE YOUR EYES!
SPHINX TELEIA... IT IS FEEDING TIME!
RAARR!
UGH
MY CELTIC GUARDIAN... NO!
RIP SHRED

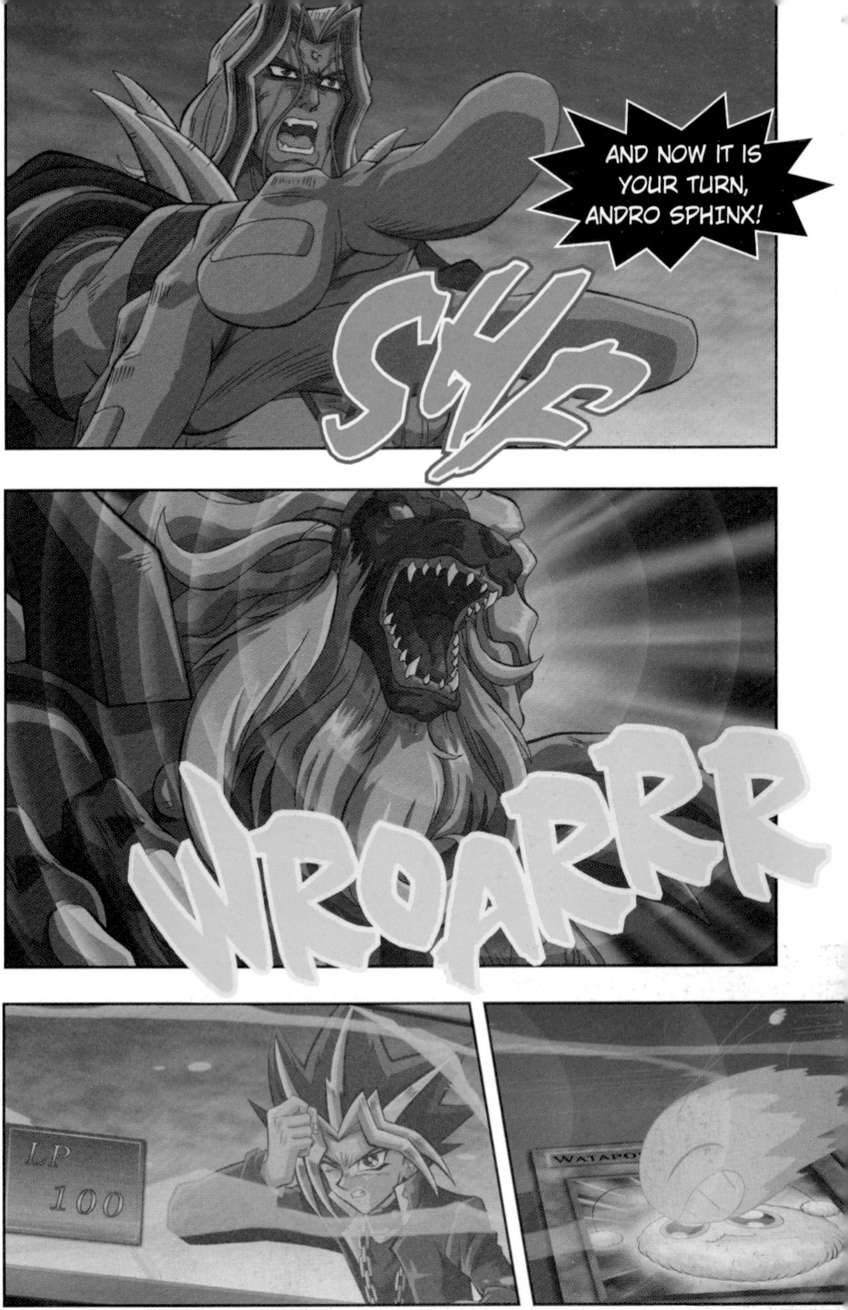
AND NOW IT IS YOUR TURN, ANDRO SPHINX!
WROARRR
LP
100

READ THIS WAY

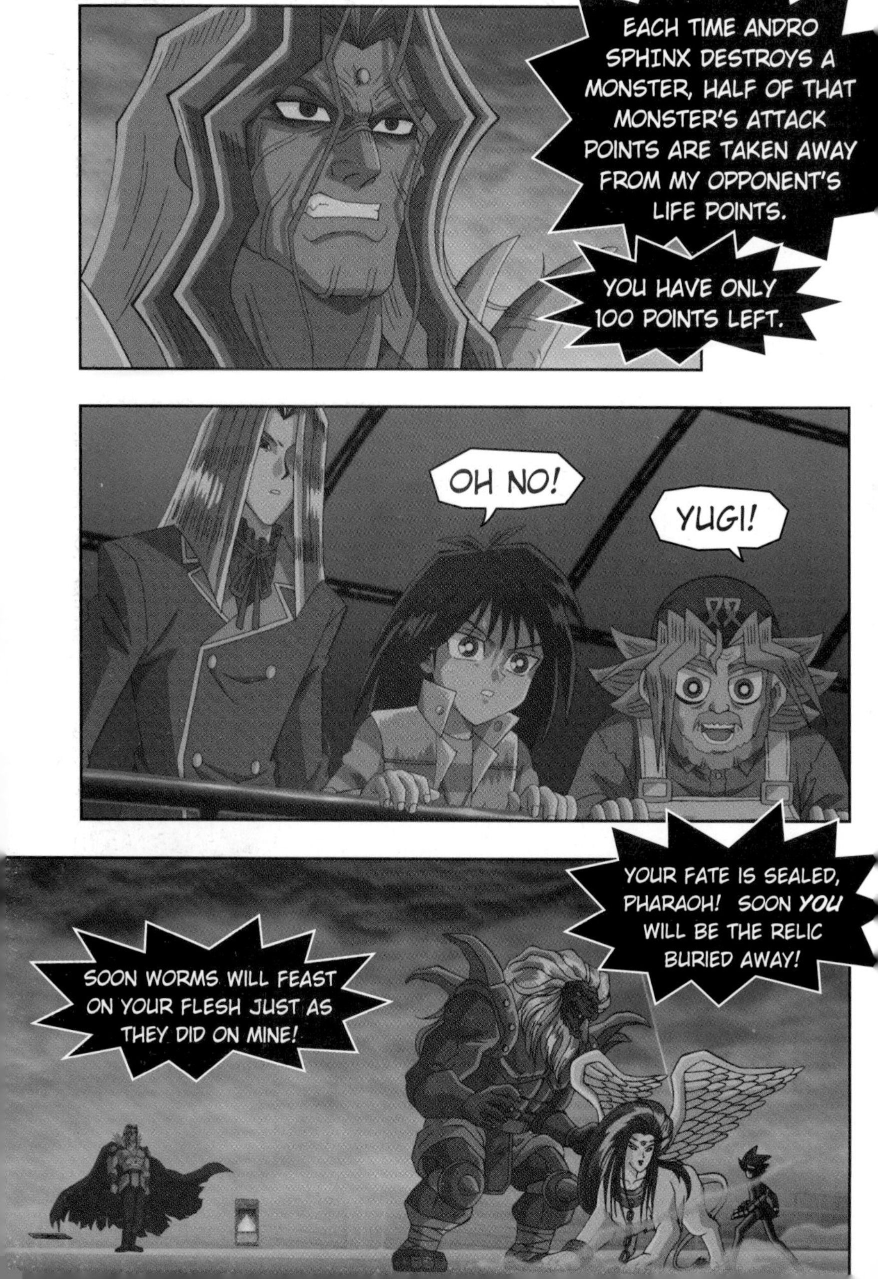
EACH TIME ANDRO SPHINX DESTROYS A MONSTER, HALF OF THAT MONSTER'S ATTACK POINTS ARE TAKEN AWAY FROM MY OPPONENT'S LIFE POINTS.
YOU HAVE ONLY 100 POINTS LEFT.
YUGI!
OH NO!
YOUR FATE IS SEALED, PHARAOH! SOON *YOU* WILL BE THE RELIC BURIED AWAY!
SOON WORMS WILL FEAST ON YOUR FLESH JUST AS THEY DID ON MINE!

READ THIS WAY

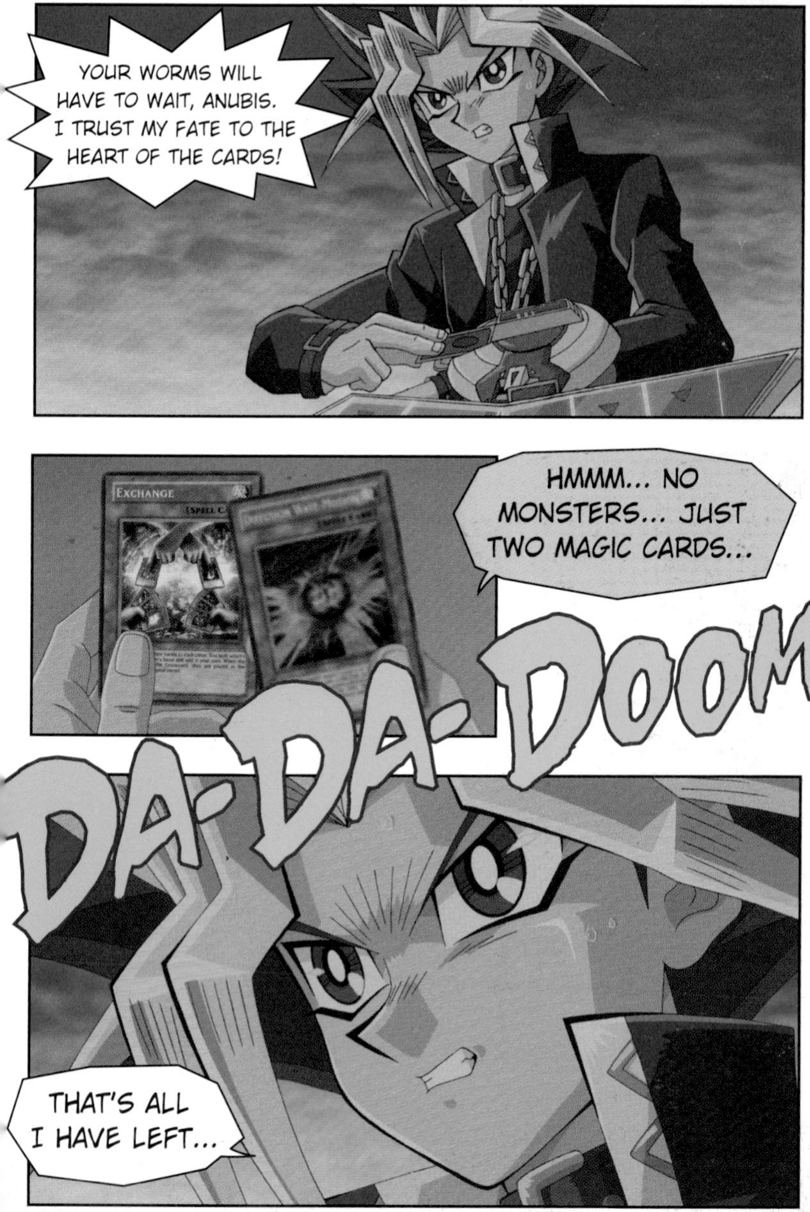
YOUR WORMS WILL HAVE TO WAIT, ANUBIS. I TRUST MY FATE TO THE HEART OF THE CARDS!
HMMM... NO MONSTERS... JUST TWO MAGIC CARDS...
EXCHANGE
DA-DA-DOOM
THAT'S ALL I HAVE LEFT...

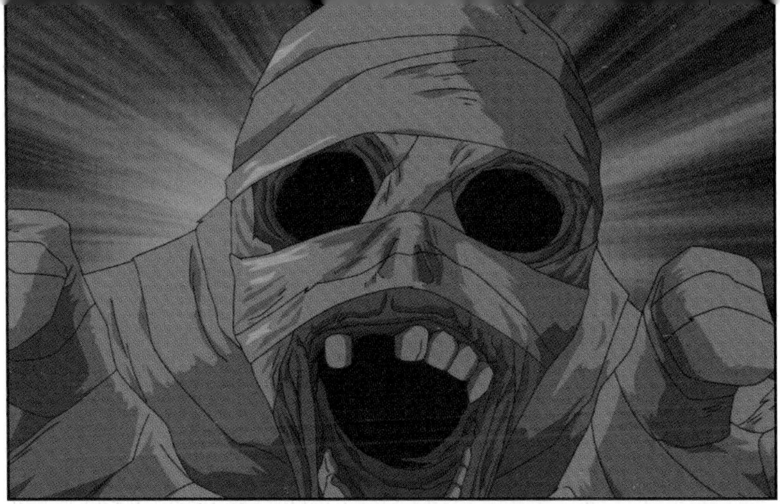

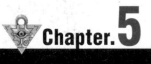

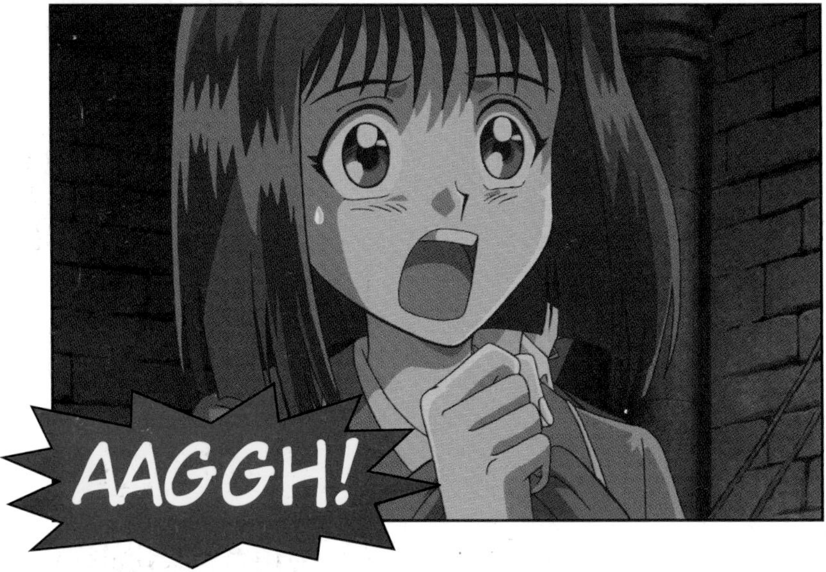
AAGGH!

Chapter. 5
Shining Nova

READ THIS WAY

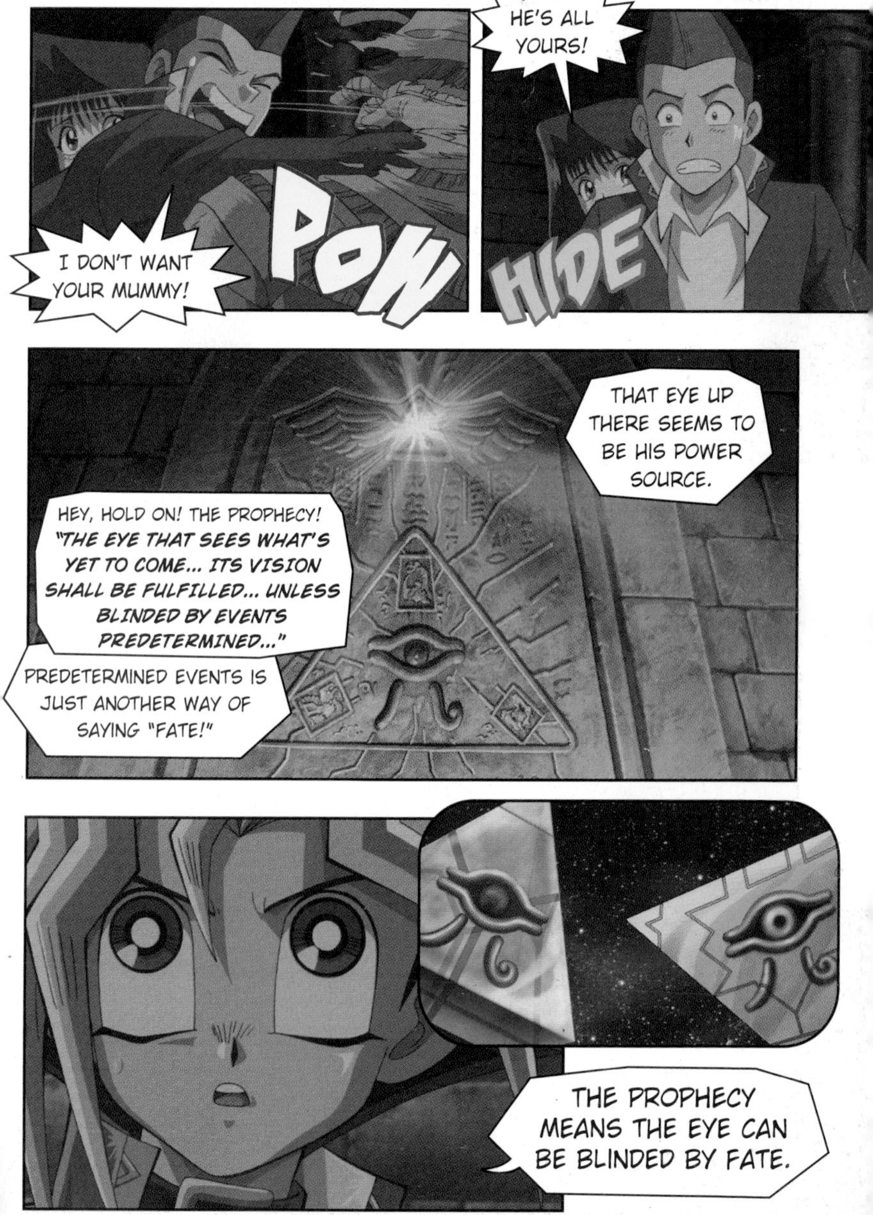

HE'S ALL YOURS!
HIDE
I DON'T WANT YOUR MUMMY!
POW
THAT EYE UP THERE SEEMS TO BE HIS POWER SOURCE.
HEY, HOLD ON! THE PROPHECY! *"THE EYE THAT SEES WHAT'S YET TO COME... ITS VISION SHALL BE FULFILLED... UNLESS BLINDED BY EVENTS PREDETERMINED..."*
PREDETERMINED EVENTS IS JUST ANOTHER WAY OF SAYING "FATE!"
THE PROPHECY MEANS THE EYE CAN BE BLINDED BY FATE.

READ THIS WAY

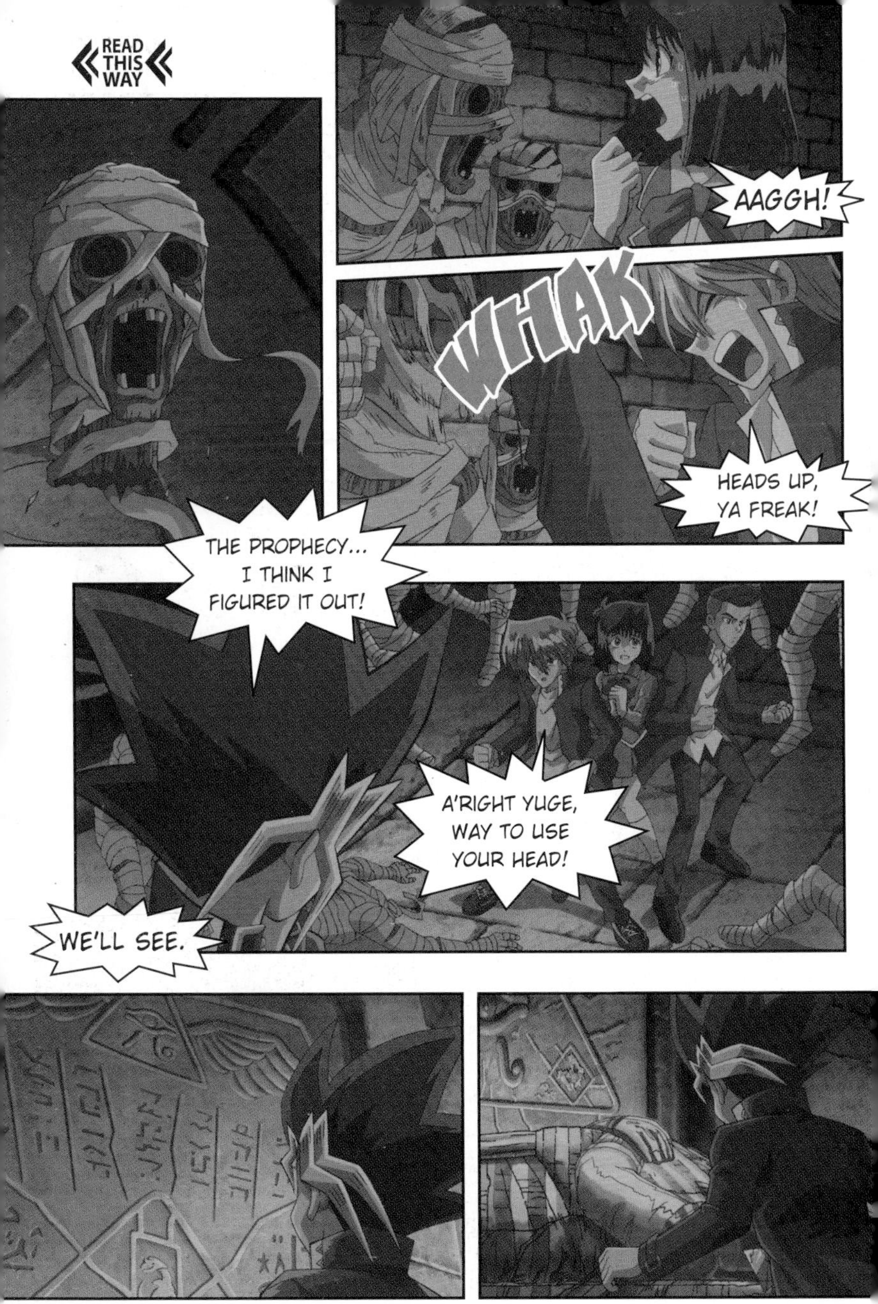

AAGGH!
WHAK
HEADS UP, YA FREAK!
THE PROPHECY... I THINK I FIGURED IT OUT!
A'RIGHT YUGE, WAY TO USE YOUR HEAD!
WE'LL SEE.

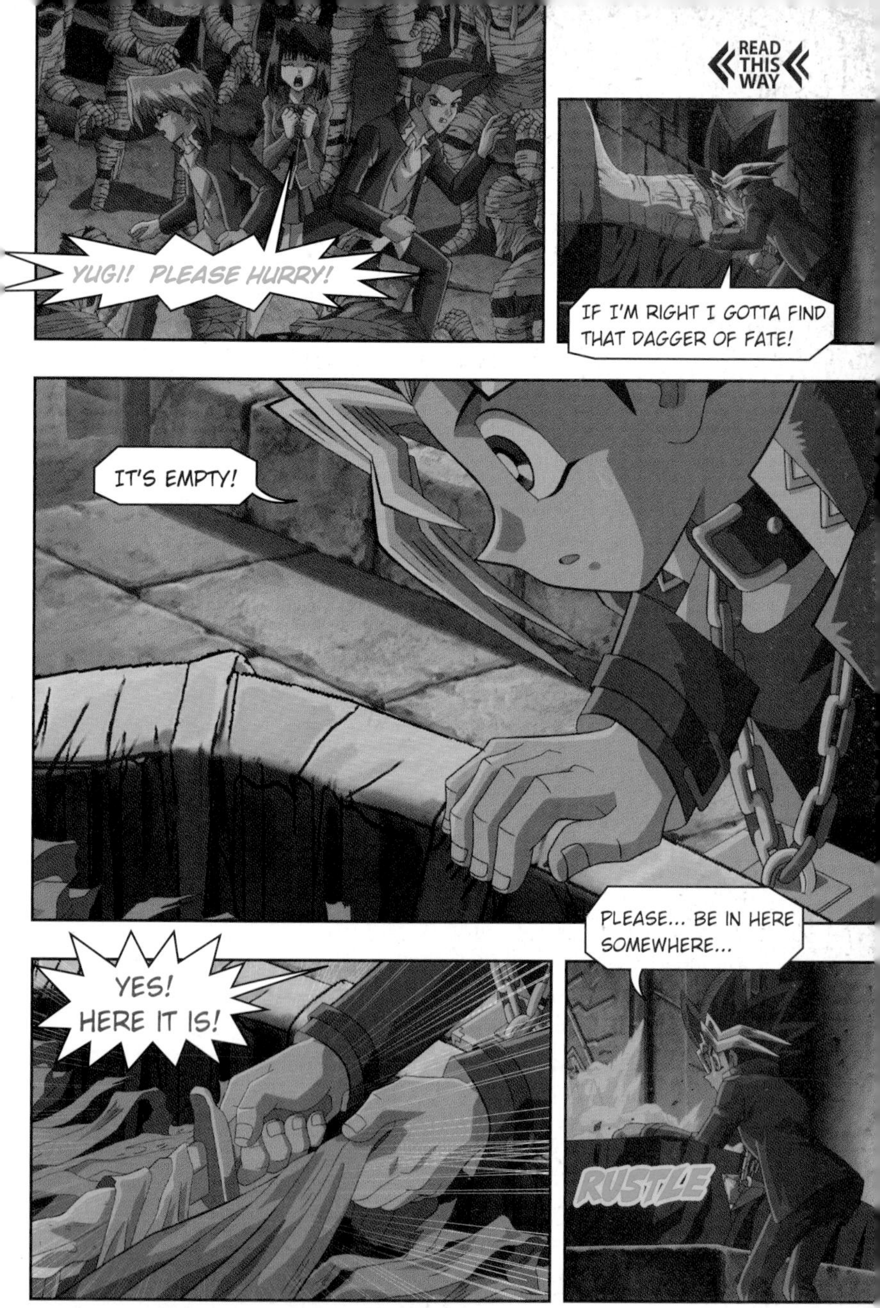
READ THIS WAY
IF I'M RIGHT I GOTTA FIND THAT DAGGER OF FATE!
YUGI! PLEASE HURRY!
IT'S EMPTY!
PLEASE... BE IN HERE SOMEWHERE...
RUSTLE
YES! HERE IT IS!

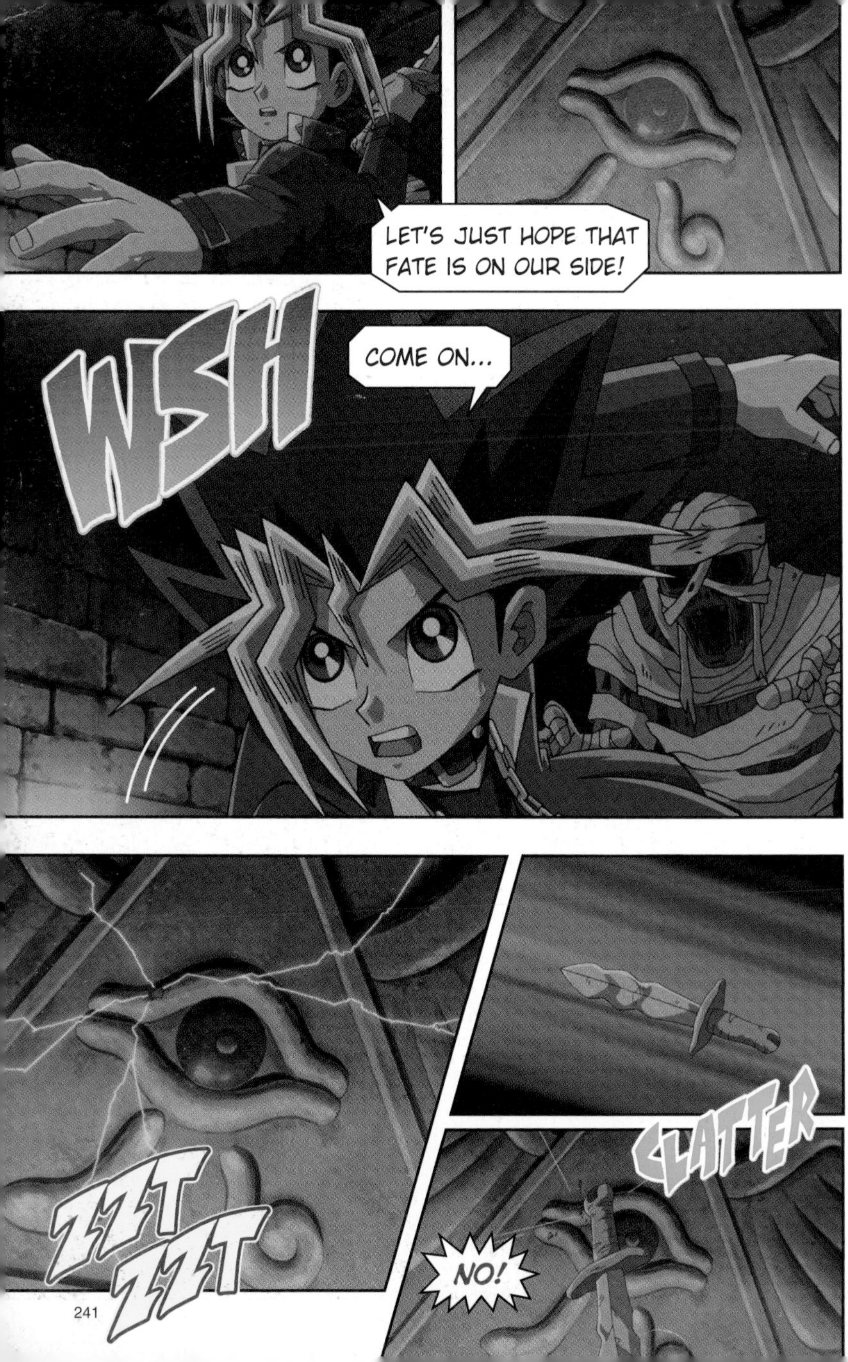
LET'S JUST HOPE THAT FATE IS ON OUR SIDE!
COME ON...
WSH
CLATTER
NO!
ZZT
ZZT

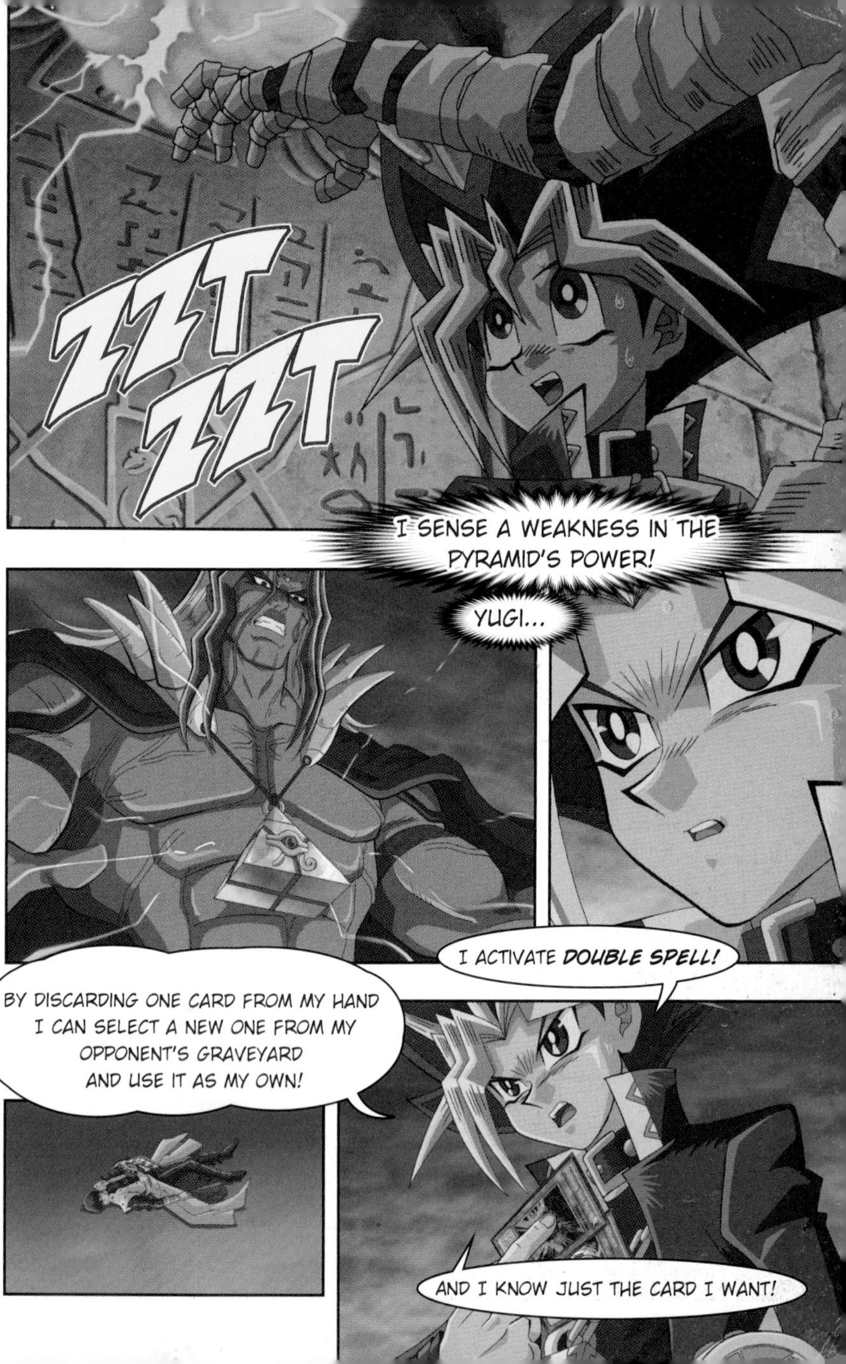
ZZZT
ZZZT
I SENSE A WEAKNESS IN THE PYRAMID'S POWER!
YUGI...
I ACTIVATE **DOUBLE SPELL!**
BY DISCARDING ONE CARD FROM MY HAND I CAN SELECT A NEW ONE FROM MY OPPONENT'S GRAVEYARD AND USE IT AS MY OWN!
AND I KNOW JUST THE CARD I WANT!

READ THIS WAY

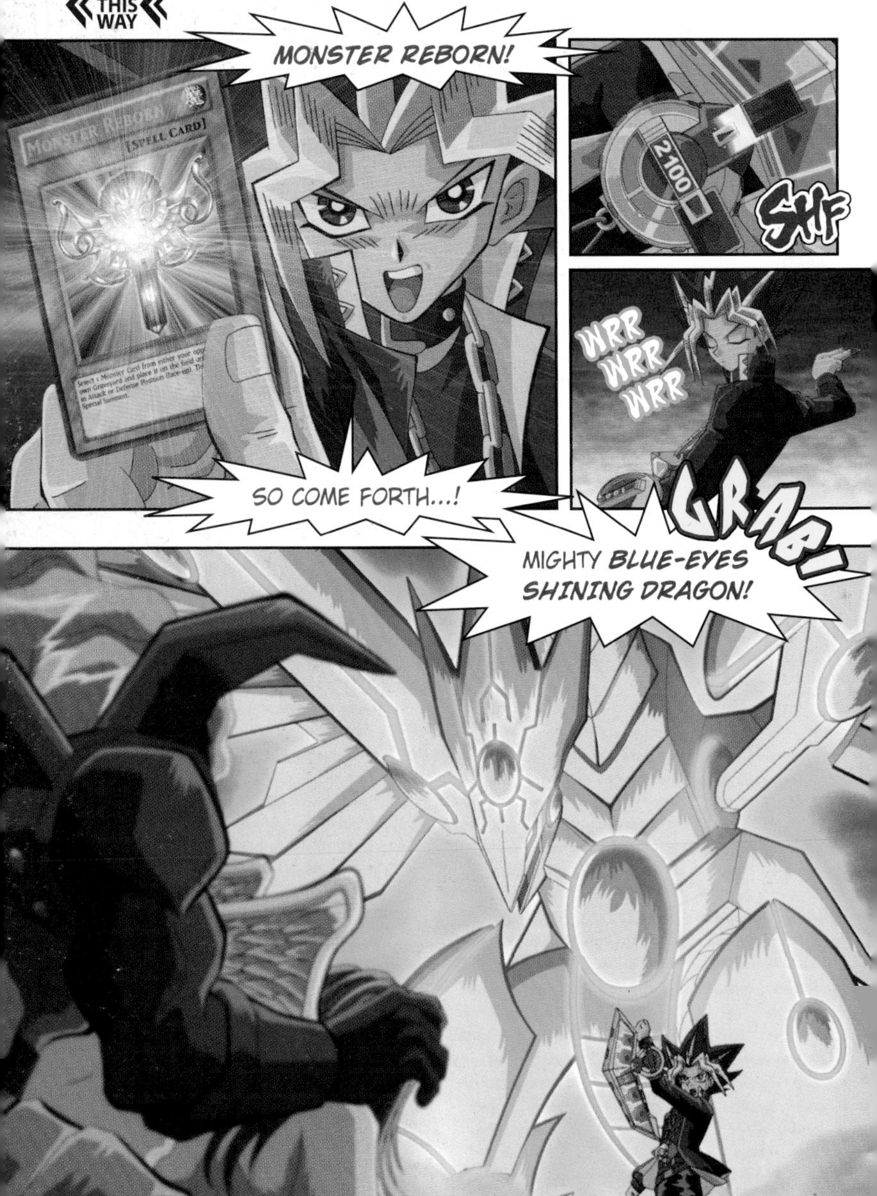

2100
SHF
WRR
WRR
WRR
GRAB!
MONSTER REBORN!
MONSTER REBORN
[SPELL CARD]
SO COME FORTH...!
MIGHTY BLUE-EYES SHINING DRAGON!

READ THIS WAY

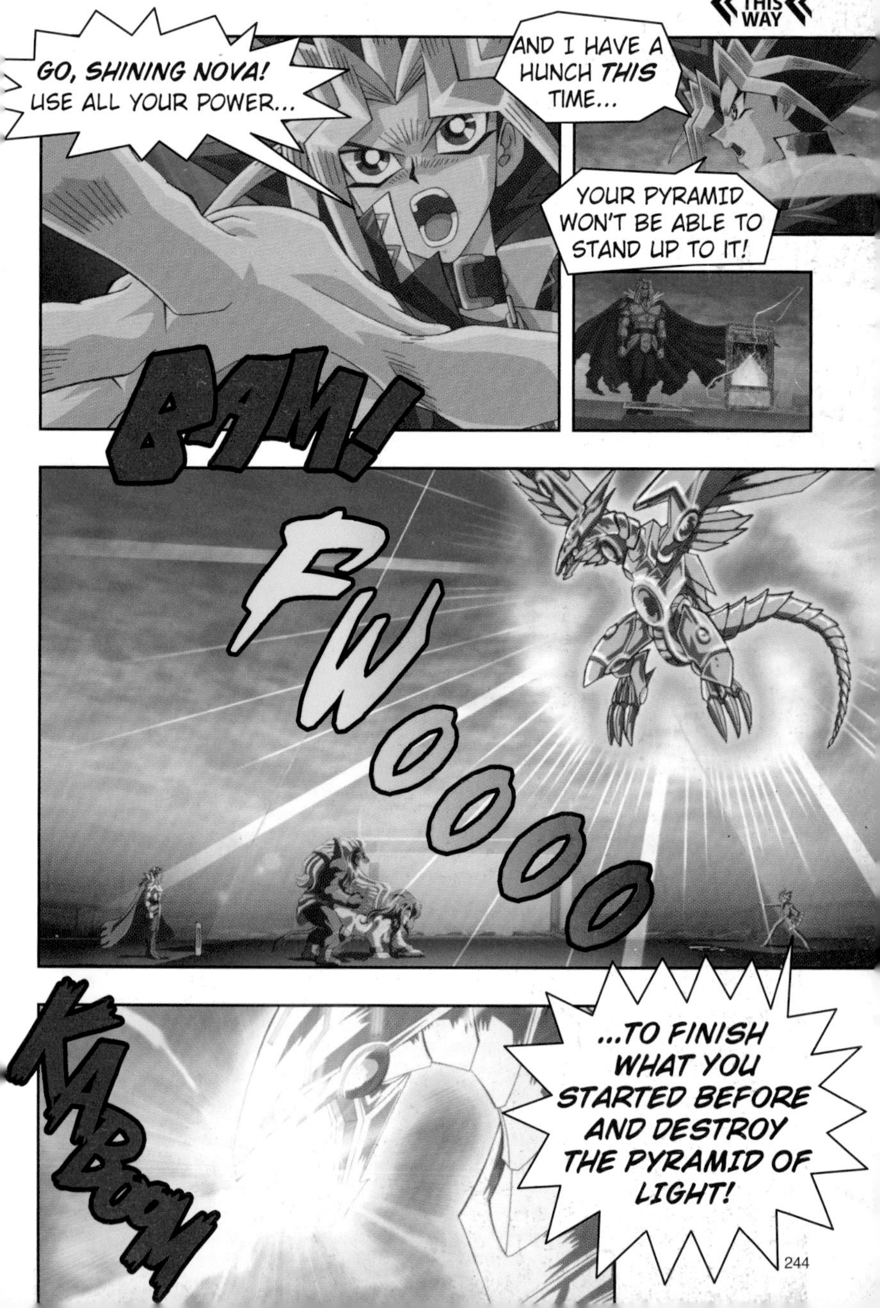
AND I HAVE A HUNCH THIS TIME...
YOUR PYRAMID WON'T BE ABLE TO STAND UP TO IT!
GO, SHINING NOVA! USE ALL YOUR POWER...
BAM!
FWOOOOOO
KABOOM
...TO FINISH WHAT YOU STARTED BEFORE AND DESTROY THE PYRAMID OF LIGHT!

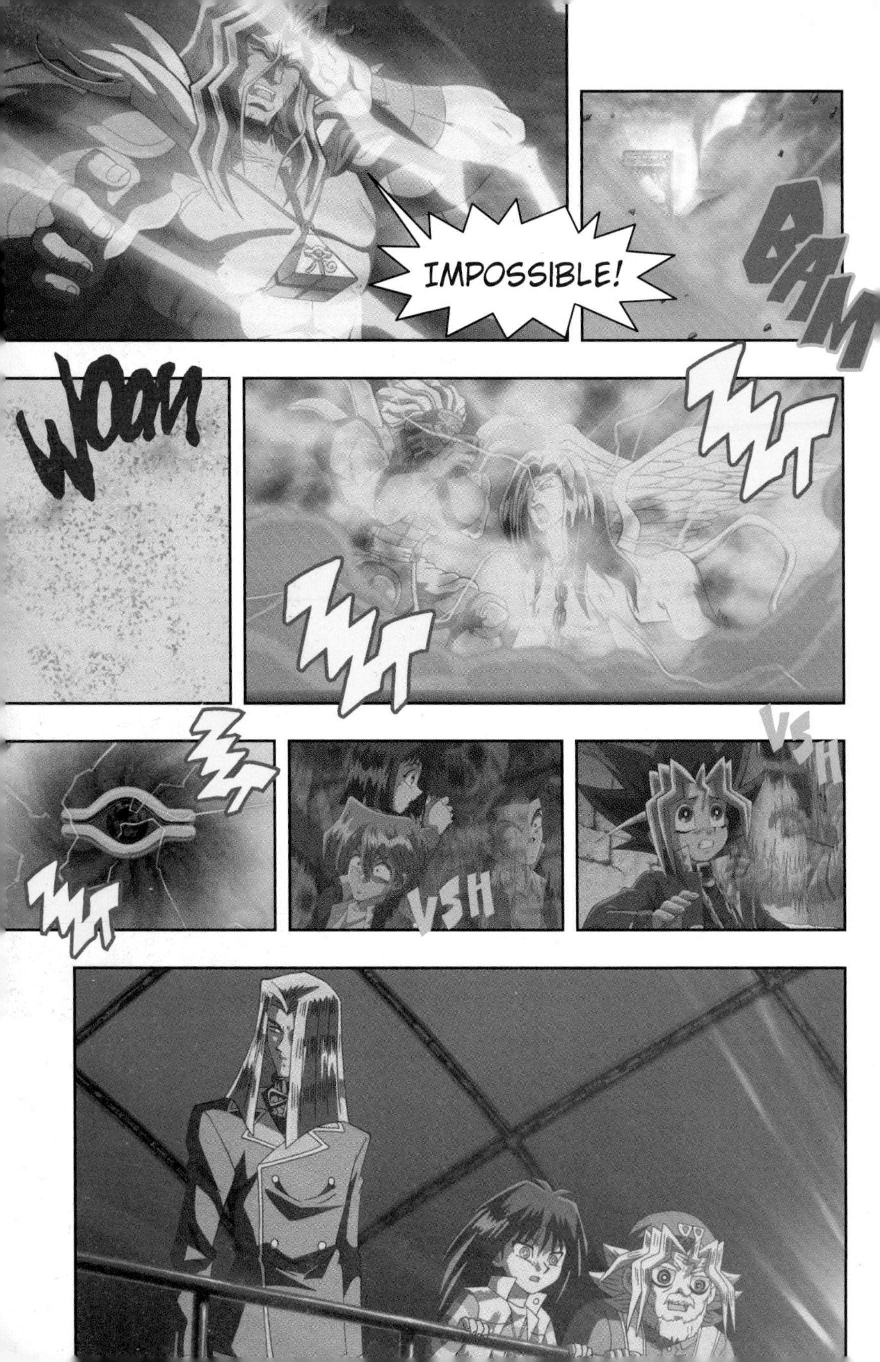
BAM
IMPOSSIBLE!
ZZZT
ZZZT
WOOM
VSH
VSH
ZZZT
ZZZT

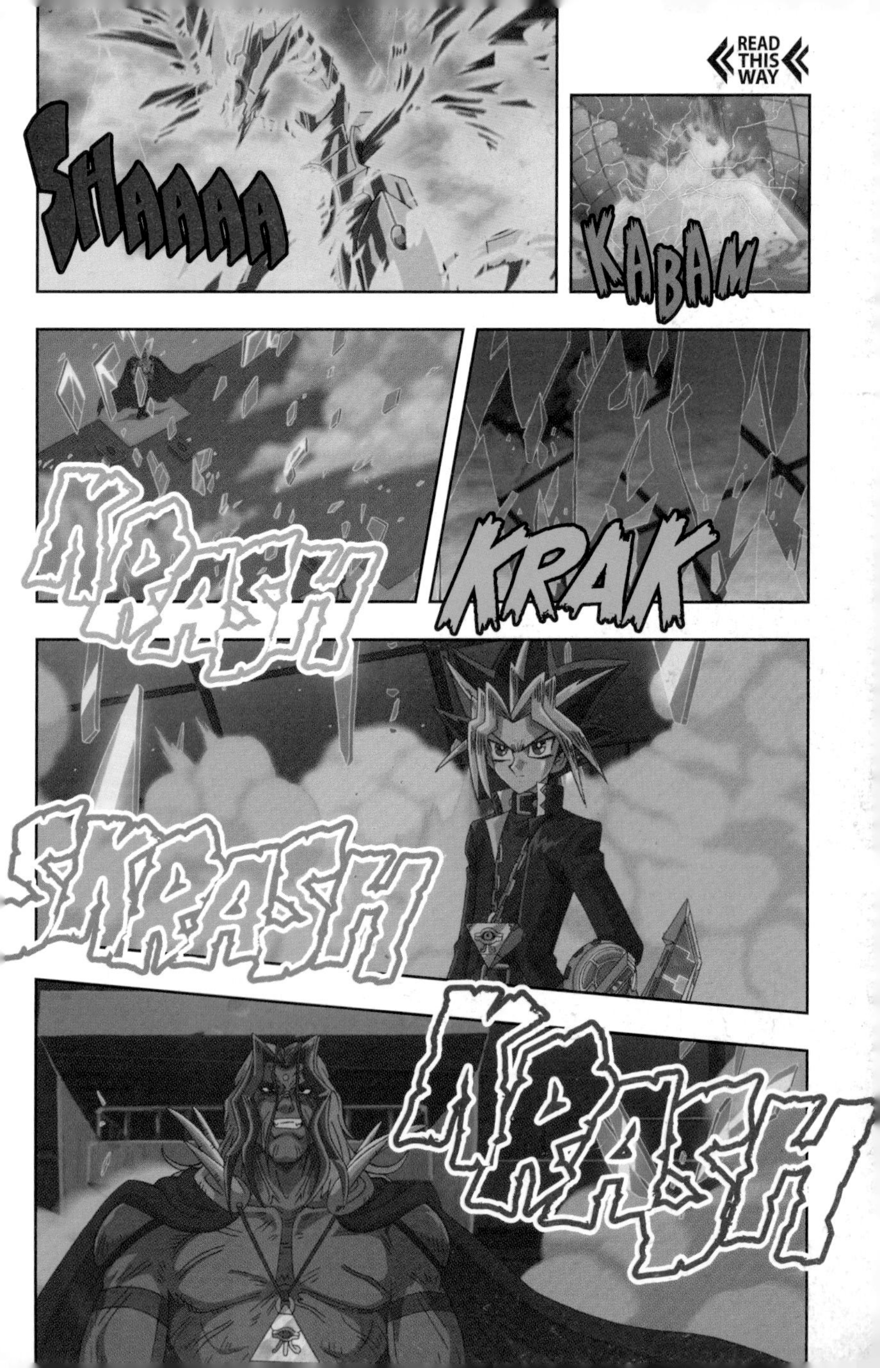
READ THIS WAY
KABAM
SHAAAA
KRAK
KRASH
SKRASH
KRASH

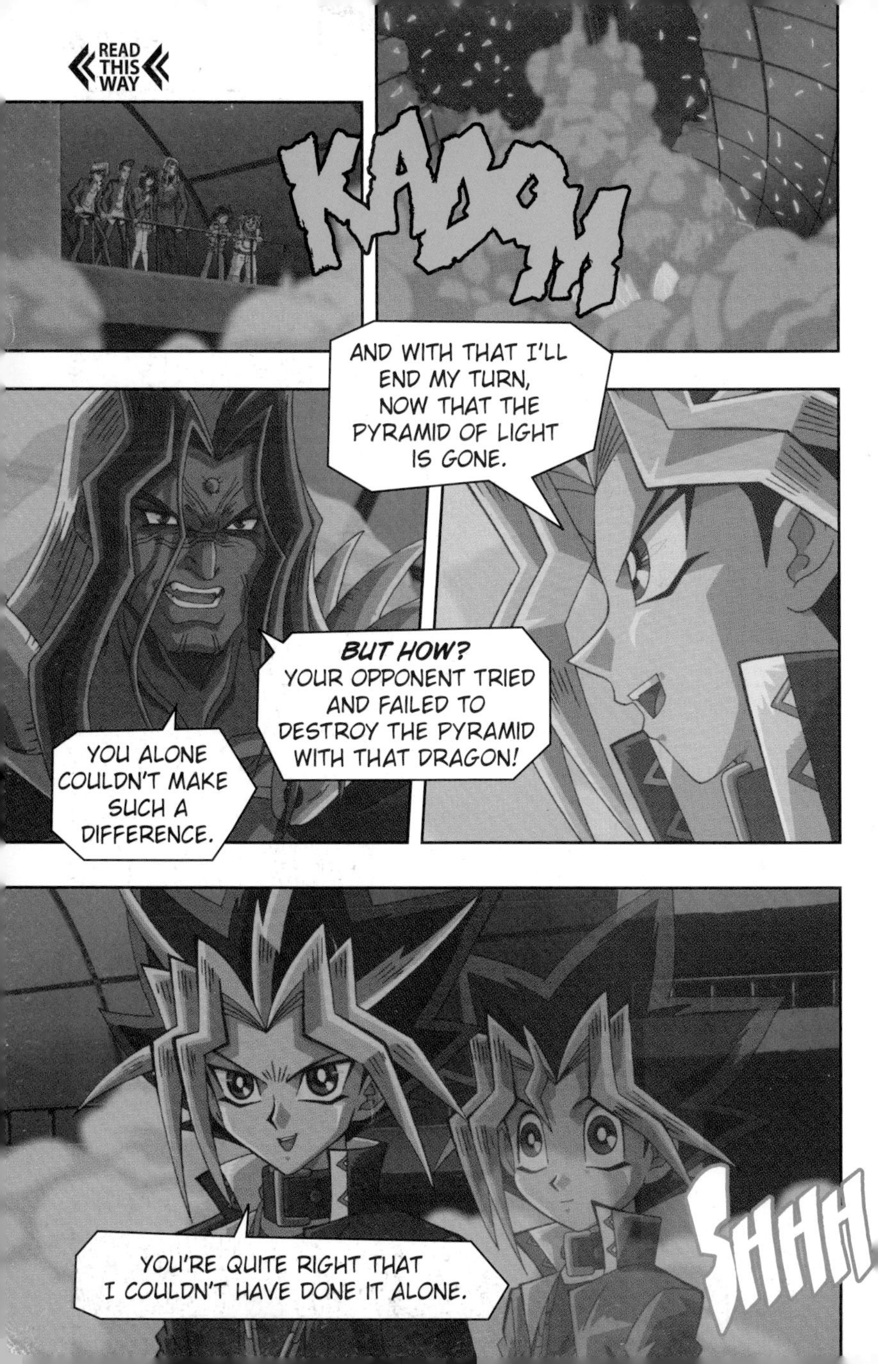
READ THIS WAY
KADOM
AND WITH THAT I'LL END MY TURN, NOW THAT THE PYRAMID OF LIGHT IS GONE.
BUT HOW? YOUR OPPONENT TRIED AND FAILED TO DESTROY THE PYRAMID WITH THAT DRAGON!
YOU ALONE COULDN'T MAKE SUCH A DIFFERENCE.
SHHH
YOU'RE QUITE RIGHT THAT I COULDN'T HAVE DONE IT ALONE.

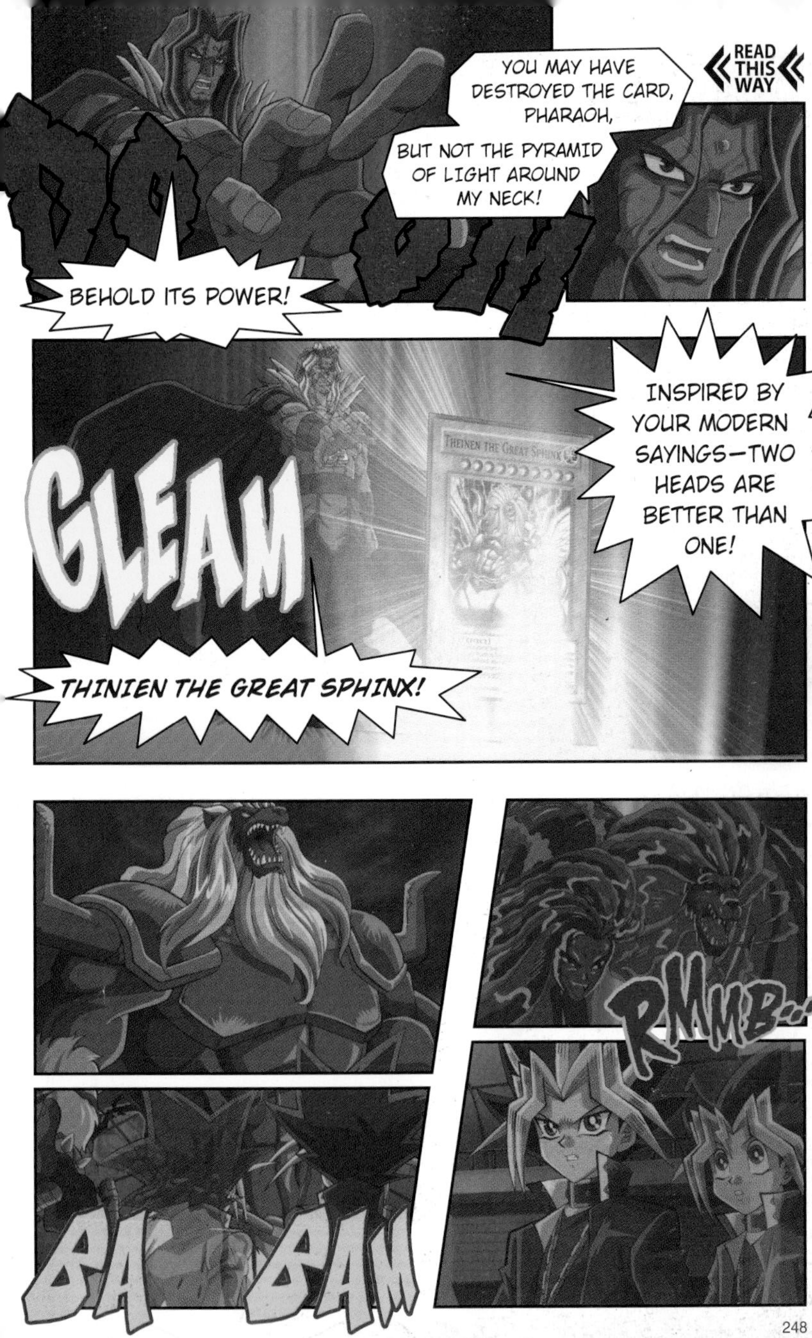
READ THIS WAY
YOU MAY HAVE DESTROYED THE CARD, PHARAOH,
BUT NOT THE PYRAMID OF LIGHT AROUND MY NECK!
BEHOLD ITS POWER!
INSPIRED BY YOUR MODERN SAYINGS—TWO HEADS ARE BETTER THAN ONE!
GLEAM
THEINEN THE GREAT SPHINX
THINIEN THE GREAT SPHINX!
RMMB...
BA BAM

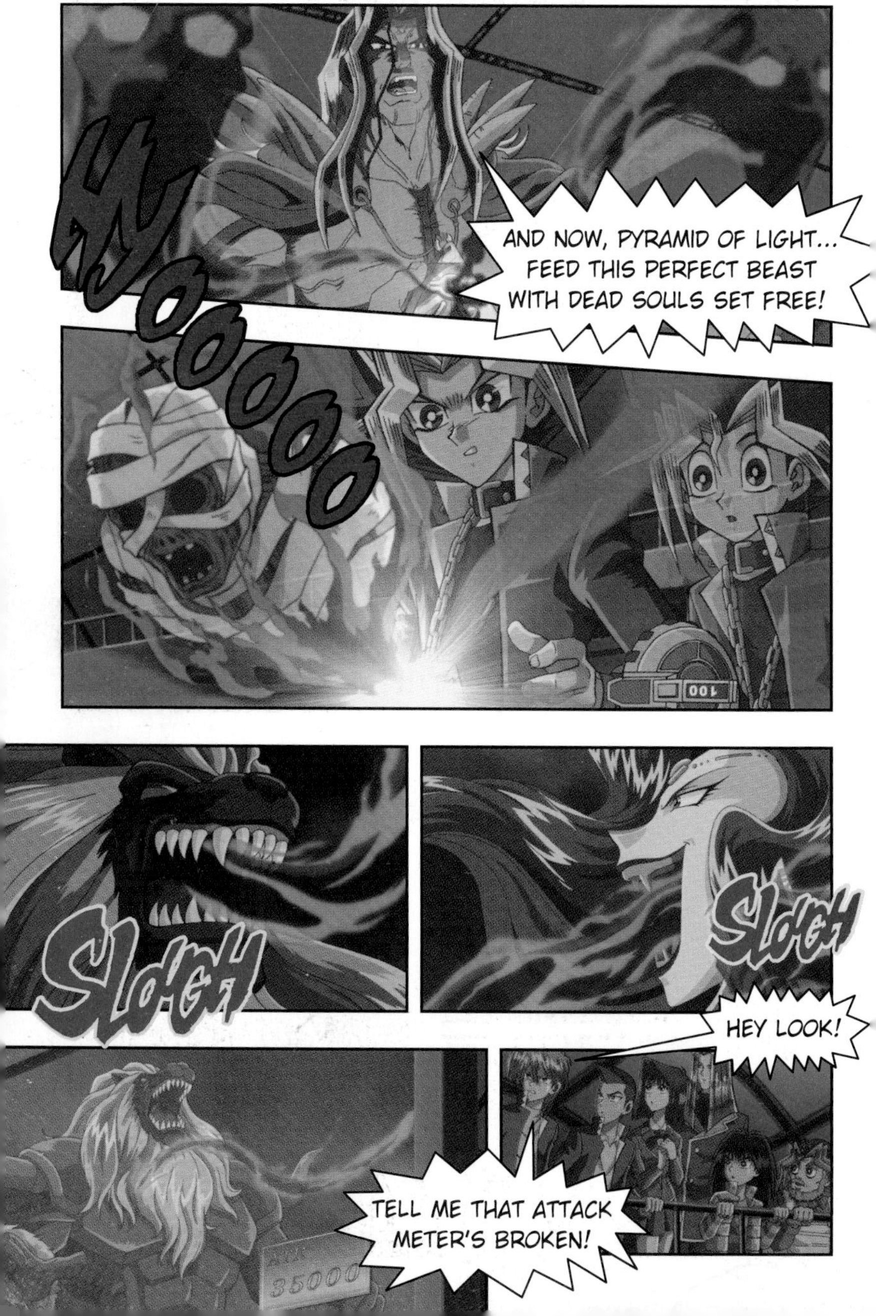
AND NOW, PYRAMID OF LIGHT... FEED THIS PERFECT BEAST WITH DEAD SOULS SET FREE!
HYOOOOOO
SLOGH
SLOGH
HEY LOOK!
TELL ME THAT ATTACK METER'S BROKEN!
35000

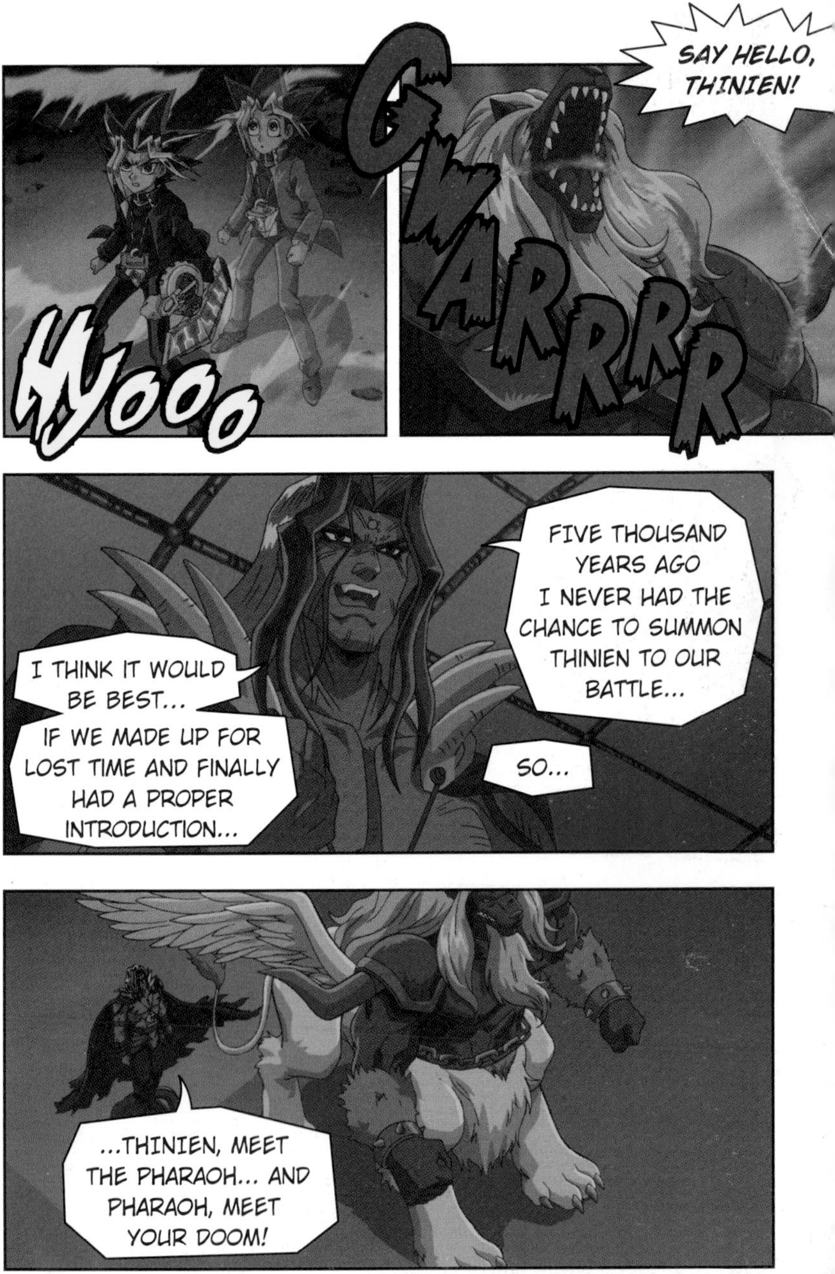
SAY HELLO, THINIEN!
GWARRRR
HYOOO
FIVE THOUSAND YEARS AGO I NEVER HAD THE CHANCE TO SUMMON THINIEN TO OUR BATTLE...
SO...
I THINK IT WOULD BE BEST... IF WE MADE UP FOR LOST TIME AND FINALLY HAD A PROPER INTRODUCTION...
...THINIEN, MEET THE PHARAOH... AND PHARAOH, MEET YOUR DOOM!

READ THIS WAY

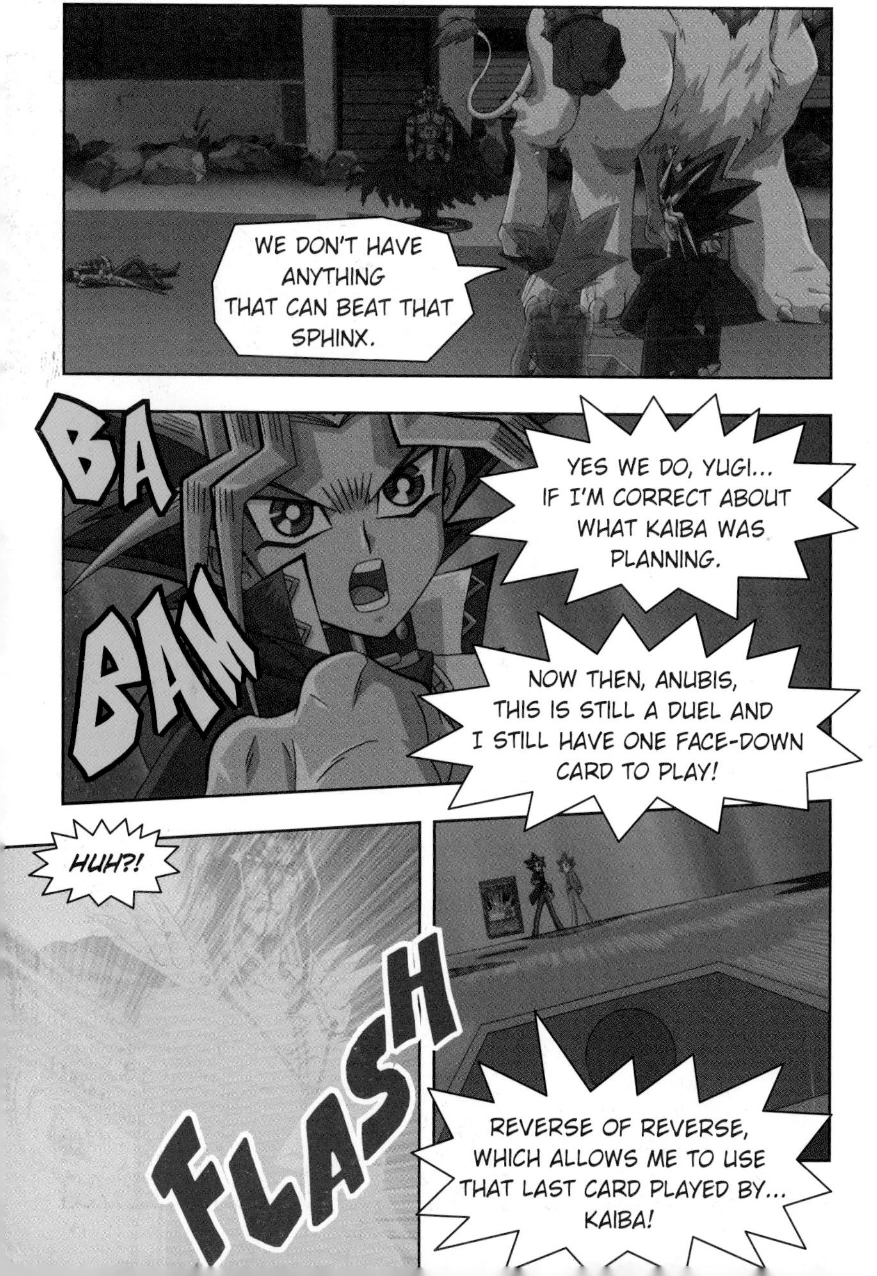
WE DON'T HAVE ANYTHING THAT CAN BEAT THAT SPHINX.
YES WE DO, YUGI... IF I'M CORRECT ABOUT WHAT KAIBA WAS PLANNING.
BA
NOW THEN, ANUBIS, THIS IS STILL A DUEL AND I STILL HAVE ONE FACE-DOWN CARD TO PLAY!
BAM
FLASH
REVERSE OF REVERSE, WHICH ALLOWS ME TO USE THAT LAST CARD PLAYED BY... KAIBA!
HUH?!

READ THIS WAY

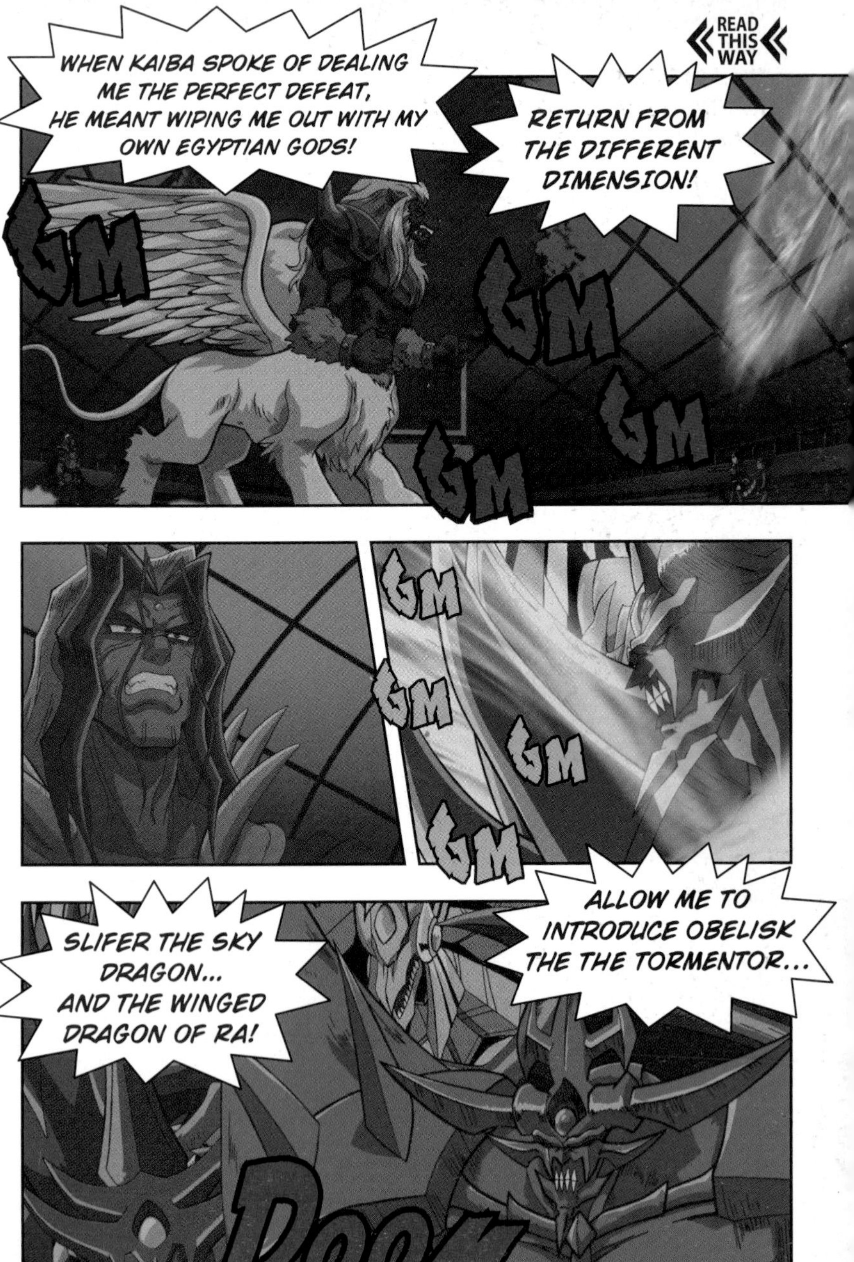
RETURN FROM THE DIFFERENT DIMENSION!
WHEN KAIBA SPOKE OF DEALING ME THE PERFECT DEFEAT, HE MEANT WIPING ME OUT WITH MY OWN EGYPTIAN GODS!
GM
GM
GM
GM
GM
GM
GM
GM
ALLOW ME TO INTRODUCE OBELISK THE THE TORMENTOR...
SLIFER THE SKY DRAGON... AND THE WINGED DRAGON OF RA!
DOOM

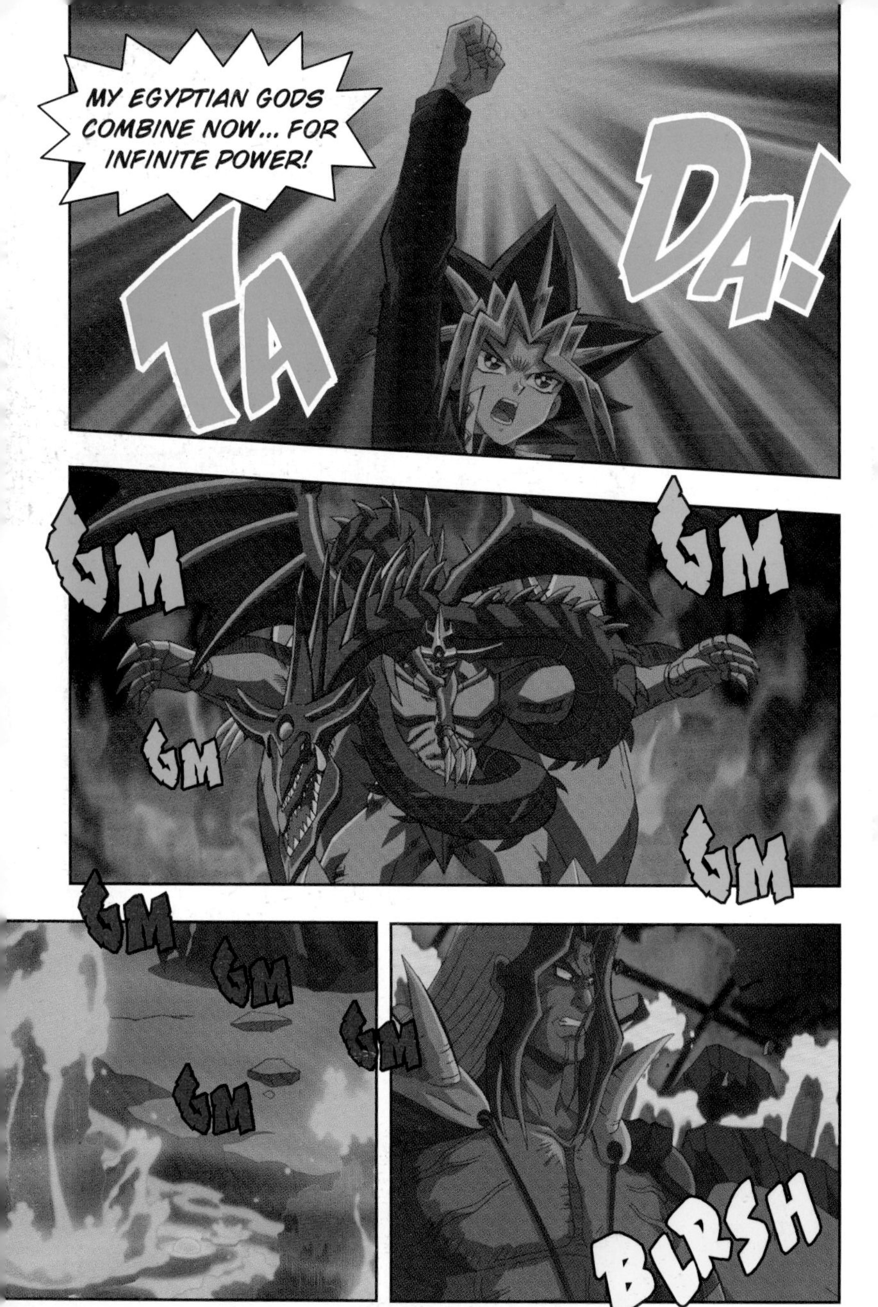
MY EGYPTIAN GODS COMBINE NOW... FOR INFINITE POWER!
TA
DA!
GM
GM
GM
GM
BLRSH
GM
GM
GM
GM

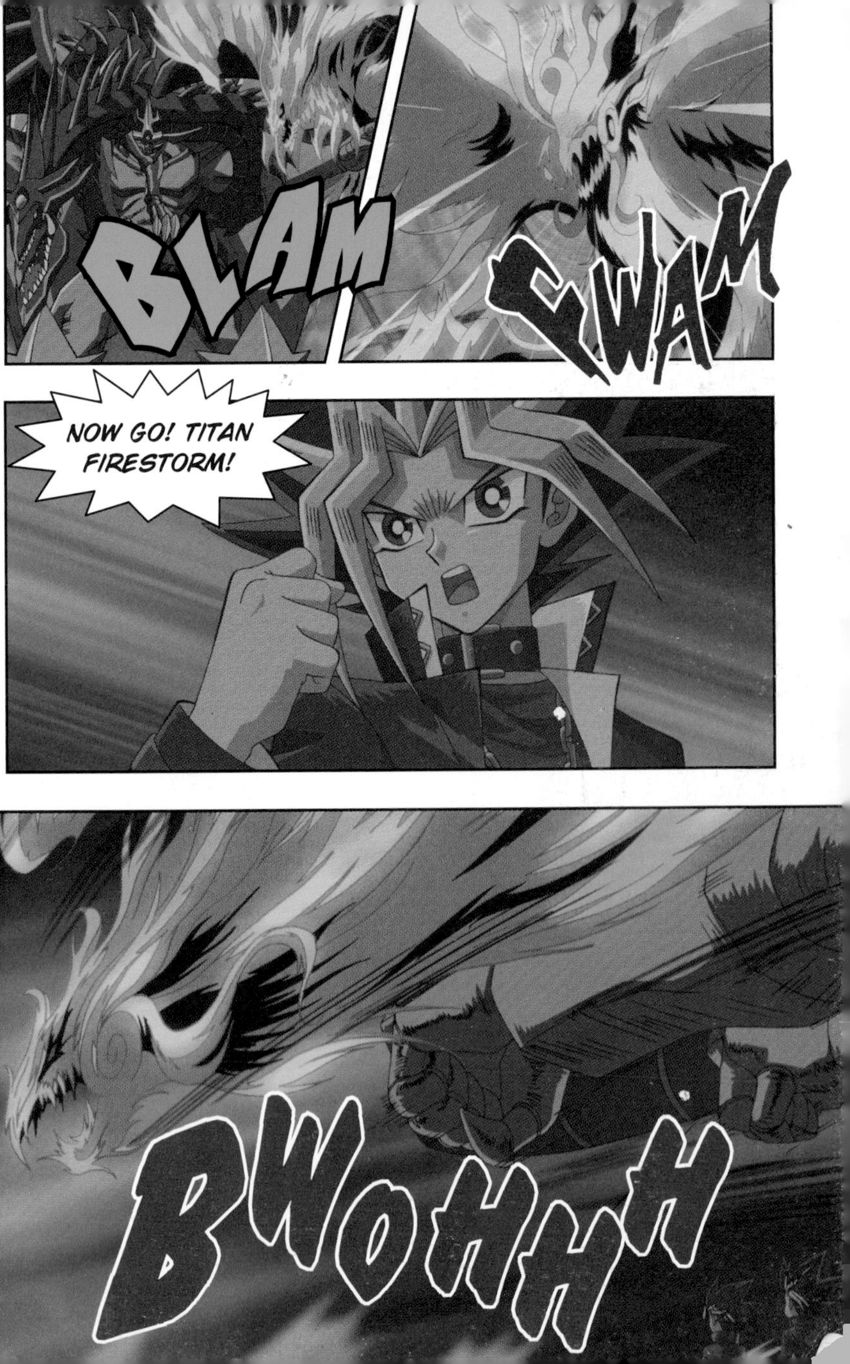
CWAM
BLAM
NOW GO! TITAN FIRESTORM!
BWOHHH

READ THIS WAY

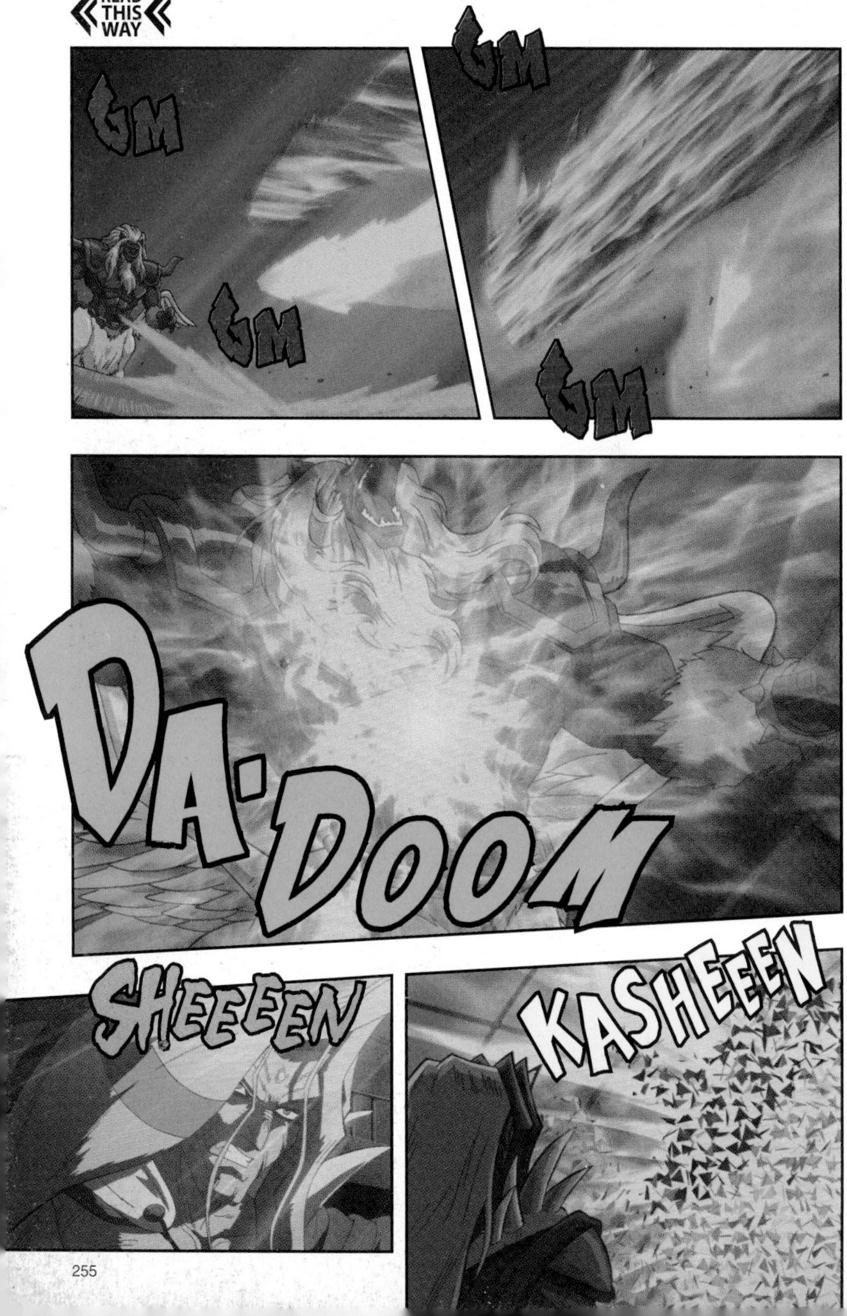
GM
GM
GM
GM
DA-DOOM
KASHEEEN
SHEEEEN

READ THIS WAY

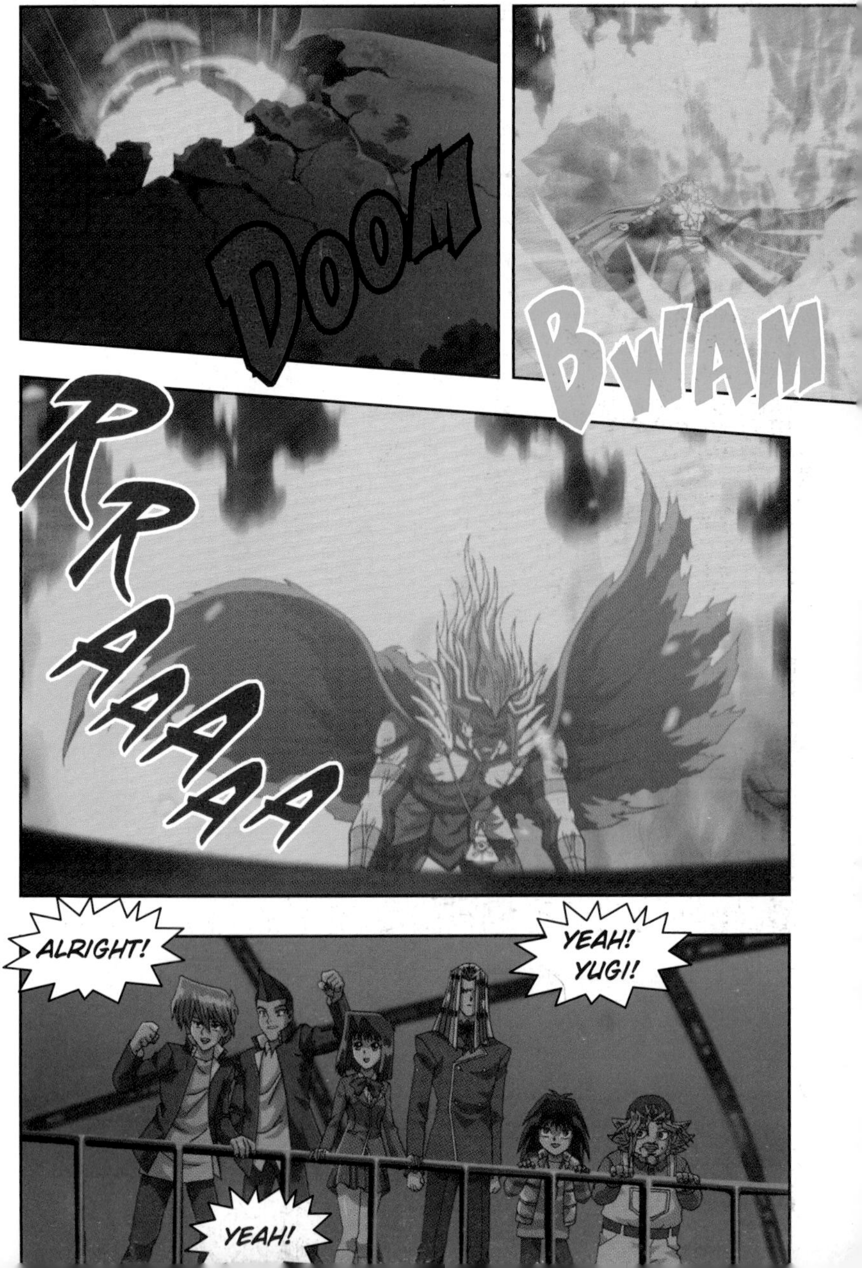
BWAM
DOOM
RRAAAAA
YEAH! YUGI!
ALRIGHT!
YEAH!

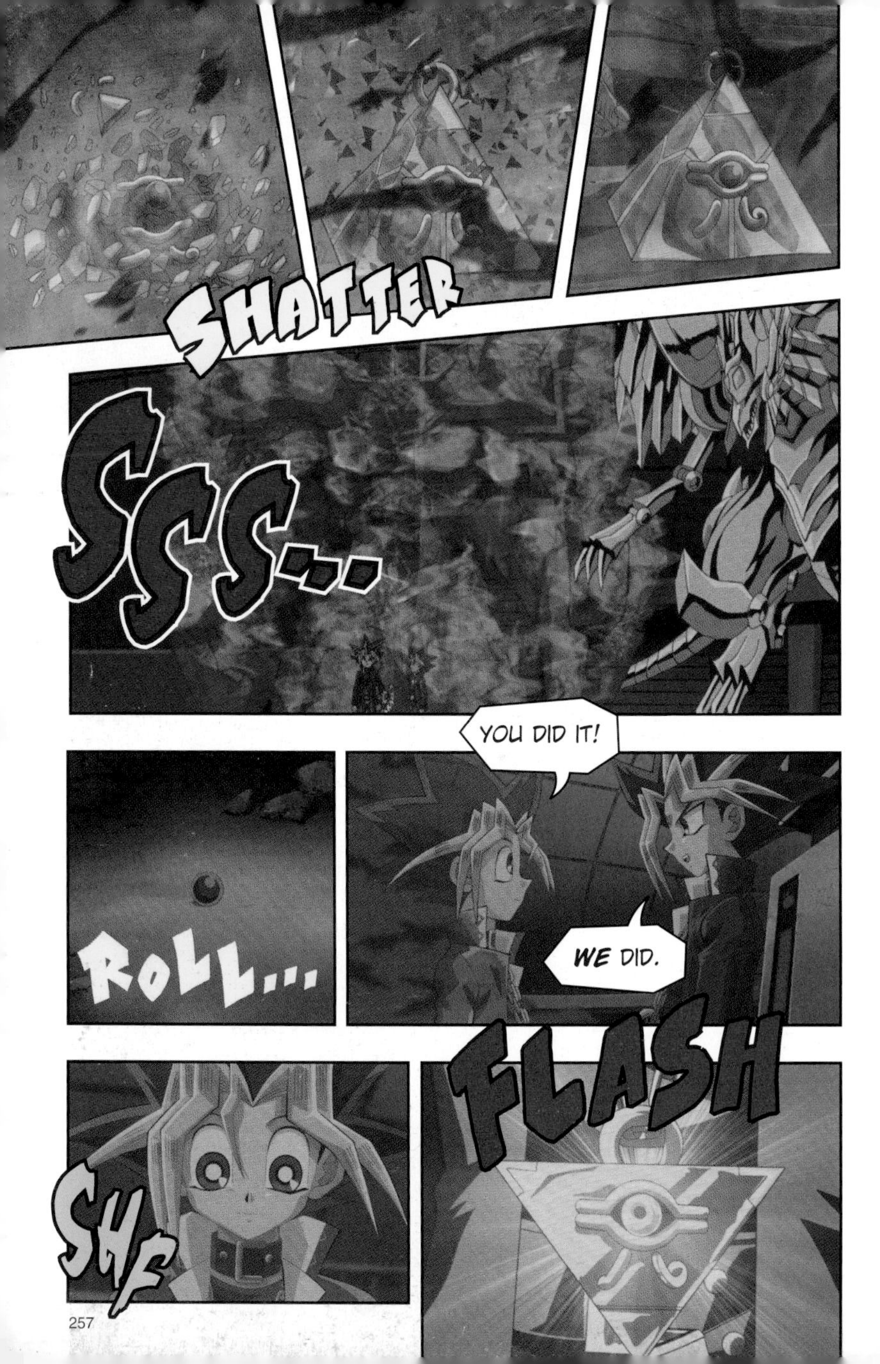
SHATTER
SSS...
YOU DID IT!
WE DID.
ROLL...
FLASH
SHF

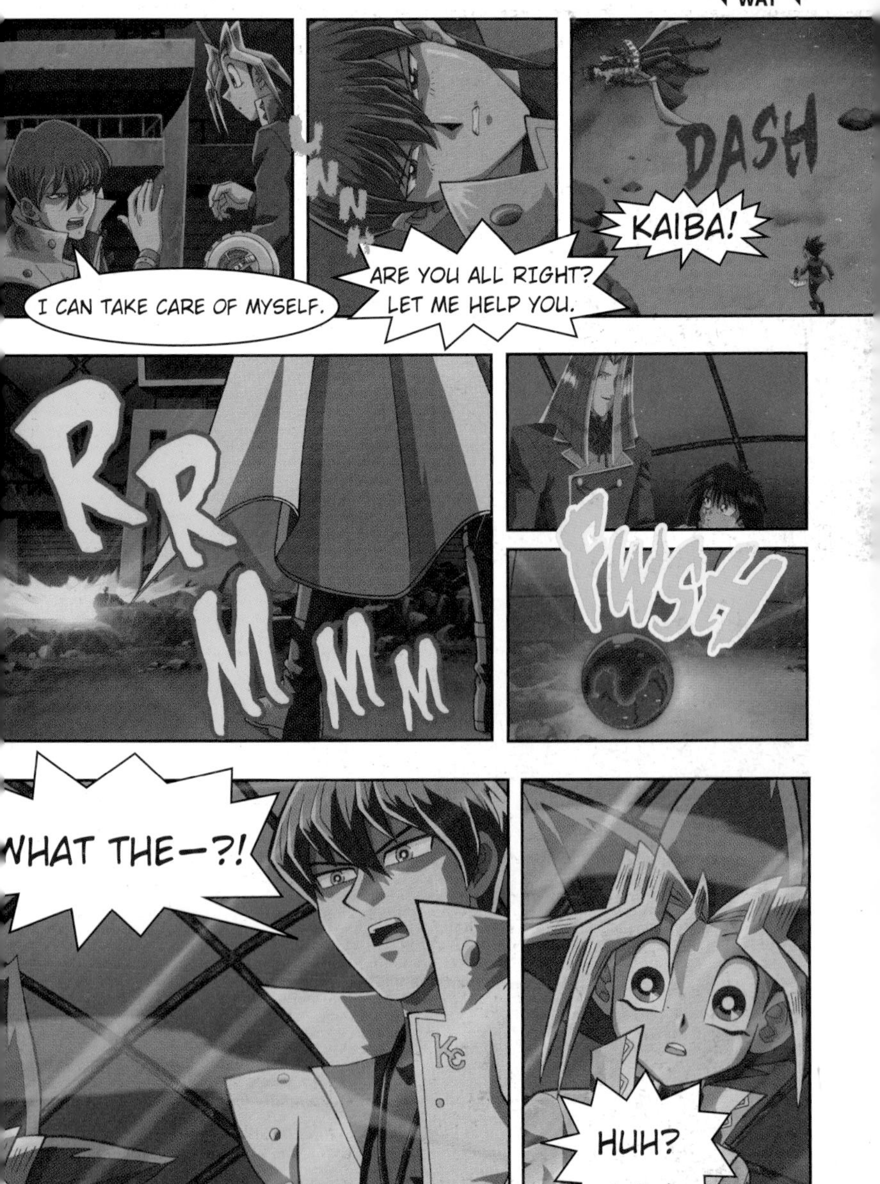
DASH
KAIBA!
UNNH
ARE YOU ALL RIGHT? LET ME HELP YOU.
I CAN TAKE CARE OF MYSELF.
FWSH
RRMMM
HUH?
WHAT THE—?!

READ THIS WAY

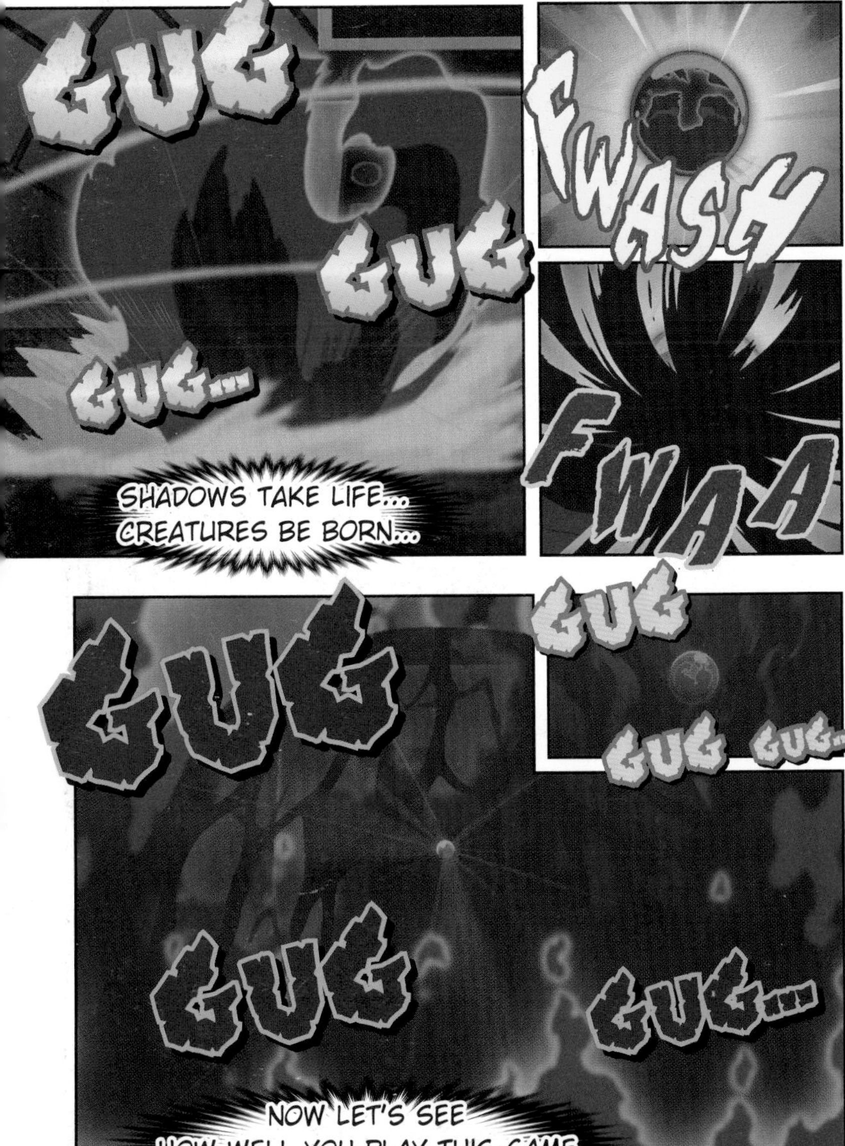
FWASH
FWAA
GUG
GUG
GUG...
SHADOWS TAKE LIFE... CREATURES BE BORN...
GUG
GUG GUG...
GUG
GUG
GUG...
NOW LET'S SEE HOW WELL YOU PLAY THIS GAME WHEN THE MONSTERS ARE REAL!

READ THIS WAY

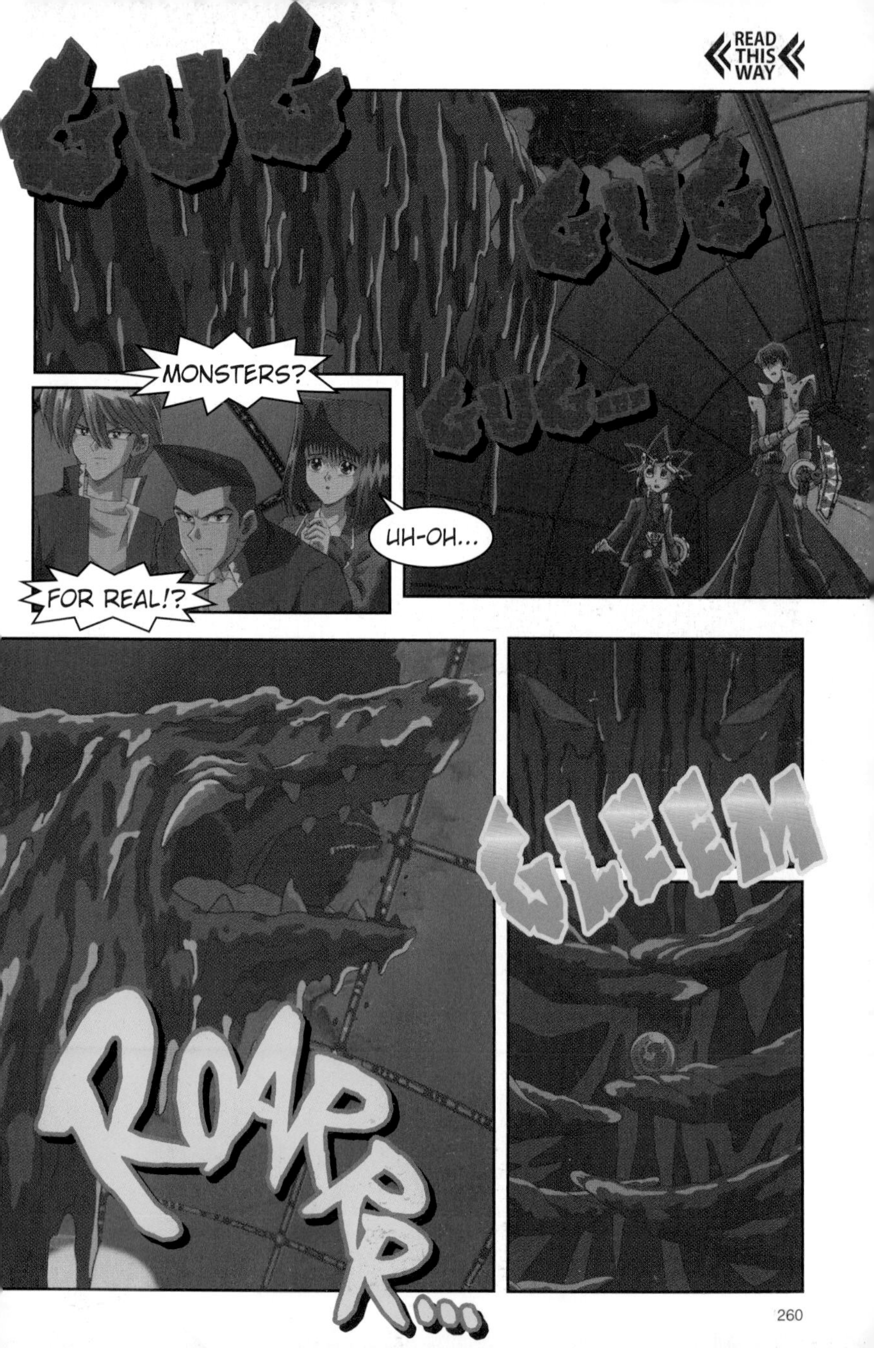
GUG
GUG
GUG...
MONSTERS?
UH-OH...
FOR REAL!?
GLEEM
ROARRR...

READ THIS WAY

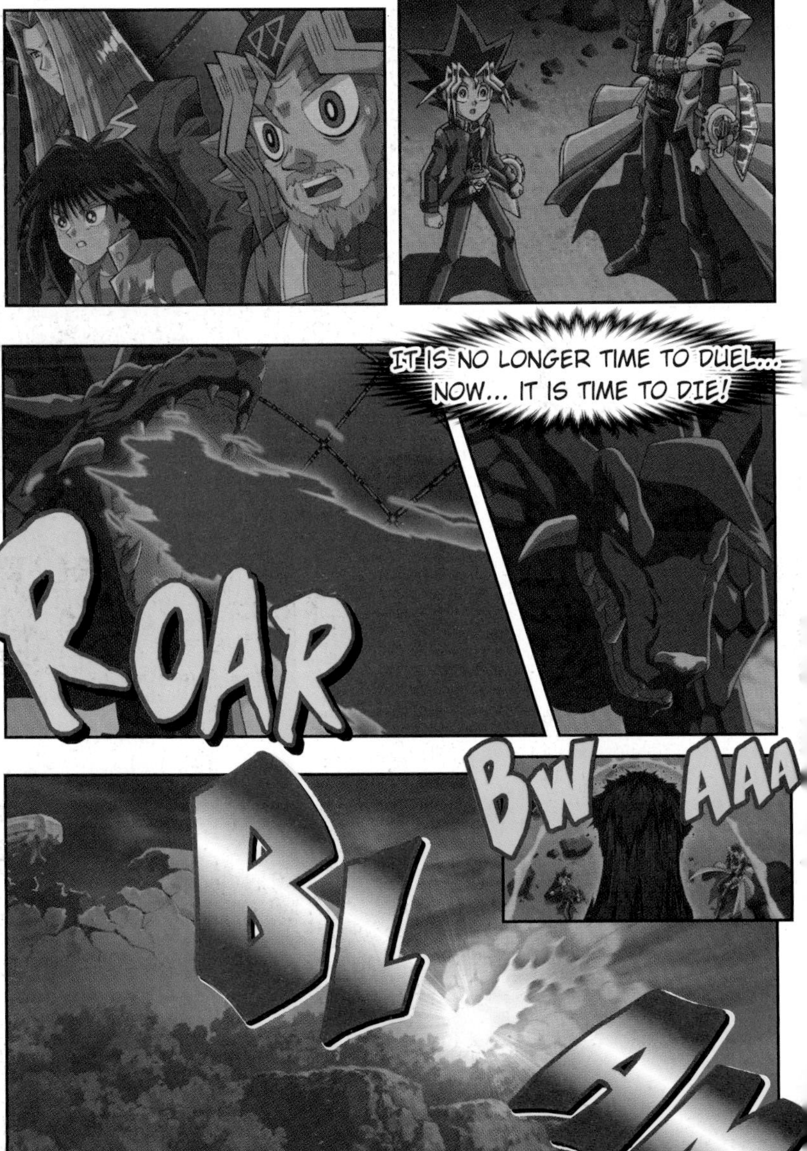
IT IS NO LONGER TIME TO DUEL... NOW... IT IS TIME TO DIE!
ROAR
BWAAA
BLAM

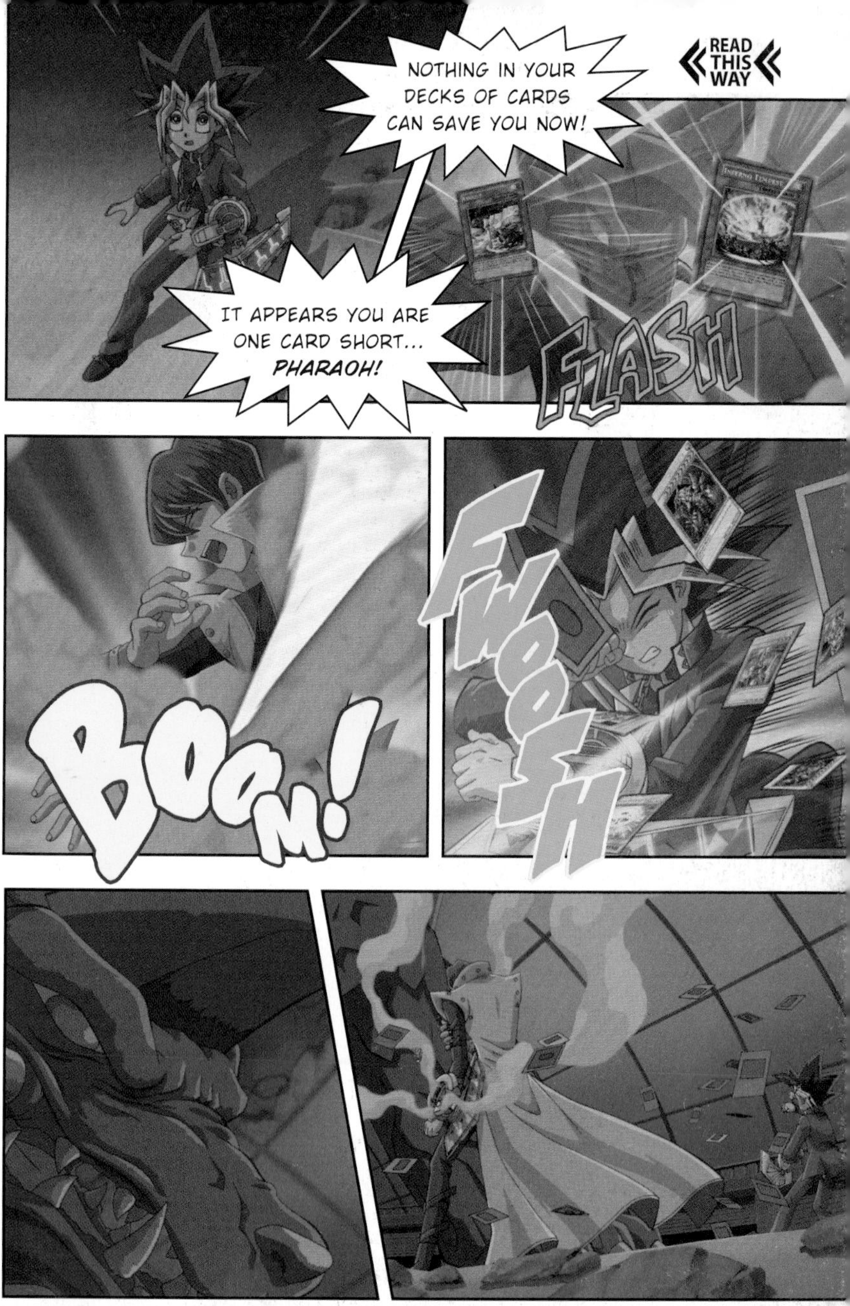
READ THIS WAY
NOTHING IN YOUR DECKS OF CARDS CAN SAVE YOU NOW!
FLASH
IT APPEARS YOU ARE ONE CARD SHORT... *PHARAOH!*
FWOOSH
BOOM!

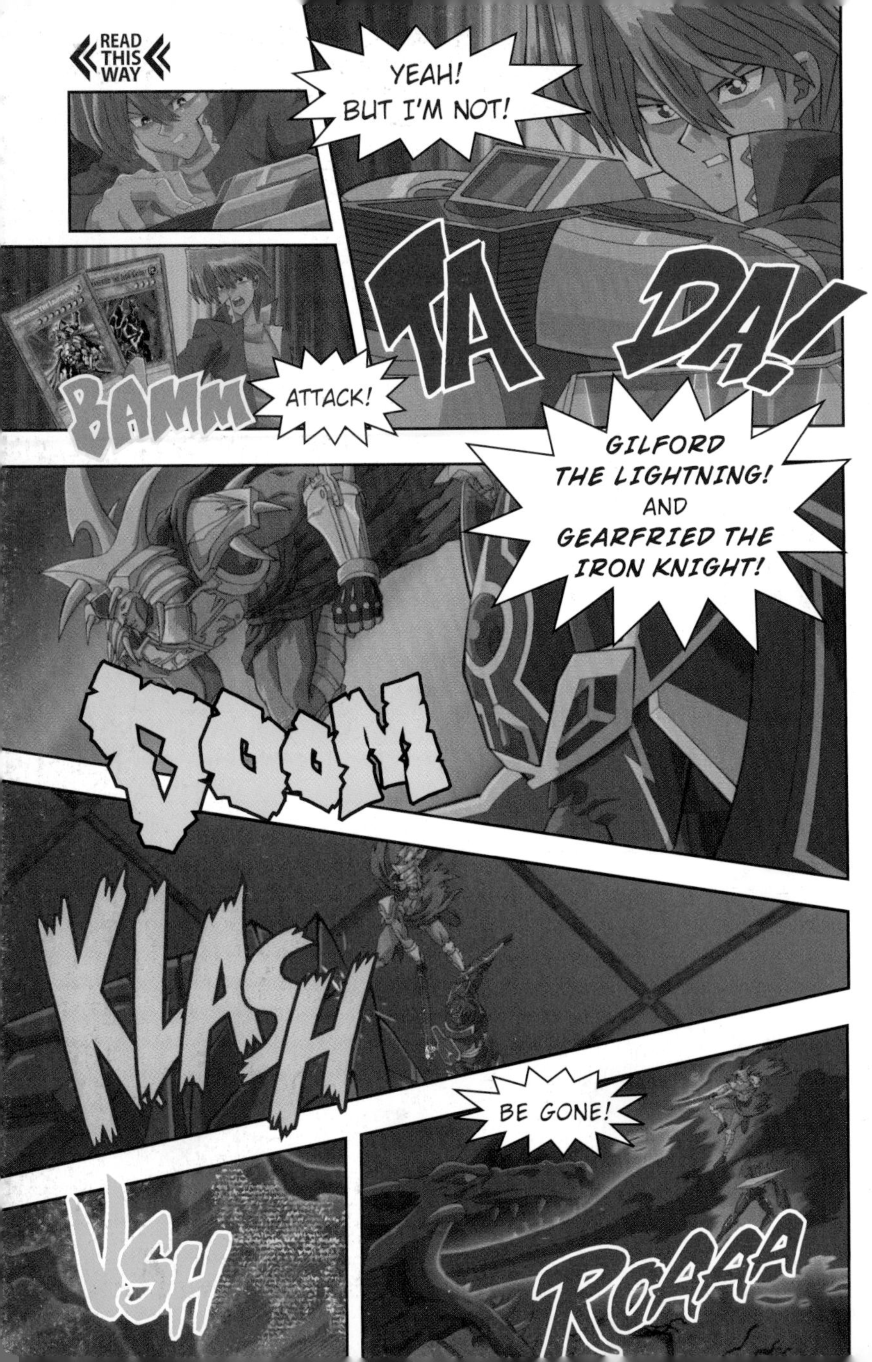
READ THIS WAY
YEAH! BUT I'M NOT!
TA DA!
BAMM
ATTACK!
GILFORD THE LIGHTNING! AND GEARFRIED THE IRON KNIGHT!
DOOM
KLASH
BE GONE!
ROAAA
VSH

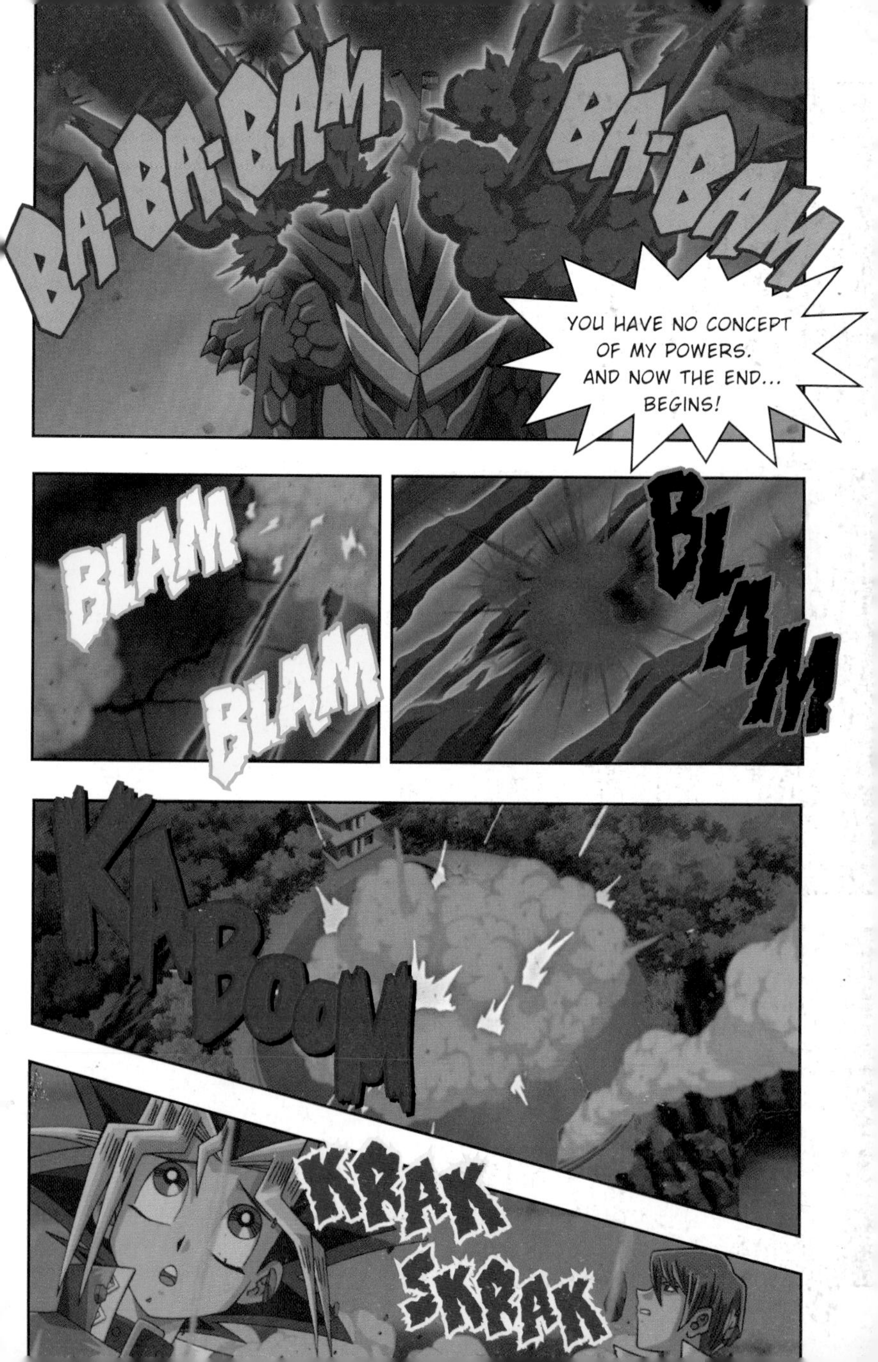
BA-BAM
BA-BA-BAM
YOU HAVE NO CONCEPT OF MY POWERS. AND NOW THE END... BEGINS!
BLAM
BLAM
BLAM
KABOOM
KRAK
SKRAK

READ THIS WAY

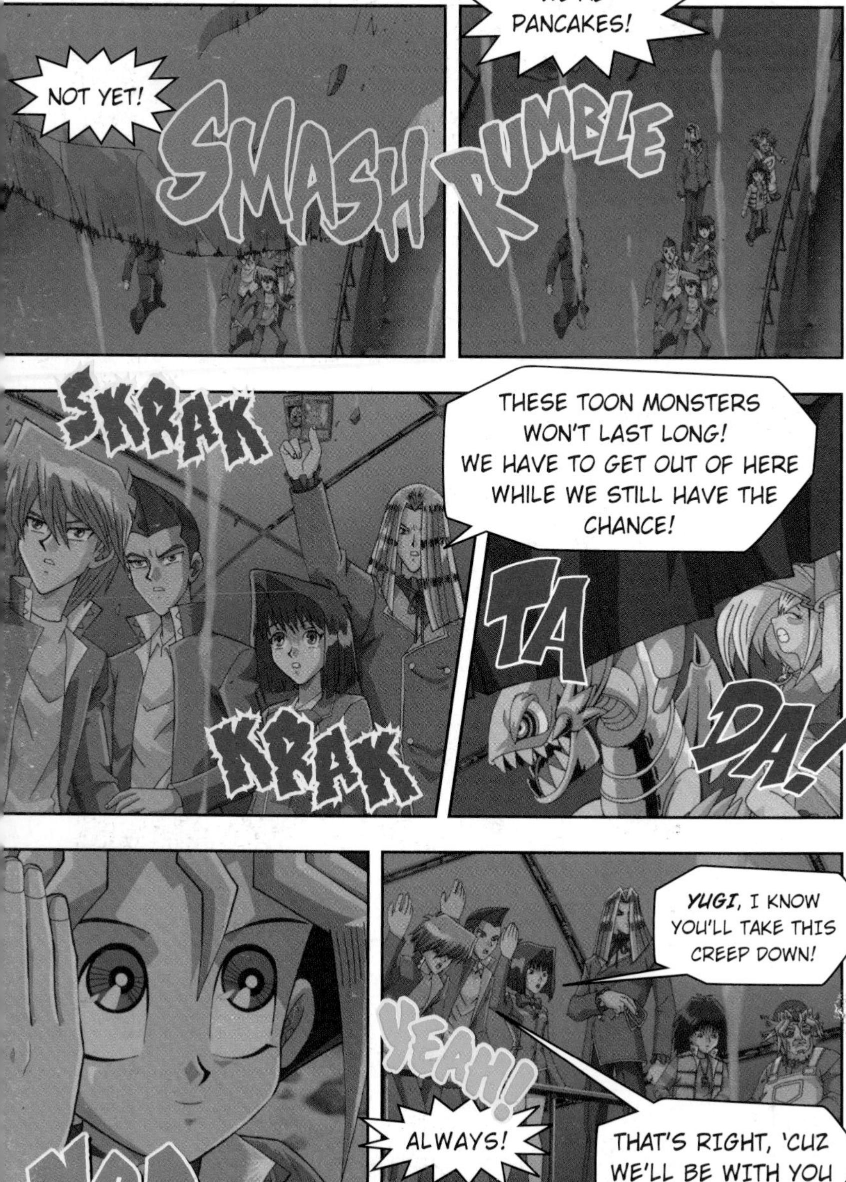
WE'RE PANCAKES!
RUMBLE
NOT YET!
SMASH
THESE TOON MONSTERS WON'T LAST LONG! WE HAVE TO GET OUT OF HERE WHILE WE STILL HAVE THE CHANCE!
TA
DA!
SKRAK
KRAK
YUGI, I KNOW YOU'LL TAKE THIS CREEP DOWN!
YEAH!
ALWAYS!
THAT'S RIGHT, 'CUZ WE'LL BE WITH YOU ALL THE WAY!
NOD

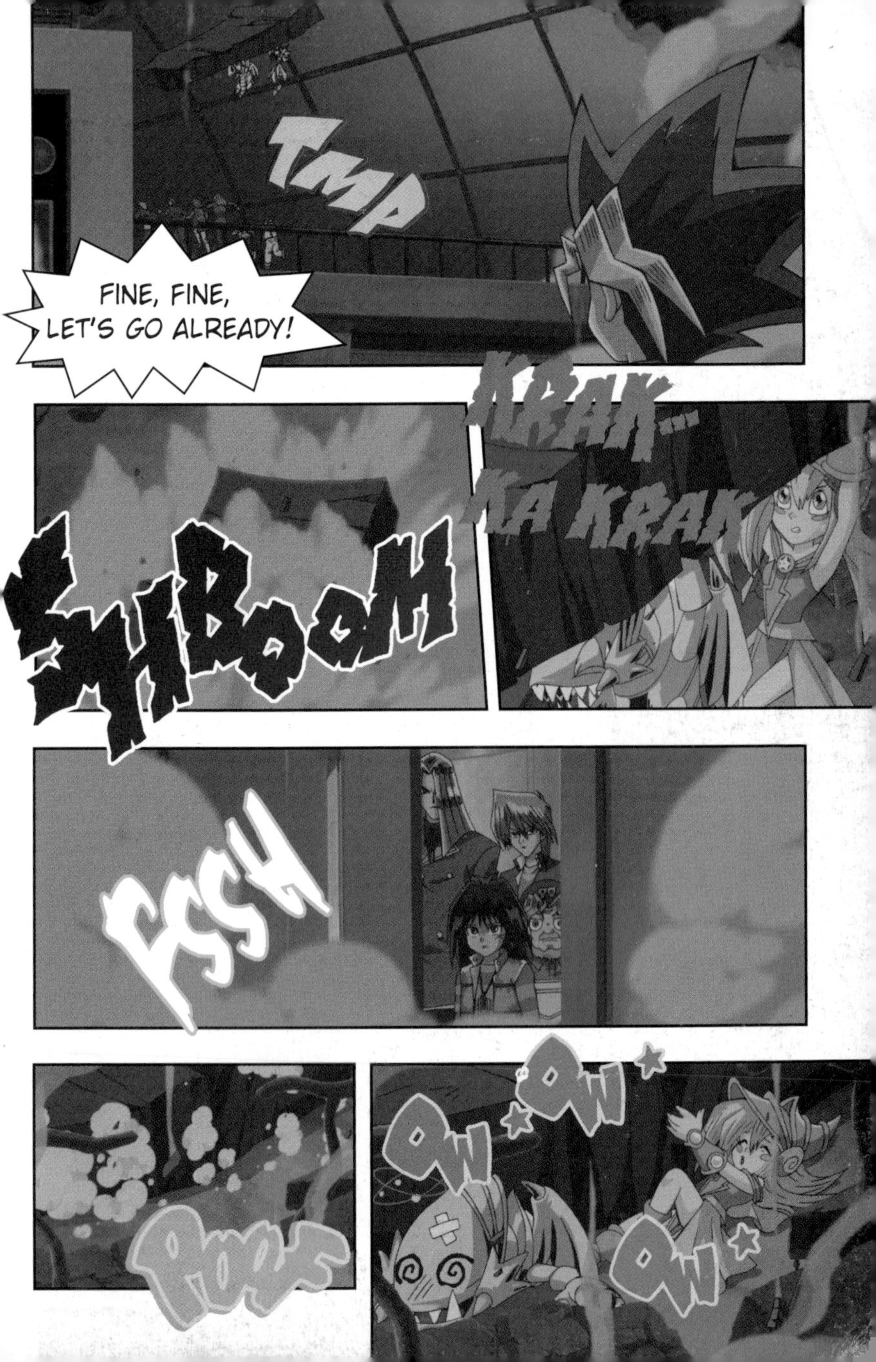
TMP
FINE, FINE, LET'S GO ALREADY!
KRAK...
KA KRAK
SHBOOM
FSSH
OW
OW
OW
POOF

READ THIS WAY

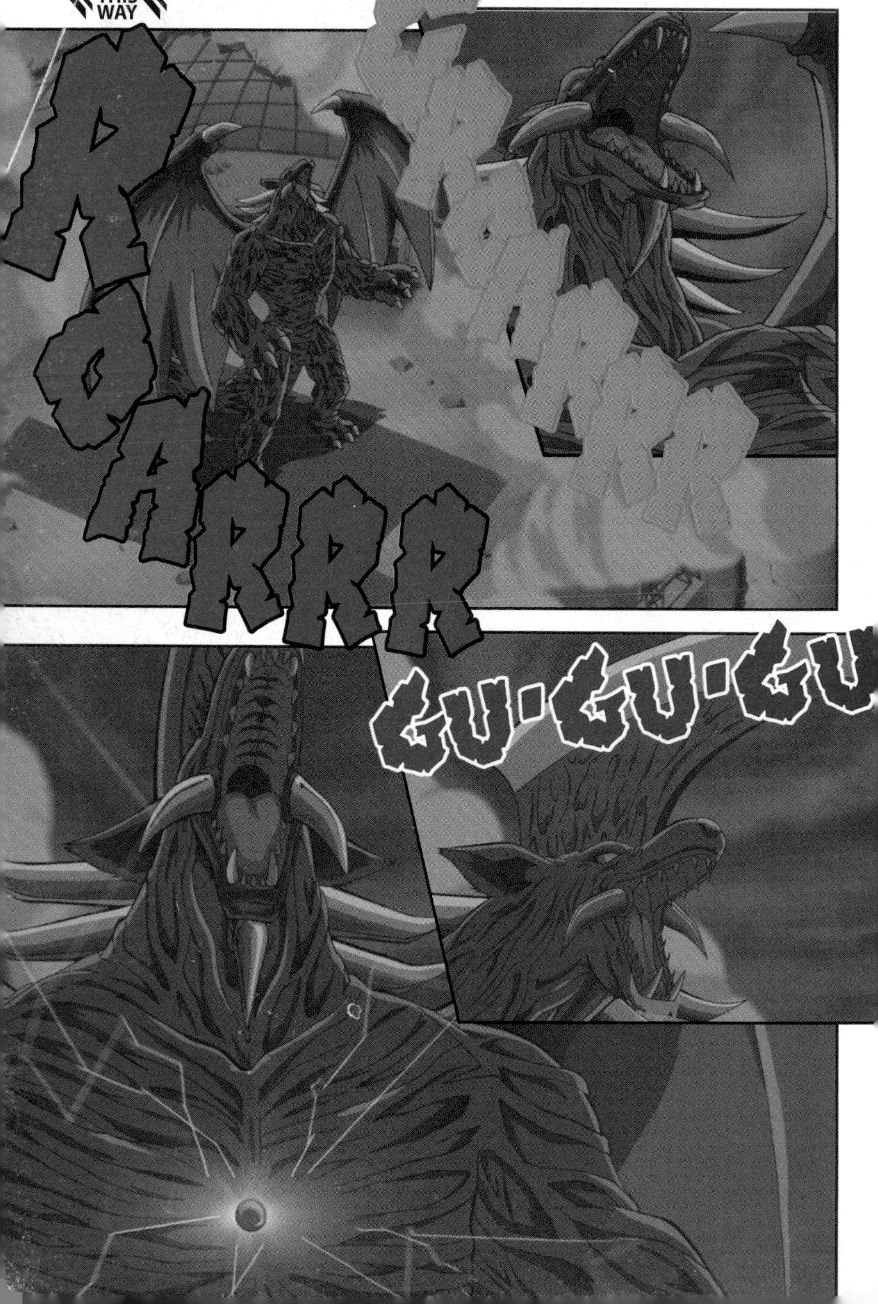
ROARRRR
GU·GU·GU

READ THIS WAY

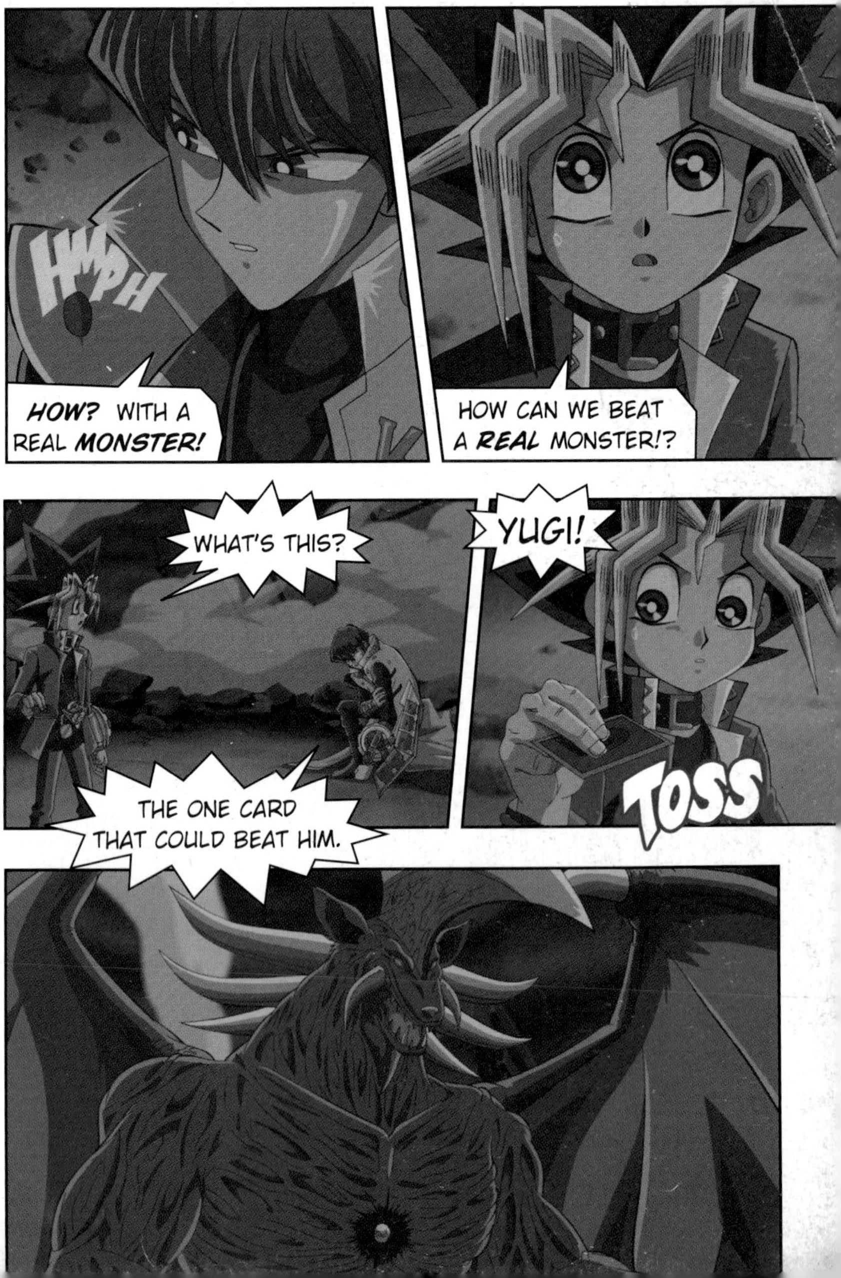
HOW CAN WE BEAT A REAL MONSTER!?
HMPH
HOW? WITH A REAL MONSTER!
YUGI!
TOSS
WHAT'S THIS?
THE ONE CARD THAT COULD BEAT HIM.

READ THIS WAY

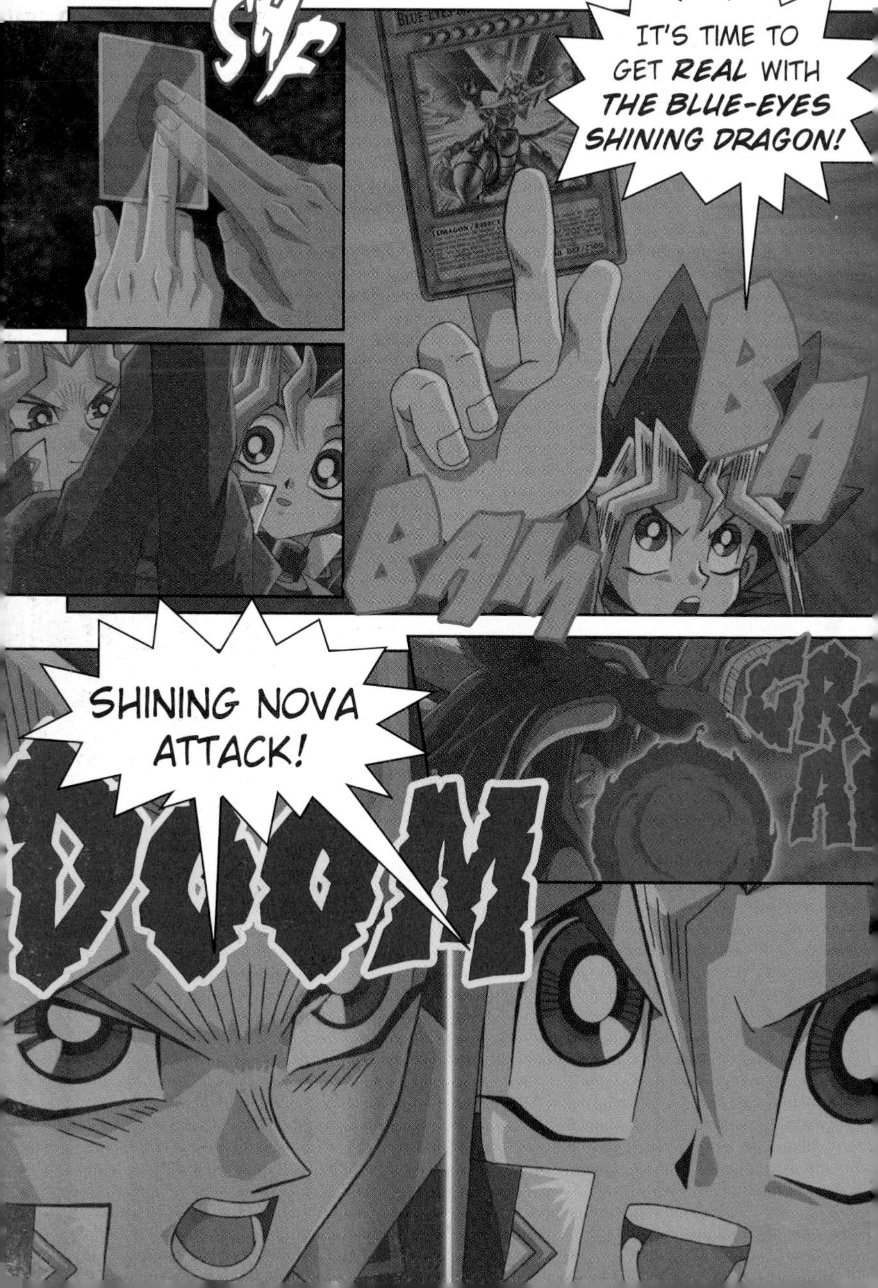
IT'S TIME TO GET *REAL* WITH *THE BLUE-EYES SHINING DRAGON!*
BA BAM
SHF
GRA
SHINING NOVA ATTACK!
BOOM

READ THIS WAY

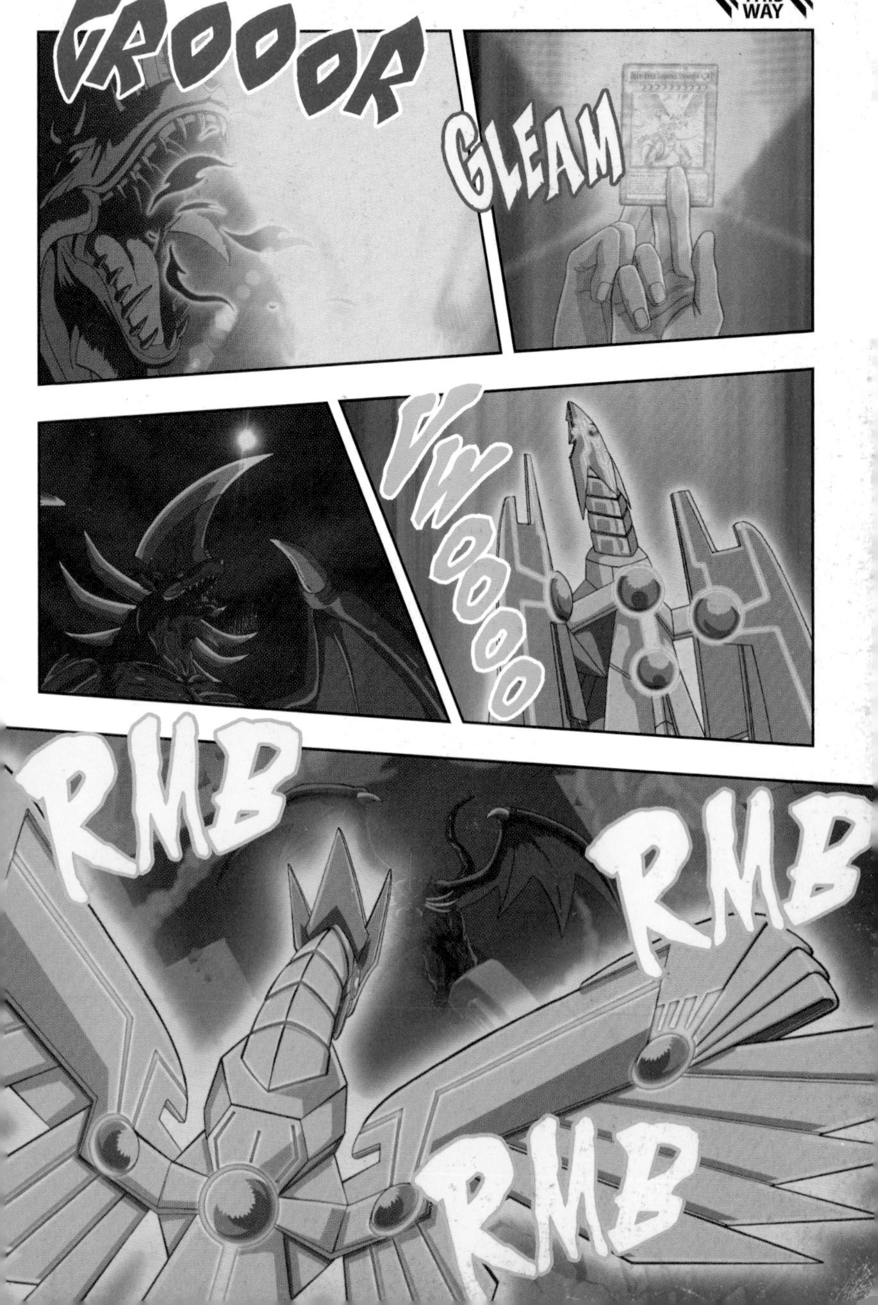
GLEAM
GROOOR
VWOOOOO
RMB
RMB
RMB

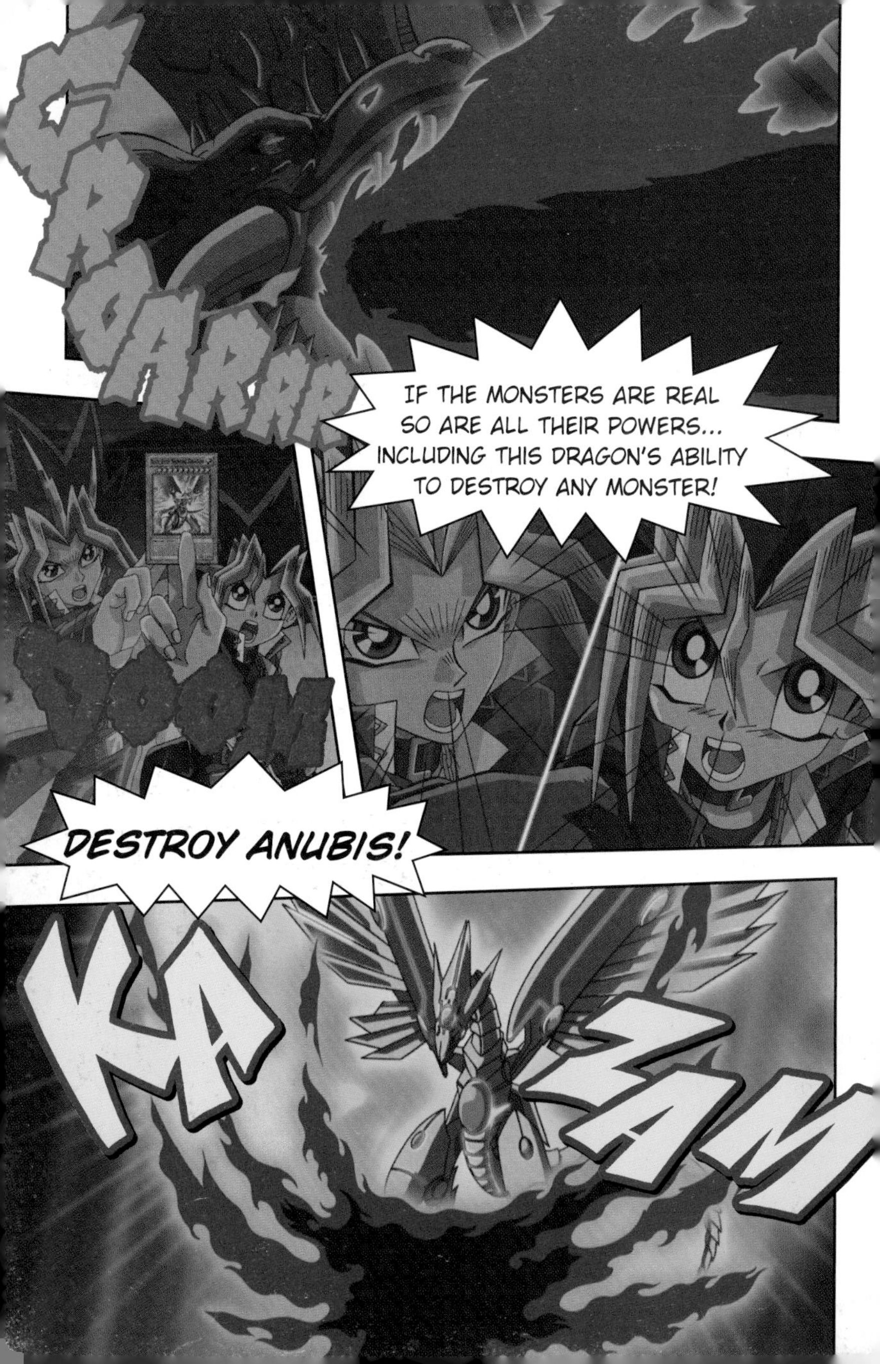
IF THE MONSTERS ARE REAL SO ARE ALL THEIR POWERS... INCLUDING THIS DRAGON'S ABILITY TO DESTROY ANY MONSTER!
DOOM
DESTROY ANUBIS!
KAZAM

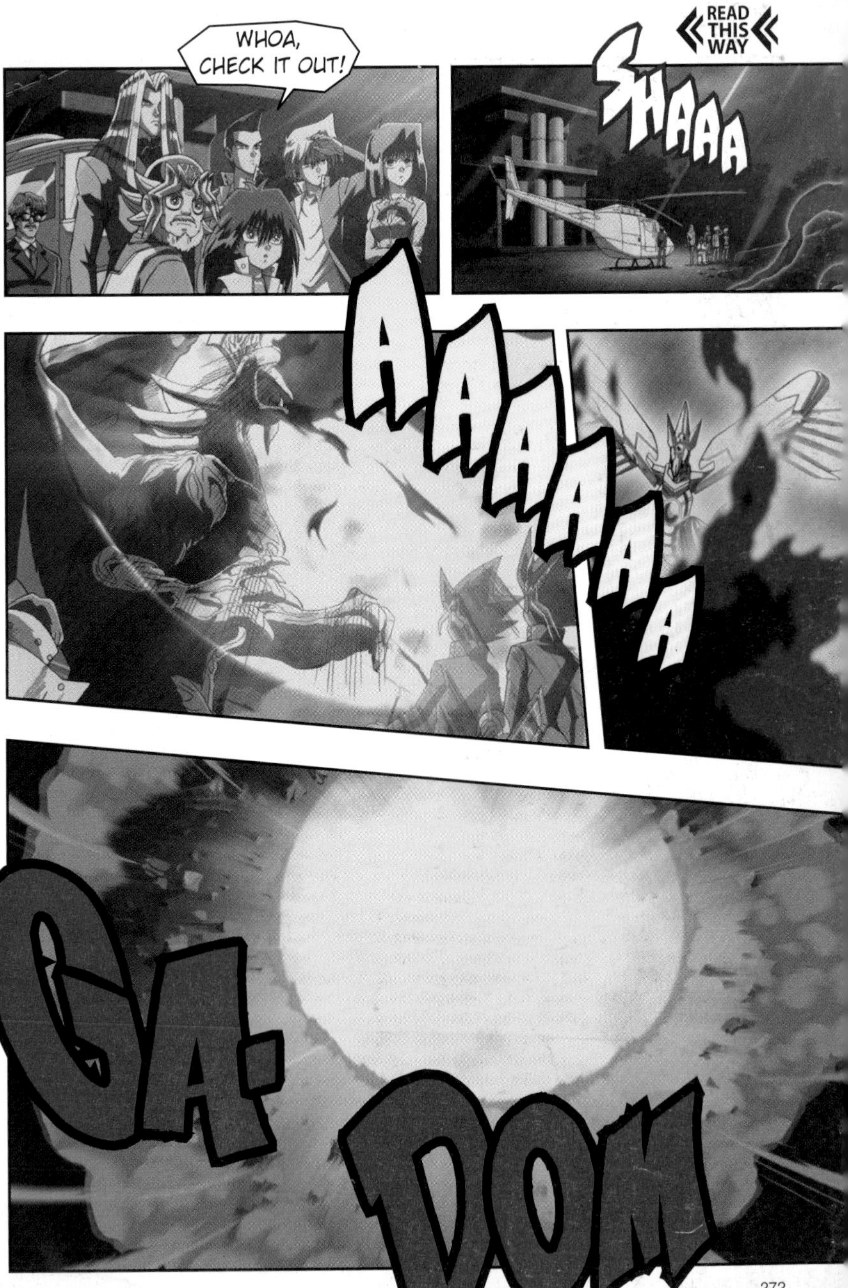
READ THIS WAY
SHAAA
WHOA, CHECK IT OUT!
AAAAAAAA
GA-DOM

READ THIS WAY

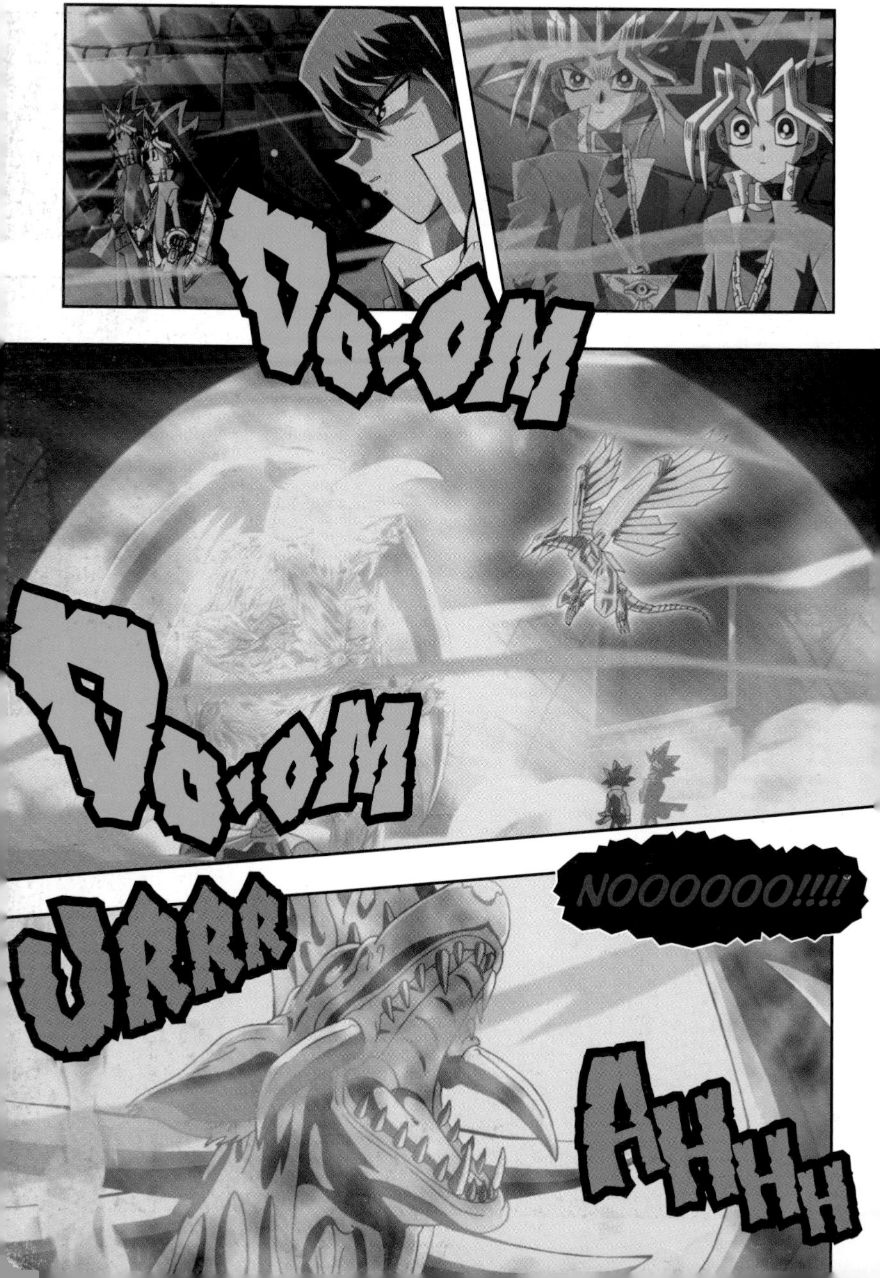
DOOM
DOOM
NOOOOOO!!!!
URRR
AHHHH

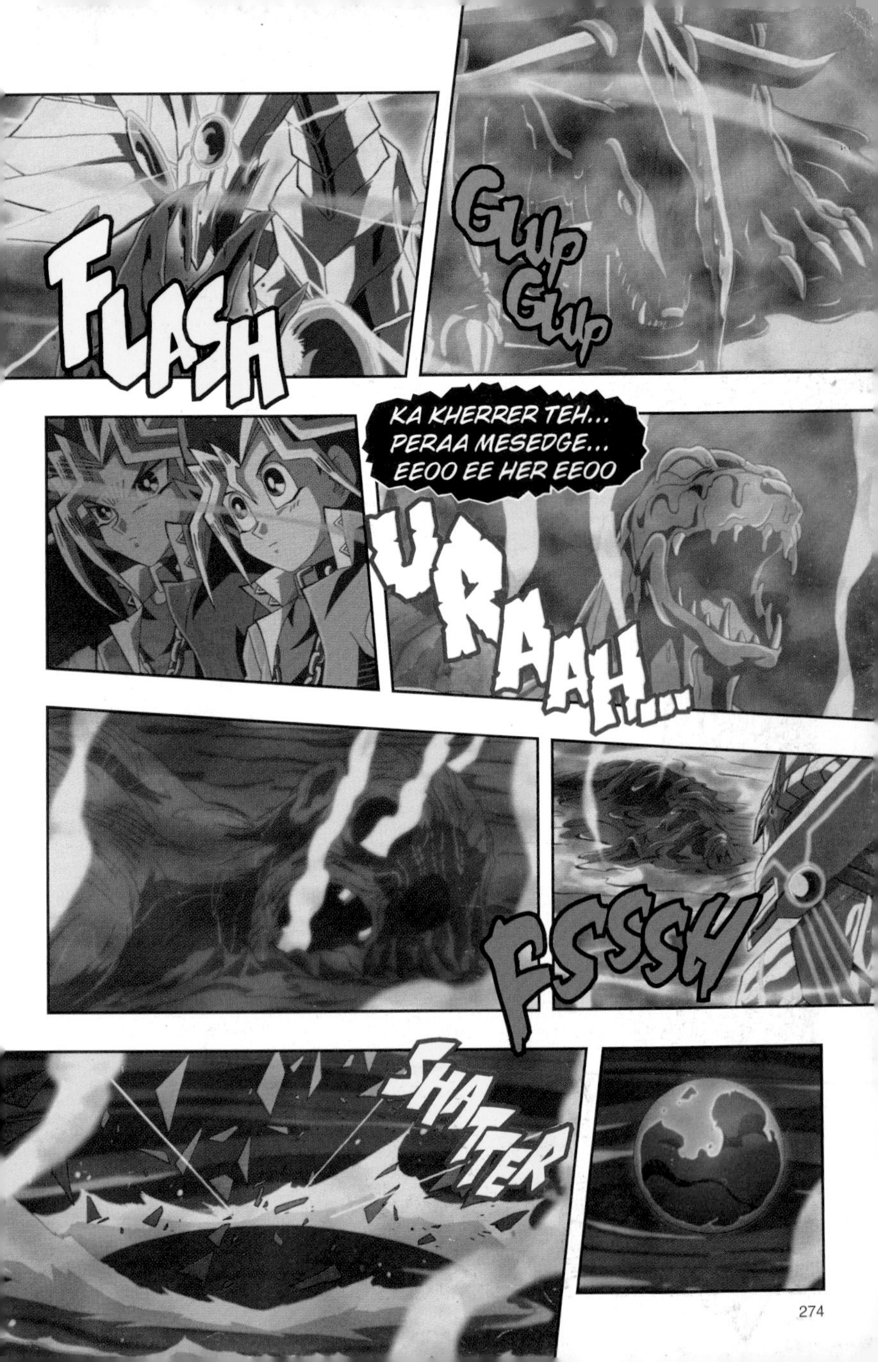
GLUP GLUP
FLASH
KA KHERRER TEH... PERAA MESEDGE... EEOO EE HER EEOO
URAAH...
FSSSH
SHATTER

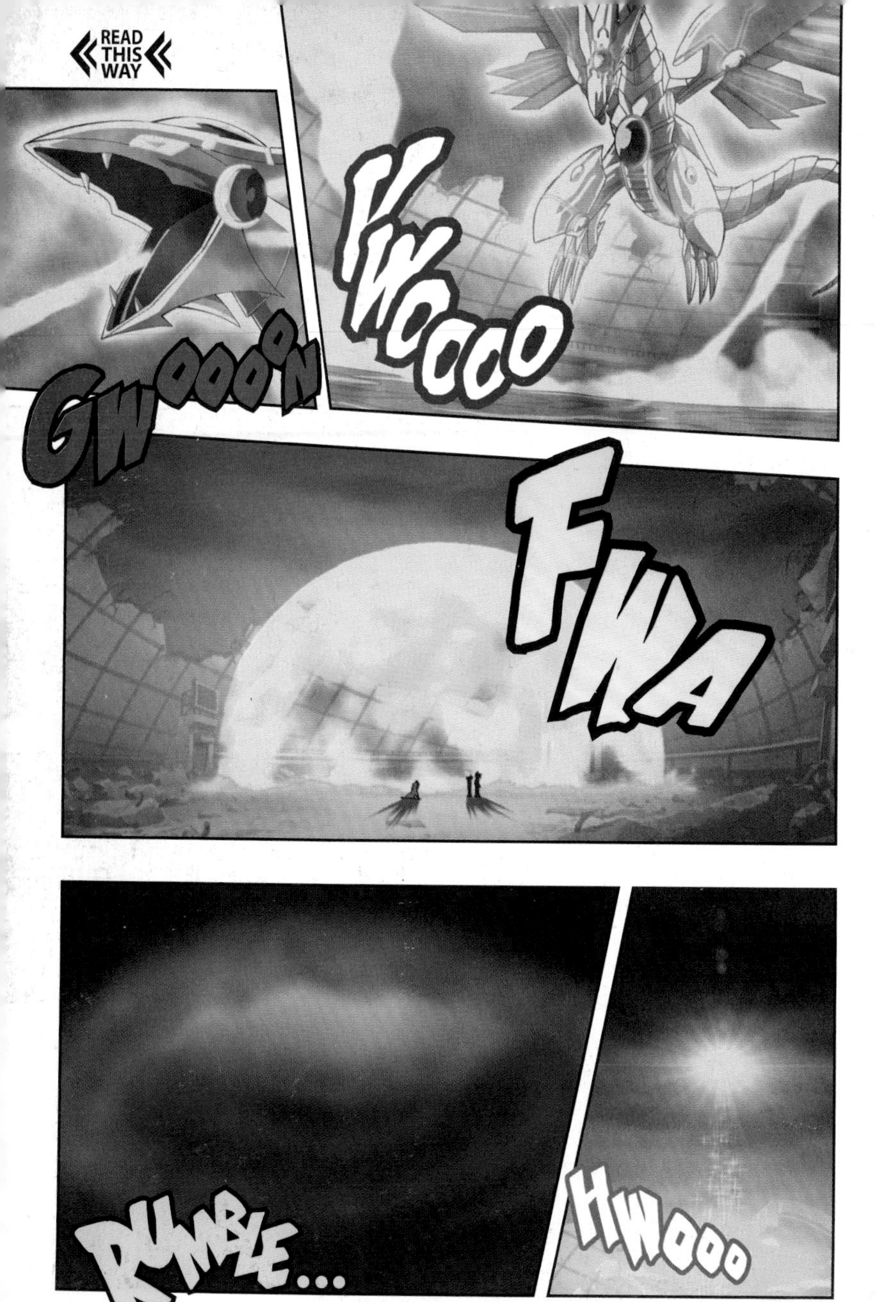
READ THIS WAY
HWOOOOO
GWOOOON
FWA
HWOOO
RUMBLE...

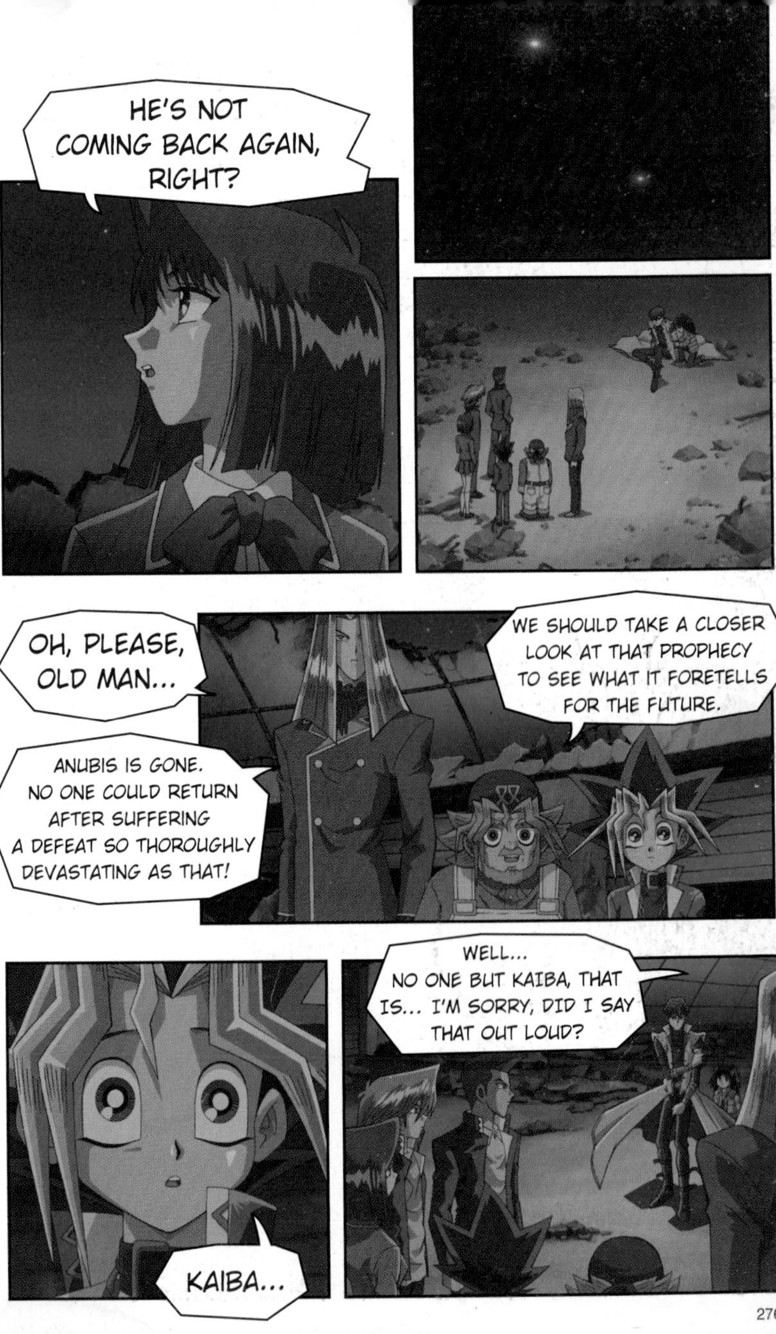
HE'S NOT COMING BACK AGAIN, RIGHT?
WE SHOULD TAKE A CLOSER LOOK AT THAT PROPHECY TO SEE WHAT IT FORETELLS FOR THE FUTURE.
OH, PLEASE, OLD MAN...
ANUBIS IS GONE. NO ONE COULD RETURN AFTER SUFFERING A DEFEAT SO THOROUGHLY DEVASTATING AS THAT!
WELL... NO ONE BUT KAIBA, THAT IS... I'M SORRY, DID I SAY THAT OUT LOUD?
KAIBA...

READ THIS WAY

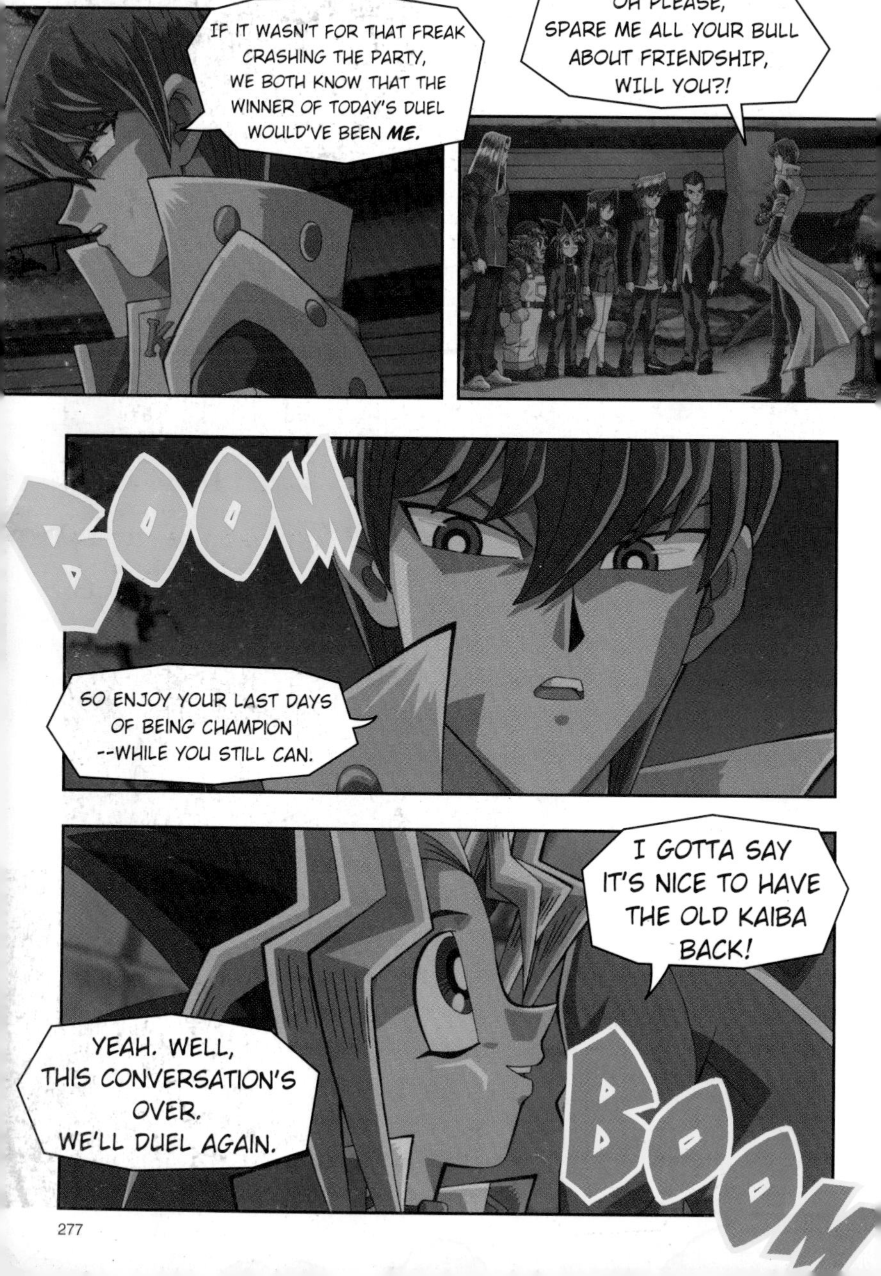
OH PLEASE, SPARE ME ALL YOUR BULL ABOUT FRIENDSHIP, WILL YOU?!
IF IT WASN'T FOR THAT FREAK CRASHING THE PARTY, WE BOTH KNOW THAT THE WINNER OF TODAY'S DUEL WOULD'VE BEEN *ME.*
BOOM
SO ENJOY YOUR LAST DAYS OF BEING CHAMPION --WHILE YOU STILL CAN.
I GOTTA SAY IT'S NICE TO HAVE THE OLD KAIBA BACK!
YEAH. WELL, THIS CONVERSATION'S OVER. WE'LL DUEL AGAIN.
BOOM

READ THIS WAY

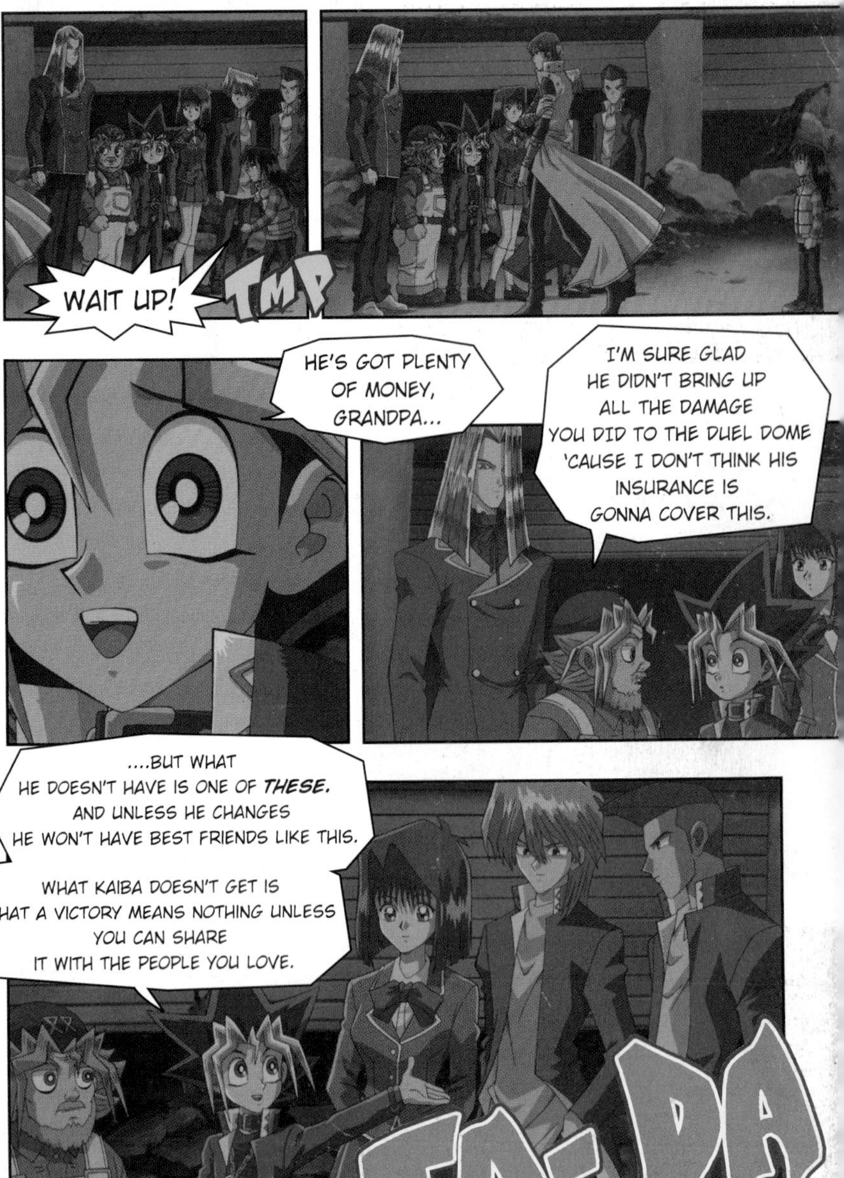
TMP
WAIT UP!
I'M SURE GLAD HE DIDN'T BRING UP ALL THE DAMAGE YOU DID TO THE DUEL DOME 'CAUSE I DON'T THINK HIS INSURANCE IS GONNA COVER THIS.
HE'S GOT PLENTY OF MONEY, GRANDPA...
....BUT WHAT HE DOESN'T HAVE IS ONE OF ***THESE.*** AND UNLESS HE CHANGES HE WON'T HAVE BEST FRIENDS LIKE THIS.
WHAT KAIBA DOESN'T GET IS THAT A VICTORY MEANS NOTHING UNLESS YOU CAN SHARE IT WITH THE PEOPLE YOU LOVE.
TA-DA

READ THIS WAY

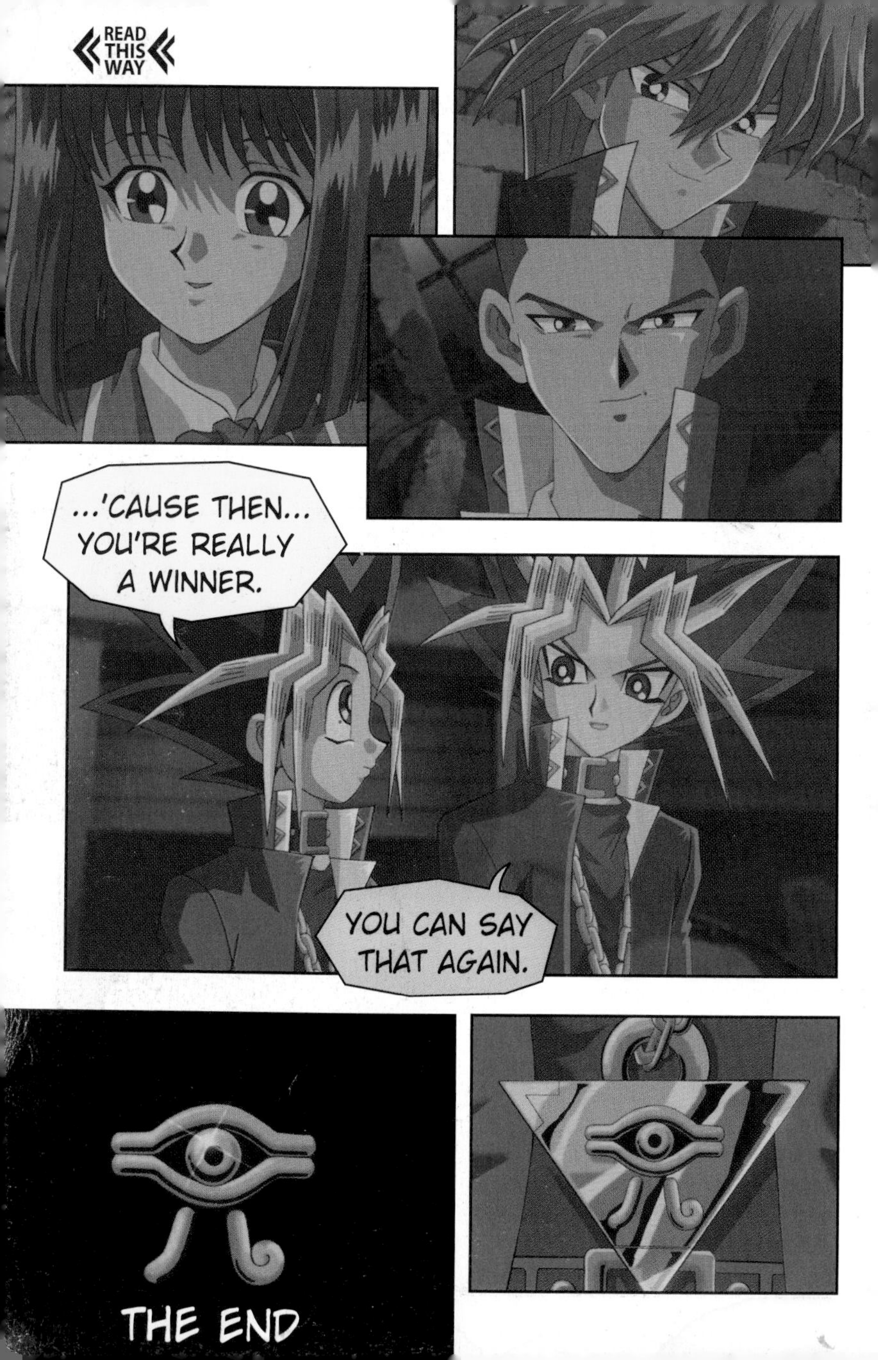
...'CAUSE THEN... YOU'RE REALLY A WINNER.
YOU CAN SAY THAT AGAIN.
THE END

ated by
AZUKI TAKAHASHI
TUDIO DICE

s seen in Shonen Jump Magazine
oundtrack Available on 4Kids
ane Records

irected by
IATSUKI TSUJI

roduced by
ORIKO KOBAYASHI (TV TOKYO)
IAOKI SASADA (NAS)

LOYD GOLDFINE
ÁTIA MILANI
ICHAEL PECORIELLO

riginal Story by
UNKI TAKEGAMI
IASAHIRO HIKOKUBO

creenplay by
IATTHEW DRDEK
LOYD GOLDFINE
ORMAN J. GROSSFELD
ICHAEL PECORIELLO

xecutive Producers
IDEYUKI NAGAI (NAS)
AMIZO SUZUKI (TV TOKYO)
IDEKI YAMASHITA (SHUEISHA)

LFRED R. KAHN
ORMAN J. GROSSFELD

dited by
IASAO NAKAGAWA

irectors of Photography
IROAKI EDAMITSU
UK GYU CHOI
AE HEE HEO
ANG OK KIM

nimation Production
TUDIO GALLOP

riginal Score Composed by
LIK ALVAREZ
OHN ANGIER
OEL DOUEK
ALPH SCHUCKETT
AYNE SHARPE
REDDY SHEINFELD
IL TALMI

usic Produced by
ULIAN SCHWARTZ
OHN SIEGLER

ast
AN GREEN
RIC STUART
COTTIE RAY
AYNE GRAYSON
OHN CAMPBELL
MY BIRNBAUM
ARA JAYNE
IADDIE BLAUSTEIN
ARREN DUNSTAN
EN BARON
IKE POLLOCK
NDREW PAULL
D PAUL
ISA ORTIZ
IARC THOMPSON
EBASTIAN ARCELUS

.S. Production

roduction
KIDS PRODUCTIONS, INC.

DR Director
RIC STUART

dditional ADR Direction
HRIS COLLET

ssociate Producers
HANE GUENEGO
HRIS GUIDO

roduction Coordinator
RENDA DILLON

tory and Gameplay Advisor
RTHUR "SAM" MURAKAMI

roduction Assistants
AKASHI OTANI
RISTEN THORNE

ssistant to the Executive Producer
IATASHA ALLAIRE

roduction Associates
ASON LAM
HERENE SHARPE

Egyptology Consultant
NICOLE DOUEK

Post Production Coordinators
AKI OHNUKI
JESSICA ALLEN

Assistant Film Editor
KEITH CROKET

Supervising Sound Editor
A. MADDY SHIRAZI, M.P.S.E.

ADR Editor
ELIZA PALEY

Sound FX Editors
BRUCE KITZMEYER
BRIAN LANGMAN
PAUL SOUCEK

Foley Editor
WILLIAM SWEENEY

Background Editor
DAVID FISHER

1st Assistant Sound Editor
DAN "DIEGO" FULTON

Assistant Sound Editor
ERIC STRAUSSER

ADR Recording Engineers
MIKE KNOBLAUCH
SHAWN CONRAD

Additional ADR Recording
QUESTAR WELSH

Re-Recording Mixer
PETER WAGGONER

Technical Support Services
AVI LANIADO
NICK CHURCH

Re-Recording Engineers
MIKE PATRICK
ROBERT OLARI

Foley Artist
NANCY CABRERA

Foley Recording
RYAN COLLISON

Post Production Sound Facilities
SOUND ONE CORP.

Dolby Sound Consultant
DUSTIN HUDSON

Compositing/Design
RYAN KELLY

3D Design
PAUL J. BACCASH
LUCIALIE C. DUMAGUING

2D Design
JENNIFER OBROTKA

2D Compositing
ROB BRUCE

HD Conform Editor
BRANDON BUSSINGER

HD Finishing Services Provided by
ORBIT DIGITAL

Digital Film Record Coordinator
MATTHEW REEDY
TRACEY SOAST

Digital Film Recordist
JEFF HUSTON

Digital Film Record provided by
POSTWORKS, NY

Musicians
CHRIS BLETH - Duduk
SANDRA PARKS – Solo Violin

Music Mixed by
LARRY ALEXANDER

Music Editor
KEITH GOLDSTEIN

Music Production Assistant
MIKE BRADY

Video Post
ABEL BAUTISTA
DAVE ETZOLD
JORDAN PODOS

Business Affairs
SAMUEL R. NEWBORN
KRISTEN GRAY

Production Accounting
FRAN SAPORITO
DORIS CAPET
WAZIDA RAMDEEN
ANNA ORLOVSKAYA
BRANDON CHUNG

Marketing
ROZ NOWICKI
JULIE DILL
ANIETRA GUZMAN

Color Timer
CATHY RAIT

Color by
DELUXE

Japan Production

Production
SHUEISHA
TV TOKYO
NAS

Character Design
HATSUKI TSUJI

Monster Design
HIDEKAZU SHIMAMURA

Animation Directors
NAK SOO CHOI
HEE NAM CHO
KOUNG TAE KIM

Storyboard Artists
HATSUKI TSUJI
NAOKI HISHIKAWA
MASAHIRO MINAMI

Line Producer
AYAO WAKANA (STUDIO GALLOP)

Production Manager
KUM NAM CHO

Assistant Directors
YOSHIAKI TSUTSUI
WOO HYUN PARK
SUNG WOON KO
CHI MAN PARK

Production Direction
JU HEE SHIN

Key Animators
DONG HWAN OH
YOO SIK JANG
IN JUNG
HOON JUNG
BANG WON LEE
TAE SUN IN
HYUN SOO WI
YOUNG DUK KIM
MIN UK KANG
SUNG SOO HWANG
SOON HO HONG
SOON YOUNG SUNG
SOOK JUNG HAN
HYOUNG JIN LIM
JAE HYUN CHO
SUNG MI HA
HYE JUNG KIM
JAE HO AN
BONG HYUN YOO
KI CHUL SHIN

Animators
SUN KYOUNG HA
SE JIN LEE
CHUN HWA SHIN
YUN JIN SUNG
JOO SUN CHO
WON SUH
HYUN NAM YANG
YOUNG SUN LEE
KYOUNG AE KIM
JUNG OK HWANG
JUNG AH KIM
YOUNG SIN KIM
MYOUNG HEE LEE
YUN JUNG HAN
EUN KYOUNG CHOI
TAE KYOUNG LEE
JUNG OK JUEN
IN YOUNG HEO
SUNG HEE JOO
HYOUNG SOOK LIM
MI AH HEO
SOO YEON KIM
SOON IM YUN
EUN AH KIM
SUNG KWANG PARK
HYUN JOO JEUN
YOUNG MI KIM
SOO KYOUNG PARK
SANG HEE OK
YOUNG HEE CHOI
CHUNG IL HAN
MI JUNG KWAK

JI YOUNG LEE
YUN YOUNG LEE
BYOUNG SUK CHA
SEUNG OK CHOI
YEON HEE KIM
HYE SUNG LEE
RAN HEE KIM
GUI YOUNG KIM
MYOUNG JOON PARK
MI HEE KIM
NAN YOUNG PARK
REE SUN KIM
DO KWUAN KIM

Model Check
YOUNG HOON KIM
HYE RYUNG PARK
HYUN JOO SONG
SANG HEE LEE
SOON JA JUNG
OK SUN KIM
SOOK HEE KIM
MI KYOUNG KIM

Scan • Clean Up Animation
MIN YONG YOO
OK JA YOO
YOUNG HEE SHIN
BOK SOON BAE
JUNG HYUN PARK
GIL JA OH
SOON HWAN LEE
NAM HEE KIM
PIL SUN LEE
HYUN YOUNG UM
JUNG SOON KIM
MI OK JEUN
KYOUNG SOOK KIM
BO SUN HWANG
MIN HO YOO
SUNG HEE YOO
MYOUNG HEE KANG
SOO JIN HWANG
OH SOOK KWUAN
SUNG SUL JEUN
OK YOUNG LEE
YEUN HUI AN
DAE HYUN NAH
YEON JIN KIM
MAN GYUN PARK
IN SUNG SONG
SEUNG YEUP BAN
MYOUNG HEE YEO
CHAN MI KIM
JUNG HYE KIM
YOO SUN KIM
GYU DONG KIM
HEE JUNG KIM

"You're Not Me"
Written by John Siegler and Norman J. Grossfeld
Produced by John Siegler
Performed by Marty Bags

"One Card Short"
Written by John Siegler and Norman J. Grossfeld
Produced by John Siegler and Norman J. Grossfeld
Performed by James Chatton

"Step Up"
Written by Jean Rodriquez and Eddie Montilla
Produced by Eddie Montilla and Jean Rodriquez
Executive Producer: Tu Casa Entertainment
Performed by Jean Rodríguez

"Blind Ambition"
Performed by The Deleted
Written and Produced by Russell Velázquez

"It's Over"
Written by Ron Riley, Eddie Brickerson,
Gabrielle Travis and Kiana Allison
Produced by Herminio Quiroz and Ron Riley
Performed by Fatty Koo

"How Much Longer"
Written and Produced by
Jen Scaturro and Julian Schwartz
Performed by Jen Scaturro

Special Thanks
JAY RUBIN
IRWIN SIMON
CARLOS BU
ELSAYED ALY
BOBBY MILLER
CARLA FIRBY

Background Art Director
HOI YOUNG LEE

Backgrounds
JOON PIL HWANG
TAE WON HEO
JUNG HWAN LEE
WON GOO LEE
EUN KYOUNG KIM
YUN SOOK YEUM
YOUNG JOO HAN
SOOK HEO
EUN MI PARK
KYOUNG AH KIM

Animation Camera Shooting Staff
DONG PIL CHOI
JUNG YUL KIM
JONG SOO YOO
HEE CHAN KANG
HYE WON SUH
JI WON PARK
EUN YOUNG NAH
JIN SUK CHOI
UN SIK KIM
JIN YOUNG LEE
EUN JOO CHOI
YOUNG RAN CHO
SANG RAE LEE

Final Animation Check
GI SUK LEE
MYOUNG HEE YOO
JONG MIN CHOI
YOUNG RA CHO

Color Keys
CHIHO NAKAMURA

Colorist
MI HYUN AHN

Assistant Line Producer
MASANOBU HACHIDA (STUDIO GALLOP)

Planning
KEISUKE IWATA (TV TOKYO)
TAKASHI HARADA (TV TOKYO)
HIDETAKA IKUTA (NAS)

Assistant Coordinators
YOUNG TAE KIM
WON SOOK KWAK
CHI YOUNG KANG

SECRETS OF Yu-Gi-Oh!

BEFORE THE ANIME...BEFORE THE CARDS...THERE WAS THE MANGA!

THE MAGAZINE **SECRET** WHERE IT ALL STARTED!

Kazuki Takahashi's **Yu-Gi-Oh!** manga appears in English every month in America's **SHONEN JUMP** magazine. (Other **SHONEN JUMP** manga include **One Piece**, **YuYu Hakusho**, **Shaman King** and **Dragon Ball Z**, on sale first Tuesday of each month.) After the manga appears in the magazine, it is reprinted in graphic novels.

SECRET YU-GI-OH! GRAPHIC NOVELS: 200 PAGES OF ACTION!

VOLUMES 1 TO 7 AVAILABLE NOW!

Kazuki Takahashi volume 4
Kazuki Takahashi volume 5
Takahashi volume 6
Takahashi volume 7

If you saw the anime before you read the manga, you may be surprised to know that **Yu-Gi-Oh!** wasn't always about cards. Originally, Yugi fought enemies with all kinds of "shadow games": board games, dice games, yoyos, table tennis, even RPGs! The manga includes lots of stories that weren't in the anime, including how Yugi solved the Millennium Puzzle; how Yugi met his friends; and the origins of Shadi, Bakura and Kaiba! Graphic Novels are available at local bookstores nationwide.

SECRET YU-GI-OH! FIRST APPEARED IN 1996 IN JAPAN!

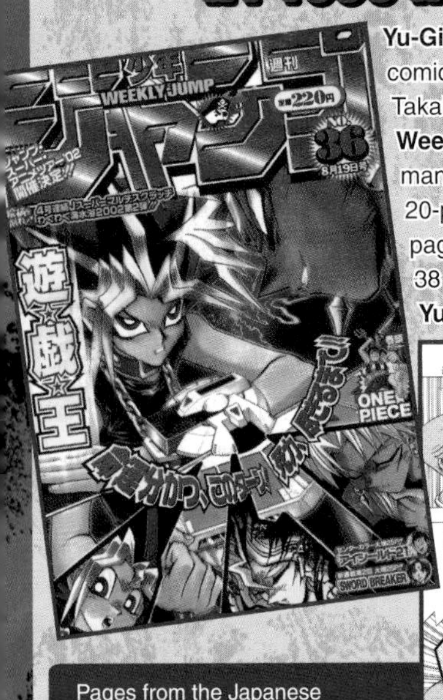
週刊少年ジャンプ
WEEKLY JUMP
220円
No.36
8月19日号
遊☆戯☆王
ONE PIECE
SWORD BREAKER

Yu-Gi-Oh! is a *manga*—a Japanese comic—created by the artist Kazuki Takahashi. It first appeared in 1996 in **Weekly Shonen Jump**, Japan's No.1 manga magazine. Takahashi drew a new 20-page chapter every week—that's 80 pages a month! After eight years and 38 graphic novels full of adventures, **Yu-Gi-Oh!** is more popular than ever!

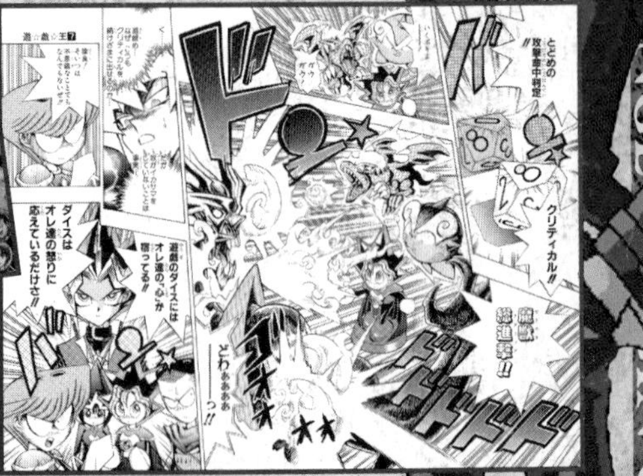
遊☆戯☆王7
とどめの攻撃命中判定!!
クリティカル!!
魔獣総進撃!!
遊戯のダイスにはオレ達の心が宿ってる!!
ダイスはオレ達の怒りに応えているだけさ!!
どわぁぁぁぁーっ!!

Pages from the Japanese **Yu-Gi-Oh!**. Of course, the dialogue is in Japanese!

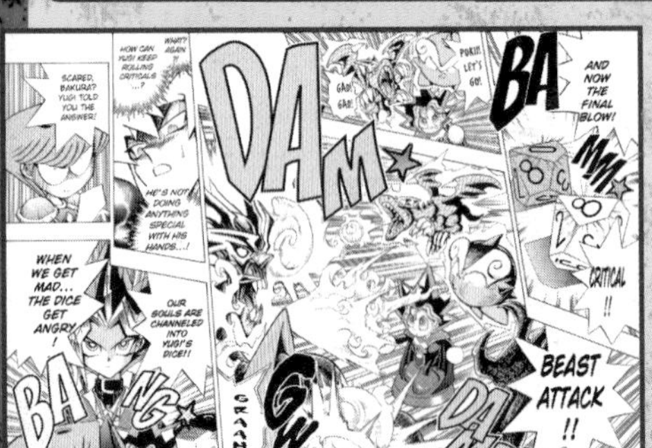
AND NOW THE FINAL BLOW!
BA
POW!! LET'S GO!
CRITICAL!!
BEAST ATTACK!!
DAMDADADAM
GWAAA
GRAAHHH!
WHAT!? AGAIN?!
HOW CAN YUGI KEEP ROLLING CRITICALS...?
SCARED, BAKURA? YUGI TOLD YOU THE ANSWER!
DAM
HE'S NOT DOING ANYTHING SPECIAL WITH HIS HANDS...!
WHEN WE GET MAD... THE DICE GET ANGRY!
OUR SOULS ARE CHANNELED INTO YUGI'S DICE!!
BANG

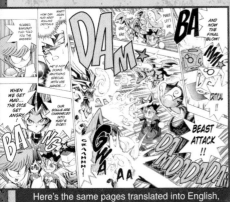

Here's the same pages translated into English, from **Yu-Gi-Oh!** graphic novel volume 7!

Sound effects in manga are different from the ones in American comics. In American comics, sound effects always indicate an action, like a door slamming (SLAM!) or a punch (POW!). But in manga, sound effects are like the soundtrack of an anime, it gets louder when something dramatic happens. Typical manga sound effects are "DON!", usually the sound of an important closeup, or "GO GO GO GO," a dramatic rumble of anticipation.

HOW TO DRAW YUGI

Do you want to be a manga artist? Kazuki Takahashi, the creator of *Yu-Gi-Oh!*, told us his secrets of how to draw Yugi. Try it yourself!

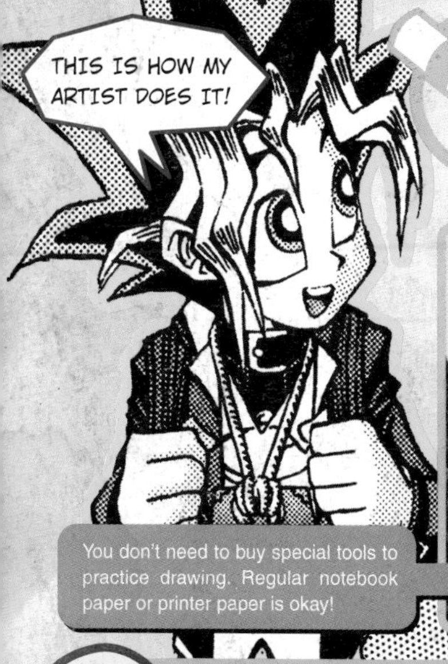
THIS IS HOW MY ARTIST DOES IT!

1 GET YOUR TOOLS!

To do a basic drawing of Yugi, all you really need is paper and a pencil. You can use a pen if you want, but the nice thing about a pencil is that you can erase!

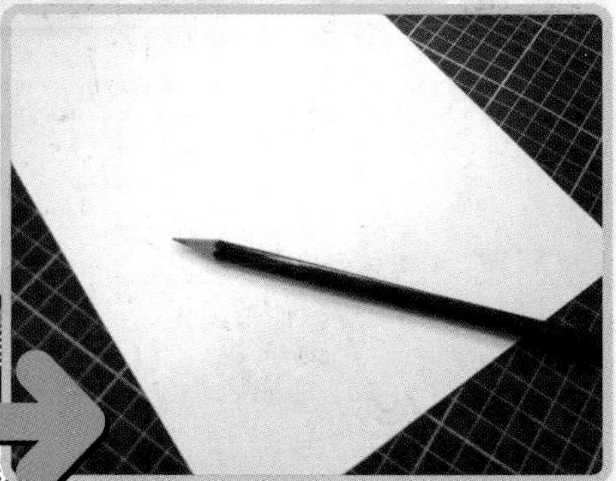

You don't need to buy special tools to practice drawing. Regular notebook paper or printer paper is okay!

WHAT KIND OF TOOLS DO PROFESSIONAL MANGA ARTISTS USE?

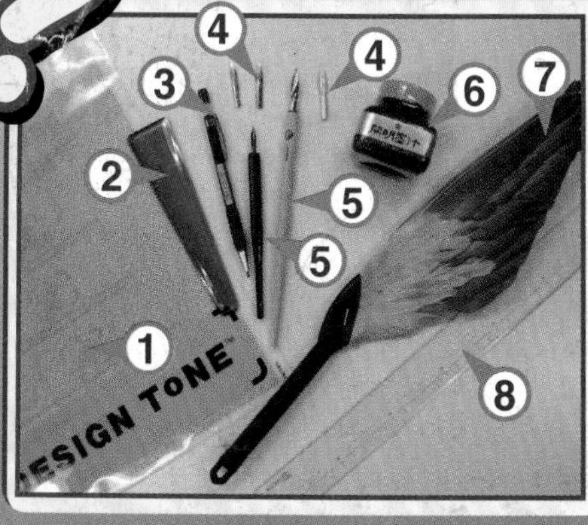
4
4
3
6
7
2
5
5
1
ESIGN TONE
8

First, the manga artist sketches with a pencil. Then, they ink the pencil lines with one of several type of pens and erase the pencil lines. (Special "gum erasers" or "plastic erasers" do a better job than the erasers on the ends of pencils.) Then, they fill in the large black areas with ink.

Finally, the manga artist puts "screentones" on the paper to fill in the gray areas. Screentones are adhesive sheets of plastic with special dot patterns that look like gray when you print it in a manga. Recently, old-fashioned plastic screentones have been mostly replaced by computer effects.

❶Screentone ❷Screentone applicator
❸Pencil ❹Pen nib (different sizes) ❺Pens
❻Ink ❼Feather brush (to brush off eraser dust)
❽Ruler

Translation/Joe Yamazaki

READ THIS WAY

2 DRAW YUGI STEP-BY-STEP!

Yu-Gi-Oh! creator Kazuki Takahashi has drawn Yugi thousands, perhaps millions, of times. Follow his step-by-step lessons to sketch the King of Games!

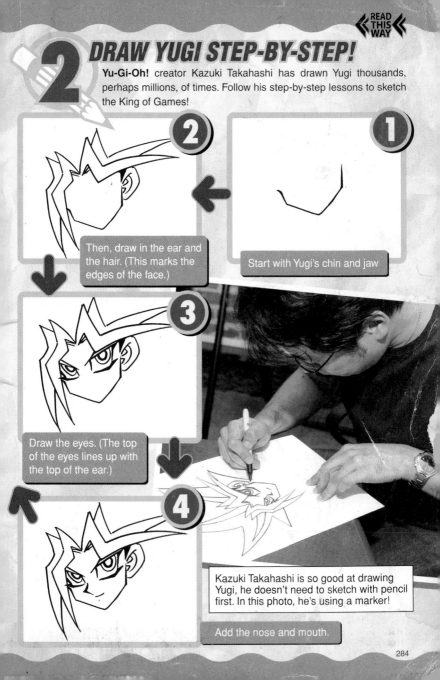

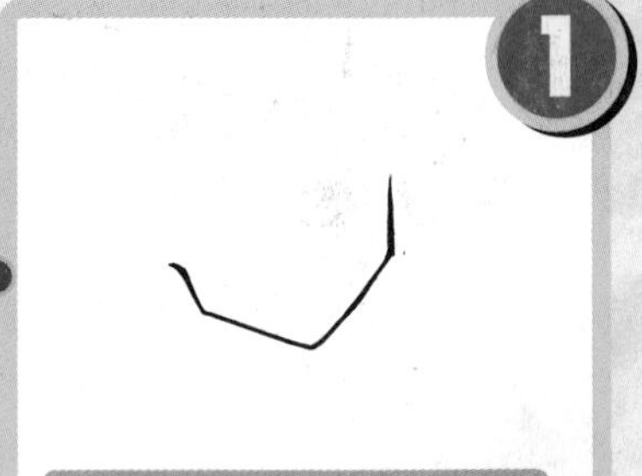
1

Start with Yugi's chin and jaw

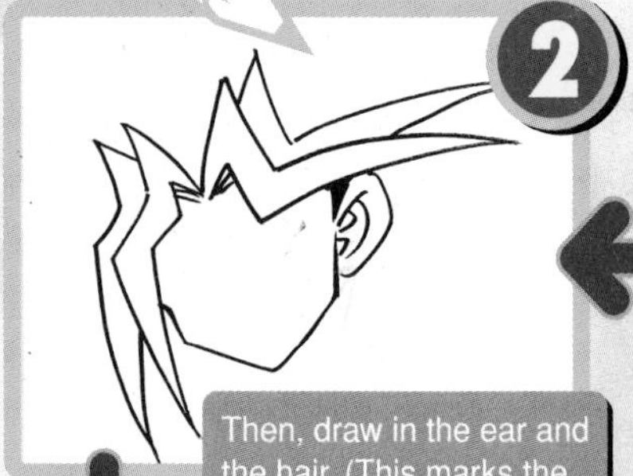
2

Then, draw in the ear and the hair. (This marks the edges of the face.)

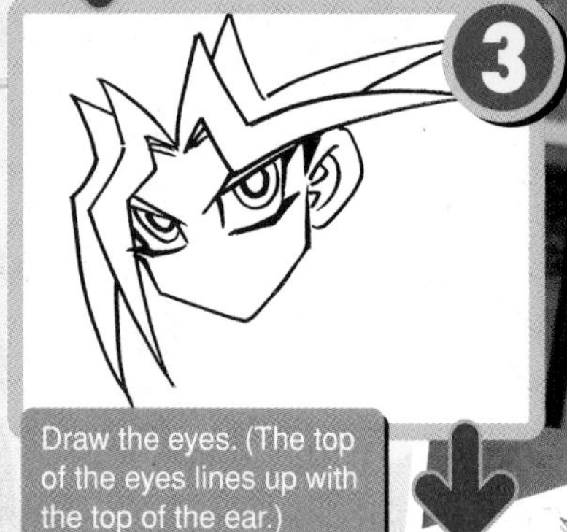
3

Draw the eyes. (The top of the eyes lines up with the top of the ear.)

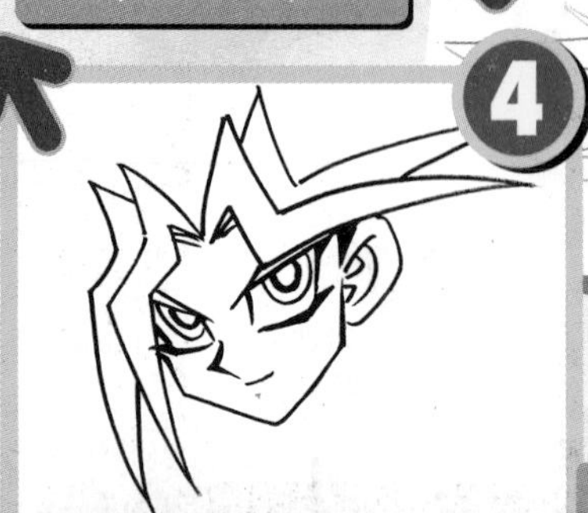
4

Add the nose and mouth.

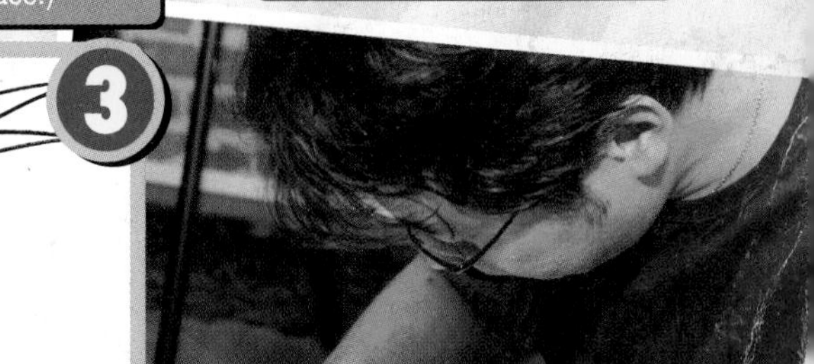

Kazuki Takahashi is so good at drawing Yugi, he doesn't need to sketch with pencil first. In this photo, he's using a marker!

5

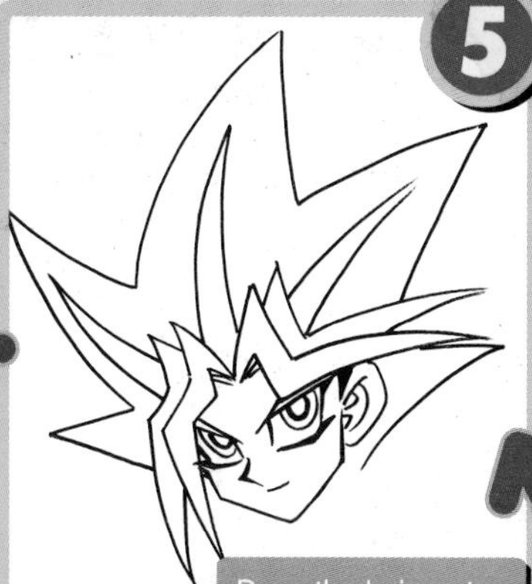

Draw the hair on top of Yugi's head.

6

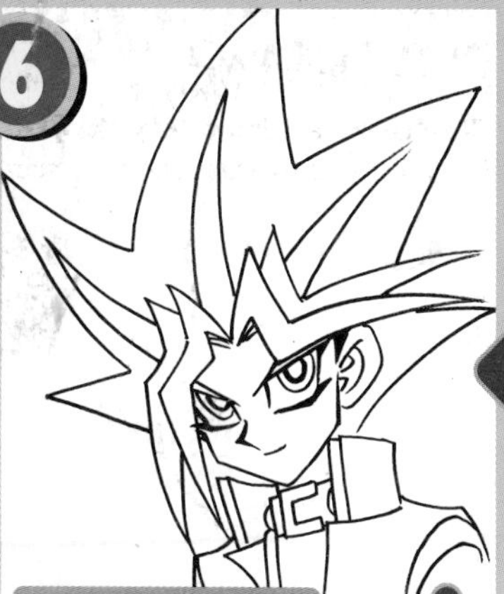

Then, fill in his neck and shoulders.

7

YOU'RE DONE!

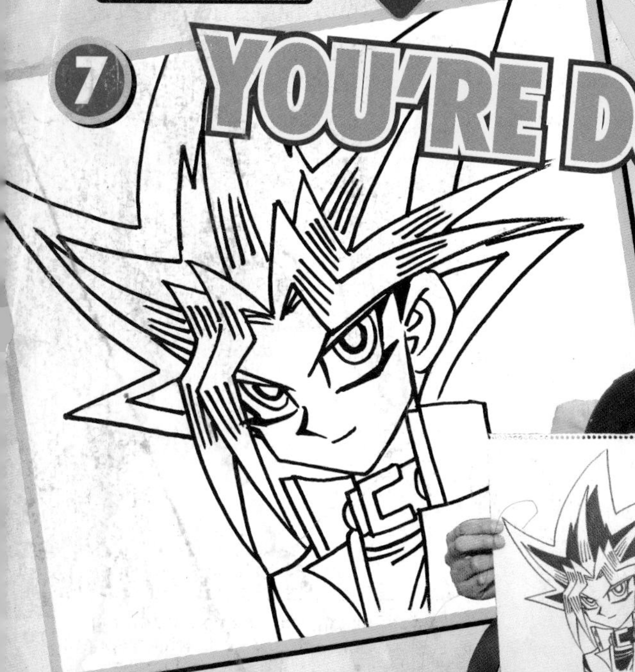

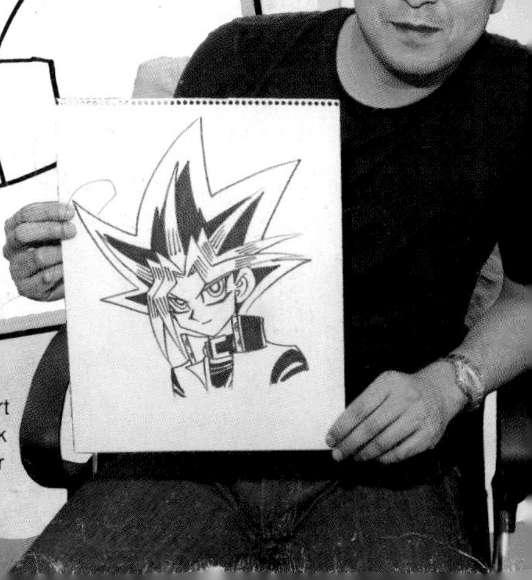

Finally, fill in the details like his shirt and the shiny marks on his hair, and fill in the black areas. You're done! Thanks to Kazuki Takahashi for showing us how to do it!

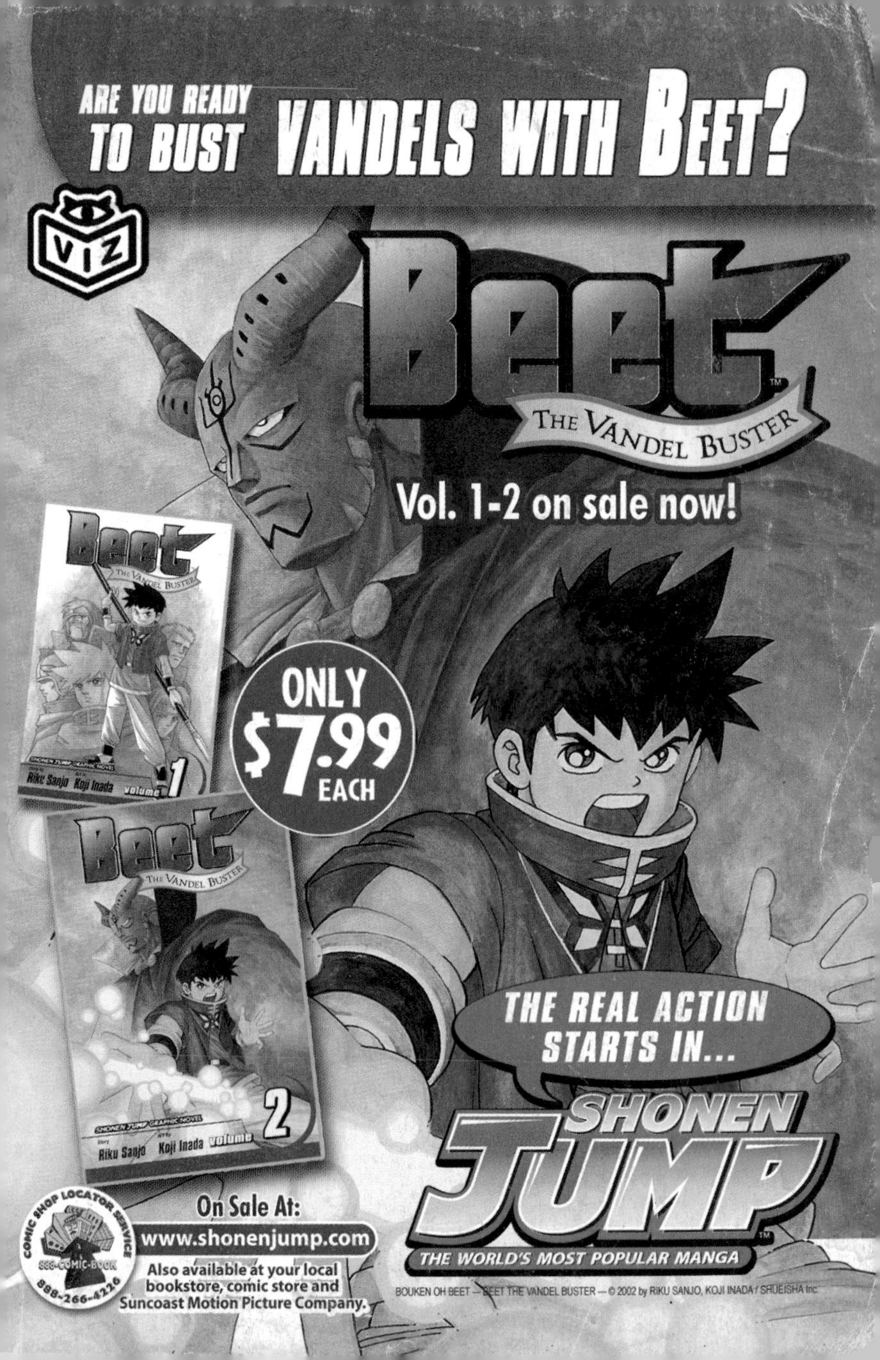
ARE YOU READY TO BUST VANDELS WITH BEET?
VIZ
Beet™ THE VANDEL BUSTER
Vol. 1-2 on sale now!
ONLY $7.99 EACH
Beet THE VANDEL BUSTER
Riku Sanjo Koji Inada volume 1
Beet THE VANDEL BUSTER
SHONEN JUMP GRAPHIC NOVEL
Riku Sanjo Koji Inada volume 2
THE REAL ACTION STARTS IN...
SHONEN JUMP™
THE WORLD'S MOST POPULAR MANGA
COMIC SHOP LOCATOR SERVICE
888-COMIC-BOOK
888-266-4226
On Sale At:
www.shonenjump.com
Also available at your local bookstore, comic store and Suncoast Motion Picture Company.
BOUKEN OH BEET — BEET THE VANDEL BUSTER — © 2002 by RIKU SANJO, KOJI INADA / SHUEISHA Inc.

SHONEN JUMP
GRAPHIC NOVELS

ALL NEW SHONEN JUMP GRAPHIC NOVELS!

Dragon Ball VOL. 16
Dragon Ball Z VOL. 17
Yu-Gi-Oh! VOL. 6
YuYu Hakusho VOL. 5
One Piece VOL. 5
Naruto VOL. 4
Shaman King VOL. 4
Rurouni Kenshin VOL. 8
Knights of the Zodiac VOL. 6
Hikaru No Go VOL. 2
The Prince Of Tennis VOL. 4
Bleach VOL. 3
Whistle! VOL. 2
Beet The Vandel Buster VOL. 1

All Books $7.99 and Under